SECOND EDITION

RUPP'S
Insurance & Risk Management
GLOSSARY

Richard V. Rupp, CPCU

D0880598

NILS Publishing Company
Chatsworth, California

Printed in the United States of America.
International Standard Book Number: 0-89246-446-1
Library of Congress Catalog Number: 95-072441

Dedication

This Second Edition is dedicated to my loving wife, Coleen, who has continually encouraged me. Now it is time for that long-awaited trip to Ireland.

Contents

Preface to the Second Edition

When *Rupp's Insurance & Risk Management Glossary* was first published, I had no idea how it would be received. My intent was to offer a more comprehensive insurance glossary than was currently available for the benefit of insurance and risk management professionals and to further the standardization of industry terms. I was very pleased that the *Glossary* received excellent reviews from both insurance trade publications and from the legal community.

From the correspondence and comments I have received, it is apparent that the book is used by a broad range of individuals, from those who have just entered the business and need a basic lexicon, to seasoned underwriters and risk managers who need a handy reference for unusual or new terms. It is also used as a reference in settling and litigating claim disputes.

This Second Edition, five years in the making, has proved to be more fun and interesting to work on than the First. The reason is that, rather than relying principally on the research files I have collected over the years, I was incorporating suggestions from flesh-and-blood readers. Due to their input, changing industry terminology, and my own continuing research, this edition includes over 1600 new terms, as well as many amendments to original terms.

I am grateful for the contributions, assistance, and wise counsel of all the colleagues, fellow CPCUs, and industry friends (in addition to those named in the Acknowledgments) who took the time to offer suggestions.

A few examples of terms that were originally omitted are *alternative dispute resolution, bed pan mutual, earthquake sprinkler leakage, and stop gap endorsement.* Examples of terms emerging from the development of new insurance products include *clinical trials product liability insurance,* developed for the biotechnology industry, and *employment practices liability insurance,* developed to incorporate discrimination, sexual harassment, and wrongful termination liability coverages into a single policy.

President Clinton's Council on Health Insurance affected the expansion and popular usage of health insurance terms, such as *health purchasing alliance* and *managed care.* I suspect that over the next few years many additional health insurance terms will ensue as businesses, Congress, and state legislatures struggle to deal with problems of an aging population and the high cost of health care.

The growth of international and global insurance programs has resulted in an expanded *International* insurance category. Terms such as *blocked currency* and *global insurance program* are among the additions. It is my belief that more international insurance terms will enter our professional language as global programs replace traditional domestic ones.

As in the First Edition, subject categories provide a context for the definitions; and these, too, have undergone changes to more accurately reflect the classifications currently used in the insurance and risk management communities. The former category *Casualty* has been replaced by *Liability* and *Professional Liability*, both because casualty insurance is such a broad line and because professional liability is a growing class of insurance, justifying a separate category.

Also, the catch-all category *General* has been substantially reduced. Many terms included there before are more correctly placed in one of two new categories, *Accounting* and *Law* —both subjects greatly important to the insurance profession.

In addition, a new *Personal* category has been added. Personal lines (e.g., homeowners insurance) represent a major segment of the industry, and sometimes there is a difference between usages of a term in personal lines and in commercial lines. I hope readers will find this subject category to be useful; however, rather than splitting several other categories between their personal and commercial applications, the basic classification of terms as *Property* and *Liability* (formerly *Casualty)* has been retained from the First Edition.

From locating and defining new terms for this edition, some interesting conceptual windows have opened for me. A technique of some futurists —identifying and counting words and phrases in trade publications to discover industry trends —appears applicable to the information I've gathered. Based on recurring terms, I have identified a number of major risk management and insurance trends. They are as follows:

1. Risk management is moving into the mainstream of organizational management and away from being an isolated division. It is being accepted as a discipline to be learned by senior management and incorporated into an organization's financial and operating structure. This is resulting in the downsizing of risk management departments and the outsourcing of some of the risk management function to risk management consultants.

2. Alphabet brokers, partly in response to this change in organizational risk management, are moving toward becoming consultants, as opposed to insurance brokers, and are becoming management consultants, as opposed to risk management consultants. They are also becoming involved in investment banking to provide risk securitization products.

3. Accounting firms and management consulting firms are incorporating risk management into their practices. Their financial and nontraditional risk management backgrounds are affecting how insurance and risk management are presented to and applied by organizations. Also, risk securitization and finite risk plans often require tax or accounting advice available only from accounting firms.

4. Traditional insurance for risk management accounts is being replaced or blended with risk securitization plans and finite risk plans to fund accidental loss exposures. These concepts were initially designed for large organizations to handle their catastrophic

loss exposures but now appear to be developing into standard risk funding techniques (in the form of pre-funded deductibles and multiyear policies) that can be applied to mid-market accounts. It is similar to the captive insurance movement several years ago. It should be noted that the finite risk concept has been around in one form or another for years under such names as a banking plan, chronological stabilization plan, or spread loss plan.

5. Insurance delivery system costs for personal lines and commercial mid-market accounts are being reduced though affinity groups and direct marketing programs. This is changing the market share mix among various types of insurers. Traditional low-cost exclusive agency insurers, such as State Farm, Allstate, and the Farmers Insurance Group, are facing real competition from traditional direct marketing companies, such as The California Casualty Group, GEICO, and USAA, and from newly established direct marketing facilities developed by such companies as AIG/20th Century, Progressive Insurance Company, and Zurich Life. The exclusive agency companies are finding their corporate cultures more difficult to change than that of the independent agency companies.

6. Catastrophic losses during the past five years in areas especially subject to wind and earthquake exposures have also changed the personal lines market share mix. Some smaller regional insurers in these areas were forced into insolvency by catastrophic losses. Several multi-line insurers who dabbled in personal lines have withdrawn from these areas. This has left the three large exclusive agency companies (State Farm, Allstate, Farmers) with increased market share in areas where they do not want it and in fact are attempting to decrease their market share. This has increased the interest in government-sponsored solutions, such as joint underwriting authorities or even government-operated facilities, to offer insurance in areas subject to catastrophic losses. It could eventually result in the passage of some form of federal catastrophic insurance legislation, such as that sponsored by the National Disaster Coalition.

7. More and more commercial lines property and casualty insurers and their agents are target marketing through group and association programs. These affinity group commercial insurance programs are reducing acquisition and service costs and are incorporating tailored risk management concepts as value added features.

8. Information technology is affecting every aspect of insurance and risk management, as it is most other businesses. We are moving toward the time when we no longer can afford the cost or time of referring to paper documents or waiting for mail. We have begun a movement away from static information on databases and CD-ROMs toward real-time data over the Internet from anywhere in the world. We are communicating globally with branch offices, clients, and industry friends by e-mail. Cellular or wireless phones and laptop computers with modems are standard means of communication. The World Wide Web is overflowing with industry information on web sites and bulletin boards maintained by risk managers, insurers, brokers, and other industry service vendors. We are doing more work with fewer people at a faster pace.

9. Professional liability is a rapidly growing area of insurance, with changes in directors' and officers' liability insurance and the introduction of employment practices liability insurance. This growth is evidenced, too, by the formation of the Professional Liability Underwriting Society.

10. Risk management and insurance have gained in professionalism during the last five years. Many new entrants into the business during this period possess advanced degrees in finance, business or law. This trend is being pushed by changes in organizational management, consumers' concerns about insurance, legislators' passage of new laws affecting the industry, regulators' tightening of license requirements, and court judgments against agents for errors and omissions claims. Society in general is examining the availability and efficiency of insurance and risk management services and demanding more from the industry, which is slowly but effectively responding.

I look forward to working on future editions of the *Glossary* knowing I will continue to receive comments from you who have invested your money in it. Please feel free to send your comments and suggestions to me care of NILS Publishing Company, P.O. Box 2507, Chatsworth, CA 91313, or to my Internet address: Rupprisk@aol.com.

Richard V. Rupp, CPCU

Acknowledgments

Many readers and users of the First Edition suggested new terms or revisions. For example, the term *alternative dispute resolution* was noted in a review by James Whitaker, CPCU, in *Smart's Insurance Bulletin* (November 15, 1991). The term *bed pan mutual* was noted by David M. Katz in his review in *National Underwriter* (August 5, 1991).

Foreign terms have been deleted from this edition as the result of a letter from Jacques Lesobre, Director, Risk and Insurance Dep't, Groupe Matra, Paris. I now realize that this *Glossary* cannot do justice to the variations foreign terms can take when used in business. A complete source for French/English/American terms is Mr. Lesobre's *Lexicon: Risk, Insurance, Reinsurance* published by Berger-Levrault, Paris.

EDITOR
David Heinze, Senior Editor, NILS Publishing Co., worked long and hard to refine the manuscript. His suggestions and advice were always helpful.

PRINCIPAL REVIEWERS
Special thanks go to three individuals who were of tremendous assistance in keeping me on the straight and narrow path needed for this type of publication:

Douglas H. Hartman, ARM; Risk Management Consultant, Ernst & Young LLP, New York, NY.

Larry L. Klein, CPCU; Director Risk Management Services, Price Waterhouse LLP, Dallas, TX.

Donn McVeigh, CPCU, ARM; Managing Director, Creative Risk Concepts International, Oakland, CA.

The following individuals provided valuable overall counsel:

Richard M. Duvall, PhD, CPCU; Vice President, Sedgwick James, Inc., Nashville, TN.

Karen J. Golden, J.D., CPCU, ARM; Risk Manager, Sears, Roebuck and Co., Hoffman Estates, IL.

Donald S. Malecki, CPCU; President, Donald S. Malecki & Associates, Inc., Cincinnati, OH.

Lawton Swan III, CPCU, CLU; Interisk Corporation, St. Petersburg, FL.

Coleen Ann Mulhern Rupp, Sedgwick, San Francisco, CA.

The following reviewers checked terms in the subjects indicated:

Richard F. Adams, Vice President, California Casualty Insurance Group, San Mateo, CA (*Workers' Compensation*).

Dick Bendten, PE, CSP; Manager of Loss Control, California Casualty Insurance Group, San Mateo, CA (*Loss Control*).

Warren G. Brockmeier, J.D., CPCU, Oak Park, IL (*Professional Liability*).

Wayne T. Browne, CPCU, Vice President, Claims, SAFECO Insurance Co., Seattle, WA (*Automobile*).

Daniel M. Crawford, J.D.; Carroll, Burdick, McDonough, San Francisco, CA (*Law*).

Joseph P. Decaminada, J.D., CPCU, CLU, ChFC; Executive Vice President, The Atlantic Mutual Companies, New York, NY (*Insurer Operations, Law, Regulation*).

Edward W. Frye, Jr., CPCU; Underwriting Consultant Service of Connecticut, Stamford, CT (*Reinsurance*).

Paul E.B. Glad, J.D., Sonnenschein Nath & Rosenthal (*Law*).

Ted O. Hall, CPA, J.D.; Insurance Consultant, Auburn, CA (*Accounting*).

Jerrol L. Harris, CPCU, CLU; Executive Vice President, California Casualty Management Co., San Mateo, CA (*Health, Life*).

Stephen Horn II, CPCU, ARM, AAI; Vice President, Calco Insurance Brokers, San Francisco, CA (*Risk Management*).

Leo Kane, CPCU; Consultant, San Francisco, CA (*Workers' Compensation*).

Lynne M. Miller, President, Environmental Strategies Corporation, Reston, VA (*environmental terms*).

Barbara L. Nielsen, CPA; Partner, Ernst & Young, Los Angeles, CA (*Accounting*).

Joseph C. Sampson, CPCU; Manager, Zurich-American Insurance Co., San Francisco, CA (*Property*).

Brian M. Smith, ARM, CPCU; Director, Fireman's Fund Insurance Company, Novato, CA (*Workers' Compensation*).

Roger L. Smith, CPCU; President, Insurance Education Association, San Francisco, CA (*Agency, Organizations*).

Sawyer Stern, CPCU, ARM, CIC; Assistant Risk Manager, DeKalb Genetics Corporation, Santa Claus, IN (*Loss Control*).

Robert V. Scholes, Engineering Manager, Kemper National Insurance Companies (*Loss Control*).

Judith Tornese, CPCU; Vice President of Risk Management, Transamerica Corp., San Francisco, CA (*Risk Management*).

Pat Warder, PE, CPCU; Pacific Western Safety Services, Snowflake, AZ (*Loss Control*).

David Warren, CPCU; Risk Management Consultant, Orinda, CA (*Property, Risk Management*).

Richard V. Rupp

Richard V. Rupp, CPCU, is Vice President of Risk Management for Calco Insurance Agents & Brokers the brokerage division of the California Casualty Group (San Mateo, CA) and General Manager of American Technology Excess & Surplus Insurance Services, the Group's excess and surplus lines division. He joined the California Casualty Group in May, 1992.

Dick began his insurance career in 1961 with the Pacific Fire Rating Bureau and in 1963 joined Marsh & McLennan, where he spent thirteen years assisting in the development of many risk management concepts widely used today. He was an officer of both Marsh & McLennan and the Continental Insurance Companies, where he headed the western operations of Continental Risk Services. He was also a principal consultant with the risk management consulting firm of Warren, McVeigh & Griffin.

He is an active member of the CPCU Society, Professional Liability Underwriting Society, and the Society of Insurance Research. He serves on the CPCU Publications Committee and is past chair of the CPCU Research Activities Committee. He has conducted seminars for the Society of CPCU, Society of Insurance Research, Risk and Insurance Management Society, Professional Insurance Agents, and the Self-Insurance Institute of America.

He teaches Associate in Risk Management classes and conducts seminars on international insurance for the Insurance Education Association. He also leads seminars on the alternative insurance market for the Society of CPCU. In addition, he is an instructor at the Insurance School of the Pacific, which is sponsored by the Non-Life Insurance Association of Japan, teaching Japanese insurance executives about the U.S. industry.

He edited the New CGL Book, published by the CPCU Society, and co-authored The Alternative Market, published by International Risk Management Institute.

Dick and his wife, Coleen, reside in San Mateo, CA.

Using the Glossary

Subject Categories

Each term is categorized in one or more subject areas, providing the context of the term's usage. The subject categories are:

Accounting	Life Insurance
Agency	Loss Control
Automobile Insurance	Mortgage Insurance
Aviation Insurance	Ocean Marine Insurance
Crime Insurance	Organizations
Employee Benefits	Personal Lines
Financial Guarantee Insurance	Professional Liability Insurance
Financial Planning	Property Insurance
General	Regulation
Health Insurance	Reinsurance
Inland Marine Insurance	Risk Management
Insurer Operations	Surety
International Insurance	Title Insurance
Law	Workers' Compensation
Liability Insurance	

Cross References

Cross-references often follow the definition of a term, referring to other terms. The signals employed for these references are:

synonym: other terms that are used interchangeably with the defined term.
compare: (a) opposites, or antonyms, of the defined term; or (b) terms that are similar in meaning but are distinct.
see: (a) conceptually related terms; or (b) the entry term's primary synonym, where the definition is located.

Form Numbers

Some definitions include a number for the policy or endorsement form that provides the coverage or exclusion described by the defined term. The number includes an abbreviation for the organization that prescribes the form, as follows:

ISO: Insurance Services Office
NCCI: National Council on Compensation Insurance
AAIS: American Association of Insurance Services
ACORD: Agency-Company Organization for Research and Development

There are tables of these selected form numbers in the back.

Abbreviations and Acronyms

An abbreviation or acronym commonly used for a defined term is given in parentheses following the term. If you know an abbreviation but not the term, consult the table in the back.

A

"A" rates
Insurer Operations. Rates that are established by judgment and do not have loss experience statistics as a foundation for their development. These rates are developed by the underwriter or company based on what is believed equitable for the particular risk involved.

compare: manual rates; *see:* account premium modification plan, judgment rates, schedule rating

A.M. Best rating
General.
see: Best's rating

AAA
Organizations.
see: American Automobile Association

AAA tenant
Financial Planning.
see: triple A tenant

abandonment
Ocean Marine/Property. The relinquishing of property by its owner to an insurance company in order to claim a total loss when, in fact, the loss is less than total. This is generally not allowed by property insurance policies, but under certain conditions it is allowed by ocean marine policies.
see: abandonment clause

abandonment clause
Ocean Marine. A provision in some ocean marine policies, allowing the insured to abandon lost or damaged property to the insurance company and claim a total loss. The abandonment clause applies to actual and constructive total losses.
see: abandonment, constructive total loss, salvage, total loss

abatement
Ocean Marine. The refund of duties on damaged or imported goods. The goods may be damaged during importation or while in a bonded warehouse.
see: bonded shipment, bonded warehouse, duty

abatement schedule
Loss Control.
see: compliance schedule

ability to earn
Workers' Compensation. In state workers' compensation laws, an employee's fair average weekly or monthly wage, or an injured worker's earning capacity. In the event of a temporary partial disability, if the injured worker is able to earn less than his or her pre-injury wages, workers' compensation covers a part of the difference (typically two-thirds, but more in some states).
see: reduced earnings, rehabilitation, workers' compensation law

abnormal use
Liability. Use of a product in a manner or for a purpose other than as intended by the manufacturer or seller. Abnormal use may constitute a defense in product liability cases where an injury was caused by using a product in a way that could not have been reasonably foreseen by the manufacturer or seller.
see: product liability insurance

abortion clinics' professional liability insurance
Professional Liability. Insurance that protects abortion clinics from general and professional liability claims. Generally, coverage is written on a hospital liability form and includes coverage for the clinic and its staff. Coverage is usually written on a claims-made basis.

abortion coverage
Health. Coverage under health insurance policies for abortions that are involuntary or necessary to preserve the mother's health. Some policies also

1

cover voluntary abortions by not specifically excluding them.

above-normal loss (ANL)
Insurer Operations. A loss enhanced by secondary conditions or circumstances, such as weather.
see: probable maximum loss

aboveground storage tank pollution liability insurance
Liability. Pollution liability insurance for owners of aboveground storage tanks that provides coverage for third-party bodily injury, property damage, and cleanup expenses arising from the release of hazardous materials from an insured container. Coverage is on a claims-made basis and can apply to a specific site or taks that are scheduled. Excluded are any known pollution conditions existing prior to the inception of the policy and intentional release of pollutants.
see: pollution insurance, underground storage tank pollution liability insurance

absolute assignment
Life. The transfer of all control and rights in a life insurance policy to another party, which cannot be reacquired except by action of the assignee. Such transfers cannot be made to the individual insured by the policy.
see: assignment

absolute beneficiary
Life.
see: irrevocable beneficiary

absolute liability
Law.
see: strict liability

absolute title
Title. An unconditional, indisputable title or right of ownership in real estate; an exclusive title free of any conditions or restrictions.
see: adverse title, fee simple, real estate, title

absorption rate
Property. A rate once used by factory mutuals for their property insurance policies; after January 1, 1986, its use was abandoned. An initial premium deposit was charged, equal to three to five times the net annual premium. On an annual basis, an "absorption"—which equaled the annual premium—took place, which resulted in the premium deposit being reinstated for the following period.
see: Factory Mutual System

abstract
Title.
see: abstract of title, title, title insurance

abstract company
Title. A company that performs title searches or specializes in providing or assisting in abstracts of bids or abstracts of title.
see: abstract of bids, abstract of title

abstract of bids
Surety. An owner's summary of unit prices, allowing the owner to select a contractor by comparing the contractors' bids with the owner's unit price list.
see: bid bond

abstract of title
Title. A written chronological summary of the public records relating to the title of land, including conveyances of the title (such as wills and deeds) and legal proceedings (such as liens). The abstract provides the names of all involved parties and their legal descriptions, as well as a description of the property and its location. An attorney or title insurance underwriter reviews an abstract to determine if there are any title defects that must be cleared before a buyer can purchase a clear title to the property.
see: chain of title, title

abstract plat
Title. A summary of records showing the size, location and owner's name of each lot, parcel, or plot of land within a specified area.
see: plat

abstractors' professional liability insurance
Professional Liability/Title. Insurance that protects title abstractors against claims for negligent acts, errors or omissions. Coverage is often written in conjunction with title agents' errors and omissions insurance. Coverage is usually written on a claims-made basis.
see: abstract company, errors and omissions insurance, title agents' errors and omissions insurance

abuse of minority shareholders
Law/Professional Liability. Actions of corporate directors or officers taken for personal reasons, rather than to further the company's interests, which treat minority shareholders unfavorably. *Examples*: Shares issued to insiders to gain greater control, or excessive compensation paid to favored individuals.
see: directors' and officers' liability insurance, dissenting shareholder

abuse of process
Law.
see: process

abutment
Property. The part of a structure that directly receives thrust or pressure; the area or point where a supporting member touches or adjoins the member it supports.

Academy of Producer Insurance Studies
Organizations. Members: Members of the Society of Certified Insurance Counselors and the Society of Insurance Service Representatives, who are termed "Fellows." Associate memberships are available to other individuals, and a Research Associate membership is available to business organizations. *Objectives:* To provide a comprehensive practical education system for insurance professionals. *Founded:* 1985. *Headquarters:* Austin, TX.

accelerated cost recovery system (ACRS)
Accounting. A method of accelerated depreciation permitted by the U.S. Internal Revenue Code for assets placed in service after 1980 and prior to 1987.
see: accelerated depreciation

accelerated death benefits
Life.
see: living benefits

accelerated depreciation
Accounting. Any method of accounting for depreciation whereby greater depreciation is taken in the early life of an asset and smaller amounts toward the end of the period. Accelerated depreciation permits larger tax deductions in early years.
compare: straight line depreciation; *see:* depreciation

accelerated option
Life. A life insurance policy provision allowing the policyholder to use accumulated policy dividends and cash value to create an endowment, or to pay off the policy premium.
see: accelerative endowment

acceleration clause
Financial Planning. A condition in a loan or mortgage that causes the entire balance of the loan to become due immediately if regular payments are missed or if other contract provisions are breached.

accelerative endowment
Life. One of the accelerated options under a life insurance policy; the endowment elected under this option.
see: accelerated option

acceptance
Insurer Operations. The acceptance of a risk by an underwriter or other person authorized to act on behalf of an insurer. The risk is accepted when the underwriter or other person expresses a willingness to issue an insurance policy.
synonym: assume; *compare:* rejection; *see:* submitted business
Law. The expressed agreement or assent to an offer; one of the elements needed to form a legal contract, with an offer, consideration, competence of the parties, and a legal purpose. In an insurance transaction, acceptance occurs when an applicant indicates agreement to the terms of a binder or policy, usually by paying the premium.
see: consideration, contract, offer

accepted bid
Surety. The quotation that an owner accepts as the basis for entering into a contract with the offeror (contractor) who submitted the bid.
see: bid

accession
Title. An augmentation of title to real estate so the title includes any permanent improvements or betterments to the property.
see: adverse possession, real estate, title

accident
Liability. A sudden, unplanned and unexpected event, not under the control of the insured, resulting in injury or damage.
compare: occurrence; *see:* accidental occurrence, fortuitous event, occupational accident
Property. The peril covered by boiler and machinery insurance; the sudden breakdown of an insured object or a part thereof, which must manifest itself by physical damage to the object requiring repair or replacement.
see: boilers fired vessels and electric steam generators—limited coverage, object, one accident

accident analysis
Loss Control. The analysis of a specific accident by separating or breaking it down into segments, in order to determine its nature, proportion, function or relationship. From this analysis, a report is developed that identifies and evaluates the unsafe conditions or actions associated with the accident in order to prevent reoccurrences.

accident and health insurance (A&H)
Health. A class of insurance that pays benefits for losses caused by disease, accidental injury or accidental death.
see: group accident and health insurance, accident only insurance

accident and sickness insurance
Health.
see: health insurance

3

accident control

Loss Control. Steps taken or procedures implemented to reduce accident potential or to limit accident frequency or severity. Techniques employed often include premises and equipment inspection, education through safety meetings, personal protective equipment, and loss engineering.

see: loss control, loss prevention, loss reduction

accident experience

Loss Control. A loss experience report that relates a risk's frequency of accidents to selected units of measurement, thereby making the loss experience more meaningful to management. For example, the accident experience report may list such things as the rate of disabling injuries, number of lost work days due to accidents, or the number of first-aid cases.

see: loss experience, loss run

accident frequency

Loss Control. The rate at which accidents occur compared to a specific number of exposure units, such as length of time, miles driven, or units produced. This allows an organization to compare its accident frequency between different periods of time or to the frequency of other organizations.

synonym: accident rate; *compare*: accident severity, loss frequency, loss severity

Automobile. The frequency of automobile accidents expressed as the number of accidents per miles driven during a specific period of time.

Liability. The frequency of general or product liability accidents expressed as the number of accidents per a number of units produced or of sales during a specific period of time.

Workers' Compensation. A measurement of workers' compensation accidents expressed as the number of accidents per a given number of hours worked per employee or per employee-years. This has been largely replaced by an incidence rate formula developed by the Occupational Safety and Health Administration.

see: incidence rate, Occupational Safety and Health Act

accident insurance

Health. Insurance under which benefits are payable after a disabling accident. Benefits include lost earnings, medical expenses, and indemnity for death or loss of limbs or sight.

see: business travel accident insurance, health insurance, student accident insurance, travel accident insurance, truckers occupational accident insurance, war risk accident insurance, youth group accident insurance

accident only insurance

Health. Policies providing coverage for death or dismemberment caused by, or hospital and medical services necessitated because of an accident.

see: accident and health insurance, accidental death and dismemberment

accident prevention

Loss Control. A term which has largely been replaced by terms such as "loss prevention" or "loss control." Accident prevention still is used frequently to refer to the loss prevention and control efforts of the National Safety Council and of workers' compensation insurers.

see: loss control, loss prevention, loss reduction

accident rate

Loss Control.

see: accident frequency, incidence rate

accident report

Loss Control. Documentation of an accident prepared by those involved or by third parties; a report of a law enforcement officer following an accident.

see: incident report, notice of loss

accident severity

Loss Control. A measure of the severity or seriousness of loss caused by reported accidents that have occurred over a specific period of time. It can be expressed as the dollar amount of paid or reserved claims or the length of time lost by employees during the time period compared to a specific number of exposure units, such as length of time, miles driven, or units produced. This allows an organization to compare its accident severity between different times or to other organizations.

compare: accident frequency, loss frequency, loss severity

Workers' Compensation. The severity of workers' compensation accidents expressed as days lost per thousand hours of work.

accident year experience

Risk Management. A comparison of all losses (paid or reserved) during a twelve-month period, with all premiums earned for the same period. The losses included in the report are those that occurred during the period (regardless of when reported); premiums included in the report are those earned during the period (regardless of when written). Once calculated for a given period, accident year experience never changes. *Formula*: total losses during a twelve-month period ÷ earned premium for the same period.

see: calendar year experience, policy year experience

accident year statistics

Insurer Operations/Risk Management. Used by insurers and risk managers in forecasting future losses, these statistics show incoming premium and outgoing losses for a 12-month period. Since they show the percentage of the premium that is paid out, these statistics are also important in setting future premiums.

see: loss ratio

accidental bodily injury

Health. An injury to the human body that results from a sudden, unplanned and unexpected event. Often there is a fine line between accidental bodily injury, which would be covered by an accident only insurance policy, and nonaccidental bodily injury, which would not be covered. *Example*: If a person is injured while changing tires of a car because the jack slipped, the injury is accidental; however, if the person strains his back while changing a tire, the injury is not considered accidental.

see: accident, accident only insurance, accidental means

accidental death

Life. A death caused by unexpected and unintended means.

see: death

accidental death and dismemberment (AD&D)

Health. Insurance coverage that pays either a specified amount, or a specified number of weekly disability benefit payments, when the insured dies, loses sight, or loses limbs as the result of an accident.

see: accident only insurance

accidental death benefit

Life. A provision added to a life policy that pays an additional benefit if a person is killed in a serious accident. An extra premium is often, but not always, charged.

synonym: additional death benefit, double indemnity

accidental death insurance

Health/Life. An insurance policy that pays its benefit when an insured is killed in an accident. Most commonly combined with dismemberment insurance and offered as accidental death and dismemberment insurance.

see: accidental death and dismemberment, accident only insurance

accidental means

Health. The unexpected or undesigned cause or instrument of an accident or loss that must be present to trigger coverage under some accident insurance policies.

see: accidental bodily injury

accidental occurrence

Liability. An event or series of events happening by chance or unexpectedly that causes injury or damage. An occurrence can be the result of continuous or repeated exposure to conditions, with no single event causing the injury. On the other hand, an "accident" is generally sudden and at a definite place in time and location.

see: accident, occurrence

accommodation

General. An obligation offered or assumed as a favor to another. There is no consideration required or expected for an accommodation.

compare: consideration, contract

accommodation line

Agency/Insurer Operations. Insurance policies written for an agent or policyholder, covering risks that normally would be rejected based on normal underwriting criteria, but for which coverage is granted because the agent's or policyholder's other business is desirable.

synonym: accommodation risks; *see*: substandard risk

accommodation party

Surety. A person or party signing a commercial document in any capacity (e.g., as a cosigner), for the purpose of lending his or her name to another party to the instrument.

accommodation risks

Agency/Insurer Operations.

see: accommodation line

accord and satisfaction

Insurer Operations. The process of adjusting a previously disputed amount, and paying that amount, to discharge a claim. *Accord* is the agreement to the adjustment; *satisfaction* is the performance and execution of that agreement.

account current

Agency/Insurer Operations. A method of transmitting insurance premiums by an agent to the insurer. The agent prepares a periodic statement showing the premiums due after deducting appropriate commissions and transmits the balance to the insurer.

compare: item basis premium payment, statement basis premium payment; *see*: agent's balances, direct bill

account executive

Agency. An individual—employed by either an insurance agency or brokerage—who is directly responsible for servicing accounts. Often, an account executive specializes in a particular type of coverage or insured or provides account service for a single large organization having numerous policies.

see: servicing broker

Reinsurance. An individual employed by either the

5

reinsurer or the reinsurance intermediary who is responsible for managing the reinsurance account of a particular insurer (the reinsured).
Financial Planning.
see: registered representative

account premium modification plan

Property. An insurance rating plan for large commercial property accounts that considers such factors as prior losses, maintenance, housekeeping and quality of management. Under this rating plan, credits or debits of up to 25% can be applied to the standard (manual) rates.
see: "A" rates, judgment rates

account underwriting

Insurer Operations. A form of underwriting where each prospective insured is considered on its own merits without regard to the class of business involved. This type of underwriting is usually only used on large accounts that qualify for some form of a loss-sensitive insurance program.
compare: class underwriting, loss-sensitive insurance program

accountant

Accounting. A person skilled in the art or system of keeping financial records.
see: Certified Public Accountant

accountants' materiality test

Accounting/Risk Management. A guideline used by accountants to determine the significance of an event's financial impact on a business. The amount most commonly used is 5% of net income before taxes from continuing operations. Any event that has an impact of 5% or greater is considered "material." This test is sometimes used to determine a self-insured's risk retention level.
see: retention

accountants' professional liability insurance

Professional Liability. Professional liability insurance for negligent acts, errors or omissions of accountants or accounting firm officers, partners or employees in connection with professional services. Coverage generally includes protection against loss caused by dishonesty, fraud and misrepresentation. Policies do not cover liability based upon intent to deceive by the insured or any partner. Coverage against liability imposed by the Securities Act of 1933 and its amendments may be added. Coverage is usually written on a claims-made basis.
see: antitrust law violations exclusion, Generally Accepted Accounting Principles, investment product sales exclusion, securities law exclusion

accounting

Accounting. A system or method of recording financial transactions and reporting, verifying and analyzing the results. The surveying of pertinent data and subsequent preparation of statements representing the financial condition of an enterprise. The two most common accounting methods are the cash basis and the accrual method.
see: accrual basis of accounting, cash basis of accounting, cost accounting, Generally Accepted Accounting Principles, tax accounting

accounting controls

Accounting. Procedures used to prevent embezzlement losses, such as internal auditing, physical inventories, and audit trails.

accounting cycle

Accounting. The full sequence of procedures that occur during each accounting period; the recording and posting of transactions.
synonym: accounting period

accounting depreciation

Accounting.
see: depreciation

accounting earned premium

Insurer Operations. The amount of premium that results from calculating the unearned premium reserve of an insurer at the beginning of the period plus the written (booked) premium during the period, minus the unearned premium reserve at the end of the period. Accounting earned premium is the figure indicated in the insurer's annual statement.
compare: exposure earned premium; *see*: earned premium

accounting period

Accounting.
see: accounting cycle

accounting postulates

Accounting. Theoretical assumptions on which modern accounting principles are based.
see: Generally Accepted Accounting Principles

accounting principles

Accounting. The doctrine and principles that serve as an explanation of accounting practices.
see: Generally Accepted Accounting Principles, Statutory Accounting Principles

accounts receivable

Accounting. The amounts that a customer owes a business on a current account for completed sales of goods or services. Deposit accruals and other items not arising out of everyday transactions are not considered accounts receivable.
see: accounts receivable insurance, agency bill,

aging accounts receivable, collection ratio, receivables

accounts receivable insurance

Inland Marine. Insurance covering uncollectible sums, extra collection fees, and costs associated with the reconstruction of records due to destruction of accounts receivable records by an insured peril. (ISO form CM 00 66 or AAIS form IM 660.) The value of blank media upon which records were stored (records, disks or computer tapes) are usually not covered. The coverage includes interest on loans to offset collections, and additional expenses resulting from impaired or damaged records. Large-limit policies can be written on a monthly reporting basis.

see: accounts receivable

accreditation

Regulation.

see: Financial Regulations and Accreditation Program

Accredited Advisor in Insurance (AAI)

Organizations. A professional designation earned after successfully completing three national examinations given by the Insurance Institute of America. The curriculum was developed in conjunction with the Independent Insurance Agents of America consisting of the principles of insurance production, multiple-lines insurance, agency operations and sales management.

see: Insurance Institute of America, Independent Insurance Agents of America

Accredited Record Technician (ART)

Organizations. A professional designation of the American Health Information Management Association based on education and experience.

see: American Health Information Management Association

accredited reinsurer

Regulation/Reinsurance. An insurer that is otherwise unauthorized to do business in the same state as the ceding insurer but which is granted approval to assume reinsurance by meeting requirements of the insurance department. These requirements usually are to file a formal acknowledgment of the jurisdiction of the state; to submit to financial examinations by the state; to provide evidence that the reinsurer is licensed as an insurer or reinsurer in at least one other state or, in the case of an alien insurer, it is lawfully entered through another state; to meet specified surplus requirements; and to file annual financial statements.

compare: admitted insurer; *see*: authorized reinsurance

accretion

Financial Planning. The added principal or interest accruing as a result of investment income.

Property. The gradual accumulation of land (including sand bars and deposits, delta land, etc.) by natural causes, such as alluvial deposits or the flow of rivers. Accretion is of two kinds: alluvial (the deposit of soil), and dereliction (the sinking of water levels).

see: alluvion, avulsion

Title. A title to real estate that includes land that has gradually accumulated from natural causes.

see: real estate, title

accrual

Employee Benefits. The accumulation of benefits under a pension plan from years of employee service.

see: vesting

General. Something that comes about as a natural growth, increase or advantage; that which accumulates or issues after a period of time. *Example*: Profits of mutual companies accrue to policyholders.

see: accumulation

accrual basis of accounting

Accounting. A method of recording earnings and expenses as they occur or are incurred, without regard to the actual date of collection or payment.

compare: cash basis of accounting; *see*: accounting, accrued expense, accrued income, accrued interest

accrual of discount

Insurer Operations. Adjustments made to the original purchase price of bonds when those bonds were purchased for less than par value, in order to increase the book value to par at the maturity date.

accrued benefit cost method

Employee Benefits.

see: unit credit actuarial cost method

accrued expense

Accounting. An expense that has been incurred but not yet paid.

see: accrual basis of accounting; *compare*: accrued income

accrued future service benefit

Employee Benefits. The portion of an employee benefit plan participant's retirement benefit attributable to service after the plan's effective date and prior to a specified current date.

see: employee benefit plan

accrued income

Accounting. Income that has been earned but not

yet received.

compare: accrued expense; *see*: accrual basis of accounting

accrued interest

Accounting. Interest that has been earned but not yet received.

compare: accumulated interest; *see*: accrual basis of accounting

accumulated benefit cost method

Employee Benefits.

see: unit credit actuarial cost method

accumulated depreciation

Accounting. The total reduction in an asset's value as of a given date as the result of accounting or financial depreciation.

see: depreciation

accumulated funding deficiency

Employee Benefits. A deficiency in a pension plan's funding standard account. This is caused by a failure to meet the minimum funding standards established by ERISA for pension plans.

see: funding standard account, minimum funding standard

accumulated interest

Accounting. Interest payments that are past due and unpaid.

compare: accrued interest

accumulated plan benefit method

Employee Benefits.

see: unit credit actuarial cost method

accumulation

Life. Increases made to a life insurance policy's benefits, such as interest on accumulated dividends left with the company or increased cash values. The benefits are a reward to the insured for continuous renewal of the policy.

synonym: accumulation benefits; *see*: accumulation period

Health. Increases made to health insurance policy benefits as the result of continuous policy renewals.

accumulation benefits

Life.

see: accumulation

accumulation period

Health. The period of time during which the insured accumulates covered expenses to satisfy the policy deductible, usually either a calendar year or the policy period.

see: deductible, policy period

Life. The period during which the insured makes premium payments on a life insurance policy; the

time prior to the commencement of income payments under an annuity.

compare: liquidation period; *see*: accumulation

accumulation trust

Financial Planning. A trust established for a limited time to distribute the accumulated income and gains from the sale of another trust's assets.

see: trust

accumulation value

Life. A value accumulated in a universal life insurance policy calculated by taking the sum of all premiums paid and interest credited to the account, less deductions for expenses, loans and surrenders.

see: cash surrender value, level death benefit option, universal life insurance

acid and chemical damage insurance

Property. Coverage of property losses caused by acids and chemicals.

acid rain

Property. Precipitation containing pollutants. It is formed by the combination of rain, fog or snow with sulfur dioxide and nitrogen oxide from volcanic eruption, coal-burning utilities and other industrial and transportation sources. It causes damage to forests, aquatic systems, and buildings. Such damage is excluded from most property and casualty insurance policies.

see: pollution exclusion, pollution insurance

acid-test ratio

Financial Planning/Surety.

see: quick ratio

acknowledgment

Law. Admission, confession, avowal, affirmation, or declaration of responsibility. Most states have adopted a uniform standard of acknowledgment, the Uniform Acknowledgment Act.

see: admission, affirmation, stipulation

ACORD Corporation

Organizations.

see: Agency-Company Organization for Research and Development Corporation

ACORD forms

Agency/Insurer Operations. Industry-wide, standardized forms developed by insurance companies and agency groups for insurance applications, certificates of insurance, quotations, etc.

see: Agency-Company Organization for Research and Development Corporation, uniform forms

acquiescence

Law. The act of implying consent by remaining silent. When there has been an infringement of rights, either implied or specific, and the victim of the infringement agrees to continue as though nothing has occurred, the victim's acquiescence may be considered an assent to the alleged infringement.

see: estoppel, laches, reservation of rights, waiver

acquired immune deficiency syndrome (AIDS)

Health. A disease that progressively weakens the immune system, making it impossible to fight off infections. The causative agent is called the human immunodeficiency virus (HIV), which is transmitted in body fluids, such as blood or semen. As yet, there is no known cure for the disease.

see: AIDS/HIV risk coverage, blood bank professional liability insurance, communicable disease exclusion, extra percentage tables, human immunodeficiency virus, limited policy, living benefits, specified disease insurance, viatical settlement

acquisition cost

Insurer Operations. The expense incurred by an insurance company to solicit and underwrite new insurance policies. These expenses include advertising expenses, commissions paid to agents or brokers, inspection expenses, credit and motor vehicle report fees, medical examination fees, and rating and underwriting expenses.

see: administrative expenses

Reinsurance. The expenses (administrative, commissions, etc.) incurred by a reinsurer that are directly related to acquiring business from ceding companies.

see: ceding commission

act of God

Property. A natural disaster or force of nature, such as an earthquake, hurricane or flood.

Liability. If negligence is alleged in a tort action, proof that an act of God is the direct or proximate cause of the injury or damage may relieve the defendant of responsibility or may limit liability to the portion of harm caused by negligence.

see: act of God bond, catastrophe loss, commercial impracticability, force majeure coverage, natural perils, proximate cause, vis major

act of God bond

Financial Planning/Reinsurance. A bond issued by an insurer with repayment terms linked to the company's losses from natural disasters. Investors are paid a higher rate of return than on most corporate bonds, and they share the insurer's risk of catastrophe losses. Interest on the bond may be a certain number of points above U.S. Treasury bonds or other benchmark investments. If a large disaster strikes, bondholders may be required to forgive some or all of the principal, or the bonds might be

automatically converted into stock of the insurer.

see: act of God, catastrophe loss, corporate bond, risk securitization

acting insurer

Insurer Operations. An insurer performing duties for another, or performing temporary services.

see: fronting

acting representative

General. A person with authority to act on behalf of another person or organization while performing temporary service or holding temporary rank or position.

see: agency

action

Law. A proceeding in a court of law. Insurance policies usually restrict actions against the insurer with time limits on the commencement of a suit. The time limit is usually one year from the date of the occurrence of the loss or one year after the cause of action begins.

see: cause of action, statute of limitations

action over

Workers' Compensation.

see: third-party-over suit

active life fund

Life. An unallocated fund maintained for active participants included under a deposit administration plan. As participants retire, individual annuities are purchased with money from this fund.

synonym: deposit account, deposit administration fund, deposit fund, purchase payment fund; *see*: deposit administration plan

active life reserve

Health/Life.

see: policy reserve

active malfunction

Liability. A product defect that does not simply render the product ineffective, but makes it counterproductive by causing damage to the user. Active malfunction claims are insured under product liability insurance. *Example*: An insecticide effective on pests but which also kills the crops.

see: bench error, latent defect, product liability insurance

active retention

Risk Management.

see: retention, self-insurance

acts of independent contractor

Liability. An independent contractor is free to do a job in his or her own way, subject to no other person's direct control. Therefore, one who employs an independent contractor is generally not liable for the acts of the independent contractor.

see: agency, contingent liability, general contractor, independent contractor, respondeat superior

actual authority

Agency. An insurance agent's authority that the insurer (the principal) intentionally confers on the agent in writing.

compare: expressed authority, implied authority; *see*: agency, principal (*Agency*)

actual cash value (ACV)

Property. Valuation of property based on the cost of repairing or replacing it with property of like kind and quality. Usually, actual cash value equals the current replacement cost minus depreciation (based on age, condition, time in use, and obsolescence). Other factors, such as the nature and market value of the property, may be considered.

Automobile. An insurance valuation method used for automobiles which is based on the cost of repairing or replacing the damaged auto with one of like kind and quality, or its replacement cost less physical depreciation. The replacement cost is based on market value replacement cost, which varies by geographic region.

Crime. The definition is expanded in some crime insurance forms when applied to material being processed and finished merchandise ready for sale. For material being processed, actual cash value includes the processing charge less unincurred expenses. For merchandise ready for sale, it includes the selling price minus discounts and unincurred expenses.

synonym: cash value; *compare*: depreciated value, functional replacement cost, manufacturer's selling price, market value, replacement cost, reproduction cost, tax-appraised value; *see*: valuation of potential property loss

actual cash value loss settlement roof surfacing endorsement

Personal. An endorsement (ISO form HO 04 93) to the Insurance Services Office's homeowners policies that substitutes actual cash value for replacement cost for roof surfacing damaged by windstorm or hail.

see: homeowners policy—property coverage

actual damage clause

Surety. A surety provision providing that an architect or engineer will arbitrate between the owner and contractor in determining damages from a proved breach of contract by the contractor.

see: arbitration

actual damages

Law.

see: compensatory damages

actual loss sustained

Property. Under a business income or other time element form, the value of loss due to suspension of business and lost income caused by physical damage to the insured property, plus expenses that would not have been incurred had the property not been damaged.

see: business income coverage form

actual total loss

Ocean Marine/Property.

see: total loss

actuarial

Risk Management. Pertaining to statistical calculations that are usually done by an actuary.

see: actuary, open group actuarial cost method, unit credit actuarial cost method

actuarial adjustment

Risk Management. A change in premiums, size of reserves, rates of reserve buildup, and other calculations that reflect actual loss experience and expenses and expected, but unpaid, benefits.

actuarial assumptions

Risk Management. The facts or suppositions utilized by an actuary to forecast uncertain future events. Assumptions on such subjects as future interest rates, claims costs, payrolls, etc. are indicated in the actuary's report.

actuarial benefit equivalence

Risk Management. A comparison of benefits under different plans.

see: actuarial equivalence tables

actuarial cost method

Risk Management. A method to determine a pension plan's future benefits based on current fixed contributions or the contributions required to reach a desired benefit level at a future time. Several different factors are considered in this calculation, such as mortality forecasts, expenses, interest, labor turnover, salary scales and retirement rates.

see: actuarial funding method, open group actuarial cost method, unit credit actuarial cost method

actuarial department

Insurer Operations. The employees and operations of an insurance company whose principal functions are developing premium rates and rating procedures, determining reserve adequacy, and assisting in the drafting of policy language.

actuarial equivalence tables

Risk Management. Tables of numbers that provide factors to be assigned to various coverages for comparing the actuarial benefit equivalence across plans.

see: actuarial benefit equivalence

actuarial equivalent

Employee Benefits/Risk Management. Two or more benefits that are of equal actuarial present value. When two series of payments have equal present values, assuming a given interest rate and mortality according to a specified mortality table, they are actuarially equivalent.

see: present value

actuarial funding method

Risk Management. A funding method selected by an actuary to determine the amount and timing of contributions needed to meet a specified financial obligation.

see: actuarial cost method

actuarial gains and losses

Employee Benefits/Risk Management. A comparison between a past event predicted by actuarial methods and the event that actually occurred. Actuarial gains result when experience under the plan is better than the actuary's estimates. Actuarial losses result when experience is less favorable than the actuary's estimates. In the case of a pension plan, this comparison is used to calculate funding needs.

actuarial liability

Risk Management.

see: present value

actuarial present value

Risk Management.

see: present value

actuarial report

Risk Management. A report prepared and signed by an actuary, indicating current conditions or future requirements of an insurer, self-insured or pension fund to meet its obligations.

actuarial science

Risk Management. The technical and mathematical aspects of insurance, including the determination of premium rates, premium and loss reserves, dividends, and other management statistical studies.

see: statistics

actuarial soundness

Employee Benefits. A written, signed report prepared by an actuary stating that, in the actuary's opinion, reserves established to fund a pension plan are adequate to make projected benefit payments.

see: actuarial cost method

Risk Management. The degree of confidence that an actuary expresses in his or her opinion.

actuarial valuation

Employee Benefits. The determination by an actuary as to whether pension plan contributions are being accumulated at a sufficient rate to fund promised benefits. The actuarial valuation indicates the plan's actuarial liabilities and identifies the plan assets available to meet such liabilities.

see: actuarial cost method

Risk Management. The determination by an actuary at a specific date of the value of an insurance company's or self-insured's reserves or liabilities.

actuaries' and pension consultants' professional liability

Professional Liability. A form of errors and omissions insurance for actuaries and pension consultants. This coverage is generally designed to meet the requirements under the Employee Retirement Income Security Act, which created specific responsibilities for fiduciaries and standards of competence for actuaries and pension consultants working with pension and employee benefit plans. Coverage is usually written on a claims-made basis.

see: errors and omissions insurance

actuary

Risk Management. An individual, often holding a professional degree, who uses mathematical skills to define, analyze, and solve complex business and social problems involving insurance and employee benefit programs. Actuaries analyze many of life's contingencies (e.g., birth, marriage, sickness, accidents, loss of property, third-party liability, retirement, death) and the financial effects that these have on insurance and benefit programs. Many of these programs involve long-range financial obligations, for which actuarial forecasts are fundamental in maintaining a sound financial basis: rate-making, premium determination, loss reserves, investment valuation, pension benefits, and insurance statistics.

see: Fellow of the Casualty Actuarial Society, Fellow of the Society of Actuaries, Fellow of the Society of Pension Actuaries

actuary enrolled

Risk Management. An actuary who has been professionally certified by the Internal Revenue Service and the Department of Labor and is thereby authorized to sign actuarial reports mandated by Title II of the Employee Retirement Income Security Act.

see: actuary

acupuncture professional liability insurance

Professional Liability. A form of professional liability insurance designed for acupuncture specialists that provides coverage for claims arising from the failure of a professional skill or learning, misconduct, negligence, or incompetence in the performance of services. Coverage is usually written on a claims-made basis.

see: professional liability insurance

acute health care facility

Health. A hospital or clinic that is equipped to provide medical and surgical care for seriously ill or injured people. It includes equipment and facilities for emergency treatment and surgical and extensive diagnostic procedures.

compare: skilled nursing facility, transitional care facility

acute toxicity

Loss Control.

see: LD$_{50}$

ad valorem bill of lading

Ocean Marine.

see: valued bill of lading

add-on no-fault benefits

Automobile. A policy provision that adds no-fault benefits, where permitted, to automobile liability coverages without restricting the right of the victim to sue the wrongdoer.

see: no-fault insurance

addendum

Surety. A document issued prior to the opening of bids that clarifies, corrects, or changes bidding documents or contract documents.

see bid

additional coverage

Property.

see: coverage extension

additional death benefit

Life. A benefit payable in addition to the face amount of a life insurance policy in the event of death by accident. A once-common provision doubled the face amount, so the provision was called *double indemnity.*

synonym: accidental death benefit, double indemnity, multiple indemnity; *see*: death benefit (*Life*)

additional deposit privilege

Life. A clause in universal life insurance policies allowing the policyholder to make unscheduled premium payments at any time prior to the policy's maturity date.

see: universal life insurance

additional expense insurance

Property.

see: additional living expense insurance, extra expense insurance

additional extended coverage

Property. Coverage for property damage caused by

such perils as vandalism and malicious mischief; water from ruptured plumbing and heating systems; glass breakage; ice, snow, and freezing; falling trees and collapse. These coverages are in addition to extended coverage and are often provided in conjunction with a fire insurance or package policy.

compare: coverage extension, extended coverages; *see*: package policy

additional insurance

General. Any added coverages or increased limits to an existing policy.

additional insured

General. A person or entity, other than the named insured, who is protected by the policy, most often in regard to a specific interest.

Life. A person, other than the individual whose life the policy was originally intended to cover, who is added to a life insurance policy as an additional insured. *Example:* A child may be added to the policy of a parent. This method of providing life insurance is generally less expensive than the purchase of a separate policy.

synonym: additional interest; *see*: family life policy

additional insured—lessor

Automobile. An endorsement (ISO form CA 20 01) to a commercial auto policy that adds the owner of a leased or rented vehicle as an insured under the lessee's policy. The endorsement insures the lessor on the same basis as if the auto were owned rather than hired or borrowed.

see: automobile insurance

additional interest

Life.

see: additional insured

Property. The interest of another party or entity in an insurance policy, usually because that party has provided financing for an insured property or automobile. The additional interest is usually stated in an endorsement attached to, or a certificate issued under, the policy.

see: additional insured, insurable interest, loss payee

additional living expense insurance

Personal. Coverage included in residential property insurance policies (for homeowners, condominium owners, renters) that provides payments when a property loss results in extraordinary living expenses for the insured. It covers expenses such as hotel rooms, restaurant meals, and laundry costs to permit the insured household to maintain its normal standard of living.

synonym: additional expense insurance; *compare*: extra expense insurance

additional medical coverage
Workers' Compensation. An endorsement attached to a workers' compensation policy that provides medical benefits above those described by the workers' compensation law. In a small number of states, medical benefits are still subject to a statutory limit; this endorsement extends that limited coverage.
see: coverage A, workers' compensation law

additional perils
Ocean Marine.
see: Inchmaree perils

additional premium (AP)
Insurer Operations. The premium due to an insurer on an insurance policy in addition to the initial premium, as a result of increased coverage, increased rates, retrospective rate calculations, or a premium audit.
compare: initial premium, return premium; *see*: audit, premium

additional provisions
General. Any clauses added to the existing insuring and benefit provisions of a policy, or to the standard or uniform provisions, to further define, extend, or limit the coverages.
synonym: general provisions

additur
Law. A judge's increase to an award of damages made by a jury. The judge can deny a plaintiff's motion for a new trial provided the defendant accepts a specified additur. If the defendant does not consent, the court grants the plaintiff's motion for a new trial, and the defendant may appeal this ruling. If the defendant accepts the additur, the court denies the new trial motion, and the plaintiff may appeal the denial.
compare: punitive damages; *see*: damages, nominal damages

adequate
Regulation. Most state insurance laws or regulations require that an insurer's rates be adequate to cover the cost of doing business, pay claims, and provide a reasonable profit.
compare: excessive; *see*: nondiscriminatory, rate making

adhesion contract
Law.
see: contract of adhesion

adit
Loss Control. A horizontal tunnel built into a hillside for mining, exploration or drainage.
see: cross-cut, raise

adjacent building
Loss Control/Property. A building situated very close to, but not in contact with, another building.
compare: adjoining building; *see*: exposure

adjoining building
Loss Control/Property. A building that touches another building.
compare: adjacent building; *see*: party wall

adjudicate
Law. To settle or decide a controversy through the presentation of a claim and evidence to a court.
see: arbitration, litigation

adjustable barrier guard
Loss Control. An enclosure attached to the frame of a machine with adjustable sections that protect workers using the machinery from injury.
see: barrier guard

adjustable life insurance
Life. A life insurance policy that allows the policyholder to change the face value, premiums, and certain other terms at his or her own discretion.
compare: universal life insurance

adjustable policy
Property. A policy that covers property with changing values, such as the inventory of retail stores. The insured reports the value of all items to be covered by the policy to the insurance company at stated periods. The premium is adjusted to reflect the increased or decreased value of the property.
compare: adjustable premium; *see*: insurable value, reporting form

adjustable premium
Health/Life. A premium that can vary. An insurer retains the right to change the premium or premium rate structure on a class of insureds or business during the year and apply the new rates to renewal policies.
compare: adjustable policy, retrospective rating plan (*Insurer Operations*); *see*: annualization

adjustable rate mortgage (ARM)
Financial Planning.
see: variable rate mortgage

adjusted base cost
Property. The cost (per square foot of building space) that is subject to adjustment if alternative components are used.

adjusted earnings
Insurer Operations. An estimate of insurance company earnings that considers written premium, income growth and net earnings from operations.

13

adjusted net worth

Insurer Operations. An insurer's adjusted net worth is calculated by taking the total of the company's capital, surplus, voluntary reserves, estimated value of in-force policies, and unrealized capital gains, less any income tax due on the capital gains.

adjuster

Insurer Operations.
see: claims adjuster

adjusters' errors and omissions insurance

Professional Liability. A form of profession liability insurance designed for an individual claims adjuster or claims adjusting firm for breach of duty by reason of any alleged negligent act, error or omission committed by the adjuster or adjusting firm. Coverage is usually written on a claims-made basis.

see: errors and omissions insurance

adjustment

Insurer Operations.
see: claim adjustment

adjustment bond

Financial Planning. A corporate bond issued to assist in funding a corporate reorganization.
see: corporate bond

adjustment bureau

General. An organization that provides loss adjustment services to insurers. It is used to supplement staff adjusters and by insurers that do not employ their own staff adjusters.

see: allocated claim expense, claims adjuster

adjustment expenses

Insurer Operations. Expenses associated with adjusting an insurance claim, such as investigation and usual expenses, but excluding actual claim payments or adjustments.

see: claim expense

adjustment income

Life. Benefits payable to a surviving spouse or other beneficiary as a part of the life insurance policy when the primary wage earner dies. Such a payment is intended to provide for the beneficiary until the beneficiary becomes self-sufficient. Adjustment income is the amount and period of time over which such payments are made. This coverage can be purchased at the same time as the original policy, or it can be added for an extra premium at a later date.

see: readjustment income

administration bond

Surety. A form of fiduciary bond that guarantees the faithful performance and fidelity of an executor

or administrator of a will, trust or estate.
see: fiduciary bond

administrative agent

Risk Management.
see: third-party administrator

administrative expenses

Insurer Operations. Costs incurred in operating an insurance company, excluding loss adjusting expenses, acquisition costs, and investment expenses.

see: acquisition cost

administrative law

Law. The body of law created by state or federal executive or independent agencies pursuant to legislative authority. Administrative law usually takes the form of rules, regulations, orders, and decisions. Insurance department regulations are a form of administrative law.

compare: civil law (1), common law, criminal law; *see*: administrative law judge, administrative order

administrative law judge

Law. An official who performs judicial functions at administrative hearings, having the power to administer oaths and affirmations, rule on questions of evidence, take testimony, make determinations of fact, and impose legislatively authorized penalties for violations of laws or regulations.

synonym: hearing officer; *see*: administrative law

administrative order

Regulation. A regulation issued by an administrative agency, such as an insurance department, that clarifies or implements a law or public policy. Orders must be based on statutes passed by the legislature.

see: administrative law

administrative procedure

Regulation. Rules governing practice and procedure allowed before federal or state administrative agencies, as distinguished from the judicial procedure usually applied to courts.

see: emergency rules and regulations

administrative services arrangement

Health/Life/Risk Management.
see: administrative services only

administrative services only (ASO)

Health/Life/Risk Management. An arrangement whereby an insurer agrees to provide services to a self-insured entity, such as providing printed claim forms, and processing and auditing claims. The insurer does not assume any insurance risk under an ASO arrangement.

synonym: administrative services arrangement;

see: deposit administration plan, third-party administrator

administrator
Law. An individual legally vested with the right of controlling an estate.
Risk Management. An individual or firm appointed by a self-insured employer to administer its plan.
see: third-party administrator

admiralty
Law/Ocean Marine. Maritime law, or a court with jurisdiction over cases arising from incidents in navigable waters.
see: maritime

admiralty court
Law/Ocean Marine. The court or system of courts having jurisdiction over maritime questions and offenses, including suits involving marine insurance policies and general average adjustments.
see: admiralty proceeding

admiralty liability
Law/Ocean Marine. Liability that arises or results from any type of maritime activity.
see: Jones Act, seaman's remedies

admiralty proceeding
Ocean Marine. A proceeding involving questions of admiralty law, generally settled by an admiralty court. In the U.S., federal courts have jurisdiction over admiralty and maritime actions.
see: admiralty court

admission
Law. In a criminal proceeding, an acknowledgment by the accused regarding the existence of matters of fact that on their own are insufficient to establish guilt. In a civil proceeding, a positive affirmation of fact or of an allegation, usually made during pretrial discovery by either party.
see: acknowledgment, affirmation, allegation, civil law (1), criminal law, discovery, stipulation

admission certification
Health. A medical utilization review procedure for assessing an individual's physical and psychological condition and whether that condition requires admission to a hospital or other inpatient institution.
see: utilization review

admission temporaire
International. The free entry into a country of goods usually subject to tax for the purpose of processing them for re-export to other countries.
synonym: temporary admission; *see*: ATA carnet

admitted assets
Insurer Operations. Assets of an insurer that the state insurance department or other regulatory authority include in determining the insurer's financial condition. Usually, assets must be convertible into cash at reasonably predictable values, and a portion must be quickly convertible (i.e., it must have a high degree of liquidity).
compare: excluded assets, nonadmitted assets; *see*: annual statement, assets, legal list, Statutory Accounting Principles

admitted company
Insurer Operations.
see: admitted insurer

admitted insurance
International/Regulation. Insurance written on locally approved policy forms by an insurer licensed, registered or authorized to do business in the country where the insured risk is located.
compare: nonadmitted insurance; *see*: admitted insurer

admitted insurance regulations
International. Legislation or rules that govern whether nonadmitted insurance policies are permitted in a country or jurisdiction.
see: admitted insurance, nonadmitted insurance

admitted insurer
Regulation. An insurance company authorized to do business in a state by the state's insurance department. While the procedure may vary from state to state, approval is usually granted when an insurer presents financial information demonstrating its financial stability.
synonym: admitted company, authorized insurer; *compare*: accredited insurer, nonadmitted insurer; *see*: authorized reinsurance
International. An insurance company authorized to do business in a country by being licensed or approved to conduct business there. Many countries require the use of local or admitted insurance companies to insure risks within their country.
compare: nonadmitted insurer; *see*: admitted insurance

admitted liability
Aviation. In aviation insurance, payments to an injured passenger made without the need of establishing liability.
see: aviation insurance

admitted market
Regulation. The market provided by insurers that are admitted to do business in a state or jurisdiction.
compare: nonadmitted market; *see*: admitted insurer

15

admitted reinsurance
Insurer Operations/Reinsurance.
see: authorized reinsurance

adult day care
Health. Daytime services such as health, medical, psychological, social, nutritional or educational care that allow an elderly or disabled adult to function in his or her own home, rather than having to be admitted to an inpatient institution.
compare: convalescent care; *see*: custodial care, dependent adult

advance deposit premium plan
Reinsurance. A reinsurance contract premium that is paid in advance and held in a fund by the reinsurer for payment of the reinsured's losses. Upon termination of the contract, the fund balance, minus paid losses and any agreed reinsurer expenses, is returned to the ceding insurer.
synonym: banking plan

advance directive
Health. A signed document stating the declarant's wishes regarding the use of medical interventions in the event of a loss of decision-making capacity. It may contain a refusal of extraordinary treatment (as in a living will) and may appoint a person as a proxy or surrogate to make health care decisions on behalf of the declarant.
see: brain death, do not resuscitate order, living will, Patient Self-Determination Act

advance discount for mortality
Employee Benefits/Life.
see: discounting for mortality

advance discount for severance
Employee Benefits/Life.
see: discounting for severance

advance freight
Aviation/Inland Marine. The partial payment of a freight bill-of-lading prior to shipment. Typically, payment is made when the freight is accepted for shipment by the carrier.
compare: free on board; *see*: freight

advance payment
Insurer Operations. An amount tendered with an application for coverage, or any premium paid before the beginning of a policy period. Advance payment on some policies may result in a discount.
see: deposit premium

advance payment bond
Surety. A guarantee that a principal will repay or liquidate any money advanced to it that is related to construction, supply bonds, or other contracts.
see: bond (*Surety*)

advance premium
Insurer Operations.
see: deposit premium

adventure
Ocean Marine. The commercial enterprise in which a vessel and its cargo are subjected to the hazard of a loss at sea.
see: adventure clause, common venture, venture

adventure clause
Ocean Marine. An accurate description in the declarations of an insurance policy of a proposed trip or voyage, so that insurance may precisely cover the insured.
see: adventure

adverse possession
Law/Title. A method whereby someone other than the true legal owner of a property takes title to the property by openly possessing it for a period of time prescribed by statute.
see: adverse title, possession

adverse selection
Insurer Operations. The demand for insurance coverage by those with the greatest loss exposures, which is greater than the demand for coverage by those with average or lesser exposures. The insuring of risks that are more prone to losses than the average results in a higher general level of premiums.
compare: anti-selection; *see*: benefit of selection, ultimate mortality table
Reinsurance. The ceding of high-risk business to reinsurers and the retention of more desirable business.

adverse title
Title. A title to real estate that stands in opposition to or in defeasance of another title, or a title acquired or claimed by adverse possession.
see: adverse possession, real estate, title

adverse underwriting decision
Insurer Operations. An unfavorable decision regarding an individual insurance application. It includes refusal to accept a risk, termination or restriction of coverage, acceptance only at a higher rate, or placement through an assigned risk or other risk-sharing plan.

advertisement to bid
Surety. Public notice of construction or demolition work to be undertaken, giving contractors an opportunity to bid for the work.
synonym: invitation to bid, request for proposal

16

advertiser's liability coverage
Liability.
see: advertising injury coverage

advertisers' and advertising agency liability insurance
Professional Liability. A form of professional liability insurance designed for advertisers and ad agencies that provides coverage for loss imposed by law or assumed under contract resulting from libel, slander, infringement of copyright, piracy, or invasion of privacy committed in any advertisement, publicity article, or broadcast or telecast of the insured's advertising.
see: advertising injury coverage, libel, slander

advertising injury coverage
Liability. Coverage for advertising injury provided by the commercial general liability policy under coverage Part B and by some umbrella policies. *Advertising injury* is a statement made in the course of advertising activities that causes loss to another person or business by libel, slander, defamation, violation of a right of privacy, piracy or misappropriation of ideas, or infringement of copyright, trademark, title or slogan. Coverage can also be purchased as a separate advertiser's liability policy or as an endorsement to another business policy form.
see: advertisers' and advertising agency liability insurance, broadcasters' liability insurance, commercial general liability policy, copyright, defamation, patent insurance, personal and advertising injury liability, trademark

advisory loss cost rating
Insurer Operations.
see: loss cost rating

advisory organization
General. An organization that provides support services to insurer rating bureaus or governmental agencies (e.g., rates, forms or statistics).
see: Insurance Services Office, rating bureau

Advocates for Highway and Auto Safety
Organizations. Members: Consumers, law enforcement groups, and insurance organizations dedicated to highway and auto safety. *Objectives*: To promote highway safety legislation, standards, and programs to reduce highway accidents. *Founded*: 1989. *Headquarters*: Washington, D.C.

affiant
Law.
see: affidavit

affidavit
Law. A voluntary, written statement of fact made under oath or affirmation before an authorized official. The affiant (the person making the statement)

is not questioned or interviewed in the document by attorneys; it is simply the affiant's statement.
compare: deposition; *see*: affidavit of claim, affirmation, oath

affidavit of claim
Insurer Operations. A statement containing the facts on which an insurance claim is based.
see: proof of loss

affiliated insurers
Insurer Operations. Insurance companies that are closely tied to each other through common stock ownership or interlocking directorates.
see: fleet of companies, intercompany transaction, parent company, pup company, subsidiary company

affiliation of health providers
Health. Health care providers that are linked together under a formal or informal agreement to provide services to certain patients, either as a subcontractor or backup facility.
see: backup facility agreement

affinity group
Insurer Operations. Insureds or potential insureds with common, distinct characteristics, activities or interests (e.g., members of a social organization, people in a particular business or industry) that insurance companies can use to design targeted marketing strategies, coverages (often multiple lines), and other services.
compare: fictitious group; *see*: group insurance, target marketing

affirm
Law. To assert, ratify, or repeat a solemn declaration of fact or trust; to agree with an earlier judgment; to agree that an affidavit is true.
see: affirmation, attest, stipulation

affirmation
Law. A solemn, formal pledge to tell the truth by persons with religious or conscientious objection to swearing an oath.
compare: oath; *see*: acknowledgment, admission, stipulation

affirmative defense
Law. An assertion in the defendant's answer to a complaint that the plaintiff's suit is barred, even assuming the alleged injury or loss, on certain legal grounds. These grounds include the defendant's duress or necessity, the plaintiff's assumption of risk, the plaintiff's contributory negligence, the expiration of a statute of limitations, or other legal justification of the defendant's conduct. Affirmative defenses must be separately identified and asserted in

the defendant's answer.

see: accord and satisfaction, answer, assumption of risk, contributory negligence, defendant, duress, duty to defend, estoppel, statute of limitations

affirmative warranty
Insurer Operations.
see: warranty (1)

affreightment
Ocean Marine. A charter party or bill of lading contract to transport goods by an ocean vessel.
synonym: contract of carriage; *see*: bill of lading, charter party

after-acquired property
Financial Planning. Property acquired after the date of a loan or mortgage, which becomes additional security for the loan.

after-market replacement parts
Automobile.
see: non-original equipment manufacturer's replacement parts

aftercare
Health. A contact made with a patient following a surgical procedure or other health treatment process to support the gains made in the treatment.
see: convalescent care

aftercharge
Property. A premium charge added to a commercial fire insurance policy that can be deleted if the insured complies with certain fire prevention recommendations (e.g., providing fire extinguishers or smoke alarms).
compare: increased hazard; *see*: fault of management

age
General. For most legal documents, age is the whole number of years since birth, as determined by the most recent birthday. Automobile insurance applications and annuities use this method of determining age in their underwriting and rating formulas.
Life. For life insurance rating, two common age options are used: 1. age closest to the insured's birthday; 2. age at the insured's last birthday.
see: age change, age discrimination, age limits, attained age, misstatement of age, original age

age-adjustment clause
Life. A provision in life insurance policies that allows for the adjustment of the amount payable at the death of the insured, if it is shown that the age of the insured was misrepresented. Usually, the amount payable at death in such cases is the amount of coverage that the premium would have

purchased for the applicant at his or her true age and sex when the insurance was taken out.
see: age, misstatement of age

age change
Life. For life insurance rating purposes, the date, midway between natural birth dates, when a person's age is deemed to advanced to the next higher.
see: age

age discrimination
Automobile. The use of age as a rating factor in automobile insurance, where drivers between 30 and 60 years of age are considered preferred risks; drivers under 30 and over 60 have a difficult time obtaining coverage and pay significantly higher premiums. Insurers treat age groups differently because statistics indicate that very young and very old drivers have a greater number of accidents than those in the middle years of life. Older drivers may receive a rate discount based on substantially reduced driving, but the rate adjustment for age is likely to increase the insurance cost per mile driven.
Health/Life. The use of age as a component affecting rates and premiums. Usually, premiums increase as an individual's age increases. For some policies, there is an upper limit on age, above which the insurer will not accept an application for insurance.
see: age limits, uniform premium
Liability. Liability for claims alleging age discrimination may or may not be covered by the definition of "personal injury" in a liability policy. Some policies specify the types of discrimination claims that are covered, which may include discrimination based on age.
see: discrimination, employment practices liability insurance, personal injury
Regulation.
see: Age Discrimination in Employment Act

Age Discrimination in Employment Act (ADEA)
Regulation. Federal legislation adopted in 1967 and amended in 1978 that prohibits discrimination against workers over 40 years of age. Employers involved in interstate commerce or who have 20 or more employees may not discriminate on the basis of age in hiring, job termination, compulsory retirement, adverse job assignments, or employee benefits.

age "rate up"
Life.
see: substandard life expectancy

age limits
Health/Life. Underwriting age limits established

for life and health policies. Applicants can be declined because they are younger or older than specified age limits.

see: age, age discrimination

age of development
Risk Management.
see: maturity

age-to-age factor
Risk Management. The ratio of the value of losses for one year of an insurance program to the value of losses for the same risk exposures for the year earlier.

see: cumulative factors

agency
Agency/Insurer Operations. A group of persons working together to sell and service insurance policies based on contractual agreements with insurance companies.

synonym: insurance agency; *see*: actual authority, agency agreement, agent, agent's authority, agent's certificate of authority, agent's license, apparent agency, appointment, authorization, expressed authority, implied authority, special circumstances

Law. A legal relationship between two parties who agree that one (the agent) is to act on behalf of another (the principal), subject to the latter's general control. The principal is held liable for the agent's actions.

see: agent, employee, independent contractor, principal, vicarious liability

Agency Administration Section, CPCU Society
Organizations. An interest section of the CPCU Society that promotes new and efficient ways to operate insurance agencies.

see: CPCU Society

agency agreement
Agency/Insurer Operations. The contract establishing the legal relationship between an insurance agent or agency and an insurer. The contract specifies the degree of authority given to the agency, the types of insurance the agency may write for the insurer, what commission is to be paid, and the payment terms between the agency and insurer.

see: agency, agent's authority, agent's certificate of authority, expressed authority, ownership of expirations

agency bill
Agency. A statement of insurance premiums due that is completed by an agent and sent to the policyholder. The agent transmits the premium payment (minus commission) to the insurer on one of three bases: item basis, statement basis, or account

current basis.

compare: direct bill; *see*: account current, collection ratio, item basis premium payment, premium, statement basis premium payment, trust position ratio

agency by estoppel
Agency.
see: apparent agency

agency company
Agency/Insurer Operations. An insurance company that uses independent agents to solicit its insurance business.

compare: captive agent, exclusive agency system; *see*: independent agency system

Agency-Company Organization for Research and Development (ACORD)
Organizations. Members: Insurers, agents, brokers, producers associations, and service providers. *Objectives*: Development of standard insurance industry forms known as ACORD forms, provides a help desk, and publishes forms and supporting informational materials. *Headquarters*: Pearl River, New York.

agency plant
Insurer Operations. An insurance company's sales organization, usually meaning all agents and marketing representatives working for or on behalf of the insurer.

agency reinsurance
Agency/Reinsurance. A contract of reinsurance between an insurer and a reinsurer that concerns or is confined to the business produced by a named agent of the ceding insurer, and administered with the reinsurer by the named agent with the permission of the ceding insurer.

see: reinsurance

agency superintendent
Insurer Operations. An officer of an insurer who supervises agents within a given territory or region.

see: agency

agency system
Agency.
see: captive agent, direct selling system, exclusive agency system, independent agency system

agent
Agency. Any person authorized to act for, or who is recognized as, the legal representative of another (the principal). An insurance agent represents the insurer in negotiating, servicing, or effecting insurance policies. An agent may be an independent contractor or employee of the insurer.

compare: principal (*Agency*); *see*: agency, agent of record, agent's authority, broker, captive agent, debit agent, exclusive agency system, general agent, independent agent, local agent, managing general agent, nonresident agent, policywriting agent, resident agent, recording agent, special agent, special circumstances, state agent, sub-agent

agent of record
Agency. An insurance agent who has the policyholder's approval to order insurance from an insurer; an agent designated in writing by a policyholder to service certain policies on behalf of the policyholder with a company represented by the agent.
compare: broker of record

agent's authority
Agency. The authority granted to an agent by an insurer. In addition to express contractual authority, any agent (whether in insurance or general business) may legally be deemed to have *apparent agency*, which is the authority that a person dealing with the agent reasonably supposes the agent to have. An ordinarily prudent person is entitled to rely on an agent's apparent authority regardless of agency contract provisions.
synonym: agent's power; *see*: actual authority, agency agreement, apparent agency, delegation, expressed authority, implied authority, respondeat superior

agent's balances
Agency/Insurer Operations. The amount due to an insurance company from an agent, which is calculated by taking the premiums paid to the agent by policyholders, less the agent's commissions and policy fees. In some instances, the agent will also be responsible for uncollected premium from a policyholder. It is often required that these funds be held in a trust account until they are paid to the insurer.
see: account current, agent's trust

agent's certificate of authority
Agency. A document evidencing an agent's appointment to represent a specific insurer. Usually this document must be filed by the insurer with the insurance department of each state in which the agent transacts business.
see: agency agreement, agent's authority

agent's commission
Agency. An amount paid to an agent by an insurer for placing and servicing their policies. It is usually expressed as a percentage of premium. New commissions are those paid for the first policy year, and renewal commissions are those paid for subsequent policy years.
see: acquisition cost, expense allowance, first-year commission, flat commission, graded commission, lead fee, level commission, overriding

commission, renewal commission, unlevel commission, variable commission, vested commissions

agent's general lien
Surety. The right of an agent to retain possession of a principal's (insurer's) goods and papers until the entire balance of all accounts between the principal (insurer) and the agent are settled.

agent's license
Agency. A certificate of authority issued by the state, allowing an insurance agent to engage in the sale and servicing of insurance.
see: agent's qualification regulations

agent's power
Agency.
see: agent's authority

agent's qualification regulations
Agency. Laws or regulations in many states that require that an insurance agent or broker meet certain educational or experience requirements to be initially licensed or to renew a license.

agent's trust
Agency. Most states require an insurance agent to establish a trust account with a financial institution for depositing any funds due to insurers that are not yet remitted. Usually, agents are permitted to retain the interest earned on such accounts, but the funds may not be used for any purpose other than paying insurers.
see: agent's balances, broker's float

agents' errors and omissions insurance
Agency/Professional Liability. A form of professional liability coverage for damages claimed against an insurance agent due to any act or omission of the agent (or of any other person for whose acts or omissions the agent is legally responsible), arising out of services as an insurance agent. Coverage is usually written on a claims-made basis.
synonym: insurance agents' liability insurance; *see*: errors and omissions insurance, life underwriters' professional liability insurance

aggravation of a previous condition
Workers' Compensation. A worsening of a preexisting medical condition. An employee who sustains a work-related injury that aggravates a prior injury or impairment, whether or not the prior condition arose out of employment, is entitled to full workers' compensation benefits. The employer must assume the responsibility for preexisting conditions of the employee except to the extent that a state second injury law apportions compensation between prior and later injuries.
synonym: aggravation of injury; *see*: cumulative

trauma, preexisting condition, recurrent disability, second injury fund

aggravation of injury
Workers' Compensation.
see: aggravation of a previous condition

aggregate benefits
Health. The aggregate policy amount payable to an insured or claimant under two or more policies or two or more coverages of a single policy. The maximum amount of benefits an insured or claimant may receive under a policy regardless of the number of claims.
see: limit of liability

aggregate deductible insurance
General.
see: aggregate excess insurance

aggregate excess insurance
Liability/Property. Coverage for large insureds that is effective only when losses exceed a predetermined amount (in the form of self-insurance or a deductible) during an annual period. After this aggregate amount is reached, the insurer is liable for any further claims. *Example:* An insured with a $500,000 aggregate excess policy suffers three $200,000 losses. The insurer is responsible for $100,000 of the third loss and for any more losses that occur during the annual period up to the policy limit.
synonym: aggregate deductible insurance; *compare:* specific excess insurance; *see:* aggregate excess of loss reinsurance, aggregate excess unemployment compensation coverage, aggregate excess workers' compensation insurance, basket aggregate excess insurance, excess insurance, maintenance deductible

aggregate excess of loss reinsurance
Reinsurance. A form of excess of loss treaty reinsurance whereby the reinsurer responds when a ceding insurer incurs losses on a particular line of business during a specific period (usually 12 months) in excess of a stated dollar amount.
synonym: excess aggregate reinsurance, nonproportional reinsurance, stop loss reinsurance; *compare:* excess loss-ratio reinsurance; *see:* treaty reinsurance

aggregate excess unemployment compensation insurance
Employee Benefits. Insurance coverage for nonprofit organizations that elect to self-insure their unemployment compensation losses. The coverage insures losses in excess of a specified, self-insured aggregate amount during an annual period. It places a cap on the maximum amount the insured will have to pay during a twelve-month period.

Coverage can be written for unemployment losses caused by loss of a physical facility or for loss caused by an economic condition.
see: self-insurance

aggregate excess workers' compensation insurance
Workers' Compensation. Insurance coverage for organizations that self-insure their workers' compensation benefits. It indemnifies the insured for claims in excess of a specific annual aggregate retention. The coverage places a cap on the maximum amount the insured will have to pay during a twelve-month period. Coverage (i.e., who is covered, what accidents are covered, etc.) is based on the insurance provided by standard workers' compensation policies.
compare: specific excess workers' compensation insurance; *see:* self-insurance

aggregate indemnity
Health. The maximum amount that may be collected under a health insurance policy for any single disability, or for any period of disability.

aggregate limit
Liability. The maximum coverage under a liability policy during a specified period of time—usually one year or the policy period—regardless of the number of separate losses that may occur. Losses paid under coverages subject to aggregate limits reduce the amounts available for future losses. Aggregate limits may apply to a specific type of coverage, or they may apply to all losses under the policy.

The ISO commercial general liability coverage form contains both a general aggregate limit and a products and completed operations aggregate limit. The ISO business owners' liability coverage form also has two aggregate limits. The first is for all injury or damage during the policy period from the products and completed operations coverage, and the second is an aggregate limit applying to all other injury or damage during the policy period except for legal liability losses.
compare: automatic reinstatement clause; *see:* commercial general liability policy, general aggregate limit, limit of liability, products-completed operations aggregate limit

aggregate operations liability limit
Liability. The maximum limit of liability available to respond to claims for damages caused by the insured in the operation of a business. The aggregate limit usually applies only to property damage liability.
see: limit of liability

aggregate product liability limit
Liability. The maximum limit of liability payable

under a liability policy during the term of the policy or in any one policy year for all product liability claims covered by the policy.

see: aggregate limit, commercial general liability policy, limit of liability, products-completed operations aggregate limit

aggregate protection liability limit

Liability. The maximum limit of liability available to respond to claims that arise from activities of independent contractors working for the insured.

see: aggregate limit, limit of liability

aggregate working excess reinsurance

Reinsurance. A form of treaty reinsurance under which the ceding insurer retains a portion of each risk as well as an aggregate amount of losses in excess of each retention.

see: aggregate excess of loss reinsurance

aggressive portfolio

Financial Planning. An investment portfolio that contains investments made on the assumption that they will greatly appreciate in value, or investments that are riskier than those that have defensive qualities (i.e., are expected to produce a lower, but more certain, yield).

compare: defensive portfolio; *see*: high-yield bond, portfolio

aging accounts receivable

Accounting. The process of classifying accounts receivable in terms of how long they have been outstanding, for the purpose of estimating the amount of uncollectible accounts. The longer a receivable amount remains unpaid, the less likely it is ever to be paid.

see: accounts receivable

aging schedule

Accounting. A report that indicates how long accounts receivable have been outstanding. It gives the percentage and amount of receivables not past due and the percentage and amount of receivables that are past due for 30 days, 60 days, 90 or more days.

see: accounts receivable

agreed amount

Property.

see: agreed value

agreed amount clause

Property. A provision in a property policy under which the insurer agrees with the insured that the amount of insurance purchased will automatically satisfy the coinsurance, average, or contribution clause of the policy.

compare: coinsurance clause; *see*: agreed value, statement of values

agreed amount endorsement

Property. An endorsement to a property insurance policy containing an agreed amound clause.

synonym: agreed value provision; *see*: agreed amount clause, agreed value, statement of values

agreed value

Property. An agreement between the insurer and the insured that the limit of insurance on a scheduled item of property equals the property's value. For some items, such as jewelry and fine arts, the insurer may require an appraisal.

synonym: agreed amount; *see*: agreed value clause, statement of values

agreed value clause

Property. A method of avoiding a coinsurance penalty in business interruption coverage, entailing a two-step procedure: 1. The insured completes a business income report showing financial data for the previous twelve months and an estimate of financial results for the next twelve months; 2. The agreed value is entered in the declarations and becomes part of the policy. The agreed value must at least equal the coinsurance percentage multiplied by the estimated net profit and operating expenses shown for the next twelve months in the report.

see: coinsurance clause

agreed value option clause

Property. A coverage modification provision available under the Insurance Services Office building and personal property coverage policy. The provision suspends the coinsurance clause for a period of one year. Underwriters generally require a signed statement of values indicating full actual cash or replacement costs.

see: building and personal property coverage form, statement of values

agreed value provision

Property.

see: agreed amount endorsement

agreement for sale

Law. An agreement obligating the purchasing party to complete a promise to buy.

compare: agreement to sell

agreement to sell

Law. An agreement obligating the vendor to complete a promise to sell. The other party is not obligated to buy.

compare: agreement for sale

agricultural cooperative

General. An organization formed and collectively owned and operated for the mutual benefit of farmers, usually to sell and process their crops or to purchase seed. Many of these cooperatives formed mutual insurance companies to insure their members.

see: farmers mutual insurer

agricultural equipment insurance

Inland Marine. Coverage for mobile agricultural equipment and machinery, including apparatus such as saddles, straps, harnesses and liveries, against specified perils (usually fire, lightning, vandalism, malicious mischief and removal). Excludes aircraft, watercraft, crops and feed.

synonym: agricultural machinery insurance

agricultural machinery insurance

Inland Marine.

see: agricultural equipment insurance

agricultural worker

Workers' Compensation. An employee involved in farming in any of its forms, including orchards, vineyards or nurseries, dairies, bee keeping, poultry and livestock, farm fishing, fur-bearing animals, etc.

synonym: farm laborer

AIA documents

Surety. Standard construction-related agreements developed by the American Institute of Architects (AIA) for separate performance and payment bonds (A311) and for bid bonds (A370).

see: American Institute of Architects, bid bond, labor and material bond, performance bond

AIDS

Health/Life.

see: acquired immune deficiency syndrome

AIDS/HIV risk coverage

Health. Health insurance coverage for persons who work in the health care industry who may become infected with HIV (human immunodeficiency virus) or AIDS (acquired immune deficiency syndrome) by contact with patients or fluid specimens. Indemnification may be made monthly to cover expenses or it may be payable in a lump sum (e.g., $150,000).

see: acquired immune deficiency syndrome, human immunodeficiency virus

air bag

Automobile/Loss Control. A passive restraint system in automobiles with an inflatable bag packaged in the steering wheel hub or passenger-side dashboard. A frontal collision at or above 12 miles per hour deploys the air bag to prevent occupants from striking the windshield or interior surfaces. Some vehicles are equipped with side-impact air bags.

synonym: air cushion restraint system; *see:* passive restraint system

air bill

Aviation/Inland Marine.

see: air waybill

air cargo insurance

Aviation. A form of aviation insurance covering an air carrier's liability arising from damage, destruction or loss of cargo during shipment.

see: aviation insurance

air cushion restraint system

Automobile/Loss Control.

see: air bag

air passenger insurance

Aviation/Life.

see: air travel insurance

air pollutant

Loss Control. As defined in the Clean Air Act, any polluting agent or combination of agents, including physical, chemical, biological, or radioactive substances emitted into the air. It also includes air pollutant precursors as determined by the Administrator of the Environmental Protection Agency.

see: air sampling, Clean Air Act, pollutant

air rights

Aviation/Law. Rights vested in real estate, allowing the owner to use all or a portion of the air space above the property. Airlines have a right to pass overhead; however, an owner may recover damages if flight paths interfere with the use of land.

air sampler

Loss Control. A measuring device designed to collect samples of airborne particles as small as .01 microns. It has special filters to sample various types of environmental and industrial dust, radioactive particles, and other airborne hazards to human health.

see: air pollutant

air sampling

Loss Control. The scientific testing of a representative sample of air to determine the quantities and types of atmospheric contaminants.

see: air pollutant, air sampler, Clean Air Act

air taxi

Aviation. An aircraft principally used in the business of carrying passengers or freight for hire, but excluding aircraft used for instruction, unscheduled service, or rental to others. Also called *charter aircraft*, air taxis differ from airlines in that the entire aircraft is hired by a single individual or organization.

synonym: charter aircraft

air transport insurance
Aviation.

see: aviation insurance

air travel insurance
Aviation/Life. A form of life insurance that may be purchased by passengers of scheduled airlines. The policy face value is paid to the named beneficiary in the event that death results from a particular flight.

synonym: air passenger insurance, aircraft passenger insurance; *compare*: aviation passenger liability insurance; *see*: charter fare protection insurance, travel accident insurance

air waybill
Aviation/Inland Marine. A bill of lading issued by an airline, acknowledging receipt of merchandise and indicating conditions for carriage.

synonym: air bill; *see*: bill of lading, waybill

aircraft damage coverage
Property. A covered peril under most basic property insurance policies. Coverage is provided for damage caused by direct contact between insured property and an aircraft and usually also covers damage caused by objects falling from an aircraft. Most policies combine this coverage with vehicle damage coverage.

see: falling objects coverage, vehicle damage coverage

aircraft hull insurance
Aviation.

see: hull coverage

aircraft insurance
Aviation. A specialized segment of the insurance industry that covers both physical damage to the hull or parts of an aircraft and liability for bodily injury or property damage to others arising out of the operation of the aircraft.

see: aircraft damage coverage, aviation insurance, falling objects coverage

aircraft nonowned coverage
Aviation.

see: nonowned aircraft liability insurance

aircraft passenger insurance
Aviation/Life.

see: air travel insurance

aircraft premium endorsement
Aviation/Workers' Compensation. A workers' compensation policy endorsement (NCCI form WC 00 04 01A) that, for an additional premium, covers an insured who operates or leases an aircraft on a regular basis. The premium is usually based on the

number of passenger seats in the aircraft.

see: workers' compensation insurance

aircraft product liability insurance
Aviation. A form of product liability insurance designed for manufacturers and dealers of aircraft and for fixed base operators who repair and maintain aircraft. Most insurance companies do not write this insurance because of the catastrophic loss potential of a key aircraft component failing while in flight. The coverage is usually written by special aviation insurers or specialized Lloyd's of London syndicates.

see: aircraft insurance, fixed base operators, product liability insurance

aircraft spare parts insurance
Aviation. All-risk coverage on leased aircraft parts—including aircraft engines, spare parts, and equipment—while the property is on the ground or is being carried as cargo by air, land or waterborne transit.

airport owners' and operators' liability insurance
Aviation. A form of general liability insurance tailored to the needs of airport owners and operators and underwritten by aviation insurers.

see: commercial general liability insurance, fixed base liability coverage, hangarkeepers' liability insurance

alarm system
Loss Control.

see: local alarm system

alcohol bond
Surety. A bond that guarantees that the principal complies with federal or state laws or regulations administering the sale, manufacture, or warehousing of alcohol. If the alcohol is for beverages, the bond is frequently called a liquor bond, or intoxicating liquor bond.

synonym: intoxicating liquor bond, liquor bond, principal (*Surety*)

alcoholic beverage liability insurance
Liability. A form of general liability coverage for owners of businesses that sell or serve alcoholic beverages for liability arising from injuries or loss caused by intoxicated customers.

see: dram shop liability insurance, liquor liability coverage

alcoholic beverages market value endorsement
Property. A commercial property coverage endorsement (ISO form CP 99 05) that amends the valuation of covered alcoholic beverages held for

24

sale to provide a loss settlement based on the current market value.

synonym: distilled spirits and wines market value endorsement; *see*: market value clause

alcoholic intoxication

Health. A temporary state of impaired physical or mental ability caused by ingesting alcohol. Under some policies, coverage is denied if an accident or sickness results from alcoholic intoxication.

compare: alcoholism

alcoholism

Health. Addiction to alcohol; chronic, excessive use of alcoholic beverages (often involving an increased adaptation to the effects of alcohol over time and therefore greater consumption), resulting in impaired health.

compare: alcoholic intoxication; *see*: substance abuse

aleatory contract

Law. A contract whose value to either or both of the parties depends on chance or future events, or where the monetary values of the parties' performance are unequal. An insurance policy is an aleatory contract because the insurer's obligation to pay a loss depends on uncertain events, while the insured must pay a fixed premium during the policy period.

see: contract, policy

alien bond

Surety.

see: immigrant bond

alien carrier

Insurer Operations.

see: alien insurer

alien insurer

Insurer Operations. An insurer or reinsurer is considered *alien* in any country other than its place of domicile or incorporation.

synonym: alien carrier, alien company, alien reinsurer; *compare*: admitted insurer, foreign insurer, domestic insurer

alien reinsurer

Reinsurance.

see: alien insurer

Alien Reporting Information System (ARIS)

Regulation. A database of the National Association of Insurance Commissioners to help monitor insurers' solvency which provides financial reports on reinsurance ceded to domestic or alien reinsurers, federal employer identification numbers, alien reinsurers' identification numbers, and the locations of reinsurers

see: alien insurer, cede, foreign insurer, insolvency, National Association of Insurance Commissioners, reinsurance

alienate

Title. To convey or transfer title to property by will or voluntary sale or gift, as opposed to passing title by operation of law.

see: alienation clause, title, will

alienation clause

Law. A provision in a contract or other document that provides, restricts, or nullifies the right to transfer property that is the subject of the contract.

see: alienate

Mortgage Insurance. A provision in a mortgage requiring that the entire loan balance be paid upon the sale of the property.

see: mortgage

Property. A provision in a fire insurance policy that voids coverage in the event the property is transferred to another owner.

all causes deductible

Employee Benefits/Health. A health insurance plan deductible that applies to all covered expenses incurred by a covered participant as a result of the same or related causes within the accumulation period.

see: accumulation period (*Health*), deductible

all causes maximum limit

Employee Benefits/Health. The maximum benefits payable under a health insurance plan for covered expenses incurred by covered plan participant(s) during a specific period of coverage.

see: maximum plan limits

"all in" condominium

Property.

see: single entity condominium

All-Industry Research Advisory Council (AIRAC)

Organizations. Members: Insurance companies. *Objectives*: To promote interests of property and casualty insurance companies. *Founded*: 1977. *Headquarters*: Oakbrook, IL.

all lines insurer

Insurer Operations. An insurer that writes both life/health and property/casualty lines. Because of regulatory restrictions and market considerations, it is rare for insurers to offer literally all coverages.

see: line (*General*)

All Nations

Organizations. Members: Cooperative insurance

facilities. *Objectives:* Provide financial and technical assistance to new and developing cooperative insurance facilities. *Founded:* 1966. *Headquarters:* Columbus, OH.

all-payer system

Health. A health care system in which all public and private third-party payers of medical bills are subject to the same rules and rates for payment. The uniform fees, in effect, bar health care providers from charging more to persons or firms who are more able to pay in order to make up losses from artificially low payment caps by some payers.

compare: capitation, fee for service, health care provider, single payer plan

all-risk insurance

Inland Marine/Property. A property or inland marine insurance form that covers all risks of loss except risks that are specifically excluded. All-risk policies always have some exclusions or limitations regarding the insured property, persons or protected interests, and some policies may exclude certain causes of loss.

see: broad form property insurance endorsement, named perils, open perils, risk, special form

all risks—ground and flight

Aviation. A form of aircraft hull coverage on an all-risk basis. The aircraft is covered both on the ground and in flight.

see: all-risk insurance, aviation insurance, hull coverage, in flight

all risks—not in motion

Aviation. A form of aircraft hull coverage on an all-risk basis while the aircraft is not in motion under its own power.

see: all-risk insurance, hull coverage, in motion

all-states coverage

Workers' Compensation. An obsolete endorsement used with older workers' compensation policies to extend benefits to the insured's business activities in any state. This coverage is now included in the body of the standard workers' compensation policy and is triggered by indicating "all-states" in the policy declarations.

compare: extraterritoriality; *see:* other states insurance

all-terrain vehicle

Personal. A motorized vehicle fitted with balloon tires or crawler tracks designed to travel through water, snow, mud, sand and rough terrain. Generally, they are not required to be licensed as automobiles and must be driven off public highways.

see: all-terrain vehicle coverage

all-terrain vehicle coverage

Personal. Coverage can be obtained for all-terrain

vehicles under one of three policies: 1. If it is licensed for highway use, it can be endorsed to the personal auto policy. 2. If it is not licensed for highway use, it can be endorsed to a homeowners policy. 3. A separate all-terrain vehicle policy can be purchased.

see: all-terrain vehicle, automobile insurance

allegation

Law. A statement, especially in a pleading submitted in court, concerning facts yet to be proved; an unsupported assertion or complaint.

see: complaint, evidence, pleading

allergy and susceptibility

Law/Liability. A defense sometimes offered in response to a claim involving a product for intimate bodily use (e.g., cosmetics, deodorants) whereby the manufacturer is not liable for injury caused by an individual's rare allergy or abnormal sensitivity to the product.

see: affirmative defense, defective product, product liability insurance, products-completed operations insurance

Alliance of American Insurers (AAI)

Organizations. Members: Property and casualty insurers. *Objectives:* Promote the interests of property and casualty insurers. Sponsors educational and research programs. *Founded:* 1922. *Headquarters:* Schaumburg, IL.

allied lines

Property. Coverages that are frequently written with property insurance. Allied lines include insurance for data processing, demolition, earthquake, increased cost of construction, radioactive contamination, sprinkler leakage, standing timber, vandalism and malicious mischief, and water damage.

see: date processing coverage, demolition cost endorsement, earthquake insurance, increased cost of construction endorsement, line, radioactive contamination insurance, sprinkler leakage coverage, standing timber insurance, vandalism and malicious mischief coverage, water damage clause

allision

Ocean Marine. Collision of a moving vessel with a stationary vessel or object.

allocated benefits

Health. A health insurance policy provision that pays certain expenses (usually miscellaneous hospital and medical charges such as x-rays, dressings and drugs) according to rates set in a schedule in the policy. There is usually a maximum total that will be paid for all allocated expenses.

allocated claim expense

Insurer Operations. An expense assigned to and

---

recorded with a specific claim, including defense and investigation costs. Allocated claim expenses have more significance in liability insurance because of the legal costs involved in defending liability claims.

synonym: allocated loss expense, paid expense; *compare*: unallocated claim expense; *see*: claim expense

allocated funding instrument
Employee Benefits.
see: deferred group annuity

allocated loss expense
Insurer Operations.
see: allocated claim expense

allocation of claims costs
Professional Liability. The division of legal costs and claim payments associated with a suit brought against one or more directors and officers and against the business entity itself. Most directors' and officers' (D&O) policies cover only the liability of the directors and officers, not the entity's direct liability for wrongful acts participated in by its directors and officers; but D&O policies typically do cover the corporation's indemnification of its directors and officers. Because legal defense costs and claim payments are usually borne by the business and are usually uninsured, allocation often requires negotiations between the D&O insurer and the business. Sometimes a court orders proportional allocation based on the damages or settlement attributable to the directors or officers and the amount attributable to the company, and policies sometimes include an express allocation clause.

see: corporate indemnification coverage, directors' and officers' liability insurance, entity coverage, larger settlement rule, relative exposure rule

allotment
Title. Apportionment; land divided into smaller parts and often sold without improvements; a subdivision.
see: real estate

allowed costs
Health. Fees for services, medicine or supplies that qualify as covered expenses for a health benefit plan to pay in whole or in part.
see: health benefit plan

alluvion
Loss Control. The wash or flow of water against a shore; the gradual accumulation of land by the addition of clay, silt, sand, gravel or similar material deposited by running water.
compare: avulsion; *see*: accretion

alphabet broker
Agency. A term for a large insurance broker widely known by an acronym or abbreviation. *Examples*: Marsh & McLennan (M&M); Alexander & Alexander (A&A).
synonym: alphabet house

alphabet house
Agency.
see: alphabet broker

alteration
Crime/Surety.
see: alteration bond, forgery or alteration coverage form

alteration bond
Surety. A bond that indemnifies the insured for loss sustained by reason of alterations to stated instruments, documents or securities. Alteration coverage is included in a forgery bond.
see: forgery bond, lost instrument bond

alternate employer endorsement
Workers' Compensation. A workers' compensation endorsement (NCCI form WC 00 03 01A) that is added to the policy for a temporary employment agency. It extends workers' compensation coverage and employers' liability coverage to the insured's customers named on the endorsement.
synonym: master-servant endorsement

alternative dispute resolution (ADR)
Law. The methods of attempting to settle disputes other than by litigation—i.e., mediation, arbitration, or settlement conferences. Many firms prefer some type of ADR because it is generally less costly and time-consuming than a lawsuit; therefore, contracts with vendors, suppliers, etc., often provide that disputes are to be resolved through either arbitration or mediation. Most states require their courts to accept the results of such proceedings.
see: arbitration, litigation, mediation

alternative energy plants
Property. Power generating facilities that use sources of energy other than hydropower or fossil fuels. Examples of alternative sources of energy are cogeneration (using waste energy to produce electricity), geothermal, windmill, and waste-to-energy plants. Some insurers have special energy departments to coordinate property, boiler and machinery, casualty and special coverages, and technical services for these facilities because they are often tied to other major industrial insureds who use the heat or waste from their manufacturing or processing facilities to generate power.

alternative market

Risk Management. The demand for all risk financing techniques or mechanisms that compete with traditional commercial insurance (self-insurance, captive insurers, finite risk insurance, etc.). In the mid-1990s the market for insurance alternatives was estimated to be 25% of worldwide commercial insurance premiums.

see: alternative risk financing techniques

alternative medical treatments

Health. Health care treatments other than traditional or conventional Western allopathic medicine and surgery, such as acupuncture, herbalism or homeopathy. Some health plans cover such treatments.

see: alternative treatment benefit

alternative risk financing techniques

Risk Management. All risk management techniques that compete with commercial insurance, such as self-insurance, risk retention groups, pools, captive insurers, and finite risk insurance.

see: captive insurance company, finite risk insurance, pool, retrospective rating plan, risk retention group, self-insurance

alternative treatment benefit

Health. A coverage in some health plans for beneficiaries who wish to utilize alternatives to traditional medicine or surgery.

see: alternative medical treatments

ambiguity

Law. Uncertainty of meaning; a lack of clarity in an insurance policy's provisions, allowing the policy to be interpreted in more than one way. In coverage litigation, courts generally construe ambiguity in a policy against the insurer and in favor of the insured.

see: contract of adhesion, contra proferentem, reasonable expectations doctrine

ambit

Ocean Marine. The geographic scope of a voyage, including time extensions.

see: adventure, voyage

ambulance service malpractice insurance

Professional Liability. A form of professional liability insurance designed for ambulance drivers and attendants that covers injury to or death of a patient caused by error, omission or negligence in professional services.

compare: paramedics' professional liability insurance; *see*: medical malpractice

ambulatory care facility

Health. A health care facility, either autonomous or contained within a hospital, that provides diagnostic or medical services including minor surgery on an outpatient basis. *Ambulatory* means capable of walking, i.e., patients are able to leave after the medical procedure without requiring overnight confinement.

see: ambulatory surgical center, outpatient

ambulatory surgical center

Health. A facility designed to provide elective surgical care in which the patient is admitted and discharged the same day.

see: ambulatory care facility, outpatient

amendment

Insurer Operations. A provision added to an original insurance policy that changes, corrects or improves the benefits and coverages.

see: endorsement, rider

American Academy of Actuaries (AAA)

Organizations. Members: Actuaries. *Objectives*: Facilitate relations between actuaries and governmental bodies. Promulgate professional standards for actuaries. *Founded*: 1965. *Headquarters*: Washington, D.C.

American Academy of Insurance Medicine

Organizations. Members: Medical directors of life insurance companies. *Objectives*: To advance the science of medicine as applied to insurance; continuing education of members and public relations. *Founded*: 1889. *Headquarters*: Portland, ME. (Formerly, Association of Life Insurance Medical Directors of America.)

American agency system

Agency.

see: independent agency system

American Agents Association (AAA)

Organizations. Members: Insurance agents. *Objectives*: Promotes interests of insurance agents and compiles statistics. *Founded*: 1980. *Headquarters*: Indianapolis, IN.

American Annuitants Mortality Table

Life. A table comprised of statistics provided by twenty American insurance companies in 1918, comparing mortality rates for males and females.

see: American Experience Table of Mortality, mortality table

American Arbitration Association (AAA)

Organizations. Members: Law firms, businesses, trade and educational associations, arbitrators, unions and other interested individuals. *Objectives*: Encourages arbitration as an alternative to litigation for purposes of resolving disputes. Recommends individuals to arbitrate or mediate certain controversies. Its accident and claims tribunal handles no-fault and automobile liability claims. *Founded*: 1926. *Headquarters*: New York, NY.

American Association of Crop Insurers (AACI)

Organizations. Members: Crop insurers and agencies selling multiple peril crop insurance. *Objectives*: Promotes interests of crop insurers. *Founded*: 1981. *Headquarters*: Washington, D.C.

American Association of Dental Consultants (AADC)

Organizations. Members: Dental insurance consultants and others concerned with dental insurance plans, from administrative and design perspectives. *Objectives*: Increasing knowledge in the area of dental insurance plans, including the interrelationships between insurers, the dental profession and consumers. *Founded*: 1977. *Headquarters*: North Babylon, NY.

American Association of Insurance Management Consultants (AAIMC)

Organizations. Members: Insurers, agents, brokers, attorneys and others with advanced management degrees. *Objectives*: Promotes interests of insurance management consultants; offers a referral service and educational seminars. *Founded*: 1978. *Headquarters*: Estes Park, CO.

American Association of Insurance Services (AAIS)

Organizations. Members: Property and casualty insurers, mutual, stock and reciprocal insurers. *Objectives*: Develops rates, rules and forms for fire, multiple lines, inland marine and casualty insurance. *Founded*: 1936. *Headquarters*: Bensenville, IL. (Formerly known as the Transportation Insurance Rating Bureau.)

American Association of Managing General Agents (AAMGA)

Organizations. Members: Managing general agents. *Objectives*: Presents chairman awards, maintains speakers' bureau, offers educational programs and compiles statistics. *Founded: 1926. Headquarters*: Kansas City, MO.

American Automobile Association (AAA)

Organizations. Members: Individual members of associated automobile clubs throughout the United States. *Objectives*: Promotes traffic safety, better highways, more efficient and safer cars, energy conservation and improvement of motoring and travel conditions. *Founded*: 1902. *Headquarters*: Heathrow, FL.

synonym: AAA, automobile club, Triple A

American Bar Association (ABA)

Organizations. Members: Attorneys in good standing, admitted to the bar of at least one state. *Objectives*: Fostering professional improvement; providing public services; improving the availability of legal services to the public; and bettering the administration of civil and criminal justice. *Founded*: 1878. *Headquarters*: Chicago, IL.

American Bureau of Shipping (ABS)

Organizations. Members: Shipowners, shipbuilders, naval architects, marine underwriters and others associated with the marine industry. *Objectives*: Classification society that surveys vessels and grants their "class" if the vessel meets the standards of construction, material and workmanship. *Founded*: 1862. *Headquarters*: Paramus, NJ.

see: American Bureau of Shipping Record

American Bureau of Shipping Record

Ocean Marine. A register prepared by the American Bureau of Shipping of all United States ocean-going vessels in alphabetical order containing the complete description of each vessel.

see: American Bureau of Shipping, Lloyd's Register of Shipping

American Cargo War Risk Reinsurance Exchange (ACWRRE)

Organizations. Members: Ocean marine insurers. *Objectives*: Spread war risks through reinsurance on cargoes in ocean commerce. *Founded*: 1939. *Headquarters*: New York, NY.

American College

Organizations. The accrediting body for both the CLU (Chartered Life Underwriter) and the ChFC (Chartered Financial Consultant) designations. Formerly it was known as the American College of Life Underwriters.

see: American Society of Chartered Life Underwriters and Chartered Financial Consultants, Chartered Financial Consultant, Chartered Life Underwriter

American Corporate Counsel Institute (ACCI)

Organizations. Members: Attorneys in corporate legal departments. *Objectives*: Provides information on various issues, including an in-house legal department's liability exposure. *Founded*: 1984. *Headquarters*: Washington, D.C.

American Council of Life Insurance (ACLI)

Organizations. Members: Life insurers, including legal reserve life insurance companies. *Objectives*: Promotes interests of life insurers. Conducts economic and social research programs; compiles statistics. *Founded*: 1976. *Headquarters*: Washington, D.C. (Formerly Institute of Life Insurance.)

American Depository Receipt (ADR)

Financial Planning/International. A special certificate that represents stock issued in a foreign country. Most countries do not allow corporate stock certificates issued in their country to be taken from the country. Therefore, to transfer these shares to a U.S. investor, a foreign company deposits shares of stock with a branch of a U.S. bank located in the country of issue. The bank then issues an American Depository Receipt to represent these shares in the United States. Each ADR is equivalent to a specified number of shares and can be traded by investors.

synonym: American Depository Shares

American Depository Shares (ADS)
Financial Planning/International.

see: American Depository Receipt

American Excess Insurance Association (AEIA)
Organizations. Members: Excess liability insurers. *Objectives:* Provide large U.S. companies with excess liability insurance. *Founded:* 1986. *Headquarters:* East Hughes, CT.

American Experience Table of Mortality
Life. A table published in 1868 of expected mortality rates, based on data accumulated from twenty American insurance companies. This table was widely used by life insurers until the 1950s to establish rates. It was superseded by the Commissioners' Standard Ordinary Table.

see: Commissioners' Standard Ordinary Table, mortality table

American Health Information Management Association (AHIMA)
Organizations. Members: Registered Record Administrators, Accredited Record Technicians, other health care professionals, and students enrolled in an AHIMA study program. *Objectives:* To set national standards for education in health information management, administer national certification examinations, and award professional credentials for Registered Record administrator, Accredited Record Technician, and Certified Coding specialist. *Founded:* 1928. *Headquarters:* Chicago, IL. (Formerly, Association of Record Librarians of North America until 1932 and Association of Medical Record Librarians until 1970.)

see: Accredited Record Technician, Certified Coding Specialist, Registered Record Administrator

American Hospital Association
Organizations. Members: Individuals and health care institutions, including hospitals, health care systems, and pre-acute and post-acute health care delivery organizations. *Objectives:* To promote the welfare of the public through leadership and assistance to its members in providing improved health care service. *Founded:* 1898. *Headquarters:* Chicago, IL.

American Hull Insurance Syndicate (AHIS)
Organizations. Members: U.S. insurance firms and foreign countries, acting as a syndicate for writing coverage on ocean-going and Great Lakes vessels, foreign hulls and builders' risks. *Objectives:* Promotes the American Merchant Marine; offers protection to shipowners, shipbuilders and maritime interests worldwide. *Founded:* 1920. *Headquarters:* New York, NY. Until 1943, known as the American Marine Syndicate.

American Industrial Hygiene Association (AIHA)
Organizations. Members: Industrial hygienists. *Objectives:* Promotes the study and control of environmental factors affecting the health and well-being of industrial workers. *Founded:* 1983. *Headquarters:* New York, NY.

American Institute for Chartered Property Casualty Underwriters
Organizations. Members: Property and casualty underwriters. *Objectives:* Conducts examinations and awards the Chartered Property Casualty Underwriter (CPCU) professional designation. *Founded:* 1942. *Headquarters:* Malvern, PA. (Previously called American Institute for Property and Liability Underwriters.)

see: Chartered Property Casualty Underwriter, Insurance Institute of America

American Institute of Architects (AIA)
Organizations. Members: Architects. *Objectives:* Develops standard agreements, including insurance provisions, for construction contracts. *Founded:* 1857. *Headquarters:* Washington, D.C.

see: AIA documents

American Institute of Marine Underwriters (AIMU)
Organizations. Members: Marine insurers authorized to conduct business in one or more states of the United States. *Objectives:* To analyze international conventions and agreements of marine insurance. Provides training and educational seminars and assists in developing the curriculum for the Associate in Marine Insurance Management designation. *Founded:* 1898. *Headquarters:* New York, NY.

see: Associate in Marine Insurance Management

American Insurance Association (AIA)
Organizations. Members: Property, casualty and surety insurance companies. *Objectives:* Promotes the interests of participating companies. *Founded:* 1964. *Headquarters:* Washington, D.C. Formed by a merger of the National Board of Fire Underwriters, the Association of Casualty and Surety Companies and the earlier American Insurance Association.

see: Association of Casualty and Surety Companies, Fire and Theft Index Bureau

American Insurance Services Group, Inc. (AISG)

Organizations. Members: Property and casualty insurers. *Objectives:* Assist in the proper resolution of property claims; serve as a clearinghouse for insurance claims; maintain an index of property and theft loss reports. *Founded:* 1984. *Headquarters:* New York, NY.

American Insurers Highway Safety Alliance (AIHSA)

Organizations. Members: Automobile insurance companies. *Objectives:* Conducts programs on accident prevention and traffic safety. Publishes safety leaflets, fleet safety materials and conducts community safety campaigns. *Founded:* 1920. *Headquarters:* Schaumburg, IL.

American Land Title Association

Organizations. Members: Title insurers, abstractors and agents. *Objectives:* Perform statistical research and lobbying services. *Founded:* 1906. *Headquarters:* Washington, D.C.

American Land Title Association Standard Loan Policy

Title. A policy issued to a mortgagee covering against loss of precedence for repaying the mortgage lien.

American Life Convention (ALC)

Organizations. A former association of life insurers; it is now part of the American Council of Life Insurance.

see: American Council of Life Insurance

American Lloyd's

Insurer Operations. A type of insurer consisting of a syndicate of individuals who have banded together to assume insurance risks. Though these groups are patterned after Lloyd's of London syndicates, they have no connection with that British institution. American Lloyd's are authorized to operate in a limited number of states.

compare: insurance exchange, Lloyd's of London

American Managed Care and Review Association

Organizations. Members: Managed care organizations (health maintenance organizations, preferred provider organizations, etc.). *Founded:* 1971; merged into Group Health Association of America in 1995. *Headquarters:* Washington, D.C.

see: Group Health Association of America

American Marine Insurance Clearinghouse (AMIC)

Organizations. Members: Ocean marine insurance underwriting groups. *Objectives:* Acts as a secretarial organization for providing risk-sharing arrangements. *Founded:* 1938. *Headquarters:* New York, NY.

American Marine Insurance Forum (AMIF)

Organizations. Members: Ocean marine insurance underwriters insuring hulls, cargoes and similar risks. *Objectives:* Promotes education and friendship among ocean marine underwriters. *Founded:* 1955. *Headquarters:* New York, NY.

American Medical Association

Organizations. Members: County medical societies and physicians. *Objectives:* To disseminate scientific information for members and the public. *Founded:* 1847 *Headquarters:* Chicago, IL.

American National Standards Institute (ANSI)

Organizations. Members: Engineers and safety design experts. *Objectives:* Promotes the use of approved standards for industry, engineering and safety design. *Founded:* 1918. *Headquarters:* New York, NY.

see: ANSI Standard

American Nuclear Insurers (ANI)

Organizations. Members: Liability and property insurance companies. *Objectives:* Provides property and liability coverage for the nuclear energy industry. *Founded:* 1957. *Headquarters:* Farmington, CT.

American Prepaid Legal Services Institute

Organizations. Members: Attorneys, insurance companies, administrators, marketers, and consumers. *Objectives:* Provide technical assistance on group and prepaid legal service plans. *Founded:* 1975. *Headquarters:* Chicago, IL.

American Risk and Insurance Association (ARIA)

Organizations. Members: Insurance educators, and others interested in risk and insurance education and research. *Objectives:* Operates as a professional society; offers a placement service for academic positions. *Founded:* 1932. *Headquarters:* Orlando, FL.

American Salvage Pool Association

Organizations. Members: Salvage companies, storage pool companies and related industries. *Objectives:* Promote the interests of salvage companies including the "pool" sales of damaged vehicles for the insurance industry at competitive prices. *Founded:* 1990 *Headquarters:* Phoenix, AZ.

American Society of Chartered Life Underwriters and Chartered Financial Consultants (ASCLU & ChFC)

Organizations. Members: Individuals who have

been awarded the Chartered Life Underwriter (CLU) or the Chartered Financial Consultants (ChFC) designations. *Objectives*: Provides education programs for continued professional development. *Founded*: 1927. *Headquarters*: Bryn Mawr, PA.

> *see*: American College, Chartered Financial Consultant, Chartered Life Underwriter

American Society of Industrial Security (ASIS)

Organizations. Members: Security managers. *Objectives*: Sponsors the Certified Protection Professional (CPP) examinations. *Founded*: 1955. *Headquarters*: Arlington, VA.

American Society of Mechanical Engineers, Inc. (ASME)

Organizations. Members: Mechanical engineers. *Objectives*: Promotes safety to prevent loss of life. *Founded*: 1880. *Headquarters*: New York, NY.

American Society of Pension Actuaries (ASPA)

Organizations. Members: Individuals involved in the consulting, administration, and design aspects of the employee benefit business. *Objectives*: Promotes high standards for pension actuaries. Awards designations to its members. *Founded*: 1966. *Headquarters*: Washington, D.C.

American Society of Personnel Administration (ASPA)

Organizations. Members: Individuals and organizations interested in the personnel profession. *Objectives*: Provide leadership in the development of the personnel profession, research and accreditation. *Founded*: 1948. *Headquarters*: Alexandria, VA.

> *see*: Personnel Accreditation Institute, Professional in Human Resources, Senior Professional in Human Resources

American Society of Safety Engineers (ASSE)

Organizations. Members: Safety engineers. *Objectives*: Promotes safety and health in the workplace. Sponsors conferences and continuing education seminars. *Founded*: 1911. *Headquarters*: Des Plaines, IL.

American Surety Association (ASA)

Organizations. Members: Surety agents, attorneys, consultants and firms operating in the surety field. *Objectives*: Improving the efficiency of surety bonding and reducing bonding costs. *Founded*: 1980. *Headquarters*: Washington, D.C.

American Table of Distances for Storage of Explosives

Loss Control. A table, developed by the Institute of Makers of Explosives, of distances from surrounding facilities that a given quantity of specific explosives can be safely stored.

> *synonym*: quantity distance tables

American Tort Reform Association (ATRA)

Organizations. Members: Law firms, professional groups, business and trade associations and state legislators. *Objectives*: Promoting reform of the U.S. tort law system. Sponsors educational programs for reform of the civil justice system. *Founded*: 1986. *Headquarters*: Washington, D.C.

American Trial Lawyers Association

Organizations.

> *see*: Association of Trial Lawyers of America

American Trust Fund

Insurer Operations. A trust fund established by Lloyd's of London and maintained in the United States to pay claims. Started in 1939, when there was concern about claims payments during World War II, the fund has been maintained to reduce the exchange problems between the U.S. dollar and English pound and to maintain the confidence of U.S. brokers. Initially funded for $40 million, today it is well in excess of $1 billion.

> *see*: guaranty fund, Lloyd's of London, Lloyd's Premium Trust Fund

Americans with Disabilities Act (ADA)

Regulation. Federal legislation (U.S. Code Title 42, Chapter 126) that prohibits discrimination against persons with physical or mental disabilities by employers with 25 or more employees and by state and local governments. Disabled employees must be provided with reasonable accommodations and equal opportunities. A disability is defined as a physical or mental impairment that substantially limits one or more major life activities, a record of such an impairment, or being regarded as having such an impairment.

amicus curiae

Law. An individual or organization that is not a party to a lawsuit but is allowed by the court to provide views on the case. The submitted document, containing legal arguments, is an "amicus curiae brief" or "amicus brief." (Latin for "friend of the court.")

ammonia contamination coverage

Property. Extended coverage under a boiler and machinery policy for the contamination of a building or personal property by the leakage of ammonia gas used as a coolant in an insured refrigeration system. The leakage must be caused by a covered accident, and coverage is usually subject to a special limit (e.g., $5,000 or $25,000). Higher limits can be obtained for an additional premium.

amortization

Risk Management. The liquidation of a debt on an installment basis; the reduction of a liability by making periodic payments until the outstanding liability reaches zero; recovery of the cost of an intangible capital asset over its useful life or a shorter time permitted by tax laws or generally accepted accounting practices.

see: capital charges, depletion, depreciation, intangible property, negative amortization

amortization period

Reinsurance. In the rating of per-occurrence excess coverages, the amortization period represents the number of years necessary to accumulate total premiums equal to the indemnity.

synonym: payback period

amortized value

Insurer Operations. A method of valuing certain premium bonds carried on an insurance company's financial statement. The value of a bond under this method is the amount to which the purchase price of the bond has increased or decreased from its discount or premium price.

see: amortization

amotion

Professional Liability. Ouster or dispossession; removal of a corporate director or officer before the end of the term of office.

see: directors' and officers' liability insurance

amount at risk

Liability/Property. The policy limit or the probable maximum loss, whichever is less.

compare: amount subject, probable maximum loss

Life. The amount of its own funds that a life insurance company has at risk on a whole life insurance policy; the difference between the policy's face value and cash value.

amount limit

Crime. The amount of insurance specified in an open stock burglary policy, beyond which the coinsurance percentage limit does not apply. This is not the same as the policy limit, which is usually greater.

see: mercantile open-stock burglary insurance

amount of insurance

Insurer Operations.

see: limit of liability

amount subject

Loss Control/Property. The maximum amount expected to be lost in any one fire or other casualty. Its determination depends on the protection and construction of the risk and the distribution of values within the risk. Determining the amount subject is a major responsibility of loss prevention specialists and property underwriters.

see: amount at risk, fire division, probable maximum loss

analyst

Financial Planning.

see: securities analyst

analytic schedule

Property.

see: analytic system

analytic system

Property. A system for measuring the probability of fire loss to property and of determining fire insurance rates. The analytic system was used for many years but has been replaced, for the most part, by other rating methods used by the Insurance Services Office.

synonym: analytic schedule

anchor tenant

Property. A store or merchant in a shopping mall or retail center that draws a large number of consumers to the mall who also shop at nearby stores. Sears, Macy's and J.C. Penney are examples.

see: triple A tenant

ancillary benefits

Health. Benefits that pay for miscellaneous hospital charges, including ambulance service to and from a hospital, drugs, blood, operating room, medicines, bandages, X-rays, diagnostic tests, and anesthetics.

ancillary services

Health. Hospital departments that provide patient services such as radiology and laboratories. Excluded from ancillary services are routine services such as housekeeping, dietary needs, nursing and supplies.

anemometer

Loss Control. A device designed to measure wind direction and velocity.

animal insurance

Inland Marine. Insurance coverage for the health or life of animals and livestock.

see: animal mortality insurance, bloodstock insurance, domestic livestock auction market form, livestock commercial feedlot reporting form, livestock floater, livestock mortality insurance, livestock transit insurance, pet insurance, poultry insurance

animal mortality insurance

Inland Marine. Insurance on domesticated animals

33

that covers death from any cause, including voluntary destruction for humane reasons when the necessity for such destruction is certified by a veterinarian.

see: animal insurance, domestic pet insurance, exotic bird insurance, livestock mortality insurance

anniversary date
Insurer Operations. The month and day of policy issue, renewal, and expiration, as shown in the policy declarations.

see: policy anniversary, policy period, renewal

anniversary rating date
Workers' Compensation. The month and day that manual rules, rates and the experience modifier apply to a workers' compensation policy. Usually it is the policy effective date and each anniversary thereafter, but it may be a different date if a policy had been issued for a term different from the normal anniversary date.

synonym: normal anniversary rating date; *see*: anniversary rating date endorsement, experience rating modification factor, group anniversary rating date, manual rates

anniversary rating date endorsement
Workers' Compensation. An endorsement (NCCI form WC 00 04 02) to a workers' compensation policy that advises the insured that the premium, rates, and experience rating modification factor may change on the anniversary rating date.

see: anniversary date, experience rating modification factor, workers' compensation insurance

annual aggregate deductible
Insurer Operations.
see: deductible, maintenance deductible

annual bond
Surety. A bond that covers a contract or bid awarded or submitted during a twelve-month period or during a fiscal year.

see: bond *(Surety)*

annual financial statement
Insurer Operations/Regulation.
see: annual statement

annual implementation plan (AIP)
Health. A written plan prepared by a hospital or clinic indicating its objectives during the next 12 months to accomplish its long-term (multiple-year) goals indicated in the health systems plan (HSP) for its region of operation. The HSP is produced by a regional planning agency—a health systems agency (HSA)—under the National Health Planning and Resources Development Act of 1974. Directed by consumers and health care providers from within the health service area, HSAs assess health care needs within their region and monitor quality with the goal of preventing duplication of effort and maximizing the effectiveness of health care resources.

synonym: health systems plan

annual payments annuity
Life. An annuity requiring annual premium payments to maintain the contract in force.

see: annuity

annual policy
Insurer Operations. A policy issued for a twelve-month period.

see: policy year

annual renewable term insurance (ART)
Life. Term life insurance that may be renewed from year to year without evidence of insurability by acceptance of a premium for a new policy term. These policies usually increase in cost each year.

synonym: yearly renewable term; *see*: guaranteed renewable, renewable term life insurance, re-entry term life insurance

annual renewal agreement
Life. A life insurance policy provision that the policy will be renewed under specified conditions at each anniversary date.

see: anniversary date, renewal

annual report
Accounting. A formal financial statement issued annually by a corporation to its shareholders. This statement may include comments from management concerning events of the prior fiscal year and the events that may be expected during the next fiscal year.

see: financial statement, Generally Accepted Accounting Principles

annual statement
Insurer Operations/Regulation. A report of an insurance company's financial operations for a particular year, including a balance sheet supported by detailed exhibits and schedules, filed with the state insurance department of each jurisdiction in which the company is licensed to conduct business. The form used was developed by the National Association of Insurance Commissioners.

synonym: annual financial statement, blank, convention blank; *see*: financial statement, gain and loss exhibit, Schedule P, Statutory Accounting Principles

annual supply contract bond
Surety. A bond guaranteeing that a contractor will furnish contracted commodities during a twelve-

34

month period.

see: manufacturer's penalty insurance

annual yield

Financial Planning. The percentage of a capital investment returned as dividends or interest in a year.

compare: average annual dividend yield; *see*: yield

annualization

Insurer Operations. A policy provision that allows the insurer to adjust the annual premium of a policy issued for more than one year to the rate prevailing at each anniversary date.

see: adjustable premium

annuitant

Life. A person entitled to receive the benefits from an annuity.

compare: grantor; *see*: annuity

annuity

Life. A contract that provides for periodic payments starting after a stated period or on a contingent date and continuing for a fixed period or for the remaining life of the annuitant.

synonym: life annuity; *see*: accumulation period, annual payments annuity, annuitant, annuity certain, annuity conversion rate, annuity due, annuity period, annuity purchase fund, annuity starting date, annuity table, annuity with period certain, charitable annuity, cost-of-living variable annuity plan, deferred annuity, equity variable annuity plan, fixed annuity, flexible premium annuity, grantor, group annuity, guaranteed annuity payments, immediate annuity, increasing annuity, insured variable annuity plan, investment annuity, joint and survivor annuity, joint life and survivor annuity, liquidation charge, liquidation period, modified refund annuity, normal annuity form, optional annuity form, pure annuity, refund annuity, retirement annuity, reverse-annuity mortgage, tax deferred annuity, temporary life annuity, temporary life annuity due, variable annuity

annuity certain

Life. An annuity contract under which the benefits are paid for a specific number of years, regardless of whether the annuitant lives or dies.

synonym: installment refund annuity, payment certain; *compare*: annuity with period certain; *see*: annuity

annuity conversion rate

Life. A rate that usually varies by age and sex of the annuitant used to determine the amount an annuity will pay to the annuitant for each dollar of

contribution accumulated to the date of retirement.

see: annuity

annuity due

Life. An annuity that disburses benefit payments at the start of the benefit period, rather than at the end.

see: annuity

annuity period

Life. The interval of benefit payments under an annuity contract (e.g., monthly or quarterly).

see: annuity

annuity purchase fund

Life. A fund established under a deposit administration plan to retain annuity purchase payments transferred from the unallocated active life fund.

synonym: retired life fund; *see*: annuity, deposit administration plan

annuity starting date

Life. The first day of the first annuity period in which an annuity payment has been made.

see: annuity

annuity table

Life. A chart, similar to mortality tables, used in calculating life insurance risks and premiums, showing for a defined group of people (grouped by age, sex, etc.) the number living at the beginning of a particular year and the number dying during that year. The yearly probabilities derived from an annuity table are used to calculate annuity premium payments and future income payments.

compare: mortality table

Annuity Table for 1949

Life. A table, published by Jenkins and Lew, of projection factors that affect reductions in mortality rates.

see: annuity

annuity with period certain

Life. An annuity contract under which the benefits are payable for a specified period in any event, and after that period for as long as the annuitant lives.

compare: annuity certain; *see*: annuity

ANSI Standard

Loss Control. Specifications established by the American National Standards Institute as a guide to aid manufacturers, consumers and regulatory agencies.

see: American National Standards Institute

answer

Law. The response by a defendant to a summons or complaint by a plaintiff. A defendant must file an answer within a time prescribed by law, or a default judgment may be entered.

see: complaint, counterclaim, default judgment, defendant, plaintiff, pleading, summons and complaint

answering services' errors and omissions insurance

Professional Liability. Insurance for firms that operate a telephone answering service which covers negligent acts, errors or omissions. Coverage is usually written on a claims-made basis.

antedate

General. To use a date in a document before the date on which it actually was written or executed.

synonym: backdate; *compare*: postdate; *see*: warranted no known or reported losses

anthropometric evaluation

Loss Control. The study of human body types, sizes and movements to determine their relationship to efficiency of operation and safety.

see: ergonomics

anti-arson application form

Property/Regulation. A fire insurance application that includes additional questions not on most applications concerning the applicant's past losses, legal convictions for arson or other fraud, the property's safety or construction code compliance, unpaid or overdue taxes, mortgage payments or other liens on the property, etc. Use of such a form is sometimes mandatory in areas identified by the state insurance commissioner or other authority as having a high incidence of arson.

see: arson

anti-coercion law

Regulation. A provision in most states' insurance statutes prohibiting coercive methods of selling insurance. Usually, the provision is part of an act on unfair trade practices, which also prohibits boycott and intimidation.

synonym: unfair trade practices; *see*: twisting

anti-compact laws

Regulation. Antitrust laws that prohibit or place limits on agreements that could prevent or restrict competition among businesses.

see: antitrust laws, tying arrangement

anti-discrimination laws

Regulation. State laws prohibiting insurance companies from extending preferential terms or rates to certain policyholders or classes of insureds, when a preference is not warranted by normal underwriting standards.

see: discrimination

anti-rebate laws

Regulation. Statutes enacted by most states that prohibit agents from offering or returning any portion of the commission they receive from insurance companies to policyholders as an inducement to purchase insurance from the agent. Some states allow partial rebates in certain lines of business.

see: rebate

anti-selection

Insurer Operations. The adverse impact upon insurers that occurs when insureds select insurance coverage for only those risks that are likely to generate losses.

see: adverse selection

antifreeze automatic sprinkler system

Loss Control. An automatic sprinkler system with pipes containing an antifreeze solution connected to a water supply. The antifreeze solution, followed by water, discharges from sprinklers opened by a fire. This type of system is used in locations subject to freezing.

see: automatic sprinkler system

antique and classic aircraft insurance

Aviation. Insurance for vintage aircraft or aircraft no longer in production. These aircraft are underwritten by specialty aviation underwriters because they require pilots with special qualifications, and repairs and replacement of parts are difficult. Parts must sometimes be specially fabricated.

antique and classic automobile insurance

Personal. A personal auto policy designed for autos that are more than 25 years old, are maintained for use in exhibitions, club activities, parades, etc., and are only occasionally driven on public highways. Specialty automobile underwriters provide all-risk physical damage coverage for a stated amount. The vehicles have substantial values and are expensive to repair, as replacement parts often must be specially fabricated. Liability coverage is similar to a standard auto policy, but rates are generally much lower because of the limited exposure.

see: coverage for damage to your auto (maximum limit of liability), personal auto policy, stated amount

antique and classic boat insurance

Personal. A form of boat owner insurance for antique boats (constructed between 1919 and 1942) and classic boats (constructed between 1942 and 1968). Specialty marine underwriters provide all-risk physical damage coverage for a stated amount. Full marine coverage is written on boats that are still seaworthy, and only hull coverage is written on those that are displayed only on land.

see: boatowners' package policy, outboard motor and boat policy, stated amount, yacht insurance

antitrust law violations exclusion

Professional Liability. An exclusion in most accountants' professional liability policies for defense costs and any judgment arising out of accounting advice to clients that results in a violation of antitrust law.

see: accountants' professional liability insurance

antitrust laws

Regulation. Federal and state statutes that protect trade and commerce from price fixing, price discrimination, monopolies and unlawful restraints of trade. State laws are usually modeled on federal antitrust laws.

see: anti-compact laws, Clayton Act, McCarran-Ferguson Act, Sherman Antitrust Act

any auto

Automobile. A classification of covered vehicles under the business auto coverage form, garage coverage form, or truckers' coverage form. It is the broadest classification available.

see: business auto coverage form, garage coverage form, truckers' coverage form

any willing provider law

Health/Regulation. A statutory requirement, adopted in some states, for managed care plans to accept any health care provider willing to meet the plan's terms and conditions. The requirement eliminates a managed care plan's screening process in developing quality and cost control programs.

see: health care provider, managed care (1), out-of-network services

apparent agency

Agency. A legal principle that an agent is deemed to have whatever power or authority a person would reasonably infer, either from the principal's (employer's) representations concerning an agent's (employee's) authority or from the agent's holding himself out as having proper authority. The principal or insurer may be obligated as if it had expressly granted the authority to the agent.

synonym: agency by estoppel; *see:* estoppel, expressed authority, implied authority

apparent partner

Law. An individual who is not a partner in fact who represents herself to a third party as a partner and undertakes actions on behalf of the partnership. If all partners consent to the apparent partner's representations or acts, they are considered done by the partnership, which is then bound or liable to the same extent as for actions of an actual partner. If not all partners consent, the representation or act is a joint obligation only as to the partners who consent, not an obligation of the partnership itself.

see: partnership

appeal

Law. A pleading to a higher court requesting and stating legal grounds for a review of a lower court's order or ruling. An appeal is generally reviewed by a panel of judges, who either affirm or reverse the lower court decision. In certain situations, the court of appeal may ask the trial court to conduct a new trial or to reconsider its verdict.

see: appeal bond, appellate court, certiorari, pleading

appeal bond

Surety. A bond filed with a court by a party against whom a judgment has been rendered. The bond stays the execution of the judgment, pending appeal to a higher court. An appeal bond guarantees that the appellant will pay the original judgment (sometimes with interest) if the appeal fails or is denied.

see: appeal, court bond, judicial bond

appellant

Law. A person who appeals a lower court decision.

compare: appellee; *see:* appeal

appellate court

Law. A court of law having the power to hear appeals from and review cases litigated in lower courts.

see: appeal, per curiam

appellee

Law. The party against whom an appeal is sought.

compare: appellant; *see:* appeal

Appleton Rule

Regulation. A provision of the New York Insurance Code requiring insurance companies licensed in that state to follow specific New York laws even when operating outside of the state. Violation can result in the suspension or termination of the operations of a New York-licensed insurer.

application

Insurer Operations. A printed form developed by an insurer that includes questions about a prospective insured and the desired insurance coverage and limits. It provides the insurer's underwriter with information for accepting or rejecting the prospective insured and rating the desired policy. Some policies—especially life, health and professional liability policies—make the application part of the policy, and misrepresentations in the application can void the policy.

see: anti-arson application form, representation, simplified application

37

application for payment
Surety. A form that a contractor, in requesting payment for work completed up to the date of application, submits to an owner. The application for payment includes documents required by the contract before payment will be made.

appointment
Agency. Authorization of an individual to act for or represent an insurance company. The appointment is formalized by the signing of an agency agreement.
see: agency agreement

apportionment
Insurer Operations. A provision for dividing a loss among insurance policies when more than one policy is in force. It provides that a loss will be divided proportionally among the policies. *Example*: Policy A = $10,000; policy B = $20,000; policy C = $70,000, making total coverage of $100,000. Under the the most common apportionment clause, policy A pays 10% of any loss ($10,000 ÷ $100,000), policy B pays 20%, and policy C pays 70%.
see: contribution by limits, contribution by equal share
Property. A property insurance provision that divides a loss proportionally among all policies in force relative to the total amount of coverage. Differences in coverage among the policies may reduce an insured's recovery to less than 100% of the loss. *Example*: Two $10,000 property insurance policies apply to a building, but only one covers the peril of windstorm. Because each policy's share of total coverage limit is 50%, on a $5,000 windstorm loss, the insured recovers $2,500—50% of the loss.
see: contribution clause, other insurance provision, pro rata liability clause

appraisal
Accounting/Property. An expert's judgment or estimate of the value or quality of property as of a given date; a report, prepared and signed by a specialist, on the value of property or of an ongoing business. An *insurance appraisal* is specifically designed to determine the appropriate amount of insurance to be purchased or the amount of a loss to be paid.
see: actual cash value, appraisal clause, appraisal inventory, appraised value, appraiser, replacement cost
Title. An expert judgment or estimate of the value or quality of real estate as of a given date.
see: appraisers' errors and omissions insurance, assessed valuation, cost approach appraisal, income approach appraisal, market approach appraisal

appraisal clause
Property. A property insurance policy provision that allows an insured and insurer who cannot reach an agreement on the amount of a loss settlement to each select their own appraiser. The appraisers then select a neutral umpire. Disagreements between the appraisers are settled by the umpire, whose decisions are usually binding on both parties.
see: arbitration clause, umpire

appraisal inventory
Property. A detailed record of individual items that constitute a property. An appraisal inventory is included in an appraisal report, and lists the values set by the appraiser.

appraised value
Property. A value assigned to a property after an appraisal of it is completed. The appraised value is used to ascertain the appropriate amount of insurance to be purchased or the amount of loss to be paid.
see: appraisal

appraiser
Loss Control. A person who determines the value of property or the amount of a disputed loss.
compare: claims adjuster; *see*: appraisal

appraisers' errors and omissions insurance
Professional Liability. A form of professional liability insurance for an appraiser or appraisal firm that covers damages from negligent preparation of an appraisal. Coverage is usually written on a claims-made basis.
see: appraisal, professional liability insurance

appreciation
Financial Planning. An increase in the value of an investment, which is the fundamental investment objective. *Example*: A stock that increases from $30 to $40 per share has appreciated by 10 points.
see: point
General. An increase in the conversion value of a specific property or medium of exchange, caused by economic or related factors that may be either temporary or permanent.
compare: depreciation; *see*: inflation

appreciation rate
Financial Planning/Risk Management. A rate or index figure that is applied against the value of a property or investment at one date, to bring it up to its present or future value.

approach
Agency. The part of an agent's sales presentation that creates openings for further discussion with prospective insureds.
see: agent

approved cargo

Inland Marine/Loss Control/Ocean Marine.
Goods transported by ship, rail, air, etc., that are
not particularly susceptible to loss or damage due
to their nature or packaging.

synonym: approved merchandise

approved charges

Health.
see: fee schedule

approved merchandise

Inland Marine/Ocean Marine.
see: approved cargo

approved roof

Loss Control/Property. A roof constructed of fire-
resistive materials, rather than more flammable
wood shingles. Tile, metal and asphalt shingles are
approved roofing materials.

see: construction

approved sprinkler system

Loss Control/Property. An automatic sprinkler system installed in accordance with fire or building
codes that uses the proper automatic sprinkler
heads for the structure's occupancy and construction, that has an adequate and reliable supply of
water, that has been tested and shown to be in
working order, and has been found acceptable to
the appropriate governmental authority. Buildings
protected by such systems usually qualify for discounts on their fire insurance premiums.

see: automatic sprinkler system, protection

appurtenant structure

Property. An auxiliary structure of lesser value on
the same premises as the main insured structure,
such as a garage or shed. Some property insurance
policies provide additional coverage for appurtenant structures up to a percentage of the main
building's coverage.

see: coverage extension

arbiter

Law.
see: arbitrator

arbitrage

Financial Planning. The simultaneous purchase of
securities in one market and their sale in another in
order to profit from price discrepancies between the
two markets.

see: arbitrage bond

arbitrage bond

Financial Planning. A bond that guarantees the
performance of an arbitrage agreement.

see: arbitrage

arbitration

Law. A method of resolving a controversy instead
of litigation. The matter is submitted to a specified
number of disinterested persons (arbitrators), who
make an award, which is usually binding upon the
parties. Arbitration is sometimes nonbinding,
which allows a party to pursue the matter in court.

compare: litigation, mediation; *see*: alternative
dispute resolution, appraisal clause, arbitration
award, arbitration clause, arbitrator

arbitration agreement

Law. The document specifying that a particular dispute will be arbitrated and, usually, the method of
arbitration.

see: arbitration, arbitration clause, arbitrator

arbitration award

Law. The final decision of an arbitrator in settling a
dispute between the parties.

compare: judgment; *see*: arbitration, arbitrator

arbitration clause

Law. A provision included in many contracts that
the parties will settle any controversies arising
under the contract by arbitration instead of by lawsuit.

see: alternative dispute resolution, arbitration

Property. A clause in property insurance policies
providing that if the insured and the insurer cannot
agree on an appropriate claims settlement, each
will appoint an arbitrator, who in turn will then select an independent umpire. A decision by any two
of the three prescribes a settlement. The arbitration
clause binds both parties to this procedure, as well
as to the final decision.

see: appraisal clause, umpire

Reinsurance. A provision in reinsurance contracts
in which the parties agree to submit any dispute or
controversy to an official tribunal of their choosing,
in lieu of other proceedings (e.g., civil litigation)
provided for by the law. Although wording of arbitration clauses may vary, it normally provides for
an appointment of two arbitrators, one selected by
each party, who in turn appoint an umpire. The decision of any two of the three is binding on the parties to the reinsurance treaty.

Arbitration Forums, Inc.

Organizations. Members: Insurance companies,
self-insurers, commercial insureds with large retentions, third-party administrators and municipalities.
Objectives: A nonprofit corporation that arbitrates
and mediates disputes over insurance related matters. *Founded*: 1943. *Headquarters*: Tampa, FL.

arbitrator

Law. A person chosen or appointed to decide a

controversy through arbitration rather than litigation.

synonym: arbiter, umpire; *compare*: mediator, referee; *see*: arbitration

arbitrators' errors and omissions insurance

Professional Liability. A form of professional liability coverage for arbitrators and mediators that covers their liability for negligence in arbitration proceedings. Coverage is usually written on a claims-made basis.

synonym: mediators' errors and omissions insurance; *see*: errors and omissions insurance

archaeologist

Risk Management.

see: insurance archivist

architects' professional liability insurance

Professional Liability. Coverage for an architect or architectural firm for liability for damages arising out of the performance of professional services including errors, omissions or negligent acts. Coverage is usually written on a claims-made basis.

see: professional liability insurance

archivist

Risk Management.

see: insurance archivist

area

Liability/Property. The measure of a planar region or zone. Area is used as a rating basis for several types of liability insurance coverage (e.g., premises liability), and is also useful in verifying insurance-to-value calculations in property insurance. In rating formulas using square feet, the number of square feet is expressed in thousands of square feet of floor space (excluding open spaces such as mezzanines, courtyards, parking areas, and the non-public parts of buildings used for maintenance or for heating, or air conditioning equipment).

see: exposure unit

arising out of and in the course of employment

Workers' Compensation. The usual statutory phrase describing the injuries and illnesses covered by workers' compensation and typically used in policy forms to describe the coverage. "Arising out of employment" means that there must be a causal relationship between the job and its duties and how the injury or disease occurred. "In the course of employment" refers to the time, place and circumstances of the injury or disease.

see: covered injury, employee, occupational accident, occupational disease, workers' compensation insurance

arithmetic mean

Risk Management.

see: mean

armored car and messenger service insurance

Inland Marine. Insurance against losses incurred during the transfer of money, securities, precious metals, and certain kinds of valuables by armored cars.

Armstrong Investigation

Regulation. An investigation by New York State, conducted in 1905, of the life insurance industry, which resulted in the regulation by many states of life insurance policy forms and provisions. The regulations required life insurance companies to provide minimum benefit levels and to write policies in understandable language.

arrears

Insurer Operations. An insurance policy with past-due premiums but within the grace period and therefore not yet subject to cancellation for nonpayment.

see: bucking arrears, grace period

arson

Property. An act of actual or attempted malicious and deliberate destruction of property by fire. If the person committing this crime (the arsonist) is not the insured, property insurance policies cover the damage that results. If it is proved that the arsonist is either the insured or someone acting at the insured's direction, most property insurance policies are voided.

synonym: incendiarism; *see*: anti-arson application form, arson fraud

arson fraud

Property. Arson committed by or at the behest of the insured is usually considered fraud. Property insurance policies do not exclude loss by arson, but public policy does not allow profit by wrongdoing or provide coverage for intentional acts. Homeowners policy forms developed by the Insurance Services Office have specific exclusions dealing with intentional loss.

see: arson, fraud, homeowners policy, intentional loss

articles of association

Regulation.

see: articles of incorporation

articles of dissolution

Regulation. A document filed with the Secretary of State or other appropriate governmental agency, prior to dissolution of a partnership or corporation. The dissolution will not be approved until after provisions have been made for the distribution of assets, and after debts have been satisfied.

compare: articles of incorporation; *see*: distribution of assets

articles of incorporation

Regulation. An official document, filed with the Secretary of State or other appropriate governmental agency, that outlines a corporation's purpose and the rights and liabilities of shareholders and directors.

synonym: articles of association; *compare*: articles of dissolution; *see*: bylaws, charter, corporation

articles of merger or consolidation

Regulation. Documents filed with the Secretary of State or other governmental agency that specify the terms and conditions of a merger or consolidation of corporations.

as if

Insurer Operations. The recalculation of prior loss experience to show what underwriting results would have been if a particular program had been in force.

synonym: what if

Reinsurance. A term used by reinsurers to describe the recalculation of prior years' loss experience to determine what the underwriting results of a particular program would have been if the proposed program had been in force during that period.

as interest may appear

Inland Marine/Ocean Marine/Property. A phrase used in a policy to describe the insurable interest in a property when it is unknown. It is avoided by most underwriters, because disputes can arise as to whom a loss should be paid.

compare: full interest admitted; *see*: insurable interest

asbestos

Loss Control/Workers' Compensation. An incombustible fibrous material made from magnesium silicate, once used for fireproofing, electrical insulation, and chemical filters. Because it can cause cancer or asbestosis when its small particles are inhaled, its use has been banned in the United States.

see: asbestos abatement bond, asbestos abatement contractor, Asbestos Hazard Emergency Response Act, asbestosis, fire resistive

asbestos abatement bond

Surety. A performance bond for contractors who specialize in the removal and transportation of asbestos. The bond is usually only available from specialty bonding companies.

see: asbestos, asbestos abatement contractor, asbestos abatement liability, asbestosis

asbestos abatement contractor

Liability. An environmental remediation contractor that specializes in the safe removal and disposal or permanent encapsulation of asbestos from older buildings.

see: asbestos, asbestos abatement bond, asbestos abatement liability, asbestosis

asbestos abatement liability

Liability. A form of pollution liability coverage for property owners or asbestos abatement contractors for third-party bodily injury, property damage, and cleanup costs arising out of asbestos abatement activities.

see: asbestos, asbestos abatement bond, asbestos abatement contractor, asbestosis

Asbestos Hazard Emergency Response Act

Regulation. Federal legislation adopted in 1986 and subsequently amended that requires the removal or control of asbestos in schools and some public buildings. The federal government recognizes that asbestos is only hazardous to humans when it is in a crumbling, friable form, which allows airborne particles to enter the lungs. Generally, it is better to contain and monitor rather than attempt to remove it from a building.

see: asbestos

asbestosis

Workers' Compensation. A characteristic fibrotic condition of the lungs caused by inhalation of asbestos dust or fibers. The disease makes breathing progressively more difficult and can lead to death. Sometimes the term is used to include all asbestos-related diseases, such as interstitial pulmonary fibrosis and bronchial or laryngeal carcinomas.

compare:' silicosis; *see*: asbestos, continuous trigger theory, exposure theory

asked price

Financial Planning. The lowest price anyone will accept in payment for a security at a given time.

see: asking price

asking price

Financial Planning. A commercial term indicating the formal price at which goods or services are offered. This may not be the final price, as that is often negotiable.

synonym: asked price, offered price, offering price

assailing thieves

Ocean Marine. Thieves, other than the officers or crew of a vessel, using violence or force to steal a ship or its cargo.

see: barratry, piracy (*Ocean Marine*)

assessable policy
Insurer Operations.
see: assessment insurance

assessable value
Property. The value of real estate or personal property set by a governmental entity or official (e.g., county or state tax assessor) to determine the owner's property tax liability.

assessed valuation
Financial Planning. The value of real estate as established by a governmental agency for tax purposes. It has no close relationship to the property's market or insurable value.
compare: insurable value, market value; *see*: appraisal

assessment
General. Charges made to members of an association or other group, to fund losses, special projects, or ongoing operations.
see: deficiency assessment
Insurer Operations. An additional premium charged to policyholders by an assessment company to meet losses greater than anticipated.
see: assessment company

assessment company
Insurer Operations. An insurer with the right to assess policyholders in addition to the annual stipulated premium in the event of unexpectedly large losses.
compare: legal reserve life insurance company; *see*: assessment insurance, reciprocal insurance exchange

assessment insurance
Insurer Operations. A type of insurance whereby the insurer can charge policyholders additional premiums if actual losses exceed those originally expected at policy issue. When specific premium payments are not fixed in the policy (as is often the case with fraternal organizations), an assessment from the insurer increases the total premiums paid by the insureds whenever necessary to meet claims.
synonym: assessable policy; *compare*: nonassessable policy; *see*: contingent liability, deficiency assessment

assessment mutual insurance company
Insurer Operations. A mutual insurer with the right to assess policyholders additional amounts of premium to meet operational needs.
see: assessment company, mutual insurance company

assessment rolls
Title. A verified list of taxable property and persons constructed and maintained by cities or towns.

assessor
Title. A public official who appraises and values properties for tax purposes.

asset
Accounting. Anything of commercial value, including real or personal, tangible or intangible property.
compare: liability (*Accounting*); *see*: assets, capital asset, current assets, intangible property, personal property, real estate, tangible property

asset adjusted tax basis
Accounting.
see: book value

asset allocation fund
Financial Planning. A mutual fund that spreads its investments over stocks, bonds and short-term instruments.
see: mutual fund

asset composition ratio
Financial Planning. A financial ratio that considers the composition of an organization's total assets to evaluate solvency. The higher the ratio, the greater the organization's ability to raise money to pay debt. *Formula*: total current assets ÷ total assets.
see: current assets, financial ratios, financial underwriting

asset share value
Insurer Operations. The value of a class of insured business to an insurance company.
Life. The actual share of a life insurance company's assets represented by the policyholder's equity, based on the policyholder's contributions to assets (actual gross premiums minus actual costs, dividends and expenses related to the class of business involved).

assets
Accounting/Insurer Operations. The assets of an insurance company include real estate holdings, stocks, bonds, and other securities, cash, mortgages, and deferred and unpaid premiums. For statutory annual statement purposes, an insurer's assets do not include accounts receivable that are over 90 days in arrears or office equipment.
see: admitted assets, asset, nonadmitted assets, Statutory Accounting Principles

assign
Law. To transfer property, rights, or interests to another.
see: assignee, assignment, assignor

assigned risk
Insurer Operations. A risk insured through a pool

of insurers and assigned to a specific insurer. Generally, these risks are deemed by underwriters to be undesirable, but because of state law or otherwise, they must be insured. The best known assigned risk programs are those that provide automobile insurance to drivers that cannot obtain it through conventional means.

synonym: automobile insurance plan; *compare*: Fair Access to Insurance Requirements; *see*: assigned risk premium differential endorsement, assigned risk premium surcharge endorsement, automobile shared market, Boston Plan, joint underwriting association, market assistance plan, residual markets

assigned risk premium differential endorsement

Workers' Compensation. An endorsement (NCCI form WC 00 04 11) attached to a workers' compensation policy that has been issued through an assigned risk plan to apply any residual market loading to the estimated standard premium.

see: assigned risk, residual markets, workers' compensation insurance

assigned risk premium surcharge endorsement

Workers' Compensation. An endorsement (NCCI form WC 00 04 13) to a workers' compensation policy that has been issued through an assigned risk plan to apply a residual market surcharge to the standard premium.

see: assigned risk, residual markets, workers' compensation insurance

assignee

Law. The individual or entity to whom property, rights or interests have been transferred.

compare: assignor; *see*: assign

assignment

Law. The transfer of a legal right or interest in property or a contract. Transfer may be by sale or hypothecation—that is, the pledge of rights or benefits under a contract as security for a debt.

see: hypothecate

Liability/Property. Most property and casualty policies require prior written consent of the insurer for an assignment.

see: nonassignable

Life. Most life insurance policies allow a policyholder to assign benefits freely. Educational and nonprofit institutions often ask donors for such assignments, although simply changing the beneficiary is usually the preferred method.

Financial institutions often ask to be assigned life insurance policies held by a debtor. If the insured dies before the loan has been repaid, the creditor receives benefits up to the outstanding debt amount, with any remaining balance going to the beneficiary.

compare: nonassignable; *see*: absolute assignment, assign, assignee, assignment of benefits, assignment of lease, assignment quota, assignor, collateral assignment

assignment fee

Life. An administrative fee, usually a nominal flat dollar charge on each assignable annuity policy, where the periodic payment option is assigned to a third party.

assignment of benefits

Health. An insured's authorization for health insurer to pay policy benefits directly to a medical provider.

assignment of lease

Law. The transfer by a tenant or lessee of all interest in a leasehold to another party. Such a transfer may require the landlord's approval.

assignment provision

Property. A provision in most property insurance policies that allows the policy to be transferred to another party in two situations. The first allows transfer with the insurer's consent if the named insured sells the insured property. The second automatically transfers the policy to anyone taking legal temporary custody of the property if the named insured dies.

see: assignment

assignment quota

Property. The sharing by insurers in losses by percentage (or quota) with other insurance policies covering the same risk.

see: quota share

Reinsurance. An arrangement whereby a ceding insurer is reinsured for a fixed percentage of any loss expense.

assignor

Law. The individual or entity who assigns or transfers a property, right, or interest to another.

compare: assignee; *see*: assign

Associate, Customer Service (ACS)

Organizations. A professional designation earned after completing five examinations administered by the Life Management Institute. The curriculum covers life and health insurance.

see: Life Management Institute

Associate in Claims (AIC)

Organizations. A professional designation earned after successfully completing four national exams given by the Insurance Institute of America. The curriculum covers insurance claims practices, human relations and bad faith issues, the writing of

43

claims reports, and review of claims files. The curriculum was developed in conjunction with the National Association of Independent Insurance Adjusters.

see: Insurance Institute of America, National Association of Independent Insurance Adjusters

Associate in Fidelity and Surety Bonding (AFSB)

Organizations. A professional designation earned after successfully completing five national examinations given by the Insurance Institute of America. The curriculum was developed in conjunction with the National Association of Surety Bond Producers and the Surety Association of America. It covers principles of suretyship, contract surety, fidelity and noncontract surety.

see: Insurance Institute of America

Associate in Insurance Accounting and Finance (AIAF)

Organizations. A professional designation earned after successfully completing four national exams given by the Insurance Institute of America. Two different curricula are available: one for individuals in property and casualty insurance, and one for those in life insurance. The life insurance curriculum was developed in conjunction with the Life Management Institute. The curriculum covers statutory accounting for property and liability insurers, insurance information systems, insurance company finance, and insurance operations.

see: Life Management Institute, Insurance Institute of America

Associate in Insurance Services (AIS)

Organizations. A professional designation earned after successfully completing four national examinations given by the Insurance Institute of America. The curriculum covers insurance principles and practices, common insurance contracts, and terms, tools and ideas of quality management and how they apply to the insurance business.

see: Insurance Institute of America

Associate in Loss Control Management (ALCM)

Organizations. A professional designation earned after successfully completing five national exams given by the Insurance Institute of America. The curriculum covers accident prevention, property protection and occupational health and hygiene.

see: Insurance Institute of America

Associate in Management (AIM)

Organizations. A professional designation earned after successfully completing three national examinations given by the Insurance Institute of America. The curriculum covers recognizing strengths and weaknesses of existing management

practices, human behavior in organizations, systematic decision-making processes, managerial problems that get in the way of organization goals, and effective leadership in a wide variety of organizational goals.

see: Insurance Institute of America

Associate in Marine Insurance Management (AMIM)

Organizations. A professional designation earned after successfully completing six national examinations given by the Insurance Institute of America. The curriculum was developed in conjunction with the Inland Marine Underwriters Association and the American Institute of Marine Underwriters and covers ocean and inland marine insurance.

see: American Institute of Marine Underwriters, Inland Marine Underwriters Association, Insurance Institute of America

Associate in Premium Auditing (APA)

Organizations. A professional designation earned after successfully completing six national examinations given by the Insurance Institute of America. The curriculum was developed in conjunction with the National Society of Insurance Premium Auditors.

see: Insurance Institute of America, National Society of Insurance Premium Auditors

Associate in Reinsurance (ARe)

Organizations. A professional designation earned after successfully completing four national exams given by the Insurance Institute of America. The curriculum—developed in conjunction with the Reinsurance Section, the CPCU Society, and the Brokers and Reinsurance Markets Association—covers the reinsurance business, insurer exposures, statutory accounting, financial analysis, reinsurance program design, reinsurance regulation, reinsurance contracts, and pricing.

see: Brokers and Reinsurance Marketing Association; Insurance Institute of America; Reinsurance Section, CPCU Society

Associate in Research and Planning (ARP)

Organizations. A professional designation earned after successfully completing six national examinations given by the Insurance Institute of America. There is a curriculum for property and casualty insurance and one for life insurance. The basic curriculum was developed in conjunction with the Society of Insurance Research. The course includes insurance principles and operations and major insurance and economic issues. The life insurance curriculum was developed in conjunction with the Life Management Institute of the Life Office Management Association.

see: Insurance Institute of America, Life Management Institute, Society of Insurance Research

Associate in Risk Management (ARM)

Organizations/Risk Management. A professional designation earned after successfully completing three national examinations given by the Insurance Institute of America. The curriculum covers the risk management decision process as it applies to any organization.

see: Insurance Institute of America

Associate in Society of Actuaries (ASA)

Organizations. A designation awarded to a life, health or pension actuary by the Society of Actuaries for those who pass a series of examinations.

see: Society of Actuaries

Associate in Underwriting (AU)

Organizations. A professional designation earned after successfully completing four national exams by the Insurance Institute of America. The curriculum covers insurance exposure identification, commercial liability and property coverage, underwriting considerations, and loss control techniques.

see: Insurance Institute of America

Associate Insurance Data Manager (AIDM)

Organizations. A professional designation awarded by the Insurance Data Management Association after an individual successfully passes four of the courses in the curriculum.

see: Insurance Data Management Association

Associate, Life and Health Claims (ALHC)

Organizations. A professional designation awarded by the International Claim Association after an individual has passed five examinations administered by the Life Management Institute. The curriculum covers medical and dental aspects of claims, life and health insurance law, and claims administration.

see: International Claim Association, Life Management Institute

Associate of the Casualty Actuarial Society (ACAS)

Organizations. A designation awarded by the Casualty Actuarial Society for persons passing a series of examinations on actuarial mathematics.

see: Casualty Actuarial Society

Associated Aviation Underwriters

Aviation. An underwriting syndicate specializing in aircraft risks.

Associated Risk Managers International (ARMI)

Organizations. Members: Insurance agencies providing property and casualty insurance, risk management services and life and health insurance programs. *Objectives*: Serves as a marketing organization to develop and market specialized insurance and risk management services for trade associations, professional groups and other industry organizations. *Founded:* 1970. *Headquarters*: Austin, TX.

association captive insurance company

Risk Management. A captive insurance company established by members of an association to underwrite their own collective risks. An association captive usually only insures members of the sponsoring association.

compare: group captive insurance company; *see*: captive insurance company

Association for Advanced Life Underwriting (AALU)

Organizations. Members: Advanced life underwriters specializing in estate analysis, business insurance, pension planning, employee benefit plans and other subjects relating to life insurance. *Objectives*: Promotes interests of members; lobbies legislatures for issues concerning life underwriters. *Founded*: 1957. *Headquarters*: Washington, D.C.

association group insurance

Health/Life. Group insurance that covers a trade or business association and its members, rather than an employer or union providing the coverage.

see: group insurance

Association of Average Adjusters of the United States (AAA)

Organizations. Members: Marine insurance adjusters, marine insurers, admiralty lawyers and ship and cargo appraisers. *Objectives*: Maintains a library on marine insurance and bestows awards to marine insurance adjusters. Provides information to its members and produces publications. *Founded*: 1979. *Headquarters*: New York, NY.

Association of Casualty and Surety Companies (ACSC)

Organizations. An organization that was merged in 1964 with the National Board of Fire Underwriters to form the American Insurance Association.

see: American Insurance Association

Association of Defense Trial Attorneys (ADTA)

Organizations. Members: Attorneys who regularly represent insurance companies and companies that self-insure. *Objectives:* Gathering and distributing information to further insurer and self-insurer defense efforts. Continuing education of its members in matters pertaining to defense of claims involving insurance companies. *Founded:* 1941. *Headquarters:* Peoria, IL. Known until 1988 as the Association of Insurance Attorneys.

Association of Health Care Internal Auditors

Organizations. Members: Health care auditors.

Objectives: Exchange of information and educational programs. *Headquarters*: Skokie, IL.

Association of Insurance Attorneys
Organizations.
see: Association of Defense Trial Attorneys

Association of Life Insurance Counsel (ALIC)
Organizations. Members: Legal counsel of life insurance companies. *Objectives*: Promoting interests of legal representatives of life insurance companies. *Founded*: 1913. *Headquarters*: New York, NY.

Association of Life Insurance Medical Directors of America
Organizations.
see: American Academy of Insurance Medicine

Association of Mill and Elevator Mutual Insurance Companies (AMEMIC)
Organizations. Members: Mutual insurance companies. *Objectives*: Holds seminars and provides an exchange of information among its members concerning grain handling and grain processing plants. *Founded*: 1897. *Headquarters*: Itasca, IL. Also known as the Mill Mutuals.

Association of Professional Insurance Women (APIW)
Organizations. Members: Women in the insurance and reinsurance industry. *Objectives*: Provides professional networking and educational assistance. *Founded*: 1976. *Headquarters*: New York, NY.

Association of Trial Lawyers of America (ATLA)
Organizations. Members: Plaintiffs' attorneys. *Objectives*: To promote effective representation of plaintiffs' legal claims by developing litigation and settlement strategies and educating members through meetings, lectures, seminars and publications. *Founded*: 1973. *Headquarters*: Cambridge, MA. (Formerly known as the American Trial Lawyers Association.)

association professional liability insurance
Professional Liability. Coverage for nonprofit associations that includes professional liability and directors' and officers' liability for all directors, officers, employees, and other association member while acting on behalf of the association. Coverage is usually written on a claims-made basis.
see: directors' and officers' liability insurance

assumability clause
Financial Planning. A provision in a mortgage that allows it to be transferred or assumed by another party. Lenders generally require a credit review of the new borrower and may charge a fee for the assumption.
compare: due-on-sale; *see*: mortgage

assume
Reinsurance. To accept (reinsure) insurance risk from another insurer (the ceding company) or from a self-insurer.
compare: cede; *see*: assumed reinsurance, ceding insurer, reinsurer, reinsurance
Risk Management. To retain some degree of risk or exposure.
see: assumption of risk, self-insurance

assumed liability policy
Insurer Operations. A policy providing business liability coverage for risks assumed or transferred by agreement or contract.
see: contractual liability insurance

assumed portfolio
Financial Planning. The assumption of all securities held by a person or an institution.
see: portfolio

assumed reinsurance
Reinsurance. The amount of insurance assumed by a reinsurer from a ceding insurer in an ordinary facultative or treaty reinsurance arrangement.
synonym: assumption; *compare*: assumption reinsurance, ceded reinsurance; *see*: facultative reinsurance, reinsurer, treaty reinsurance

assuming insurer
Reinsurance.
see: reinsurer

assumption
Insurer Operations. An archaic term for *gross line*.
see: gross line

assumption of risk
Law/Workers' Compensation. The legal doctrine that a plaintiff is not entitled to compensation if, knowing of a dangerous condition, he voluntarily exposed himself to the risk that resulted in injury. It is a common law defense, which was widely used in employee injury cases prior to the enactment of workers' compensation laws. The theory was that an employee implicitly assumes all of the ordinary and usual risks of a job, but workers' compensation laws abolished the defense. Some states with no-fault insurance laws have abolished the defense in automobile cases as well.
see: affirmative defense, common law defense, guest law, Priestly v. Fowler, workers' compensation law

assumption reinsurance
Reinsurance. A relatively uncommon form of reinsurance whereby the reinsurer is substituted for the

ceding insurer and becomes directly liable for policy claims. This ordinarily requires a notice and release from affected policyholders. In the more typical reinsurance arrangement, the reinsurer has an obligation to indemnify the ceding insurer, which remains liable for claims on policies it has issued, and policyholders' approval is not required.

compare: assumed reinsurance; *see*: ceding insurer, facultative reinsurance, reinsurer, treaty reinsurance

assurance
Insurer Operations. 1. A term used interchangeably with *insurance*, especially in European and British markets, although *insurance* is the preferred term in the United States.
2. A guarantee or declaration of full confidence.
see: insurance, warranty (3)

assurance company
Insurer Operations.
see: insurance company

assured
Insurer Operations. An insured; the person or entity named in the policy that is insured against specified losses or perils.
see: insured, policyholder

assurer
General. Insurer; the underwriter or indemnifier for specified losses.
see: insurance company

asymmetrical curve
Risk Management.
see: skewed curve

ATA carnet
International. A customs document issued by a national Chamber of Commerce that is recognized in place of national customs documents as security for import duties to cover the temporary admission of goods and, sometimes, their transit. The International Chambers of Commerce guarantee payment of duties under the ATA carnet in the event of failure to re-export. (ATA is a combined French/English abbreviation for admission temporaire/temporary admission.)
see: admission temporaire

Atmospheric Release Advisory Center (ARAC)
Loss Control. A government sponsored facility established in 1974 at the Lawrence Livermore National Laboratory in Livermore, California. Its purpose is to predict the path of radioactive material released in a nuclear accident and to study radioactive releases from atomic bomb tests.

Atomic Energy Act
Regulation. Federal legislation adopted in 1954 that makes it unlawful for any person to transfer, manufacture, acquire, possess, or use any nuclear material without a license from the Nuclear Regulatory Commission.
see: nuclear energy liability insurance

atomic energy reinsurance
Liability.
see: American Nuclear Insurers, MAERP Reinsurance Association

attachment
Insurer Operations. An addition to a basic insurance policy that explains, adds or excludes coverages. It can also add or delete locations. An endorsement or rider that is added to an insurance policy.
see: endorsement, rider
Law. The seizure of property pursuant to a court order, or the document (writ of attachment) that effects a seizure in order to subject the person in possession of the property to the court's jurisdiction or to secure payment of a judgment in favor of a creditor of the property owner.
see: attachment bond, foreclosure

attachment bond
Surety. A bond that guarantees payment of damages by the principal if property has been wrongfully attached.
see: attachment

attachment point
Reinsurance. The dollar amount under an excess of loss reinsurance contract at which a ceding (primary) insurer's retention requirements have been met, and the point at which the reinsurance will respond to a loss.
see: excess of loss reinsurance

attained age
Life. The insured's age at a specified point in time, often based on the previous or next birthday, whichever is closer.
see: age, misstatement of age, original age

attending physician's statement (APS)
Health. A statement made to an underwriter by a proposed insured's personal physician with the permission of the patient. Information obtained in this manner generally concerns illnesses and injuries that may have a bearing on the insurability of the proposed insured.
see: warranty (1)

attest
Law. To bear witness to a fact; to affirm to be genuine or true; to authenticate.

see: affirm, attestation clause

attestation clause
Insurer Operations. The final clause of an insurance contract where an officer or officers of an insurance company place their signature(s) to officially authenticate it as a binding contract.

see: insurance contract

attorney-in-fact
General. A person authorized by another (the principal) to act in the principal's place or stead for a particular purpose. This authority is usually conferred through an instrument called *power of attorney*.

see: power of attorney

Insurer Operations. An individual or organization that manages a reciprocal insurance exchange for the benefit of its members. Through a *subscriber's agreement* signed by each of the exchange members, the attorney-in-fact is given authority to conduct the day-to-day business of the exchange, including the exchange of insurance among the members.

see: Lloyd's of London, reciprocal insurance exchange

attorneys' professional liability insurance
Professional Liability. A form of professional liability insurance designed for attorneys that provides coverage for damages and expenses arising from alleged neglect, error or omission in the performance of legal services. Coverage is usually written on a claims-made basis.

synonym: lawyers' professional liability insurance; *see*: employed counsel professional liability insurance, public service exclusion

attractive nuisance doctrine
Law. There is normally no particular care required of property owners to safeguard trespassers from harm, but an attractive nuisance is an exception. An attractive nuisance is any inherently hazardous object or condition of property that can be expected to attract children to investigate or play (for example, construction sites and discarded large appliances). The doctrine imposes upon the property owner either the duty to take precautions that are reasonable in light of the normal behavior of young children—a much higher degree of care than required toward adults—or the same care as that owed to "invitees"—a higher standard than required toward uninvited, casual visitors (licensees).

see: degree of care, invitee, licensee, negligence, nuisance, trespasser

auctioneers' errors and omissions insurance
Professional Liability. A form of professional liability insurance designed for auctioneers, providing coverage for negligent acts, errors or omissions in the conduct of their business. Coverage is usually written on a claims-made basis.

see: errors and omissions insurance

audible alarm
Loss Control.

see: burglar alarm

audio, visual and data electronic equipment coverage
Automobile. An endorsement to a commercial automobile policy (ISO form CA 99 60) that covers physical damage to any permanently installed electronic equipment that receives or transmits audio, visual, or data signals and is not designed solely for the reproduction of sound. Coverage includes removable units that are contained in permanently installed housing.

see: physical damage coverage

audio, visual and electronic data equipment and tapes, records, discs and other media endorsement
Personal. An endorsement (ISO form PP 03 06) to the personal auto policy that extends coverage to electronic equipment excluded under part D of the policy. Coverage can be provided for audio, visual and electronic equipment with specifically scheduled limits on the endorsement, and the endorsement includes a $200 limit for tapes, records, discs and other media.

see: personal auto policy

audit
Accounting.

see: Generally Accepted Accounting Principles

Insurer Operations. Insurers commonly review the financial records of their commercial insureds, to determine premiums for business interruption, workers' compensation, manufacturing, contracting, product liability, and other risks, where premiums are based upon payroll, gross receipts, and other auditable factors. Auditors (either employees of the insurer or independent contractors) survey insured businesses' records to determine premiums due, based upon expenses and conditions stated in the policy. Audits are usually performed annually, after the policy period in question has expired, and after the items to be audited can be considered final.

If the audit determines that an insured's initial premium was too low (i.e., the estimates for audited exposures were lower than actuals), the audit will result in an *additional premium*. If the audit shows that the initial premium was too high (i.e., exposures were over-estimated), the insured will

receive a *return premium.*
see: additional premium, audit policy, audit provision, initial premium, inspection, payroll audit, return premium
Regulation.
see: examination

audit bureau
Insurer Operations. A central bureau where companies submit daily reports and copies of issued endorsements for auditing before transmittal to the insurance company. If errors are discovered, the originating office is informed and corrections are requested.
synonym: stamping office; *see*: examination bureau, rating bureau

audit policy
Insurer Operations. An expired policy examined by an insurer, usually to determine the adequacy of the premium charged by the underwriter.
see: audit

audit provision
Insurer Operations. An insurance policy provision that explains the insurer's right to examine and audit the insured's books and records at any time during the policy period and within three years after expiration, insofar as such records relate to the policy. The calculation of the estimated and final premium are explained, as well as the determination of premium upon policy cancellation.
see: audit

audited financial statement
Accounting. An organization's financial statement that has been audited by a Certified Public Accountant, who has expressed an opinion as to the accuracy of the statement in accordance with Generally Accepted Accounting Principles.
see: Certified Public Accountant, financial statement, Generally Accepted Accounting Principles

authorization
Insurer Operations. Information and guidance given to agents by underwriters that specify the amounts and types of insurance that will be accepted on a risk of a given class or at a specific location.
see: agency, agency agreement, agent's certificate of authority

authorized insurer
Regulation.
see: admitted insurer

authorized reinsurance
Insurer Operations / Reinsurance. Reinsurance ceded to a reinsurer either admitted to write insurance directly in the state or approved (accredited)

by the state regulator to assume reinsurance. The ceding insurer may take credit for authorized reinsurance on its statutory annual statement. If the reinsurer is not admitted to do business or is not accredited, reinsurance credit is not allowed unless ceded reserves are funded by cash or letters of credit.
synonym: admitted reinsurance; *compare*: unauthorized reinsurance; *see*: accredited reinsurer, reinsurance credit

auto club
Organizations.
see: American Automobile Association

auto loan receivables insurance
Financial Guaranty. Insurance that guarantees the repayment of an auto loan to a financial institution. Should a lessee stop payments to the lessor, the insurer makes the outstanding installment payments over the balance of the lease period. The insurance remains in force until all of the insured obligations have been paid. Generally, coverage is provided for all forms of debtor insolvencies and for the non-payment of all past-due accounts filed with the insurer within ninety days after their original due date.
see: financial guaranty insurance

automatic cover
Liability/Property. A policy provision permitting increases in coverage, changes in interest, and coverage of newly-acquired property. The amount and duration of automatic coverage are usually limited. For continued and full protection, the insured must report changes to the insurer and obtain an amendment to the policy.

automatic increase in insurance endorsement
Property.
see: inflation guard endorsement

automatic insured
Insurer Operations. An individual or entity closely associated with the named insured (e.g., a family member, officer of a firm, employee) who is automatically considered an insured under a policy.
see: insured

automatic premium loan (APL)
Life. A feature in life insurance policies that uses the cash value accumulated by the insurance policy to pay for past due premiums at the end of the grace period. This prevents a lapse of coverage.
see: cash surrender value

automatic reinstatement clause
Liability/Property. A provision in an insurance policy that reinstates the original limits of the policy

after a covered loss has been paid. Not all coverages may be subject to automatic reinstatement of limits (for example, coverage subject to aggregate limits).

synonym: loss clause; *compare*: aggregate limit, first loss insurance, restoration premium

automatic reinsurance

Reinsurance. A reinsurance agreement under which the insurer cedes those portions of a specified class of risks that exceed the retention limits set by contract (treaty) with the reinsurer. The reinsurer must accept all risks ceded to it under the treaty with the insurer.

synonym: automatic treaty; *compare*: facultative reinsurance; *see*: assume, cede, reinsurance, retention, treaty reinsurance

automatic retirement

Employee Benefits.

see: compulsory retirement

automatic safety belt

Automobile/Loss Control. A passive restraint device in a vehicle that automatically positions a shoulder belt around the driver or front passenger when the car door closes. It is safer than a manual seat belt because it works without requiring the occupant to take any action.

see: passive restraint system, seat belt

automatic sprinkler clause

Property. A provision in a property insurance policy (written on a building equipped with an automatic sprinkler system) that requires the insured to maintain the system in working order and to notify the insurer whenever the system is not operational, even when only briefly inoperative during maintenance. Coverage may be suspended if the insured fails to comply.

see: automatic sprinkler system, emergency impairment, preplanned impairment, protective safeguards clause

automatic sprinkler system

Loss Control. An integrated system of underground and overhead piping connected to sprinkler heads (usually mounted in the ceiling) which are activated at a relatively low temperature (the initial stage of a fire). The sprinkler heads release a spray of water to extinguish the fire or prevent it from spreading. Insurance underwriters typically require automatic sprinkler systems in certain types of buildings or occupancies, and sprinkler water supply systems usually must be independent of normal water service to the protected building. Periodic inspection and testing of sprinklers is required. The existence of an approved sprinkler system normally reduces premiums for the insured property.

see: antifreeze automatic sprinkler system, approved automatic sprinkler system, automatic sprinkler clause, cold weather valve, control valve, deluge automatic sprinkler system, dry pipe automatic sprinkler system, emergency impairment, fire extinguishing system, halon, indicator post, outside screw and yoke valve, preplanned impairment, preaction automatic sprinkler system, present value of automatic sprinkler reduction, scuppers, sprinkler leakage coverage, sprinkler leakage liability insurance, wet pipe automatic sprinkler system

Property. Under a property insurance policy, an automatic sprinkler system includes sprinkler heads, piping, tanks, pumps, standpipes and associated valves.

see: earthquake sprinkler leakage, sprinkler leakage coverage

automatic treaty

Reinsurance.

see: automatic reinsurance

automatically convertible term life insurance

Life. A life insurance policy designed to be converted to permanent insurance at a predetermined date without the express instructions of the insured at that time.

see: convertible term life insurance

automobile

Automobile. In business auto and truckers' coverage, an automobile is defined as a motor vehicle designed for use on public roads and includes a land motor vehicle, trailer, or semitrailer. "Mobile equipment" is not considered an automobile.

see: automobile insurance, business auto coverage form, mobile equipment, truckers' coverage form

Personal. In personal auto coverage, an automobile is a private passenger automobile, pick-up truck, sedan, panel truck, or trailer not used in any business or occupation.

compare: all-terrain vehicle, moped, personal auto policy, private passenger automobile, snowmobile

automobile club

Organizations.

see: American Automobile Association

automobile dealers rating plan

Automobile.

see: dealer class plan

automobile exclusion

Inland Marine. Licensed automobiles are excluded in most contractors' equipment policies, as they are expected to be covered by automobile policies. Occasionally, the exclusion is modified to provide physical damage coverage on vehicles used principally in construction operations.

see: contractors' equipment

automobile fleet

Automobile. A group of automobiles, owned and managed by the same owner. The economies for an insurer of covering a significant number of vehicles under a single policy allows a discounted premium to be offered on automobile fleet policies.

see: fleet policy

automobile insurance

Automobile. Insurance that provides coverage for physical damage to the insured's vehicle, liability coverage for bodily injury and property damage to others arising out of the insured's operation of a vehicle, and coverage for medical treatment of the insured's or operator's own injuries.

see: all-terrain vehicle coverage, automobile liability bond, automobile liability coverage, basic standard automobile policy, business auto coverage form, collision coverage, comprehensive coverage, family automobile policy, Mexican automobile insurance, personal auto policy, physical damage coverage, special package automobile policy, uninsured motorist coverage

automobile insurance identification card

Automobile. An information card (ACORD form 50) provided by an insurer that is required in some states to be carried by the insured or in the insured auto and produced on demand as evidence of insurance.

see: evidence of coverage, financial responsibility law

automobile insurance plan

Automobile.

see: assigned risk

Automobile Insurance Plans Service Office (AIPSO)

Organizations. Members: Automobile insurance companies. *Objectives*: A nonprofit organization that compiles statistics and calculates rates for automobile assigned risk plans and provides other services for auto insurance plans. *Headquarters*: Johnston, RI.

see: assigned risk

automobile liability bond

Automobile. A surety bond maintained in lieu of automobile liability coverage to satisfy a state's financial responsibility or compulsory insurance law when an organization self-insures its auto liability exposure.

see: automobile liability coverage, compulsory

insurance law, financial responsibility law, surety bond

automobile liability coverage

Automobile. Insurance against financial loss because of the insured's liability to others for vehicle-related injuries or property damage.

compare: personal injury protection, physical damage coverage; *see*: business auto coverage form, personal auto policy, third-party liability

automobile medical payments

Automobile.

see: medical payments coverage (*Automobile*)

automobile physical damage insurance

Automobile.

see: physical damage coverage

automobile racing spectator coverage

Liability. A form of special event insurance that covers the insured race track or road course owner and event sponsors for injuries to spectators because of hazards of the premises or event (for example, the collapse of bleachers and flying debris from a racing vehicle). Coverage is excluded for participating drivers, pit crews, and owners of racing vehicles.

synonym: drag strip spectator coverage

automobile reinsurance facility

Automobile/Regulation. One of several types of automobile shared market mechanisms, used to make auto insurance available to persons who are unable to obtain it in the regular market. Policies written under the plan are reinsured by a pool.

see: automobile shared market

automobile repossessors' liability insurance

Professional Liability. Insurance for auto repossessors, consisting of general liability coverage, including personal injury coverage, towing and driveaway coverage (while repossessing a vehicle by the use of duplicate keys). It includes garagekeepers' legal liability to insure against damage to vehicles while in the insured's care, custody or control.

automobile service contract

Personal. A contract issued by an automobile manufacturer or dealer (sometimes backed by insurance) that promises to perform (or pay for) certain repairs or services to a specific automobile. It differs from a manufacturer's warranty, which comes with a new vehicle and is included in the original price. A service contract may be purchased at any time at a separate cost.

see: warranty (3)

automobile shared market

Automobile/Regulation. Programs available in every state and the District of Columbia in which all state-licensed automobile insurers participate to make coverage available to car owners who are unable to obtain insurance in the regular market. (An exception is Maryland, which operates a state-funded mechanism where losses are subsidized by private insurers.) One of three systems is used to guarantee the availability of insurance: an auto insurance plan (also called an *assigned risk plan*), a joint underwriting association, or an auto reinsurance facility.

see: assigned risk, automobile reinsurance facility, joint underwriting association

automobile use policy statement

Risk Management. A document that sets out the guidelines for employees of an organization concerning the use of company vehicles, personal vehicles used for business purposes, rental cars used on business, personal auto insurance requirements, and motor vehicle report review and corrective procedures. The document is usually approved by senior management and distributed to employees likely to travel on business.

see: business auto coverage form, business use

automotive products in outside containers

Crime. An endorsement (ISO form CR 15 07) to crime coverage forms E or H that covers loss or damage to automotive products (e.g., gasoline) in an enclosed and locked outside container adjacent to the premises. The loss must be caused by forcible entry into the container (e.g., gas pump) or the premises.

see: crime coverage form A (B, etc.)

autopsy provision

Health.

see: physical examination and autopsy provision

autos left for service, repair, storage or safekeeping

Automobile. A classification of covered vehicles under the garage coverage form.

see: garage coverage form

auxiliary alarm system

Loss Control. A system that transmits a fire alarm from a detection device to a municipal fire alarm box, which transmits the alarm to the public fire service communication center.

compare: central station alarm system, local alarm system, proprietary alarm system, remote station alarm system

auxiliary fund

Employee Benefits.

see: conversion fund

available seat miles (ASM)

Aviation. A measure of an airline's seating capacity available for sale. Each available seat mile is one seat flown one mile. This is one factor used by aviation underwriters to measure an airline's exposure to liability risks.

see: revenue passenger miles

average

Risk Management.

see: mean, median, mode

Ocean Marine. Any loss or damage due to insured perils that is less than a total loss.

see: average agreement, free of particular average, general average, general average bond, general average contribution, particular average

average adjuster

Ocean Marine.

see: general average adjuster

average agreement

Ocean Marine. A document signed by a cargo insurer, to allow release of the cargo after the occurrence of an average loss which is covered by the insurer. Prior to the release, the owner must post a bond or cash deposit for the amount of the assessment against the owner's shipment, or provide a guarantee from an acceptable insurance company.

see: general average bond, general average

average annual dividend yield

Financial Planning. The total common dividends declared per share, divided by the average stock price, for a given fiscal year. It is expressed as a percentage.

see: yield

average blanket rate

Property. When property insurance is blanketed, this is the rate applied against all the property insured by the policy, and is the rate used to determine premiums on mid-term endorsements (e.g., increases in insured values). The rate is developed by determining premiums in the usual manner (i.e., multiplying each location's specific rate by the value at that location), totaling these premiums, and dividing this sum by the total of all values insured.

synonym: average rate; *compare*: specific rate; *see*: blanket insurance

average clause

Property. When multiple properties are covered by a single policy, an average clause provides that each property is insured in the same proportion that its value bears to the total of all values insured. The clause is used to prevent an insured from underinsuring one of the properties.

compare: coinsurance, coinsurance clause; *see*:

insurance to value, pro rata distribution clause
International. A coinsurance clause, so called in
some countries. If insured property values are inadequate to meet the average clause (coinsurance) requirement, the insured will bear a proportional
share of any loss.
see: coinsurance

average cost
Risk Management. A business inventory valuation
method that develops an inventory value by dividing the total costs of goods available for sale
throughout the year by the total quantity purchased.
compare: first in, first out; last in, first out

average daily census
Health. The average number of hospital inpatients,
calculated by dividing the number of patient-days
during a period by the number of calendar days in
the period. An inpatient charged for occupying a
bed for one day constitutes one patient-day.
Newborns are excluded from this calculation.
see: average length of stay, inpatient

average indexed monthly earnings (AIME)
Employee Benefits. A method whereby a worker's
earnings are indexed according to changes in national average wages, so that retired workers maintain the same relative income level in their Social
Security benefits.
see: average monthly wage, Social Security

average length of stay (ALOS)
Health. The average number of inpatient days
spent by patients in a hospital during a given period. It is used to measure health care facility utilization. Newborns are excluded from the calculation.
see: average daily census, inpatient

average monthly earnings
Employee Benefits.
see: average monthly wage

average monthly wage (AMW)
Employee Benefits. A weighted average of an individual's Social Security wages. *Formula*: 1. Determine the total number of years that the individual
paid the Social Security tax, starting with the year
beginning in their 21st birthday, subject to a maximum of 40 years; 2. Select the 35 years (420
months) of highest Social Security wage earnings;
3. Divide the total wages subject to Social Security
earned during those 35 years by 420 to calculate
the average monthly wage.
The AMW is then used when referring to a table
published by the Social Security Administration
(the Social Security Wage Index) to find the corresponding primary insurance amount that will be

paid.
synonym: average monthly earnings; *see*: average indexed monthly earnings, primary insurance amount, Social Security Wage Index

average rate
Property.
see: average blanket rate

average risk
Insurer Operations.
see: standard risk

average weekly benefits
Workers' Compensation. A percentage of the average weekly wage, calculated or prescribed by state
workers' compensation laws. It is subject to minimum and maximum amounts.
synonym: weekly compensation; *see*: average
weekly wage, disability benefit, workers' compensation law

average weekly wage (AWW)
Workers' Compensation. The average rate of remuneration per week, computed or prescribed by
state workers' compensation and disability benefits
laws, and used for determining weekly workers'
compensation or disability benefits.
synonym: weekly compensation; *see*: average
weekly benefits, workers' compensation law

average weekly wage loss
Workers' compensation. The difference between
an injured employee's average weekly wage prior
to a workers' compensation injury and the average
weekly wage paid by workers' compensation.
compare: wage loss, reduced earnings; *see*: average weekly wage

averaging
Financial Planning.
see: dollar cost averaging

aviation accident insurance
Life. Life insurance that protects passengers, pilots,
or flight employees while on scheduled air flights
against losses connected with airline accidents.
Non-scheduled or foreign flight coverage generally
requires higher premiums.
see: aviation insurance

aviation clause
Life. An exclusion found in many life insurance
policies that denies coverage for a loss resulting
from an aviation accident, unless the insured was a
passenger on a regularly scheduled airline.
see: aviation hazard

aviation hazard
Life. The increased life insurance risk associated

with flight on aircraft other than commercial airlines. Many life insurance policies exclude coverage for such risks by use of the aviation clause.

see: aviation clause

Risk Management. The increased hazard of death or disability arising from travel on other-than-commercial aircraft.

aviation insurance

Aviation. Protection of an insured against losses arising out of the manufacture, use or operation of aircraft. The insured is likely to be an airport, aircraft manufacturer, airline, pilot, flight instructor, fixed base operator, or transportation company that uses aircraft. Coverages may include liability for bodily injury, property damage or medical payments, and various types of first-party property loss, including hull coverage.

synonym: air transport insurance; *see*: air cargo insurance, aircraft insurance, aircraft product liability insurance, aircraft spare parts insurance, airport owners' and operators' liability insurance, air travel insurance, all risks—ground and flight, aviation passenger liability insurance, crop dusting and spraying insurance, FAA special waiver endorsement, fixed base liability coverage, hangarkeepers' liability insurance, hull coverage, in flight, in motion

Aviation Insurance Rating Bureau (AIRB)

Organizations. Members: Aviation insurers. *Objectives*: Promulgating rates for aircraft hulls, aircraft property damage liability and employers' aviation indemnity. Establishes and administers plans to secure statistical data for creating underwriting rules, classification of risks, rating plans, rates or premiums. *Founded*: 1948. *Headquarters*: New York, NY.

aviation passenger liability insurance

Aviation. Coverage for aircraft operators in the event a passenger is injured, killed or disabled during an accident while aboard an insured aircraft. Aviation policies divide liability coverage into two parts—general liability (excluding passengers), and passenger liability.

compare: air travel insurance

avocations

Life.

see: hobbies or avocations

avoidable consequence

Law. An adverse result that arises from a lack of care, especially on the part of a person who suffers a harm or loss. Under this concept, a plaintiff cannot recover damages for injuries or losses that could have been avoided or mitigated by using reasonable care.

see: comparative negligence, negligence

avoidance

Financial Planning.

see: tax avoidance

Risk Management.

see: risk avoidance

avulsion

Loss Control. The sudden cutting off of land by flood, currents, or change in course of a body of water.

compare: alluvion; *see*: accretion

B

back end load

Financial Planning. A fee charged at the time of the sale, transfer, disposition of, or withdrawal from annuities, life insurance policies, mutual funds, or securities. The front end is the purchase, and the back end is the sale.

synonym: exit fee, redemption fee; *compare*: front end load; *see*: no load fund

backdate

General.

see: antedate

backup facility agreement

Health. A formal or informal agreement between health care providers or health service plan sponsors to render services to the other's patients or enrollees. The agreement can involve either specific medical services or overflow patients. Such agreements can be between two similar health care providers (two hospitals or two clinics, for example) or two quite different health care facilities (a hospital for inpatient care, and a clinic for outpatient follow-up visits).

Risk Management. A formal agreement between two businesses for one to provide the other with some form of assistance in the event of a breakdown of equipment or damage to property. *Example*: An agreement between two newspapers to print the other's paper in the event of a breakdown or loss.

see: disaster plan

bad faith

Law. In general, dishonesty, unfair dealing or deceit; failure by an insurer to act according to the terms of an insurance policy, for example, not paying a valid claim after proof of loss has been submitted. In most states, bad faith is more culpable than an honest mistake or mere negligence, but the action need not constitute fraud, malice or oppression.

see: excess judgment loss, fraud, negligence, punitive damages, unfair claims practice

baggage coverage

Personal. Coverage on the personal effects owned by and for the personal use, adornment or amusement of the insured (or a family member of the insured) while traveling. Coverage is written on an all-risk basis and applies anywhere in the world.

compare: personal effects floater

baghouse filter

Loss Control. A large fabric bag, usually made of glass fibers, that captures intermediate and large particles (greater than 20 microns in diameter) as air passes through it.

bail

Law. A security given to a court guaranteeing the later appearance of a person in police custody in order to obtain his release.

see: bail bond

Surety. To deliver property in trust to another for a special purpose and for a limited period.

see: bailee

bail agents

Surety. Persons appointed by a surety to execute or countersign bail bonds.

bail bond

Surety. A bond provided to a court for the release of an individual (principal) who has been placed under arrest because of a civil action or criminal offense. The face value of the bond is forfeited if the principal fails to appear in court at an appointed time.

bailee

Inland Marine. An individual or business that has been given temporary custody of another's property. A bailee, such as a dry cleaner or appliance repair shop, will often provide a receipt when accepting a bailor's property. A bailee must exercise a high degree of care in protecting property in their care, custody or control.

compare: bailor; *see*: bailment, fiduciary

bailee's customer insurance

Inland Marine. Insurance that protects a bailee for loss or damage to a customer's (bailor's) personal property while in the bailee's care, custody or control.

see: carriers' legal liability

bailment

Inland Marine. A temporary transfer of property from a bailor to a bailee. *Example:* A customer leaves a personal computer with a technician for repair. Most often a receipt signifying this temporary transfer of property is given by the bailee to the owner (bailor), although a receipt is not necessary for a bailment to exist.

see: bailee, bailor, care custody or control, intrust policy

bailor

Inland Marine. The owner of property which has been temporarily entrusted to a bailee.

compare: bailee; *see:* bailment

balance

Accounting. The difference between credits and debits. If the balance is negative, it is a debit balance; if positive, it is a credit balance.

see: credit balance, debit balance

Reinsurance. A surplus share reinsurance concept concerning the relationship between written premium under the treaty and the maximum limit of liability to which the reinsurer is exposed. If the desired ratio for a treaty is achieved, the treaty is said to be balanced.

see: surplus relief reinsurance

balance sheet

Accounting. One of an organization's financial statements, which summarizes the nature and values of an organization's assets, liabilities and capital as of a specific date. It shows what the organization owns, what is owes, and its ownership interests.

see: assets, balance, financial statement, liability

balance sheet reserves

Accounting. A funded or unfunded reserve established as a liability on an employer's books so that it will be taken into account in determining the corporation's profits and stockholders' equity.

Insurer Operations. Reserves for benefits owed to policyholders established by an insurer. They are shown as a liability on the insurer's balance sheet. Regulations require adequate reserves so an insurer will be able to pay the benefits for which it has received premiums.

see: loss reserve

balanced mutual fund

Financial Planning. A mutual fund that invests in a diverse mixture of bonds and preferred and common stocks. The goal is to blend a high return with a low risk.

see: mutual fund

balloon loan

Financial Planning. A loan containing a repayment schedule of periodic payments insufficient to fully amortize the loan within its time limit. At the end of the loan term, a balance payment is due. This "balloon" payment may be made in cash or by refinancing.

see: amortization, balloon mortgage

balloon mortgage

Mortgage Insurance. A mortgage for a three-to-five-year period used in the belief that interest rates will drop during that period of time and a conventional mortgage can be arranged before the balloon payment becomes due.

see: balloon loan

banding

Life. A method of life insurance pricing where the premium rate depends on the amount of coverage purchased. The larger the amount, the lower the premium per $1,000 of coverage.

bank burglary and robbery insurance

Crime. An insurance package that combines coverage for burglary, robbery, and vandalism or malicious mischief in a single policy. It is written on a primary basis for smaller banks, and on an excess basis for larger banks.

see: crime coverages

banker's acceptance

International/Financial Planning. A bank draft used as a short-term security in international trade. The acceptance is a draft drawn on a bank that has pre-approved its payment when presented.

banker's blanket bond

Crime. A standard bond form of the Surety Association of America that covers a financial institution for dishonest or fraudulent acts of employees, inside and outside theft of property, and losses resulting from reliance upon a document later discovered to be counterfeited or forged.

synonym: Financial Institution Bond form 24; *see:* crime coverages, electronic and computer crime coverage

banking plan

Risk Management. A formalized self-insurance program where arrangements are made to obtain a policy with an insurer that spreads the cost of losses over a period of time and at the same time build a reserve fund to pay larger losses.

see: chronological stabilization plan, spread loss

plan

Reinsurance.

see: advance deposit premium plan

bankrupt

General. A financial condition of an individual or business wherein the individual or business is unable to meet its current or future obligations and is liable to be proceeded against by creditors. Under certain circumstances, an individual or entity is entitled to seek court protection of certain financial or corporate assets.

see: bankruptcy, default, deficiency judgment, foreclosure

bankruptcy

General. A court proceeding allowing for the distribution of property of an insolvent person or entity to creditors. Although payment to some creditors is often made for less than full value, the debtor is discharged of all liability to those creditors receiving any payments. Bankruptcy is "voluntary" if the debtor initiates the petition seeking bankruptcy protection; it is "involuntary" if the debtor is forced into it by the petition of a sufficient number of creditors.

Bankruptcy is regulated by the federal Bankruptcy Act. Since insurance is a subject primarily regulated by the states, insolvencies and liquidations of insurance companies are generally under the authority of state insurance commissioners.

compare: insolvency; *see*: insolvency, liquidation, voidable preference

bare bones coverage

Health.

see: basic benefits (2)

bare wall condominium

Property. A condominium unit in which the condominium association has no ownership interest within the bare walls. Everything within the walls—including paint and wall coverings, carpet and floor coverings, drapes, cabinets, appliances, non-load-bearing interior walls, doors, plumbing, and electrical fixtures—are the property of the unit owner.

compare: single entity condominium; *see*: condominium

bareboat charter

Ocean Marine. A charter arrangement under which the individual hiring the vessel provides his or her own crew.

synonym: demise charter; *compare*: voyage charter; *see*: charter party

barge

Ocean Marine. A large, flat-bottomed open deck type vessel that usually is towed or pushed by a

tug.

synonym: lighter; *see*: lighter aboard ship

barratry

Ocean Marine. A fraudulent act or other breach of duty committed by a master or crew of a vessel which damages the vessel or its cargo.

see: assailing thieves, piracy (*Ocean Marine*)

barrier guard

Loss Control. A shield or device covering hazard points on a machine to prevent accidental contact that may injure or catch fingers or limbs of workers or to control flying objects from machinery. Barrier guards may be part of the original machine or installed later.

synonym: guard, machine guard; *see*: adjustable barrier guard, fail-safe, fixed barrier guard, in-running nip point, interlocked barrier guard, machine tool, movable barrier guard, point of operation, retrofit

base period

Employee Benefits. Generally, the 52-week or four-quarter period before a period of unemployment. It is used to limit benefits to workers currently or recently a part of the labor force. A period used to ascertain qualifying wages.

base premium

Reinsurance.

see: subject premium

base rate

Insurer Operations. The rate for a specific coverage indicated in a rating manual to which other factors are applied (i.e., exposure units, increased limits factor, experience modification factors, etc.) to arrive at a final rate to be used in rating a policy.

see: exposure unit, experience rating modification factor, increased limits table, rate making

baseline data

Risk Management. Benchmark statistics or data of expected losses. Actual losses and other pertinent data are then compared against this data.

see: benchmarking

basic benefits

Health. 1. The minimum benefit package required for Medicare supplement insurance in most states. Typically, coverage must be provided for the coinsurance for Medicare Part A (hospitalization), plus coverage for an additional year after Medicare benefits end. Required for Part B (supplementary medical expenses) are the coinsurance (usually 20% of Medicare-approved expenses) and the first three pints of blood each year.

see: Medicare supplement insurance

2. The minimum coverages required by law of a

57

health benefit plan in many states, with the aim of providing affordable coverage to employees of small employers and, sometimes, other uninsured people. If individuals have been uninsured or if small employers have not provided a health plan to employees for a specified period of time before policy issuance, they qualify to buy the low-cost package of basic coverages.

synonym: bare bones coverage, minimum coverage; *compare*: mandated benefits

basic extended reporting period
Liability. A provision found in most claims-made liability policy forms. Provides for a specified time following policy expiration, during which claims arising out of occurrences during the policy period may be made against the policy at no extra cost. The ISO commercial general liability claims-made form provides an additional 60 days to report claims.

synonym: mini-tail; *see*: claims-made form, extended reporting period, maxi-tail, midi-tail, supplemental extended reporting period, tail, tail coverage

basic form
Property.
see: causes of loss—basic form

basic homeowners policy
Personal.
see: homeowners policy form 1

basic limits
Liability. The lowest limits of liability coverage that can be purchased by a policyholder—often the same as the minimum amount of insurance required by law. The basic limits are those for which the base rate is developed. If higher limits are requested by the insured, the insurer applies an increased limits factor to the base rate and other factors used to calculate the premium.

see: base rate, increased limits table

basic medical expense
Health. Coverage for hospital, surgical, and physician expenses, usually provided on a "first dollar" basis. Some policies now contain deductibles or coinsurance schedules or are subject to specified restrictions, limitations and exclusions.

compare: major medical insurance; *see*: corridor deductible

basic perils
Property.
see: causes of loss—basic form

basic premium
Liability/Life/Workers' Compensation. A factor used in retrospective premium calculations for casualty, workers' compensation and life insurance. It is a percentage of the standard premium and is used to provide the insurer with up-front money for agents' commissions, engineering service, administrative service, and profit. An insurance charge for a stop loss or a maximum limitation can be included.

see: retrospective rating plan, standard premium

basic protection insurance
Automobile.
see: Keeton-O'Connell Plan

basic standard automobile policy
Automobile/Personal. A policy introduced in 1935 that was once widely used but was replaced by the family automobile and business auto policies.

compare: business auto coverage form, family automobile endorsements, family automobile policy, personal auto policy

basis point
Financial Planning. One-hundredth of a percentage point (0.01%), used when referring to interest rates; the smallest measure of interest rates or yield on investment.

see: yield

basket aggregate excess insurance
Insurer Operations. An aggregate excess insurance policy that covers a commercial insured for more than one line (e.g., general liability, professional liability and property). Coverage starts when the combined losses for all covered lines exceed a retained amount. *Example*: An insured has a $500,000 basket aggregate excess policy that includes auto liability, general liability and property insurance. Within the policy period, the insured suffers a $200,000 auto liability loss, a $200,000 general liability loss, and a $200,000 property loss. After the insured's retained losses of $500,000, the insurer is responsible for $100,000. Any further losses in covered lines during the policy year would be covered by the insurer up to the excess insurance policy limit.

see: aggregate excess insurance, maintenance deductible

beach coverage plan
Property/Regulation. A FAIR plan formed in the states of Alabama, Florida, Louisiana, Mississippi, North Carolina, South Carolina and Texas that requires insurers to write homeowners coverage on homes located close to the coast, where they are subject to high winds, flooding and wave wash.

compare: beachfront coverage plan; *see*: Fair Access to Insurance Requirements

beachfront coverage plan

Property. An assigned risk property insurance program established in response to heavy windstorm losses caused by hurricanes. Beachfront plans provide coverage for fire and windstorm but generally exclude losses from high waves.

compare: beach coverage plan; *see*: hurricane insurance

bear market

Financial Planning. A period of generally falling prices for stocks or bonds.

compare: bull market

bearer bond

Financial Planning. A financial bond payable to its holder, so it can be transferred without having to be registered with the issuer.

Beaufort scale

Loss Control. A scale of observable wind damage running from 0 (no damage; calm) to 12 or more (severe damage, such as that caused by a hurricane).

see: hurricane

bed pan mutual

Insurer Operations. An informal term for one of the many mutual insurance companies that were formed by hospital groups during the malpractice insurance crisis of the 1970s to cover their medical malpractice exposures.

see: mutual insurance company

bell curve

Risk Management.

see: normal probability distribution, symmetrical curve

bench error

Liability. A mistake made by a worker in the assembly of a product, or the incorrect measurement of materials used to manufacture the product, which causes a product liability loss. Bench errors are typically covered by product liability insurance.

see: active malfunction, latent defect, product liability insurance

benchmarking

Risk Management. A firm's use of information (e.g., output and revenue, operational methods) about other firms in the same industry to set standards and goals for itself. A monitoring program examines changes in the operations or risk management programs of other firms, and adjustments are made to remain competitive.

synonym: competitive benchmarking; *compare*: baseline data, performance assessment review, outsourcing analysis

beneficial interest

General. A financial interest in the proceeds of an insurance policy, as distinct from the policyholder's legal ownership or control of the policy contract.

compare: insurable interest

beneficiary

Life. A person, other than the insured, who is entitled to receive the proceeds on the death of the policyholder. Beneficiaries can be designated as primary or contingent, and irrevocable or revocable.

see: beneficiary change, beneficiary clause, beneficiary of trust, change of beneficiary provision, class beneficiary, contingent beneficiary, creditor beneficiary, irrevocable beneficiary, primary beneficiary, revocable beneficiary, secondary beneficiary, spendthrift trust clause, tertiary beneficiary, third-party beneficiary

beneficiary change

Employee Benefits/Life. Replacing the person eligible to receive benefits under a life insurance policy or employee benefit plan with another. Two conditions must be present. First, the policy must give the right to change the beneficiary to the policyholder, and second, the law must permit the change.

see: change of beneficiary provision, irrevocable beneficiary, revocable beneficiary

beneficiary clause

Life. A life insurance policy provision allowing the insured to name anyone as primary and contingent beneficiaries. It also allows the insured to change beneficiaries at any time by proper written notice to the insurance company.

see: beneficiary, change of beneficiary provision, contingent beneficiary, primary beneficiary, revocable beneficiary

beneficiary of trust

Life. The person who receives the benefits of a trust. Often the trust is created to prevent the dissipation of property or money left to minors or ill or disabled persons who may be unable to conduct business for themselves.

see: trust

benefit

Employee Benefits. The right of a pension plan or other benefit plan participant to receive payments or services after meeting eligibility requirements.

see: employee benefit plan, normal retirement benefit, past service benefit, pension, vested benefit

Insurer Operations. The advantage, profit, gain or monetary sum paid or payable to a policyholder or beneficiary by an insurer in exchange for premiums paid by the insured.

see: accidental death benefit, aggregate benefits, alternative treatment benefit, assignment of benefits, basic benefits, beneficiary, coordination of benefits, death benefit, disability benefit, dismemberment benefit, elective benefits, living benefits, mandated benefits, maternity benefit, medical benefit, nonforfeiture benefit, survivorship benefits, unallocated benefit

benefit administration

Workers' Compensation. A division within a state's workers' compensation board or industrial commission that is responsible for administering laws and promulgating regulations concerning the settlement of claims for injured workers' benefits.

see: workers' compensation law

benefit formula

Employee Benefits. The actuarial method used to determine a pension plan participant's benefits.

synonym: pension benefit formula, plan benefit formula; *see*: career average, employee benefit plan, pension

benefit funds

Employee Benefits. Funds set aside by an employee benefit plan's sponsor (e.g., the employer or union), usually deposited with the plan's trustee or an insurance company, for present and future benefit obligations.

see: employee benefit plan, funding instrument, funding standard account, minimum funding, unfunded actuarial accrued liability

benefit of selection

Insurer Operations. The business advantage gained by an insurance company, through the careful selection by its underwriters, to insure only those risks it feels are desirable and to decline those risks it considers as potentially adverse.

compare: adverse selection; *see*: underwriting

benefit plan

Employee Benefits.
see: employee benefit plan
Health.
see: health benefit plan

benefits of survivorship

Employee Benefits/Life.
see: survivorship benefits

Bermuda market

Insurer Operations. The insurance market in Bermuda, including captive insurers that write insurance for unaffiliated companies and special insurers. Similar markets have been established in Barbados, the Cayman Islands, and other offshore locations.

see: captive domicile

berth

Ocean Marine. The mooring place for a vessel.

Best's rating

General. An evaluation published by the A.M. Best Company of all life, property and casualty U.S.-domiciled insurers and U.S. branches of foreign property insurer groups that are active in the United States. These ratings are often used by agents, brokers and commercial insureds to determine the suitability, service record, and financial stability of insurance companies.

synonym: A.M. Best rating

betterments

Property.
see: improvements and betterments

beyond a reasonable doubt

Law.
see: burden of proof

bicycle floater

Personal. An all-risk inland marine policy used to insure all types of bicycles except motorized bicycles. The floater is usually used to insure expensive bicycles and is often written through bike dealers, who issue certificates to a master policy issued to them.

see: floater policy, inland marine insurance, master insurance policy

bid

General/Surety. An offer to perform a contract for work, labor, goods, materials or coverage at a specific price.

synonym: quote; *see*: abstract of bids, bid bond

bid bond

Surety. A surety bond filed by contractors, guaranteeing that in the event a bid is accepted, the successful contractor will sign the contract and furnish a performance bond.

see: abstract of bids, performance bond

bid price

Financial Planning. The highest price anyone will pay for a security at a given time.

compare: asked price

bilateral contract

Law. A contract, such as a contract of sale, that includes rights and duties from both contracting parties; an exchange of promises in which one party's promise is the consideration given to the other.

compare: unilateral contract; *see*: acceptance, contract, consideration, offer

bilateral mistake

Law. The same mistake of fact made by both contracting parties, usually voiding an agreement if the mistake relates to a material fact (that is, one of such substance or importance that the parties relied upon it in deciding to make the contract).

see: contract

bill of interpleader

Law.

see: interpleader

bill of lading

Inland Marine/Ocean Marine. A contract for the transport of goods between the shipper and the carrier. This document also specifies the carrier's duties and responsibilities for the property.

see: affreightment, bill of lading number, clean bill of lading, commercial invoice, delivery receipt, dock receipt, endorsement in blank, manifest, on board bill of lading, order bill of lading, released bill of lading, short form bill of lading, valued bill of lading, waybill

bill of lading number

Inland Marine/Ocean Marine. A unique number appearing on a bill of lading, used to identify the bill of lading and the shipment it represents.

bill of sale

General. A written agreement between a seller and a buyer, assigning the rights and interest in personal property to the buyer.

binder

Agency/Insurer Operations. An agreement (ACORD form 75-S) issued usually in writing, but occasionally orally, by an agent or an insurer providing temporary coverage until a policy can be issued. A binder should include a specified effective time limit, be in writing, and clearly designate the company to which the agent is binding the coverage. The amount, the perils insured against, and the type of insurance must also be included.

Reinsurance. A temporary record of a reinsurance agreement's provisions, used while the formal reinsurance contract is being drawn.

see: certificate of reinsurance

General. A preliminary agreement, secured by the payment of earnest money, between a buyer and seller as an offer to purchase real estate. It secures the right to purchase the property upon agreed

terms for a limited time. If the buyer changes his or her mind or is unable to purchase, the earnest money is forfeited unless the binder expressly provides for a refund.

synonym: offer to purchase

binder log

Agency. A log (ACORD form 76) used by an agent to keep a manual record of all binders issued by the agency. By documenting that coverage was bound on a specific date, the log confirms that the binder was not prepared after a loss occurred.

see: binder

binding authority

Agency/Insurer Operations. The power of an insurance agent to bind one of his or her insurers to a risk.

see: actual authority, agency

binding receipt

Health/Life. A receipt issued by life and health agents, acknowledging the prospective insured's payment of the premium and providing evidence of a temporary contract. Such a receipt binds the company to the contract if the insurer accepts the risk and accompanying application.

synonym: binding slip

binding slip

Health/Life.

see: binding receipt

bioagent

Loss Control. A biological cause of an occupational disease or illness. The agent can be viral, bacterial, fungal or parasitic.

see: occupational disease

bioremediation

Loss Control. A soil treatment technology where oxygen and nutrients are injected into soil to enhance the growth of natural bacteria that break down contaminants. In some cases, specially grown bacteria may be used to break down contaminants that would otherwise resist degradation.

see: prepared-bed bioremediation, stabilization/solidification bioremediation

birth rate

Life. The number of people born (expressed as a percentage of the total population) in any given period of time. It is usually expressed as births per 100,000 people in one year.

Black Lung Act

Regulation/Workers' Compensation. Federal legislation incorporated into Title IV of the Federal Coal Mine Health and Safety Act of 1969 by amendments in 1972, 1978, and 1981. It provides benefits for total disability or death due to respiratory illness (black lung disease) attributable to coal mining. The Act is administered by the Division of Coal Mine Workers in the U.S. Department of Labor's Office of Workers' Compensation Programs and by the Social Security Administration.

synonym: Coal Mine Health and Safety Act; *see*: black lung disease, brown lung disease, occupational disease, silicosis

black lung disease

Workers' Compensation. A morbid condition of the lungs caused by inhalation of coal dust. A disease in the pneumoconiosis family, black lung afflicts many coal miners and causes total disability or death. It is covered under a federal law (Black Lung Act) that prescribes benefit payments to victims and survivors and dependents.

synonym: coal miners' pneumoconiosis; *see*: Black Lung Act, brown lung disease, byssinosis, occupational disease, silicosis

blackout period

Life. Under the Social Security Act, the period during which Social Security benefit payments to a widow with children are suspended. The blackout period runs from the eighteenth birthday of the youngest child until the widow's sixty-second birthday.

see: Social Security, spouse's benefit

blank

Insurer Operations/Regulation.

see: annual statement

blank forms

Insurer Operations. Printed forms (applications, certificates of insurance, policy declarations, endorsements, etc.) used by insurers and agents, such as ACORD forms and standard forms published by the Insurance Services Office. They contain blank spaces for entering specific information.

see: ACORD forms, Insurance Services Office

blanket basis

Property.

see: blanket insurance

blanket contract

Health. An accident or health insurance contract that provides benefits for all individuals designated in a special group that are not individually identified. *Example*: The purchase by an employer of a travel accident policy that covers all executive and sales staff employees while on business-related travel.

blanket contractual liability coverage

Liability. A form of contractual liability insurance that covers all contracts not specifically excluded that are entered into by the named insured. This

coverage is automatically included in the basic provisions of the Insurance Services Office 1986 and 1988 commercial general liability forms. Prior to that time, this coverage had to be added by endorsement.

synonym: broad form contractual liability coverage; *see*: broad form liability coverage, commercial general liability policy, contractual liability coverage

blanket coverage

Property.

see: blanket insurance

blanket crime policy

Crime. A policy with the broadest coverage possible against crime hazards, written on a package basis under a single limit of liability. It covers the same hazards available on an optional basis under a comprehensive dishonesty, disappearance and destruction policy (e.g., employee dishonesty, loss inside and outside the premises, lost money orders and counterfeit paper currency and depositor's forgery).

see: combination crime—single limit, crime coverages

blanket employee dishonesty coverage form

Crime. The same coverages as provided under the employee dishonesty forms A, CR 00 01, or CR 00 02, but with a single limit applying to each loss.

see: employee dishonesty coverage form, public employee dishonesty coverage form (blanket), welfare and pension plan ERISA compliance (blanket) coverage form

blanket fidelity bond

Crime. A fidelity bond that covers loss of money, merchandise or other property owned by the insured, when such loss is due to employee dishonesty. The bond covers all employees unless any are specifically excluded.

see: crime coverages

blanket group

Property. Boiler and machinery insurance that covers objects by grouping them together according to a broad class, rather than specifying each object.

see: boiler and machinery insurance, object

blanket group policy

Health/Life. A policy that covers members of a natural group—such as employees of a particular business, members of a union or association—with no individual designation of the group's members. The insurance applies to the entire group.

blanket insurance

General. Any insurance policy that covers one or more broad classes of persons or property, without identifying the specific subjects of insurance in the contract.

Health. A broad medical expense policy that covers all medical expenses (except those that are specifically excluded), up to a maximum limit without any limitation on specific types of medical expenses.

Property. A single property insurance policy that provides coverage for multiple classes of property at one location or one or more classes of property at multiple locations. Coverage under this form is written for one total amount of insurance. No single item (e.g., a building or machine) is assigned a specific amount of insurance, although different amounts may be shown for buildings in general, equipment in general, and other items.

synonym: blanket basis, blanket coverage; *compare*: specific insurance; *see*: average blanket rate

blanket medical expense

Health. A policy that covers an individual for all covered necessary and reasonable medical expenses up to a maximum limit established in the policy, without limitation for any specific procedure.

blanket position bond

Crime. A blanket fidelity bond insuring an employer against losses from dishonest acts by employees, with the same amount of coverage applied separately to each covered job position. The maximum coverage is the per-employee coverage limit multiplied by the number of employees involved in the loss.

see: commercial blanket bond, crime coverages, fidelity bond

blasting and explosion exclusion

Liability. An exclusion in the 1973 Insurance Services Office comprehensive general liability rating program that was triggered when the rating classification for a particular risk was followed by an "X." For risks so designated, liability coverage for property damage arising from blasting or explosion was excluded by endorsement. If the policyholder needed coverage for these exposures, they could be bought by paying a surcharged rate.

see: collapse exclusion, comprehensive general liability policy, underground exclusion, XCU exclusions

blended finite risk insurance

Financial Guaranty/Risk Management. A finite risk insurance contract that includes a risk transfer feature, usually to gain business benefits, including possible tax deductibility.

synonym: hybrid finite risk insurance; *see*: finite risk insurance, risk transfer

blind thrust fault

Loss Control/Property. A geological thrust fault that does not break the earth's surface, making it difficult to identify. Thrust and strike-slip are the other two types of geological faults.

compare: strike-slip fault, thrust fault; *see*: earthquake

block cancellation

Insurer Operations. Cancellation or refusal to renew an entire class or line of insurance coverage by an insurer.

block limit

Property. A maximum amount of insurance that an insurer will write within a specific city block, which limits the company's risk of a large loss should a fire destroy the entire block.

see: fire map

block policy

Inland Marine. A single property insurance policy that covers all of an insured's property on an open perils basis. Coverage is generally extended to include property in transit and the property of others in the insured's care, custody, or control. *Examples*: Jewelers' block, camera and musical instrument dealers' block, and equipment dealers' block.

blocked currency

International/Financial Planning. A discriminatory exchange rate that some governments use against foreign creditors. A blocked currency is exchanged at a less favorable rate than other foreign currencies.

see: exchange rate

blood bank professional liability insurance

Professional Liability. Professional liability insurance designed to protect the operators of blood banks against injury arising from malpractice, error or mistake in the taking of blood donations, or the mishandling or misuse of, or existence of any condition in, blood products handled or distributed by the insured. Most such policies include coverage for AIDS-related claims. Coverage is usually written on a claims-made basis.

see: acquired immune deficiency syndrome, medical malpractice

blood pressure

Health/Life. A factor used in evaluating the risk for health and life insurance coverage. High blood pressure may result in a higher incidence of illness and accident and lead to less favorable morbidity and mortality factors.

see: sphygmomanometer

bloodstock insurance

Inland Marine. A form of livestock mortality insurance designed for thoroughbred, standardbred, quarterhorses, and show horses. The coverage is also available for stallions and for blood mares.

see: animal insurance, breeder's policy

blowout and cratering

Liability/Property. An accident resulting from a penetration of a gas or oil reservoir during drilling operations under higher-than-calculated pressure. Blowouts are dangerous because of the risk they pose to workers and firefighters; blowouts can also be expensive, due to the cost of fighting the fire and the value of the oil or gas consumed. Cratering occurs when the circulation system, dug around the drilling rig to prevent blowouts, collapses. Often, the drilling rig itself is lost during a cratering incident.

see: blowout prevention insurance

blowout prevention insurance

Property. Coverage for drilling operations against losses associated with penetration of reservoirs containing high-pressure gas or oil.

see: blowout and cratering

blue chip stock

Financial Planning. A stock of a well-known corporation that has a long record of profits and dividend payments.

compare: high-yield bond; *see*: stock

Blue Cross and Blue Shield Association (BCBSA)

Health/Organizations. Members: An association of local Blue Cross and Blue Shield Plans. *Objectives*: Contracts with the federal government to act as the administrative agency for federal health programs. Promotes acceptance of voluntary, nonprofit prepayment of health services. *Founded*: 1982. *Headquarters*: Chicago, IL.

see: Blue Cross Plan, Blue Shield Plan

Blue Cross Plan

Health. An independent, nonprofit, voluntary membership organization formed principally for the purpose of prepaying hospital medical care expenses for its members. Hospitals that participate in the Blue Cross Plan agree to accept payment based on a predetermined fee schedule and bill the plan directly for services provided to members.

synonym: Blue Plan, Blues; *compare*: Blue Shield Plan; *see*: fee schedule

Blue Plan

Health.

see: Blue Cross Plan, Blue Shield Plan, Blues

Blue Shield Plan

Health. An independent, nonprofit, voluntary membership organization formed principally for the purpose of prepaying the physician and surgeon expenses for its members. Physicians and surgeons that participate in the Blue Cross Plan agree to accept payment based on a predetermined fee schedule and bill the plan directly for services provided to members.

synonym: Blue Plan, Blues; *compare*: Blue Cross Plan; *see*: fee schedule

blue sky laws

Regulation. State statutes that limit and control the sale of new securities to protect potential investors from fraud. Blue sky laws compel sellers of new stock issues or mutual funds to register their offerings and provide information to investors.

compare: Securities Act of 1933; *see*: security

Blues

Health. An informal term for Blue Cross or Blue Shield plans.

synonym: Blue Plan; *see*: Blue Cross Plan, Blue Shield Plan

board certified physician

Health/Liability. A physician who passes an examination administered by a medical specialty board, requiring expert knowledge in a particular area of medical practice. In addition to treating difficult or special conditions, board certified specialists are often requested to provide expert testimony in court trials.

see: expert witness, medical licensing board, medical malpractice, primary care physician

Board of Certified Safety Professionals of the Americas, Inc. (BCSP)

Organizations. Members: Safety engineers, industrial hygienists, safety managers, fire protection engineers and others who have received the Certified Safety Professional (CSP) designation by passing two exams and meeting other criteria set by the board. *Objectives*: Certifies the professional and technical competence of individuals in the safety field. *Founded:* 1969. *Headquarters*: Savoy, IL.

see: Certified Safety Professional

board of directors

Financial Planning/Professional Liability.

see: director, directors' and officers' liability insurance

board of education liability insurance

Professional Liability. Professional liability insurance for members of a board of education, administrative staff, teachers and other employees of a school district for liability for wrongful acts. Coverage is usually written on a claims-made basis.

boatowners' package policy

Personal. A package policy similar to the personal

auto policy in that it provides coverage for incidents arising out of the use of recreational watercraft for third-party liability, first-party physical damage and bodily injury, and, often, uninsured boaters. Physical damage coverage includes the boat and miscellaneous equipment permanently attached to the boat (spars, sails, rigging, and machinery). This insurance is generally used for recreational watercraft over 16 feet in length but less than 28 feet.

compare: antique and classic boat insurance, outboard motor and boat policy, yacht insurance

bobtail coverage

Automobile. Vehicle liability coverage for truckers that covers a tractor returning empty from a trip, which therefore may not be insured by a contracting shipper's policy. *Bobtail* is a trucking term for a tractor being operated without a trailer.

see: automobile liability coverage

bodily injury and property damage liability

Liability. Coverage Part A of the ISO commercial general liability policy, which combines both bodily injury and property damage in a single insuring agreement and limit of liability.

see: bodily injury, bodily injury liability, commercial general liability policy, property damage liability coverage

bodily injury (BI)

Liability. The destruction or impairment of living human tissue by an outside force; physical harm, disease or impairment (excluding the natural aging process), sometimes including resulting required care, loss of services, and death.

compare: personal injury; *see*: bodily injury liability, damages, illness

bodily injury liability

Liability. Liability for physical harm or death of a person caused by negligent or intentional acts or omissions of an insured. It includes sickness or disease contracted by the injured person as a result of an injury.

compare: personal injury liability; *see*: bodily injury, bodily injury and property damage liability, bodily injury liability endorsement

bodily injury liability endorsement

Liability/Property. A boiler and machinery endorsement that covers liability for injuries to persons caused by an accident involving an insured object. Coverage is excess over any other valid insurance. This was formerly part of standard boiler and machinery policies, but because it usually duplicated coverage available under general liability policies, it is no longer included.

see: boiler and machinery insurance

boiler and machinery

Property. Any refrigeration or air conditioning system; any piping and its accessory equipment; any compressor, pump, engine, turbine, motor, generator, gear set, fan or blower, including any shaft forming a part of the object, together with any coupling, clutch, wheel or bearing on that shaft; any transformer or electrical distribution equipment; and any other mechanical or electrical equipment used for maintenance or service of premises.

see: boiler and machinery insurance

boiler and machinery insurance (B&M)

Property. Coverage for the failure of a boiler, machinery and electrical equipment (ISO form BM 0025). Such coverage can be extended to include consequential and business interruption losses. Insurance benefits are provided up to the limit per accident in the following order: 1. all property of the insured that is directly damaged by the accident; 2. reasonable costs of temporary repairs and expediting expenses; 3. liability for damage to property of others.

see: accident; ammonia contamination limitation; blanket group; boilers, fired vessels and electric steam generators—limited coverage; covered boiler and machinery property; expediting expenses; hazardous substance limitation; joint loss agreement; object; suspension of coverage provision; small business boiler and machinery broad coverage form; testing exclusion

boilers, fired vessels and electric steam generators—limited coverage

Property. A boiler and machinery coverage endorsement (ISO form BM 99 25) occasionally used for older boilers, fired vessels and electric steam generators. The endorsement modifies the definition of *accident* to include only losses arising from a sudden tearing asunder of the object or part of the object. This tearing asunder must be caused by water or steam pressure within the object.

see: accident, boiler and machinery insurance

bona fide

General. An act done without deceit, fraud, dishonesty or pretense; a sincere effort made with earnest intent. (Latin for "good faith.")

compare: bad faith; *see*: faithful performance of duty, uberrima fides

bond

Financial Planning. A debt instrument secured by a lien on some or all of the issuing organization's property (as opposed to a *stock*, which is an equity, or ownership, share in the issuing company). Typically, either a bond is payable to the bearer, and coupons representing annual or semi-annual payments of interest are attached (these are called *coupon bonds*), or it is registered in the name of the owner as the principal only (*registered bonds*).

The word *bond* is sometimes used in a broader sense to signify an unsecured debt instrument, with the interest obligation limited or tied to the corporate earnings for the year. *Participating bonds* are another variation of debt instrument, with the interest obligation arranged so that holders are entitled to receive additional amounts from excess earnings or from excess distributions, depending on the terms of the participating bond.

Bonds are often described according to the issuing body (U.S. government, state, municipal, or corporate bonds); the currency in which the bonds will be paid (dollars, gold, etc.); any special privileges (participatory or convertible bonds); the types of liens that are the subject of the bond (junior, first or second mortgage bonds); the bond's investment grade (safe versus high-yield or "junk" bonds); or its maturity (long- or short-term).

compare: stock; *see*: adjustment bond, arbitrage bond, bearer bond, bond fund, callable bond, corporate bond, coupon bond, current bond yield, debt security, guaranteed bond, high-yield bond, mortgage bond, mortgage-backed security, municipal bond, participating bond, treasury bond, zero-coupon bond

Surety. An agreement by which a party (called the *surety*) obligates itself to a second party (the *obligee*) to answer for the default, acts or omissions of a third person (the *principal*). A bond can guarantee the performance of the principal under a contract with the obligee (i.e., a performance bond), or it can protect against the dishonesty of employees (i.e., a fidelity bond).

see: administration bond, advance payment bond, alcohol bond, alteration bond, annual bond, annual supply contract bond, appeal bond, bail bond, bid bond, blanket fidelity bond, blanket position bond, commercial blanket bond, contract bond, convertible bond, coupon bond, court bond, customs bond, defendant's bond to dissolve, depositor's forgery bond, depository bond, ejectment bond, family forgery bond, federal bond, fidelity bond, fiduciary bond, financial guaranty bond, forgery bond, general average bond, hospital bond guaranty insurance, indemnity bond, industrial development bond guaranty insurance, injunction bond, judicial bond, labor and material bond, lender's bond, license bond, lost instrument bond, maintenance bond, movie completion bond, municipal bond insurance, name position bond, name schedule bond, partnership financial bond, penalty, performance bond, permit bond, plaintiff's bond to secure, plaintiff's replevin bond, position schedule bond, probate bond, public official bond, registered bond, schedule bond, surety bond, warehousemen's bond

bond fund
Financial Planning. A mutual fund that invests in corporate, municipal, or U.S. Treasury bonds.

see: bond (*Financial Planning*), mutual fund

bonded shipment
Inland Marine/Ocean Marine. A shipment on which duty is payable, but which is permitted to travel to inland destinations before customs inspection is made and duty is actually paid. Until the duty is paid, such goods must be kept in a bonded warehouse.

see: abatement, bonded warehouse, customs bond, duty, federal bond

bonded warehouse
Inland Marine/Ocean Marine. A warehouse where bonded shipments are stored, pending customs inspection. Such warehouses must be secure, with dutiable goods segregated from nondutiable, and their operators must usually provide a customs bond.

see: bonded shipment, customs-bonded warehouse, federal bond, warehouse receipt

bonding
Loss Control. A method of preventing the accumulation and eventual discharge of static electricity, by connecting containers of hazardous materials or equipment with a grounded conductor that continuously drains the static charge.

see: electrical grounding

Surety. The act of issuing a surety bond.

see: surety bond

bonus commission
Agency.

see: variable commission

bonus shares
Financial Planning. Par value shares of stock usually issued in connection with preferred or senior securities or debt instruments, often issued free. Bonus shares are considered a type of watered stock and may impose a liability on the recipient equal to the amount of par value.

see: watered stock

bonus yield
Life. An incentive to purchase a fixed annuity. Some insurers offer higher interest rates or additions to the principal for a limited time. When a bonus yield is offered, the insurer generally reduces later yields, includes a large surrender charge, or restricts the method by which money can be withdrawn at retirement.

see: fixed annuity, surrender charge

book of business
Agency/Insurer Operations. The policies that an

insurance agent or company has in force at a given point in time.

book value

Accounting. 1. The value of an asset as carried on an organization's balance sheet. For most fixed assets, this is the acquisition cost minus accumulated depreciation. Inventory is usually booked at the lower of cost or market value.

2. A company's total net worth; the firm's assets (excluding intangible assets) minus liabilities and equity shares with prior claims. The total net worth divided by the number of outstanding shares is the *book value per share*, which may vary significantly from the market value.

compare: market value; *see*: net worth

book value per share

Accounting. A company's net worth minus the value of its preferred stock (at its liquidation or redemption value), divided by the number of common shares outstanding.

boom

Inland Marine. A long beam projecting from the mast of a derrick to support or guide an object to be lifted or swung.

compare: crane; *see*: derrick, upset coverage

boom coverage exclusion

Inland Marine. An exclusion found in most contractors' equipment policies written on an all-risk basis. It eliminates coverage for loss or damage to crane and derrick booms over 25 or 50 feet in length while they are in operation. The exclusion can usually be eliminated for an additional premium.

see: boom, crane

bordereau

General. A detailed listing of accounts or documents.

see: marine insurance certificate

Reinsurance. A listing supplied by a ceding insurer that provides the loss and premium histories of all or certain types of risks ceded or proposed to be ceded to a reinsurer. It is used by the reinsurer in establishing terms of the reinsurance agreement or in monitoring the business ceded under an existing treaty, or in establishing the premium.

see: ceding insurer, reinsurance

borderline risk

Insurer Operations. From an underwriting viewpoint, a risk of doubtful quality; bordering between acceptable and not acceptable.

see: accommodation line, substandard risk

borrowed employee

Workers' Compensation. An employee who has been loaned by one employer (the general employer) to another (the special employer) for a specific job. *Example*: The subcontractor (general employer) to a large aircraft manufacturer loans an employee to the manufacturer (special employer) to complete the installation of equipment in a unique order of airplanes.

synonym: seconded employee; *compare*: leased employee; *see*: employee leasing, general employer, special employer

Boston plan

Property. A plan first implemented by the city of Boston by which insurers agreed not to reject property coverage in lower socioeconomic residential areas if property owners agreed to correct faults.

see: assigned risk, Fair Access to Insurance Requirements

both to blame collision clause

Ocean Marine.

see: running down clause

bottomry

Ocean Marine. The oldest known form of risk transfer. It was used by the ancient Greeks and provided that a ship not returning to port is absolved of any debt on the ship itself or on its cargo. Lloyd's of London refined this concept when it began insuring the shipment of goods across the Atlantic to the Americas. From this, modern property and casualty insurance evolved.

see: insurance

brain death

Life. The termination of life as determined by a physician based on irreversible brainstem damage or lack of cerebral functioning in a person with a heartbeat.

see: advance directive, death, living will

braking distance

Automobile/Loss Control. The distance a motor vehicle travels from the moment the brakes are applied until the vehicle completely stops.

compare: braking time; *see*: reaction distance, stopping distance

braking time

Automobile/Loss Control. The time required for a motor vehicle to be brought to a complete stop after the driver applies the brakes.

compare: braking distance; *see*: reaction time, stopping time

branch manager

Insurer Operations. An individual responsible for managing an insurance company's branch office.

see: branch office

branch office

Insurer Operations. A local business office supplying certain services and performing specified company functions, but which reports to a regional or home office.

see: regional office

breach

Law. A violation or breaking of a law, promise, obligation, duty, contract, warranty, or trust, either by omission or commission.

see: default, trust, warranty

breach of warranty endorsement

Aviation. An endorsement to an aviation hull policy that protects a lienholder's or lessor's interest in the aircraft should the insured breach a condition in the policy, which would void coverage. The amount of recovery under this provision is limited to the amount due to the lienholder or lessor.

see: hull coverage

break bulk cargo

Ocean Marine. Loose cargo, such as cartons, stowed directly in a vessel's hold as opposed to containerized or bulk cargo.

compare: bulk cargo, containerized cargo

break-even point

Accounting. The point where sales or income equals incurred costs, so an organization neither earns a profit nor incurs a loss.

break in service

Employee Benefits. Under a pension plan, an employee may lose benefits if a minimum number of hours (usually 500 hours) of service are not completed during a calendar year. Some pension plans contain a provision whereby an employee whose service has been interrupted can have such a break credited toward retirement.

see: employee benefit plan, leave of absence, pension, Social Security

break point

Financial Planning. The amount of individual investment required for a mutual fund to reduce its fees (load).

see: load, mutual fund

breakage exclusion

Personal. An exclusion in homeowners and personal articles floaters covering art objects. Coverage is excluded for the breakage of art glass windows, glassware, statuary, marble, bric-a-brac, porcelains and similar fragile articles unless the breakage was caused by fire, lightning, aircraft, windstorm, malicious damage, theft, explosion, earthquake, flood, or collision, derailment, or overturn of a conveyance. This exclusion can usually be deleted by endorsement for an additional premium.

see: fine arts coverage, personal articles floaters

breeder's coverage

Inland Marine. A policy providing coverage on livestock owned by breeders from specified perils.

see: animal insurance, bloodstock insurance, livestock mortality insurance

brick building

Property. A building of brick construction with a roof structure of combustible sheathing or combustible roof supports is a brick building for underwriting purposes.

see: brick construction

brick construction

Property. A building or structure with 75% or more of the exterior walls made of some type of masonry material—such as brick, stone, poured concrete, hollow masonry block, etc.—is considered to be of brick construction for underwriting purposes. Walls usually must be of a minimum thickness, depending on the material used.

see: construction

brick veneer construction

Property. A building with outside supporting walls constructed of combustible materials such as wood, and covered (faced) with a single layer of brick not exceeding a specified thickness is of brick veneer construction for underwriting purposes.

see: construction

bridge insurance

Inland Marine. Coverage for damage and destruction to bridges. Normally it is written on an all-risk basis, subject to exclusions for war, wear and tear, inherent defect, and nuclear damages.

British business interruption insurance

International/Property. A form of business interruption insurance used in many international insurance programs. Recovery is based on the application of gross profit to the amount by which the insured's turnover during the indemnity period falls short of the standard turnover. *Turnover* is the amount paid or payable to the insured for goods sold and delivered and for services rendered at the damaged premises. *Gross profit* is the sum of the net profit plus those categories of expenses that the insured elects to include. The insured selects an indemnity period ranging from a few months to two years or more. This is the most common form used outside the United States and is generally more flexible than the U.S. business income forms.

synonym: English loss of profits form, loss of profits form, consequential loss form; *see*: business income coverage form

broad form

General. A general term designating policies that provide additional coverages beyond standard coverages.

see: money and securities broad form insurance, storekeepers broad form

Property.

see: causes of loss—broad form

Liability. A vendor's endorsement that extends a manufacturer's liability policy to include a vendor of the manufacturer's product as an additional insured against product liability claims. The broad form does not contain many of the exclusions found in the limited form, such as the unauthorized sale or distribution of the product, acts that change the condition of the product, or failure to maintain the product in a merchantable condition. But it does exclude intentional changes to the product, injury from its repacking and demonstration, and its installation, servicing or repair away for the vendor's premises.

compare: limited form vendor's endorsement; *see*: product liability insurance, vendor's endorsement

broad form all-states endorsement

Workers' Compensation. An endorsement that became obsolete when all-states coverage was added to the workers compensation policy in 1993. This form was broader than the standard all-states form in use prior to 1993 because it paid benefits on behalf of the insured instead of reimbursing the insured for claims paid.

see: all-states coverage

broad form comprehensive general liability endorsement

Liability.

see: broad form liability endorsement

broad form contractual liability coverage

Liability.

see: blanket contractual liability coverage

broad form drive other car coverage

Automobile.

see: drive other car coverage

broad form liability endorsement

Liability. An endorsement to the 1973 ISO comprehensive general liability form that added twelve coverages: blanket contractual; personal and advertising injury; medical payments; host liquor liability; fire liability; broad form property damage liability; incidental medical malpractice; nonowned watercraft liability; limited worldwide coverage; additional persons insured; extended bodily injury coverage; and automatic coverage on newly acquired locations. Most of these coverages have been incorporated into the 1986 ISO commercial general liability policy.

synonym: broad form comprehensive general liability endorsement; *see*: comprehensive general liability policy

broad form personal theft insurance

Crime. All-risk coverage for loss due to theft or mysterious disappearance of personal property. It also covers damage to premises and property resulting from theft, and damage resulting from vandalism and malicious mischief to the interior of the premises. Sublimits apply to property that is highly susceptible to theft (e.g., money, securities, paintings, coins, and jewelry).

synonym: personal theft insurance; *see*: all-risk insurance

broad form product liability

Automobile. Coverage that can be added to the garage coverage form, removing the exclusion for "property damage to any of your products" and covering damage to products (subject to a deductible of $250). This coverage does not guarantee the fitness or quality of a product, but covers property damage to a vehicle resulting from a defective product. (ISO form CA 25 01.)

see: defective product, garage coverage form, products-completed operations insurance

broad form property damage (BFPD)

Liability. Coverage that can be endorsed to the 1973 ISO comprehensive general liability policy and other older general liability forms, to reduce the restrictive scope of the "care, custody, or control" and "injury to work performed" exclusions contained in these contracts. The endorsement is needed by contractors, manufacturers, processors and service firms that work on the property of others. The 1986 ISO commercial general liability coverage form includes much of the coverage provided by the old broad form property damage endorsement.

see: care, custody or control; care, custody or control exclusion; comprehensive general liability policy

broad form property insurance endorsement

Property. An endorsement to a property insurance policy covering perils such as breakage of glass, falling objects, weight of snow, ice, sleet, or water damage, in addition to the basic perils.

see: all-risk insurance, named perils

broad named insured definition endorsement

Liability. An endorsement to a commercial liability policy, providing automatic coverage for all owned or controlled entities existing at policy inception or formed or acquired during the policy period.

see: named insured

broad theft coverage endorsement

Personal. An endorsement (ISO form DP 04 72) to a dwelling policy that adds theft coverage for personal property belonging to the dwelling's owner. This coverage also includes property belonging to resident relatives of the owner.

compare: limited theft coverage endorsement; *see*: dwelling policy

broadcasters' liability insurance

Professional Liability. Professional liability insurance designed to protect radio and television stations from errors and omissions in the production, use or dissemination of program or advertising material. Coverage is usually written on a claims-made basis.

see: community antenna television liability insurance, professional liability insurance

broker

Agency. An individual or entity who represents the consumer in negotiating, servicing or obtaining coverage with insurers; a person who negotiates contracts of insurance on behalf of an insured for a fee or agreed commission from an insurer. Many brokers are also agents of the insurers with which they do business.

compare: agent

broker network

Agency/International. A group of jointly owned or affiliated insurance brokerage offices that work together to develop, implement, and service their clients' international and global insurance programs.

see: controlling broker, corresponding broker

broker of record

Agency. The broker designated and authorized to conduct and handle specified insurance business on behalf of the policyholder.

compare: agent of record

broker's float

Agency. Premiums held by a broker until they are remitted to insurers, upon which the broker earns interest.

see: agent's trust, float

brokerage

Agency. A group of individuals working to sell and service insurance policies. Also used to describe the fee or commission received by a broker.

compare: agency; *see*: broker

Financial Planning. The commission or fee charged by a broker-dealer for the execution of a securities transaction.

brokerage business

Agency/Insurer Operations. Insurance coverage placed by a broker with an insurance company, as opposed to business placed with the company by one of its agents.

see: broker

brokerage department

Insurer Operations. A division of an insurance company that negotiates with brokers in placing insurance coverage.

brown lung disease

Workers' Compensation. A disease of the lungs caused by excessive inhalation of dust. The disease is in the pneumoconiosis family and frequently afflicts textile workers.

see: black lung disease, byssinosis, occupational disease

Brussels Tariff Nomenclature (BTN)

International.

see: Customs Cooperation Council Nomenclature

bucking arrears

Agency/Insurer Operations. A falsification of records and subsequent embezzlement of premiums by an agent who applies advance payments of one policy to another policyholder's past due balance that is still within the grace period.

see: arrears, out of trust

budget

Accounting. A formal statement of future activities, especially income and expenses during a specific time.

see: budgeting, capital budgeting, cash budget

budgeting

Accounting. The process of developing formal plans for future business activities to provide an organization's management with a clear understanding of all the activities that need to be undertaken and completed in order to accomplish the objectives of the organization.

see: budget, capital budgeting, cash budget

buffer layer

Liability. Coverage that lies between the upper limits of the primary insurer and the beginning of the umbrella or excess policy. *Example*: Total policy limits of $10 million constructed as follows: primary layer = $1 million; buffer layer = $1 million excess of $1 million; and umbrella layer = $8 million excess of $2 million.

synonym: gap layer; *compare*: working cover; *see*: excess liability insurance, layering

Risk Management. One of the three categories to which losses are normally assigned. It includes those losses that do not normally fit into either the working layer or catastrophe layer. It includes relatively large losses that do not occur annually but do occur with some regularity.

compare: catastrophe layer, working layer

builders' risk hull insurance

Ocean Marine. A marine property insurance policy providing direct damage coverage on ships while they are under construction and until possession is transferred to the owners. Coverage is on an all-risk basis and includes protection during launch and sea trials. The policy may be written on a completed value (100% of final values) or reporting form (values reported as completed) basis.

see: all-risk insurance, builders' risk insurance, hull policy

builders' risk insurance

Inland Marine/Property. A property insurance policy (ISO form CP 00 20) that provides direct damage coverage on buildings or structures while they are under construction. It also covers foundations, fixtures, machinery and equipment used to service the building, and materials and supplies used in the course of construction. Coverage may be written on a completed value (100% coinsurance) or reporting form (values reported as completed) basis, using either a property form or a broader inland marine form.

synonym: course of construction insurance; *see*: delayed opening coverage, duration of coverage clause, efficacy coverage, occupancy clause, off-site storage coverage, ripping and tearing insurance, scaffolding and forms coverage, temporary structures coverage, testing coverage

building and personal property coverage form (BPP)

Property. The basic commercial property policy (ISO form CP 00 10), designed to cover the building, personal property used in business, and personal property of others. Coverage applies to each category of property for which a limit of liability has been indicated in the policy declarations. Coverage is included for debris removal, fire department service charges, and preservation of property.

see: agreed value option clause, causes of loss—basic form, personal property, personal property of others

building code

Loss Control. Municipal or governmental regulations, laws and ordinances concerning construction and maintenance standards within a specific area.

building line

Title. The limit within a parcel of land beyond which construction may not extend. The building line may be established by a filed plat of subdivision, by restrictive covenants in deeds or leases, by building codes, or by zoning ordinances.

synonym: setback; *see*: encroachment, ordinance

or law coverage endorsement, plat

building ordinance or law coverage

Property.

see: ordinance or law coverage endorsement

building rate

Property. Fire insurance rates are usually developed by considering the building or structure separately from the contents. The building rate is used for premiums on real property, tenants' improvements, and business income coverages. Whether for buildings or contents, rates usually apply per $100 of property value. Separate rates apply to fire, extended coverages, vandalism and malicious mischief, sprinkler leakage, earthquake and all-risk coverages.

compare: contents rate; *see*: buildings

building standards

Loss Control. Construction standards for buildings and structures.

see: building code, construction

buildings

Property. In commercial property insurance, those structures that are principally used for business or institutional purposes, including additions and extensions. The policy definition of "buildings" often includes fixtures, machinery, and equipment used in servicing a building.

Personal. In personal lines insurance, buildings include the primary residence and appurtenant structures (garages, sheds, etc.). In most property insurance policies, separate coverage limits are provided for buildings and for contents.

see: property insurance

bulk cargo

Ocean Marine. Unpackaged, loose cargo loaded directly into a vessel's hold (such as grain).

compare: break bulk cargo, cargo, containerized cargo

bulk reinsurance

Reinsurance. The transfer of over 50% (or some other substantial portion defined by law or regulation) of a ceding insurer's liabilities to an assuming insurer. Such a transfer often requires the approval of the state insurance commissioner.

see: portfolio reinsurance

bull

Automobile. A driver of an automobile that intentionally causes it to strike another in a staged accident for the purpose of filing a fraudulent claim.

synonym: hammer; *compare*: cow; *see*: fraud

bull market

Financial Planning. A period of generally rising

prices for stocks or bonds.

compare: bear market

bumbershoot

Ocean Marine. A marine umbrella liability insurance policy that provides coverage for ocean marine risks and can also include general liability, protection and indemnity, and Longshore and Harbor Workers' Compensation Act coverages. "Bumbershoot" is a British word for umbrella and is used in this context to indicate the broad nature of this type of policy.

compare: parasol policy, umbrella liability insurance

burden of proof

Law. The responsibility of a plaintiff in a lawsuit to provide evidence supporting the claim against a defendant; the burden of persuasion, which always begins with the plaintiff but may shift to the defendant for particular issues as the case proceeds.

The term often means the *standard of proof*, or the quantity of evidence required to win the case. In a criminal case, the prosecution must prove each element of the crime "beyond a reasonable doubt" to establish the defendant's guilt. To prevail in a civil case, a party must demonstrate its claim by a "preponderance" of evidence, meaning that offered proof must have more credibility or weight or be more likely than the other party's.

see: civil law (1), criminal law, directed verdict, due process of law, evidence

bureau insurer

Insurer Operations. An insurance company that uses a rating bureau's rates and forms. Bureau insurers usually do not have a large enough data base or sufficient resources of their own to develop rates.

see: rating bureau

bureau rate

Insurer Operations. The rate developed on specific risks by a rating bureau for its member companies.

see: building rate, rate, rating bureau

burglar alarm

Loss Control. An audible or silent alarm, activated by unauthorized entry. Often, properties protected by burglar alarms can receive a discount on their property and crime insurance premiums.

see: contact switch, infrared detector, lacing detection system, microwave detector, object protection, photoelectric detector, proximity detector, ultrasonic detector, vibration detector, window tape

burglary

Crime. The forcible entry or exit of the premises of another person with the intent to deprive the rightful owner of personal property.

compare: theft; *see*: burglary divided coverage, burglary insurance

burglary divided coverage

Crime. Burglary insurance in which covered items are grouped by class, with a stipulated maximum payable for loss or damage for losses within each of the specified classes.

compare: divided coverage; *see*: burglary insurance

burglary insurance

Crime. Coverage for property taken or destroyed by breaking and entering into an insured premises. The break-in must be made with felonious intent, and visible signs of forced entry should be present in order for the policy to pay.

see: burglary, crime coverages, theft

burn facility

Health. A specialized medical facility or center for treating burn injuries.

burning cost

Reinsurance.

see: pure loss cost

burning layer

Insurer Operations. The first layer of insurance in property and casualty coverage that will respond to losses. It is usually insurance above low deductibles but provides less than catastrophe limits.

see: layering

burning ratio

Insurer Operations. The ratio of actual losses to the total amount of insurance in effect; the ratio of losses that can reasonably be expected to the amount of insurance in effect. By contrast, the *loss ratio* is the ratio between actual losses and earned premiums.

compare: loss ratio

business

Insurer Operations. For property/casualty and health insurers, *business* usually refers to premium volume; for life insurers, the face amount of all life policies written.

see: book of business

business and pleasure

Aviation. A general aviation rating classification that applies when the aircraft operator is an individual, business or corporation owning and operating an aircraft for both business and pleasure, but not employing professional, full-time pilots.

compare: fixed base operators, flying club, industrial aid operators; *see*: general aviation

business auto coverage form

Automobile. An Insurance Services Office policy (ISO form CA 00 01) that provides selected liability and physical damage coverages on vehicles used for commercial purposes. The form uses simplified wording and must be combined with the appropriate declarations, conditions and endorsements to constitute a commercial vehicle policy. It was introduced in 1977 to replace the basic standard auto policy. The ISO business auto policy has nine classifications of covered vehicles, coded by numbers, as follows:

1. Any auto: the broadest classification, providing coverage for owned, hired, and nonowned vehicles.

2. Owned autos only: vehicles owned by the insured, including any acquired during the policy period.

3. Owned private passenger autos only: vehicles defined as private passenger (for example, a sedan or station wagon). Coverage is not provided on vans or pickup trucks even if they are used only to transport people.

4. Owned autos other than private passenger autos only: vehicles not designed as private passenger vehicles (for example, pickup trucks, vans, trucktractors), including newly acquired vehicles.

5. Owned autos subject to no-fault: coverage only for no-fault or personal injury protection on vehicles located in no-fault states.

6. Owned autos subject to compulsory uninsured motorist law: vehicles located in a state where uninsured motorist coverage is compulsory. The required coverage is provided under the policy form.

7. Specifically described autos: vehicles listed in the policy. Coverage is limited to 30 days for newly acquired vehicles.

8. Hired autos only: vehicles that are leased, rented or borrowed.

9. Nonowned autos only: vehicles belonging to employees and partners or their household members, which are covered while being used for the insured's business purposes.

compare: garage coverage form, truckers' coverage form; *see*: automobile insurance, no-fault insurance, personal injury protection, uninsured motorist law

business continuation insurance

Property.
see: business income coverage form

business income and extra expense coverage

Property. A commercial property policy (ISO form CP 00 03) that combines business income and extra expense coverages. A single limit applies to both, and the extra expense coverage has no monthly limitation.

see: business income coverage form, extra expense insurance

business income coverage form

Property. Commercial property coverage (ISO forms CP 00 30 and CP 00 32, which excludes extra expenses) that reimburses lost earnings when normal business operations are temporarily suspended because of property loss caused by insured perils. Coverage usually includes salaries, taxes, rents, net profits, and necessary operating expenses during the period required to restore operations with due diligence. This policy replaced previous business interruption forms.

synonym: business continuation insurance, business income insurance, loss of income insurance, loss of time insurance; *see*: business income and extra expense coverage, business income report and work sheet, business interruption insurance, chomage, contingent business income coverage, continuing expenses, contributing location, critical path analysis, extended period of indemnity, gross earnings form, maximum period of indemnity, monthly limit of indemnity, per diem business interruption coverage, period of restoration, profits and commissions insurance, time element insurance, tuition and fees insurance, use and occupancy insurance

business income from dependent properties

Property.
see: contingent business income coverage

business income insurance

Property.
see: business income coverage form

business income premium adjustment

Property. A commercial property coverage endorsement (ISO form CP 15 20) that puts business income coverage on a reporting basis. This allows the insured to select a conservatively based limit for the policy period without being penalized with a high premium. A provisional maximum premium is charged at the policy inception, and the final premium is based on the actual exposure subject to the maximum.

see: business income coverage form, reporting form

business income report and work sheet

Property. A commercial property coverage form (ISO form CP 15 15) designed to assist the insured in determining the required business income coverage limit. The form is required to be filed with the insurer to obtain coverage according to an agreed value.

see: agreed value, business income coverage form

business insurance
Insurer Operations. Any insurance for commercial or business enterprises, as opposed to *personal insurance*, which is for the protection of individuals; a policy written for business purposes, such as key employees, partnerships, and corporations.

see: commercial lines

business interruption insurance
Property. An insurance coverage form that was replaced in 1988 by the Insurance Services Office business income coverage form.

see: business income coverage form

business interruption value
Property. The amount of business income insurance needed to cover estimated business interruption losses. This amount is developed by completing a business income worksheet. The term also refers to the dollar amount of gross earnings to which the policy's contribution clause applies.

see: business income coverage form

business judgment rule
Law/Professional Liability. Immunity from liability on the part of directors and officers if their actions are in good faith and within the authority of management and the power of the firm or the nonprofit organization. Directors and officers have a duty to exercise reasonable care in making business decisions, but they are not liable for honest mistakes of judgment made with reasonable prudence that result in a financial loss. They are expected to assume the ordinary risks of their business or industry, but not reckless, unnecessary, or highly speculative risks.

see: directors' and officers' liability insurance, intra vires, ultra vires

business legal expense insurance
Liability. Legal expense insurance for covered expenses related to the insured's business.

see: legal expense insurance

business life insurance
Life. Life insurance that is purchased by a business enterprise on the life of a member of the organization. It is often purchased by partnerships to protect the surviving partners against loss caused by the death of a partner, or by a corporation to compensate for loss caused by the death of a key employee.

see: disability overhead expense insurance, key employee insurance, partnership insurance

business of insurance
Regulation. To be exempt from federal regulations and qualify for the "business of insurance" provisions of the McCarran-Ferguson Act, an insurer must meet the following criteria: 1. it must spread policyholder risk; 2. it must be an integral part of

the relationship between the insurer and the insured; and 3. it must be limited to entities within the insurance business. Mergers, securities regulation, and insurer contracts with health providers are not the "business of insurance."

see: insurance, McCarran-Ferguson Act, transacting insurance

business owners' policy (BOP)
Property. A commercial insurance program that has been replaced by the business owners' policy program. In a package policy, it provided broad property, liability, and business interruption coverage.

see: business owners' policy program

business owners' policy program
Liability/Property. A package of property and liability coverages for small and medium-size businesses, such as retail stores, offices, apartments, and residential and office condominium associations.

business personal property—special limit
Personal. The ISO homeowners policy coverage C (personal property) "special limits of liability" section applies to business personal property. It limits coverage on business personal property to $2,500 on the resident premises and $250 away from the premises. This limitation does not apply to electronic equipment, which has a separate special limit. The limit can be increased by using the "increased limits on business property" endorsement.

see: electronic equipment—special limit, homeowners policy—special limits of liability, increased limits on business property endorsement

business pursuits endorsement
Personal. An endorsement (ISO form HO 24 71) to the Insurance Services Office's homeowners policies that extends the personal liability and medical payments coverage (section II) to some business pursuits (sales, clerical, and instructional occupations) by eliminating the exclusion for liability arising from an insured's business activities.

see: homeowners policy

business risk
Risk Management. The basic risk inherent in a firm's operations. Business risk plus financial risk (resulting from a company's use of debt) equals total corporate risk.

see: financial risk, hedging, loss of market, risk

business travel accident insurance
Health. A form of travel accident insurance that covers accidents that occur while away from home for business purposes. Coverage usually includes all accidents occurring while on a business trip, not

just those occurring while in transit.

see: travel accident insurance

business use

Personal. A personal auto policy rating classification signifying that the principal driver uses the vehicle for occupational, business or professional purposes.

see: drive to or from work, farm use, pleasure use, personal auto policy, principal driver

business-use personal property

Property.

see: personal property

Butterfield v. Forrester

Law/Workers' Compensation. An 1809 English court decision that first applied the common law defense of contributory negligence, which had applied to personal injury cases outside of employment, to a workers' compensation case. Barring recovery if the employee himself had been negligent in any degree made it difficult for injured workers to win compensation.

see: common law defense, contributory negligence, workers' compensation law

buy and sell agreement

Law. An agreement among owners of a closely held business or among partners that the firm or partnership will buy the interest of an owner or partner who withdraws or dies, and the withdrawing individual or surviving heirs will sell to the firm or partnership, at a price fixed by amount or by formula.

see: close corporation, partnership

buy-back deductible

Insurer Operations. A deductible that can be deleted from a policy by paying an additional premium.

see: deductible

buy-down

Financial Planning. Payment by a seller of property (usually a developer) to a lender in order to reduce the interest rate charged to the buyer.

see: mortgage

buy hedge

Financial Planning. A technique used in commodities trading, where a commodities futures contract is purchased to protect against future increases in the price of the commodity.

synonym: long hedge; *see*: futures contract, hedging

buyer's market

General. A market in which prices are suppressed or tending downward, favoring the buyer rather than the seller.

compare: hard market, tight market; *see*: soft market, underwriting cycle

bylaws

Law. An organization's rules as adopted by its board of directors.

see: charter

bypass trust

Financial Planning.

see: credit shelter trust

byssinosis

Workers' Compensation. A disease of the lungs caused by excessive inhalation of cotton, flax or hemp dust. It afflicts mill workers and takes several years of exposure before manifestations are noticed. It can progress to chronic bronchitis and emphysema.

synonym: mill fever; *see*: black lung disease, brown lung disease, occupational disease

C

cable television liability
Professional Liability.
    see: community antenna television liability

cafeteria benefit plan
Employee Benefits. An employee benefit program under which employees of a company may choose the benefits program that best fits their needs, based on the individual's marital status, age, dependents, and income level. Normally, a firm allocates a stipulated amount of money and permits the employee, subject to some limits, to choose or assemble the program that best fits their needs. If the employee's allocation is not used up, in some cases the worker receives the difference in cash. Such a program is similar to, but usually more limited than, a flexible benefit plan.
    compare: flexible benefit plan; *see*: employee benefit plan, flexible spending account, medical savings account

caisson
Loss Control. A temporary watertight box or cofferdam used as a work chamber during construction of foundations, piers, and other structures below water.

calendar year experience
Insurer Operations. An analysis of losses that matches incurred losses during a defined calendar year with premium earned during the same twelve-month period.
    see: annual, accident year experience, policy year experience

call option
Financial Planning. An order to buy a fixed amount (usually in blocks of 100 shares) of a particular stock, currency or commodity at a predetermined price within a specified period of time. The option expires if the order cannot be executed at the call price.
    compare: put option; *see*: call price, exercise price, option

call price
Financial Planning. The predetermined price at which a corporation or other obligor is permitted to redeem securities containing call provisions.
    see: callable bond, callable preferred stock, call option, call provision

call provision
Financial Planning.
    see: callable bond

callable bond
Financial Planning. A bond that contains a provision allowing all or part of it to be redeemed prior to the indicated maturity date.
    synonym: redeemable bond

callable preferred stock
Financial Planning. Shares of preferred stock that contain a provision allowing them to be redeemed for a specified price.
    see: preferred stock

camera and musical instrument dealers' coverage
Inland Marine. Insurance for retail dealers of camera equipment or of musical instruments to insure their merchandise on an open perils basis. (ISO form CM 00 21 or AAIS form IM 700.)
    see: commercial articles coverage

camera coverage
Personal. Coverage for one of the nine classes of property that can be included in a personal articles floater. The property includes cameras, projection machines, film and related articles of equipment. It can also include sound recording equipment used in conjunction with motion pictures, home video cameras, playback recorders, and miscellaneous property such as binoculars and telescopes used with insured camera equipment.
    see: camera and musical instrument dealers' coverage, camera floater, film coverage insurance, personal articles floater

camera floater

Inland Marine. A personal articles floater insuring most photographic equipment, including projection machines, portable sound and recording equipment, binoculars, and telescopes against direct loss on an all-risk basis. Each item must be individually described and valued.

see: floater policy, personal articles floater

Canadian Association of Accident and Sickness Insurers

Health/Organizations. *Members:* Accident and sickness insurers in Canada. *Objectives:* Fosters the development of voluntary insurance providing sound protection against loss of income and financial burdens resulting from accident and sickness. *Founded:* 1959.

Canadian Council of Superintendents of Insurance

Organizations. *Members:* Superintendents of Insurance in the nine common-law Provinces of Canada (except the Quebec Province). *Objectives:* Promote uniformity in the regulation of insurance matters and the provision of a forum for consultation. *Founded:* 1917. *Headquarters:* Toronto, Canada. Formerly known as the Association of Superintendents of Insurance of the Provinces of Canada.

Canadian Federation of Insurance Agents and Brokers Association

Organizations. *Members:* Canadian insurance agents and brokers. *Objectives:* Encourages special educational qualifications for general insurance agents. Cooperates with provincial insurance departments, fire marshals and other organizations dedicated to conservation of life, limb and property by preventing disasters. *Founded:* 1921. *Headquarters:* Toronto, Ontario

Canadian Fraternal Association

Organizations. *Members:* Canadian fraternal benefit societies. *Objectives:* Promotes the interests of the fraternal benefit system in Canada. *Founded:* 1891. *Headquarters:* Ontario, Canada.

Canadian Home Office Life Underwriters Association

Organizations/Life. *Members:* Home office underwriters in Canada. *Objectives:* Holds informal discussions on issues facing underwriters. *Founded:* 1949. *Headquarters:* Toronto, Canada.

Canadian Institute of Actuaries

Organizations. *Members:* Canadian actuaries. *Objectives:* Advance and develop actuarial science in Canada. *Founded:* 1965. *Headquarters:* Ottawa, Canada.

Canadian Life Insurance Association, Inc.

Organizations/Life. *Members:* Life insurance companies in Canada. *Objectives:* Promotes the interests of life insurers. *Founded:* 1894. *Headquarters:* Toronto, Canada.

Canadian Life Insurance Medical Officers Association

Organizations/Life. *Members:* Life insurance medical officers in Canada. *Objectives:* Advance the science of medicine as applied to insurance. *Founded:* 1946. *Headquarters:* Toronto, Canada.

cancelable policy

Insurer Operations. A contract of insurance that may be canceled at any time by either the insured or the insurer upon notification to the other party and in accordance with the provisions of the contract.

see: cancellation

cancellation

Insurer Operations. The termination of an in-force insurance contract by either the insured or the insurer. Termination may be voluntary, involuntary, or mutual in accordance with provisions contained in the contract.

see: block cancellation, cancellation notice, cutoff provision, evidence of cancellation, expiration date, flat cancellation, lapse, pro rata cancellation, run-off cancellation, short-rate cancellation, stripped building cancellation provision, taxes and utilities cancellation provision, unrepaired damage cancellation provision, vacant or unoccupied cancellation provision

cancellation notice

Insurer Operations. *By the insured:* A written notice delivered to the insurance company requesting cancellation of the insurance contract. Only the first named insured listed in the declarations may give notice of cancellation.

By the insurer: The insurer must give notice of cancellation, in most cases, a minimum of ten days before the date of the cancellation's effect, for nonpayment of premiums. Generally, 30 days' notice before the cancellation date is required for other reasons. Some states now require insurers to provide the canceled policyholder with reasons for the cancellation.

synonym: notice of cancellation; *see:* cancellation request/policy release, cancelable policy, expiration notice, flat cancellation, premium financing, pro rata cancellation, short-rate cancellation

cancellation request/policy release

Agency. A form (ACORD form 35) used by an agent or insurer to obtain permission from an insured to cancel a policy. The form must be signed by the insured prior to cancellation. It releases the insurer from responsibility for any losses that occur after the date the policy is canceled.

see: cancellation notice, release

cancer insurance

Health. A health insurance policy that specifically provides coverage for medical expenses resulting from cancer treatment.

see: extra percentage tables, specified disease insurance

Life.

see: living benefits

cap

Financial Planning. 1. The upper limit on a floating rate note or variable rate mortgage.

2. A contract (usually traded on a stock exchange) that protects the holder of some form of financial derivative from a rise in interest rates or in the value of some other underlying asset or rate beyond a certain point.

compare: floor; *see*: collar, financial derivative, payment cap, variable rate mortgage

capacitance detector

Loss Control.

see: proximity detector

capacity

Insurer Operations. 1. The total amount of insurance coverage available in a defined market (e.g., a region or country or the world) for a class of insurance or a single risk.

2. The maximum amount of insurance available from a single insurer (including that insurer's reinsurers) for a class of insurance or a single risk.

3. The maximum amount of insurance available from a single insurer excluding reinsurance (net line) for a class of insurance or a single risk.

see: naive capacity, premium to surplus ratio, tight market, underwriting cycle

capital

Accounting. The accumulated assets of a business; an owner's equity in a business.

see: capital asset, capital budgeting, owner's equity, paid-in capital

Insurer Operations. The aggregate par value of an insurance company's stock.

capital asset

Accounting. An asset with a useful life of more than one year that is held for investment or used for producing income and is not consumed or sold in the ordinary course of business. Most types of capital assets are eligible for depreciation.

see: capital gain (or loss), depreciation

capital budgeting

Accounting/Financial Planning. The planning of expenditures on capital assets (i.e., assets with a useful life or returns on which are expected to extend beyond one year).

see: cost of capital, cut-off point, internal financing, internal rate of return, net present value, payback, profitability index

capital charges

Accounting. Charges against interest and amortization of monies invested in an enterprise.

see: amortization

capital expenditures

Accounting. Expenditures that involve assets that will either generate receipts or require cash disbursements in future accounting periods or years.

compare: operating expenses; *see*: capital asset, depreciation

capital gain (or loss)

Accounting. Profit (or loss) from the sale of a capital asset, which is subject to special income tax provisions.

see: capital asset, capital gains distribution

Insurer Operations. The excess (or deficiency) of the sales price of an asset compared to the asset's book value. The total of all such amounts is shown on an insurance company's annual statement.

capital gains distribution

Financial Planning. The payment by a mutual fund to its shareholders of the realized gains on assets sold by the fund.

see: capital gain (or loss), mutual fund

capital market line

Financial Planning. A graphic representation of the relationship between risk and the required rate of return on an efficient investment portfolio.

see: portfolio

capital rationing

Accounting. The establishment of a limit on the total capital investment that a business will make during a particular period of time.

see: capital

capital requirement

Accounting. The investment necessary to equip, promote and operate an enterprise.

see: capital, organizational expenses

capital stock

Accounting/Financial Planning. The sum of all outstanding shares of common and preferred stock, which represents the total ownership interest (or equity) in a corporation.

compare: debt security; *see*: common stock, equity (*Financial Planning*), preferred stock, treasury stock

capital stock insurance company
Insurer Operations.

see: stock insurance company

capital sum
Life. The maximum amount payable in one sum to the beneficiary in an accident policy in the event of accidental death or dismemberment of the insured.

see: principal sum

capital surplus
Accounting. A contribution to a corporation's capital that is made by its stockholders in excess of capital raised by the sale of stock or earned as business profits.

see: capital, owner's equity

capitalization
Accounting. The total amount received from the sale of all equity securities issued by a corporation. Preferred and common shares may be par or stated values.

see: capital stock, equity (*Financial Planning*)

capitalization appraisal method
Financial Planning.

see: income approach appraisal

capitalization rate
Accounting. An assumed rate of return on investment used by financial officers to determine the investment of available capital in a project.

see: return on investment

capitation
Health. A method of payment to a provider of medical services according to the number of members in a health benefit plan that the provider contracts to treat. The plan sponsor agrees to pay a uniform periodic fee for each member. (*Capitation* means by the head, or per person.) Because the fee is independent of how many services are performed, the doctor has an incentive to keep costs low. The doctor's incentives not to render only minimal treatment include professional integrity, the risk of malpractice suits, loss of business if patients are dissatisfied, and the risk of simple illnesses becoming more severe and costly to treat.

synonym: fee per person; *compare*: community rating, fee for service; *see*: health benefit plan, managed care

capper
Workers' Compensation. A person who solicits fraudulent personal injury or workers' compensation claimants and receives kickbacks from unethical attorneys or doctors or clinics for referrals.

see: fraud, ten percenter

captive agent
Agency/Insurer Operations. A person who represents only one insurance company and is restricted by agreement from submitting business to any other company unless it is first rejected by the agent's captive company. Captive agents are not employees of the company, but they usually receive financial assistance in the form of allowances for office expenses and some employee benefits.

compare: broker, independent agent; *see*: agent, exclusive agency system, marketing representative, policywriting agent

captive broker
Agency/International. An insurance brokerage owned by a parent company and used to arrange the parent's insurance. Through this arrangement, the parent receives the commission on policies issued to it, reducing its insurance costs. In effect, the parent firm's insurance department becomes a profit center. This practice is common in northern European countries.

captive domicile
Regulation. A state, country or U.S. possession that allows the formation of captive insurance companies within its borders.

see: Bermuda market, captive insurance company

Captive Insurance Companies Association (CICA)
Organizations. Members: Insurance companies originally formed for the purpose of providing insurance for their sponsoring corporations. *Objectives*: Promotes interests of captive insurance companies. *Founded*: 1973. *Headquarters*: New York, NY.

captive insurance company
Risk Management. A risk-financing method or form of self-insurance involving the establishment of a subsidiary corporation or association organized to write insurance. Captives are domiciled either in a country outside the United States or in one of the few U.S. states that authorize them. Captive insurance companies are formed to serve the insurance needs of the parent organization and to escape uncertainties of commercial insurance availability and cost. A captive insurer owned by one company is generally called a *single parent* captive. A captive owned jointly by two or more companies is a *multiple-owned, group* or *association* captive.

synonym: offshore insurer; *see*: association captive insurance company, group captive insurance company, risk retention group, self-insurance, underwriting cycle

car pool
Personal.
 see: public or livery exclusion

car seat
Automobile/Loss Control.
 see: child safety seat

carbon dioxide
Loss Control. A gas used in fire extinguishing systems which is nontoxic and nonpolluting. When directed at a burning flammable liquid or when used to flood an enclosure (oven or dip tank), it extinguishes a fire by depriving it of oxygen.
 compare: carbon monoxide; *see*: fire extinguishing system

carbon monoxide
Loss Control. A colorless, odorless, toxic gas generated by combustion of common fuels with an insufficient air supply or where combustion is incomplete. It causes poisoning in humans and animals.
 compare: carbon dioxide

carcinogen
Health. A substance or agent that produces or encourages the growth of cancer cells.
 see: cancer insurance

CARE Alliance
Organizations.
 see: Concerned Alliance of Responsible Employers

care, custody or control
Liability. The status of property temporarily placed in the possession of another person or company, called a *bailee*. Use of the term in a contract transfers responsibility for the safekeeping of the property to the bailee, pending its return to the owner (the bailor). Liability policies usually exclude coverage for damage to property in the insured's care, custody or control, but they can be endorsed to afford protection. Sometimes separate property or inland marine insurance policies are purchased, covering only property held under contract.
 see: bailee; bailee's customer insurance; broad form property damage; care, custody or control exclusion; trust and commission clause

care, custody or control exclusion
Liability. A provision in most liability insurance policies that eliminates coverage for damage or destruction to property of others under the care, custody or control of the insured.
 see: bailee, broad form property damage

career average
Employee Benefits. A method of basing pension benefits on the credited compensation of an employee over the total period of plan participation.
 see: benefit formula

cargo
Inland Marine/Ocean Marine. Goods, merchandise or commodities of every description that may be carried by a vessel, train, truck or airplane. A vessel's stores or provisions are not included.
 see: break bulk cargo, bulk cargo, containerized cargo, deck cargo

cargo insurance
Inland Marine/Ocean Marine. A general term for a marine insurance policy that covers goods being transported by ship, truck, railroad, or airplane. This coverage insures against most perils to which the property may be subject.
 synonym: cargo policy; *see*: cargo, marine insurance, officers' protective policy, open cargo policy, special cargo policy, warehouse-to-warehouse coverage

cargo legal liability
Inland Marine. A special insurance form covering a shipper's or handler's legal liability for loss or damage to cargo or baggage.

cargo policy
Inland Marine/Ocean Marine.
 see: cargo insurance

Cargo Reinsurance Association (CRA)
Organizations. Members: Reinsurers of American cargo insurance companies. *Objectives*: Reinsures American cargo insurance companies. *Founded*: 1965. *Headquarters*: New York, NY.

carpal tunnel syndrome
Health/Workers' Compensation. An inflammation or disorder of the tendons in the wrist which results from repetitive movement and causes pain or tingling in the wrist and hand.
 see: cumulative trauma, repetitive motion injury

Carpenter Plan
Reinsurance. A concept developed by reinsurance executive Guy Carpenter where, under an excess of loss reinsurance contract, each year's final reinsurance premium is based on the ceding insurer's excess losses over a specified period. A type of retrospective rating formula is used to determine the policy's renewal premium, using losses from the previous three to five years.
 synonym: spread loss reinsurance

Carriage of Goods by Sea Act (COGSA)
Ocean Marine. Federal legislation that pertains to various phases of maritime ventures, particularly

the rights and responsibilities of carriers and shippers and the bill of lading. This legislation encompasses the Harter Act and defines the liability of vessels carrying cargo to and from United States ports. The act provides that a carrier's liability is limited to $500 per shipping package and that the time limit for filing a claim against a carrier is one year.

see: Hague Rules, Harter Act

Carriage of Goods by Water Act (COGWA)

Ocean Marine. A Canadian act which is the equivalent of the Hague Rules concerning the shipment of cargo for which bills of lading are issued between Canada and foreign ports.

see: Hague Rules

carrier

Inland Marine/Ocean Marine. A business that transports merchandise from one point to another. The carrier can be a vessel's owner, manager, operator, an airline, a truck operator or a railroad.

see: common carrier, contract carrier, private carrier

Insurer Operations. An entity that assumes or carries insurance risk, i.e., an insurance company, a reinsurer, a managed care organization, or a self-insurer.

see: insurance company, managed care, quasi-insurance institutions, self-insurance

Automobile.

see: motor carrier

carrier's form

Inland Marine.

see: motor truck cargo insurance

carriers' legal liability

Inland Marine. An insurance coverage form that protects the insured carrier against the bailee liability that arises out of damage to property in the carrier's care, custody or control.

see: care custody or control exclusion

Ocean Marine.

see: Carriage of Goods by Sea Act, Hague Rules, Harter Act

case law

Law.

see: common law

case management

Health. A cost control method, usually employed by health maintenance organizations and other managed care plans but sometimes also by insurers, that directs individual members or insureds to the most appropriate amount, duration and type of health services and monitors medical outcomes. The managed care plan or insurer may employ a case manager or may contract with an independent

case management agency.

see: integrated care (2), managed care, outcomes program

cash assets

Accounting. The sum of cash on hand plus short-term demand certificates and securities (such as Treasury bills) that can readily be converted into cash without disrupting normal operations. (Cash assets do not include marketable securities.)

see: assets, demand deposit

cash basis of accounting

Accounting. An accounting method in which income is recognized only upon the receipt of a cash payment without considering the period for which payments are due. Also, expenses are accounted for only upon their cash payment. This accounting method is rarely applied to commercial businesses, but it may be used by professionals and small private enterprises. Government accounts are usually maintained on this basis.

compare: accrual basis of accounting; *see*: accounting

cash budget

Accounting. A budget showing the expected cash receipts and disbursements during each period covered by the budget, including receipts from loans necessary to maintain an adequate cash balance and repayments of loans.

see: budget, cash flow

cash cycle

Accounting. The length of time between the purchase of raw materials and the collection of accounts receivable generated in the sale of the final product that is produced from those raw materials.

cash flow

Accounting. The cash account of a business; money available, even if not required, for current expenses; income and expenditures traceable (through a "cash flow statement") from their first appearance in an organization's bank accounts through their final disposition.

see: cash budget, cash flow program, cash flow underwriting, negative cash flow, net net income

cash flow program

Risk Management. An insurance program where premium payment is deferred over the policy term or until losses are paid. This allows the insured to utilize or gain investment income on funds for a greater period of time.

see: cash flow, cash flow underwriting, paid loss retrospective rating plan

cash flow underwriting

Insurer Operations. An underwriting practice where coverage is provided for a premium level that is actuarially less than necessary to pay claims and expenses. The insurer that engages in cash flow underwriting believes that it can make an investment profit on the premiums to compensate for the underwriting loss.

see: financial underwriting, investment income, underwriting cycle

cash-on-cash return

Financial Planning. The ratio produced by dividing the annual cash flow of a property by the original cash payment for the property.

synonym: equity capitalization rate, equity dividend rate; *see*: financial ratios

cash out

Employee Benefits/Life. To accept a lump sum payment and give up a claim to future benefits. This may be done by a participant in an employee pension plan or by a life insurance policyholder.

see: cash surrender value, employee benefit plan, pension

cash payment option

Life.

see: lump sum option

cash refund annuity

Life. A life annuity contract that pays to a beneficiary, upon the death of the annuitant, a lump sum equal to the difference between the amount of premium paid for the annuity and the income benefits already paid to the annuitant. Income payments simply continue if the annuitant lives past the point where the total income equals the premiums paid.

synonym: lump sum refund annuity; *see*: lump sum option, refund annuity

cash sale

Financial Planning. A securities transaction that requires the traded securities to be delivered on the day of the trade, as opposed to the usual requirement of delivery on the fifth day following the trade.

see: delivery

cash surrender value

Life. The amount payable to a life insurance policyholder or deferred annuity contract holder in the event of termination or cancellation of the policy or annuity before its maturity or the insured event. The cash value may be specified in a table attached to the policy, and there may be a waiting period before payment is made. (Sometimes called the *policyholder's equity.*)

Premiums paid in the early years of a life policy are greater than actuarially required to provide coverage, and they accumulate earnings over the years, building a reserve for a time late in the policy term

when premium payments become less than required to provide the coverage. If a policy is canceled or surrendered before maturity, the premiums and accumulations are greater than the coverage actually purchased by the insured. The cash surrender value represents this amount minus a surrender charge and any outstanding balance on a policy loan the insured may have taken.

synonym: cash value, nonforfeiture cash surrender value benefit, policyholder's equity; *compare*: maturity value; *see*: nonforfeiture benefit, policy loan

cash value

Life.

see: cash surrender value

Property.

see: actual cash value

cash value insurance

Life. A life insurance policy that combines death benefits with a savings or investing plan. A premium is paid in early years that is higher than actuarially required in order to build up a tax-advantaged "savings account" or reserve that makes up for the actuarially deficient premiums in later years. Examples are whole, universal, and variable life insurance.

see: cash surrender value, universal life insurance, variable life insurance, whole life insurance

cashier's check

General. A check drawn by a bank on itself, giving the payee authorization to collect the amount represented on the check.

compare: certified check, draft

cast insurance

Professional Liability. A special form of entertainment insurance that combines life and health with casualty coverages for on-screen movie and television personnel. Coverage is provided to the production company for losses resulting from abandoning a movie or television production or extra expenses incurred in completing the production following illness, disability or death of designated cast members. The coverage is written on a valued per diem loss of income basis.

synonym: film and television producers' indemnity insurance; *see*: business interruption insurance, entertainment insurance, nonappearance insurance

Casualty Actuarial Society (CAS)

Organizations. Members: Insurance actuaries. *Objectives*: Promotes actuarial and statistical science as applied to insurance problems, other than

82

life insurance. *Founded*: 1914. *Headquarters*: Arlington, VA.

see: Associate of the Casualty Actuarial Society, Fellow of the Casualty Actuarial Society

casualty catastrophe reinsurance
Reinsurance.

see: clash reinsurance

casualty insurance
Liability. Casualty is a legal and accounting term for nearly any accident or a sudden, unexpected loss. Casualty insurance traditionally refers to many different lines or coverages other than life or health, including automobile and general liability; employers' liability; plate glass insurance; professional liability; errors and omissions insurance; burglary, robbery and forgery insurance; aviation insurance; and workers' compensation insurance. Boiler and machinery insurance was historically included but is increasingly classified as property insurance. A typical characteristic of casualty insurance is indemnity for bodily injury or property damage to third parties caused by negligent acts or omissions of the insured. This is the central meaning of *liability insurance*, which is the term used more often.

see: liability insurance, line

casualty loss
Accounting. An unexpected, usually sudden event or accident in which property is destroyed or damaged or its value is reduced.

see: casualty insurance, funded reserve

catalyst
Loss Control. A substance that initiates or alters the speed of a chemical reaction without changing its own composition. It may accelerate or retard the reaction.

catastrophe
General. An event causing severe loss, injury or damage. Most often associated with natural disasters, the term usually is used when there is concentrated or widespread damage.

see: act of God, catastrophe insurance futures contract, catastrophe loss, force majeur, natural perils

catastrophe insurance futures contract
Financial Planning. A type of futures contract traded on the Chicago Board of Trade since December, 1992, used to hedge an insurer's exposures from the catastrophe perils of wind, hail, earthquake, riot or flood over a quarterly period. Some of the contracts (or options thereon) cover specific geographic areas, reflecting different probabilities of various types of natural disasters, and some are national. The settlement value of the contract is determined by an index, or composite, of applicable loss data reported by many insurers for the contract period. If losses are greater than expected, the value of the contract increases. The buying insurer partly compensates for its unanticipated claim losses with the profit on the futures contract. If catastrophe losses are less than expected, the buyer incurs an investment loss on the contract (but has been spared significant catastrophe losses).

see: futures contract, hedging, risk securitization

catastrophe layer
Risk Management. One of the three categories to which losses are normally assigned. As the highest layer of losses, it includes those that do not occur with regularity and may not ever occur but are especially destructive.

compare: buffer layer, working layer

catastrophe loss
Property. An incident or series of related incidents causing insured property losses of more than $5 million.

see: force majeure, natural perils

Risk Management. An exceptionally large loss that cannot accurately be predicted and therefore should be transferred by an individual or organization to an insurer.

see: catastrophe insurance futures contract, catastrophe reinsurance, insurable risk

catastrophe number
Property. A number assigned by the National Board of Fire Underwriters to severe losses (i.e., those exceeding $5 million) for insurance statistical purposes.

catastrophe plan
Loss Control.

see: disaster plan

catastrophe policy
Health. A term formerly used for *major medical insurance.*

see: major medical insurance

catastrophe reinsurance
Reinsurance. A type of excess of loss treaty reinsurance that protects the ceding insurer against a loss or losses in excess of a specified retention, from an accumulation of losses resulting from a single catastrophic event or a series of events, subject to the reinsurance contract limit.

synonym: catastrophe treaty; *see*: excess of loss reinsurance

catastrophe treaty
Reinsurance.

see: catastrophe reinsurance

catastrophic loss fund

Insurer Operations. Any special fund or reserve held for extraordinary or catastrophic losses (e.g., losses incurred by a fire insurer due to an extensive, general conflagration).

catastrophic peril

Property. The cause of a catastrophe loss; a peril that has the potential to result in a major disaster (such as earthquakes, floods and nuclear accidents).

see: catastrophe loss, natural perils, peril

cathodic protection

Loss Control. A technique used to prevent electrolytic corrosion of a metal surface. An example of its use is to protect an underground metal storage tank.

cause

General.

see: cause of action, cause of loss, concurrent causation, immediate cause, proximate cause

cause of action

Law. The asserted basis for a legal claim against another; the alleged facts that give rise to the plaintiff's right to sue.

see: action, complaint, demurrer

cause of loss

Property. The event or condition that produces a loss covered by an insurance policy. Some policies use this term instead of "peril" to describe an event that is insured against, but "peril" is still widely used by insurance personnel.

compare: exposure, hazard, risk; *see*: peril

causes of loss—basic form

Property. A named perils policy (ISO form CP 10 10) in the Insurance Services Office commercial property program that covers the perils of fire, explosion, lightning, windstorm or hail, smoke, riot or civil commotion, vandalism, sprinkler leakage, sinkhole collapse, and volcanic action. Coverages are subject to certain exclusions and restrictions.

compare: causes of loss—broad form, causes of loss—special form, causes of loss—earthquake

causes of loss—broad form

Property. A named perils policy (ISO form CP 10 20) under the Insurance Services Office commercial property program that provides the same coverages as the basic form plus breakage of glass; falling objects; weight of snow, ice or sleet; water damage from leakage from appliances; and collapse. Coverages are subject to certain exclusions and restrictions.

compare: causes of loss—basic form, causes of loss—special form, causes of loss—earthquake.

causes of loss—earthquake form

Property. An endorsement (ISO form CP 10 40) under the Insurance Services Office commercial property program that extends the covered causes of loss to include the perils of earthquake and volcanic eruption. The form specifically excludes loss for fire, explosion, landslide, tidal wave, flood, and mudslide or mudflow even if they are directly attributable to an earthquake or volcanic eruption. Coverage for exterior masonry veneer (except stucco) on wood frame walls is excluded, but this exclusion can be deleted for an additional premium.

see: earthquake, earthquake insurance, earthquake shock

causes of loss—special form

Property. An all risks policy (ISO form CP 10 30) under the Insurance Services Office commercial property program that covers risks of direct physical loss unless the loss is excluded.

compare: causes of loss—basic form, causes of loss—broad form, causes of loss—earthquake.

caveat emptor

Law. Latin for "let the buyer beware"; a maxim admonishing a buyer to examine, judge, and test an item before buying it. The implication is that the seller in an arm's length transaction cannot be assumed to be completely candid, that there is no guaranty of quality, and that a buyer must accept any deficiencies he could have discovered by careful inspection. However, the consumer rights movement, reflected in court opinions and statutes, has substantially modified this principle.

compare: uberrima fides; *see*: warranty of merchantability

cease and desist

Law/Regulation. A court order, or the order of a government agency authorized to issue such an order, to stop a potentially dangerous, injurious or fraudulent act. *Example*: A state insurance department may issue a cease and desist order to an insurance company to stop false advertising, redlining (bias in the selection of risks), or unfair claims practices.

see: injunction

cede

Reinsurance. To transfer insurance risk from an insurer (the ceding insurer, or cedent) to another insurer (the reinsurer).

compare: assume; *see*: ceding insurer, reinsurance

ceded leverage

Insurer Operations/Reinsurance. A ratio used in evaluating an insurer's solvency. Reinsurance premiums ceded, plus net ceded reinsurance balances for unpaid losses and unearned premium reserves recoverable, plus ceded reinsurance balances payable for nonaffiliates are compared to policyholders' surplus.

see: policyholders' surplus, reinsurance

ceded reinsurance
Reinsurance. The amount of insurance transferred from a ceding insurer to a reinsurer.

compare: assumed reinsurance; *see*: ceding insurer, reinsurance

cedent
Reinsurance.
see: ceding insurer

ceding commission
Reinsurance. The commission paid to a ceding insurer by a reinsurer on reinsurance contracts, in order to obtain business.

synonym: reinsurance commission; *see*: acquisition cost, management expense, sliding scale commission

ceding insurer
Reinsurance. An original or primary insurer that purchases reinsurance; in so doing, the primary insurer cedes part of its business to the reinsurer.

synonym: cedent, primary insurance company, reassured, reinsured; *compare*: reinsurer; *see*: reinsurance

cemetery professional liability insurance
Professional Liability. Insurance designed to protect cemetery operators from third-party claims for injury or loss (including mental anguish) resulting from the actions of a cemetery, management or staff. Included is coverage for damage to property of others, such as caskets, human remains, urns, and clothing in the insured's custody for use in burial or cremation.

center of gravity
Law.
see: center of influence

center of influence
Law. In a lawsuit, one of the considerations used to resolve a conflict of laws between states or countries. The jurisdiction with the most significant relationship to the parties or matter at issue is the one whose law will apply to the case in the absence of outweighing factors. The law applied in a tort case is generally that of the state where the accident or injury occurred. In a contract dispute, a court would consider factors such as where the parties reside, where the contract was signed, and where the contract is to be performed.

synonym: center of gravity; *see*: conflict of laws, diversity jurisdiction, tort

central limit theorem
Risk Management. An actuarial principle that if a series of samples is collected from a stable population, the distribution of the means (averages) of the samples will result in a normal distribution, where the mean approaches the population as the number of samples increase.

see: mean

central loss fund
Insurer Operations. A fund maintained in certain states by contributions from insurers in order to pay claims against insolvent insurance companies.

see: guaranty fund

central station
Loss Control. A fire resistive secure facility operated 24 hours a day by a professional alarm company, usually approved by Underwriters Laboratories. Client alarms, connected to the central station by electrical or electronic circuits, are continually monitored. When an alarm is received, the local fire or police department is notified and a security guard is often dispatched.

see: central station alarm system

central station alarm system
Loss Control. An alarm system that is controlled and operated by a central station, which upon receipt of a signal will take the necessary action. Actions may include notifying the fire or police department, calling the subscriber, or sending its own investigator to the scene of the alarm.

compare: auxiliary alarm system, local alarm system, proprietary alarm system, remote station alarm system; *see*: central station

Centre for the Study of Insurance Operations (CSIO)
Organizations. *Members*: Canadian insurance companies and brokers. *Objectives*: To promote automation of the insurance distribution system. *Headquarters*: Toronto, Ontario.

certain payments
Life.
see: guaranteed annuity payments

certain period
Life. The period over which an annuity's payments will be made, regardless of whether the annuitant is living. If the annuitant dies within the certain or guaranteed period, payments remaining in the certain period are made as to the annuitant's estate.

synonym: guaranteed period; *see*: annuity, annuity certain

certificate
General. A written authorization or official representation or assurance attesting to compliance with

a legal requirement.

see: agent's certificate of authority, certificate of authority, certificate of convenience, certificate of deposit, certificate of insurance, certificate of occupancy, certificate of reinsurance, certificate of sale, certificate of title, group certificate, marine insurance certificate, renewal certificate

certificate of authority

Agency. A document enumerating the powers granted by an insurance company to its agents.

see: license

Insurer Operations. A state-issued document empowering an insurer to write insurance contracts and perform certain business within its borders.

certificate of convenience

General. A certificate issued by an administrative agency granting temporary operating authority for utilities and transportation companies.

Regulation. A license issued by a state insurance department on a temporary basis which allows an individual to act as an insurance agent, though not having completed the normal licensing process. It usually is issued where a spouse or parent has died, has become disabled or has been called to serve in the military, and the spouse or children must step in to run an existing insurance agency.

see: license, limited license

certificate of deposit (CD)

Financial Planning. A written acknowledgment by a chartered financial institution giving proof of a specific deposit amount with a promise to pay the amount indicated on the certificate to the order of the depositor, or to pay that amount to some other person.

see: time deposit

certificate of insurance

Employee Benefits/Health/Life. Written evidence that an individual is a participant in a group life or health insurance program or employee benefit plan. In most group programs, only the employer or sponsoring organization receives a complete copy of the policy; members (employees, union members, etc.) receive only certificates of insurance.

synonym: group certificate; compare: group contract, master insurance policy

Inland Marine/Ocean Marine.

see: marine insurance certificate

Liability/Property. Written evidence that an insurance policy has been issued, indicating both the amounts and the types of insurance. It is used when general contractors or property owners require subcontractors to provide evidence of insurance. It is sometimes requested by mortgage companies or other lenders, although such parties usually require loss payable clauses, because a certificate of insurance does not obligate the insurance company to the individual or organization to which the certificate is issued.

see: loss payable clause, master insurance policy, policy certification log, underlying insurance policy

certificate of occupancy

General. A document issued by a municipality, certifying that a given premises complies with zoning and building ordinances and codes.

certificate of origin

International. An international trade document that includes a signed statement showing the origin of imported goods. This document is required for all imports entering the United States.

see: customs entry form

certificate of purchase

General.

see: certificate of sale

certificate of reinsurance

Reinsurance. An abbreviated documentation of a reinsurance transaction, usually incorporating standard terms and conditions by reference.

see: binder, reinsurance

certificate of sale

General. A document issued by a public official to the successful bidder at a judicial sale, which will entitle the bidder to a deed upon confirmation of the sale by the court.

synonym: certificate of purchase

certificate of title

Title. A certificate issued by a title company or a written opinion rendered by an attorney that the seller has good marketable and insurable title to the property that is offered for sale. A certificate of title offers no protection against any hidden defects in the title that an examination of the records could not reveal. The issuer of a certificate of title is liable only for damages due to negligence. The protection offered by a certificate of title is not as great as that offered by title insurance.

see: paper title, title, title insurance

certification form

General. A preprinted form that confirms or attests to attaining some standard of compliance with a specified requirement.

certified check

Financial Planning. A check that has been authorized by a bank, causing the bank to be liable to the holder of the check, in effect debiting the drawer's account and placing the sum in a separate account.

Certified checks are often required by payees because payment cannot be stopped.

compare: cashier's check, draft

Certified Coding Specialist (CCS)

Organizations. A professional designation awarded by the American Health Information Management Association based on education and experience.

see: American Health Information Management Association

Certified Employee Benefit Specialist (CEBS)

Organizations. A professional designation granted jointly by the International Foundation of Employee Benefit Plans and the Wharton School of the University of Pennsylvania. The designation requires the completion of ten college-level courses and examinations in pension planning, Social Security, health insurance, economics, finance, labor relations, group insurance and other employee benefit-related concepts.

see: International Foundation of Employee Benefit Plans

Certified Financial Planner (CFP)

Organizations. A professional designation granted by the College for Financial Planning. It requires successful completion of a two-year curriculum in financial planning, insurance, investment, taxation, employee benefit plans, and estate planning.

Certified Hazard Control Manager (CHCM)

Organizations. A professional designation for a person who has satisfied the educational and administrative requirements of the Board of Certified Hazard Control Management, at either the senior or master level, as qualified to manage a comprehensive safety and health program.

Certified Insurance Data Manager (CIDM)

Organizations. A professional designation awarded by the Insurance Data Management Association after successful completion of all of the courses offered in its curriculum.

see: Insurance Data Management Association

Certified Manager of Patient Accounts (CMPA)

Organizations. A professional designation awarded by the Health Care Financial Management Association after successful completion of a national examination.

see: Health Care Financial Management Association

Certified Public Accountant (CPA)

Accounting. An accountant who has met the licensing requirements of a state.

see: accountant, audited financial statement

Certified Safety Professional (CSP)

Loss Control/Organizations. A professional designation awarded by the Board of Certified Safety Professionals of the Americas, Inc. which certifies an individual as having achieved professional competence by remaining abreast of technical, administrative, and regulatory developments in the safety fields.

see: Board of Certified Safety Professionals of the Americas, Inc.

certiorari

Law. A writ issued by an appellate court requesting a certified record of proceedings from a lower court to review for possible errors. (Latin for "to be informed of.")

see: appeal

cession

Reinsurance. The insurance coverage transferred to a reinsurer by a ceding insurer. It corresponds with policy units of an insurance company. A cession may be all or a portion of a single risk, a group of defined policies, or defined portions of a policy.

see: assumed reinsurance, ceding insurer, reinsurance

cession number

Reinsurance. An assigned number used to identify reinsurance premium transactions.

cestui que vie

Life. The person whose life measures an estate or is the subject of a life insurance policy. (French for "the one whose life.")

chain

Title. A land measurement used by surveyors that is equal to 66 feet, or 100 links, or 4 rods. (An engineer's chain is equal to 100 feet)

chain of title

Title. The successive conveyances that affect a particular parcel of land, from an accepted starting point to where the present holder of real property derives his or her title.

see: abstract of title

chain stores multiple location insurance

Property. A type of business insurance coverage for stores under common ownership and management that sell uniform merchandise at multiple locations.

change in conditions insurance

Property.

see: difference in conditions insurance

change in occupancy or use

Liability/Property. A provision in many property and casualty policies that a change of occupancy, purpose or use of a premises can void the policy if the changes increase the hazards. The insurer may cancel the policy outright or charge additional premium to cover the additional hazards.

see: increased hazard, occupancy permit

change in ownership

Workers' Compensation. Most workers' compensation rating bureaus define a change in the ownership of an organization to include sales, purchases, transfers, mergers, consolidations, dissolutions and formations of new entities. Such a change can result in a revision in the experience rating modification factor.

see: experience rating modification factor, notification of change in ownership endorsement, rating bureau, workers' compensation insurance

change of beneficiary provision

Life. The provision in a life insurance policy that permits the policyholder to change beneficiaries at will, unless a beneficiary has been designated as irrevocable in the policy.

see: beneficiary change, beneficiary clause

change of occupation provision

Health. A provision in a health insurance policy that if the insured changes to a more hazardous occupation, benefits will automatically be reduced to those that could be purchased by the premium paid by an individual in the more hazardous occupation. If the change is to a less hazardous occupation, the premium will be reduced at the insured's request.

chaplain or priest professional liability insurance

Professional Liability.

see: clergy professional liability insurance

chargeable offense

Automobile. An action or violation committed while driving a motor vehicle for which insurers are permitted to charge an additional premium or to deny, terminate, or refuse to renew coverage. Parking tickets are not chargeable against a driving record.

see: safe driver plan

charitable annuity

Life. An annuity paid by a charitable organization in exchange for property or a sum of money. Part of the value of the contribution (or purchase price of the annuity) is tax deductible to the grantor, provided the recipient organization is operated for a qualified charitable, religious, scientific or educational purpose and the gift or purchase price is greater than the annuity's present value, calculated according to Internal Revenue Service rules.

see: annuity, grantor, present value

charitable lead trust

Financial Planning. A trust that pays income to a charity for a set number of years, after which the principal is paid to the inheriting heirs.

see: trust

charter

Aviation.

see: air taxi

Law. A document describing the rights granted by a government to a business organization, or to a lower public agency, to conduct and transact certain business.

see: articles of incorporation, bylaws, intra vires, ultra vires

Ocean Marine. The mercantile lease of a ship or some principal part of it.

see: charter party

charter aircraft

Aviation.

see: air taxi

charter fare protection insurance

Health. A special form of accident and health insurance that reimburses an insured individual for the cost of a tour if the insured is unable to participate due to a covered accident or sickness. Coverage extends if the insured is unable to make a return flight on a scheduled date because of illness. In this case, the insured is reimbursed for the specific cost of a later return flight.

synonym: trip cancellation insurance; *see*: air travel insurance, travel accident insurance

charter party

Ocean Marine. A document between the individual, group, or company chartering a ship and the owner of the vessel, stating the terms and conditions of the charter.

see: affreightment, bareboat charter, charterer's liability insurance, time charter, voyage charter

Chartered Financial Consultant (ChFC)

Organizations. A professional designation granted by the American College. The designation requires the successful completion of national examinations in financial planning, insurance, investments, taxation, employee benefits, estate planning, accounting and management.

see: American College, American Society of Chartered Life Underwriters and Chartered Financial Consultants

Chartered Life Underwriter (CLU)

Life/Organizations. A professional designation granted by the American College. Those seeking the designation must successfully complete ten college-level courses and examinations in insurance, investments, taxation, employee benefits, estate planning, accounting, management and economics.

see: American College, American Society of Chartered Life Underwriters and Chartered Financial Consultants, special circumstances

Chartered Property Casualty Underwriter (CPCU)

Organizations. A professional designation granted by the American Institute for Property Casualty Underwriters. Successful candidates are those who complete ten college-level courses and examinations in insurance, risk management, economics, finance, management, accounting and law.

see: American Institute for Property Casualty Underwriters, CPCU Society, special circumstances

charterers liability insurance

Ocean Marine. Coverage that insures against the liability of a person who leases a vessel from another. The lessor may assume full responsibility for the vessel and crew (as in a bareboat charter), or limit insurable interest to partial responsibility (as in a time charter) and leave most insurance requirements for the vessel owner to handle.

see: bareboat charter, charter party, time charter

chattel

Property.

see: personal property

chattel mortgage

Mortgage Insurance. A mortgage on personal (movable) property, as opposed to a mortgage on real property.

see: mortgage

chattel mortgage nonfiling insurance

Mortgage Insurance. Insurance coverage that protects banks, credit unions and other lending institutions, against their financial loss due to the inability of the institution to obtain possession of property represented by a chattel mortgage or similar security instrument in the granting of the loan. This coverage also insures against the inability of the lending institution to enforce its rights under the instrument due to the intentional nonfiling of the instrument with the proper public official.

check alteration and forgery insurance

Crime.

see: forgery bond

Chemical Abstracts Service registry number

Loss Control. The identification number assigned to a chemical that is registered with the Chemical Abstracts Service.

chemical recovery boiler exclusion

Property. A boiler and machinery policy exclusion for any explosion within the furnace of a chemical

recovery boiler or any accident that results from the explosion.

Chemical Referral Center (CRC)

Loss Control. A facility established in 1985 by the Chemical Manufacturers' Association to provide nonemergency information about chemicals and chemical products to the public, transportation workers, and users of chemicals.

chemical release sheet

Loss Control.

see: Material Safety Data Sheet

cherry picker

Automobile. A traveling crane equipped with a boom designed to raise or lower workers. As respects a business auto policy, this is considered a type of mobile equipment that is specifically excluded from coverage unless it is mounted on an automobile or truck chassis.

see: business auto coverage form, mobile equipment

child labor

Workers' Compensation. Employment of, or work performed by, minors. The definition of a child or minor varies by state from under 14 to under 18 years of age. Children are covered by the workers' compensation laws of all states. In many states, if a child is employed illegally, the workers' compensation benefits are increased by 50% to 200%.

see: double compensation, illegal employment, workers' compensation law

child's benefit

Health. A benefit provided under Social Security, payable to the child of a disabled, deceased, or retired worker. In order to receive these benefits, the child must be under 18 years of age, or be a full-time student between 18 and 22 years of age, or must be disabled and have suffered the disability prior to 22 years of age.

see: Social Security

child safety seat

Automobile. A seat for use in automobiles to protect or restrain an infant or young child in the event of a collision. Seats are subject to federal Child Seating Systems regulations. To be effective, the seat must be properly anchored to the automobile seat by a safety belt. The seat may face rearward (for infants up to 9-12 months old) or forward (for children from 9-12 months up to 4 or 5 years and weighing up to 40 pounds).

synonym: car seat; *see*: infant car carrier, passive restraint system, safety belt

childbirth

Health.

see: maternity benefit

Chinese retro
Liability/Workers' Compensation.
see: retrospective penalty insurance

chiropodists' professional liability insurance
Professional Liability. A form of professional liability insurance designed for chiropodists that covers injuries arising from malpractice in rendering professional services. Coverage is usually written on a claims-made basis.

see: malpractice insurance, medical malpractice, professional liability insurance

chiropractors' professional liability insurance
Professional Liability. A form of professional liability insurance designed for chiropractors that covers injuries arising from malpractice in rendering professional services. Coverage is usually written on a claims-made basis.

see: medical malpractice, professional liability insurance

chomage
Property. An early form of business interruption insurance that based the insured's business interruption recovery on a percentage of the fire loss to a building or its contents. *Example*: If the fire loss was $50,000, the chomage amount might be 2%, or an additional $1,000.

see: business income coverage form, business interruption insurance

chose in action
Law. A right of ownership in a tangible thing that carries the right to take legal action on it. The right itself is intangible. A written contract is evidence of a chose in action because the destruction of the writing does not destroy the contract right. Examples are claims, debts, insurance policies, negotiable instruments, contract rights, copyrights, and bills of lading.

compare: chose in possession; *see*: intangible property, personal property

chose in possession
Law. A tangible or physical article of which one has possession.

compare: chose in action; *see*: personal property, tangible property

Christmas tree lot coverage
Liability. A special insurance coverage for operators of both pre-cut and cut-your-own Christmas tree lots. Coverage includes third-party liability for injuries occurring on the premises and inland marine coverage (usually excluding theft) for the value of the trees. The policy term is usually 30 to 60 days or expires on December 31st.

see: standing timber insurance

chronic toxicity
Loss Control/Workers' Compensation. The ability of a substance to harm human health with long-term exposure. In general, toxicity depends on both length and level of exposure. With prolonged exposure, even low levels or doses may be toxic.

compare: LD50

chronological stabilization plan
Risk Management. An insurance program intended to level losses or stabilize costs, similar to some reinsurance plans or retrospective rating plans. Losses are actuarially projected to arrive at a premium figure that includes a small loading factor. Claims paid for the five- to fifteen-year term of the plan will approach 85% to 95% of paid premium, depending on the terms and type of coverage. If the amount of payable losses falls short of actuarial expectations, a retrospective refund of the excess premium is paid. If losses exceed the calculated amount, an upward adjustment is made.

see: banking plan, spread loss plan

church members', officers' and volunteers' coverage
Liability. An endorsement (ISO form CG 20 22) to the commercial general liability policy for places of worship to include members, officers and volunteer workers as additional insureds.

see: clergy professional liability insurance, commercial general liability policy

churning
Financial Planning. The illegal practice by a securities broker of excessive trading, in size or frequency, of a client's account in order to increase the broker's commissions. Excessive trading is determined in light of the client's resources and investment objectives.

see: discretionary account

circulating main
Loss Control. A water main or piping used for fire protection that is fed from two directions.

see: deadend main

civil authority clause
Property. Coverage included in most business income forms. If access to an insured's premises is denied by order of a civil authority as the result of damage or destruction of neighboring or adjacent property belonging to others, and the damage or destruction is due to an insured peril, then the insured's loss of income is covered for up to two weeks.

synonym: ingress or egress clause; *see*: governmental action exclusion, ordinance or law exclusion

civil commotion

Property. A general disturbance or uprising of a number of people who threaten or commit acts of violence and destroy property. Civil commotion is an insurable peril under most property insurance policies and is fundamentally the same as *riot*.

see: civil commotion exclusion, riot and civil commotion coverage

civil commotion coverage

Property.

see: riot and civil commotion coverage

civil commotion exclusion

Property. A property insurance exclusion for losses caused by uprisings, riots and civil commotion.

compare: riot and civil commotion coverage

civil commotion insurance

Property.

see: riot and civil commotion coverage

civil damages

Law.

see: civil law (1), damages

civil law

Law. 1. The legal principles, rights and remedies that apply to the private relations between people, as opposed to criminal law. A private wrong is called a *tort*, while a public wrong is a *felony* or *misdemeanor*, depending on its severity.

2. In international law, the tradition of public law based on codes or written legislation, as opposed to the Anglo-American tradition of common law, which is based on judicial opinions and custom.

compare: criminal law; *see*: common law, tort

civil liability

Law. Liability under civil law; an obligation to compensate another person for harm or loss.

see: civil law (1), liability, damages, tort

Civil Rights Act

Regulation. Federal legislation (U.S. Code Title 42, Chapter 21) adopted in 1964 that prohibits employers who engage in interstate commerce and have fifteen or more employees from discriminating on the basis of race, national origin, color, religion or sex. A 1991 amendment permits recovery of compensatory and punitive damages for intentional discrimination. Fines range from $50,000 to $300,000, depending upon the size of the employer, even absent an actual economic loss to the individual.

see: Pregnancy Discrimination Act

civil rights exclusion

Professional Liability. An exclusion in most police professional liability policies relating to defense costs and judgments for violating the rights of a person in police custody.

see: police professional liability insurance

claim

Insurer Operations. A demand by an insured or another party for indemnification of a loss under an insurance contract or bond; sometimes, the actual or estimated amount of a loss.

see: notice of loss, proof of loss

claim adjustment

Insurer Operations. The process used by an insurer to evaluate and settle a claim. This includes determining whether and to what extent the loss is covered by the policy, determining the cause of loss, and valuing the loss.

synonym: adjustment; *see*: claims adjuster

claim agent

Ocean Marine. A claims representative of an ocean marine insurer, located in ports and cities throughout the world, whom a claimant can contact in the event of a loss or damage to an insured shipment.

see: claims adjuster

claim expense

Insurer Operations. Expenses related to adjusting and settling a claim, excluding the claim payment. Claim expenses include both allocated and unallocated claim expenses.

see: adjustment expenses, allocated claim expense, defense costs, economic loss, ex gratia payment, legal expenses, loss adjustment expense, loss development, paid claim count, paid expense, trending, unallocated claim expense

claim number

Insurer Operations. A reference number that is assigned by an insurance company or third-party administrator to each claim.

claimant

Insurer Operations. One who claims or asserts a loss and his or her right to demand payment of compensation or benefits.

see: insured, plaintiff

claims adjuster

Insurer Operations. An individual who acts on behalf of, or is employed by, an insurance company to settle claims.

synonym: adjuster, claims representative; *compare*: public adjuster; *see*: adjustment bureau, claim adjustment, claim agent, drop check procedure, field adjuster, general average, independent adjuster, inside adjuster, staff adjuster, third-party administrator

claims administration

Risk Management. The management of claims that have occurred. This includes certifying a claimant's eligibility; monitoring adjusters, attorneys and medical service providers; and preparing reports.

see: third-party administrator

claims deductible workers' compensation plan

Workers' Compensation. A deductible workers' compensation plan where the policy deductible applies to both medical and indemnity or disability benefits.

see: deductible workers' compensation plan, disability benefit, medical benefit

claims department

Insurer Operations. The division of an insurance company that administers the handling and payment of claims.

see: claim, claim adjustment

claims frequency

Risk Management.

see: loss frequency

claims-made form

Liability. A liability policy that provides coverage for an injury or loss if the claim is first reported or filed during the policy period. This is in contrast to the broader *occurrence* policy forms, which cover injury or loss that occurs during the policy period, regardless of when the claim is first made. Generally, medical malpractice, professional liability, and high hazard product liability policies are written on a claims-made basis.

see: commercial general liability policy, extended reporting period, immature policy, laser endorsement, manifestation theory, mature policy, maxi tail, midi-tail, mini-tail, prior acts coverage, retroactive date, tail

claims-made trigger

Liability. Under a claims-made policy, coverage is activated upon the filing of a claim. The coverage trigger is the first notification of a claim against the insured during the policy period.

compare: continuous trigger theory, exposure theory, occurrence trigger; *see*: claims-made form, manifestation theory

claims management

Workers' Compensation. A process or system of reviewing and handling claims for benefits, designed to control hospital costs, provide the best medical care, and produce early return-to-work dates.

claims processing

Insurer Operations. Activities routinely involved in administering claims, from first receiving notice of loss to final settlement.

see: claim, claims adjuster, third-party administrator

claims report

Agency.

see: loss run

claims representative

Insurer Operations.

see: claims adjuster

claims reserve

Insurer Operations.

see: loss reserve

claims run

Insurer Operations/Risk Management.

see: loss run

Claims Section, CPCU Society

Organizations. An interest section of the CPCU Society that promotes the principles and practices associated with good claims management and customer service.

see: CPCU Society

claims severity

Risk Management.

see: loss severity

clash reinsurance

Reinsurance. A form of casualty excess of loss treaty reinsurance for catastrophe coverage in the event that two or more policies (perhaps from different lines of business) of the primary insurer are involved in the same loss occurrence. The ceding insurer's retention on this coverage will be more than the limits on any one reinsured policy.

synonym: casualty catastrophe cover; *see*: excess of loss reinsurance

class

Insurer Operations.

see: classification

Property.

see: protection class

class A fire

Loss Control. One of four categories of fires. Class A fires involve solid combustibles (such as wood or paper), which are best extinguished by water or dry chemicals. A portable fire extinguisher using water or dry chemicals is called a "class A extinguisher."

see: class B fire, class C fire, class D fire, fire extinguisher

class action

Law. A lawsuit that joins a large number of people

affected by a matter in dispute, rather than making each bring suit separately. Only one or a few named plaintiffs represent all members of the class.

synonym: representative action; *see*: derivative suit, strike suit

class B fire

Loss Control. One of four categories of fires. Class B fires involve flammable liquids, which are best extinguished by foam, carbon dioxide or dry chemicals. Portable extinguishers using these agents are called "class B extinguishers."

see: class A fire, class C fire, class D fire, dry chemical fire extinguisher, fire extinguisher, foam

class beneficiary

Life. A specific but unnamed individual or member of a group receiving the proceeds of an insurance policy, such as "children of the insured."

see: beneficiary

class C fire

Loss Control. One of four categories of fires. Class C fires involve live electrical equipment which must be extinguished by a nonconductive extinguishing agent such as carbon dioxide or dry chemicals. An extinguisher using either of these agents is called a "class C extinguisher."

see: class A fire, class B fire, class D fire, dry chemical fire extinguisher, fire extinguisher

class code

Workers' Compensation.

see: classification code

class D fire

Loss Control. One of four categories of fire. Class D fires involve combustible metals such as magnesium or titanium, which must be extinguished by special dry chemical extinguishers. Extinguishers designed to extinguish such fires are called "class D extinguishers."

see: class A fire, class B fire, class C fire, dry powder fire extinguisher, fire extinguisher

class rate

Insurer Operations. The rate assigned to similar risks or a class of risks, based on its classification code.

see: classification, classification code, governing classification

class rating

Property. A property insurance rating method where the type of building or occupancy is used to determine the rate. The rating bureau establishes rates for various building construction types (e.g., wood frame, brick, etc.) and protection classes and for occupancy by hazard categories (e.g., office,

computer manufacturing, etc.). This information is published in a manual used by underwriters. If the rate classification is not listed in the manual, the risk must be specifically rated.

compare: specific rate, tariff rate; *see*: construction, occupancy (*Property*)

class underwriting

Insurer Operations. An underwriting process where certain classes of business (e.g., auto dealers, truckers) are automatically rejected because they are not the types of business the insurer believes will be profitable, or because the insurer does not have the facilities (e.g., loss control, claims) to properly handle them.

compare: account underwriting

classification

Insurer Operations. Categorization on the basis of established criteria for rating risks, establishing premiums and tabulating statistical experience.

synonym: class; *see*: classification code, homogeneity, rating class, risk classification, underwriting

classification code

Insurer Operations. A code used in commercial lines rating to determine a specific rate. The *Commercial Lines Manual* published by the Insurance Services Office includes a table listing over 1,000 types of operations, each with a classification code.

see: class rate, classification, Insurance Services Office, rate manual

Workers' Compensation. A specific industry classification published in a workers' compensation rate manual. Such classifications are used to identify the activities of insureds and place them into underwriting and rating groups. Class codes are tied to premium rates based on underwriting experience for the class. Insureds may be rated using more than one class code if their activities fall into more than one category.

synonym: class code; *see*: class rate, governing classification, rate manual

classification endorsements

Insurer Operations. Endorsements that either restrict or expand coverages under a liability policy to meet the specific needs of special classes of business, or a specific insured.

see: XCU exclusions

classified insurance

Health/Life. The writing of life or health insurance on substandard risks.

see: substandard risk

clause

Insurer Operations. A provision or section of an

insurance policy describing its terms and conditions, such as the insuring agreement, exclusions, insured locations, insured's duties, and the policy period.

Life. A provision added to a life insurance policy, usually requiring an additional premium. Typical clauses include the waiver of premium clause, the disability income clause, the accidental death clause, and the settlement option.

see: accidental death benefit, disability income insurance, settlement options, waiver of premium

Clayton Act

Regulation. Federal legislation (U.S. Code Title 15, Chapter 1) enacted in 1914 that amended the Sherman Antitrust Act to prohibit price-fixing conspiracies in interstate commerce.

see: antitrust laws, McCarran-Ferguson Act, Sherman Antitrust Act

Clean Air Act

Regulation. Federal legislation (U.S. Code Title 42, Chapter 85) adopted in 1963 that assigns to each state primary responsibility for ensuring outdoor air quality. The states are required to submit a plan to the Environmental Protection Agency that specifies the manner in which they will achieve and maintain air quality. The Environmental Protection Agency also has authority to specially regulate hazardous pollutants and new sources of pollutants in the air through federal programs and federally approved state programs.

see: air pollutant, Environmental Protection Agency, National Ambient Air Quality Standards, National Emission Standards for Hazardous Air Pollutants

clean bill of lading

Inland Marine/Ocean Marine. A bill of lading with indication of any problems with the cargo's condition when it was accepted for carriage.

compare: clean receipt; *see*: bill of lading

clean change room

Loss Control. A room designed to allow workers to change into clean clothing or protective equipment in an environment free of toxic or hazardous substances. Often such rooms include shower facilities.

clean receipt

Inland Marine/Ocean Marine. A delivery receipt with no exceptions from damage or shortage noted by the party receiving the merchandise.

compare: clean bill of lading

Clean Water Act

Regulation.

see: Federal Water Pollution Control Act, National Pollutant Discharge Elimination System, Spill Prevention Control and Countermeasure Plan

cleanup fund

General. An insurance provision that pays for expenses associated with the principal insured event.

Examples: A life insurance provision that pays funeral expenses; extra expense coverage in a property insurance policy.

see: extra expense insurance

clear title

Title.

see: marketable title

clergy professional liability insurance

Liability. Coverage for clergy members (priests, ministers, rabbis, chaplains, etc.) for injuries or loss caused by the negligent or malfeasant performance of their professional duties, such as counseling. Lawsuits have been brought for emotional or physical suffering from wrong or inadequate advice, as well as for sexual and other misconduct. Coverage is usually written on a claims-made basis.

synonym: chaplain or priest professional liability; *see*: church members', officers' and volunteers' coverage; malfeasance; negligence; professional liability insurance

cliff vesting

Employee Benefits.

see: ten-year vesting

clinical trials product liability insurance

Professional Liability. Liability coverage for manufacturers of medical devices or pharmaceutical products for injuries resulting from product tests on humans in clinical trials approved by the Food and Drug Administration, National Institutes of Health or similar authority. Coverage is written on a claims-made basis.

see: product liability insurance

close corporation

Law. A corporation with relatively few shareholders and no regular market for its shares. Close corporations usually have made no public offering of shares, and the shares themselves are often subject to restrictions on transfer.

synonym: closely held corporation; *see*: corporation, limited liability company, partnership

closed circuit television interruption insurance
Property.
see: television closed circuit breakdown insurance

closed-end mutual fund
Financial Planning. A mutual fund whose charter limits the number of shares issued. The value of the shares are determined by trading on a major stock exchange or over-the-counter.
compare: open-end mutual fund; *see*: mutual fund

closed panel health maintenance organization
Health. One of two types of HMO approved by the Health Maintenance Organization Act. (The other is the independent practice association.) Under this form, the HMO employs a group of medical professionals at a central location or contracts with a medical group to provide services exclusively for the HMO's members. Tight control of medical services is maintained because of the close affiliation between the employer HMO and its medical personnel.
synonym: staff-model plan, group-practice association; *compare*: independent practice association; *see*: health maintenance organization

closely held corporation
Law.
see: close corporation

closing costs
Financial Planning. Expenses in addition to the purchase price that the buyer or seller of real estate normally incurs to complete the sale. Costs are paid on the closing day and include expenses such as deed or mortgage recording, escrow fees, title insurance premiums, appraisal and inspection fees, and realtor's commission.
see: escrow, mortgage

closure
Loss Control. In reference to hazardous waste management, securing a treatment, storage and disposal facility pursuant to Environmental Protection Agency regulations. The facility must be closed in a manner that minimizes the potential escape or runoff of hazardous waste. The owner or operator must provide financial assurance for closure and post-closure, which may satisfied by insurance, a trust fund, a surety bond, a letter of credit, or by meeting net worth standards.
see: closure and post-closure insurance, Environmental Protection Agency, hazardous waste, post-closure, treatment storage and disposal facility

closure and post-closure insurance
Liability. Insurance coverage for operators of hazardous waste treatment, storage and disposal facilities to meet the requirements of the Resource Conservation and Recovery Act requiring proof of financial responsibility for the closure and post-closure maintenance of waste and disposal sites. The regulations require site owners to provide the federal Environmental Protection Agency with evidence that they will be able to close and monitor the site, usually for a period of 30 years.
see: financial responsibility law, Resource Conservation and Recovery Act

cloud on title
Title. An outstanding claim or encumbrance that adversely affects the marketability of the title to real estate.
compare: marketable title; *see*: defective title, encumbrance, real estate

club members' coverage
Liability. Members of social clubs can be added by endorsement (ISO form CG 20 02) as additional insureds to a club's commercial general liability policy to cover liability arising from club activities or activities of members acting on behalf of the club.
see: commercial general liability policy

cogeneration plants
Property.
see: alternative energy plants

cognitive impairment
Health. A peril that can be covered under a long-term care policy. Coverage is triggered if the insured individual has a loss of awareness and judgment, such as with senility or Alzheimer's disease
see: long-term care insurance

coin and stamp dealers' insurance
Inland Marine.
see: stamp and coin dealers' insurance

coin collections coverage
Personal. One of the nine classes of property that can be covered under a personal articles floater. Coverage is included for rare or current coins, medals, paper money, bank notes, tokens of money, and other numismatic property. Coverage is also provided for coin albums, containers, frames, cards, and display cabinets containing such collections whether or not owned by the insured. Special exclusions relating to coin collections include fading, creasing, denting, scratching, tearing, or thinning; transfer of colors, inherent defect, dampness, extremes of temperature, and depreciation; being handled or worked on; and the disappearance of individual coins.
see: personal articles floater, stamp and coin

dealers insurance

coinsurance

Health. The insured's share of covered health insurance benefits. Coinsurance has become common as costs to insurers have risen, and it is considered both a cost-sharing and cost-containment technique. *Example:* In some policies the insurer pays 80% of the covered medical expenses, and the insured pays the remainder.

see: copayment

Insurer Operations. An agreement between the insured and the insurer to share in the settlement of any covered losses in a proportion agreed upon in advance.

Property.

see: agreed amount clause, coinsurance clause

coinsurance clause

Property. A provision in most property and inland marine policies that requires property to be insured at a specified percentage of its full value (usually 80%, 90% or 100%) in exchange for a rate credit. If at the time of a loss it is determined that the insured carried inadequate limits, the loss recovery will be a percentage of the total loss amount, calculated by dividing the actual insured amount by the required amount. *Example:* A building valued at $100,000 has a 90% coinsurance clause and is insured for $45,000. It suffers a $20,000 loss. The insured would recover $45,000 ÷ (.90 × 100,000) × 20,000 = $10,000 (less any deductible).

synonym: average clause, coinsurance, contribution clause; *see:* agreed amount clause, agreed value clause, foundation exclusion clause

coinsurance deficiency coverage

Property. Insurance coverage that indemnifies the insured against financial loss sustained through the unintentional failure of the insured to purchase adequate insurance to comply with the provisions of a coinsurance clause in a property insurance policy.

see: coinsurance clause

coinsurance penalty

Property. A provision in property insurance policies that if an insured did not have adequate insurance relative to the property value at the time of a partial loss, the loss payment is determined by the following formula: loss payment = (amount of insurance carried ÷ amount of insurance required) × (loss − the deductible amount, if any).

see: coinsurance clause

cold call

Agency. Solicitation of a prospective insurance buyer without a prior appointment.

synonym: cold canvassing; *see:* marketing

cold canvassing

Agency.

see: cold call

cold weather valve

Loss Control. An automatic sprinkler system with an indicating type of control valve that controls ten or fewer sprinkler heads in a wet pipe system protecting an area subject to freezing. The valve is normally closed and the system drained during freezing weather.

see: automatic sprinkler system, wet pipe automatic sprinkler system

collapse

Property. To fall down or inward; the abrupt failure or imminent fundamental weakening of a wall or foundation of a structure. Collapse is covered in most property policies when it is due to an insured peril. Collapse does not include settling, cracking, shrinkage, bulging or expansion.

see: fallen building clause

collapse exclusion

Liability. An exclusion in the 1973 ISO comprehensive general liability rating program that was triggered when the rating classification for a particular risk was followed by a "C". For risks so designated, liability coverage for property damage arising from collapse claims was excluded by endorsement. Insureds could purchase coverage for this hazard for an additional charge.

see: blasting and explosion exclusion, underground exclusion, XCU exclusions

collar

Financial Planning. An upper and lower limit (cap and floor) on a floating price note that protects the holder from a large change in interest rates.

see: cap, financial derivative, floor, floating rate note, payment cap

collateral

General. Property used to secure a loan.

see: chattel mortgage, collateral protection insurance, mortgage, real chattel, real estate

collateral assignment

Life/Property. The transfer of benefits or payments under a life or property insurance policy to a creditor as part of the security for a loan. The creditor has a right only to the portion of the policy's proceeds equal to the creditor's remaining interest or value in the loan.

see: assignment, credit life insurance, mortgage insurance

collateral estoppel

Law. The principle that any fact or issue that has

96

been decided in a previous suit should not be litigated by the same parties in another suit. The earlier determination is binding, and a party is estopped, or prevented, from disputing the matter.

see: estoppel

collateral protection insurance

Property. Insurance coverage for financial institutions, providing physical damage coverage on collateral held by the lender in support of a loan. (This may include automobiles, trucks, vans, motorcycles, campers, motor homes, boats, etc.) Coverage includes reimbursement for mechanics' liens and repossession expense.

see: lender's single interest coverage

collateral source rule

Law. The legal doctrine that there should be no reduction in damages due to an injured person merely because there are other sources of partial indemnity (such as insurance) for the same harm or loss. The rule prevents a tortfeasor from escaping full responsibility.

compare: indemnification; *see*: damages, tortfeasor

collect freight

Inland Marine/Ocean Marine. Freight for which the charges are not payable to the carrier unless and until the merchandise arrives at the port of discharge named in the bill of lading.

compare: prepaid freight; *see*: freight

collection agents' errors and omissions insurance

Professional Liability. A form of professional liability insurance for a collection agency that covers losses on accounts in collection caused by a negligent act, error or omission. Coverage is usually written on a claims-made basis.

see: professional liability insurance

collection guaranteed endorsement

General. The endorser of a note that contains the words "collection guaranteed" agrees to pay only after the note holder is unable to collect on a judgment, or after the maker or acceptor has become insolvent.

collection ratio

Agency. A financial ratio used to evaluate the effectiveness of an insurance agency's collection program. *Formula*: premium receivables ÷ premiums payable + pre-billed payables.

see: agency bill, trust position ratio

collective bargaining

Employee Benefits. Negotiations between an employer and a union done in good faith to resolve issues of mutual interest.

see: collectively bargained contribution plan, collectively bargained plan

collective bargaining contract

Employee Benefits. A contractual agreement between an employer and a union on wages, benefits, hours and conditions of employment.

see: collective bargaining, collectively bargained contribution plan, collectively bargained plan

collectively bargained contribution plan

Employee Benefits. A defined contribution pension plan under which the employer contributions have been established by a collective bargaining agreement, usually involving a union. Generally, such a plan covers the employees of several firms and is administered by a board of trustees made up of employer and union representatives.

see: negotiated contribution plan

collectively bargained plan

Employee Benefits. An agreement reached through collective bargaining that is approved by the U.S. Secretary of Labor.

compare: nonqualified plan

College of Insurance

Organizations. An accredited educational institution in New York City that specializes in insurance education. It offers the degrees Master of Business Administration (MBA), Bachelor of Business Administration (BBA), Bachelor of Science (BS), and Associate in Occupational Studies (AOS). It also offers certificate courses in insurance and financial services.

see: Insurance Society of New York

collision clause

Ocean Marine.

see: running down clause

collision coverage

Automobile. Physical damage coverage that can be part of an automobile, garage, or truckers' policy. It covers damage to the insured's vehicle caused by collision or overturn of the vehicle.

compare: automobile liability coverage, comprehensive coverage; *see*: garage coverage form, personal auto policy, physical damage coverage, truckers' coverage form

collision damage waiver (CDW)

Automobile. A provision in many auto rental contracts charging an extra fee to the person renting a vehicle, and in exchange the rental company waives its right to recover physical damage losses from the renter.

synonym: loss damage waiver, limited damage waiver

collision diagram

Loss Control. A schematic drawing prepared after a traffic accident that indicates street intersections and other roadway locations, vehicle and pedestrian movements, and accidents that have occurred in a given time period. Symbols represent items such as the vehicle types, travel directions, pedestrians, bicycles, manner of collision, any injuries or deaths, and the extent of property damage.

color code

Loss Control. A system of coding by which piping, wiring and equipment in a building are identified by various colors.

combination crime—separate limits

Crime. A crime coverage plan developed under the 1986 Insurance Services Office crime program that is similar to a dishonesty, disappearance and destruction policy. This program offers any combination of coverage forms A through J, with each coverage subject to a separate limit.

synonym: crime plan 1; *see*: dishonesty disappearance and destruction policy

combination crime—single limit

Crime. A crime coverage form developed under the 1986 ISO crime program that provides coverage similar to a blanket crime policy. Crime forms A, B, C and D are used with a single coverage limit.

see: blanket crime policy

combination foreign credit insurance policy

Financial Guaranty/International. A form of foreign credit insurance written by the Foreign Credit Insurance Association that combines the short- and medium-term policies. It provides coverage on parts and accessories up to 180 days, on inventory up to 220 days, and on accounts receivable up to three years.

see: export credit insurance, Foreign Credit Insurance Association, medium-term foreign credit insurance policy, short-term foreign credit insurance

combination plan reinsurance

Reinsurance. A reinsurance contract that combines quota share and excess of loss reinsurance. The premium is based on a percentage of the ceding insurer's premium on the risks to be reinsured, for which the reinsurer will indemnify the ceding company for the amount of loss on each risk in excess of a specified retention, subject to a specified limit. After deducting the excess recoveries on each risk, the reinsurer will indemnify the ceding insurer for a fixed quota share percentage of all remaining losses.

see: excess of loss reinsurance, quota share reinsurance

combined ratio

Insurer Operations. A formula used by insurance companies to relate premium income to claims, administration and dividend expenses. It is used in the annual statement filed by an insurer with the state insurance department. It is calculated by dividing the sum of incurred losses and expenses by earned premium. It indicates the profitability of the insurer's operations by combining the loss ratio with expense ratio (including dividends if any). *Formula*: (1) loss ratio + expense ratio + dividend ratio; or (2) (incurred losses + incurred underwriting expenses) ÷ earned premiums. This is termed the *statutory combined ratio* and measures the amount that an insurer must pay to cover claims and expenses per dollar of earned premium. The combined ratio does not take account of investment income. *Examples*: A ratio of .98 means the insurer has made two cents (2%) of underwriting profit; a ratio of 1.17 means it has an underwriting loss of 17 cents (17%) for each premium dollar.

synonym: operating ratio, statutory combined ratio; *compare*: trade basis combined ratio; *see*: dividend ratio, expense ratio, loss ratio

combined single limit (CSL)

Automobile/Liability. An aggregate limit of liability coverage for bodily injury and property damage in one accident or occurrence.

synonym: single limit; *compare*: split limits

combined stock and mutual insurer

Insurer Operations. An insurer that has issued capital stock and allows both shareholders and participating policyholders to have voting rights.

combustible

Loss Control. A material or structure that will burn. It is a relative term, as many materials that will burn under some conditions will not burn under others.

compare: fire resistive; *see*: construction, fireproof

commercial aircraft

Aviation. Aircraft used principally in an insured's business, including student instruction, carrying passengers or freight, carrying for hire or reward, and rental to others.

compare: air taxi

commercial articles coverage

Inland Marine. Coverage on an open perils basis, designed for cameras and musical instruments owned by, or in the care, custody, or control of a commercial insured.

see: camera and musical instruments dealers' coverage

commercial automobile policy

Automobile. An insurance contract that covers vehicles owned and used by a business, government, or nonprofit organization in its operations.

compare: personal auto policy; *see*: business auto coverage form, commercial use

commercial blanket bond

Crime. A bond providing a single amount of coverage for any one loss caused by dishonest acts of employees, regardless of the number of employees involved in the embezzlement or other activity.

see: blanket position bond

commercial common policy conditions

Insurer Operations. Under the Insurance Services Office's simplified commercial policies, a common form is used that contains the conditions that apply to commercial lines of insurance. In a commercial package policy, this form is included only once regardless of the number of different coverage sections included in the policy.

see: commercial package policy, policy conditions

commercial common policy declarations

Insurer Operations. Under the Insurance Services Office's simplified commercial policies, a common declarations form is used that contains the declarations that apply specifically to commercial lines of insurance. In a commercial package policy, this form is included only once regardless of the number of different commercial coverage sections included in the policy.

see: commercial common policy conditions, policy declarations

commercial domiciles

Insurer Operations. Jurisdictions in which an insurer writes more business than in its state of domicile.

compare: domiciliary state; *see*: domestic insurer, foreign insurer

commercial fire and allied lines insurance

Property.

see: commercial property insurance

commercial general liability policy (CGL)

Liability. A policy form introduced by the Insurance Services Office in 1986, and subsequently amended, to replace the comprehensive general liability policy. The two basic coverage forms available under the CGL are an occurrence form (ISO form CG 00 01), patterned after the 1973 CGL form, and a claims-made form (ISO form CG 00 02), providing an extended reporting period. These include the following coverages: Coverage A, bodily injury and property damage liability; Coverage B, personal injury and advertising injury liability;

Coverage C, medical payments; and, as applicable, products-completed operations coverage. An aggregate limit applies to coverages A, B and C, and a separate aggregate limit applies to the products-completed operations coverage.

Coverage is provided for most of the premises, products, completed operations, personal injury, advertising, and contractual liability exposures of an organization. Unlike older forms that required endorsements to broaden coverage, the CGL provides very broad coverage that can be narrowed by endorsement. It is a modular policy that can provide several coverages in combinations. There are five basic parts: 1. Common policy declarations; 2. Common policy conditions; 3. Commercial general liability declarations; 4. Coverage section (either the occurrence or claims-made form); 5. Broad form nuclear exclusion.

see: aggregate limit, bodily injury and property damage liability, claims-made form, commercial package policy, comprehensive general liability policy, faulty work exclusion, fire damage liability, general aggregate limit, laser endorsement, liability insurance, long-tail liability, medical payments coverage (*Liability*), occurrence policy, personal and advertising injury liability, pollution exclusion, products-completed operations insurance

commercial impracticability

Law. A legitimate excuse for nonperformance or breach of a contract. The impracticability must be caused by an unexpected contingency that affects or creates conditions that neither party contemplated, such as a natural disaster, war, or shortage of materials caused by an embargo.

see: act of God, force majeure coverage

commercial inland marine conditions

Inland Marine. A form (ISO form CM 00 01) attached to a commercial inland marine policy that adds general conditions concerning claims reporting and losses.

see: policy conditions

commercial insurance

Risk Management. Contractual risk transfer by the use of conventional insurance policies purchased by an organization or individual from a licensed insurance company.

see: risk transfer

commercial invoice

Inland Marine/Ocean Marine. An invoice issued by the seller to the buyer that specifies the merchandise being sold, its packaging, number of units, per-unit cost, and total cost.

see: bill of lading

International. An international trade document that

includes the addresses of the buyer and seller, shipment details, unit and total price, date, order number, quantity, weight, number of packages, and shipping marks. It is required in letter of credit transactions and is used for customs declarations and to prepare an ocean bill of lading.

see: certificate of origin, customs entry form, bill of lading

commercial lease payment insurance

Financial Guaranty. A form of financial guaranty insurance that guarantees periodic commercial lease payments owed by the tenant (lessee). If the lessee ceases paying rent, the insurer makes installment payments over the balance of the lease period. The insurance is irrevocable and remains in effect until all of the insured obligations have been paid.

see: financial guaranty insurance

commercial lines

Insurer Operations. A general term for any type of insurance (property, casualty, health, life, etc.) purchased by businesses, organizations, institutions, governmental agencies or other commercial establishments to protect risks associated with their operations.

compare: personal lines; *see*: business insurance

commercial lines manual

Insurer Operations. A manual developed and maintained by the Insurance Services Office that contains rating divisions for most commercial insurance coverages (excluding workers' compensation and some specialty lines of insurance).

see: Insurance Services Office

commercial package policy (CPP)

Insurer Operations. A coverage plan that includes a wide range of essential liability and property coverages for a commercial enterprise. The package policy usually features common policy conditions, common declarations, and two or more coverage sections.

see: commercial common policy declarations, commercial general liability policy

commercial paper

Financial Planning. Short-term, unsecured promissory notes issued by a corporation, usually one with an excellent credit rating, to borrow capital for a term up to 270 days, often at a slightly lower interest rate than that charged by commercial banks. It is usually backed by a line of credit at a bank.

see: commercial paper insurance, debenture, debt security, note

commercial paper insurance

Financial Guaranty. Insurance guaranteeing the prompt payment of principal and interest on commercial paper issued by large firms. The insurer's financial rating affords the commercial paper a higher investment rating than that of the issuing party's rating, which allows the commercial paper to be issued at a lower interest rate.

see: commercial paper

commercial perils

Financial Guaranty/International. A group of perils under an export credit insurance policy that includes insolvency of the debtor and inability or unwillingness of the debtor to pay.

compare: political perils; *see*: export credit insurance

commercial property insurance

Property. Coverage of real or personal property exposures of businesses, governmental agencies, and private nonprofit organizations, as opposed to residential or personal types of property.

synonym: commercial fire and allied lines insurance

Commercial Risk Services, Inc. (CRS)

Organizations. A subsidiary of the Insurance Services Office that conducts property rating surveys to help insurance companies develop accurate premiums.

see: Insurance Services Office

commercial speech

Liability. A communication (spoken, written, or broadcast) intended to promote or market a business enterprise, product or service. Commercial speech does not generally have the same degree of constitutional protection under the First Amendment as political speech. Damages may be awarded in cases of false or misleading comparative advertising or product disparagement (also called *trade libel*).

see: advertising injury coverage, damages, libel

commercial use

Automobile. A business-use automobile rating classification that applies to vehicles used for the transportation of property other than those vehicles in the retail use or service use classifications.

compare: business use, farm use, pleasure use, retail use, service use

commission

Agency.

see: agent's commission

Reinsurance.

see: ceding commission, overriding commission

commissioner

Regulation.

see: insurance commissioner

Commissioners Standard Ordinary Table (CSO Table)

Life. A mortality table prepared for the National Association of Insurance Commissioners in the years 1938 to 1941. Most states have adopted it as the minimum standard for calculating nonforfeiture values and policy reserves.

see: American Experience Table of Mortality, mortality table, nonforfeiture benefit, policy reserve

commitment fee

General. The fee paid by a borrower to a lender for a formal line of credit.

see: line of credit

Committee for National Health Insurance (CNHI)

Organizations. Members: Representatives from the health care field, government, labor, academic, business, economic and citizen organizations. *Objectives*: Conduct research and promote education regarding the health care system in the United States. Promotes reform measures by enactment of a comprehensive national health insurance program. *Founded*: 1969. *Headquarters*: Washington, D.C.

Committee of Lloyd's

Insurer Operations. A committee established by Lloyd's of London, to assure that Lloyd's is properly run and that its reputation for integrity is maintained. Comprised of sixteen members who are elected by Lloyd's underwriters and brokers, no member may be on the Committee for more than four years. A chairman and two deputy chairmen are elected to office, usually for two years each.

see: Lloyd's of London

Commodity Futures Trading Commission (CFTC)

Organizations. A federal regulatory agency established in 1974 by the Commodity Futures Trading Commission Act to regulate futures trading in all commodities. The five commissioners are appointed by the President, and one is designated the chairperson.

see: futures contract

common area

Property. Areas under the control of a landlord or condominium association, which serve the community or the public (such as shopping center parking areas, greenbelts, walkways, etc.).

see: condominium

common carrier

Automobile/Inland Marine. An airline, busline, railroad or trucking company that furnishes transportation services to the general public. Common carriers are regulated by the Interstate Commerce Commission or by state public utilities commissions and are liable to shippers for the safe delivery of freight entrusted to them (except for losses arising from certain named perils).

compare: contract carrier, private carrier; *see*: carrier

common conditions form

Insurer Operations.

see: common policy conditions

common disaster clause

Life. A life insurance policy provision or a settlement arrangement to take effect in the event that the insured and beneficiary die nearly simultaneously due to the same accident. Unless the beneficiary survives the insured for a stated, relatively short period of time, proceeds are payable to the insured's estate rather than first to the beneficiary.

see: secondary beneficiary, uniform simultaneous death act

common equity

Financial Planning. The sum of the value of common stock at par, the surplus of capital received (over par) from the sale of common (i.e., capital surplus), and retained earnings (i.e., earned surplus). *Retained earnings* in this context equals net profits earned in all years, less dividends paid in all years.

see: equity (*Financial Planning*), retained earnings

common equity ratio

Financial Planning. Common equity divided by total capital. *Total capital* in this context includes long-term debt, preferred equity, and common equity.

see: financial ratios

common law

Law. The legal principles, rights and remedies that are based on Anglo-American custom and prior court decisions, as opposed to statutory law (though statutes are imbued with common law principles); judge-made law.

synonym: case law; *compare*: administrative law, criminal law; *see*: civil law (1), common law defense

common law defense

Law/Workers' Compensation. Before workers' compensation laws were enacted, employers being sued by employees often defended themselves by claiming that the employee contributed to the accident, that the risk of injury was assumed by the employee when he or she agreed to the employment, or that fellow workers were responsible for the employee's injury. Such common law defenses are not available under workers' compensation laws, which generally make statutorily prescribed benefits the exclusive remedy for injured workers, except in cases of an employer's gross negligence, criminal behavior, or other aggravating factors.

see: assumption of risk, common law, compulsory compensation law, contributory negligence, exclusive remedy, fellow servant rule, workers' compensation law

common policy conditions

Insurer Operations.

see: commercial common policy conditions

common shares outstanding

Financial Planning/Risk Management. The number of shares of common stock actually outstanding at the end of the calendar (or fiscal) year, excluding any shares held in the company's treasury. The figures for common shares outstanding in previous years are fully adjusted for all subsequent stock splits and stock dividends.

see: capital stock

common stock

Financial Planning. A share or shares of ownership in a corporation with rights to vote on management and corporate policy but not preferred over other classes of stock in regard to the payment of dividends or distribution of assets. It is usually the only class of stock with voting rights.

compare: preferred stock; *see*: dissenting shareholder, dividend, equity (*Financial Planning*)

common stock to surplus

Insurer Operations. The market value of the common stock held in the insurance company's investment portfolio divided by statutory net worth.

common stock to total investment

Insurer Operations. The market value of the common stock portion of an insurance company's investment portfolio divided by the reported value of the total portfolio, expressed as a percentage.

common venture

Ocean Marine. The combination of a vessel and its cargo involved in an adventure.

see: adventure, venture

common wall

Loss Control.

see: party wall

communicable disease exclusion

Personal. An endorsement added to some older homeowners policies providing that the coverages for personal liability and medical payments to others do not apply to the transmission of a communicable disease by an insured.

see: homeowners policy

communications supply services

Inland Marine. Off-premises telecommunications utility services that can be covered for a business income loss. The off-premises utilities coverage endorsement includes communications facilities such as transmission lines, coaxial cables, and microwave radio relays for telecommunications. Coverage is usually excluded for overhead communication lines and satellites.

see: off-premises services—time element, power interruption insurance, overhead transmission lines coverage

community antenna television liability insurance (CATV)

Professional Liability. A form of broadcasters' liability insurance for the cable TV industry. Coverage is provided for general liability; libel, slander or defamation; infringement of copyright, literary title or slogan; plagiarism, misappropriation or piracy of intellectual property; and invasion of privacy arising out of programming distributed over the cable system. Coverage is extended for contractual liability with sponsors and advertising agencies and franchise agreements with public entities.

synonym: cable television liability; *see*: broadcasters' liability insurance

community rating

Health. A health insurance rating method whereby premiums are based on the average cost of providing medical services to all people in a specified geographic area without adjusting for each person's medical history or likelihood of using services.

compare: fee for service, capitation; *see*: health benefit plan, managed care

commutation clause

Reinsurance. A provision in most finite risk insurance/reinsurance contracts that if the contract is canceled by mutual agreement, all outstanding obligations will be discharged including future obligations between the parties. Usually, all known and unknown claim obligations must be assumed back by the insured. In exchange, all claims fund balances and any profit-sharing earnings are returned to the insured by the insurer. For most primary finite risk programs, the commutation provision can only be exercised at specified dates (i.e., anniversary date).

see: finite risk insurance

comparative negligence

Law. The apportionment of fault when both the plaintiff and the defendant contributed to a loss by failing to exercise the required degree of care. Damages for the plaintiff are decreased in proportion to his or her own negligence.

see: avoidable consequence, contributory negligence, damages, negligence

comparison statement

Agency. A document that compares benefits of an existing policy to those of a proposed new policy.

see: specimen policy, twisting

compensable injury

Workers' Compensation. An accidental injury or occupational disease that requires medical services or results in disability or death and arises out of and in the course of employment and is therefore subject to workers' compensation laws.

see: arising out of and in the course of employment, occupational accident, workers' compensation law

compensating balance

General. A required minimum noninterest-paying bank account balance that an organization must maintain with a commercial bank in order to obtain a loan or line of credit. The required bank balance is generally equal to 15% to 20% of the amount of loans outstanding. Compensating balances can raise the effective rate of interest on bank loans.

compensation agreement

Agency/Insurer Operations. An agreement between an employer and employee, insurer and agent, etc., fixing the rate of compensation to be paid.

compensatory damages

Law. Money awarded in a civil lawsuit to make an injured person whole, including recompense for damaged property, lost wages or profits, pain, bereavement, medical expenses, etc.; pecuniary compensation for a person's out-of-pocket losses and future expenses due to injury, disability, disfigurement, pain and suffering, and all actual losses, whether economic or noneconomic.

synonym: actual damages; *compare*: nominal damages, punitive damages; *see*: damages, economic loss, noneconomic loss

competence

Law. Legal fitness to enter into a contract or perform some other social action; intellectual or moral capacity to understand the effects of one's actions or the nature of a commercial transaction. Attaining legal age is an element of competence to enter into contracts. Most states permit 15-year-olds to contract for most forms of insurance.

compare: insanity; *see*: age, contract

competitive benchmarking

Risk Management.

see: benchmarking

competitive replacement parts

Automobile.

see: non-original equipment manufacturer's replacement parts

competitive state fund

Workers' Compensation. Several states operate a state fund in competition with private insurance. Employers in these states may choose to purchase workers' compensation insurance from a private insurer or from the state fund.

compare: monopolistic state fund; *see*: state fund, workers' compensation insurance

complaint

Law. The pleading that initiates a civil suit; a written claim for legal relief or compensation. It is filed in court by the plaintiff and must include the grounds for the court's jurisdiction, a statement of the claim (i.e., a brief statement of the alleged facts and reason for the defendant's liability), and a demand for judgment.

see: allegation, answer, counterclaim, petition, pleading, summons, summons and complaint

completed operations coverage

Liability. Liability insurance for injury or damage resulting from real or alleged faults in work completed by the insured. Completed operations insurance is purchased by commercial insureds who provide services (e.g., plumbers, painters, carpenters), whereas manufacturers require product liability insurance. In most commercial liability forms, products and completed operations coverages are combined.

see: product liability insurance, products-completed operations insurance, turnkey insurance

completed-value builders' risk form

Property.

see: builders' risk insurance

completion bond

Surety.

see: lender's bond

compliance schedule

Loss Control/Regulation. 1. In regard to environmental cleanup, a negotiated agreement between an organization that generates pollution and a regulatory agency which describes specific dates and procedures for the organization to reduce emissions and comply with regulations.

2. In regard to the safety of working conditions, a schedule to comply with regulations of the Occupational Safety and Health Administration which

describes specific dates and actions required to correct violations.

synonym: abatement schedule; *see*: environmental audit, environmental site assessment, Occupational Safety and Health Act

compound interest

Financial Planning. A rate that results when interest in succeeding periods is earned not only on the initial principal, but also on the accumulated interest of prior periods.

compare: simple interest; *see*: compounding, cumulative rate of return, interest

compounding

Financial Planning. The mathematical process of determining the final value of a payment or series of payments after all interest has been applied.

compare: discounting; *see*: continuous compounding, interest, present value

comprehensive coverage

Automobile. Physical damage coverage that can be part of an automobile, garage, or truckers' policy. It covers damage to the insured's vehicle from causes other than collision or overturn—which are insured separately under collision coverage—such as theft, vandalism or fire.

synonym: other-than-collision coverage; *compare*: automobile liability coverage, collision coverage; *see*: physical damage coverage, specified causes of loss

comprehensive coverage excluding production machines

Property. A boiler and machinery object coverage form (object definitions no. 5 or ISO form BM 00 30), which is the broadest coverage available for nonproduction machinery. It covers any accidental damage to any machinery or equipment not excluded (as compared to listed covered objects) except machinery used in the insured's production process.

compare: comprehensive coverage including production machines; *see*: object

comprehensive coverage including production machines

Property. A boiler and machinery object coverage form (object definitions no. 6 or ISO form BM 00 31), which is the broadest coverage available, as it provides coverage for any accidental damage to any machinery or equipment not excluded (as compared to listed covered objects), including machinery used in the insured's production process.

compare: comprehensive coverage excluding production machines; *see*: object

Comprehensive Environmental Response, Compensation and Liability Act (CERCLA)

Regulation. Federal legislation (U.S. Code Title 42, Chapter 103) enacted in 1980 that created a federal authority to clean up spills and other releases of hazardous substances into the environment. Funds are raised through taxes on chemical and petroleum companies. The Act has been interpreted to impose strict liability on generators, transporters, treaters and disposers of hazardous wastes, including all costs of removal or remedial action, any other necessary response expense, and damages to natural resources, with maximum liabilities of up to $50 million. The liability for cleanup expenses is joint and several on all parties in the chain of handling the substance.

synonym: Superfund Act; *see*: hazardous waste, joint and several liability, National Oil and Hazardous Substances Contingency Plan, pollutant, pollution exclusion, pollution insurance, potentially responsible party

comprehensive general liability policy (CGL)

Liability. The comprehensive general liability policy form was initially developed by the Insurance Services Office (ISO) in 1940 and revised several times thereafter. It was the first commercial liability form to combine many coverages under a single contract. Coverage included bodily injury and property damage liability insurance for operations at (or emanating from) described premises. Any new locations or operations added during the policy year were automatically insured. Although some insurers still use this form, it has been largely replaced by the commercial general liability policy (which has the same abbreviation CGL) introduced by ISO in 1986.

compare: commercial general liability policy; *see*: liability insurance

comprehensive glass insurance

Property. A policy that covers breakage of windows and plate glass from any cause except war and fire. Coverage can be extended to include the value of special lettering, etching and frames.

see: glass coverage form, glass insurance, glass insurance 50/50 basis

comprehensive medical expense policy

Health. Medical expense coverage that combines hospital-surgical expense coverage and major medical coverage. These plans are usually provided on a group basis with a relatively small deductible, and they usually contain some coinsurance provision.

see: hospital-surgical expense insurance, major medical insurance, coinsurance

comprehensive outpatient rehabilitation facility

Health.

see: transitional care facility

comprehensive personal liability policy (CPL)

Personal. A personal liability policy that covers an individual's or family's liability for bodily injury or property damage. This coverage is included in the homeowners policy but is written as a separate policy when a person is not covered by homeowners or renters insurance.

see: farmowners personal liability policy, homeowners policy, personal umbrella, ranchowners personal liability form

compulsory compensation law

Workers' Compensation. A state workers' compensation statute that requires both employers and employees to accept its provisions as the exclusive remedy for work-related injuries.

compare: elective compensation law; *see*: exclusive remedy, workers' compensation law

compulsory insurance

General. Insurance required by law. Automobile insurance, workers' compensation and employers' liability insurance are compulsory in most of the United States and in most countries.

compare: voluntary insurance; *see*: compulsory insurance law, compulsory unlimited automobile bodily injury coverage, mandated benefits

compulsory insurance law

Automobile/Regulation. A law enacted in several states requiring a vehicle owner or operator to have minimum automobile liability coverage before the vehicle can be registered or licensed.

compare: financial responsibility law; *see*: automobile liability coverage

compulsory retirement

Employee Benefits. Prior to the mid-1980s, many organizations required an employee to retire upon reaching a specified age. Such a practice now constitutes illegal age discrimination.

synonym: automatic retirement, mandatory retirement; *see*: Age Discrimination in Employment Act, normal retirement age

compulsory unlimited automobile bodily injury coverage

International. A form of automobile insurance required in some countries (e.g., northern Europe, India) where liability coverage must be provided for the full value of any claim. Therefore, there is no maximum limit of liability.

see: compulsory insurance

computer equipment coverage

Property.

see: data processing coverage

computer fraud

Crime. The use of computerized systems and equipment to illegally transfer money, securities or other property.

see: computer fraud coverage form, electronic and computer crime coverage

computer fraud coverage form

Crime. A crime coverage policy (ISO form CR 00 07, or form F) that covers loss of, and loss from damage to, money, securities and other property by computer fraud.

synonym: crime coverage form F; *see*: computer fraud, crime coverages, electronic and computer crime coverage

concealment

Insurer Operations. The intentional withholding of information that will result in an imprecise underwriting decision. For example, concealment of an existing medical condition by an insured when applying for life or health insurance can be grounds for an insurer to void the policy or reduce the benefits.

see: contribute-to-the-loss statute, election to avoid a policy

Law. The intentional withholding from another party to a transaction or negotiations of information or of a material fact that is important in making a decision.

see: material misrepresentation

concentration ratio

Insurer Operations. The insurance market share held by the leading insurers for a class of business. A low percentage indicates a competitive market for that class of business.

Concerned Alliance of Responsible Employers (CARE)

Organizations. Members: Companies and trade associations interested in employee benefits. *Objectives*: Lobbies against mandated health insurance and parental leave legislation. *Founded*: 1987. *Headquarters*: Washington, D.C.

synonym: CARE Alliance

concrete tilt-up construction

Loss Control. A type of masonry construction where the building's floor slab is first poured and allowed to dry. Exterior walls are then cast on the floor slab; once dried, the walls are raised (tilted) into place. While this type of structure is fire resistive, it can be susceptible to earthquake damage if the panels are not properly anchored to a supporting structural system.

see: fire resistive construction

concurrent causation

Law. The action of more than one cause to produce a particular harm or loss. The predominant legal rule is that if a loss is caused by both an insured peril and an uninsured peril, coverage is deemed to apply.

see: cause of loss, immediate cause, proximate cause

concurrent insurance

Liability. Coverage provided under two or more policies, all of which are identical except that they may vary in amount or policy periods.

compare: nonconcurrency; *see*: layering, other insurance provision

concurrent joint tortfeasors

Law.

see: joint tortfeasors

condemnation

Law. 1. The taking of private property for public use through the power of eminent domain, usually against the owner's will but with payment of compensation.

2. A governmental declaration that a building or vessel is unsafe or unfit for use.

see: condemned building cancellation provision, confiscation, eminent domain, inverse condemnation

condemned building cancellation provision

Property. A provision in some property insurance policies that allows cancellation with prior written notice (usually 5 days) by the insurer if the insured building is under a demolition order, an order to vacate, or has been declared unsafe by a governmental authority.

see: governmental action exclusion

condition

Insurer Operations. An insurance policy provision specifying the rights and obligations of the insured or the insurer as respects the policy.

see: policy conditions

condition precedent

Law. A future event or contingency that must occur or be done by a party to a contract before another party is required to perform their duty or promise. *Example*: An insurer is not obligated to pay a claim until the insured provides proper notice and proof of a loss.

compare: condition subsequent

condition subsequent

Law. A future event that may or may not occur after a contract becomes legally enforceable. The condition terminates certain rights under provisions of contract.

compare: condition precedent

conditional delivery

Life. A condition making it clear that no coverage exists until the terms of that condition have been met. *Example*: Mailing a policy with an accompanying letter stating the policy will become effective when the applicant pays a stated fee to the agent.

compare: conditional receipt

conditional receipt

Health/Life. A written acknowledgment that a completed application and initial premium payment have been received for life or health insurance and that coverage is provided until the company issues a policy or declines coverage.

compare: conditional delivery

conditional sales floater

Inland Marine. Insurance coverage for retail and wholesale merchants, manufacturers, banks and finance companies who sell or use personal property as collateral for a loan or a conditional sales contract, deferred payment plan, or installment payment plan. Coverage is for named perils for the interest of the seller, lessor or finance company. The loss payable is the unpaid balance under the sales contract or loan.

synonym: installment sales floater; *see*: floater policy, named perils

conditional vesting

Employee Benefits. A pension plan participant's right to receive benefits from a contributory pension plan may have limitations as to when and to what extent an employee is vested. The participant's receipt of benefits will be subject to these conditions.

see: pension, vesting

condominium

Personal. A dwelling unit in a multiple unit building or complex which is individually owned. The unit owner also has an ownership interest in the common areas and facilities. There is a separate title to the real estate for each unit.

compare: cooperative housing; *see*: homeowners unit owners' form

Property. Business space in a multiple-unit commercial building or office complex which is individually owned. As with a personal condo, the unit owner of a commercial condominium has an ownership interest in common areas.

see: condominium commercial unit owners' coverage

condominium association directors' and officers' liability insurance

Professional Liability. A form of insurance for condominium association directors and officers. The coverage is usually broader than the standard D&O policy because the exposure involves a non-profit association with a limited number of condominium owners (possible plaintiffs). Unlike typical D&O insurance, the policy generally includes coverage of the condominium association as a whole (entity coverage). This coverage is written on a claims-made basis.

see: condominium, directors' and officers' liability insurance, entity coverage

condominium association insurance

Property. An insurance policy designed to protect condominium association property held in common (such as the buildings) or personal property used to maintain or furnish common areas. It excludes coverage for personal property or improvements owned or used by, or in the care, custody or control of an individual unit owner.

see: common area

condominium commercial unit owners' coverage

Property. An insurance form (ISO form CP 00 18) designed to protect the owner of a business or commercial condominium unit against loss or damage to furniture, fixtures, stock, improvements and alterations owned by the insured.

see: condominium, loss assessment coverage

condominium forms

Property. Special coverage forms, differing from forms used for buildings and personal property, that contain specialized language to account for the unique legal characteristics of condominiums.

see: condominium commercial unit owners' coverage, homeowners unit owners' form

condominium unit owners' form

Liability/Property.

see: homeowners unit owners' form

Conference of Actuaries in Public Practice (CAPP)

Organizations. Members: Consulting actuaries, governmental actuaries. *Objectives:* To advance the knowledge of actuarial science, to promote and maintain high professional and ethical standards among its members, and to keep the public informed of the professional actuary in public practice. *Founded:* 1950. *Headquarters:* Itasca, IL. CAPP is affiliated with the American Academy of Actuaries and the Society of Actuaries.

Conference of Casualty Insurance Companies (CCIC)

Organizations. Members: Casualty insurance companies. *Objectives:* Sponsors educational programs for executives of member firms. *Founded:* 1930. *Headquarters:* Indianapolis, IN.

Conference of Insurance Legislators

Organizations.

see: National Conference of Insurance Legislators

confidence level

Risk Management. The degree of certainty about an actuarial forecast or calculation. *Example:* A 95% confidence level indicates that only 5 occurrences in 100 will not fall within a stipulated range.

confining illness

Health. An illness that requires the insured individual to remain at home or in a hospital.

see: house confinement

confiscation

International. The taking of property by a government. Sometimes it means seizing property without compensating the owner; sometimes it means the legal power of a government to take private property for public use, with or without compensation, which is known in the United States as *eminent domain*. If property is confiscated but full market value is paid, the owner has no loss from an insurance standpoint.

compare: deprivation, expropriation, nationalization; *see*: condemnation, confiscation and expropriation insurance, confiscation of contractor's plant or consignment stocks insurance, eminent domain, inverse condemnation, political risk insurance

confiscation and expropriation insurance

International. A form of political risk insurance that covers confiscation, seizure, expropriation, requisition of title, or willful destruction to property in a foreign country by government order. Coverage is may be written by the Overseas Private Investment Corporation, private insurers, or Lloyd's of London.

synonym: expropriation insurance; *see*: confiscation, deprivation, expropriation, nationalization, Overseas Private Investment Corporation, political risk insurance

confiscation of contractor's plant or consigned stock insurance

International. A special form of political risk insurance designed for contractors working in or selling to foreign countries. It covers the contractor's plant or consigned stock against loss by expropriation, confiscation and nationalization. Coverage for deprivation can be added.

see: confiscation, confiscation and expropriation insurance, deprivation, expropriation, nationalization, political risk insurance

conflict of laws

Law. An inconsistency between the laws of different states or countries. When more than one state has some relationship to the parties or matters at issue in a suit and the state laws differ, a decision is required as to which law should govern. A "center of influence" (or "most significant relationship") test often determines which law applies.

see: center of influence, diversity jurisdiction, due process of law

conformity with statute clause

Insurer Operations. A provision in many policies that any terms of the policy that are not in conformity with local statutes are amended to conform, thereby enabling the insurer to use a standard, countrywide form.

consent order

Law. A court order banning an alleged unlawful trade practice that is issued before a hearing is held. The party receiving the order may accept the entry of the order, waiving the right to appeal, and the effect is the same as if it had been issued after a formal hearing.

see: enjoin

consent to settle provision

Professional Liability. Some professional liability policies provide that the insurer is allowed to settle a claim without the consent of the insured; others provide that the insured has the right to veto a proposed settlement by the insurer. Since a settlement can affect the reputation and earning ability of the insured, this type of clause is an important consideration in selecting a policy.

see: professional liability insurance, settlement

consequential damage

Property. Property loss from a peril that is not the immediate cause of loss; an indirect loss (e.g., a business interruption loss, extra expense, lost rent, etc.) arising out of an insured's inability to use property damaged by another peril. *Example*: A burglar destroys records of accounts receivable during the burglary, causing further loss because the accounts cannot be collected.

synonym: indirect damage, indirect loss, special damage; *compare*: direct damage; *see*: business income coverage form, consequential damage endorsement

consequential damage endorsement

Property. A boiler and machinery coverage endorsement (ISO form BM 15 18) that covers a personal property loss due to spoilage from lack of power, light, steam, heat, or refrigeration as a consequence of an insured accident.

compare: spoilage coverage endorsement; *see*: consequential damage

consequential loss form

International.

see: British business interruption insurance

consideration

Insurer Operations. For purposes of the insurance transaction, the consideration is the premium paid by the insured for the insurer's promise to pay claims in accordance with the terms of the policy.

see: premium

Law. The exchange of something of value for a promise of performance; one of the elements needed to form a contract.

see: acceptance, contract, offer

consignee

Inland Marine/Ocean Marine. The party that is to receive the goods listed on a bill of lading.

compare: consignor; *see*: consignment

consignment

International/Property. Transfer or delivery of goods from one person (consignor or exporter) to another (consignee or importer) under an agreement that the consignee will sell the goods and pay the consignor. After a specified time, unsold goods are returned. During the consignment period, the consignor keeps legal title to the goods.

see: bailee, care custody or control

consignment insurance

Inland Marine.

see: in-trust policy

consignor

Inland Marine/Ocean Marine. The party that initiates the shipment of the goods listed on a bill of lading.

synonym: shipper; *compare*: consignee; *see*: consignment

consolidated financial statement

Accounting. A financial statement for an organization that combines the results of all operations under its control, including subsidiaries, as if the organization where a single entity. Assets and liabilities of all affiliates are reported on a single balance sheet; revenues and expenses are reported on a single income statement; cash flows are reported on a single statement of cash flow.

see: financial statement

consolidated insurance program
Liability/Workers' Compensation.
see: owner-controlled insurance program

Consolidated Omnibus Budget Reconciliation Act (COBRA)
Health/Regulation. Federal legislation, a major part of which addressed health insurance, adopted in 1985 that applies to firms with more than 20 employees. It provides: 1. Employees are allowed to remain covered under their group medical plan for 18 months after leaving their job. Employees must pay their own premium, but the rates will remain the same as for others in the group. 2. A group medical plan cannot require Medicare to be the primary provider for participants 70 years of age and over. 3. Medicare was expanded to include state and local government employees.
see: Technical and Miscellaneous Revenue Act

consolidated tax return
Financial Planning. An income tax return that combines the income statements of affiliated firms.
see: affiliated insurers

consolidation condition
Property. In a unification or merger of properties, this provision in a property insurance policy extends coverage automatically to the new premises provided the insured notifies the insurer of the acquisition within a specified time (e.g., 30 days) and pays the additional premium.

consolidation endorsement
Ocean Marine. An endorsement to an open cargo policy that provides coverage on merchandise while in transit and while at a common consolidation point for the purpose of preparing or consolidating the merchandise for transit.
see: open cargo policy

consolidation of plans
Employee Benefits.
see: merger of plans

consortium
Law. The legal entitlement of one spouse to the companionship and assistance of the other.
see: loss of consortium

construction
Property. In fire underwriting, the types of materials used in the building and roof of the insured structure. Construction types include fire resistive, semi-fire resistive, and combustible, depending on the materials used. Other construction factors that an underwriter considers include the number of fire divisions in the building, the adequacy of electrical circuits for the occupancy, the number of stories, the building's age, and the type of heating system.

Most underwriters recognize seven classes of construction: 1. frame; 2. joisted masonry (which includes ordinary construction and mill construction); 3. incombustible; 4. masonry incombustible; 5. modified fire resistive; 6. fire resistive; 7. mixed.
compare: exposure, occupancy, protection; *see*: brick construction, brick veneer construction, class rating, fire resistive construction, frame construction, joisted masonry construction, masonry incombustible construction, mill construction, mixed construction, modified fire resistive construction, incombustible construction, ordinary construction

construction wrap-up
Liability.
see: owner-controlled insurance program

constructive receipt
Accounting/Financial Planning. Under Internal Revenue Service rules, a person is deemed to have received funds when there is control over the disposition of money, when the present value of money is specifically set aside for use by the person, or when the funds are available to the person. Funds are not constructively received if something of value must be relinquished to obtain them, if the right to receipt is legally contested, if the obligor is financially insolvent or cannot make payment, or if a valid contract requires that payment be postponed.

constructive total loss
Property. Damage to property that does not totally destroy it but renders it valueless to the insured or prevents it from being restored to the original condition except at a cost exceeding its value; therefore, it is deemed a total loss.
see: partial loss, total loss
Ocean Marine. A constructive total loss occurs when the damage or destruction of the cargo is not total, but the cost of salvaging the cargo would be greater than the cargo's remaining value.
see: total loss only clause

consular invoice
Inland Marine/International/Ocean Marine. A special invoice that is required by some countries to control imported merchandise that must be notarized or validated by the country's consulate prior to shipment.

Consumer and Professional Relations Division of Health Insurance Association of America
Organizations. Members: Health insurance companies. *Objectives:* Provide information and technical assistance to hospitals, physicians and allied health care groups. *Founded:* 1946. *Headquarters:* Washington, D.C.

109

consumer credit compliance insurance

Financial Guaranty. Insurance for a financial institution that pays judgments, defense costs, and plaintiff's attorney fees from actions brought against the financial institution for alleged noncompliance with Federal Consumer Credit Regulations, Truth in Lending Act, Fair Credit Billing Act, Equal Credit Opportunity Act, or Electronic Fund Transfer requirements.

Consumer Credit Insurance Association (CCIA)

Organizations. Members: Insurers underwriting consumer credit insurance in areas of life, accident and health and property insurance. *Objectives:* Bestowing the Arthur J. Morris Award for outstanding contributions to the consumer credit insurance industry. *Founded:* 1951. *Headquarters:* Chicago, IL.

contact switch

Loss Control. A device used to trigger a burglar alarm. When a door or window is opened, a magnetic field is removed, which activates the switch, turning on the alarm.

synonym: door switch, window switch; *see:* burglar alarm

container

Inland Marine/Ocean Marine. A large box made of steel, aluminum or fiberglass-reinforced plywood in which merchandise is shipped. Containers are made in standard lengths of 8, 20, 25, 35, 40, and 45 feet; each has an identification number assigned to it.

see: containerized cargo

container seal

Inland Marine/Ocean Marine. A steel, aluminum or plastic device affixed to the locking mechanism of a shipping container door, to protect against unauthorized opening. The seal, which is designed to readily show signs of tampering, is attached by the party packing the container.

see: container, containerized cargo

container seal number

Inland Marine/Ocean Marine. Each container seal has a unique identifying number assigned to it which should be noted on all documents issued in conjunction with a shipment. In addition, the container number to which the seal is attached is noted.

containerized cargo

Ocean Marine. Cargo shipped in large containers (up to 45 feet long) that can be lifted by crane onto and off trucks, trains and ships.

compare: break bulk cargo, bulk cargo; *see:* container

contaminant

Property/Liability. An excluded pollutant that was added to most property insurance forms issued after 1988 as respects the additional coverage for the cost of cleanup and removal of pollutants.

see: pollutant cleanup and removal additional coverage, pollutant, product contamination

contamination and pollution cleanup coverage

Property.

see: pollutant cleanup and removal coverage

contents rate

Property. Fire insurance rates are usually developed separately for contents of buildings and the buildings themselves. The contents rate is for stock, furniture and fixtures, equipment, electronic data processing equipment, and accounts receivable. Rates are usually applied per $1000 of insurance value. Separate rates apply to fire, extended coverages, vandalism and malicious mischief, sprinkler leakage, earthquake, earthquake sprinkler leakage, and all-risk coverage.

see: building rate

contingency commission

Reinsurance. A commission paid by a reinsurer to a ceding insurer based on a predetermined percentage of the profit realized by the reinsurer on the ceded business.

synonym: profit commission; see: variable commission

contingency fee

Law.

see: contingent fee agreement

contingency reserve

Accounting. A cash amount set aside to fund a contingent liability. Such reserves are generally not considered a liability for income tax purposes, and funds placed in them are not tax deductible.

see: contingent liability

contingent beneficiary

Life. The person entitled to life insurance or annuity benefits if the primary beneficiary dies before the insured.

compare: secondary beneficiary; *see:* beneficiary clause, irrevocable beneficiary, primary beneficiary, revocable beneficiary

contingent business income coverage

Property. Insurance for lost business income caused by a loss at a specific location not owned by the insured but on which the insured depends for business operations. The loss must be caused by an insured peril. *Example:* A supplier suffers a major fire, making it impossible for the insured to continue to manufacture its product.

There are two forms for this coverage: business income from dependent properties—broad form (ISO form CP 15 08), which extends the insured business income limit to include the dependent property, and business income from dependent properties—limited form (ISO form CP 15 09), which specifies the limit of coverage that is to apply to the dependent property.

synonym: business income from dependent properties; *see*: business income coverage form, dependent property, extra expense from dependent properties endorsement, power interruption insurance, tax interruption insurance

contingent experience rating modification factor endorsement

Workers' Compensation. An endorsement (NCCI form WC 00 04 12) attached to a workers' compensation policy when a contingent experience rating modification factor is used instead of a rating bureau-approved experience modification factor.

see: experience rating modification factor, rating bureau, workers' compensation insurance

contingent extra expense coverage

Property.

see: extra expense from dependent properties endorsement

contingent fee agreement

Law. A contract between an attorney and client by which the attorney's fee is paid only if the client wins a judgment or settlement. Nearly all personal injury cases are handled in this way. The fee is usually a percentage of the recovery, commonly one-third.

compare: retainer; *see*: personal injury

contingent liability

Insurer Operations/Law. Liability that depends on uncertain events. All insurance is a contingent liability of the insurer because its indemnity obligations are triggered by uncertain events specified in the insurance contract. A contractual agreement wherein one party agrees to reimburse the other should an act of the first party give rise to a suit against the second creates a contingent liability for the first party.

Policyholders of assessment insurance are contingently liable for assessments if premiums are inadequate to meet losses.

see: assessment insurance, contingency reserve, contingent liability from operation of building laws endorsement, deficiency assessment, leasing or rental concerns—contingent coverage

contingent liability from operation of building laws endorsement

Property. An optional endorsement (ISO form CP 04 05) to a property policy on a building to insure against loss caused by the enforcement of building laws. When rebuilding a damaged structure, laws may require the demolition of all or part of the undamaged portions of an insured building; repairing, remodeling or rebuilding to conform with codes that have changed since the building was first constructed which now require more expensive materials or installation. The insurable value of the undamaged portions of the property is covered by this endorsement. Under the Insurance Services Office's Commercial Property Program, this coverage has been incorporated into the ordinance or law coverage endorsement.

see: ordinance or law coverage endorsement

continuation of coverage
Health.
see: conversion privilege

continuing care facility
Health.
see: life care facility

continuing expenses
Property. Expenses that continue during a business interruption, such as insurance, taxes, payroll of key employees, and debt service.
see: business income coverage form

continuous compounding
Financial Planning. Interest that is added continuously (daily) rather than at longer specified intervals (e.g., quarterly).
see: compound interest, discounting, interest

continuous loss
General.
see: progressive loss

continuous trigger theory
Law/Liability. A legal theory that a loss is charged against any liability insurance policy in effect for any period from the time a covered person was first exposed to a harmful substance to the time the injury is finally manifested (i.e., when symptoms of an illness, such as asbestosis, are discovered). It is sometimes called the *triple trigger* or *multiple trigger* theory, because coverage is invoked by initial exposure, by continuing exposure or "exposure in residence" (the gestational phase of the disease between first exposure and manifestation), and by manifestation of loss. Any policy in effect at any one of these stages is liable. Not all courts or jurisdictions apply this theory.

synonym: multiple trigger theory, triple trigger theory; *compare*: exposure theory, injury-in-fact theory, manifestation theory; *see*: asbestosis, Keene doctrine, long-tail liability, progressive loss

continuum of care services

Health. A comprehensive program of home and in-patient care to meet the physical, emotional, and social needs of families and patients during the final stages of a terminal illness.

contra proferentem

Law. The legal principle that if the meaning of a contractual provision is ambiguous, that meaning is preferred which operates against the party who drafted the contract or supplied the particular provision. (Latin for "against the proffering person.") In lawsuits involving insurance contracts, most courts construe ambiguities against the insurer and in favor of the insured, because it is assumed that the insurer could have written the contract more plainly. Some courts are reluctant to apply this rule in cases where the insured equals or surpasses the insurer in business sophistication, knowledge of possible risks, and assistance of legal counsel.

see: ambiguity, contract of adhesion

contract

Law. A legally enforceable promise made by agreement between two or more parties to create reasonably specific mutual obligations. Required elements of a contract are legally competent parties, a purpose that is not illegal or against public policy, an offer, an acceptance of the offer within a reasonable time, and consideration (which is any value or benefit acquired by a party, or actions undertaken or a sacrifice by a party with the purpose of fulfilling an obligation).

compare: accommodation; *see*: acceptance, aleatory contract, bilateral contract, blanket contract, chose in action, collective bargaining, competence, consideration, contra proferentem, contract of adhesion, discharge of contract, executed contract, executory contract, group contract, guaranteed investment contract, implied contract, insurance contract, land contract, modification of contract, novation, offer, optionally renewable contract, personal contract, privity of contract, quasi-contract, unconscionability, unilateral contract

contract bond

Surety. A surety bond that guarantees the faithful performance of a contract, including the payment for all labor and material involved with completing the contract. In some instances, two bonds are used, one to cover performances and the other to cover payment of labor and material.

compare: labor and material bond, performance bond; *see*: lender's bond, surety bond

contract carrier

Automobile/Inland Marine. A shipping firm that enters into specific written agreements with one or more parties to carry their goods, and generally does not accept business from other parties.

compare: common carrier, private carrier; *see*: carrier

contract fulfillment insurance

Health. A form of accident insurance that indemnifies a professional athletic team for contractual obligations to a player if the player is injured. Typically, the policy covers 60% to 80% of the obligations, subject to a waiting period.

contract of adhesion

Law. A contract drafted by one party and offered on a take-it-or-leave-it basis or with little opportunity for the offeree to bargain or alter the provisions. Contracts of adhesion typically contain long boilerplate provisions in small type, written in language difficult for ordinary consumers to understand. Insurance policies are usually considered contracts of adhesion because they are drafted by the insurer and offered without the consumer being able to make material changes. As a result, courts generally rule in favor of an insured if there is an ambiguity in policy provisions.

synonym: adhesion contract, unilateral contract; *compare*: manuscript policy; *see*: contra proferentem, contract, offer, reformation, unconscionability

contract of carriage

Inland Marine/Ocean Marine.

see: affreightment

contract ratification indemnity insurance

International. A form of political risk insurance designed for contractors who have agreed to work in a foreign country and have made financial commitments (e.g., purchased materials) to fulfill the contract. It covers a portion of expenses should the contract be canceled (not ratified) for any reason beyond the contractor's control.

compare: contract repudiation indemnity insurance; *see*: political risk insurance

contract repudiation indemnity insurance

International. A form of political risk insurance designed for contractors who have an existing (ratified) contract with a foreign government. It covers financial loss if the foreign government illegally cancels or repudiates the contract.

compare: contract ratification indemnity insurance; *see*: political risk insurance

contractors' equipment

Inland Marine. Mobile equipment, tools and implements of a building, road or bridge contractor, including excavating and grading machinery, cranes, hoists and derricks.

see: automobile exclusion, contractors' equipment floater, mobile equipment

contractors' equipment floater

Inland Marine. An inland marine form covering contractors' equipment on an all-risk or specified perils basis. Normal wear and tear, war, and nuclear damage are excluded.

see: contractors' equipment, floater policy, inland marine insurance, mobile equipment

contractors' installation floater

Inland Marine. see: installation floater

contractors' pollution liability coverage

Liability. A coverage designed for environmental, remediation, general or trade contractors for third-party bodily injury and property damage liability claims from a hazardous materials release. It usually includes coverage for the clean-up costs following an incident.

see: pollution insurance

contractual liability insurance

Liability. Coverage for losses incurred by an insured's express or implied assumption of liability under a contract. Contractual coverage was added by endorsement prior to 1973. It is now automatically included in the basic provisions of the 1986 and 1988 commercial general liability forms.

see: assumed liability policy, blanket contractual liability coverage, broad form liability endorsement, commercial general liability policy, incidental contract, liability insurance

contribute-to-the-loss statute

Regulation. When misstatements of fact or breaches of warranty are material contributions to a loss, some states permit insurance companies to deny payment of claims resulting from the insured's loss.

see: concealment, material misrepresentation, warranty

contributing location

Property. A business that furnishes materials or services that are key to the insured's business. Contingent business income insurance covers losses resulting from an interruption of supplies due to insured perils.

synonym: contributing property; *see*: contingent business income coverage, dependent property, recipient property

contributing property

Property.

see: contributing location

contribution by equal share

Insurer Operations. In cases where two or more insurance policies provide coverage at the same level (i.e., primary or excess), the contribution by each insurer of an equal amount to the loss settlement until the loss is paid or until each insurer has exhausted its limit of coverage, whichever comes first.

compare: contribution by limits; *see*: excess insurance, layering, other insurance, primary insurance, proration of benefits

contribution by limits

Insurer Operations. When two or more insurance policies provide coverage at the same level (i.e., primary or excess), the payment by each insurer of the same proportion of the loss that its limit bears to the total of all applicable insurance. Paid losses never exceed the insurer's limit of insurance.

compare: contribution by equal share; *see*: excess insurance, layering, limit of liability rule, other insurance provision, primary insurance, proration of benefits

contribution clause

Property. A policy provision that when more than one policy covers a loss, insurers will share the loss proportionally. The clause is most often associated with business income forms.

synonym: other insurance provision; *see*: business income coverage form, contribution by limits, contribution by share

contributory group insurance

Employee Benefits. A group insurance plan requiring employees to contribute toward the cost of coverage. Statutes vary from state to state, but generally a minimum of 75% of eligible employees are required to participate in this type of plan.

compare: noncontributory group insurance, split dollar insurance

contributory negligence

Law/Liability/Workers' Compensation. An injured person's failure to exercise due care, which along with another person's (the defendant's) negligence, contributed to the injury. A common law defense, originating in England, that one who negligently harms another cannot be found liable if the injured person himself was negligent in the slightest degree.

This defense was often used by employers in suits brought by injured workers. Workers' compensation laws made the defense inapplicable to claims for compensation; it is available only if an employee waives his compensation claim and instead sues an employer in tort.

Many states have adopted a comparative or proportional form of contributory negligence whereby negligence of the injured person is not a complete defense, but reduces the defendant's liability according to the degree of the plaintiff's negligence. *see*: assumption of risk, Butterfield v. Forrester, common law defense, comparative negligence, fellow servant rule, last clear chance, negligence, tort, workers' compensation law

contributory value
Ocean Marine. The value of property saved as the result of a general average act during an ocean voyage which forms the basis for determining each party's general average contribution.
see: general average

controlled master insurance program
International. A centralized and uniform international insurance program by a single international insurer to provide coverage of all of an organization's foreign locations. The insurance is replicated in each country by issuing locally admitted policies that provide coverage as identical as possible. A master insurance policy is issued to the parent organization to fill coverage gaps and provide additional limits that cannot be obtained in the local admitted policies.
compare: coordinated program, global insurance program, uncontrolled insurance program; *see*: master insurance policy

controller
General. The chief accounting officer of a business enterprise or institution, who usually reports to the chief financial officer.
compare: chief financial officer, treasurer

controlling broker
Agency/International. The brokerage firm that produces an international or global insurance program and is responsible to the parent organization (insurance purchaser) for overseeing its design, implementation and servicing.
compare: account executive; *see*: broker network, corresponding broker, servicing broker

convalescent care
Health. Care in a skilled nursing facility or an institution that meets certain standards for medical care. Patients continue to receive skilled nursing care or therapeutic services following hospital confinement. This care is included in some health insurance plans.
compare: custodial care; *see*: skilled nursing facility

convention blank
Insurer Operations/Regulation.
see: annual statement

conversion
Law. The intentional, unlawful use of another person's property; the taking of property without the owner's permission.
see: deprivation, embezzlement, involuntary conversion
Health/Life.
see: conversion privilege

conversion clause
Financial Planning. A variable rate mortgage provision that allows it to be changed to a fixed rate mortgage during its term. When converted, interest is set at a rate then prevailing. An additional charge is usually made to include a conversion clause in a mortgage.
see: mortgage, variable rate mortgage

conversion, embezzlement, or secretion exclusion
Automobile. An older version of the current "false pretense" exclusion, found in commercial automobile coverage forms.
see: false pretense exclusion, trick and device exclusion

conversion fund
Employee Benefits. An unallocated employee benefit plan fund maintained by an employer trustee or an insurance company to purchase annuities that supplement annuities purchased through individual insurance contracts.
synonym: auxiliary fund

conversion parity
Financial Planning. The price of common stock at which a convertible security can be exchanged for common shares; the equality in market values between a convertible security and the underlying common stock.
see: convertible bond, convertible preferred stock

conversion privilege
Health/Life. The right of a person covered under a group health or life insurance contract to purchase individual insurance of a comparable type and amount when the group coverage terminates (for example, when an employee leaves a job). The person may continue coverage without evidence of insurability or a medical examination. The conversion period is usually limited to 31 days.
synonym: continuation of coverage; *see*: Consolidated Omnibus Budget Reconciliation Act, evidence of insurability, portability

converted losses
Automobile/Liability/Workers' Compensation. A loss factor used in retrospective rating and retention plans which is developed by multiplying incurred

losses by a loss conversion factor. *Formula*: incurred losses × loss conversion factor (LCF). *Example*: $100,000 (incurred losses) × 1.20 (LCF) = $120,000 (converted losses).

see: incurred losses, loss conversion factor, retrospective rating plan

convertible bond

Financial Planning. A bond that, under the terms of the contract, may be exchanged for equity securities, usually from the same company.

see: bond (*Financial Planning*), conversion parity, debt security

convertible preferred stock

Financial Planning. Preferred stock that can be exchanged for a corporation's common stock, allowing the shareholder to benefit if the common stock increases sufficiently in value.

see: conversion parity, preferred stock

convertible term life insurance

Life. A form of term life insurance that offers the policyholder the option of exchanging the term policy for some form of permanent insurance without evidence of insurability.

see: automatic convertible term life insurance, evidence of insurability, renewable and convertible term life insurance, term life insurance

cooperative housing

Personal. Dwelling units in a multiple unit building or complex owned by a corporation, the stockholders of which are the residents of the dwelling. It is operated for their benefit by their elected board of directors. The corporation owns the title to the real estate, and each unit resident has an absolute right of occupancy for as long as they own stock in the corporation.

compare: condominium; *see*: homeowners unit owners' form

cooperative insurer

Insurer Operations. An insurer, usually formed as a nonprofit organization, that is owned by its policyholders and provides insurance protection to its members at minimum cost. Examples are mutual insurance companies, reciprocal insurance exchanges, and fraternal benefit societies.

compare: proprietary insurer; *see*: fraternal benefit society, mutual insurance company, reciprocal insurance exchange

coordinated program

International. An international or global insurance program that is controlled by a single broker who coordinates all insurance placements and servicing at the direction of the parent organization's home

office or risk manager. The broker is usually located in the same country as the parent organization.

compare: controlled master insurance program, global insurance program, uncontrolled insurance program

coordination of benefits (COB)

Health. A provision in group health insurance policies that the insurer will not pay benefits covered by other policies or that coverage will be provided in a specific sequence when more than one policy covers the claim.

see: nonduplication of benefits, other insurance provision, proration of benefits

copayment

Health. Under a health maintenance organization or preferred provider organization program, the payment that a member must pay in addition to their premiums. *Example*: A $5 charge for each visit regardless of the cost of the services rendered.

compare: percentage participation; *see*: coinsurance

Professional Liability. A provision in some professional liability policies (such as directors' and officers' liability) that requires the insured to pay a percentage (e.g., 5%) of all claim expenses, awards or settlements.

see: professional liability insurance

copyright

Law/Professional Liability. The exclusive legal right granted by the federal government to reproduce, publish and sell a literary, musical, or artistic work.

compare: patent, trademark; *see*: intangible property (1)

corporate bond

Financial Planning. A bond issued by a corporation. Bonds guarantee repayment at a specified time or intervals, and corporate bonds generally pay a higher rate of return than government bonds.

see: adjustment bond, bond (*Financial Planning*), debt security, government bond, mortgage bond

corporate bond fund

Financial Planning. A mutual fund that invests in corporate bonds.

see: mutual fund

corporate indemnification coverage

Professional Liability. Coverage of a corporation's indemnification of its directors or officers for their personal liability and defense costs. The corporation's indemnification may be required by the corporate charter or bylaws or by state law or may be a provision of the employment contract. Most directors' and officers' liability policies have two insuring provisions: A is the direct coverage of directors and officers; B is the corporate indemnification coverage, which usually has a separate deductible significantly higher than the deductible for coverage A.

see: directors' and officers' liability insurance

corporate risk
Risk Management.
see: business risk

corporation
Law. An entity or artificial person chartered by a government to act as a single enterprise although constituted of one or more natural persons. It is endowed with various rights and duties, including the capacity of succession, the right to form contracts, to sue and be sued, etc. The distinctive characteristics are limited liability of the owners (shareholders, who do not generally participate in management), easily transferred ownership rights, and continuous existence despite changes in ownership.
compare: limited liability company, partnership; *see*: articles of incorporation, bylaws, charter, close corporation, de facto corporation, derivative suit, insider, intra vires, perpetual succession, person, ultra vires

corpus bond
Financial Planning. A coupon bond that has had the coupons removed from the body (corpus) of the bond. In this form the bond has the same characteristics as a zero-coupon bond.
see: bond (*Financial Planning*), coupon bond, zero-coupon bond

correlation
Risk Management. An actuarial term for the degree of interaction between two or more attributes of a group of elements.

corresponding broker
Agency/International. A broker residing in a foreign country who acts as the agent for the controlling broker and assists in servicing the controlling broker's clients who have locations or business activities in the corresponding broker's country. The controlling and corresponding broker usually have regular commercial relations on a number of accounts.
see: foreign correspondent

corridor deductible
Health. A major medical policy deductible applied in the transitional area between basic coverage and the major medical expense coverage. Benefits are paid by the basic health policy first; when these benefits are exhausted, the corridor deductible is applied before benefits under the major medical plan are paid. The corridor deductible is usually a fixed dollar amount per loss.
see: basic medical expense, deductible, major medical insurance

corrosion
Property. The deterioration or destruction of property caused by chemical or electrochemical action, as contrasted with erosion, which is caused by mechanical means.
compare: erosion

cosmetic surgery
Health. Plastic surgery undertaken with the primary purpose of improving an individual's appearance, usually on an elective basis. Cosmetic surgery is generally excluded from health insurance policies, except when it is necessary due to an accident or to correct a congenital anomaly.
see: elective surgery

cost accounting
Accounting. The accounting process used to determine and control an organization's costs, including assessing the performance of managers who are responsible for costs. This can involve accounting for the costs of production or services or of performing any other specific function.
see: accounting, direct expenses

cost approach appraisal
Financial Planning. One of three methods used to appraise real estate for investment purposes. It is similar to insurance actual cash value, as the cost to replace or reproduce the property is determined, then obsolescence and functional or economic depreciation is deducted.
compare: actual cash value, income approach appraisal, market approach appraisal; *see*: real estate, appraisal

cost center
Accounting. A department or unit of an organization that incurs costs (or expenses) but does not directly generate revenues.
compare: profit center

cost index
Life. A way to compare the costs of various life insurance policies. A policy with a smaller index number is generally a better buy than a comparable policy with a greater number.
see: index

cost of capital
Accounting. The discount factor that is used in the capital budgeting process; a business's cost of funds (e.g., prime rate, interest rate on corporate

bonds, etc.).
see: capital budgeting, discount factor

cost of goods sold

Accounting. The section of a financial statement that includes all of the purchasing or production costs and expenses, both direct and indirect, of the merchandise sold during that period. These expenses include raw materials, direct and indirect labor costs, plant costs (such as depreciation), electricity, water and shipping costs.

cost of hire

Inland Marine.
see: rental cost reimbursement

cost-of-living rider

Life. A rider to a term life policy that permits the insured to purchase increasing insurance limits. The limits increase by a stated amount each year, to coincide with an estimated increase in the cost of living.
see: term insurance

cost-of-living variable annuity plan

Life. A variable annuity where the plan's benefits are tied to a specific index, such as the Consumer Price Index.
see: variable annuity

cost of risk

Risk Management. All of an organization's costs created by risk. Cost of risk is the sum of: (1) the cost of accidental casualty losses not reimbursed by commercial insurance or other contractual transfers of risk, (2) cost of commercial insurance or other risk financing or transfer payments, (3) loss prevention and loss control program costs, and (4) all risk management and claims administration costs.
see: cost of risk survey

cost of risk survey

Risk Management. A periodic survey conducted jointly by the Risk and Insurance Management Society and Tillinghast, a Towers Perrin Company, that analyzes the cost of commercial organizations' insurance and risk management programs. It summarizes information on property and liability insurance, retained property and liability loss, workers' compensation costs, and company demographics and administration. It does not include loss control costs.
see: cost of risk, Risk and Insurance Management Society

Council of Insurance Agents and Brokers

Organizations. Organizations: *Members*: Insurance agents and brokers with annual gross revenues of at least $2.5 million. *Objectives*: To safeguard the public's insurance interests, to preserve a stable competitive insurance market, to foster self-regulation and good public relations, and to lobby state and federal governments. *Founded*: 1913. *Headquarters*: Washington, D.C. (Formerly, National Association of Casualty and Surety Agents)

Council on Employee Benefits (CEB)

Organizations. Members: Employers interested in employee benefits. *Objectives*: Exchanges ideas, information and statistics on employee benefits. *Founded*: 1946. *Headquarters*: Akron, OH.

Council on Environmental Quality (CEQ)

Regulation. A council established by the National Environmental Policy Act in 1970 to advise the President on environmental quality, gather information concerning the environment, and review actions of the federal government.
see: National Environmental Policy Act

counsel selection provision

Professional Liability. A policy provision or endorsement in some professional liability insurance policies (particularly directors' and officers') that allows the insured to participate in selecting attorneys who will defend claims.
see: directors' and officers' liability insurance, duty to defend, professional liability insurance

counterclaim

Law. A defendant's answer to the plaintiff's complaint that includes a cause of action against the plaintiff.
see: answer, complaint, pleading

counterparty

Financial Planning. Each party to a financial derivative transaction. The term implies that if one party gains, the other must lose.
see: financial derivative, open interest, swap

countersignature

Agency/Insurer Operations. The signature of a licensed agent or broker, required to validate an insurance contract.
see: countersignature law, nonresident agent, resident agent

countersignature law

Agency/Insurer Operations. A law in most states that all insurance policies covering persons or property in the state must be countersigned by a licensed agent, broker or other resident representative of the insurer.
see: countersignature, nonresident agent, resident agent

county clerks' and recorders' errors and omissions insurance

Professional Liability. Insurance coverage that indemnifies county clerks and recorders against claims from breach of official duties made against the insured by reason of negligent acts, errors or omissions committed or alleged to have been committed by the insured or members of the insured's staff. The coverage is required by legislation in some states.

see: errors and omissions insurance, public entity insurance

coupon bond

Financial Planning. A bond that makes regular payments of the bond principal (corpus) and of interest in dated installments (coupons). The coupons are tickets or certificates attached to the bond that, at their due date, are cut off and presented for payment.

compare: zero-coupon bond; *see*: bond (*Financial Planning*), corpus bond

course of construction insurance

Property.

see: builders' risk insurance

court bond

Surety. A bond required of a party in a lawsuit (litigant) as a condition for the litigant to pursue his or her rights in court.

synonym: litigation bond; *see*: judicial bond

court of equity

Law. A trial court with jurisdiction in cases of equity, or exercising powers considered to be equitable, as opposed to jurisdiction in common law. The historical distinction in Anglo-American law between "legal" and "equitable" forms of action has been abolished in the United States. However, for some purposes, certain remedies and procedures are still considered to be equitable rather than legal, for example, reformation of contracts, injunctions, temporary restraining orders, and other decrees and special orders.

see: civil law, common law, criminal law

covenant

Law. A contractual pledge by one party that something has been or will be done to protect the interests of the other party. In a loan agreement, a covenant may protect the lender's interest by limiting the borrower's total indebtedness, dividend payments, or self-insurance, or by requiring the purchase of a certain type of insurance.

see: lender's single interest coverage

covenant of good faith and fair dealing

Law.

see: good faith

covenants for title

Title. Covenants contained in a document used to transfer the title to real estate by which the grantor pledges completeness, security and continuance of the title transferred to the grantee.

see: real estate, restrictive covenants

cover note

Agency.

see: binder

coverage

Insurer Operations. The protection afforded by insurance. The term can be applied either to the amount of indemnity provided or the perils insured against, or both.

see: coverage extension, exclusion, indemnification, insuring agreement, peril

coverage A (B, etc.)

Personal.

see: dwelling policy, homeowners policy—liability coverage, homeowners policy—property coverage

coverage A

Professional Liability. Under a directors' and officers' liability policy, coverage A provides direct reimbursement to a director or officer for third-party claims.

see: directors' and officers' liability insurance

Workers' Compensation. Prior to the 1983 workers' compensation form, this was the section of a workers' compensation policy that provided the statutory workers' compensation benefits.

compare: coverage B; *see*: part one

coverage B

Professional Liability. Under a directors' and officers' liability policy, coverage B reimburses the corporation for any amounts it is required to pay as indemnification to an officer or director for third-party claims.

see: directors' and officers' liability insurance

Workers' Compensation. Prior to the 1983 workers' compensation form, this was the section of a workers' compensation policy that provided employers' liability benefits.

see: employers' liability insurance, part two

coverage C increased special limits of liability endorsement

Personal. An endorsement (ISO form HO 04 65) that increases three homeowners policy special limit categories: jewelry, watches and furs; silverware, goldware, and pewterware; and firearms.

see: homeowners policy—special limits of liability, personal property floater

coverage extension

Property. An extension of the coverage provided by a policy that may be applied to a specific type of loss, which is in addition to the amount indicated in the policy declarations. Some extensions—such as providing limited extra expense coverage in addition to a fire loss—increase the total amount of insurance. *Example*: Many commercial property forms add an off-premises extension of up to 2% of the amount of insurance applicable to each item of insurance—but not exceeding $5,000—to be applied to each item. Other additional coverage provisions extend a percentage of the main structure limit to appurtenant structures and fences. Such additional coverage usually does not increase the total amount of insurance provided by the policy.

synonym: additional coverage; *compare*: additional extended coverage, extended coverages; *see*: appurtenant structure, debris removal clause, off-premises coverage

coverage for damage to your auto (maximum limit of liability)

Personal. An endorsement (ISO form PP 03 08) to the personal auto policy that limits the coverage amount for physical damage to a specified owned auto. This endorsement is used by insurers on vehicles that are difficult to value, such as antique or custom-built cars.

see: antique and classic automobile insurance, personal auto policy

coverage form

Insurer Operations. Those portions of an insurance policy in which the insuring agreement and exclusions are contained.

see: basic form, coverage part, insuring agreement

coverage part

Insurer Operations. Those portions of an insurance policy that make up a specific line of insurance, including conditions, declarations, coverage forms, causes of loss forms, endorsements, and any other mandatory parts.

see: coverage form, insuring agreement, package policy

coverage territory

Insurer Operations.

see: geographic limitation

coverage trigger

Liability. The event or series of events that activates the obligation of an insurer to provide the benefits it has promised in a policy. The trigger varies between an occurrence and claims-made policy.

see: claims-made trigger, continuous trigger theory, exposure theory, Keene doctrine, manifestation theory, occurrence trigger

covered boiler and machinery property

Property. Any property owned by the named insured or in the named insured's care, custody or control and for which the named insured is legally liable. Boiler and machinery insurance is intended to cover damage to any property of the named insured as long as a "covered cause of loss" is responsible.

see: boiler and machinery insurance, object

covered injury

Workers' Compensation. An injury or disease covered under a workers' compensation policy and therefore eligible for benefits.

see: arising out of and in the course of employment

covered instrument

Crime. In a crime insurance policy, a legal document creating an obligation that is covered by the policy, such as a written promise or order to pay a certain sum (a check, promissory note, bill of exchange, etc). Coverage applies to losses caused by forgery of a payee's name, falsifying documents and altering documents.

see: forgery

cow

Automobile. The automobile that is struck in an accident staged in order to file a fraudulent claim.

synonym: nail; *compare*: bull

CPCU—Harry J. Loman Foundation

Organizations. Members: Individuals who hold the CPCU designation. *Objectives*: A nonprofit foundation that sponsors insurance and risk management research. *Headquarters*: Malvern, PA.

CPCU Society

Organizations. Members: Insurance professionals who are awarded the CPCU designation by the American Institute for Property and Casualty Underwriters. *Objectives*: Promote professionalism, social responsibility, education and research in the insurance industry. Assists in developing the curriculum for the Associate in Fidelity and Surety Bonding designation. *Founded:* 1944. *Headquarters*: Malvern, PA.

see: Agency Administration Section, CPCU Society; American Institute for Property and Liability Underwriters; Associate in Fidelity and Surety Bonding; Chartered Property Casualty Underwriter; Claims Section, CPCU Society; CPCU—Harry J.Loman Foundation; Excess/Surplus/Specialty Lines Section, CPCU Society; International Insurance Section, CPCU Society; Loss Control Section, CPCU Society; Regulatory and Legislative Section, CPCU Society; Reinsurance Section, CPCU Society; Risk Management Section, CPCU Society; Senior CPCU Section,

CPCU Society; Underwriting Section, CPCU Society

crane

Inland Marine. A machine for raising, shifting, and lowering heavy objects by means of a projecting swinging arm or with a hoisting apparatus supported on an overhead track.

compare: boom; *see*: derrick, upset coverage

cratering

Liability/Property.

see: blowout and cratering

credibility

Risk Management. In general, the predictive value associated with a given body of data; an actuarial term for the input data used in a calculation. High credibility indicates sufficient input data is available, and the distribution of results falls within a narrow range.

see: dispersion, distribution curve, mean

credit

Accounting. An accounting entry on the liability (right) side of the ledger. It decreases assets, increases liabilities, or increases owner's equity.

compare: debit

credit balance

Accounting. An amount of money owed to an individual or organization due to overpayment on an invoice, refund, or other adjustment.

compare: debit balance; *see*: balance

credit bureaus' errors and omissions insurance

Professional Liability. A form of professional liability insurance designed for credit bureaus for third-party injury or loss arising from errors or omissions in the conduct of their operations. Covered acts include wrongly assigning a bad credit rating to an individual. Coverage is usually written on a claims-made basis.

see: errors and omissions insurance

credit, debit, or charge card forgery

Crime. A endorsement (ISO form CR 10 12) that amends crime coverage forms B and CR 00 03 to include coverage for loss resulting from forgery of the authorized signature under the insured's credit, debit, or charge card accounts.

see: forgery or alteration coverage form

credit health insurance

Health. Disability or health insurance sold by a lender to cover payment of a debt or an installment loan, in the event the debtor is disabled.

synonym: credit insurance; *see*: credit life insurance, creditor beneficiary, mortgage insurance

credit insurance

Financial Guaranty. Insurance against loss resulting from failure of debtors to pay their obligations to the insured. It guarantees to manufacturers, wholesalers and service organizations payment for goods shipped or services rendered. Generally, it provides coverage against all forms of debtor insolvencies and against nonpayment of all past-due accounts filed with the insurer within 90 days after their original due date. There are two basic forms: general coverage policies that insure all of an insured's accounts receivable, and specific coverage for accounts receivable submitted to the insurer by name.

see: credit health insurance, credit life insurance, lease payment insurance

Health/Life.

see: credit health insurance, credit life insurance

credit life insurance

Life. Life insurance coverage on a borrower designed to repay the balance of a loan in the event the borrower dies before the loan is repaid.

synonym: creditor life insurance; *see*: collateral assignment, credit health insurance, creditor beneficiary, group credit life insurance, mortgage insurance

credit line

Risk Management.

see: line of credit

credit report

Insurer Operations.

see: retail credit report

credit risk

Insurer Operations. A term used when an insurer provides a form of insurance that involves risk financing (e.g., fronting, paid loss retrospective rating plan, finite risk insurance) and the insurer has paid claims based on a financial guaranty of the insured, and the insured does not or can not reimburse the insurer for the paid losses.

see: finite risk insurance, fronting, paid loss retrospective rating plan

credit shelter trust

Financial Planning. A trust containing the amount of funds in an estate that are exempt from federal estate and gift taxes. The trust provides income to a surviving spouse for life, after which the principal goes to surviving heirs.

synonym: bypass trust; *see*: estate tax, gift tax, inter vivos trust

creditor beneficiary

Health/Life. In credit health and life insurance, the creditor is named as beneficiary, and will receive the balance due on a loan in the event of death or disability.

see: credit health insurance, credit life insurance, group credit life insurance

creditor group life insurance

Life. A form of group life insurance issued to a creditor (e.g., a bank, credit union) to insure the lives of its debtors in the amount of their unpaid debt. Coverage is provided for both the debtor's estate and the creditor's benefit, as the proceeds are used to discharge all of the indebtedness to the creditor.

see: credit life insurance, group life insurance

creditor life insurance

Life.

see: credit life insurance

crime

Crime. A violation of law or an offense against the government.

see: crime coverages, criminal law, felony, misdemeanor

crime coverage form A (B, etc.)

Crime.

form A: *see* employee dishonesty coverage form

form B: *see* forgery or alteration coverage form

form C: *see* theft, disappearance and destruction of money and securities coverage form

form D: *see* robbery and safe burglary coverage form—property other than money and securities

form E: *see* premises burglary coverage form

form F: *see* computer fraud coverage form

form G: *see* extortion coverage form

form H: *see* premises theft and outside robbery coverage form

form I: *see* lessees of safe deposit boxes coverage form

form J: *see* securities deposited with others coverage form

form K: *see* liability for guests' property—safe deposit coverage form

form L: *see* liability for guests' property—premises coverage form

form M: *see* safe depository liability coverage form

form N: *see* safe depository direct loss coverage form

form O: *see* public employee dishonesty coverage form (blanket)

form P: *see* public employee dishonesty coverage form (per employee)

form Q: *see* robbery and safe burglary coverage form—money and securities

crime coverages

Crime. A broad term that applies to insurance for the taking of money, securities and other property. Included are employee dishonesty, forgery, theft, robbery, burglary and fraud coverages.

see: bank burglary and robbery insurance, blanket crime policy, blanket fidelity bond, blanket employee dishonesty coverage form, blanket position bond, computer fraud coverage form, depositor's forgery bond, employee dishonesty coverage form, extortion coverage form, forgery or alteration coverage form, hotel safe deposit box liability, innkeepers' legal liability, lessees of safe deposit boxes coverage form, liability for guests' property—premises coverage form, liability for guests' property—safe deposit coverage form, mercantile open-stock burglary insurance, mercantile robbery insurance, mercantile safe burglary insurance, paymaster robbery insurance, premises burglary coverage form, premises theft and outside robbery coverage form, property other than money and securities, robbery and safe burglary form, safe depository direct loss coverage form, safe depository liability coverage form, securities deposited with others coverage form, storekeepers' broad form, storekeepers' burglary and robbery coverage, telephone fraud coverage

crime plan 1 (2, etc.)

Crime.

plan 1: *see* combination crime—separate limits

plan 2: (withdrawn by ISO in 1988)

plan 3: *see* storekeepers' broad form

plan 4: *see* storekeepers' burglary and robbery coverage

plan 5: *see* office burglary and robbery insurance

plan 6: *see* guests' property—safe deposit box

plan 7: *see* guests' property—premises

plan 8: *see* safe depository direct loss coverage form, safe depository liability coverage form

criminal law

Law. The legal principles and procedures that pertain to the enforcement of social order. Though a private person may be the victim, a crime is considered an offense against the order of the state or against the community as a whole. An offense is ordinarily categorized as a *felony* or a *misdemeanor*, depending on its seriousness.

compare: administrative law, civil law (1), common law; *see*: felony, misdemeanor

critical path analysis

Risk Management. A risk management identification tool that is of particular value in identifying business income loss exposures. What a business needs to be restored to its pre-loss operational level is analyzed to identify those steps that are most critical or would take the longest time to restore. This includes identifying the fundamental or instrumental components of business operations (those that are a "condition precedent" to other components), allowing the firm to concentrate loss prevention and control efforts on the identified components.

see: business income coverage form, loss control

criticality

Loss Control. The value of a security (crime) loss. The term is used by security specialists and has the same meaning as the risk management term *loss severity*.

see: loss severity

Cromie rule

Insurer Operations. A guide used to apportion losses among nonconcurrent policies.

see: nonconcurrency, nonconcurrent apportionment rules

crop dusting and spraying insurance

Aviation. A special aviation coverage that takes into account the special hazards of crop dusting, the flying risk, and the possibility of spraying the wrong location or applying too much insecticide or herbicide.

crop hail insurance

Property. Specialized property insurance underwritten by National Crop Insurance Services for farmers. While hail damage to crops is the basic coverage, the coverage may be written for perils ranging from basic named perils to open perils, depending on the crop and the state in which it is grown.

synonym: hail insurance; *see*: crop insurance, hail, National Crop Insurance Services, windstorm and hail coverage

Crop-Hail Insurance Actuarial Association (CHIAA)

Organizations. Members: Insurers covering agricultural crops against hail damage. *Objectives*: Serves as a statistical and rating organization and statistical agents. *Founded*: 1947. *Headquarters*: Chicago, IL.

crop insurance

Property. Growing crops are subject to numerous perils—bad weather, hail, fire, flood, insects, disease. Policies may cover one or more of these perils through the Federal Crop Insurance Corporation or private insurers. Generally, coverage is effective 24 hours after an application is received. Coverage is reduced proportionally as harvesting progresses and terminates when the harvest is complete.

see: American Association of Crop Insurers, crop hail insurance, Crop Hail Insurance Actuarial Association, Crop Insurance Research Bureau, Federal Crop Insurance Corporation, hail, multi-peril crop insurance, National Association

of Crop Insurance Agents, National Crop Insurance Association, National Crop Insurance Services, open perils crop insurance

Crop Insurance Research Bureau (CIRB)

Organizations. Members: Crop insurance companies and other organizations related to the crop insurance field. *Objectives*: Supports research through joint sponsorship of programs. Increases the accuracy of hail loss settlements. Monitors the Federal Crop Insurance Corporation. *Founded*: 1964. *Headquarters*: Overland Park, KS.

cross-cut

Loss Control. A mining tunnel, generally running horizontally and at right angles to a vertical shaft.

see: adit, raise

cross liability clause

Insurer Operations.

see: severability of interest

cross liability exclusion

Professional Liability.

see: insured vs. insured exclusion

cross purchase plan

Life. A plan where each partner or stockholder in a closely held corporation purchases life insurance policies on each of the other partners or stockholders, in amounts sufficient to purchase the partners' or stockholders' interests in the concern in the event of their death.

see: key employee insurance, partnership insurance

cross-selling

Insurer Operations. The marketing of an unrelated form of insurance to existing policyholders (such as offering life insurance to property insurance clients).

see: marketing

cryogenics

Loss Control. The science that deals with the production of very low temperatures and their effect on the properties of matter.

cumulative dividend

Financial Planning. A preferred stock dividend that, if not paid due to insufficient earnings or any other reason, accrues as an obligation that must be paid before common share dividends can be declared.

see: cumulative preferred stock, dividend, preferred stock

cumulative factors

Risk Management. Adjustments (e.g., inflation) that are applied to currently evaluated losses to calculate their ultimate cost level. These factors are derived as the product of the individual age-to-age factors.

see: age-to-age factor, trending

cumulative liability

Reinsurance. The liability of a reinsurer that accumulates under policies from several ceding insurers (covering similar or different lines of insurance), all of which are involved in a common event or disaster.

see: catastrophe loss

cumulative preferred stock

Financial Planning. Preferred stock that accumulates unpaid dividends. Any unpaid dividends must be paid before dividends are paid on common stock.

see: cumulative dividend, preferred stock

cumulative rate of return

Financial Planning. The compounded rate of return that covers more than one period or year.

see: compound interest, rate of return, yield

cumulative trauma

Health/Workers' Compensation. A chronic or continuous injury or disability that results from a series of minor injuries or illnesses or from repetitive activity over a period of time.

see: aggravation of a previous condition, carpal tunnel syndrome, ergonomics disorder, repetitive motion injury

cumulative voting

Financial Planning. A method of stock voting that permits shareholders to cast all votes for one candidate. *Example*: With 100 shares and three board members to be elected, the shareholder may cast 300 votes for one director, 150 votes for each of two directors, or 100 votes for each of three. Under the more common *statutory voting* rule, the shareholder is permitted only to cast 100 votes either for or against each of the three directors. Cumulative voting improves minority shareholders' chances of electing a director.

compare: statutory voting; *see*: common stock, proxy

cure

Ocean Marine. Medical expenses paid by a shipowner to a seaman disabled by illness or injury. Such payments are made until recovery, or until the individual's condition has stabilized.

see: cure, Jones Act, maintenance, seaman's remedies, wages, maintenance and cure

currency swap

Financial Planning. A financial derivative in the form of a swap where the counterparties agree to convert an obligation in one currency to an obligation in another currency. This is a financial risk management technique used by organizations that operate internationally to counteract currency fluctuations.

see: counterparty, financial derivative, swap

current assets

Accounting. Cash or other assets that are expected to be (or could be) converted into cash or consumed within twelve months or within an organization's normal operating cycle. Current assets include marketable securities, notes receivable, accounts receivable, inventory and prepaid items.

synonym: quick assets; *see*: accounts receivable, assets, current ratio prepaid expense, net quick assets

current assumption whole life insurance

Life. A form of universal life insurance with fixed premiums and death benefits and a cash value growth that depends on market conditions. With favorable market conditions and large enough premium payments in the initial years, the premiums for one or more of the following years may be reduced to zero.

see: universal life insurance

current bond yield

Financial Planning. A bond's annual interest amount divided by its current market value, expressed as a percentage.

see: bond (*Financial Planning*), rate of return, yield

current expensing

Accounting/Risk Management. The charging of specific expenses, such as self-insured claims, to the current accounting period without establishing a funded or unfunded reserve for them. *Example*: The charging of owned automobile physical damage losses to the current operating budget.

see: funded reserve, unfunded reserve

current liabilities

Accounting. Liabilities that must be satisfied within the next twelve months. Current liabilities include trade accounts payable, taxes, wage accruals, current installments on long-term debt, and notes payable.

see: current ratio, liability

current ratio

Risk Management. A financial analysis ratio that indicates the liquidity or ability of an organization to pay current bills. *Formula*: total current assets ÷ total current liabilities. The higher the current ratio, the better an organization's debt paying ability.

see: current assets, current liabilities, financial ratios, financial underwriting

currently insured status

Employee Benefits. A Social Security provision that the dependents of a deceased individual who has not reached fully insured status can obtain survivor benefits.

see: fully insured status, Social Security

curtain wall

Loss Control/Property. An exterior non-bearing wall more than one story in height, usually supported by the structural frame, which protects from weather, sound or fire.

see: construction, panel wall

custodial care

Health. Assistance with activities of daily living, whether in a residential care facility or at home, including help in walking, bathing, preparing meals and special diets, and supervising use of medications. These services normally do not require trained medical professionals, though residential care facilities often must be state licensed. Custodial care is usually not covered by health insurance plans.

compare: convalescent care; *see:* adult day care, integrated care, residential care facility

custodian

Crime. A person who has care and custody of insured property on an insured premises. Most crime policies that provide burglary coverage define a custodian as the named insured or a partner or employee of the named insured who has custody of insured property. Generally, a watchperson retained by the named insured whose only duties are to have custody of the property inside the premises is excluded from the definition, however some burglary policies include coverage for robbery of a watchperson.

compare: messenger; *see:* care, custody or control

Financial Planning. A bank or other organization that is responsible for holding and safekeeping securities or other assets of a mutual fund or trust but does not have any fiduciary responsibility for them.

see: fiduciary

customer's broker

Financial Planning.

see: registered representative

customhouse broker

International. A broker licensed by the U.S. Treasury Department who enters and clears goods through customs. The broker prepares customs documents, handles duty payments, arranges inland transportation, and frequently handles placement of transit insurance.

customs bond

Surety. A bond that guarantees the payment of import duties and taxes and also guarantees compliance with regulations governing the import of merchandise into the United States.

synonym: customs house bond; *compare:* ATA carnet; *see:* bonded shipment, bonded warehouse, federal bond

customs-bonded warehouse

International/Inland Marine/Ocean Marine. A bonded warehouse where imported goods may be stored for up to five years without the payment of customs duty or taxes.

see: bonded warehouse

customs broker

Inland Marine/Ocean Marine. A firm that specializes in the clearance of imported merchandise and that arranges subsequent inland transit, documentation and payment of all related charges.

see: customs brokers' and freight forwarders' errors and omissions insurance, freight forwarder

customs brokers' and freight forwarders' errors and omissions insurance

Professional Liability. A form of professional liability insurance for customs brokers that covers claims for negligence in arranging for the clearance and forwarding of imports on behalf of the importer. These are often written separately, as a customs broker's bond for importers and a freight forwarder's E&O liability policy for exporters.

see: customs broker, errors and omissions insurance

customs entry form

Inland Marine/Ocean Marine. A U.S. customs form required for all merchandise entering the country indicating the country of origin, a description of the merchandise, and the estimated duty.

see: certificate of origin, customs bond, import

customs house bond

Surety.

see: customs bond

cut-off

Loss Control. Masonry or brick walls (which may or may not have doors or openings) designed to limit the area exposed to fire.

see: fire division, fire wall

cut-off point

Financial Planning. In the capital budgeting process, the rate of return established by a business's management as the minimum rate that will be accepted on investment opportunities.

see: capital budgeting

cut-off provision

Reinsurance. A reinsurance contract termination provision stipulating that the reinsurer is not liable for a loss resulting from occurrences after the termination date.

compare: run-off cancellation; *see*: cancellation

cut-through clause

Reinsurance. A provision of a reinsurance contract that if the ceding (primary) company becomes insolvent, the reinsurer is liable for its assumed coverage directly to original policyholders. It also usually provides that any such payment is a complete discharge of the reinsurer's obligations, so it will have no further obligation to a liquidator or receiver handling the ceding company's affairs.

synonym: insolvency clause; *compare*: cut-through endorsement; *see*: reinsurance

cut-through endorsement

Insurer Operations/Reinsurance. An attachment to a policy issued by a ceding insurer that makes a reinsurer liable for its assumed coverage directly to the policyholder in the event the ceding company becomes insolvent. It is normally used for commercial insureds who want to deal directly with the reinsurer rather than have their claims possibly delayed by a liquidator. This provision is part of the policy issued to the insured, while a *cut-through clause* is part of the reinsurance agreement between the ceding and assuming insurers.

compare: cut-through clause; *see*: reinsurance

cyclical stock

Financial Planning. The stock of corporations whose profits are closely tied to economic swings, such as steel, textile, and construction companies.

compare: defensive stock

cyclone

Property.

see: tornado

D

daily report (DR)

Agency/Insurer Operations. A document that includes important information on a specific insurance policy in a shortened form, for use by an insurer, agent or broker.

daily value deductible

Property. A deductible used with business income coverage which is expressed as a number of days. After a loss, a determination is made as to the amount that would have been earned each working day (daily value) if the loss had not occurred. The deductible amount is the specified number of days multiplied by the daily value.

see: business income coverage form, deductible

damage from strikers insurance

Property. A form of commercial insurance coverage that indemnifies employers for property losses due to sabotage by strikers.

see: strike insurance

damages

Law. Money awarded in a suit or legal settlement as compensation for an injury or loss caused by a wrongful or negligent act or a breach of contract. Most often, damages are intended as compensation to an injured person for both economic and noneconomic losses, but damages occasionally include a noncompensatory award to punish intentional or wanton wrongdoing, called *punitive* (or exemplary) damages.

synonym: money damages, pecuniary damages; *compare*: specific performance; *see*: additur, compensatory damages, consequential damage, incidental damages, liquidated damages, nominal damages, post-judgment interest, prejudgment interest, punitive damages

damper control

Loss Control. An adjustable metal plate that controls airflow in furnaces and fireplaces.

data

Property. Intangible personal property consisting of facts, concepts or instructions converted into a form that can be used in a data processing operation. Computer programs are also considered data.

compare: media; *see*: data processing coverage, intellectual property

data processing coverage

Property. A type of property insurance (usually an all-risk form) covering data processing equipment, magnetic tapes and disks, and extra expenses incurred to restore the system to its prior working condition.

see: special computer coverage endorsement

data processors' errors and omissions insurance

Professional Liability. A form of professional liability coverage for organizations that perform data processing services for others, against claims arising out of a negligent act, error or omission. Generally, coverage is available for organizations that process financial data as opposed to those doing scientific, engineering or mathematical calculations. Coverage is usually written on a claims-made basis.

see: errors and omissions insurance

date of grace

Insurer Operations.

see: grace period

date of issue

Insurer Operations. The date that a contract was issued by the insurer, which may be different from the effective date.

synonym: issuance date; *see*: effective date

de facto corporation

Law. A corporation formed with a good faith attempt to comply with the law but which fails to meet a minor requirement. A corporation "in fact" is a valid legal entity for most purposes and in its dealings with most people except the state. It can sue and be sued, and its contracts are enforceable.

see: corporation, ultra vires

deadend main

Loss Control. A water main or pipe used for fire protection that is fed from one direction and has a closed end.

see: circulating main

dealer class plan

Automobile. A rating plan developed for automobile dealers under the ISO commercial auto insurance program, garage coverage section.

synonym: automobile dealers rating plan; *see*: floor plan insurance, garage coverage form, lemon aid insurance, limited coverage for customers

dealer's autos and autos held for sale by nondealers or trailer dealers

Automobile. A classification of covered vehicles under the garage coverage form.

see: garage coverage form

Dean analytic schedule

Property. An obsolete commercial fire insurance rating method that was developed by A. F. Dean in 1902. It was the first comprehensive rating method to consider the numerous physical factors that can affect a fire exposure.

death

Life. The termination of life; an irreversible cessation of vital biological functions. If there is continued cardiac activity, some jurisdictions permit death to be determined by a cessation of brain function. For a life insurance policy benefit to be paid, the insurer must receive a death certificate.

synonym: demise; *see*: accidental death, advance directive, brain death, death benefit, decedent, do not resuscitate order, living will

death benefit

Employee Benefits. A payment made upon the death of an employee benefit plan participant of the participant's share in an investment plan or group life insurance.

see: employee benefit plan

Life. A payment made according to a life insurance policy when the insured dies. The benefit is the policy's face amount plus amounts due because of riders, minus outstanding loans and interest thereon.

see: additional death benefit, double indemnity, face amount, living benefits

Workers' Compensation. The payment to the spouse, children or other qualified survivors of an employee who dies from an injury or illness incurred in the course of employment. The amount depends on the employee's wages during the year or other specified period preceding death. Unless a lump sum settlement is arranged, payments are made periodically until a terminating event (e.g., the death or remarriage of the surviving spouse or the attainment of majority age by the children). The death benefit may include a sum for burial expenses prescribed by statute.

compare: disability benefit, medical benefit; *see*: arising out of and in the course of employment, workers' compensation law

Death on the High Seas Act (DOHSA)

Ocean Marine/Regulation/Workers' Compensation. Federal legislation (U.S. Code Title 46, Chapter 21) passed in 1920 that specifies the method of recovery for survivors of persons who suffer wrongful death on the high seas. Suit may be brought in a federal court based on unseaworthiness of a vessel, or negligence or strict liability of vessel owners or operators. The Act defines the "high seas" as being beyond three nautical miles from the coastline of the United States, its territories, or dependencies. The Act also applies to airline crashes in international waters.

see: maritime coverage endorsement

death rate

Life.

see: mortality, mortality assumption

death waiver

Life.

see: payer disability

debenture

Financial Planning. A document evidencing a loan to a company on general credit with no specific pledged collateral. A certificate evidencing an obligation to pay is issued that bears a fixed rate of interest and a principal repayment schedule. Other provisions are sometimes included to protect the holder of a debenture, such as limits on the corporation's further borrowing or limits on the payment of dividends to shareholders.

synonym: unsecured bond; *see*: debt security

debit

Accounting. An accounting entry on the asset (left) side of the ledger. It increases assets, decreases liabilities, or decreases owner's equity.

Life. A term for the premium on an industrial life insurance policy.

see: industrial life insurance

debit agent

Life. An agent who sells industrial life insurance policies.

see: industrial life insurance

debit insurance

Life.

see: industrial life insurance

debit system

Life. A system established by industrial life insurers to have agents or collectors personally collect policy premiums on a weekly or monthly basis.

see: industrial life insurance

debris removal clause

Property. Insurance coverage for the expense of removing debris that results from a loss covered by the policy if the limit of insurance is insufficient to cover both the amount of direct loss and the added cleanup. Many property policies provide an additional $5,000 for each insured location. Higher limits must be purchased separately.

see: coverage extension, demolition clause

debt adjuster

Financial Planning. An individual or firm that provides a service by assisting in the valuation of debt, often in bankruptcy proceedings. Debt adjusters receive periodic payments from debtors, which are then distributed among creditors.

see: bankruptcy

debt cancellation contract

Financial Planning. An agreement whereby a debt is canceled upon the death of the borrower.

debt security

Financial Planning. A bond, note, debenture, or other form of commercial paper issued by a corporation to borrow money, as opposed to capital stock, which represents the shareholders' ownership, or equity. Holders of debt securities have priority in secured assets (the corporation's general property or assets specified in the debt obligation) over unsecured general creditors.

compare: capital stock, equity (*Financial Planning*); see: bond (*Financial Planning*), commercial paper, corporate bond, debenture, note

debt service

Financial Planning. The amount of money needed on a periodic basis to repay an organization's outstanding debt and interest; the funds needed on a monthly, quarterly, or annual basis, to pay the principal and interest on debt.

debt-to-assets ratio

Financial Planning. A measurement of assets financed by creditors, expressed as a percentage. *Formula*: total debt ÷ total assets.

see: financial ratios

debt-to-equity ratio

Financial Planning. A measurement of the proportion of funds provided from investors and from

lenders. *Formula*: total liabilities ÷ total equity. The smaller the ratio, the greater the organization's long-term solvency.

see: financial ratios, financial underwriting

deceased human body

Professional Liability. A term in morticians' professional liability policies for a human corpse, the ashes of a deceased person after legal cremation, or a severed body part.

see: morticians' professional liability insurance

decedent

Law. A dead person, especially one who has died recently. Any property owned by a person at the time of death is called an *estate*.

see: estate planning

deceit

Law. An action or communication intentionally based on falsehood or the withholding of material facts that induces another person to part with a legal right or property; generally used interchangeably with *fraud* or *misrepresentation*.

see: action in deceit, fraud

decennial liability insurance

International. A form of products-completed operations insurance sometimes required of contractors doing work in a foreign country. It provides ten years of coverage to the owner of a construction project for repair or replacement costs in the event of a complete or partial collapse. (*Decennial* means lasting ten years or occurring every ten years.)

see: products-completed operations insurance

decentralization

Insurer Operations. The dispersion of functions and control from a central authority to regional and local authority. *Example*: An insurance company can give authority to local branches instead of controlling underwriting from its home office.

decibel (dB)

Loss Control. A measure of sound expressed as the logarithmic ratio of two amounts of pressure, power, or intensity, between a measured quantity and a reference quantity. The two most frequent applications of decibel involve the measurement of sound intensity level and sound pressure level.

see: hearing level, noise level

decision tree

Risk Management. A device for graphically showing the relationships between decisions and chance events.

see: fault tree analysis, hazard logic tree analysis

deck cargo

Ocean Marine. Cargo carried outside (on the deck) rather than within the enclosed cargo spaces of a vessel. Typically, cargo carried outside a ship's holds are more exposed to both the risk of foul weather and being lost overboard. It is less expensive to ship goods as deck cargo.

synonym: on-deck cargo; *see*: cargo

declarations

Inland Marine/Ocean Marine. A form provided by an insurance company to insureds for reporting payments under an open cargo policy when no marine insurance certificates are issued.

see: marine insurance certificate

Liability.

see: policy declarations

declaratory judgment

Law. A court ruling as to the rights of parties involved in a controversy but without an order of damages or other substantive relief.

see: judgment

declination

Insurer Operations. An insurance underwriter's rejection of an application for insurance.

see: substandard risk, underwriting

decreasing term life insurance

Life. A term life insurance policy where the face amount declines by a stipulated amount on a periodic basis. *Example*: A $250,000 policy may decrease by $10,000 annually so that after 10 years the face amount will be $150,000.

see: term life insurance

decree

Law. A decision or judgment of a court of equity or civil court exercising equitable powers.

see: court of equity, judgment

decrement

Accounting. The amount (usually quantity, but possibly quality) lost by waste.

see: depletion, depreciation

dedicate

Title. To set aside private property for a public use. *Example:* The setting aside of private property for a public sidewalk or street.

compare: eminent domain; *see*: easement, public easement

deductible

Insurer Operations. The amount of an insured loss for which the insured is financially responsible before an insurance policy provides coverage. Though a deductible is usually a monetary amount (a *flat deductible*), a waiting period can function as a deductible, for example, when an injured person must be unable to work for a specified period of

time before disability income coverage is payable.

see: accumulation period (*Health*), all causes deductible, annual aggregate deductible, buy-back deductible, claims deductible workers' compensation plan, corridor deductible, daily value deductible, deductible average, deductible clause, deductible liability insurance, deductible workers' compensation plan, disappearing deductible, family deductible, flat deductible, franchise deductible, indemnity deductible workers' compensation plan, medical deductible workers' compensation plan, memorandum clause, percentage of loss deductible, percentage of value deductible, retention limit, split deductible, straight deductible

deductible average

Ocean Marine. An ocean marine deductible that is either a percentage of the insured value of a shipment or a specified dollar amount.

deductible clause

Insurer Operations. A provision in an insurance policy that indicates a specified deductible amount and states how the deductible applies in the event of a loss.

see: deductible

deductible liability insurance

Liability. Liability insurance where the policy contains a deductible that applies to each claim. The insurer settles the claims and charges back to the insured the amount of each settlement up to the deductible amount. Sometimes, the insurer requires the insured to establish a claims trust account or a letter of credit to guarantee payment of claims within the deductible. (ISO form CG 03 00.)

see: deductible, liability insurance

deductible workers' compensation plan

Workers' Compensation. A form of workers' compensation insurance introduced in 1990 and approved for use in some states. The employer/policyholder pays a reduced premium but must reimburse the insurer for claims that fall within the deductible amount. There are three types of deductible workers' compensation plans: indemnity deductible, medical deductible, and claims deductible.

see: claims deductible workers' compensation plan, indemnity deductible workers' compensation plan, large deductible plan, medical deductible workers' compensation plan, workers' compensation insurance

deed

Title. A document that transfers title to real estate from one party to another party.

compare: mortgage; *see*: administrator's deed, general warranty deed, quit claim deed, trust deed, warranty deed

deed of trust
Title.
see: trust deed

deep well injection
Loss Control. A method of hazardous waste disposal where waste fluids are injected into a well below the ground water level, where geological formations filter the waste or prevent waste water from contacting the ground water.
see: hazardous waste disposal

defalcation
Surety. An archaic term for the embezzlement of money.
see: embezzlement

defamation
Law. The intentional misrepresentation of a person's or an organization's behavior or character so as to invite contempt or ridicule. Defamation includes both libel and slander—that is, both written and spoken defamatory statements. No one can be held liable for a true statement even though it may injure a person's reputation.
see: advertising injury coverage, commercial speech, employment-related practices exclusion, libel, noneconomic loss, personal injury liability, slander

default
Law. The failure of a party in a legal proceeding to make a required pleading or appearance, which can result in a default judgment.
see: default judgment, pleading
Financial Guaranty. An omission or failure to fulfill an obligation, especially failure to make timely payments of principal and interest on a loan, mortgage, bond or other debt.
see: deficiency judgment, financial guaranty insurance, foreclosure, mortgage guaranty insurance, municipal bond guaranty insurance

default judgment
Law. A final judicial decision against a party who fails to file a required pleading or make an appearance in court.
see: pleading

defeasance
Financial Planning. The termination of a corporation's bond liability by purchasing new securities with a cash flow that covers payments on the old bonds. Also, outstanding bonds can be purchased and exchanged for an equivalent market value of new stock. A defeasance transaction clears debt

from the corporation's financial statement.
see: corporate bond
Law. An instrument accompanying a deed specifying conditions that, when performed, end (or defeat) the deed; a document or clause that cancels a contract or obligation when a future action is done.
see: defeasance clause, deed

defeasance clause
Mortgage Insurance. The provision in a mortgage contract that ends the mortgage when all payments are made, transferring title to the property back to the mortgagor or terminating the lender's interest in the property.
see: mortgage, mortgagor

defective product
Liability. A product that does not perform as reasonably expected or poses unreasonable dangers to the user or others who may come into contact with it. There are two main types of product defects: A *manufacturing defect* occurs in the course of production or assembly and is likely to affect only a small percentage of finished goods; a *design defect* is a flaw inherent in the design or engineering of a product, making it unreasonably dangerous regardless of the quality of the manufacturing process. Liability may also be imposed for a manufacturer's or seller's failure to warn of known hazards associated with a product.
see: defective products exclusion, duty to warn, product liability insurance, products-completed operations insurance, strict liability, warranty (3)

defective products exclusion
Automobile. An exclusion in the garage coverage form for a manufacturing defect in a product or part installed by the garage.
see: defective product, faulty work exclusion, garage coverage form

defective title
Title. A title to real estate that is not clear, is encumbered, or is subject to litigation and therefore cannot be transferred.
compare: marketable title; *see*: encumbrance, real estate

defendant
Law. The person in a legal proceeding who is accused of wrongdoing, which may be either civil or criminal.
compare: plaintiff; *see*: affirmative defense, civil law (1), criminal law, defense clause, duty to defend

defendant's bond to dissolve
Surety. One of two forms of injunction bonds. As the result of a judicial process, an order dissolving an injunction may be issued conditioned upon the

defendant providing a bond of this type, guaranteeing to pay such damages as the plaintiff may sustain as a result of the performance of the act or acts originally enjoined.

compare: plaintiff's bond to secure; *see*: injunction bond, judicial bond

Defense Base Act

Regulation/Workers' Compensation. Federal legislation adopted in 1943 that extends benefits under the Longshore and Harbor Workers' Compensation Act to civilian non-nationals of the United States who work on a military, air or naval base acquired after January 1, 1941, from a foreign government. The Act also extends benefits to employees on public works projects outside the continental United States.

see: Defense Base Act coverage endorsement, Longshore and Harbor Workers' Compensation Act

Defense Base Act coverage endorsement

Workers' Compensation. An endorsement (NCCI form WC 00 01 01A) to a workers' compensation policy that provides U.S. Longshore and Harbor Workers' coverage to the employees of contractors performing work at domestic and foreign military bases scheduled on the endorsement. Employers' liability coverage is also included in this endorsement.

see: Defense Base Act, Longshore and Harbor Workers' Compensation Act

defense clause

Liability. A liability insurance policy provision that the insurer has the right and duty to defend any suit against the insured, even if the suit is false or fraudulent. In most policies, the defense expenses are covered in addition to policy limits; however, some policies include this expense in the limit, effectively reducing the amount available for damages by the costs of defense.

see: damages, duty to defend, liability insurance

Defense Research Institute, Inc. (DRI)

Organizations. Members: Attorneys involved with insurer and policyholder defense. *Objectives*: To improve the administration of justice and defense lawyers' skills. *Founded*: 1960. *Headquarters*: Chicago, IL.

defensive portfolio

Financial Planning. An investment portfolio that contains mostly investments made on the assumption that they will not fluctuate much in value, so they are expected to be safer than investments with high growth potential.

compare: aggressive portfolio; *see*: portfolio

defensive stock

Financial Planning. The stock of corporations whose profits are relatively unaffected by economic swings, such as food and utility companies.

compare: cyclical stock

deferred annuity

Life. An annuity whose benefits begin after a given number of years or at an age or age choices specified in the contract. The contract may be purchased by a single premium or, more commonly, by periodic premiums.

compare: immediate annuity; *see*: annuity

deferred dividend policy

Life. An old form of whole life insurance where dividends were postponed for several years. If the insured died or coverage was canceled before the dividend date, dividends were forfeited.

see: whole life insurance

deferred group annuity

Employee Benefits. A funding method for an insured pension plan where the benefits are funded by a single-premium deferred annuity for each plan participant in an amount equal to the participant's accrued benefits each year.

synonym: allocated funding instrument, group deferred annuity; *see*: deferred annuity

deferred life insurance

Life. Policies providing higher death benefits after a period of vesting.

see: life insurance

deferred premium

Life. Life insurance policy premiums that are not currently due, such as monthly or quarterly payments of an annual premium.

see: premium

deferred premium payment plan (DPP)

Insurer Operations. Initially this concept was developed for multi-year (three- or five-year) policies, where the premium could be paid in annual installments. As policy premiums increased, this concept was expanded to include annual policies, where the premium payment is made over the course of the year in quarterly or monthly payments.

see: premium financing

deferred retirement

Employee Benefits. The election by a pension plan participant to work beyond the normal retirement age. Such a deferral may or may not result in an increase of pension benefits.

see: pension, retirement age

deferred stock grant
Employee Benefits/Financial Planning. An agreement by a corporation to give to another party (e.g., an employee) a specified number of shares of stock at a specified future time. Generally, the grantee collects dividends from the initial date of the award, but no taxes are due until the grantee's actual or constructive receipt.

compare: stock purchase plan; *see:* constructive receipt, tax deferral

deferred vesting
Employee Benefits. A pension plan participant's right to receive benefits from a plan that requires a minimum age and a minimum number of service years before the participant is vested in the benefits.

see: vesting

deficiency assessment
Regulation. An assessment levied on insureds under an assessable policy when policy losses exceed those originally expected.

see: assessment, assessment insurance

deficiency judgment
Law. A judgment against a borrower in favor of the lender in an amount equal to the difference between the funds received from a court sale of property and the balance remaining on a mortgage or other loan.

see: default, foreclosure, judgment, mortgage

deficiency reserve
Life/Regulation. A reserve that must be maintained by life insurers when the gross premium charged on a class of policies is less than the net level premium reserve or modified reserve.

see: valuation premium

Deficit Reduction Act (DEFRA)
Regulation. Federal legislation adopted in 1984 as part of the Tax Reform Act that (1) prohibits tax deductions for contributions to 501(c)(9) trusts or premiums paid to experience-rated plans if reserves for benefits exceed specified benefit levels; (2) excludes most taxable benefits from being offered for flexible benefit plans and flexible spending accounts; (3) requires that employers provide retirement-age employee spouses with the opportunity to enroll in employee health insurance programs.

see: flexible benefit plan, flexible spending account, Tax Reform Act of 1984

defined benefit plan
Employee Benefits. Any benefit plan other than an individual account plan. It is primarily a means of funding for retirement and uses a formula to determine the benefit amount. Employer contributions to these plans are actuarially determined.

compare: defined contribution plan; *see:* employee benefit plan, target benefit plan

defined contribution plan
Employee Benefits. An employee benefit plan under which each participant's benefits are based solely on the contributions made to the participant's account. Income or gains are credited to the account, and expenses, losses or forfeitures assigned to a participant's account are deducted.

synonym: individual account plan; *compare:* defined benefit plan; *see:* employee benefit plan, money purchase plan

degree of care
Law. The level of caution, prudence or forethought legally required to avoid causing harm or loss to another person. In determining liability, depending on the circumstances and the relationship of the persons involved, a person may be required to exercise degrees of care variously described as "ordinary," "due," "reasonable," "great," or "utmost." Failure to meet the applicable standard constitutes a breach of duty in the corresponding degree—e.g., ordinary negligence, gross negligence, recklessness, wanton or willful misconduct, etc.

see: attractive nuisance doctrine, duty to warn, gross negligence, invitee, licensee, negligence, trespasser

degree of risk
Risk Management. The uncertainty that can arise from a given set of circumstances; the probability that actual experience will differ from what is anticipated.

see: law of large numbers, odds, probability analysis, risk

delay clause
Life. A life insurance policy provision that allows the insurer to delay policy loans or payment of the cash surrender value for a stated period (usually six months). It is intended to protect life insurers from losses from a "run," during tough economic times, on cash reserves built up in life insurance.

see: cash surrender value, policy loan

Ocean Marine. An exclusion found in ocean marine contracts that denies coverage for liability for loss of markets caused by delayed voyages.

delayed opening coverage
Property. A form of business income coverage that can be added to a builders' risk policy to pay for lost revenue resulting from a delay in the completion of a project due to damage from an insurable peril. The coverage can range from complete loss of income to the additional cost of interest that must be paid until the project is completed.

see: builders' risk insurance, business income

coverage form

delayed payment clause

Life. A life insurance policy clause designed to handle a disaster where both the insured and the primary beneficiary die in the same accident. The clause provides that the beneficiary must survive the insured's death by a specified period of time to receive benefits and that payment will be deferred for that length of time. Or, the provision may state that in the event the beneficiary is likely to die as the result of the accident, the insurer will defer the payment of benefits for a specified period of time. Should the primary beneficiary die before that period of time has elapsed, the benefits will be paid to contingent beneficiaries or the insured's estate.

see: contingent beneficiary, uniform simultaneous death act

delayed retirement credit

Employee Benefits. A gradual increase in retirement credits given to those who attain age 65 in order to encourage working beyond that age.

see: retirement age

delegation

Agency. The transfer of one party's duty to another party. The responsibility for the duty remains with the transferor.

see: agency, agent's authority

delivered business

Life. Life insurance policies that have been issued and delivered by the insurer, but for which no premium has yet been collected.

compare: examined business, issued business, paid business, placed business, written business; *see*: conditional delivery, not taken

delivery

Life. The physical transfer of a life insurance policy from the insurer or its agent to the insured.

see: conditional delivery, conditional receipt

Financial Planning. The transfer of traded securities between the buyer and the seller. A trading transaction usually requires the securities to be delivered on the fifth day following the trade.

see: cash sale, delivery versus payment, market order, scale order

delivery receipt

Inland Marine/Ocean Marine. A receipt used by carriers to prove delivery of merchandise to the intended party. Occasionally, it is a copy of the bill of lading or waybill, with the recipient's signature.

compare: dock receipt; *see*: bill of lading

delivery versus payment (DVP)

Financial Planning. A securities payment arrangement used by large institutional investors whereby the selling institution delivers the securities to the buyer's designated bank, which pays the seller and transfers the securities to the buying institution.

see: delivery, institutional investor

deluge automatic sprinkler system

Loss Control. An automatic sprinkler system where all the sprinkler heads are open and the water is held back at a main (deluge) valve. When the valve is triggered, water is discharged from all the sprinkler heads simultaneously. The triggering device is usually a heat or smoke detector. This type of system is used where it is necessary to wet down a large area quickly, such as an airplane hangar or explosives factory.

see: automatic sprinkler system

demand deposit

Financial Planning. A financial account, usually not interest-bearing, from which a depositor may withdraw by writing a check or providing an access number or code. Funds are available immediately (upon demand), with no waiting period or penalty.

compare: time deposit; *see*: cash assets

demise

Law. The death of a person.

see: brain death, death, decedent

demise charter

Ocean Marine.

see: bareboat charter

demographics

General. The study of characteristics of a given population for such factors as age, sex, birth date, buying habits, etc.

demolition clause

Property. A provision in property insurance policies that excludes coverage for any costs involved in demolishing undamaged property as the result of a covered loss. This clause is necessary because some building codes require a structure to be demolished if it sustains more than a specified percentage of damage.

see: debris removal clause, ordinance or law coverage endorsement

demolition cost endorsement

Property. An endorsement once used in conjunction with the "contingent liability from operation of building laws" endorsement to provide coverage and a separate amount of insurance for costs associated with demolishing undamaged portions of a building. Now, under the Insurance Service Office's commercial property program, the coverage is incorporated into the "ordinance or law coverage" endorsement.

see: ordinance or law coverage endorsement

demonstrative evidence

Law. In a legal proceeding, physical evidence (e.g., a weapon, contract, map, photograph, x-rays); evidence other than testimony, though testimony is usually required to explain the source and significance of demonstrative evidence.

see: documentary evidence, evidence, testimony

demurrage

Ocean Marine. The additional port charges that result from the act of detaining a vessel in port beyond the time needed for loading or unloading; ocean marine coverage for the additional port costs that can be incurred when a ship is detained in port for reasons beyond the insured's control, including delays in loading or unloading.

see: embargo

demurrer

Law. A written statement by a defendant that the plaintiff's complaint is insufficient to state a legal cause of action upon which relief can be granted. Most states and the federal courts require a demurrer to be made at the time an answer is due.

see: answer, cause of action, complaint, pleading

demutualization

Insurer Operations. The process of converting a mutual insurance company to a stock insurance company. A mutual insurer is owned by its policyholders with no outstanding stock. It may convert to a stock insurer with the approval of the insurance department of its domiciliary state. In the conversion process, a mutual insurer offers policyholders cash or stock in the new insurer. The company may then also make a public stock offering.

compare: mutualization; *see*: mutual insurance company, stock insurance company

dental benefit plan

Health.

see: dental service plan

dental hygienists' professional liability insurance

Professional Liability. A form of professional liability insurance for dental hygienists that is patterned after dentists' professional liability coverage. It covers claims for personal injury from alleged malpractice, error or mistake in the rendering of professional services. Coverage is usually written on a claims-made basis.

see: professional liability insurance

dental insurance

Health. Coverage of dental services under an employee benefit plan or as part of a health insurance policy or by a separate dental policy. Most often, it contains a coinsurance provision and may stress preventative care, for example, by fully paying for

cleanings and check-ups twice a year.

compare: dental service plan

dental plan organization

Health. An organization that sponsors one or more programs under which dental services are provided directly or are arranged for or administered on a prepaid basis.

see: dental service plan

dental service plan

Health. A program for the direct provision of dental services, as opposed to indemnification of dental expenses. The plan sponsor (dental plan organization) employs or contracts with dentists or other health care personnel to provide services to the plan members.

compare: dental insurance; *see*: dental plan organization

dentists' professional liability insurance

Professional Liability. Coverage for dentists against claims for personal injury arising from alleged malpractice, error or mistake in rendering professional services. Coverage is usually written on a claims-made basis.

see: medical malpractice, physicians' surgeons' and dentists' professional liability insurance, professional liability insurance

Department of Transportation (DOT)

Regulation. A federal regulatory department whose responsibilities include vehicle safety standards and, along with the Interstate Commerce Commission, the regulation of trucking operations. DOT sets the truckers' liability insurance standards for bodily injury, property damage and environmental impairment.

see: Hazardous Materials Transportation Act

Department of Veterans Affairs

Organizations. A federal executive department that administers programs for people who served in the U.S. armed forces. These programs include life and health insurance, mortgage loans, educational assistance, and pension benefits. Before 1991, it was called the Veterans' Administration and was not a cabinet-level department. Hospitals run by the Veterans Health Administration within the Department are still commonly known as Veterans Administration hospitals.

see: Veterans Administration hospital

dependency period

Financial Planning. The period of time during which children are growing up and are dependent on their parents. The period ranges from the birth of the oldest child until the youngest child reaches maturity. The dependency period is used in planning for the family's financial ability to provide support and education for the children and the parents' retirement thereafter.

see: dependent

dependent

Employee Benefits/Health. Most employee benefit plans define covered dependents as a plan participant's spouse and unmarried children under age 18 (or 21) who are not employed full-time, or who are full-time students at an accredited college up to age 21 or 22. The term "spouse" is sometimes expanded to include lifetime partners or others.

see: child's benefit, dependent adult, dependent coverage, spouse's benefit

dependent adult

Employee Benefits/Health. A person beyond minority age who is incapable of self-sustaining employment because of a mental or physical disability.

see: adult day care, custodial care

dependent coverage

Employee Benefits/Health. Coverage under an employee benefit plan that extends to a plan participant's dependents (spouse, minor or unmarried children, or sometimes domestic partner).

see: dependent, employee benefit plan

dependent property

Property. A facility, location or premises of a critical supplier or customer of an insured which if damaged or destroyed would cause a major business interruption to the insured. Such a loss can be insured by contingent business income coverage.

see: contingent business income coverage, recipient property

depletion

Risk Management. A lessening or diminution in quantity, content, or value.

see: amortization, decrement, depreciation

deponent

Law. An individual who testifies to facts in a legal proceeding; one who gives testimony under oath or whose deposition is taken.

see: deposition, expert witness, testimony

deposit account

Life.

see: active life fund

deposit administration contract

Life.

see: deposit administration plan

deposit administration fund

Life.

see: active life fund

deposit administration plan (DAP)

Health/Life. A pension plan administered by a life insurance company where pension funds accumulate in a master group annuity policy until a participant retires. As plan members retire, individual annuity policies are purchased with money from the fund.

synonym: deposit administration contract, group deposit administration annuity; *see*: administrative services only, annuity purchase fund, third-party administrator

deposit and minimum earned premium

Insurer Operations.

see: minimum earned premium

deposit fund

Life. Provisions under individual life or annuity contracts in which amounts are paid, in addition to premiums, to accumulate interest.

see: active life fund

deposit premium

Insurer Operations. A partial payment of premium to an insurer that may later be adjusted up or down; an initial premium, as close to the final premium as possible, that can be modified later (e.g., after the close of the policy year) by an audit of the insured's records.

synonym: advance premium; *see*: audit, estimated annual premium, initial premium, provisional premium

Reinsurance. An amount paid by a ceding insurer to a reinsurer that represents a partial or total payment of premiums expected to be earned under the contract. The premium is then adjusted at the end of the contract term (or periodically within a multi-year term) to reflect actual premiums earned at the rates charged for the coverage.

deposition

Law. A person's sworn statement, not taken in open court, as to facts in a legal proceeding; a discovery device used before a trial begins to question parties and potential witnesses.

see: deponent, discovery

depositor's forgery bond

Crime. Insurance issued to individuals (not lending institutions), protecting them against financial loss due to alteration or forgery of checks, drafts, promissory notes and the like.

see: crime coverages

depository bank

General. A bank that accepts funds to be withdrawn at the will of the depositor or pursuant to agreed conditions.

see: demand deposit

depository bond
Surety. A bond that guarantees payment of funds to depositors in accordance with the terms of a deposit in a bank.

see: Federal Deposit Insurance Corporation

depreciated value
Property. The original cost (or other accounting or tax basis) of property minus physical depreciation.

compare: actual cash value, depreciation, functional replacement cost, market value, replacement cost, reproduction cost, tax-appraised value; *see:* valuation of potential property loss

depreciation
Accounting. A noncash expense that reflects the current year's share of the cost of an asset; recovery of the cost of a tangible capital asset over its useful life or a shorter time permitted by tax laws or generally accepted accounting practices. In calculating the insurable actual cash value of an asset, insurers use physical depreciation, i.e., the non-accelerated decline in economic value.

see: accelerated depreciation, amortization, capital asset, depreciation insurance, deterioration, straight-line depreciation

depreciation insurance
Property. Coverage in case of a loss for the difference between the actual cash value of the property insured and the cost of replacement for comparable size and construction.

see: actual cash value, depreciation, replacement cost insurance

deprivation
Law. Confiscation or removal of property without just compensation.

International. A government's withholding of property located within its territory from use by the owner.

compare: confiscation, expropriation, nationalization; *see:* deprivation insurance

deprivation insurance
International. A form of political risk insurance designed for an investor or contractor with operations in a foreign country who is prohibited from exporting or returning its equipment from that country because the government will not issue an export license.

see: political risk insurance

derelict
Ocean Marine. An abandoned vessel, giving no indication that it is to be reboarded or recovered. Ordinarily, anyone finding a derelict may take possession of it.

see: flotsam, jetsam, lagan

derivative
Financial Planning.

see: financial derivative

derivative insured
General. An individual or entity, such as an executor of an estate or an heir, who is entitled to receive insurance proceeds on behalf of the insured.

see: insured

derivative suit
Law. A civil lawsuit filed by shareholders on behalf of a corporation asserting rights of the corporation in the absence of corporate action to protect such rights; a suit by shareholders to enforce corporate rights against directors or other insiders. The standing of shareholders to sue is derived from the rights of the corporation. This differs from a class action (or representative suit), where a large group of plaintiffs (shareholders or otherwise) bring suit in their own right.

synonym: shareholder derivative suit; *see:* class action, corporation, insider, strike suit

dermatitis
Health/Loss Control. Inflammation of the skin, frequently caused by contact with harmful or allergic materials.

see: allergy and susceptibility

derrick
Inland Marine. A hoisting apparatus that employs a tackle rigged at the end of a boom.

compare: crane; *see:* boom

descent
Law. The transfer of real estate to heirs of the owner upon the owner's death.

see: estate planning, real estate

design errors and omissions insurance
Professional Liability.

see: architects' professional liability insurance, design professionals' liability insurance, efficacy coverage, engineers' professional liability insurance, errors and omissions insurance, product liability insurance, turnkey insurance

design load
Loss Control. The planned amount of authorized work to be performed; the weight to be carried by a device for a specific function or purpose.

design professionals' liability insurance
Professional Liability. Coverage for individuals and organizations that are involved in the design or preparation of plans and specifications (other than architects and engineers) for third-party liability arising out of professional services, including error, omission or negligent acts. Coverage is usually

136

written on a claims-made basis.

see: professional liability insurance

Designated Planning Agency (DPA)

Health/Regulation. An agency required by the Social Security amendments of 1973 to be established by states to oversee and review the capital expenditures for health care projects partially funded with Medicaid and Medicare reimbursements.

see: Medicaid, Medicare

designated workplace exclusion endorsement

Workers' Compensation. An endorsement (NCCI form WC 00 03 02) to a workers' compensation policy that deletes coverage at specified locations where the workers are covered by another policy. The endorsement is usually used with a contractors' owner-controlled insurance program.

see: owner-controlled insurance program

desk underwriter

Insurer Operations.

see: line underwriter

destruction

Crime. One of the insured perils of a dishonesty, disappearance, and destruction (3D) policy. It is a covered peril under most money and securities policies, as well. Destruction is deemed to have occurred when the insured property is useless for its intended purpose, even though the property may not be entirely destroyed.

see: dishonesty, disappearance and destruction policy

detached structure

Property. A structure not sharing a wall with another building on the same property. Most commercial property policies cover detached structures on the same premises.

compare: adjoining building; *see*: adjacent building, appurtenant structure

Personal. Any structure on an insured location separated from the insured dwelling by clear space (often connected to the insured dwelling by only a fence or utility line). Most homeowners and dwelling property policies cover detached structures on the same premises.

see: dwelling policy, homeowners policy

deterioration

Property. The natural and expected decline in the usefulness and value of property from wear and tear and normal environmental forces. Physical deterioration results in value depreciation.

compare: inherent vice; *see*: decrement, depreciation, wear and tear exclusion

deviated rate

Insurer Operations. Rates that are usually lower than the indicated manual or bureau rates. In most states, insurers must file justification for rate deviations with the insurance department.

see: deviation insurer, rate

deviation

Insurer Operations. A rate for coverage that differs from a manual or bureau rate.

see: deviated rate

Ocean Marine. A voluntary departure by a vessel from the usual course between a port of departure and a port of destination.

see: deviation clause

deviation clause

Ocean Marine. A provision found in ocean marine insurance policies allowing a vessel to deviate from the routes indicated in the policy for reasons beyond the insured's control.

see: deviation

deviation insurer

Insurer Operations. An insurance company that writes the majority of its business at deviated (usually lower-than-bureau) rates.

see: deviated rate, deviation

devise

Law. A gift of real property by the last will and testament of the donor.

compare: escheat; *see*: estate planning, will

diagnosis related group (DRG)

Health. A medical cost reimbursement category used in the Medicare program's prospective payment system for hospitals. Each category is based on patient characteristics (e.g., age and sex), diagnosis, and medical procedures. Predetermined payment amounts are assigned to the categories. DRGs have also been utilized by employers and insurers as a cost containment technique.

see: fee schedule, Medicare, outlier, prospective payment system, reasonable and customary charge

diagnostic coverage

Health. Coverage in a health insurance policy for diagnostic procedures such as laboratory tests and radiology.

dies insurance

Property. Insurance that specifically covers a manufacturer's dies (metal or plastic forms for molding materials), which may have very high replacement value. Usually, coverage is endorsed to a property policy, but it can be provided by a separate inland marine policy.

see: pattern and die floater

dietitian and nutritionists' professional liability

Professional Liability. Coverage for dietitians and nutritionists for third-party liability resulting from malpractice, error or mistake in rendering professional services. Coverage is usually written on a claims-made basis.

  see: professional liability insurance

difference in conditions insurance (DIC)

International. A nonadmitted international insurance policy that can provide first-dollar property or liability coverage for perils not covered by admitted policies issued in a foreign country. It can also be used for excess limits over local admitted policies. A DIC policy is designed to supplement coverage purchased in a foreign country and is issued by the international department of an insurer or Lloyd's of London for a multinational corporation.

  compare: difference in limits insurance

Property. A property insurance policy, usually written on a large risk, to supplement a named-perils policy. It provides all-risk coverage (often including flood and earthquake) but excludes the named perils provided by a standard fire policy. The policy is written for a specific limit (e.g., $5 million or $10 million) without a coinsurance provision.

  synonym: change in conditions insurance; *see*: all-risk insurance, named perils

difference in limits insurance (DIL)

International. A nonadmitted international policy that provides excess limits over locally admitted primary policies issued in a foreign country. It is issued by the international department of an insurer or Lloyd's of London for a multinational corporation.

  compare: difference in conditions insurance

dike

Loss Control. A bank of earth or a masonry wall constructed around storage tanks to prevent the leakage of their contents from spreading to other areas.

dilution

Financial Planning. An increase in the number of common shares issued by a corporation without a corresponding increase in assets. The additional shares dilutes, or reduces, the value of the initial shares.

direct action statute

Regulation. A statute in some states that allows an injured party to take direct legal action against the insurer of the other party. Usually, a direct action against an insurer cannot be taken without first obtaining a judgment against the insured.

direct bill

Insurer Operations. A statement of insurance premium due that is sent directly by an insurer to the policyholder.

  compare: agency bill; *see*: premium

direct damage

Property. Property loss or destruction caused directly by an insured peril, as opposed to indirect or consequential damage.

  synonym: direct loss; *compare*: consequential damage

direct excess coverage

Automobile. A form of excess insurance available under the garage coverage form for damage to a customer's vehicle. The coverage is in excess of any other applicable insurance.

  compare: direct primary coverage; *see*: garage coverage form, excess insurance

direct excess policy

Liability. A liability policy that is issued for the sole purpose of providing excess insurance. *Examples*: A following form excess policy or an umbrella policy.

  see: following form excess liability insurance, umbrella liability insurance

direct expenses

Accounting. Those expenses that can be easily traced or associated with a cost object (i.e. the cost of materials that become part of a manufactured product, or the cost of labor that is used solely in a single processing department of a manufacturer).

  see: cost accounting

direct health care corporation

Health. A corporation providing direct health care services to its members and subscribers through contracts with licensed health service personnel and health service institutions, but not paying any cash indemnity benefits.

  see: health indemnity plan, health maintenance organization, preferred provider organization

direct loss

Property.

  see: direct damage

direct marketing

Insurer Operations.

  see: direct marketing system

Direct Marketing Insurance Council (DMIC)

Organizations. Members: Direct marketing divisions of insurers and service companies. *Objectives*: Holds educational seminars and awards the Direct Marketing Insurance Man of the Year Award. *Founded*: 1917. *Headquarters*: New

York, NY.

direct placement

Financial Planning. The purchase of an issue of securities directly from the issuer, bypassing a stock broker or investment banker. Insurance companies and other institutional investors frequently purchase securities in such a way.

see: institutional investor, public offering

direct primary coverage

Automobile. A form of primary insurance available under the garage coverage form for damage to a customer's vehicle. The coverage applies regardless of any other collectible insurance or the insured's legal liability.

compare: direct excess coverage option; *see*: garage coverage form, primary insurance

direct response marketing

Insurer Operations.

see: direct response system

direct response system

Insurer Operations. An insurance marketing system where company employees directly contact prospects by telephone or mail.

synonym: direct marketing, direct response marketing; *compare*: exclusive agency system, independent agency system

direct writer

Insurer Operations. An insurer that markets its policies directly through salaried employees or captive agents, rather than through independent agents or brokers.

compare: independent agency system; *see*: captive agent

Reinsurance. A reinsurer that markets directly to insurance companies, rather than through a reinsurance intermediary.

see: intermediary

direct written premium

Insurer Operations. The amount of an insurer's recorded originated premiums (other than reinsurance) issued during the year, whether collected or not.

see: premium

directed verdict

Law. A jury verdict ordered by the trial judge on the basis that the party with the burden of proof has failed to present a prima facie case.

see: burden of proof, dismissal, judgment, verdict

director

Financial Planning/Professional Liability. A person elected by the shareholders of a corporation to manage its affairs and establish its general policies. All of the directors together constitute the board of directors.

see: corporation, directors' and officers' liability insurance, inside director, insider, outside director

director of insurance

Regulation.

see: insurance commissioner

directors' and officers' liability insurance (D&O)

Professional Liability. A specialized form of professional liability coverage for legal expenses and liability to shareholders, bondholders, creditors or others due to actions or omissions by a director or officer of a corporation or nonprofit organization. Directors and officers are not liable for an honest mistake of business judgment made with reasonable prudence or care that results in a financial loss; but officers and directors are held personally liable for actions or omissions made with negligence, recklessness, or bad faith. Most policies have two parts: coverage A provides direct reimbursement to the directors and officers for third-party claims; coverage B reimburses the corporation if it is required or permitted, under state law or the corporate charter or by-laws, to indemnify the directors and officers. Coverage is on a claims-made basis. A few policies contain only coverage A, and some pay expenses on behalf of directors and officers, as opposed to paying on an indemnity basis.

see: abuse of minority shareholders, allocation of defense costs, amotion, business judgment rule, condominium association directors' and officers' liability insurance, corporate indemnification coverage, counsel selection provision, entity coverage, environmental directors' and officers' liability insurance, greenmail exclusion, inside director, insured vs. insured exclusion, intercompany transaction, intra vires, negligence, outside director, sale of company exclusion, ultra vires

disability

Health. A physical or psychological condition resulting from injury, illness or congenital abnormality that interferes with the activities of daily living that a nondisabled person can perform.

see: disability income insurance

Employee Benefits. For Social Security purposes, a physical or mental impairment that is expected to keep a person from doing any "substantial" work for at least a year. Generally, a job paying $500 or more per month is considered substantial. Alternatively, the person must have a condition that is expected to result in death.

see: Social Security

Workers' Compensation. An incapacity, due to a work-related injury or illness, to earn the amount of wages an employee was receiving before the injury or illness.

see: disability benefit, nondisabling injury, non-occupational disability, partial disability, permanent partial disability, permanent total disability, presumptive disability, recurrent disability, short-term disability, temporary partial disability, temporary total disability, total disability, workers' compensation insurance

disability benefit
Workers' Compensation. Compensation for an employee's income lost due to a work-related illness or injury. The amount is a portion of the worker's pre-injury wages prescribed by statute.

compare: death benefit (*Workers' Compensation*), medical benefit; *see*: arising out of and in the course of employment, 24-hour coverage, workers' compensation law

disability benefit law
Employee Benefits. A law requiring employers to pay weekly benefits to employees who are injured in non-occupational accidents or who become ill outside of employment.

compare: workers' compensation law; *see*: temporary disability benefits, 24-hour coverage

disability income insurance
Health/Employee Benefits. Insurance that provides payments on a periodic basis (usually monthly) to replace income lost because of a disability that prevents the insured from working. A separate health policy with a disability benefit normally either excludes coverage for an injury covered by workers' compensation or discounts the benefits by the amount of workers' compensation to which the insured is entitled. The Social Security program includes disability insurance as one of its benefits.

see: disability, elective benefits, group disability insurance, lifetime disability benefit, long-term disability insurance, maximum disability income policy, partial disability insurance, payer disability, pilot and crew occupational disability insurance, quarantine benefit, residual disability income policy, short-term disability insurance, Social Security, statutory disability income insurance, unemployment compensation disability insurance

Life. A rider that can be added to an ordinary life insurance policy that pays the insured 1% of the face value of the policy each month if the insured is disabled more than six months. Premiums are waived while disability payments are made.

Disability Insurance Training Council (DITC)
Organizations/Health. The education division of the National Association of Health Underwriters.

The DITC provides seminars on disability income and health insurance, as well as marketing and underwriting clinics.

see: National Association of Health Underwriters

disability overhead expense insurance
Health.
see: overhead expense insurance

disability waiver of premium
Health/Life.
see: waiver of premium

disabling injury
Workers' Compensation. A job-related physical or mental injury that prevents a person from pursuing his or her normal occupation.

see: disability benefit, occupational accident, workers' compensation law

disappearance
Aviation. An aircraft missing and not reported for a specified time (usually 60 days) after commencing a flight.

Crime/Inland Marine. A crime insurance peril that encompasses losses from a known location at a known time, resulting from a theft or burglary. If a loss occurs without knowledge about the location or time of loss, it would be a *mysterious disappearance*, which is often excluded from coverage.

see: dishonesty, disappearance and destruction coverage form; mysterious disappearance

disappearance and destruction coverage form
Crime.
see: money and securities broad form insurance

disappearing deductible
Insurer Operations. A deductible that decreases in amount as the amount of a loss increases. When the loss equals or exceeds a specified amount, the deductible no longer applies. For losses less than the deductible, an increasing proportion of the loss is paid. *Example*: For a $1,000 deductible, the insured would receive 125% of losses exceeding $1,000, 150% of losses exceeding $2,000, and at $3,000 the deductible disappears.

see: deductible, franchise deductible

disaster plan
Risk Management. A detailed plan to transfer business operations to another location, or to utilize other equipment, if an existing facility is damaged; a plan to minimize the consequences of loss at a single location.

synonym: catastrophe plan; *see*: backup facility agreement, emergency response plan

discharge of any substance

Property. A term used in sprinkler leakage coverage that expands coverage to include not only the accidental discharge of water, but also discharge of substances such as carbon dioxide gas, Halon gas, dry chemical powder, and antifreeze solution.

see: sprinkler leakage coverage

discharge of contract

Law. There are four ways by which the parties to a contract can be relieved or discharged of their obligations: 1. complete performance; 2. substitution of a new agreement; 3. the impossibility of performance; or 4. the operation of law.

see: commercial impracticability, contract

disclaimer

Liability. The denial of an obligation or a claim. As respects product liability, a disclaimer may be a statement by the seller that the product is not warranted or has a warranty only for specific consequences or costs.

compare: implied warranty

discount

Financial Planning. 1. As respects a variable rate mortgage, an initial interest rate reduction by the lender for a time (usually one year or less) to provide a lower payment as a way to attract borrowers. After the discount period, the interest rate usually increases depending on the index rate at that time.
2. The difference between a bond's selling price and its face or redemption value; any reduction in the offering price of a security from its market value.

see: variable rate mortgage

discount factor

Financial Planning/Risk Management. A number that is multiplied by a monetary value to reduce an expected future sum to its present value. *Formula:* $1 \div (1+r)^t$, where r is the interest rate expressed as a decimal and t represents the time in years for which an amount is to be discounted.

see: discounting, present value

discount rate

Financial Planning. The interest rate a U.S. Federal Reserve Bank charges on loans to member banks. If the discount rate is high, banks are discouraged from borrowing, and if it is low, banks are encouraged to borrow, making more funds available for loans. Interest rates charged by banks for both consumer and commercial loans typically rise or fall with changes in the discount rate.

synonym: federal funds rate; *see:* interest, prime rate

discounted cash flow techniques (DCF)

Risk Management. Methods of evaluating the return on a capital investment, by calculating the present value of the income flow. The analysis of the discounted cash flow is valuable when selecting from competing investments, by taking into account the time value of money.

see: cost of capital, discounting, internal rate of return, net present value method, present value

discounted premium

Life. A lump sum advance premium paid in lieu of the frequency of payments specified in the policy. Such payments may be discounted by the insurer, based upon an agreed rate of interest.

see: premium

discounting

Risk Management. The process of funding the present value of a series of future cash flows.

compare: compounding; *see:* continuous compounding, discounted cash flow techniques, discount factor, present value, risk-adjusted discount rate

discounting for mortality

Employee Benefits/Life. The discounting of pension plan contribution rates or benefit costs, under the assumption that a specified percentage of participants will die prior to qualifying for benefits.

synonym: advance discount for mortality; *see:* mortality table

discounting for severance

Employee Benefits/Life. The discounting of pension plan contribution rates or benefit costs, under the assumption that a specified percentage of participants will stop working for the employer prior to qualifying for benefits.

synonym: advance discount for severance

discovery

Law. The gathering of evidence before a trial begins by a party to a suit. Each party has a right to question or depose the other, submit written interrogatories, review evidentiary documents in the other party's possession, and inspect property owned by the other party when relevant to the case.

see: deposition, evidence

discovery period

Surety. A provision in a fidelity bond that allows the insured to report a loss to the surety company for a specified period, usually one year, after the bond has been canceled. The loss must have occurred while the bond was in force.

discretionary account

Financial Planning. A trading account with a securities broker with authorization for the broker or an investment advisor to make specific types of trades on the client's behalf (a limited trading authorization) or to make any type of trade on the customer's behalf (full trading authorization) without prior approval.

see: churning, full trading authorization

discretionary group

Regulation. In group insurance, a group not included in standard group classifications but which may be used with the insurance commissioner's approval.

compare: fictitious group; *see*: minimum group, true group insurance

discrimination

Regulation. Different treatment of persons or groups; failure to treat individuals equally when no reasonable distinction can be made between them. Treating or classifying consumers differently when they have objectively similar risks is prohibited by state insurance laws; and federal laws prohibit discrimination in employment, education, and access to public accommodations on the basis of race, sex, age, national origin, or religion.

see: age discrimination, Age Discrimination in Employment Act, Civil Rights Act, employment practices liability insurance, equity (*Insurer Operations*), life risk factors, sex discrimination, sexual harassment, sexual harassment defense coverage

Liability. Before the late 1980s, some general liability policies provided coverage for discriminatory acts under the personal injury coverage section. Virtually all forms of discrimination are now excluded, but special employment practices liability insurance policies now provide this coverage.

dishonesty, disappearance and destruction policy (DDD)

Crime/Surety. A crime insurance policy that combines fidelity insurance with crime insurance. The form contains five insuring agreements: 1. employee dishonesty; 2. premises, money, and securities coverage; 3. off-premises money and securities coverage; 4. counterfeit currency or money order coverage; and 5. depositor's forgery coverage. This policy has been replaced by the 1986 commercial crime program.

synonym: 3-D policy; *see*: depositor's forgery bond, destruction, disappearance, employee dishonesty coverage form, money and securities broad form insurance

dismemberment

Health/Life. The loss of an arm, leg, finger or toe, or eyesight in one or both eyes.

dismemberment benefit

Health/Workers' Compensation. Insurance payable in case of dismemberment.

see: dismemberment

dismissal

Law. An order ending a suit without trial of the issues. A dismissal "with prejudice" is based on a claim's lack of merit or failure to prosecute the claim in a timely fashion and bars the right to bring another action on the same claim. A dismissal "without prejudice" is without reference to the merits and allows a subsequent suit on the same claim if not barred by a statute of limitations.

see: affirmative defense, demurrer, directed verdict, judgment, statute of limitations

disparagement of goods

Liability. Untrue or misleading criticism of a firm's merchandise offered for sale in order to discourage purchases.

see: advertising injury coverage, twisting

dispersion

Risk Management. An actuarial term for the measurement of variability of data from the mean, median or mode. The farther losses occur from the point being measured (i.e., the greater the dispersion), the lower their reliability.

see: mean, median, mode

dispossess

Law. The act of depriving a person from the use of real estate.

compare: adverse possession; *see*: ejectment bond

dissenting shareholder

Financial Planning. A shareholder who objects to a proposed corporate action and demands payment for his or her shares. Under most state laws, a shareholder may dissent from specified proposed actions: a merger or consolidation, a plan of share exchange, a sale or exchange of substantially all of the corporation's assets, certain amendments to the articles of incorporation that would adversely affect the rights of shares held by the dissenter, or any action with respect to which the articles or bylaws of the corporation grant a right to dissent. The shareholder must give notice of dissent before the action is voted upon, and if the action is approved, the corporation must buy the shares of dissenters for fair value.

see: abuse of minority shareholders, common stock, corporation, proxy, statutory voting

distilled spirits and wines market value endorsement
Property.

see: alcoholic beverages market value endorsement

distraint
Law. The taking of goods of another in order to obtain satisfaction of a claim or debt, especially for unpaid rent. (Also called *distress.*)

see: default

distribution clause
Property.

see: pro rata distribution clause

distribution curve
Risk Management. An actuarial term for the scattering of data around the mean. The normal distribution curve is a symmetrical bell shape.

see: lognormal distribution, mean, Poisson distribution, skewed curve, symmetrical curve

distribution of assets
General. When an organization is being dissolved or is in bankruptcy, assets are distributed in a specified order. Solvent assets or the proceeds from such assets are distributed in the following order, unless a partnership agreement provides otherwise: 1. creditors; 2. partner's advances; 3. each partner's capital; 4. remaining surplus to partners.

compare: articles of dissolution, liquidation distribution; see: assets, bankruptcy, partnership

diversification
Risk Management. A risk management technique that can be used to avoid a catastrophic loss, by spreading an organization's risk geographically, by type of risk, or by type of coverage. Diversification makes it less likely that a single event will adversely affect a significant percentage of an organization's operations or business.

see: insurance, retention, risk avoidance, risk transfer

diversity jurisdiction
Law. The constitutional authority of federal courts to hear cases between citizens of different states, between a state and citizens of another state, between different states, or between a U.S. and a foreign citizen. A federal statute requires that the amount in controversy be $50,000 or more.

see: conflict of laws

divided coverage
General. Insurance normally covered by one company, which is instead divided between two or more companies.

compare: burglary divided coverage; see: layering

dividend
Financial Planning. A payment by a corporation to its stockholders of a portion of its net earnings.

see: cumulative dividend, dividend reinvestment plan, ex-dividend date, nimble dividend, record date, stock dividend

Insurer Operations. A percentage of premiums refunded by an insurance company to all or a segment of its participating policyholders.

Life. A part of premium on a participating life insurance policy that is returned to a policyholder after the insurer deducts for benefits, expenses and reserves for future benefit payments.

see: dividend accumulation, dividend addition, divident option, dividend ratio, factoring, participating policy, policy dividend

dividend accumulation
Life. A participating life insurance policy option allowing dividends to be left on deposit with the insurer, to accumulate at an agreed-upon interest rate.

see: dividend, taxation of interest on life insurance dividends

dividend addition
Life. An option allowing the insured to use dividends to purchase additional single premium life insurance.

see: dividend, settlement options

dividend option
Life. Any of the alternative methods by which dividends paid under participating life insurance policies can be used by a policyholder.

see: dividend (*Life*), participating policy, settlement options

dividend ratio
Insurer Operations. A formula used by insurance companies to relate income to policyholder dividends. Frequently, policyholder dividends are included in the expense ratio. *Formula*: policyholder dividends ÷ earned premiums.

see: combined ratio, expense ratio, loss ratio

dividend reinvestment plan
Financial Planning. A plan where the dividends paid on securities are automatically used to purchase additional shares of the same security.

dividend yield
Financial Planning. The year-ahead estimated dividend yield is the estimated total of cash dividends to be declared over the next twelve months per-share, divided by the recent stock price. The trailing dividend yield is the sum of the dividends declared over the last 12 months, divided by the recent stock price.

see: trailing dividend yield, yield

divisible contract clause

Property. A policy provision that a violation of policy conditions at one insured location does not void coverage at other locations.

do not resuscitate order

Health. A written order by a physician that directs emergency services personnel to withhold cardiopulmonary resuscitation from a named patient in the event of cardiac or respiratory arrest. Other medical interventions, such as oxygen, fluids, and alleviation of pain, are not to be withheld.

see: living will

do not solicit list

Insurer Operations.

see: prohibited list

dock receipt

Inland Marine/Ocean Marine. A receipt used by carriers as evidence that merchandise was, in fact, received by the carrier for shipment.

synonym: received for shipment bill of lading; *compare:* delivery receipt; *see:* bill of lading

documentary evidence

Law. Evidence in written form that is allowed to be presented in a legal proceeding.

see: affidavit, demonstrative evidence, deposition, evidence

documentary stamp

Regulation. A revenue stamp for paying tax required by federal or state law—affixed to documents such as deeds, wills, checks—before the documents can be recorded. Federal Revenue Stamps were abolished in 1968.

dollar cost averaging

Financial Planning. An investment strategy where equal amounts are invested in the same stock or group of stocks every week or month over an extended time. Under this concept the cost per unit should always be less than the average unit price in up, down, or fixed markets. Usually, the purchases are set up to operate automatically. For the strategy to be effective, investments must be continued in up and down markets.

synonym: averaging

domestic and agricultural workers exclusion endorsement

Workers' Compensation. An endorsement (NCCI form WC 00 03 15) to a workers' compensation policy that allows an employer to elect not to be responsible for providing workers' compensation benefits for farm and agricultural workers or for domestic and household workers. Some states exempt these workers from coverage on the basis that they are independent contractors.

see: workers' compensation insurance

domestic broker

Agency/International. An insurance brokerage with offices only in its own country which provides service to clients only within that country.

compare: global broker, international broker, multinational broker, transnational broker

domestic carrier

Insurer Operations.

see: domestic insurer

domestic goods in transit

Inland Marine. Domestic shipments exposed to loss while in transit by rail, motor truck, aircraft, or while in the custody of the U.S. Postal Service. (Imports and exports—nondomestic goods—are not within the scope of inland marine insurance.)

see: transit insurance, transportation insurance

domestic insurer

Insurer Operations. An insurer or reinsurer is considered *domestic* in the state (or country) where it is legally incorporated. It is considered a *foreign* insurer in another state in which it does business, and an *alien* insurer in another country.

synonym: domestic carrier; *compare:* alien insurer, assurer, foreign insurer; *see:* domiciled company, domiciliary state, home office

domestic organization

International. A business organization that limits its activities to a single country. It acquires its resources and sells all of its products or services within that country.

compare: international organization, multinational organization

domestic pet insurance

Inland Marine/Personal.

see: pet insurance

domestic worker

Workers' Compensation. A household servant, either full- or part-time.

see: employee, residence employee

domestication agreement

Insurer Operations. An agreement by which an affiliated domestic insurer assumes the assets and liabilities of the U.S. branch of an alien insurer.

see: affiliated insurers, alien insurer, domestic insurer

domicile

Insurer Operations.

see: domiciliary state

domiciled company

Insurer Operations. A company with a legal permanent residence in a particular state or country.

see: domestic insurer, domiciliary state

domiciliary state

Insurer Operations. The state in which an insurer has its permanent legal residence.

synonym: domicile; *compare*: commercial domiciles; *see*: domiciled company

domino theory

Loss Control. An accident causation theory proposed in 1931 by H.W. Heinrich, an industrial engineer, that all industrial accidents represent a series of conditions or events (analogous to dominos standing in a row): ancestry or social environment, the person's faults or personal shortcomings, a negligent act or omission or an unsafe machine or working environment, the accident, and the injury caused by the accident. Heinrich believed it was easiest to remove the unsafe act to prevent an accident.

compare: energy-release theory

donee

Financial Planning. The recipient of a gift.

compare: donor

donor

Financial Planning. A person who gives a gift; one who establishes a trust.

compare: donee; *see*: settlor, trust

door switch

Loss Control.

see: contact switch

door-to-door coverage

Inland Marine/Ocean Marine. Transit insurance that covers a shipment of merchandise from the original point of manufacture to its final destination.

synonym: house-to-house coverage; *see*: transit insurance, warehouse-to-warehouse coverage

dosimeter

Loss Control. An instrument for measuring doses of x-rays or of radioactivity.

double compensation

Workers' Compensation. A statutory provision that awards an illegally employed minor who is injured in a job-related accident twice the usual compensation benefits.

see: child labor, illegal employment, workers' compensation law

double indemnity (DI)

Life. A life insurance policy provision, contained in some policies, under which the face amount payable on death is doubled if the death is the result of an accident.

synonym: accidental death benefit, multiple indemnity

double insurance

Insurer Operations. Duplicated or redundant coverage on the same risk.

compare: dual coverage; *see*: other insurance provision

double protection life insurance

Life. A form of life insurance combining equal amounts of whole life and term insurance, with the term insurance expiring at a stated future date. The limit on the term insurance is either equal to the whole life limit ("double protection") or twice the whole life limit ("triple protection"). These policies are designed for younger insureds who cannot afford high-limit whole life insurance but still want to build some cash value.

compare: split life insurance; *see*: cash surrender value, term life insurance, whole life insurance

double trigger

Insurer Operations. A unique policy form used for large commercial accounts where coverage is not provided until two triggering events occur. The first is a loss occurrence from a covered peril (e.g., earthquake, product liability claim). The second trigger can be another loss occurrence or a stipulated financial criterion, for example, the insured has an earnings increase of less than 10% from the previous year.

dower

Title. The legal right of a widow to the interest in real estate of her deceased husband.

draft

General. A negotiable instrument written by one party, instructing a second party to pay a third party. In insurance, the draft is the written claim instructing the insurer to pay the beneficiary.

compare: cashier's check, certified check; *see*: drawee, drawer

drag strip spectator coverage

Liability.

see: automobile racing spectator coverage

dram shop act

Regulation. A law that holds taverns and bars liable for damage and injuries caused by intoxicated persons who were served intoxicating beverages by the tavern or bar.

synonym: liquor control laws; *see*: dram shop liability insurance, liquor liability law

dram shop liability insurance

Liability. Coverage for claims arising under dram shop laws, which impose liability on owners of taverns or other places where liquor is sold to be drunk on the premises, for third-party injuries caused by an intoxicated patron.

see: liability insurance, liquor liability laws, liquor liability coverage

"D" ratio

Workers' Compensation. A ratio used in calculating a workers' compensation experience rating plan. It is the ratio of primary expected losses (those losses under $2,000 that an employer is expected to control), plus a discounted value of large losses, divided by the total expected losses.

see: experience rating modification factor, experience rating plan

drawee

General. The person on whom a draft is drawn, and who is thereby ordered to pay.

compare: drawer; *see*: draft

drawer

General. The person who initially draws or creates and signs a draft.

compare: drawee; *see*: draft

dread disease insurance

Health/Life.

see: specified disease insurance

drive-away collision

Automobile. An endorsement to the garage policy that provides collision coverage on an auto dealer's vehicles driven or transported more than 50 miles from the point of purchase to their destination. Drive-away collision coverage is excluded from a dealer's garage insurance policy without this endorsement.

see: garage coverage form, limited coverage for customers

drive other car coverage

Automobile. Automobile liability coverage that protects the insured while driving a car not owned by the insured and not named in the policy. It can also be used to cover a business when an employee drives a car for business purposes but which is not owned by the business. (ISO form CA 99 10.)

synonym: broad form drive other car coverage; *compare*: hired autos liability coverage, named non-owner coverage, nonowned automobile liability

drive to or from school

Personal.

see: drive to or from work

drive to or from work

Personal. A personal auto insurance rating classification used when the principal driver uses the insured vehicle only for personal use and to drive between home and work (i.e., the driver does not use the car in business, nor strictly for pleasure). This classification also includes driving to and from school. Usually, the classification is divided between one-way trips of more than or less than 15 miles.

compare: business use, farm use, pleasure use; *see*: principal driver

driver training credit

Personal. A credit applied to the personal automobile insurance premium for insureds who have completed an approved driver education course.

see: good student discount

drop check procedure

Insurer Operations. A claim adjusting procedure where a field adjuster visits a claimant with a check and a release form to provide fast service and to avoid possible litigation.

see: field adjuster, release

drop-down provision

Liability. A provision contained in umbrella liability policies, where the policy will provide primary coverage in the event that the underlying (primary) aggregate limits of liability are exhausted or reduced. This is one of the items that distinguishes an umbrella policy from an excess policy.

see: umbrella liability insurance

drug addiction

Health.

see: substance abuse

druggists' liability coverage

Professional Liability. Professional liability insurance for drug stores, covering bodily injury or property damage arising from the sale of drugs or other products. The drug store owner is covered under this policy, but employed pharmacists must be specifically added.

compare: pharmacists' professional liability insurance

dry chemical fire extinguisher

Loss Control. A device designed primarily for class B and C fires containing dry chemical agents that extinguish fire by a chemical chain reaction. Three types of chemicals are used: sodium bicarbonate, potassium bicarbonate, and ammonium phosphate.

see: class B fire, class C fire

dry chemicals

Loss Control. A combination of fine powders used

in fire extinguishing systems which can be directed at a burning flammable liquid or flood an area (such as a restaurant cooking area) and snuff out a fire by depriving it of oxygen.

see: class A fire, class B fire, class C fire, class D fire, fire extinguishing system

dry pipe automatic sprinkler system

Loss Control. An automatic sprinkler system where all piping contains air under pressure. When a sprinkler head opens, the air is released and water flows into the system and to any open sprinkler heads. This type of system is used in areas where the sprinkler heads and the immediately adjacent piping can be exposed to freezing conditions.

compare: wet pipe automatic sprinkler system; *see*: automatic sprinkler system, dry valve, quick-opening device

dry powder fire extinguisher

Loss Control. An extinguisher designed for use on combustible metal fires (e.g., sodium, titanium, uranium, zirconium, lithium, magnesium, sodium-potassium alloys).

see: class D fire

dry season charge

Property.

see: standing timber insurance

dry valve

Loss Control. An automatic sprinkler valve under air pressure, designed to allow air to escape prior to the release of water. The air prevents freezing and bursting of pipes.

see: dry pipe automatic sprinkler system

dual capacity doctrine

Liability/Workers' Compensation. A legal doctrine that an employer who is normally immune from tort actions by employees because of workers' compensation laws may be held liable for additional damages as a party who has committed a wrongful or negligent act beyond its role as employer. *Example*: An employee of an aerosol shaving cream manufacturer is injured by an exploding can while handling stock. The manufacturer is liable to the employee under workers' compensation laws, but it may also be held responsible for manufacturing a defective can. The employee then may choose to bring a civil suit, where the potential recovery is greater than the statutory remedy of workers' compensation.

see: common law defense, exclusive remedy, tort, workers' compensation law

dual coverage

Liability. Equal liability for a loss that is caused by an occurrence or circumstance that is seemingly covered in one insurance policy and excluded in another but questionable in both. Typically, such a loss involves an automobile and a homeowners or general liability policy. *Example*: An insured has a homeowners policy, which includes general personal liability but excludes liability arising out of the use of an automobile, and he has an auto policy that covers losses arising from the use of a vehicle. The insured shoots at a deer from a moving car and strikes another hunter. The homeowners policy would usually cover this situation but for the auto exclusion; and though the auto policy could be interpreted as providing coverage, this is not a use of a vehicle normally contemplated by auto insurance. Under the dual coverage concept, a court could require both policies to respond.

see: loading or unloading, overinsurance, stacking of limits

dual life stock company

Life. A life insurer formed as a stock company that issues both participating and nonparticipating life insurance policies.

see: nonparticipating life insurance, participating life insurance

dual security

Financial Planning.

see: guaranteed stock

dual valuation clause

Ocean Marine. Hull insurance policies covering older vessels sometimes contain this clause, which provides for a lower valuation for the vessel in the event of a total loss. A higher value applies to all other (i.e., partial loss) claims.

see: hull policy

due-on-sale provision

Financial Planning/Mortgage Insurance. A provision in a mortgage that requires the entire balance to be paid if the property is sold.

compare: assumability; *see*: mortgage

due process of law

Law. The regular, customary, and fair administration of justice; a right guaranteed to people in the United States by the Fifth and Fourteenth Amendments to the Constitution and by state constitutions. Among other requirements, a person may be brought before a court only by regular service of process, the court must have proper grounds for exercising jurisdiction, the court and the trier of fact must be impartial, and parties must be given fair notice and an opportunity to be heard and to defend themselves in an orderly proceeding.

see: burden of proof, civil law (1), criminal law, litigation, process

dunnage

Inland Marine/Loss Control/Ocean Marine.
Loose packing material placed in shipping containers to prevent damage to the items being shipped.

see: container

duplication of benefits

Health. Coverage of an insured under two or more benefit plans. When this happens, benefit payments must be coordinated among the insurers or plan sponsors.

synonym: multiple coverage; *see*: coordination of benefits, nonduplication of benefits

duplication of exposure units

Risk Management. A risk control technique that involves the maintenance of a second set of assets in the form of back-up facilities, spare parts, alternative suppliers, or duplicate records to be used in the event the initial assets are damaged or destroyed.

see: risk control techniques

duration of coverage clause

Property. A builders' risk policy provision that limits the term of coverage. Usually, coverage under the policy terminates when insured property under construction has been accepted by the owner or when the interest of the insured ceases.

compare: decennial liability insurance; *see*: builders' risk insurance

duration of risk

Insurer Operations. The extent, limit, or time specifically stated in a policy for which the risk is to run; the policy period.

see: claims-made trigger, occurrence trigger, policy period

duress

Law. Compulsion, coercion or forcible restraint. An otherwise wrongful act, if done under duress, may be legally excused, and a contract agreed to under duress may be rescinded.

see: affirmative defense, rescission

duties provision

Insurer Operations.

see: evidence and duties provision

duty

Ocean Marine. A tax levied on imported goods.

see: abatement

duty to defend

Liability. A liability policy provision that the insurer has an obligation to defend the insured in a suit brought by a third party. For occurrences covered by the policy, a defense must be provided even if a suit is found to be groundless or false. However, there is no duty to defend a suit if the complaint or petition fails to state facts that potentially bring the case within the coverage of the policy.

see: defense clause, separation of insureds

duty to warn

Liability. An obligation to provide notice of a known hazard to any person who may come into contact with it. A product manufacturer has a duty to warn buyers (by warning labels, special instructions, etc.) if the manufacturer knows of an unsafe condition either inherent in the product or which may arise through foreseeable uses of the product.

see: defective product, degree of care

dwelling, buildings and contents form (DB&C)

Personal. A property insurance form designed for use with a standard fire policy or a commercial property policy to cover private residences and other types of dwelling. It provides, on a limited basis, some of the property coverages included in the homeowners or dwelling policy forms.

compare: dwelling policy, homeowners policy; *see*: homeowners policy—property coverage

dwelling policy

Personal. An insurance policy that covers buildings and the personal property inside. The Insurance Services Office has a basic form, a broad form, and a special form. The principal differences among them are the perils covered. The forms are designed to insure one- to four-family dwellings, whether owner-occupied or tenant-occupied, and can be used to insure mobile homes. Unlike homeowners policies, dwelling policies do not include theft, liability or medical payments coverage, but these coverages can be added by endorsement. The ISO policy forms have a standard format:

Coverage A—Dwelling
Coverage B—Other Structures
Coverage C—Personal Property
Coverage D—Fair Rental Value
Coverage E—Additional Living Expense (except basic form)

compare: homeowners policy; *see*: dwelling policy basic form, dwelling policy broad form, dwelling policy special form

dwelling policy basic form

Personal. A very limited dwelling policy (ISO form DP 00 01) that only covers the perils of fire or lightning and internal explosion and does not include additional living expense coverage, though this can be added by endorsement. The form includes an "other coverages" section that extends coverage to other structures; debris removal; improvements, alterations and additions; world-wide personal property coverage; rental value; reasonable repairs; and fire department service charges.

An extended coverage option adds the perils of windstorm, hail, explosion, riot, civil commotion, aircraft, vehicles, smoke, and volcanic eruption. Another option adds the perils of vandalism and malicious mischief.

compare: dwelling policy broad form, dwelling policy special form; *see*: dwelling policy

dwelling policy broad form

Personal. This dwelling policy (ISO form DP 00 02) is identical to the basic form except it includes coverage E (additional living expense) and the perils available as coverage options under the basic form. In addition, it includes the perils of damage by burglars; falling objects; weight of ice, snow or sleet; accidental discharge or overflow of water or steam; sudden and accidental tearing apart, cracking, burning or bulging; freezing; and sudden and accidental damage from artificially generated electrical current. In addition to the "other coverage" provided in the basic form, it includes coverage for trees, shrubs, and other plants; collapse; and glass or safety glazing material.

compare: dwelling policy basic form, dwelling policy special form; *see*: dwelling policy

dwelling policy special form

Personal. This dwelling policy (ISO form DP 00 03) is identical to the broad form, but it insures the dwelling and other structures on an open-perils basis and covers personal property on the same broad named-perils basis as the broad form.

compare: dwelling policy basic form, dwelling policy broad form; *see*: dwelling policy, open perils

dynamic risk

Risk Management. A risk that arises from the continuous change that exists in the business or economic environment or in technology. Dynamic risk can produce a gain (or savings) as well as a loss (or expenses).

compare: static risk; *see*: risk

dynamo clause

Property.

see: electrical apparatus exclusion

E

early retirement

Employee Benefits. Voluntary termination of employment before the normal retirement date. When an individual elects early retirement, benefits are usually less than those for normal retirement. For purposes of Social Security, early retirement age is 62.

 see: normal retirement age, pension, retirement age, Social Security

earned income

Financial Planning. The money a person or family receives from services performed, including wages, as opposed to returns on capital (such as the sale or rental of property, dividends, or interest). Earned income is required to be reported separately on income tax returns.

 compare: gross income, net income

earned premium

Insurer Operations. The portion of a premium that represents coverage already provided; the portion of premium that belongs to the insurer based on the part of the policy period that has passed. For each day a one-year policy is in force, an insurer earns 1/365th of the annual premium. For an insurer's accounting purposes, earned premium is the total of all premiums written during a period plus the unearned premiums at the beginning of the period, minus the unearned premiums at the end of the period.

 compare: unearned premium; *see*: accounting earned premium, exposure earned premium, premium

earned reinsurance premium

Insurer Operations. The portion of premiums earned on policies issued by a primary (ceding) company which is paid to a reinsurer; part of the reinsurance premium, calculated on a periodic basis and retained by the reinsurer if the coverage is canceled.

 compare: unearned reinsurance premium; *see*: earned premium

earnest money

Financial Planning. A sum given by the buyer when entering into a contract to indicate the intention and ability to carry out the contract. It is often used in the purchase of real estate. If the sale goes through, the earnest money is applied to the purchase price. If the sale is not competed, the earnest money is forfeited unless the binder or offer to purchase expressly provides for a refund.

 see: binder, escrow, mortgage

earning ability

Workers' Compensation.

 see: ability to earn

earnings insurance form

Property. A business interruption form designed for small businesses. It is similar to a gross earnings form, except there is no coinsurance clause, and there is a maximum limit on the amount of loss payment during any 30-day period.

 compare: business income coverage form, gross earnings form, simplified earnings form

earnings per share

Financial Planning. A corporation's net profit, minus preferred stock dividends, divided by common shares outstanding. This figure may be based on actual year-end shares outstanding; on average shares outstanding; on average shares outstanding plus common stock equivalents ("primary earning per share"); or on actual year-end or average shares outstanding plus all shares reserved for conversion of convertible senior securities, and exercise of all warrants and options ("fully diluted earnings per share").

 see: estimated constant dollar earnings per share, price/earnings ratio

earnings retained

Accounting.

 see: retained earnings

earnings yield

Financial Planning. A financial ratio used to evaluate stock. A stock's annual earnings are divided by its current market price.

see: financial ratios, yield

earth movement coverage

Property. A form of earthquake coverage that is extended to include landslide, mudflow, earth sinking, earth rising or shifting, and volcanic eruption.

see: causes of loss—earthquake form, earthquake insurance, volcanic action, volcanic eruption

earth movement exclusion

Property. An exclusion in most property insurance policies for any loss resulting from an earthquake, landslide, mine subsidence, or earth sinking, rising or shifting, and volcanic eruption, explosion or effusion. The exclusion does not apply to sinkhole collapse.

see: collapse coverage, earth movement coverage, earthquake insurance

earthquake

Property. A trembling or shaking of the earth that is volcanic or tectonic (seismic) in origin, often resulting in severe damage.

see: blind thrust fault, earthquake exclusion, earthquake insurance, earthquake shock, epicenter, focus, ground failure, ground motion, liquefaction, Mercalli scale, moment-magnitude scale, off-set ground motion, Richter scale, seismograph, strike-slip fault, thrust fault, volcanic action, volcanic eruption

Ocean Marine. An earthquake under the ocean or the sea is a "peril of the seas" under an ocean marine policy.

Personal. Earthquake coverage for personal property can be added by attaching endorsements to the dwelling policy (ISO form DP 04 69) or to the homeowners policy (ISO form HO 04 54).

see: dwelling policy, homeowners policy

earthquake exclusion

Property. An exclusion in some property insurance policies for any loss resulting from an earthquake or volcanic action. Most policies contain a broader earth movement exclusion, which includes earthquake.

see: earth movement exclusion, earthquake

earthquake inception extension endorsement

Property. A commercial property insurance endorsement (ISO form CP 10 41) designed to fill the gap in coverage that could exist when an older policy is replaced by a newer form that uses the term *earthquake shocks* instead of *earthquakes.* The endorsement covers damage during the policy term from a series of earthquake shocks that began up to 72 hours prior to the policy inception date.

earthquake insurance

Property. Coverage for property damage caused by the perils of earthquake or volcanic eruption. The coverage is limited to direct damage caused by an earthquake and excludes a loss resulting from another peril even if it is triggered by the earthquake, such as a fire, explosion, flood or tidal wave. Any earth tremors or aftershocks following an initial occurrence within a 168-hour period is considered the same event for claims purposes. Most forms provide earthquake coverage as earth movement coverage.

see: earthquake, earthquake exclusion, percentage of value deductible

earthquake shock

Property. The causes of loss—earthquake form (ISO form CP 10 40) refers to *earthquake shocks,* which is not defined in the form. This term is used in an attempt to avoid problems of multiple claims that can occur with earthquake losses. Major earthquakes usually involve an initial violent shake followed by a series of aftershocks. Most earthquake or earth movement policies consider the initial shock and aftershocks within a 168-hour period to be the same earthquake.

see: earthquake

earthquake sprinkler leakage

Property. A peril that can be insured under a property insurance form. An endorsement (ISO form CP 10 39) that adds coverage for direct damage to the building or contents caused by the leakage or discharge of water or other substances from an automatic sprinkler system due to earthquake or volcanic action.

see: discharge of any substance, sprinkler leakage insurance

easement

Title. An irrevocable right given by a landowner to others for the limited use of land.

compare: encroachment; *see:* dedicate

Eastern Claims Conference (ECC)

Organizations. Members: Disability examiners, including life, health and group claims personnel of insurance companies. *Objectives:* Provides education and training to examiners, managers and officers who review medical and disability claims. *Founded:* 1977. *Headquarters:* New York, NY.

easy read
Insurer Operations. A term for simplified language policies, which are not written in the traditional legal contract form, but use commonly understood words.

see: Flesch readability test, plain language laws, policy

economic loss
General. The total monetary cost, whether insured or not, of an injury or wrong, including continuing or future expenses to be incurred because of the injury. Economic loss includes costs such as property damage, medical and legal fees, funeral expenses, and actual and reasonably expected lost wages or profits.

compare: noneconomic loss; *see*: damages

economic performance
Accounting. Under the Tax Reform Act of 1994, a liability loss cannot be deducted for tax purposes until the taxpayer actually repairs or replaces the property or service required as a result of the loss, or in the event of a workers' compensation or employee benefit claim, until payment is actually made. This eliminates any deduction for self-insured loss reserves because of the requirement of actual payment.

see: Tax Reform Act of 1994

economic perils
Risk Management. One of three broad categories of perils (with *human* and *natural* perils), concerning the production, distribution, and consumption of goods and services that can cause a loss, such as currency fluctuations, recession or depression, expropriation, inflation, obsolescence, financial market decline, strike, technological advances or war.

compare: human perils, natural perils; *see*: exchange stabilization, financial risk management, peril

Economic Recovery Tax Act
Regulation. Federal legislation adopted in 1981 that establishes rules and procedures for employee stock options, deductible voluntary employee contributions, tax credit employee stock ownership plans, withdrawal from savings or thrift plans, and the availability and use of individual retirement accounts and Keogh plans.

see: employee stock ownership plan, individual retirement account, savings plan

economic value
Property. Valuation of income-producing property based on its potential earnings over a specified time instead of replacement or depreciated value. Occasionally, a risk is underwritten on the basis of economic value.

compare: actual cash value, depreciated value, functional replacement cost, going concern value, market value, replacement cost, reproduction cost

economic value of an individual life
Liability/Life.
see: human life value

educational fund
Life. A life insurance policy that is designed to fund a child's education if the insured (the family's provider) dies.

compare: emergency fund

educators' professional liability insurance
Professional Liability. Professional liability insurance for a school district from suits brought against the school board members, faculty, staff, student teachers, and volunteers for their negligent acts or omissions. Coverage is usually included for claims alleging bodily injury due to corporal punishment.

see: professional liability insurance

effective date
Insurer Operations. The date on which coverage under an insurance policy or bond begins.

see: date of issue, expiration date, policy period

effective retention
Risk Management. A self-insured retention amount used in loss forecasting that has been adjusted for the effect of loss development and trends.

see: loss development, self-insured retention, trend analysis

efficacy coverage
Financial Guaranty. A form of financial guaranty insurance for large industrial construction projects. Coverage guarantees that an installation (e.g., chemical plant, manufacturing facility) will perform efficiently (as represented or warranted). Coverage usually guarantees the loans used to finance the project, the repayment of which are contingent on the project meeting certain minimum production requirements.

synonym: inefficacy coverage; *see*: product warranty inefficacy insurance

efficiency of a vessel
Ocean Marine. An ocean marine policy provision that pays for repairing damage caused by an insured peril.

ejectment bond
Surety. A bond that may be required of a plaintiff (property owner, landlord) before a law enforcement agency will dispossess a person of property they do not want to surrender. The plaintiff in the action must furnish the agency with the bond to protect them against a suit filed by the defendant in

the event of wrongful dispossession.

see: dispossess

election to avoid a policy

Insurer Operations. An insurer's right to not fulfill a policy's obligations if the insured misrepresents or conceals certain facts or activities. The right must be exercised with reasonable promptness, and the insurer cannot remain silent, or the right to avoid the policy will be lost (estopped).

see: concealment, estoppel, misrepresentation, void

elective benefits

Health. An option allowing an insured under a disability policy to receive a lump sum benefit payment for certain injuries (e.g., fractures, dislocations) rather than receiving periodic payments.

synonym: optional benefits; *see*: disability income insurance

elective compensation law

Workers' Compensation. The states of New Jersey, South Carolina, and Texas allow an employer to opt out of the workers' compensation system in their state. An injured employee of an employer who rejects the statute (a *nonsubscriber*) must pursue a settlement or bring suit according to tort law. An employer who elects not to participate in the workers' compensation system is not permitted to offer the common law defenses of contributory negligence of the employee, negligence of a fellow servant, or assumption of risk.

compare: compulsory compensation law; *see*: assumption of risk, common law defense, contributory negligence, fellow servant rule, tort

elective surgery

Health. A surgical procedure undertaken to treat or correct a condition that is not life-threatening or that does not pose an immediate risk of serious disability; a procedure that may be scheduled at the patient's or surgeon's convenience without jeopardizing the patient's life or causing a serious bodily impairment. Elective surgery may be necessary for a patient to fully recover from an injury, illness or disability, but it is not required as an emergency procedure.

compare: emergency medical services; *see*: medically necessary

electrical apparatus exclusion

Property. A property policy provision that excludes coverage for loss or damage caused by artificially generated electric current, including electric arcing that disturbs electrical devices, appliances or wires. However, if fire results, coverage is provided for the resulting fire damage.

synonym: dynamo clause, electrical exemption clause; *see*: electrical disturbance coverage

electrical disturbance coverage

Property. Coverage designed to delete the apparatus exclusion in fire insurance policies.

see: electrical apparatus exclusion

electrical exemption clause

Property.

see: electrical apparatus exclusion

electrical grounding

Loss Control. An electrical connection between a conductive body and the earth, which eliminates any difference in potential between the object and the ground. A proper electrical ground will discharge a charged conductive body.

see: bonding, ground fault circuit interrupter

electrical objects

Property. One of the four boiler and machinery object classifications used to describe the machinery or equipment to be covered under a policy. This classification (object definitions no. 3 or ISO form BM 00 28) includes coverage for rotating electrical machines, transformers, and induction feeder regulators; miscellaneous electrical equipment; and solid state rectifier units.

see: object

electronic and computer crime coverage

Crime. Coverage designed to complement insurance available under a banker's blanket bond. Coverage is for fraudulent input of electronic data or computer instructions to the insured's computer, by unauthorized access to a terminal or a bank's communications lines, or by the fraudulent preparation of tapes or computer programs.

see: banker's blanket bond, computer fraud, computer fraud coverage form

electronic apparatus coverage

Personal.

see: electronic equipment coverage

electronic claim

Insurer Operations. An insurance claim that is maintained as data in a computer or on an electronic media storage device and can only be retrieved by use of a computer or printer.

see: claim, quill pen law

electronic equipment coverage

Personal. The standard homeowners policy provides coverage for electronic equipment, including accessories or antennas, tapes, wires, records, discs or other media for use with any electronic apparatus. The homeowners form often uses the term *electronic apparatus.*

Equipment that is permanently installed in an automobile can be covered for direct and accidental loss by an endorsement (ISO form PP 03 13) to the personal auto policy.

synonym: electronic apparatus coverage; *see*: electronic equipment—special limit, homeowners policy, personal auto policy

electronic equipment—special limit

Personal. The ISO homeowners policy coverage section C (personal property) has a "special limit of liability" provision that applies to electronic equipment that can be operated from a motor vehicle's electrical power system or operated independently from batteries or standard electrical outlets (e.g., portable tape decks, cellular telephones). Coverage is limited to $1,000 while equipment in or upon a motor vehicle is away from the insured residence, or if it is used for business purposes. This limitation does not apply to nonbusiness electronic equipment designed for use in a residence or that operates strictly by batteries.

see: business personal property—special limit, homeowners policy—special limits of liability, special computer coverage

electronic funds transfer plan

General.

see: preauthorized check plan

electronic media and records endorsement

Property. A commercial property coverage endorsement (ISO form CP 15 29) that can either extend the business income coverage limitation of 60 days for damaged computer software, or delete the limitation altogether.

see: electronic media and records limitation

electronic media and records limitation

Property. A limitation on business income coverage to 60 days after damaged computer software or electronic media has been repaired or replaced.

see: electronic media and records endorsement

electronic rate manual

Insurer Operations. A rate manual maintained as electronic data or on an electronic media storage device (CD-ROM, computer disk or tape).

see: rate manual

electrostatic detector

Loss Control.

see: proximity detector

electrostatic discharge

Loss Control. An electrical charge generated by the friction of two dissimilar bodies, either solids or liquids. It has the potential to ignite combustible dusts or vapors and cause an explosion, or it can damage electronic computer components while they are being assembled or repaired.

synonym: static electricity

electrostatic precipitator

Loss Control. Equipment that removes dust or fume particles from the air. An electrostatic precipitator ionizes the particles and collects them on negatively-charged plates.

elevator insurance

Liability.

see: elevator liability insurance

elevator liability insurance

Liability. An old form of liability insurance that was designed specifically for elevators, escalators or other hoisting devices. It provided coverage for claims brought because of bodily injury or property damage caused by the device, as well as damage to the device itself. In modern times, losses have been infrequent and the commercial general liability policy does not address (exclude) this exposure.

synonym: elevator insurance; *see*: commercial general liability policy

eligibility period

Employee Benefits. A period of time (usually the first 30 days of employment) during which an employee may elect to participate in an employee benefit plan without proving insurability (by taking a physical examination).

see: employee benefit plan

eligibility requirements

Employee Benefits. Conditions such as a minimum employment period that employees must meet to qualify for benefits.

elimination period

Health.

see: waiting period

embargo

Ocean Marine. A government order prohibiting the departure of ships or the shipment of goods from some or all of the ports under its authority.

see: demurrage

embezzlement

Crime/Surety. Theft or conversion to personal use of money or property lawfully in possession or custody of a person holding a position of trust (e.g., an employee, agent or trustee of the rightful owner).

see: conversion (*Law*), defalcation, theft

emergency

Risk Management. An urgent situation with the potential to adversely affect the operations of an organization. Emergencies include war, economic depression, major earthquakes, hurricanes, etc.

see: disaster plan, emergency response plan

Health.

see: emergency medical services

emergency exposure limit (EEL)

Loss Control. The maximum period of time an individual can be exposed to a toxic agent during an emergency situation and still be physically safe.

emergency fund

Life. A life insurance policy with a small face amount specifically maintained to cover emergency expenses after the death of the principal breadwinner in a family.

compare: educational fund; *see*: readjustment income

emergency impairment

Loss Control. All or a portion of an automatic sprinkler system that is out of service due to an unexpected occurrence, such as a ruptured pipe, opened sprinkler head, or interruption of the. water supply.

compare: preplanned impairment

emergency medical services

Health. Services medically required to be performed without delay; immediate diagnosis and treatment of a person suffering an injury or illness of a sudden, acute nature. In addition to treatment, such services include triage and emergency transportation by ambulance.

compare: elective surgery; *see*: in-area emergency services, medical emergency, triage

emergency medical technicians' error and omissions insurance (EMT E&O)

Professional Liability. Professional liability coverage for emergency medical technicians, such as fire departments, ambulance services, first aid teams, and rescue squads, that protects them individually and as a group. It covers claims for personal injury from negligence in rendering professional services. Coverage is usually written on a claims-made basis.

see: professional liability insurance

Emergency National Flood Insurance Program

Property. One of two National Flood Insurance Programs available to communities. This one provides coverage until the requirements for the Regular National Flood Insurance Program are met. Amounts of coverage available under this program are: for single family dwellings, $35,000 on the structure and $10,000 on contents; for small businesses, $100,000 on the structure and $100,000 on contents.

compare: Regular National Flood Insurance Program; *see*: National Flood Insurance Program

Emergency Planning and Community Right-to-Know Act

Regulation. Federal legislation of 1986 (U.S. Code

Title 42, Chapter 116) that expands the Superfund Amendments and Reauthorization Act. It requires facilities that produce, use or store hazardous substances to prepare emergency response plans and submit safety data to state and local emergency response agencies. It also provides procedures for residents and governments to obtain information about chemical hazards in their communities. It encourages emergency planning efforts and includes specific programs for local emergency response planning.

see: Environmental Protection Agency, Resource Conservation and Recovery Act, Superfund Amendments and Reauthorization Act

emergency response plan (ERP)

Risk Management. A written statement of procedures by an organization, approved by its management, that contains information and prescribes appropriate actions in response to emergencies.

see: disaster plan, emergency

emergency rules and regulations

Regulation. Administrative rules or regulations adopted without prior notice and hearing, or after only an abbreviated notice period and cursory hearing.

see: administrative procedure

emergency service organization liability

Liability. Liability coverage for volunteer fire departments and other emergency service organizations that incorporates professional and general liability coverages.

eminent domain

Law. The power of a government to take private land for public use without the owner's consent, requiring that the owner be fairly compensated.

compare: dedicate; *see*: confiscation, inverse condemnation

emotional distress

Law.

see: mental distress

empirical rate calculation

Insurer Operations. A judgment-based or experience-based rate loading that is added to the pure loss cost for expected increases in the number and sizes of losses, losses incurred but not reported, inflation, expenses, profits and contingencies.

see: incurred but not reported, pure loss cost, rate making

employed counsel professional liability insurance

Professional Liability. Insurance for in-house legal counsel by organizations other than law firms, covering claims for losses caused by legal services rendered on behalf of their employers and extended to cover legal services performed outside the scope of their employment. Coverage is usually written on a claims-made basis.

see: attorneys' professional liability insurance

employee

Liability/Workers' Compensation. An individual who performs services for another under an expressed or implied contract, for wages or other valuable consideration, and who acts under the direction of that party.

compare: employer, independent contractor; *see*: arising out of and in the course of employment, domestic worker, leased employee, master-servant rule, respondeat superior

Crime. Employee dishonesty coverage defines an employee as a person in the regular service of the insured in the ordinary course of the insured's business whom the insured compensates by salary, wages or commissions and has the right to direct in the performance of such service. Coverage is usually extended to any uncompensated officer of the insured, any former employee for a period of 30 days following termination of service, any person assigned to perform employee duties within the insured's premises by a temporary personnel agency, and any volunteer worker who may have custody of property belonging to the insured.

see: employee dishonesty coverage form

employee benefit

Employee Benefits. An advantage or thing of value in addition to monetary compensation that an employee receives or is entitled to because of employment.

synonym: fringe benefit; *see*: employee benefit plan

employee benefit plan

Employee Benefits. A plan created or maintained by an employer or employee organization, providing benefits to employees. The two main types are employee pension plans (for retirement benefits) and employee welfare plans (for benefits such as life insurance, health and dental insurance, and disability income insurance). A plan's cost can be completely paid by the employer or be shared by the employer and employees. A plan can also provide advantages or benefits to employees whether or not they are insured, including sick leave, disability, profit sharing or a stock purchase program.

see: cafeteria benefit plan, defined benefit plan, defined contribution plan, dental benefit plan, employee benefits manager, employee contributions, Employee Retirement Income Security Act, flexible benefit plan, flexible spending account, Internal Revenue Code § 401(k), medical savings account, money purchase plan, profit-sharing plan, stock purchase plan, target benefit plan, Welfare and Pension Plans Disclosure Act

employee benefit plan liability insurance

Professional Liability/Employee Benefits. Insurance coverage for employers against any claims by employees or former employees caused by a negligent act, error or omission in the administration of the insured's employee benefit programs. This coverage can be endorsed to a general liability policy, written as a separate policy, or included in a financial liability policy. It is usually written on a claims-made basis.

see: fiduciary liability insurance

Employee Benefit Research Institute (EBRI)

Organizations. Members: Any individual or organization with an interest in employee benefit plans. *Objectives*: Promotes development of effective and responsible public policy through research, publications, educational programs and seminars on employee benefits. *Founded*: 1978. *Headquarters*: Baltimore, MD.

employee benefits manager

Employee Benefits. The person responsible for administering pension and employee welfare programs (life, accident and sickness, dental, etc.). This individual usually is part of a firm's human resources department.

compare: human resources manager; *see*: administrative services only, third-party administrator

employee contributions

Employee Benefits. Payments made by an employee to an employee benefit plan, either to obtain coverage under contributory plans, or on a voluntary basis under a noncontributory plan to increase benefits.

see: employee benefit plan

employee dishonesty coverage form

Crime. A crime coverage form (ISO form CR 00 01 or CR 00 02) that provides coverage for loss of, and loss from damage to, money, securities and property other than money and securities caused directly by employee dishonesty.

synonym: crime coverage form A; *see*: blanket employee dishonesty coverage form, crime coverages, money, property other than money and securities, excess coverage for specified employees or positions, public employee dishonesty coverage form (per employee), trading loss exclusion form, warehouse receipts losses exclusion form, welfare and pension plan ERISA compliance (scheduled) coverage form

employee leasing

Workers' Compensation. An arrangement whereby an employment service company provides full-time employees to other employers for a fee. Some leasing companies will assume or hire the employees of an existing organization, and lease them back to that organization. The employee leasing firm handles payroll and tax reports and obtains workers' compensation and employee benefit coverages for the leased employees. Such arrangements have been entered into by some employers to avoid application of a high workers' compensation experience modification factor. Rating bureaus have, in turn, adopted rules designed to discourage this practice.

see: borrowed employee, employee, leased employee

employee leasing client endorsement

Workers' Compensation. A workers' compensation policy endorsement (NCCI form WC 00 03 19) that specifies that a client of a long-term labor contractor covered by the policy must provide the following information to the insurer within 30 days, or coverage will lapse: the effective date of contract and term, client's federal identification number, client's name, client's address, number of workers leased, description of duties and work location.

see: labor contractor endorsement, leased employee, multiple coordinated policy endorsement

employee leasing client exclusion endorsement

Workers' Compensation. A workers' compensation policy endorsement (NCCI form WC 00 03 22) that covers only the direct (not leased) workers of a labor contractor's client. The leased employees are covered by the labor contractor's workers' compensation policy.

see: leased employee

Employee Retirement Income Security Act (ERISA)

Employee Benefits/Regulation. Federal legislation (U.S. Code Title 29, Chapter 18, associated Internal Revenue Code and miscellaneous provisions) adopted in 1974 that preempts state regulation of workers' medical and pension benefits. It imposes a fiduciary responsibility on persons who administer, supervise and manage private pension plans. It regulates plan funding, participation, vesting, termination, disclosure and federal tax treatment. Under ERISA, an insurance program has been established to guarantee that employees receive their pension benefits in the event that a pension plan is terminated.

see: employee benefit plan, Pension Benefit Guaranty Corporation, self-administered plan

employee stock ownership plan (ESOP)

Employee Benefits. A form of employee benefit plan, where stock of a corporation is distributed to employees. Usually the distribution is based on a formula tied to wages and is not dependent on the corporation's profitability. It can be a qualified stock bonus plan or a qualified stock bonus and money purchase plan. Such plans are often used as a financing method for a corporation where funds are loaned to the ESOP, which are used to buy corporate treasury shares thereby increasing the corporation's capital. The stock is pledged to support the loan, and a corporate guarantee is given for its repayment. Tax benefits accrue to both the corporation and the employees under this plan.

see: deferred stock grant, employee benefit plan, profit-sharing plan

employer

Liability/Workers' Compensation. An individual, firm, partnership, association, corporation, legal representative of a deceased employer, or the receiver or trustee of a person, partnership, association, or corporation who uses or engages the services of another under a contract for hire.

compare: employee, independent contractor; *see*: respondeat superior

employer credits

Employee Benefits. Credits that apply against future contributions required under an employer's accounting and administration of a pension plan. These credits accumulate when an employee leaves prior to being fully vested or works beyond the normal retirement age. Exceptions to this requirement arise in those circumstances where the IRS requires "cash basis" accounting.

employer group life insurance

Life. Group life insurance issued to an employer on the lives of employees for the benefit of persons other than the employer.

see: group life insurance

employer mandate

Health. A legal requirement of employers to provide basic health benefits for their employees, either by directly purchasing or self-funding a health benefit plan or by paying into a government-administered purchasing pool that funds coverage. Also called *play or pay.*

synonym: play or pay; *compare*: mandated benefits; *see*: basic benefits (2), compulsory insurance, health benefit plan

employer's first injury report

Workers' Compensation. A report filed by an employer with the workers' compensation insurer and appropriate state agency immediately upon receiving knowledge from any source that an employee has been injured on the job.

synonym: employer's first report

employer's first report

Workers' Compensation.

see: employer's first injury report

Employers Council on Flexible Compensation (ECFC)

Organizations. Members: Employers currently using or considering a flexible compensation plan. *Objectives*: Promotes and improves flexible compensation plans. *Founded*: 1981. *Headquarters*: Washington, D.C.

employers' liability insurance

Liability/Workers' Compensation. Insurance that covers an employer's liability for bodily injury to employees occurring within the scope of their employment when that liability is not covered by workers' compensation. Primary coverage is provided by Part II (before 1986, Section B) of a workers' compensation policy, usually for a limit of $1 million. Self-insured employers are normally covered by an endorsement to their general liability policy. Excess coverage can be provided under most umbrella and excess liability policies. Employers' liability coverage can be added to a workers' compensation policy issued for specific states to provide coverage in additional states, including monopolistic states, by endorsement (NCCI form WC 00 03 03B).

synonym: coverage B; *see*: monopolistic state fund, workers' compensation insurance

employers' mutual liability insurance association

Insurer Operations. Any corporation, association or other entity formed by employers to mutually insure against employers' liability claims.

see: employers' liability insurance

employers' nonownership liability

Automobile.

see: nonowned automobile liability

employment agencies' errors and omissions insurance

Professional Liability. Insurance for firms that act as consultants to employers or individuals in filling job positions on a permanent basis. Coverage is provided for errors and omissions in representing an individual's qualifications, for discrimination, and for defamation of character. Coverage is usually written on a claims-made basis.

see: error and omissions insurance, temporary employment agencies' errors and omissions insurance

employment practices liability insurance (EPLI)

Professional Liability. Professional liability insurance for employers that covers wrongful termination, discrimination, or sexual harassment toward the insured's employees or former employees. Many policies include coverage for claims by applicants for employment. Some policies provide very specific coverage, such as for claims brought under the Americans with Disabilities Act or the Civil Rights Act. Before the late 1980s, some protection for wrongful or discriminatory employment practices was provided under the general liability policy or employers' liability coverage, but subsequent exclusions under these policies have virtually eliminated the coverage. Generally, it is provided by a separate policy, but coverage can be endorsed to a business liability policy or a directors' and officers' liability policy. Coverage is written on a claims-made basis.

see: defamation of character, directors' and officers' liability insurance, employers' liability insurance, employment-related practices exclusion, sexual harassment defense coverage, wrongful discharge or discrimination legal expense insurance

employment-related practices exclusion

Liability. An exclusion in most general liability policies issued after the late 1980s by endorsement (ISO form CG 21 47) or incorporated into the policy form. The exclusion applies to the following employment-related claims: refusal to employ, wrongful termination, demotion, reassignment, disciplinary action, performance evaluation, coercion, harassment, humiliation, defamation, and discrimination.

see: defamation of character, discrimination, employment practices liability insurance

enact

Regulation. To develop and establish new laws; to pass through legislative and executive action.

compare: promulgate

encroachment

Title. An obstruction, building, or part of a building that intrudes beyond a legal boundary onto neighboring land, or a building extending beyond the building line.

compare: easement; *see*: building line

encumbrance

Title. A legal term for a documented claim against property, such as a mortgage.

see: lien, mortgage

Endangered Species Act

Regulation. Federal legislation (U.S. Code Title 16, Chapters 5A and 35 and miscellaneous provisions) enacted in 1973 that prescribes criteria for declaring a species endangered. It is designed to protect animals, birds, fish, and plants that are threatened with extinction by prohibiting the import, export, taking or trading of any endangered species, including hunting, capturing, or collecting named animals and plants and destroying habitat required for their continued survival.

see: Marine Mammal Protection Act

endemic disease coverage

International/Workers' Compensation. Coverage for a disease that is native to a particular people or country. This is of concern to organizations whose employees often travel abroad. Because a disease may be rare or unknown in the home country, the cost of medical treatment can be extremely expensive. Coverage can be included under a workers' compensation policy, or special health insurance coverage can be purchased.

compare: specified disease insurance; *see*: foreign voluntary workers' compensation coverage, repatriation coverage

endorsement

Insurer Operations. A written amendment to a policy that is part of the insurance agreement. In case of conflicting provisions, an endorsement supersedes the main part of the policy. If two endorsements contradict each other, the one with the latest date prevails.

compare: rider; *see*: attachment, date of issue, effective date, insurance contract, interline endorsement

endorsement in blank

Inland Marine/Ocean Marine. The process whereby an insured may assign his or her rights to insurance on a special cargo policy for an order bill of lading by endorsing the reverse side of a certificate issued by the insurer to provide the evidence of insurance.

see: bill of lading, open cargo policy, order bill of lading

endothermic process

Loss Control. A process in which heat is absorbed.
compare: exothermic process

endowment policy

Life. A form of life insurance that pays the insured the face value on the maturity date stated in the contract. If the insured dies before the maturity date, a beneficiary receives the policy's face value.

compare: term life insurance, whole life insurance; *see*: retirement income endowment policy

enemy alien insurer

Regulation. An insurer domiciled in a country at war with the insured's nation, or an individual residing in a country at war with the insurer's country of domicile. It is against public policy for insurance to be transacted with enemy aliens in time of war.

see: alien insurer

enemy goods

Ocean Marine. Items of cargo carried on a vessel

that are shipped from or to an opponent in war. A provision of the 1856 Treaty of Paris states that cargo, excluding contraband of war, is free of capture when it is carried on a neutral ship. Contraband of war (weapons, ammunition, etc.) may be seized, while other enemy goods may not.

see: free of capture and seizure

enemy property insurance

Ocean Marine. Property insurance for goods covered by a license granted by the insurer's country to an enemy for trading goods.

energy-release theory

Loss Control. An early loss control theory developed by Dr. William Haddon, Jr. It holds that accidents are caused by the transfer of energy with sufficient force to cause bodily injury or property damage, and if this transfer of energy can be interrupted or suppressed, the chain of events leading to the accident will be broken.

compare: domino theory

engineering approach

Loss Control. A loss control approach that concentrates on the physical characteristics of the risk to reduce accidents and injuries. The approach emphasizes the use of safeguards on equipment, air bags in autos, etc.

see: loss control

engineers' professional liability insurance

Professional Liability. Coverage for an individual engineer or an engineering firm for claims arising from the performance of professional services, including negligence, errors and omissions. Coverage is usually written on a claims-made basis.

see: professional liability insurance

English loss of profits form

International.

see: British business interruption insurance

enjoin

Law. To issue an order of injunction.

see: injunction

Enrolled Actuary (EA)

Organizations. An individual who is enrolled with the federal Joint Board for the Enrollment of Actuaries.

enrollment card

Employee Benefits. An application on a card that an employee completes to enroll in an employee benefit plan.

see: employee benefit plan

entertainment insurance

Liability. Any insurance that protects against loss of revenues suffered by promoters, film companies, concert facilities, distributors, etc., resulting from the interruption, cancellation or postponement of theatrical, musical, television, motion picture or other entertainment or sports productions.

see: hole-in-one coverage, prize indemnification insurance, television closed circuit breakdown insurance

entire contract provision

Insurer Operations. A policy provision that the written policy contains all of the contractual agreements or understandings between the insured and insurer. It eliminates the possibility of either party using outside evidence to modify the contract, such as an alleged oral agreement. The policy terms can be amended or waived only by an endorsement issued by the insurer.

see: entire contract statute

entire contract statute

Regulation. A statute enacted in many states that makes the written insurance policy and its application the entire contract between the parties. It precludes any oral statement from being used as a defense by the insurer against a claim.

see: bad faith, entire contract clause, unfair claims practice

entity coverage

Professional Liability. An addition to some directors' and officers' liability policies (often added for nonprofit organizations' policies) that expands the definition of "insured" to include the organization or business entity whose directors and officers are insured by the policy. This is important because most lawsuits filed against directors and officers also name the organization itself as a codefendant.

see: allocation of defense costs, directors' and officers' liability insurance

environmental audit

Loss Control. An independent assessment of an organization's compliance with environmental regulations, or an evaluation of an organization's environmental compliance polices, practices, and controls. It includes a review of the organization's specific sites and may also include the operations of suppliers, vendors and customers. The audit also reviews pollution prevention programs and employee training.

compare: environmental site assessment; *see*: pollution prevention program

environmental consultants' errors and omissions insurance

Professional Liability. Professional liability insurance for environmental consultants for errors and omissions in risk assessment, remedial action plan design, and lab testing. Coverage is written on a claims-made basis.

see: errors and omissions insurance

environmental directors' and officers' liability insurance

Professional Liability. A professional liability policy that covers an organization's directors and officers for personal liability for environmental mismanagement. Coverage is usually written by a pollution insurance underwriter.

see: directors' and officers' liability insurance

environmental engineers' errors and omissions insurance

Professional Liability. Professional liability overage for environmental engineers for errors and omissions in risk assessment, remedial action plan design, and lab testing. Coverage is written on a claims-made basis.

see: errors and omissions insurance

environmental impairment liability insurance

Liability.

see: pollution insurance

Environmental Protection Agency (EPA)

Regulation. A federal agency established by Presidential Executive Order in 1970 that brought together fifteen governmental agencies that were involved with pollution control. It has authority to issue orders directing an individual, business, or other entity to take corrective action or refrain from an activity. An order describes the violations and actions to be taken and can be enforced in court.

see: Clean Air Act, Comprehensive Environmental Response Compensation and Liability Act, Emergency Planning and Community Right-to-Know Act, Federal Insecticide Fungicide and Rodenticide Act, Federal Water Pollution Control Act, National Environmental Policy Act, Resource Conservation and Recovery Act, Safe Drinking Water Act, Toxic Substances Control Act

environmental site assessment

Loss Control. An audit or assessment based upon standards established by the American Society for Testing and Materials (ASTM) to identify hazardous wastes at a specific site. Phase I, the most common type of assessment, is a qualitative review of the site history to determine obvious, potential or suspected environmental impact. This may be followed by Phase II, a quantitative assessment to determine if contamination has actually occurred and to establish the nature and extent of contamination. Phase III implements corrective actions. ASTM has not completed its guidelines for Phases II and III.

compare: environmental audit; *see*: Resource Compensation and Recovery Act

environmental title insurance

Title. A form of title insurance underwritten by pollution liability insurance underwriters that is similar to traditional title insurance in that it protects the purchaser or lienholder for an amount equal to the amount financed against any environmental liabilities that arise from past contamination that was undiscovered during an environmental site assessment.

see: pollution insurance, site assessment, title insurance

epicenter

Loss Control/Property. In an earthquake, the point on the earth's surface directly above the subsurface focus (or the point where slippage begins).

compare: focus; *see*: earthquake

equipment

Property. For insurance purposes, a broad term applying to mobile property, including anything used to equip a person, organization or thing that is not a building or machinery.

compare: machinery; *see*: equipment floater

equipment dealers floater

Inland Marine. An inland marine policy (ISO form CM 00 22) that provides coverage for dealers in agriculture implements and contractors' equipment, such as bulldozers, reapers, harvesters, plows, tractors, air compressors and road scrapers. Coverage is usually written on an open perils basis and includes the dealer's stock in trade, and similar property of others in the care, custody or control of the dealer.

see: floater policy, inland marine insurance

equipment floater

Inland Marine. A broad term applied to any of a number of inland marine forms for mobile property, including coverage forms for contractors' equipment, equipment dealers, film, floor plans, jewelers, and physicians' and surgeons' equipment.

see: bicycle floater, camera floater, contractors' equipment floater, equipment dealers floater, fine arts floater, floater policy, fur floater, installation floater, jewelry floater, livestock floater, neon sign floater, pattern and die floater, personal articles floater, personal property floater, physicians' and surgeons' equipment floater, salesperson's samples floater, unscheduled property floater, wedding presents floater

equipment value insurance

Financial Guaranty. A policy covering leased equipment, guaranteeing its value on a specific date (usually, but not necessarily, the lease's termination date). If the equipment's fair market value is less than the value stated in the policy on the agreed date, the insurer would pay the difference.

see: residual value, residual value insurance

equitable title

Title. A title or ownership rights resulting from considerations of equity (fairness) or contract, as opposed to formal legal title. Under a trust, the beneficiaries have equitable title while the trustee has legal title. Equitable title is also said to belong to a purchaser of real property from the time the sales contract is signed and earnest money paid until the closing.

see: escrow, inter vivos trust, title

equity

Insurer Operations. Fairness; equal treatment. State laws require insurance rates not to discriminate among consumers except according to valid underwriting criteria. Equity is accomplished by setting premium rates according to the expected losses for a group of similar insureds. Thus, all insureds with the same loss characteristics are classified together for underwriting and rating purposes.

see: discrimination, rate making

Financial Planning. The ownership interest of shareholders in a corporation, represented by stock, as opposed to an organization's debt, represented by bonds, loan notes, debentures, and commercial paper; a firm's total capital stock. Shareholders (equity interests) are repaid out of profits, which are largely unpredictable, while lenders and bondholders (debt interests) are repaid in the form of stated interest rates or bond redemption values.

compare: debt security; *see*: capital stock, common equity, owner's equity

Law.

see: court of equity

equity capitalization rate

Financial Planning.

see: cash-on-cash return

equity dividend rate

Financial Planning.

see: cash-on-cash return

equity fund

Financial Planning. A mutual fund that invests in stocks that pay high dividends, such as those of large, well established corporations.

compare: growth fund; *see*: mutual fund

equity variable annuity plan

Life. A variable annuity where the plan's benefit units or accumulation units are tied to the value of a specific portfolio of stocks or bonds.

see: accumulation, annuity, variable annuity

ergonomics

Loss Control. The application of knowledge regarding human abilities and behavior to the design of tools, machines, systems, and working environments to ensure safety, comfort, and efficiency.

see: ergonomics disorder

ergonomics disorder

Workers' Compensation. A work-related illness or injury caused by machine, equipment, or a work station poorly suited to a person's job duties.

see: cumulative trauma, ergonomics, repetitive motion injury

ERISA Industry Committee (ERIC)

Organizations. Members: Corporations that sponsor major employee pension and benefit plans. *Objectives*: Represents employers regarding policy, legislation, judicial, and regulatory matters involving the administration of private pension and benefit plans. *Founded*: 1977. *Headquarters*: Washington, D.C.

see: Employee Retirement Income Security Act

erosion

Property. 1. A gradual wearing or carrying away of soil by abrasion, disintegration, or decomposition.
2. The deterioration or destruction of property caused by mechanical means, as opposed to *corrosion*, which is caused by chemical or electrochemical action.

compare: corrosion

errors and omissions clause

Reinsurance. A provision included in some obligatory treaty reinsurance contracts that if an error or omission is made in describing a risk covered by the contract, it does not invalidate the reinsurer's liability for that risk.

see: obligatory reinsurance treaty

errors and omissions insurance (E&O)

Professional Liability. Coverage for damages arising out of the insured's negligence, mistakes, or failure to take appropriate action in the performance of business or professional duties. It often has a deductible in excess of $1,000 and usually does not require the insured's consent to settle claims (unlike *professional liability insurance*, which is a term sometimes used instead of errors and omissions insurance).

see: adjusters' errors and omissions insurance, agents' errors and omissions insurance, auctioneers' errors and omissions insurance, consent to settle provision, county clerks' and recorders' errors and omissions insurance, credit bureaus' errors and omissions insurance, customs brokers' and freight forwarders' errors and omissions insurance, data processors' errors and omissions insurance, oil landmen's and lease brokers' errors and omissions insurance, premium finance company errors and omissions insurance, professional liability insurance, real estate agents' errors and omissions insurance, registered mutual fund representative errors and omissions insurance, seedmens' errors and omissions insurance, tax preparers' errors and omissions insurance, testing and research laboratory errors and omissions insurance, transfer agents' errors and omissions insurance, trust departments' errors and omissions insurance, trustees' and fiduciaries' errors and omissions insurance

escheat

Law. The reversion of property to the state when the owner dies intestate and without any legally recognizable heirs. Bank accounts are claimed by the state government when left inactive for an extended period of time.

compare: devise; *see*: estate planning, intestate

escrow

Financial Planning/Mortgage Insurance. An arrangement for a neutral third person (escrow agent or depositary) to hold funds paid by a contracting party until a specified event, when the funds are released to the other contracting party. In most real estate sales, the deed to the property and the earnest money are placed in escrow pending the fulfillment of other contractual conditions.

see: closing costs, earnest money, escrow agents' errors and omissions insurance

escrow agents' errors and omissions insurance

Professional Liability. Professional liability insurance for firms that act as escrow agents, such as mortgage service companies, title companies, banks, and savings and loans, that covers loss from negligent acts, errors or omissions while acting in the capacity of an escrow agent. Coverage is written on a claims-made basis.

see: errors and omissions insurance, escrow

estate planning

Financial Planning. The systematic review of an individual's or family's wealth and strategies to enhance its value, conserve it, and distribute it when the owner dies. The *estate* is the total property owned by a decedent before its distribution to the decedent's spouse or heirs.

see: estate tax, intestate, probate court

estate tax

Financial Planning. A tax based on an estate's value at the time of the owner's death. A federal unified tax is assessed on the combined value of the estate and qualifying gifts so that estate taxes cannot be avoided by gifts in anticipation of death.

Special provisions apply to life insurance proceeds, and these vary by the type of life policy providing the benefits.

synonym: inheritance tax; *see:* gift tax

estimated annual premium (EAP)

Workers' Compensation. The amount of premium that an employer pays at the beginning of a policy period. EAP is determined by multiplying estimated payrolls by the rates that correspond to their classifications, and by the experience rating modification factor. At the end of the policy period, additional or return premiums will be calculated using the final payrolls.

see: deposit premium, initial premium, provisional premium; *compare:* additional premium, return premium

estimated constant dollar earnings per share

Financial Planning. An estimate of the impact of changes in the consumer price index on the cost of replacing, at current prices, previously purchased property that was depreciated at rates sufficient only to recover the original costs. This estimate also adjusts earnings per share for the impact on cost of sales and inventories.

see: earnings per share

estimated premium

Insurer Operations.

see: deposit premium, estimated annual premium, initial premium, provisional premium

estoppel

Law. A legal principle that when an individual represents a material fact to another, who alters his position in reasonable reliance on the representation, the first may not deny that the condition or fact exists. *Examples:* An insurer may be estopped from denying a claim submitted after the policy expired if the insurer (or its agent) acted as though the policy had been or would be renewed.

see: acquiescence, collateral estoppel, election to avoid a policy, laches, nonwaiver agreement, reservation of rights

Eurobond

International. A financial bond payable or denominated in the borrower's currency, but sold outside the borrower's country, usually by an international syndicate.

see: bond (*Financial Planning*)

evacuation expense

International. A form of political risk insurance that pays the expenses involved with quickly removing employees and their families from a foreign country because of an adverse change in political climate or health conditions.

see: political risk insurance

evergreen clause

General. A contractual provision that the contract is automatically renewed unless a party gives notice to the contrary. In a letter of credit, the clause prevents expiration without an affirmative action by the issuer of the letter of credit.

see: letter of credit

evidence

Law. Oral testimony, documents, or physical articles properly submitted to a court or quasi-judicial trier of fact.

see: burden of proof, demonstrative evidence, deposition, documentary evidence, expert witness, hearsay, testimony

evidence and duties provision

Insurer Operations. A policy provision requiring the insured to cooperate with the insurer in the investigation, settlement or defense of a claim or suit.

synonym: duties provision, evidence provision

evidence of cancellation

Insurer Operations. When a cancellation notice is mailed, the insurance company generally is not required to show proof that the policyholder received the notice. The company need only prove that the notice was mailed.

see: cancellation, cancellation notice, first named insured

evidence of coverage

Insurer Operations. A policy, certificate or summary provided by an insurer to an insured or by a health benefit plan sponsor to an enrollee which describes at least the essential contract provisions. Evidence of coverage is often required of motor vehicle operators.

see: automobile insurance identification card, certificate of insurance, evidence of property insurance

evidence of insurability

Health/Life. A statement or other information in an insurance application or a medical examination report that provides proof that the applicant's physical condition, occupation, etc., meet the insurer's standards of acceptability for insurance. It is a widely recognized legal right of an insured under a group policy to obtain individual insurance, upon termination of group membership, without evidence of insurability.

compare: guaranteed insurability; *see:* conversion privilege, insurable risk

evidence of property insurance

Agency. A form (ACORD form 27) used by an agent or insurer to provide a statement of coverage for mortgagees, additional insureds, and loss payees. Many lending institutions and loss payees accept this form in lieu of a complete policy as evidence that required insurance coverage is in effect.

see: evidence of coverage, certificate of insurance, loss payee

evidence provision
Insurer Operations.
see: evidence and duties provision

ex-dividend date
Financial Planning. The date by which an investor must own a stock in order to receive announced dividends or stock distributions.
see: dividend

ex gratia payment
Insurer Operations. A payment made by an insurer to an insured or claimant, even if a valid claim does not exist. (Latin meaning "from favor.") The payment is made because the insurer believes a mistake or a misunderstanding exists but desires to maintain goodwill.
see: claim expense, nuisance value

ex mod
Liability/Workers' Compensation.
see: experience rating modification factor

ex parte communication
Law. Communication concerning the subject of a pending legal proceeding between one party to the proceeding and the judge or hearing officer in the absence of and without the knowledge of the other party.

examination
Life/Health.
see: medical examination
Regulation. The audit and review by a state insurance department of an insurance company's operations, records and books of account.
synonym: audit; see: insurance examiner

examination bureau
Regulation. An organization licensed to examine policies, renewal certificates, endorsements and other forms to ensure that fair rates are charged and proper forms are used.
see: audit bureau, bureau insurer, rating bureau

examined business
Insurer Operations. Life or health insurance where an applicant has applied for coverage and has passed a required physical examination, but has not yet paid the initial premium to allow issuance of the policy.
compare: delivered business, issued business, paid business, placed business, written business;

see: medical examination

examiner
Regulation.
see: insurance examiner

excess aggregate reinsurance
Reinsurance.
see: aggregate excess of loss reinsurance

excess and surplus lines broker (E&S)
Agency. A specialty insurance broker who obtains coverage on risks that are difficult to place, unique or large through insurance companies not licensed to do business in the broker's state of domicile. These brokers are subject to special licensing requirements and usually act as wholesale brokers to agents.
synonym: excess line broker; see: nonadmitted market, surplus lines, surplus lines broker

excess bank burglary and robbery
Crime. An endorsement (ISO form CR 15 33) used with the robbery and safe burglary form to provide banks with excess burglary and robbery coverage.
see: excess insurance, robbery and safe burglary form

excess coverage for specified employees or positions
Crime. A crime coverage form (ISO form CR 10 15) that increases the limits on specifically named individuals or employment positions.
see: employee dishonesty coverage form, excess insurance

excess insurance
Insurer Operations. Coverage provided above a primary policy or a self-insured retention.
compare: primary insurance; see: excess liability insurance, excess of loss reinsurance, other insurance provision, umbrella liability insurance

excess interest
Life. In a whole life policy, that portion of the interest credited to the policy's cash values that is in excess of the guaranteed minimum interest rate.
see: cash surrender value, whole life insurance

excess judgment loss
Insurer Operations. The amount paid by an insurer in excess of the applicable policy limits for a bad faith failure to settle a claim for an amount within the policy limits.
see: bad faith, extra-contractual obligations

excess liability insurance
Liability. Insurance coverage that is written in excess of primary insurance. It is designed to increase the limits of liability, thereby providing catastrophe

coverage. Excess liability coverage does not respond to a loss until the amount of the loss exceeds (or exhausts) any existing primary policy limits. *Example*: A primary $500,000 liability policy is written, and excess insurance is written for $2 million excess of the primary. The primary policy would pay all losses within $500,000 and the excess policy would pay losses in excess of the primary coverage, up to the excess policy limit of $2 million.

compare: umbrella liability insurance; *see*: aggregate excess insurance, buffer layer, direct excess policy, following form excess liability insurance, layering

excess line broker
Agency.
see: excess and surplus lines broker

excess line reinsurance
Reinsurance. An excess of loss reinsurance contract, where the limit and deductible are expressed as "each and every loss, each and every risk."
see: excess of loss reinsurance

excess lines
Insurer Operations. The same as *surplus lines*, which is the preferred term to avoid confusion with *excess insurance*. The phrase *excess and surplus lines* is also used.
compare: excess insurance; *see*: excess and surplus lines broker, surplus lines

excess loss premium factor (ELP)
Liability/Workers' Compensation. A retrospective rating factor used when a specific loss limitation is included in the plan. A rate or flat charge is included in the plan, to limit the amount of any one loss that is to be included in the rating formula. *Example*: A plan with a $250,000 loss limitation would include only the first $250,000 of each occurrence in the plan's losses when the final premium is calculated.
see: retrospective rating plan

excess loss-ratio reinsurance
Reinsurance. A form of nonproportional treaty reinsurance, whereby the reinsurer responds when a ceding insurer's losses during a specified period (usually 12 months) on a specific line or book of business exceed a stated loss ratio—usually the ceding insurer's overall loss ratio—for the same period.
compare: nonproportional automatic reinsurance; *see*: aggregate excess of loss reinsurance

excess of loss insurance
General. Coverage for that portion of a loss which exceeds a certain amount retained by the insured or

covered by other insurance, and then only for liability in excess of that figure.
see: excess liability insurance, excess property insurance, layering, quota share reinsurance, umbrella liability insurance

excess of loss reinsurance
Reinsurance. A form of nonproportional reinsurance that indemnifies the ceding insurer for that portion of each loss occurrence in excess of a stipulated primary (ceding) company retention. This form of reinsurance is usually used with casualty risks.
see: attachment point, excess insurance, intermediate excess reinsurance, net retained lines clause, nonproportional reinsurance, retention and limits clause, treaty reinsurance, workers' compensation catastrophe policy, working cover

excess per risk reinsurance
Reinsurance. A form of treaty excess of loss reinsurance that, subject to a specified limit, indemnifies the ceding insurer for the amount of a loss in excess of a specified retention for each risk involved in each loss.
see: excess of loss reinsurance

excess property insurance
Property. A property insurance program for large commercial insureds that is layered, with a primary policy that has a stop-loss limit designed to cover most losses, after which an excess property policy covers catastrophic losses. *Example*: A primary property policy written on an all-risk basis for $5 million and an excess policy written on a "named perils" basis for $20 million excess of the primary policy's $5 million.
see: layering

Excess/Surplus/Specialty Lines Section, CPCU Society
Organizations. An interest section of the CPCU Society that offers information on all aspects of the excess, surplus and specialty lines insurance industry.
see: CPCU Society

excessive
Regulation. Most state insurance laws or regulations prohibit premium rates that generate unfair profits or are unreasonably high for the insurance benefits or compared to a reasonably efficient insurer's cost of providing the insurance services.
compare: adequate; *see*: equity (*Insurer Operations*), rate making

exchange
Insurer Operations.
see: insurance exchange, reciprocal insurance exchange

165

exchange fund
International.
see: exchange stabilization

exchange privilege
Financial Planning. A benefit offered by some mutual funds allowing an investor to transfer his or her investment between funds in the same mutual fund family. Often, such exchanges can be made for free or for a modest transfer fee.
see: mutual fund

exchange rate
International. The rate at which the currency of one country is exchanged for that of another; the price of one currency denominated in another. A global network of private financial institutions who exchange currencies for both their own account and their customers has a greater influence over the value of currencies than do central banks and governments, primarily determining the prices of most currencies. Rates commonly quoted in newspapers are wholesale rates for the exchange of large sums; when exchanging small amounts, a retail rate applies, which is less favorable.
synonym: foreign exchange rate; *see*: exchange stabilization, money

exchange risk
International. The possibility of a fall in income or a rise in expenses of an international transaction or business operation due to a change in exchange rates.
see: exchange rate, exchange stabilization

exchange stabilization
International. A function of a firm's treasury department of monitoring the exchange rates of currencies held by the business and acting to keep them within a predetermined valuation range. Actions include buying or selling currencies or purchasing gold to replace currency.
synonym: exchange fund; *see*: economic perils, exchange risk

exchange transfer embargo indemnity insurance
International.
see: exchange transfer insurance

exchange transfer insurance
International. A form of political risk insurance that indemnifies the exporter for part of the value of exported goods (usually 80% of the net loss) if the buyer's government prevents the transfer of payment. Coverage may also include financial losses resulting from the revocation of import and export licenses.
synonym: exchange transfer embargo indemnity insurance, *see*: export credit insurance

excise tax
Insurer Operations/Reinsurance. A federal tax that applies to some types of insurance placed with non-U.S. domiciled insurers or reinsurers.
Accounting. A tax levied on specific commodities or services, such as liquor, tobacco, and gasoline. A federal excise tax also applies to certain insurance premiums that are paid to non-U.S. insurers.

excluded assets
Insurer Operations/Regulation. Assets of an insurer that are not included in financial statements prepared under statutory accounting principles but would be assets in financial statements prepared under Generally Accepted Accounting Principles. *Examples*: Accounts receivable more than 90 days in arrears, or office equipment.
see: Generally Accepted Accounting Principles, nonadmitted assets, Statutory Accounting Principles

excluded period
Health.
see: probationary period

exclusion
Insurer Operations. An insurance policy or bond provision that eliminates coverage for specific hazards, perils, property or locations. It designates what the insurer does not intend to cover under the contract. There are generally six recognized legitimate purposes for exclusions: 1. to eliminate coverage for uninsurable loss exposures; 2. to assist in the management of moral and morale hazards; 3. to reduce the likelihood of coverage duplications; 4. to eliminate coverage not needed by the purchaser; 5. to eliminate coverage requiring special treatment; 6. to assist in maintaining premiums at a reasonable level.
see: blasting and explosion exclusion, care, custody or control exclusion, civil commotion exclusion, collapse exclusion, communicable disease exclusion, conversion embezzlement or secretion exclusion, electrical apparatus exclusion, face, family exclusion, faulty work exclusion, foundation exclusion clause, governmental action exclusion, impairment exclusion rider, insects, birds, rodents or other animals exclusion, insuring agreement, limitations, military service exclusion, named driver exclusion, nuclear hazard exclusion, ordinance or law exclusion, ordinary payroll exclusion endorsement, passenger hazard exclusion, policy conditions, policy declarations, pollution exclusion, products recall exclusion, quarantine exclusion, strikes, riots and civil commotions exclusion, temperature extremes exclusion, testing exclusion, trick and device exclusion, underground exclusion, water exclusion clause, watercraft exclusion, wear and tear exclusion

exclusive agency system

Agency/Insurer Operations. An insurance distribution system that contractually requires agents or agencies to sell and serve policies of only a single insurer. The exclusive representation agreement between the insurer and agent also specifies that the ownership, use and control of policy records and expiration dates belong to the insurer.

compare: independent agency system; *see*: captive agent, direct selling system

exclusive provider organization

Health. A preferred provider organization that does not provide coverage for care performed outside the PPO's network or facilities.

see: out-of-network services, preferred provider organization

exclusive remedy

Workers' Compensation. State workers' compensation statutes gave employees a definite remedy for injuries and diseases arising out of or suffered in the course of their employment. In exchange for a definite recovery, the workers' compensation remedy is exclusive, that is, with just a few exceptions, a worker's right of recovery against the employer is limited to the benefits provided by the workers' compensation law. The employee may not sue in tort.

Exceptions include cases in which the employer acts with fraud or gross negligence, assaults the employee, or where the injury is caused through the employer's activities in a capacity other than as employer (e.g., as the manufacturer of machinery sold to others, but which is also used in the employer's business operation).

see: common law defense, dual capacity doctrine, tort, workers' compensation law

exculpatory provision

Law. A contract provision that absolves one or more parties from liability resulting from the implementation of the contract.

see: hold harmless agreement

executed contract

Law. A contract under which all obligations of the parties have been performed.

compare: executory contract; *see*: contract

executor

Law. An individual who is appointed or specified in a will to execute its provisions.

see: will

executory contract

Law. A contract under which not all of the obligations of the parties have yet been performed.

compare: executed contract; *see*: contract

exemplary damages

Law.

see: punitive damages

exempt organization

General.

see: nonprofit organization

exemption

General. A provision allowing an individual or organization to be free or excluded from certain duties.

see: tax planning

exercise price

Financial Planning. The selling price of a security underlying a put or call option.

see: call option, put option

exhibition floater

Inland Marine. A trip transit policy that covers property during transit, from the original location to the place of exhibit, while the property is on exhibition, and during the return trip to the original location. Coverage is usually written on an all-risk basis.

see: floater policy, trip transit insurance

exit fee

Financial Planning.

see: back end load

exonerating provision

Insurer Operations. A type of other insurance provision that attempts to relieve an insurer from any obligation for a loss if other insurance exists. The provision takes one of the following forms: 1. prohibition of other insurance; 2. exclusion of property or coverage provided by other insurance; 3. general disclaimer of responsibility should other insurance apply; or 4. an offset that reduces the amount of recovery by the amount of the other insurance.

synonym: escape clause; *see*: offset, other insurance provision

exoneration

Surety.

see: right of exoneration

exothermic process

Loss Control. A process in which heat is produced.

compare: endothermic process

exotic bird insurance

Inland Marine. A form of animal insurance that combines comprehensive theft, animal mortality, and veterinarian fees for the owners of rare or valuable birds.

see: animal insurance, pet insurance

expected expense ratio

Insurer Operations. A formula used by an insurer to relate expected income to expected incurred expenses. *Formula*: expected incurred expenses ÷ expected written premiums.

see: expected expenses, expense ratio

expected expenses

Insurer Operations. Expense projections for a future period of time developed by an insurer, generally through the budgeting process. Expected expenses do not include claims and claims adjusting expenses

see: expected expense ratio

expected loss ratio

Insurer Operations. A formula used by insurance companies to relate expected income to expected losses. *Formula*: (expected incurred losses + expected loss adjusting expense) ÷ expected earned premiums.

see: expected losses, loss ratio

expected losses

Insurer Operations. Loss and claim expense projections based on actuarial probability calculations. An insurer uses such projections in the budgeting process.

see: expected loss ratio, incurred but not reported

expected morbidity

Health. The anticipated number of individuals within a given group who will become ill or injured within a specified period of time as indicated on a morbidity table.

see: morbidity rate; *compare*: expected mortality

expected mortality

Life. The anticipated number of individuals within a given group who will die within a specified period of time as indicated on a mortality table.

see: mortality rate; *compare*: expected morbidity

expected rate of return

Financial Planning. The rate of return an organization expects to realize from an investment.

see: return on investment

Risk Management.

see: rate of return

expected return

Risk Management. The expected return is the mean value of the probability distribution of the possible returns.

see: expected rate of return, mean

expediting expenses

Property. Coverage included in business income and boiler and machinery policies that indemnifies the insured for extra expenses required to speed the restoration of damaged property and thus resume operations more quickly.

see: extra expense insurance

expense allowance

Agency/Insurer Operations. An allowance paid to an insurance agent, in addition to commissions, to encourage the placing of business with an insurer.

see: agent's commission

expense constant

Insurer Operations. An expense factor (usually a dollar amount) added to the premium charged for a class of policies, which would otherwise produce insufficient premium to cover the cost of issuing and servicing them.

see: rate making

expense funds

Life. Funds maintained by an insurer other than a legal reserve insurer.

see: legal reserve life insurance company

expense loading

Insurer Operations. Insurance company administrative and sales expenses (e.g., commissions, taxes, advertising) that are added to the insurer's pure or basic premium to develop the final premium.

synonym: loading; *see*: field expenses, general and insurance expenses, pure premium, rate making

expense-only coverage

Liability. Liability coverage where the insurer pays only claims expenses and provides no indemnity payments.

see: claim

expense ratio

Insurer Operations. A formula used by insurance companies to relate income to administrative expenses (e.g., commissions, taxes, acquisition advertising and administration expenses). *Formula*: expenses (excluding losses, loss adjusting expenses and policyholder dividends) ÷ earned premiums.

compare: combined ratio, dividend ratio, expected expense ratio, loss ratio; *see*: underwriting margin

expense reserve

Insurer Operations. A reserve established for liabilities, resulting from incurred but unpaid expenses.

see: reserve

expenses

Insurer Operations. Any costs of doing business. Insurance companies divide expenses into two major categories: administrative expenses (overhead, commissions, etc.) and loss expenses (payable claims and legal defense costs).

see: expense ratio, loss ratio

experience

Insurer Operations.

see: loss experience

experience rating

Insurer Operations. The development of a premium for a specific policyholder by using that insured's own loss experience to apply a premium modification factor to the manual rate. If the policyholder's prior experience was favorable, a premium less than the manual rate results. If the experience was unfavorable, a higher premium results.

see: experience rating modification factor, loss-sensitivie insurance program, manual rate, rating

experience rating form

Workers' Compensation. A document produced on an annual basis that indicates an employer's premium, loss experience and experience modification factor.

see: experience rating modification factor

experience rating modification factor

Liability. A factor that attempts to reflect an insured's actual losses in relation to the same insured's premium. A factor is a number applied to the manual premium to either increase or decrease the insured's final premium. A *retrospective plan* modifies the premium after the policy period or after most of the policy period, while a *prospective plan* examines prior periods, such as the last three years, to produce a premium.

synonym: ex mod; *see*: anniversary rating date endorsement, change in ownership, contingent experience rating modification factor endorsement, experience rating, experience rating modification factor endorsement, notification of change in ownership endorsement, prospective rating plan, retrospective rating plan

Workers' Compensation. A factor (expressed as a percentage) that is developed by a rating bureau for workers' compensation insurance. The calculation relates an employer's losses, payroll, and premiums, segregated according to classifications of operations, as reported to the bureau by the employer's insurance company.

synonym: ex mod; *see*: experience rating plan, interstate experience modification, unit statistical card, workers' compensation experience rating worksheet

experience rating modification factor endorsement

Workers' Compensation. An endorsement (NCCI form WC 00 04 03) that is attached to a workers' compensation policy when the insured's experience rating modification factor is unknown at the time

the policy is issued. It advises the insured that the premium will be adjusted by the rating factor when it is available.

see: experience rating modification factor, workers' compensation insurance

experience rating plan

Liability/Workers' Compensation. A premium rating plan that considers the past loss experience of the insured to develop current policy rates. Usually, the past three to five years of loss experience are used to develop an experience credit or debit that is applied to the manual rates for the specific risk being rated.

see: "D" ratio, experience rating modification factor, loss-sensitive insurance program, rate making, retrospective rating plan

experience refund

Liability/Workers' Compensation. The return of a portion of the premium paid by an insured because of a favorable loss ratio under a retention or retrospectively rated plan.

Reinsurance. A predetermined percentage of the net reinsurance profit that the reinsurer returns to the ceding insurer as a form of profit sharing at year's end.

experimental procedures exclusion

Health. Exclusion from the coverage of most health insurance policies of experimental and investigative medical procedures, drugs or equipment on the grounds that they are not proved to be medically effective. To determine effectiveness, insurers may refer to clinical tests or reports of medical or scientific institutions or government agencies.

compare: medically necessary; *see*: health insurance

expert witness

Law. A witness whose testimony is based on specialized knowledge. The witness's expertise must be pertinent to the facts at issue, and the witness must possess sufficient education, training or experience to be accepted as an expert. A witness's evaluation of physical evidence must be based on generally accepted ideas and methods in the relevant scientific or technical profession to avoid introducing so-called "junk science" as evidence. This is the "general acceptance" standard for admissibility of scientific evidence.

see: board certified, evidence, forensic expert

expiration card

Agency/Insurer Operations. A card maintained by an agent or insurer to record the termination date of a policy. It is used to prompt the agent or insurer to solicit renewal of the policy.

see: expiration file, tickler

169

expiration date

Insurer Operations. The date on which an insurance policy or bond terminates or ceases to provide coverage.

see: cancellation, effective date, expiration notice, policy period, renewal

expiration file

Agency/Insurer Operations. A list, often maintained on a data base by an agent and insurer, of the inception and expiration dates of all policies they have written. An expiration file has the same purpose as a collection of expiration cards.

see: expiration card, tickler

expiration notice

Insurer Operations. A written notice mailed to an insured (or to a loss payee or mortgagee) prior to the expiration date of an insurance policy.

compare: cancellation notice

expirations

Insurer Operations.

see: ownership of expirations

explosion

Property. A violent bursting, accompanied by sudden burning or a violent expansion of hot gases with a great disruptive force. It includes the explosion of accumulated gases or unconsumed fuel passing through flues or passages.

see: blasting and explosion exclusion, explosion-proof, explosive atmosphere, firebox explosion, furnace explosion, inherent explosion, internal explosion coverage

explosion, collapse, and underground exclusions

Liability.

see: XCU exclusions

explosion-proof

Loss Control. A term used to describe electrical fixtures and devices which have been designed to prevent them from becoming a source of ignition for gases or dust located near the fixture or device.

see: fireproof

explosive atmosphere

Loss Control. An atmosphere containing a mixture of vapor or gas which is within the explosive or flammable range.

explosive level

Loss Control.

see: flammable limits

export bond

International/Surety. A form of federal bond that guarantees payment by dealers and handlers of goods subject to customs charges and taxes.

see: federal bond

export credit insurance

International/Financial Guaranty. A form of credit insurance that protects an exporter against losses resulting from the inability to collect on credit that has been extended to commercial customers in other countries. Coverage is divided into commercial perils (such as the debtor's insolvency or refusal to pay) and political perils (such as war or blocked currency). Most foreign credit insurance is provided through government supported programs, but some plans are jointly underwritten by governments and private insurers.

synonym: foreign credit insurance; *see*: blocked currency, commercial perils, exchange transfer insurance, Export-Import Bank, Foreign Credit Insurance Association, political perils

Export-Import Bank (EXIM Bank)

International. A joint venture between the U.S. government and the Foreign Credit Insurance Association, an association formed by major U.S. insurers to encourage export of American goods. The EXIM Bank was formed in 1934 to insure U.S. business ventures abroad against losses resulting from uncollectible foreign accounts and investments, from war or civil strife, confiscation, or currency devaluation.

see: export credit insurance, Foreign Credit Insurance Association

export restraint agreement

International. A quota agreement between the governments of two countries that limits the volume or value of specified goods traded between them.

compare: quota, tariff

exporters' embargo insurance

International. A form of political risk insurance that indemnifies an exporter for losses caused by a foreign government's interference with an export contract, including embargo or license cancellation. The inability to convert or exchange local currency or to transfer currency from the country may also be covered. The coverage can be written in conjunction with importer's embargo insurance.

compare: importers' embargo insurance; *see*: political risk insurance

exposure

Liability. The extent of exposure to loss, as measured by an exposure base, such as payroll, receipts, area, or units produced.

Loss Control. A hazardous structure or activity of others near an insured's property.

see: hazard, Prouty exposure analysis

Property. In fire underwriting, the chance of a fire

spreading to an insured risk from adjacent structures.

see: adjacent building, class rating, construction, occupancy, protection

exposure base
Liability.

see: exposure unit

exposure earned premium
Insurer Operations. The earned premium that is actually exposed to loss during a specified period of time. To develop this earned premium, the date on which premiums were booked is disregarded. The portion of the written premium exposed to loss (earned) is allocated to the exposure period whether the premiums were booked in a prior period, during the current period, or after the period. The exposure earned premium eliminates the deficiency contained in accounting earned premium that results from timing problems in the recording of the premium.

compare: accounting earned premium; *see*: earned premium

exposure in residence
Law/Liability. The period of continuous exposure to a harmful condition or substance (such as asbestos) between the initial exposure and the manifestation of loss (i.e., the discovery of symptoms of an illness).

see: continuous trigger theory, exposure theory, injury-in-fact, manifestation theory, Keene doctrine

exposure theory
Law/Liability. A legal theory that liability is based on the time of the exposure to the cause of an illness or other loss. In cases of continuous exposure (e.g., a worker's exposure to silica dust, asbestos, etc.), all insurers with a liability policy in effect during the exposure period are liable; however, the liability may be allocated among insurers according to the length of time that their policies applied. This theory is rooted in an effort to determine when an illness or loss "occurred," despite the fact that some illnesses result from a long-term exposure or series of exposures.

compare: continuous trigger theory, injury-in-fact theory, manifestation theory; *see*: Keene doctrine, occurrence policy, progressive loss

exposure unit
Insurer Operations. The unit of measure (e.g., area, gross receipts, payroll) used to determine an insurance policy's premium. Also, an individual's risk or location.

synonym: exposure base; *see*: base rate, experience rating modification factor, increased limits table, rate making

express warranty
General. A statement (e.g., a provision of a contract) guaranteeing that an item or service is of a certain quality or condition.

compare: disclaimer, implied warranty; *see*: warranty (3)

expressed authority
Agency. Authority plainly granted, either orally or in writing, to an agent by an insurance company (the principal). Written authority is granted in an agency agreement that usually allows the agent to countersign, issue and deliver policies and binders, cancel policies, collect policy premiums, and provide all customary services of an insurance agent regarding all policies accepted by the insurer from the agent.

see: actual authority, agency, agency agreement, countersign, implied authority

expropriation
International. The seizure of property or the restriction of property rights by the government of a country.

compare: confiscation, deprivation, nationalization

expropriation insurance
International.

see: confiscation and expropriation insurance

expulsion
General. Involuntary ejection or removal from membership of an organization.

extended business income
Property. An extension of coverage under a business income policy for lost income for an additional period, usually 30 days, beyond the time normally required to restore the damaged property that caused the income loss.

see: business income coverage form, extended period of indemnity, period of restoration

extended care facility (ECF)
Health. A health care facility that is intended to offer services to patients, including skilled nursing, rehabilitation, custodial and convalescent care, over a long period of time. Such a facility does not provide acute care. Many states require such a facility to be licensed in the same manner as a hospital.

synonym: long-term care facility; *see*: custodial care, integrated care (2), long-term care insurance, skilled nursing facility

extended coverages (EC)
Property. Coverage for property damage caused by windstorm, hail, smoke, explosion, riot, riot attending a strike, civil commotion, vehicle and aircraft

collision. This coverage is usually provided by endorsement to a basic policy (e.g., in conjunction with the standard fire insurance policy and various "package" policies).

compare: additional extended coverage, coverage extension

extended definition of premises to include portion of grounds enclosed by fence or wall

Crime. A endorsement (ISO form CR 15 23) that amends the definition of an insured premises in certain crime coverage forms. Coverage is extended to include outdoor property within a fenced or walled area adjacent to the insured premises.

see: premises burglary coverage form, premises theft and outside robbery coverage form

extended health insurance

Health. Health insurance for persons 65 years or older, usually provided through a joint underwriting association.

synonym: over-age insurance; *see*: joint underwriting association

extended period of indemnity

Property. An endorsement (ISO form CP 00 30) for loss of business income that reimburses the insured for reduced earnings after the premises have been restored and business has been resumed. The coverage provides protection against a delay in a business's return to full activity.

see: business income coverage form, extended business income

extended reporting period (ERP)

Liability. The period allowed under most claims-made policies for coverage of acts, errors or omissions that occurred during the policy period but are not submitted as claims until after the policy is expired. The time period may be limited (e.g., 60 days), or there may be no limit on the extended reporting period. Some policies require an additional premium to extend the reporting period.

For directors' and officers' liability policies, the extended reporting period usually applies only if the insurer cancels or does not renew the policy. If the insured cancels, there is generally a limited time (e.g., 10 days) in which to request the extension and pay the required additional premium. The option is normally not available if the insured is offered a renewal but decides not to accept it.

synonym: tail coverage; *see*: basic extended reporting period, claims-made form, maxi-tail, mini-tail, supplemental extended reporting period

extended term life insurance

Life. A nonforfeiture option in most whole life insurance policies, providing term life coverage for the face amount of the existing policy for as long as the whole life policy's cash value is adequate to pay the term life premiums.

see: cash surrender value, nonforfeiture extended term benefit, term life insurance, whole life insurance

extended wait

Reinsurance. Reinsurance of disability insurance contracts, where the reinsurer makes the monthly benefit payments after the ceding insurer has paid a specified number of monthly payments.

see: disability income insurance

extended warranty agreement

Financial Guaranty. A contract or agreement under which someone other than the manufacturer assumes the cost of repair or replacement of a product due to mechanical breakdown, wear and tear, deterioration or other reasons. Extended warranties are sold on such items as automobiles and other motor vehicles, major appliances, etc. In some states, an extended warranty agreement is considered an insurance contract.

see: warranty (3)

exterminator liability insurance

Professional Liability. Liability coverage for exterminators who use poisonous chemicals to eliminate termites, rodents and other pests. Coverage is usually written on a claims-made basis.

see: pesticide or herbicide applicator coverage

extortion

Crime. The taking of money or other valuable property by actual or threatened force, by threatening a strike or boycott, or by threatening to harm a person's business reputation or credit. Extortion usually includes blackmail, an unlawful demand for money by threatening harm or exposure of disgraceful conduct.

see: extortion coverage form, extortion insurance, kidnap insurance, kidnap-ransom-extortion insurance

extortion coverage form

Crime. A crime coverage form (ISO form CR 00 08, or form G) that covers loss of money, securities, and property other than money and securities that results directly from extortion.

synonym: crime coverage form G; *see*: crime coverages, extortion, money, property other than money and securities, securities

extortion insurance

Crime. Coverage for money surrendered in response to a threat to harm persons or damage property.

see: kidnap insurance, kidnap-ransom-extortion insurance

extra-contractual obligations (ECO)

Reinsurance. An award of damages against an insurer for its negligence (bad faith) to its insured. These awards are "extra-contractual" in that they are beyond the insurance contract between the insurer and the insured. A reinsurance treaty may be extended to cover these damages for an additional premium. The reinsurer usually limits coverage to specific types of situations.

see: bad faith, excess judgment loss, reinsurance

extra expense from dependent properties endorsement

Property. A commercial property coverage endorsement (ISO form CP 15 34) for the insured's extra expenses caused by a loss at a specific, non-owned location on which the insured depends for business operations. The loss must be caused by a peril otherwise insured under the policy. It is similar to contingent business income coverage.

see: contingent business income coverage, extra expense insurance

extra expense insurance

Property. Property insurance coverage for necessary additional expenses of continuing business operations after damage to insured premises from a covered cause of loss.

synonym: additional expense insurance; *compare*: additional living expense insurance, contingent business income coverage, expediting expenses, extra expense from dependent properties endorsement; *see*: cleanup fund

extra percentage tables

Health/Life. Mortality and morbidity tables that are used to determine, as a percentage of standard table premium, the additional premium required to insure persons impaired by serious health conditions such as cancer or AIDS.

see: acquired immune deficiency syndrome, cancer insurance, specified disease insurance

extraterritoriality

Workers' Compensation. A workers' compensation policy provision that extends coverage to pay the benefit level of a state other than where an employee is hired in the event an injury occurs in that state.

compare: all-states coverage, broad form all-states endorsement; *see;*: workers' compensation insurance

extremely hazardous substance

Loss Control. A substance listed by the U.S. Environmental Protection Agency pursuant to the Superfund law (CERCLA) based on its high toxicity. The list includes approximately 400 chemicals.

see: Comprehensive Environmental Response Compensation and Liability Act, hazardous substance, LD_{50}

F

FAA special waiver endorsement

Aviation. An endorsement that amends the aviation policy exclusions pertaining to maintenance flights, ferry flights of damaged aircraft, and flights carrying hazardous materials. The endorsement provides coverage when such a flight is conducted under a waiver or special permit issued by the Federal Aviation Administration.

see: aviation insurance, Federal Aviation Administration

face

Insurer Operations. The first page of an insurance policy, which usually includes the policy declarations.

see: exclusion, insurance contract, insuring agreement, policy conditions, policy declarations

face amount

Financial Planning. The value shown on a security. In the case of bonds, it usually represents the principal or redemption value; in the case of stock, the par value.

synonym: face value; *see*: bond (*Financial Planning*), par value, stock (*Financial Planning*)

Insurer Operations. The amount of insurance provided by the terms of an insurance policy, usually found on the policy's face or declarations.

see: limit of liability

Life. The death benefit of a life insurance policy.

see: death benefit (*Life*)

face value

Financial Planning.

see: face amount

facility-of-payment clause

Life. A provision in group life and industrial insurance policies that is designed to simplify benefit payments when there is doubt as to the policy beneficiary. It provides that the insurer may pay the benefits to any relative or person who has physical possession of the policy and who appears equitably

entitled to its benefits.

see: group life insurance, industrial life insurance

factoring

Insurer Operations. A percentage amount (up to 99%) of an earned dividend that is paid to a policyholder on a participating policy when the entire indicated dividend is not paid because of adverse underwriting or financial results.

see: participating policy, policy dividend

Factory Insurance Association

Insurer Operations/Property.

see: Industrial Risk Insurers

Factory Mutual System (FM)

Property. The Factory Mutual System—once comprised of as many as 40 individual mutual companies—has experienced consolidations and mergers over the years, resulting in just three member organizations today: Allendale Mutual Insurance Company, Arkwright Mutual Insurance Company, and Protection Mutual Insurance Company. They specialize in property coverages and loss prevention services for large industrial and institutional properties worldwide. Jointly, they own the Factory Mutual Engineering Corporation, Factory Mutual Engineering Association, Factory Mutual Research Corporation, and Factory Mutual Service Bureau.

compare: Industrial Risk Insurers; *see*: absorption rate

facultative certificate

Reinsurance. A document formalizing a facultative reinsurance cession.

see: facultative reinsurance

facultative obligatory reinsurance treaty

Reinsurance. A hybrid reinsurance agreement comprised of the facultative and treaty approaches. The reinsurer must accept all risks ceded to it under the treaty, but the primary (ceding) insurer need not cede every risk of the type covered by the treaty.

compare: facultative semi-obligatory reinsurance

treaty, obligatory reinsurance treaty; *see*: facultative reinsurance, open cover, treaty reinsurance

facultative reinsurance

Reinsurance. A reinsurance arrangement by which individual risks are offered by the ceding insurer to a reinsurer, who has the right (faculty) to accept or reject each risk.

synonym: specific reinsurance; *compare*: treaty reinsurance; *see*: facultative semi-obligatory reinsurance treaty, facultative treaty reinsurance, nonproportional reinsurance

facultative semi-obligatory reinsurance treaty

Reinsurance. A facultative obligation treaty whereby the ceding insurer may select which risks it will cede to the reinsurer who has the right to reject the risk within a certain time frame; otherwise the reinsurer is obligated to accept the risk.

compare: facultative obligatory reinsurance treaty, obligatory reinsurance treaty; *see*: facultative reinsurance

facultative treaty reinsurance

Reinsurance. A reinsurance arrangement whereby the ceding insurer may cede and the reinsurer may accept or decline individual risks within a general treaty agreement. Ordinarily, *facultative* means individual risk reinsurance and *treaty* means reinsurance of all the cedent's risks in a general line or class. A facultative treaty is used for similar risks when there are not enough of them to justify a standard treaty or there is a problem with the class, but the reinsurer has an interest in the type of business and wants to avoid contracting separately for each risk. Any single risk can be added to the treaty when approved by both parties.

see: facultative reinsurance, treaty reinsurance

fail-safe

Loss Control. Design of a guard, device, mechanism, or other equipment in such a manner that, when it fails or becomes inoperative, it will do so in a safe position or condition.

see: barrier guard

failure to maintain other valid insurance exclusion

Professional Liability. A directors' and officers' coverage exclusion for actions against the directors and officers if the corporation suffers a loss that is normally insured but does not have adequate, valid coverage for it. This exclusion can usually be deleted by providing the D&O underwriter with a summary of the corporate insurance program.

see: directors' and officers' liability insurance

Fair Access to Insurance Requirements (FAIR plan)

Property/Regulation. A state-established program that requires insurers who write property insurance to accept risks in economically depressed areas in the same proportion as their other business bears to the total property insurance market. In most states, the laws also provide for a facility that distributes risks among the participating insurers.

compare: assigned risk; *see*: automobile shared market, Boston plan, extended health insurance, joint underwriting association, market assistance plan, residual markets

Fair Credit Reporting Act

Insurer Operations/Regulation. Federal legislation requiring an insurance applicant to be informed of the purpose of a requested credit report. When insurance is declined because of information contained in a credit report, the insurer must give the credit company's name and address to the applicant.

fair market value

Property.

see: market value

faithful performance of duty

Crime. An endorsement (ISO form CR 10 09) that amends an employee dishonesty coverage form issued to a fraternal order or labor union. Coverage is extended to include the failure of an employee to faithfully perform duties prescribed by the organization's constitution or bylaws or by resolution of the governing body, and it includes losses resulting from an employee's inability to perform duties because of a criminal act committed by someone other than an employee.

see: employee dishonesty coverage form

fallen building clause

Property. A provision contained in some fire insurance policies that voids coverage in the event that the building collapses from a cause other than a fire or explosion.

see: collapse

falling objects coverage

Property. A coverage in some property insurance policies for any object that falls on a building and damages it. Coverage includes both the interior and exterior of the building, but for coverage to apply, the exterior must be damaged.

see: aircraft damage coverage

false pretense coverage

Automobile. A garage policy endorsement (ISO form CA 25 03) extending coverage for autos that the insured voluntarily parts with because of a trick, scheme, or false pretense, or acquires from a seller not possessing legal title to the vehicle. The trick and devise exclusion to the garage policy must be deleted.

see: conversion, embezzlement or secretion exclusion; trick and device exclusion

false pretense exclusion
Automobile.

see: trick and device exclusion

Family and Medical Leave Act
Employee Benefits/Regulation. Federal legislation (U.S. Code Title 29, Chapter 28) adopted in 1993 that requires an employer with more than 50 employees to provide employees with up to twelve weeks' unpaid leave each year for births, adoptions, foster care placements, and illness of family members.

see: leave of absence, sabbatical

family automobile endorsement
Personal. An endorsement to the basic automobile policy that broadens the definitions of persons insured and drive other car coverage.

see: basic standard automobile policy, drive other car coverage, personal auto policy

family automobile policy (FAP)
Personal. A standard personal automobile policy used through the 1980s that has been replaced by the personal auto policy. The family auto policy was the first to include both automobile liability and physical damage in a single form. Prior to its use, the basic standard automobile policy was the standard form.

compare: basic standard automobile policy, personal auto policy

family benefits
Employee Benefits. Family members may be eligible for Social Security payments when a covered person begins collecting retirement payments. These benefits can be paid to a husband or wife and to unmarried children under the age of 18. In some cases, payments are made to older children who are disabled or who are full-time students.

see: Social Security

family deductible
Health. A deductible in a health insurance plan that is satisfied or eliminated by the combined expenses of all covered family members. *Example*: A plan with a $150 individual deductible may limit its application to a maximum of three deductibles ($450) for the family, without regard to the number of family members.

family exclusion
Personal. An exclusion in most personal auto and homeowners policies for liability for bodily injury

or damage to property of family members.

see: family member, intra-family immunity, liability coverage exclusion endorsement

family expense insurance
Health. A type of health insurance that extends the medical coverage to all members of a insured's household.

synonym: family health policy

family forgery bond
Crime. A bond that covers all members of a family for nonbusiness financial transactions against loss by forgery of outgoing instruments, accepting forged documents, or accepting counterfeit U.S. currency.

family health policy
Health.

see: family expense insurance

family income life insurance
Life. A life insurance policy that combines whole life with decreasing term insurance. In the event of the insured's death prior to a specified date, the beneficiary is paid a monthly income benefit. If the insured lives beyond the specified date, the full face amount of the policy is paid to the beneficiary. This policy is designed to protect a family with young children.

see: family maintenance life insurance, term life insurance, whole life insurance

Family Leave Act
Employee Benefits/Regulation.

see: Family and Medical Leave Act

family life policy
Life. Life insurance combining whole life with term insurance to cover family members in a single policy. Coverage for the principal is whole life, while the spouse and children are insured on a term basis for a lesser amount.

see: additional insured, term life insurance, whole life insurance

family maintenance life insurance
Life. Life insurance based on a family income policy that combines whole life with level term insurance to provide a beneficiary with income over a specified period of time (10, 20 years) if the insured dies during that period of time. Should the insured survive the specified period, the beneficiary would receive the policy face amount.

see: family income life insurance, term life insurance, whole life insurance

family member
Insurer Operations. For insurance coverage purposes, a person related to the insured by blood, marriage, or adoption, including a ward or foster

child who is a member of the household.

see: dependent, family exclusion, spouse's benefit

Personal. As respects the personal auto and homeowners policies, a person related to the named insured or the named insured's spouse by blood, marriage or adoption, and who resides in the named insured's household.

see: liability coverage exclusion endorsement, personal auto policy

family protection endorsement

Automobile.

see: uninsured motorist coverage

farm credit system associations

Organizations. Associations comprised of the major lenders to farmers, including the federal land bank associations, the federal intermediate credit associations and the production credit associations.

farm laborer

Workers' Compensation.

synonym: agricultural worker

farm use

Automobile. An automobile rating classification for a vehicle that is principally garaged on a farm or ranch and not used in any business other than farming or ranching.

see: business use, drive to or from work, pleasure use

farmers' comprehensive personal liability policy (FCPL)

Personal. A personal liability policy similar to the comprehensive personal liability policy, adapted to cover liability exposures peculiar to farming, such as damage caused by grazing animals, farm employees, and the sale of farm products. This coverage is included in the farmowners policy but is written as a separate policy when an individual is not covered by a farmowners or homeowners policy.

compare: comprehensive personal liability policy; *see*: farmowners policy, homeowners policy

farmers mutual insurer

Insurer Operations. A mutual insurer formed by farmers to insure fire, hail and other casualty losses to farm property, stock and rural buildings.

see: agricultural cooperative, mutual insurance company

farming personal liability endorsement

Personal. An endorsement (ISO form HO 24 72) to the homeowners policy forms that applies section II coverage (personal liability and medical payments) to farming activities on the residential premises. This endorsement can only be used when farming

is incidental to the use of the property as a residence.

see: homeowners policy

farmowners and ranchowners policy

Personal. A package policy designed for family-owned ranches and farms patterned after a homeowners policy. Coverages include farm dwellings (and their contents), barns, stables and other farm structures.

see: homeowners policy

farmowners personal liability form

Personal. An endorsement covering a farmer's liability arising out of a collision between an animal owned by the farmer that has escaped its enclosure and a motor vehicle owned or operated by a third party. The collision must occur on a public highway or road and not while the animal was being transported in a vehicle.

see: animal insurance, ranchowners personal liability form

farmowners policy

Personal. A package policy designed for family-owned ranches and farms patterned after a homeowners policy. Coverages include farm dwellings and their contents, barns, stables and other farm structures.

compare: homeowners policy, ranchowners policy

farthest terminal

Automobile. As respects a zone rated commercial vehicle, the city farthest from its normal garage location to which the vehicle travels.

see: radius of operation, zone rating

fault of management

Property. As used in the schedule rating of commercial property risks, hazards that exist due to the negligence or wrongdoing of corporate officers or key personnel and to which rating penalties are applied. These additional charges can be removed when the condition is eliminated. Such hazards include poor housekeeping, general disrepair, and improper or unsafe storage—all conditions attributable to management's indifference or neglect.

compare: increased hazard; *see*: aftercharge

fault tree analysis

Loss Control/Risk Management. A safety system analysis technique developed in 1962 by Bell Laboratories that was first used to analyze the hazards associated with the Minuteman intercontinental ballistic missile. A diagram is developed that resembles a pine tree with the fault event at the top of the tree and the branches displaying subsystems. It represents the causal relationships between certain subsystem failures and a loss or undesired event.

Two types of logic gates (*and* gate, *or* gate) are used to connect the subsystems.

see: decision tree, hazard logic tree analysis

faulty work exclusion

Liability. An exclusion in products-completed operations insurance that prevents an insured from recovering for a loss to his or her own work due to the insured's poor craftsmanship. However, the exclusion does not apply to damage to other property caused by the insured's faulty work or defective product.

see: maintenance bond, products-completed operations insurance

Automobile. An exclusion in the garage coverage form for property damage, including the cost to make repairs, if the damage was caused by the garage's work on the vehicle or by parts used in the work.

synonym: work you performed exclusion; *see*: defective products exclusion, garage coverage form

feasibility study

Risk Management. A study or research project undertaken to determine whether a given plan of action will succeed. In risk management, such studies are undertaken to determine whether a business should self-insure, form a captive insurance company, or join with other businesses in a risk sharing pool.

see: risk management proces s

Federal Aviation Administration (FAA)

Aviation/Regulation. The U.S. federal agency charged with regulating air commerce, fostering aviation safety, promoting civil aviation, maintaining a national system of airports, achieving efficient use of navigable airspace, and operating a common system of air traffic control.

see: Federal Aviation Regulations

Federal Aviation Regulations

Aviation/Regulation. Rules and regulations administered by the Federal Aviation Administration, to control and maintain safety in airspace over the United States.

federal bond

Surety. A bond guaranteeing that specific acts will be performed or that obligations will be met with respect to the federal government and its laws and regulations.

see: bond (*Surety*), customs bond, export bond, immigrant bond

Federal Coal Mine Health and Safety Act

Regulation.

see: Black Lung Act

Federal Coal Mine Health and Safety Act coverage endorsement

Workers' Compensation. An endorsement (NCCI form WC 00 01 02) to a workers' compensation policy that includes federal Coal Mine Health and Safety Act coverages.

see: black lung, Black Lung Act

federal crime insurance program

Crime. A crime insurance program that protects personal property of homeowners, tenants and small businesses located in high crime areas against burglary or robbery. The program is administered by the Federal Insurance Administration.

see: Federal Insurance Administration, National Insurance Development Corporation, Urban Development Act of 1970

Federal Crop Insurance Corporation (FCIC)

Organizations. A federal agency that is part of the U.S. Department of Agriculture. It provides crop coverage for farmers.

see: crop insurance

Federal Deposit Insurance Corporation (FDIC)

Organizations. A federal agency created by Congress to insure the deposits of federally chartered banks. The insurance is financed through premiums charged the financial institution, and each insured account is covered up to $100,000.

see: Savings Association Insurance Fund, Securities Investor Protection Corporation

Federal Emergency Management Agency (FEMA)

Organizations. An agency of the federal government responsible for federal response and recovery assistance in the event of a major disaster. It provides assistance to individuals and public entities that suffer property damage in emergencies or disasters declared as such by the President. It is also the parent organization of the Federal Insurance Administration.

see: Federal Insurance Administration

Federal Employers' Liability Act coverage endorsement

Workers' Compensation. An endorsement (NCCI form WC 00 01 04) to a workers' compensation policy that includes coverage for any liability of an employer pursuant to the Federal Employers' Liability Act.

see: Federal Employers' Liability Act

Federal Employers' Liability Act (FELA)

Regulation/Workers' Compensation. A federal statute that provides to injured employees of interstate railroads the right to sue their employer for employment-related injuries. Interstate railroads are exempt from state workers' compensation laws, which normally limit an injured employee's remedies to scheduled benefits.

see: tort, workers' compensation law

Federal Environmental Pesticide Control Act
Regulation.

see: Federal Insecticide Fungicide and Rodenticide Act

federal funds rate
Financial Planning.

see: discount rate

Federal Insecticide, Fungicide and Rodenticide Act (FIFRA)
Regulation. Federal legislation adopted in 1947 and amended by the Federal Environmental Pesticide Control Act in 1972. The provisions of the Act are administered by the Environmental Protection Agency and require the registration of all pesticides prior to sale or distribution.

see: Environmental Protection Agency

Federal Insurance Administration (FIA)
Organizations. A federal agency that oversees the administration of the National Flood Insurance Program and the Federal Crime Insurance Program. It is part of the Department of Housing and Urban Development. It has no involvement in the regulation of the insurance industry.

see: federal crime insurance program, National Flood Insurance Program

Federal Insurance Contributions Act (FICA)
Regulation. A federal statute that established a payroll tax to assist in the funding of Social Security benefits.

see: Social Security

Federal Motor Carrier Act
Regulation. Federal legislation passed in 1935 and subsequently amended in 1980 that prescribes the legal liability of organizations engaged in transporting goods for hire.

see: motor truck cargo insurance

federal official bond
Surety.

see: public official bond

Federal Savings and Loan Insurance Corporation (FSLIC)
Regulation. A corporation formed by Congress to insure the deposits of federally chartered savings and loans institutions. It was abolished in 1989 and replaced by the Resolution Trust Corporation,

which in turn was replaced by the Savings Association Insurance Fund.

see: Federal Deposit Insurance Corporation, Resolution Trust Corporation, Savings Association Insurance Fund

Federal Tort Claims Act
Regulation. Federal legislation adopted in 1946 and subsequently amended that waives sovereign immunity and establishes conditions under which the United States and its agencies may be held liable for injuries caused by government employees acting within the scope of their employment. The government remains immune from suits for most intentional torts (e.g., assault, battery, false imprisonment, libel) and from punitive damages. Immunity also extends to officials exercising discretionary authority (making policy or general management decisions), as opposed to ordinary, ministerial duties.

see: sovereign immunity, tort

Federal Trade Commission (FTC)
Regulation. A federal agency that has conducted numerous investigations of the insurance industry but exercises no regulatory powers save enforcement of the Fair Credit Reporting Act, which requires insurers to notify an applicant for insurance that a credit report is required.

see: Fair Credit Reporting Act, McCarran-Ferguson Act

Federal Water Pollution Control Act
Regulation. Federal legislation (U.S. Code Title 33, Chapter 26) enacted in 1972 for the purpose of restoring and maintaining the integrity of the nation's waters. It mandates that each state adopt water quality standards for both intrastate and interstate waters. It is administered by the Environmental Protection Agency and the Army Corps of Engineers. It establishes a federal permit system for discharge of waste into U.S. waters, including wetlands. It authorizes state permit programs and regulates dredge and fill operations.

synonym: Clean Water Act; *see*: Environmental Protection Agency

Federation of Insurance and Corporate Counsel (FICC)
Organizations. Members: Attorneys involved in the legal aspects of the insurance industry, insurance company executives and corporate counsels involved in the defense of claims. *Objectives*: Conducting research through the Federation of Insurance and Corporate Counsel Foundation. Sponsoring essay competitions for students at accredited law schools and bestowing awards. *Founded*: 1936. *Headquarters*: Walpole, MA.

fee for service

Health. Payment to providers of medical services according to the services performed. The fee for each procedure or treatment is individually billed by the provider and paid in full by the patient, insurer, or other health benefit plan sponsor.

compare: all-payer system, capitation; *see*: health benefit plan, usual customary and reasonable fees

fee per person

Health.

see: capitation

fee schedule

Health. A list of medical and surgical procedures and related services with corresponding maximum fees or benefits payable to hospitals, physicians, and other health care providers by health insurers or other sponsors of a health benefit plan. For instance, under the Medicare program, every physician service is listed with a numerical value, which is multiplied by a sum of money (dollar conversion factor) to determine how much the doctor is paid. The list of payable fees is updated annually based on an economic index formula that considers medical cost inflation.

synonym: approved charges, schedule, table of allowances; *compare*: unallocated benefit; *see*: diagnosis related group, Medicare, reasonable and customary charge, usual customary and reasonable fees

Workers' Compensation. Most states publish a schedule of maximum fees that medical providers may receive for procedures covered by workers' compensation insurance.

see: workers' compensation insurance

fee simple

Financial Planning/Title. A form of property ownership where the property is owned completely and can be sold or transferred unconditionally. Upon the death of a fee simple property owner, the title passes to the owner's estate.

compare: fee tail; *see*: absolute title, freehold

fee tail

Financial Planning/Title. An estate inherited by the donor's direct descendants.

compare: fee simple; *see*: freehold

fellow employee exclusion

Automobile/Liability. An exclusion in the business auto, garage and truckers' policies that excludes liability coverage for an injury to an employee negligently caused by a fellow employee.

compare: fellow servant rule; *see*: business auto coverage form, garage coverage form, truckers' coverage form

Fellow of Patient Accounts

Organizations. A professional designation awarded by the Health Care Financial Management Association after successful completion of a national examination.

see: Health Care Financial Management Association

Fellow of the Casualty Actuarial Society (FCAS)

Organizations. A professional designation conferred by the Casualty Actuarial Society after passing twelve examinations on actuarial science, insurance mathematics, statistics, accounting and finance.

see: Casualty Actuarial Society

Fellow of the Life Management Institute (FLMI)

Health/Life/Organizations. A professional designation awarded to individuals who successfully complete ten life and health insurance examinations, in such areas as finance, marketing, law, accounting, management and personnel, employee benefits, and information (computer) systems. The courses and examinations are administered by the Life Office Management Association (LOMA).

see: Life Management Institute, Life Office Management Association

Fellow of the Society of Actuaries (FSA)

Health/Life/Risk Management. A professional designation earned by passing ten examinations on the mathematics of life and health insurance, actuarial science, accounting, and finance. In addition, successful candidates must meet other educational and experience requirements. Exams and courses are administered by the Society of Actuaries.

see: Society of Actuaries

Fellow of the Society of Pension Actuaries (FSPA)

Organizations. An advanced designation awarded to Members of the Society of Pension Actuaries who successfully complete two examinations on pensions and actuarial practice.

see: actuary, pension

fellow servant rule

Workers' Compensation. Prior to enactment of workers' compensation laws, this was a common law defense used by employers in tort suits brought by injured employees. The theory was that if the employee's injury resulted from a negligent act or omission of a fellow employee, that person was responsible, not the employer. The fellow servant rule, assumption of risk, and contributory negligence were the "unholy trinity" of defenses that left many workers uncompensated for their injuries. Statutory reforms made these defenses inapplicable to workers' compensation claims.

see: assumption of risk, common law defense, contributory negligence, Priestly v. Fowler, tort, workers' compensation law

felony

Law. A grave crime, more serious than a misdemeanor; a crime punishable by imprisonment for more than one year.

compare: misdemeanor; *see*: criminal law

fender wall

Loss Control. A wall used in buildings made of combustible material to slow the spread of fire from one section to another. The fender wall is constructed of fire resistive or slow-burning materials and protrudes from both sides of the building from the ground level to above the roof line (or parapet).

compare: fire wall; *see*: combustible, fire resistive, parapet

fictitious group

Regulation. A group organized mainly to purchase insurance at a reduced rate. Many states have laws that prohibit the formation of fictitious groups. The Liability Risk Retention Act of 1986 precludes state laws from restricting fictitious purchasing groups.

compare: affinity group, discretionary group, true group insurance; *see*: purchasing group, group insurance

fidelity bond

Surety. A bond covering an employer for a loss resulting from an employee's dishonest acts.

synonym: individual fidelity bond; *see*: blanket position bond, name position bond, position schedule bond

fiduciary

General. A person occupying a position of special trust and confidence, usually one holding the funds or items of value of another under personal care, custody, or control.

see: bailee

Regulation. Insurance by nature establishes a fiduciary relationship between the insurer (the fiduciary) and the insured. Insurers hold the funds of many and are entrusted to manage those funds prudently, so that money will be available in the event of an insured loss. Because of this, oversight and control in the form of regulation is necessary to protect the public interest.

Reinsurance. A ceding insurer's fiduciary obligation with respect to a reinsurer's interests has been recognized in some court decisions. Because the ceding insurer in a treaty reinsurance arrangement accepts risks that obligate the reinsurer, and thereby controls the fortunes of the reinsurer, courts

have determined that a ceding insurer owes the reinsurance company the same duty as any other fiduciary.

see: follow the fortunes, treaty reinsurance, uberrima fides

fiduciary bond

Surety. A type of judicial bond that guarantees the faithful performance of a fiduciary (e.g., an executor, guardian, or a trustee) as directed by the court.

compare: court bond; *see*: judicial bond, probate bond

fiduciary liability insurance

Professional Liability. Professional liability coverage for people and organizations who act as a fiduciary under the provisions of the Employee Retirement Income Security Act. Fiduciaries include anyone responsible for the investment, control or disposition of assets held by a plan covered under the Act. Coverage is sometimes included for administrative errors and omissions liability, which duplicates the employee benefit plan liability coverage often endorsed to a general liability policy. Coverage is provided on a claims-made basis.

see: employee benefit plan liability insurance, Employee Retirement Income Security Act, professional liability insurance

field

Agency. A term no longer in frequent use, referring to a geographic area or territory covered by an agent, special agent, agency or insurer.

Insurer Operations. A type or line of insurance, as "in the life insurance field."

field adjuster

Insurer Operations. A claims adjuster who works outside the office. Field adjusting is principally used for claims for real property damage, automobile physical damage, and auto liability property damage. Most liability, workers' compensation, and casualty claims are handled by inside adjusters, who may use outside adjusting firms if any field investigation is needed.

synonym: outside adjuster; *compare*: inside adjuster; *see*: claim adjustment, claims adjuster, drop check procedure

field expenses

Insurer Operations. Commissions, training allowances, agency and local office salaries and rent, and all other expenses incurred in agency supervision and the production of new business.

see: expense loading, field

field force

Agency/Insurer Operations. Employees of an insurance company or agency that work away from

the home or principal office.
see: field

field representative
Agency/Insurer Operations.
see: marketing representative, special agent

field service representative
Insurer Operations. An employee of an insurer or managing general agent who assists agents or solicitors in the soliciting or negotiating of insurance.
see: field, managing general agent

file-and-use rating
Regulation. The practice in some states of allowing insurers to implement new rates upon filing them with the insurance commissioner, without waiting for specific approval.
compare: modified prior approval rating, open competition rating, prior approval rating, use-and-file rating; *see*: rate making, rate regulation

filing requirements
Regulation. The specific information and documents that are required to be filed by an insurance company with a state department of insurance in order to write certain kinds of business or to obtain approval for new rates or coverage forms.
see: rate making

film and television producers' errors and omissions insurance
Professional Liability. Professional liability coverage for the producers of movie and TV shows that includes liability for violation of intellectual property rights, such as copyright infringement. Coverage is usually written on a claims-made basis.
see: entertainment insurance, errors and omissions insurance

film and television producers' indemnity insurance
Professional Liability.
see: cast insurance

film coverage
Inland Marine. Coverage (ISO form CM 00 45) on an all-risk basis for exposed motion picture and magnetic or video tapes, including sound tracks and records. Exclusions include loss due to faulty stock, faulty cameras and sound equipment, and faulty developing, editing and processing, but some underwriters will delete many of these exclusions for an additional premium.
synonym: negative film coverage; *see*: all-risk insurance

financed premium
Insurer Operations. Payment of insurance premiums, in whole or in part, with funds borrowed from

a financial institution. This term does not apply to payment of premiums with funds borrowed from a policy's cash value or payment terms offered by an insurer at no additional cost.
see: premium financing

Financial Accounting Standard No. 113
Accounting/Reinsurance. A standard issued by the Financial Accounting Standards Board in December 1992 saying that, for an insurer to take credit for reinsurance, it must transfer substantial insurance risk to the reinsurer, and the reinsurer must have a reasonable possibility of suffering a significant loss under the contract.
see: Financial Accounting Standards Board, financial reinsurance, reinsurance

Financial Accounting Standard No. 115
Accounting. A standard issued by the Financial Accounting Standards Board that requires insurers to value bonds held for sale at their market value on the insurer's financial statements. Statutory accounting continues to require that insurers report bond values at their amortized value. Prior to the adoption of FAS 115, bonds were valued at their value upon maturity.
see: Financial Accounting Standards Board

Financial Accounting Standard No. 5, paragraph 44
Accounting. A statement published in March, 1975, by the Financial Accounting Standards Board titled "Payments to Insurance Enterprises that May Not Involve Transfer of Risk." To the extent that an insurance contract or reinsurance contract does not, despite its form, provide for indemnification of the insured or the ceding enterprise by the insurer or reinsurer against loss or liability, the premium paid, minus the amount of the premium to be retained by the insurer or reinsure must be accounted for as a deposit by the insured or the ceding enterprise. Contracts may be structured in various ways, but if in substance all or a part of the premium paid by the insured or the ceding enterprise is a deposit, it must be accounted for as such.
see: Financial Accounting Standards Board, risk transfer

Financial Accounting Standard No. 5, paragraphs 8 and 9
Accounting. A standard published in March, 1975 by the Financial Accounting Standards Board which requires that a self-insured reserve be established for any existing condition or situation of uncertainty as to possible gain or loss to an enterprise that will be resolved when one or more future events occur·or fail to occur.
see: Financial Accounting Standards Board, reserve

Financial Accounting Standards Board (FASB)

Accounting. A professional standards board created by accountants to establish Generally Accepted Accounting Principles (GAAP), which are the accounting standards used by accountants in the U.S. The GAAP reporting method makes it possible for investors and regulatory authorities to accurately determine an organization's financial results. A previous name for this Board was the Accounting Principles Board.

see: Generally Accepted Accounting Principles, Governmental Accounting Standards Board

Financial Analysis and Solvency Tracking System (FAST)

Regulation. A system of confidential risk scoring models developed in 1995 by the National Association of Insurance Commissioners for "nationally significant" insurers to supplement the Insurance Regulatory Information System. Like the IRIS, FAST consists of a series of financial ratios based on annual statement data. It produces a score for each insurer which is used to prioritize them for audits.

see: Insurance Regulatory Information System, National Association of Insurance Commissioners

financial derivative

Financial Planning. A two-party financial contract the worth of which is derived from the value of some underlying asset (e.g., a currency, security or commodity), reference interest rate (e.g., a rate based on the prime), or index (e.g., Standard & Poor's Composite Index). Examples are futures contracts, swaps, call options, and put options.

see: call option, counterparty, currency swap, forward contract, futures contract, put option, swap

financial futures

Financial Planning. Futures contracts for interest-sensitive securities, such as Treasury bills, Treasury bonds, Treasury notes, and mortgage participation certificates.

see: futures contract, mortgage-backed security, Treasury bill, Treasury bond, Treasury note

financial guaranty bond

Surety. Any judicial bond that guarantees the payment of money, such as an appeal bond, bail bond, plaintiff review bond, or sales tax bond.

see: court bond, judicial bond

financial guaranty insurance

Financial Guaranty. A form of insurance that first appeared in the 1930s as mortgage guaranty insurance and returned in the 1970s in several different forms (municipal bond guaranty insurance, limited partnership investor bond insurance, residential value insurance, etc.). Today, most states exclude mortgage guaranty and consumer-oriented credit insurance from their definition of financial guaranty insurance. It is a descendant of suretyship and is generally recorded as surety on the annual statement that insurers file with regulators. Loss may be payable in any of the following events: the failure of an obligor on a debt instrument or other monetary obligation to pay principal, interest, purchase price or dividends when due as a result of default or insolvency (including corporate or partnership obligations, guaranteed stock, municipal or special revenue bonds, asset-backed securities, consumer debt obligations, etc.); a change in interest rates; a change in currency exchange rates; or a change in the value of specific assets, commodities or financial indices. These contracts usually involve sophisticated insureds, and therefore rates may be exempt from general statutory standards.

see: consumer credit compliance insurance, credit insurance, efficacy coverage, equipment value insurance, holder in due course insurance, investment return insurance, limited partnership investor bond insurance, manufacturer's penalty insurance, mortgage guaranty insurance, movie completion bond, municipal bond guaranty insurance, mutual fund insurance, oil and gas deficiency insurance, residual value insurance, suretyship

Financial Institution Bond Form 24

Crime.

see: banker's blanket bond

Financial Institutions Insurance Association

Organizations. Members: Financial and insurance companies, brokers, marketing and support organizations interested in selling insurance through financial institutions. *Objectives:* National trade association dedicated to the marketing of insurance services by financial institutions. *Headquarters:* Berwyn, PA.

financial lease

Accounting. A lease that does not provide for maintenance services, is not cancelable, and is fully amortized over its lifetime.

financial ratios

Financial Planning. Mathematical ratios developed from a corporation's financial statements that are used to analyze its financial strength and stability by institutions making credit or investment decisions. Making these calculations and evaluating the results is often called *ratio analysis* or *fundamental analysis.*

see: asset composition ratio, common equity ratio, current ratio, debt-to-assets ratio, debt-to-equity ratio, earnings per share, earnings yield, financial statement, financial underwriting, net worth ratio, operating ratio, price earnings ratio, quick ratio, return on investment, return on sales ratio

Financial Regulations and Accreditation Program

Regulation. A program of the National Association of Insurance Commissioners begun in 1990 that requires states and their insurance departments to have laws, regulations and procedures necessary for effective insurer solvency regulation. Independent auditors evaluate each state annually for compliance with the standards. An insurer licensed in an unaccredited state may not be admitted to do business in an accredited state until the insurer is audited by representatives of an accredited state.

see: National Association of Insurance Commissioners

financial reinsurance

Reinsurance. A form of reinsurance designed to ease the drain on the ceding insurer's surplus during a period of rapid premium growth or reduction in surplus because of unexpected claims or other financial losses.

see: ceding insurer, Financial Accounting Standard No. 113, reinsurance, reinsurance credit

financial responsibility law

Automobile/Liability/Regulation. A law that requires a person or organization to furnish evidence of ability to respond to claims for harm from a specified type of activity. The most common financial responsibility requirement applies to motor vehicle operators, who must have evidence of ability to pay for automobile-related injuries or damage. An auto liability policy is the main form of financial responsibility. Some states allow drivers to post a bond or deposit cash and acceptable securities into a trust fund held by a state official in lieu of insurance.

Financial responsibility laws, notably including federal laws, also apply to some businesses that pose a risk of large-scale damage, such as nuclear plants and facilities that generate and store or dispose of toxic waste. The financial responsibility options for these facilities are a trust fund, surety bond, letter of credit, or insurance.

compare: compulsory insurance law; *see*: automobile liability bond, closure and post-closure insurance, nuclear energy liability insurance

financial risk

Financial Planning. The risk associated with making a financial or a speculative investment, which can result in a financial gain or loss.

synonym: investment risk

Risk Management. A portion of total corporate risk, over and above basic business risk, that results from using debt.

see: business risk, hedging

financial risk management

Financial Planning. The procedures used by a business to analyze financial risks, such as changes in interest rates, cost of capital, foreign currency, commodity prices and other financial variables, and the financial techniques employed to control their effects.

see: economic perils, risk management

financial statement

Accounting. A written report summarizing the financial status of an organization for a stated period of time. It describes the organization's activities and resulting profit or loss, the flow of resources, and the distribution or retention of profits.

see: annual report, audited financial statement, balance sheet, balance sheet reserves, consolidated financial statement, financial underwriting, Generally Accepted Accounting Principles, income statement, retained earnings, statement of changes in financial position, statement of opinion

financial underwriting

Insurer Operations. The review of an organization's financial statements and related background with the belief that this will indicate the quality of its management. This financial analysis can reveal the moral and morale hazards present in an organization and the potential of the organization for growth, as well as confirm that exposures to risk exist and indicate its ability to pay premiums and comply with financial obligations or guarantees.

see: cash flow underwriting, cash flow program, financial ratios, financial statements, paid loss retrospective rating plan

fine arts coverage

Personal. One of the nine classes of property that can be covered under a personal articles floater. Fine arts include private collections of paintings, etchings, pictures, tapestries, art glass windows, and other bona fide works of art (such as valuable rugs, statuary, antique furniture, rare books, antique silver, porcelain, rare glass, and bric-a-brac). Fine arts are usually insured on a stated amount basis.

see: breakage exclusion, fine arts floater, pair or set, personal articles floater, stated amount

fine arts floater

Inland Marine. An inland marine form that provides coverage for fine arts (paintings, statues, sculptures or antiques) on an all-risk basis. Usually, items to be covered are scheduled on the form for a specified stated amount.

see: floater policy, inland marine insurance

fine print

Regulation. In an earlier period, policy benefits were presented in larger print, while small type was used for exclusions, reductions, exemptions, and limitations of coverage. Most state laws now specify a minimum type size for both benefits and exclusions. In some cases, exclusions must be printed in type that is larger than that used to illustrate benefits.

see: insurance contract

finished stock

Property. Merchandise that has been manufactured by the insured, excluding goods held for sale on the premises of a retail outlet insured for business income loss.

see: stock (*Property*)

finite risk insurance

Financial Guaranty/Reinsurance. An insurance or reinsurance contract that transfers financial risk of loss from an insured to an insurer over a specified period of time, subject to an ultimate limit of liability, and which usually includes a profit-sharing feature. The insurer holds large sums belonging to the insured in some form of savings account and a part of the investment income is rebated to the insured.

see: blended finite risk insurance, commutation clause, profit-sharing provision, time and distance reinsurance

fire

Property. A rapid, persistent chemical reaction that releases heat. For coverage purposes, a fire must be "hostile," not "friendly."

see: class A fire, class B fire, class C fire, class D fire, explosion, fire triangle, friendly fire, hostile fire

fire and theft coverage

Automobile. Physical damage coverage that can be added to an automobile, garage or truckers' policy for the specific perils of fire, lightning, explosion, theft, flood, mischief or vandalism, or the sinking, burning, collision, or derailment of a conveyance transporting the covered vehicle. The coverage is included in the specified causes of loss endorsement.

compare: comprehensive coverage, fire coverage, fire theft and windstorm coverage, limited specified perils; *see:* physical damage coverage, specified causes of loss

Fire and Theft Index Bureau

Organizations. A department of the American Insurance Association which compiles and shares fire and theft claims information with Association members in an attempt to identify and prevent fraudulent claims.

see: American Insurance Association, Insurance Crime Prevention Institute, Insurance Services Office, interinsurer claim service organization, Medical Information Bureau, National Automobile Theft Bureau, Property Insurance Loss Register

fire brigade

Property.

see: underwriters' fire patrol

fire coverage

Automobile. Physical damage coverage that can be added to an automobile, garage or truckers' policy for the specific perils of fire, lightning, explosion or the sinking, burning, collision, or derailment of a conveyance transporting the covered vehicle. The coverage is included in the specified causes of loss endorsement.

compare: comprehensive coverage, fire and theft coverage, fire theft and windstorm coverage, limited specified perils; *see:* physical damage coverage, specified causes of loss

fire damage liability

Liability. Coverage protecting an insured against liability incurred for negligent acts resulting in fire damage to a premises rented by or loaned to the insured. This coverage is included in the ISO commercial general liability coverage form, usually for a limit of $50,000, with higher limits available for an additional premium. Occasionally, this coverage is added to fire insurance policies. This coverage is usually not increased by an excess liability or umbrella liability policy.

synonym: fire liability; *see:* commercial general liability policy, fire damage limit

fire damage limit

Liability. The amount provided under the ISO commercial general liability coverage form for liability claims arising from any one fire, usually $50,000. Higher limits may be purchased for an additional premium.

see: commercial general liability policy, fire damage liability

fire department service clause

Property. A provision in most fire insurance policies that indemnifies the insured for fees charged by a fire department for responding to a fire alarm at the insured location. The provision applies to insured property located outside a fire district where an alarm will be answered only for a fee.

fire detection systems

Loss Control. A system or apparatus designed to

discover or determine the existence of a fire within a building or structure, then sounding or sending an alarm. Such systems include smoke detectors, heat detectors and fusible link monitors.

fire division

Loss Control/Property. A section of a structure formed by fire walls and fire doors designed to stop a fire from spreading beyond or into its confines.

see: cut-off, fire door, fire stop, fire wall, parapet

fire door

Loss Control/Property. A door constructed of noncombustible materials that has been tested and rated for its resistance to fire. Fire doors may be used in horizontal openings (ceilings and floors) or vertical openings (walls), and usually must remain closed under normal circumstances. They must be equipped to shut automatically in the presence of fire.

see: fire division

fire extinguisher

Loss Control. A portable or wheeled apparatus for putting out small fires by ejecting fire-extinguishing chemicals. Fire extinguishers are classified by a letter or group of letters to indicate the type(s) of fires they are designed to extinguish.

see: carbon dioxide, class A fire, class B fire, class C fire, class D fire, dry chemicals, foam, halon

fire extinguishing system

Loss Control. An apparatus or system designed to cause a fire to cease burning or to quench it. Such systems include water spray, carbon dioxide, dry chemicals, halon and foam, portable or fixed fire extinguishing systems.

see: automatic sprinkler system, carbon dioxide, dry chemicals, fire extinguisher, foam, halon

fire insurance

Property. Coverage for losses to real or personal property (usually excluding currency, securities, accounts and deeds) directly caused by fire or lightning.

see: friendly fire, hostile fire, New York standard fire policy

fire liability

Liability.

see: fire damage liability

fire liability coverage

International/Property.

see: neighbors and tenants liability coverage

fire load

Loss Control. The amount of combustibles present

in a given situation, usually expressed in terms of weight of combustible material per square foot.

fire map

Loss Control/Property. A diagram that represents an individual property, industrial complex or properties within a specific area. Fire maps usually distinguish different types of construction (e.g., frame, reinforced concrete, etc.) and indicate the proximity of fire hydrants and stations. Fire maps are principally used to present large accounts to underwriters and for loss control purposes. Historically, they were used by fire insurers to plot insured properties for the purpose of avoiding catastrophic losses.

see: block limit, map, Sanborn Map Company Inc.

fire mark

Property. A metal plaque or medallion that in times past was attached to the front of buildings to indicate which fire brigade was to extinguish a fire in that building. Each insurer had its own fire brigade and would compete for business on the brigade's ability to extinguish a fire. The original fire marks are valuable collectors items today.

see: underwriters fire patrol

fire marshal

Loss Control. A state, county or municipal official that is responsible for fire prevention and public fire safety in a specified geographic area.

Fire Office Committee forms (FOC)

International. Uniform international property insurance forms developed by the Fire Office Committee in London, England.

fire prevention

Loss Control. Measures taken to avoid a fire.

see: fire protection, loss prevention

fire protection

Loss Control. Methods of providing for fire control or fire extinguishment. Also, the prevention, detection, and extinguishment of fire.

see: fire extinguishing system, fire map, loss control specialist, protection

fire protection funds

Loss Control. Any funds collected, assessed or appropriated to support local fire departments.

fire resistance

Loss Control. A relative term, used with numerical rating or modifying adjectives to indicate the extent to which a material or structure resists the effect of fire. *Example*: Fire resistance of two hours.

see: fire resistive, fire retardant

fire resistive

Loss Control. Properties, material or equipment designed to resist fire.

compare: fireproof; *see*: fire retardant, flame retardant

fire resistive construction

Loss Control. A building or structure constructed of fire resistive materials to reduce the severity of a potential fire. Lower fire insurance rates apply to fire resistive construction.

compare: fireproof; *see*: concrete tilt-up construction, construction

fire retardant

Loss Control. Chemicals (such as boric acid, ammonium sulfate, and calcium chloride) used to treat materials or property for the purpose of reducing or delaying their flammability.

see: flame retardant

fire stop

Loss Control. A barrier of thick wood, or incombustible material used to limit the rapid spread of fire in hollow walls, floors, other concealed air spaces, and under long continuous work tables.

see: fire division

fire, theft and windstorm coverage

Automobile. Physical damage coverage that can be added to an automobile, garage or truckers' policy for the specific perils of fire, lightning, explosion, theft, or windstorm or the sinking, burning, collision, or derailment of a conveyance transporting the covered vehicle. The coverage is included in the specified causes of loss endorsement.

compare: comprehensive coverage, fire coverage, fire and theft coverage, limited specified perils; *see*: physical damage coverage, specified causes of loss

fire triangle

Loss Control. The three ingredients needed for a fire, sometimes represented as the sides of a triangle: an ignition source, oxygen and fuel. If any one of the three is not present or is removed, a fire cannot start or continue to burn.

fire wall

Loss Control. A wall separating a building into parts in order to prevent fire from spreading; a wall from floor to roof made of incombustible materials and having no open doors, windows or other spaces through which fire can pass. Fire walls and fire doors create fire divisions.

compare: fender wall; *see*: cut-off, fire division, fire door, parapet

firearms—special limit

Personal. The Insurance Services Office homeowners policy coverage C (personal property) has a special limit of liability for the theft of firearms of $2,000, which does not include such firearm accessories as detachable gun sights, carrying cases, slings, cartridges, shells, magazines, or clips.

see: homeowners policy—special limits of liability

firebox explosion

Property. The extended coverage provisions of a property insurance policy include coverage for explosion of accumulated gases or unconsumed fuel within the firebox, flues, or passages of any fired vessel. This provision can duplicate coverage provided by a boiler and machinery policy.

see: explosion, joint loss agreement

fired pressure vessel

Property.

see: pressure vessel

fireproof

Loss Control. A term historically used to describe a material or structure capable of withstanding damage by fire. It is misleading because no material or structure is totally safe from fire. The preferred term is *fire resistive.*

synonym: flameproof; *compare*: fire resistive; *see*: explosion-proof

first aid fire response

Loss Control. The immediate response to a fire by use of any means at hand, such as portable fire extinguishers, hoses, buckets of sand, etc.

first class mail coverage

Inland Marine. A form of mail insurance that provides coverage on an all-risk basis for negotiable and nonnegotiable securities and detached coupons that are shipped by first class mail.

see: mail coverage

first dollar

General. The primary amount of loss for which the insured is financially responsible.

see: deductible

first dollar coverage

Employee Benefits. An employee benefit plan that reimburses benefits from the first dollar of loss without applying a deductible.

see: employee benefit plan

Insurer Operations. An insurance coverage providing payment of claims without applying a deductible.

see: deductible

first dollar defense

Liability. Coverage under some umbrella or professional liability policies that indemnifies the policyholder for the cost of defending against claims, even when the claim falls within the policy's self-insured retention.

see: professional liability insurance, umbrella liability insurance

first-in-first-out (FIFO)

Accounting. An accounting method used to value inventory where sales are considered to be made against the earliest-purchased merchandise or inventory. During times of increasing prices, the FIFO method tends to overstate profits. FIFO, LIFO (last-in-first-out) and average cost are of importance to insurers, since inventory valuation methods are used in estimating business income losses.

compare: average cost, last-in-first-out; *see*: stock (*Property*)

first loss earthquake insurance

Property. An earthquake insurance policy that has a limit significantly less than the insured property's value and no coinsurance. It is designed to insure a portion of the 5% to 15% deductibles in standard earthquake insurance policies. First loss policies usually have a flat dollar deductible.

see: percentage of value deductible

first loss insurance

Property. A policy that covers only a single loss during the policy period or that provides coverage of multiple locations for only the first loss at each location during the policy period. Also, a policy whose limits are reduced (and not reinstated) by loss payments.

compare: automatic reinstatement clause; *see*: restoration premium, stop loss

first loss retention

Reinsurance.

see: net retention

first loss scale

Property.

see: Lloyd's property first loss scale

first named insured

Insurer Operations. The individual or entity whose name appears first in the declarations of a commercial policy. Some policy forms allow an insurer to satisfy contractual duties by giving notice (of cancellation, for example) to the first named insured, rather than requiring notice to all named insureds.

compare: additional insured, insured, named insured; *see*: evidence of cancellation

first-party insurance

Health/Life/Property. Coverage of the insured's own property (e.g., fire insurance, collision and comprehensive coverages of auto insurance) or person (life and health), as opposed to coverage for liability to others.

compare: third-party liability

first surplus reinsurance treaty

Reinsurance. The first layer of reinsurance in excess of the ceding insurer's net retention shared by the reinsurer and ceding insurer on a pro rata basis. Their respective shares can be fixed or variable, depending on the class of risk and the net retentions, which the ceding insurer retains.

see: second surplus treaty, surplus reinsurance treaty

first-year commission

Agency/Insurer Operations. The commission an insurance company pays to an insurance agent on a policy's first-year premium. In some lines of business (e.g., life, employee benefits), first-year commissions are paid at a higher rate than commissions for subsequent years.

compare: renewal commission; *see*: agent's commission, flat commission, graded commission, unlevel commission

fish coverage

Inland Marine.

see: record fish coverage, tagged fish coverage

five-percent rule

Property. A provision in a property insurance policy that covered losses less than $10,000 and less than 5% of the total amount insured do not need to be appraised or inventoried by the insurer.

see: coinsurance

five-year vesting

Employee Benefits.

see: ten-year vesting

fixed amount option

Life. An option that a life insurance beneficiary may select as a settlement whereby the policy proceeds are paid through periodic fixed installments until the principal and interest are exhausted.

compare: fixed period option, interest option, life income option, life income with period certain option; *see*: settlement options

fixed annuity

Life. An annuity that offers guaranteed or fixed benefit payments to the annuitant. A fixed annuity grows at a pre-set interest rate guaranteed by the insurer. In addition, the insurer guarantees to return the amount of principal paid in. Some insurers guarantee the interest rate only for an initial period (one to three years) but usually set a minimum guaranteed rate that will be paid regardless of economic conditions.

synonym: guaranteed annuity; *see*: annuity, bonus yield

fixed asset

Accounting. A capital asset, especially a permanent or immovable one, required for use in the operations of a business.

see: capital asset, fixed machinery, fixture

fixed barrier guard

Loss Control. A barrier guard located at a point of operation. An enclosure attached to the machine or equipment.

see: barrier guard

fixed base liability coverage

Aviation. Aircraft liability insurance specifically designed for fixed base operators such as aircraft dealers, charters, aircraft maintenance facilities, and flight instructors.

see: fixed base operators

fixed base operators

Aviation. A general aviation rating classification applying to businesses that are located (based) on the premises of airports and that own, operate, buy, sell, rent, or lease aircraft. They also may perform such services as fueling, repairs or flight instruction.

compare: business and pleasure, flying club, industrial aid operators; *see*: fixed base liability coverage, general aviation

fixed benefit

Life. A benefit from a life or annuity policy that does not vary in amount and is paid on a regular periodic basis.

fixed charges

Accounting. Costs that do not vary with the level of output, especially fixed financial costs such as interest, lease payments, and sinking fund payments.

fixed income

Financial Planning. Income that does not fluctuate, such as that derived from interest on savings, bonds, annuities, and preferred stock.

fixed income fund

Financial Planning. A mutual fund with the goal of maintaining a constant income stream by investing primarily in corporate or government bonds.

compare: growth income fund, equity fund; *see*: mutual fund

fixed machinery

Property. Machinery that is permanently affixed to

real property, including its hangings.

see: capital asset, fixed asset

fixed period option

Life. An option that a life insurance beneficiary may select as a settlement under which the policy proceeds are left on deposit with the insurer to accrue interest and are paid to the beneficiary in equal payments for a specific number of years.

compare: fixed amount option, interest option, life income option, life income with period certain option; *see*: settlement options

fixed rate mortgage

Financial Planning. A mortgage with an interest rate that remains constant over the life of the loan.

compare: graduated payment mortgage, variable rate mortgage

fixture

Property. An object attached to a building or structure as a permanent appendage, apparatus or appliance. At one time, fixtures were considered personal property, but now they are generally considered part of real property. An insurable interest can exist on the part of both the building owner and a tenant who has installed the fixtures.

see: capital asset, fixed asset, improvements and betterments, personal property, real estate, trade fixtures

flame resistant

Loss Control.

see: flame retardant

flame retardant

Loss Control. A material that has been chemically treated or has inherent properties so it not ignite readily or propagate flames under a small to moderate fire exposure.

synonym: flame resistant; *see*: fire resistance, fire resistive, fire retardant

flameproof

Loss Control. A term historically used to describe a material capable of withstanding ignition by a flame. It is a misnomer in that no material is totally flameproof. The preferred term is *flame retardant.*

compare: fire resistive; *synonym*: fireproof; *see*: flame retardant

flammable

Loss Control. Any material or substance that is easily ignited or will readily burn.

synonym: inflammable

flammable limits

Loss Control. Gases and flammable liquid vapors

that can form flammable mixtures with air or oxygen have upper and lower limits to the concentrations that will provide ignitable mixtures. The lower flammable or explosive level (LEL) is the lowest percentage of vapor in air that will burn. The upper flammable or explosive level (UEL) is the maximum percentage that will burn.

flash point
Loss Control. The lowest temperature at which a flammable mixture is formed between the vapor of a liquid and the surrounding air.

see: ignition temperature

flashover
Loss Control. A term used to describe the result of a process whereby a slowly developing fire (or radiant heat source) produces radiant energy at wall and ceiling surfaces; the radiant feedback from those surfaces gradually heats the contents of the fire area, and when all combustibles in the space have become heated to their ignition temperature, simultaneous ignition occurs.

flat amount benefit formula
Employee Benefits.
see: flat amount pension formula

flat amount pension formula
Employee Benefits. A pension plan under which all of the plan participants receive the same benefit amount on retirement. This usually requires each participant to attain a minimum number of service years and a minimum age. Upon achieving these requirements all participants receive the same dollar amount as a retirement benefit regardless of income, position, or additional years of service. *Example*: For each year of service, a participant is credited with $50 of monthly retirement income. If a person worked for 11 years, the monthly benefit would be $550.

synonym: flat amount benefit formula, flat schedule; *see*: pension

flat amount unit benefit formula
Employee Benefits. A method for determining the amount of pension benefits due an individual. *Formula*: per-year benefits amount × years of service completed = pension benefit.

see: pension

flat benefit
Health. An amount for specified medical expenses payable under certain circumstances, such as a $75 daily payment made while a person is confined to a hospital.

see: flat maternity benefit

flat cancellation
Insurer Operations. Cancellation of a policy on its

effective date as if it had never been issued. No coverage was provided and no premium is due.

compare: fully earned premium; *see*: cancellation, rescission, return premium

flat commission
Agency/Insurer Operations. A commission percentage rate that does not vary with the type of policy written, whether the policy is new or a renewal.

synonym: level commission; *compare*: first-year commission, graded commission; *see*: agent's commission

flat deductible
Property. A specific sum that is deducted from each loss or claim, regardless of the size of the loss or claim.

compare: franchise deductible, percentage of loss deductible, percentage of value deductible; *see*: deductible

flat dollar benefit formula
Employee Benefits.
see: flat amount pension formula

flat maternity benefit
Health. A maternity benefit of a specific sum, rather than one based on incurred medical or hospital expenses.

see: flat benefit, maternity benefit

flat percentage pension formula
Employee Benefits. A pension plan under which all eligible retirees receive the same percentage of annual wage.

see: pension

flat rate
Insurer Operations. An insurance rate that is not subsequently adjusted even if an insured risk suffers unexpectedly high losses.

see: rate making

Property. A property insurance rate used when no coinsurance clause appears in the policy. Usually higher than the coinsurance rate, the actual cost of a flat rated policy may be less because the insured values do not have to meet a coinsurance requirement and losses cannot be reduced by a coinsurance clause.

see: coinsurance

Reinsurance. 1. A reinsurance contract rate that is not subject to subsequent adjustment on the basis of loss experience or size of risk.

2. A reinsurance premium rate based on the entire premium income received by the ceding insurer from business ceded to the reinsurer, as distinguished from a rate applicable only to the excess limits premium.

see: reinsurance

flat schedule
Employee Benefits.
see: flat amount pension formula

fleet
Automobile. A business auto rating classification used when the insured owns five or more vehicles.
compare: nonfleet; *see*: business auto coverage form

fleet automatic
Automobile. An outdated term for blanket coverage on all commercial vehicles owned by the insured during the policy period. This is now provided by "any auto" coverage in the business auto, garage or truckers' policies.
compare: nonfleet automatic; *see*: automobile fleet, fleet policy, business auto coverage form, garage coverage form, truckers' coverage form

fleet of companies
Insurer Operations. Insurance companies that are under common ownership and, frequently, common management.
see: affiliated insurers

fleet policy
Automobile. A single automobile insurance contract that applies to a number of vehicles, usually five or more, under common ownership. Coverage may be written for specifically scheduled vehicles (nonfleet automatic, for example), or it may apply to all vehicles of the insured on a reporting or audit basis (fleet automatic).
see: automobile fleet, nonfleet automatic
Ocean Marine. A single ocean marine insurance policy that covers all ships of a single owner. A fleet policy is advantageous because older ships, which are less attractive from an underwriter's perspective, can be written at the lower average fleet rate.

Flesch readability test
Insurer Operations. A measurement of how easily a document can be read. It has been adopted by many state insurance departments to help consumers understand their policies. The test compares a document to a standard one written for a reader with an eighth-grade education. A good score requires simple words and short sentences. The simplified policy forms of the Insurance Services Office are designed to score well on this test.
see: easy read, insurance contract, Insurance Services Office, plain language laws

FLEX
International/Property. An acronym used principally in Europe for a standard group of property insurance perils covered by a policy: fire, lightning

and explosion.
compare: FLEXAC

FLEXAC
International/Property. An acronym used principally in Europe for a standard group of property insurance perils covered by a policy: fire, lightning, explosion and aircraft.
compare: FLEX

flexible benefit plan
Employee Benefits. A benefit program that complies with Internal Revenue Code § 125, allowing employees to choose between taxable benefits (including cash) and nontaxable health and welfare benefits (such as life and health insurance, child care, retirement plans and vacation pay). The allocation of the benefits is determined by the employee from the total amount provided by the employer.
synonym: flexible compensation; *compare*: cafeteria benefit plan; *see*: employee benefit plan, flexible spending account, medical savings account

flexible compensation
Employee Benefits.
see: flexible benefit plan

flexible premium adjustable life insurance
Life.
see: universal life insurance

flexible premium annuity
Life. An annuity that allows the amount of each premium payment to be determined by the insured. This type of annuity is used principally to fund individual retirement accounts and Keogh plans where payments are tied to an individual's earnings.
see: annuity, individual retirement account, Keogh plan

flexible premium life insurance
Life. A form of variable life insurance. After the payment of an initial premium, the amount and timing of each additional premium payment is determined by the insured. A minimum death benefit is guaranteed, with a higher benefit based on the actual premiums paid and the investment performance of the plan.
see: life insurance

flexible spending account (FSA)
Employee Benefits. A flexible benefit plan that allows an employee a tax exemption from federal and most state taxes to pay for approved expenses out of an account managed by the employer. Employees may have payroll deductions deposited to such an account during the year to be reimbursed at

year's end for out-of-pocket medical, dental, and day-care expenses. Since qualified expenses are paid with pre-tax funds, they are effectively less costly to the employee; however, unused funds in the account are forfeited to the government, making it important for participating employees not to overestimate their expenses.

compare: medical savings account; *see*: flexible benefit plan

flight coverage

Aviation. Coverage on a fixed-wing aircraft from its take-off run until it completes its landing roll. For a rotorcraft, coverage commences when the rotors start to revolve under power for the purpose of flight until they cease to revolve.

compare: ground coverage; *see*: in motion

flight simulator

Aviation.

see: Link trainer

float

Financial Planning. Interest earned by a bank in the time between deposit of a check and the earliest date that the bank allows the depositor to use those funds. With the advent of electronic fund transfers, many states are have laws shortening this period.

see: broker's float

floater

Financial Planning. A financial derivative in the form of a mortgage bond with a variable coupon rate tied to an index plus a spread which the counterparties agree to exchange on a specified date.

see: counterparty, coupon bond, financial derivative, mortgage bond

floater policy

Inland Marine. An inland marine policy designed to cover movable property wherever it may be located. It may be written on an all-risk, open perils or named perils form.

see: bicycle floater, camera floater, contractors' equipment floater, equipment dealers floater, equipment floater, fine arts floater, fur floater, installation floater, jewelry floater, livestock floater, pattern and die floater, personal articles floater, personal property floater, physicians' and surgeons' equipment floater, salesperson's samples floater, unscheduled property floater, wedding presents floater

floating rate note

Financial Planning. A note with an interest rate that varies depending upon the existing rate in the money market.

see: cap, collar, note

flood

Property. An overflowing of a body of water onto normally dry land or an unusual rise in the level of inland or tidal waters.

see: flood insurance, floodplain, National Flood Insurance Program

Flood Disaster Protection Act

Property. Federal legislation of 1973 that amended the National Flood Insurance Act of 1968. Major changes included making the new program mandatory for flood-prone communities and increasing the amount of coverage available.

see: National Flood Insurance Program

Flood Hazard Boundary Map

Loss Control. A flood map published by the Federal Insurance Administration for a specific community which indicates areas within the community that are subject to severe flooding. These maps are the basis for requiring a community to join the National Flood Insurance Program. If a community does not join the program, it may lose federal disaster relief in the event of flooding. Each community map is assigned an identification number which must be used when applying for flood insurance in that community.

see: National Flood Insurance Program

flood insurance

Property. Insurance that reimburses the policyholder for damage to property caused by the peril of flood.

see: flood, National Flood Insurance Program

Flood Insurance Manual

Property. A manual published by the National Flood Insurance Program that includes the program's eligibility and policy writing rules, as well as rating information.

see: National Flood Insurance Program

flood insurance rate map (FIRM)

Property. A flood map published by the Federal Insurance Administration developed from a community flood study and used to produce actuarial rates. Once this map is complete, a community is eligible for the National Flood Insurance Program. Rates developed from this map are termed *pre-FIRM* or *post-FIRM*, depending on when a building is constructed.

see: National Flood Insurance Program, post-FIRM rates, pre-FIRM rates

floodplain

Property. A relatively level area alongside a river that is periodically subject to flooding.

floor

Financial Planning. 1. The lower limit on a floating rate note.

2. A financial derivative similar to an option that protects the holder from a decline in price or some other underlying value beyond a specified point.

compare: cap, collar; *see*: financial derivative, floating rate note, option

floor plan insurance

Inland Marine. Inland marine insurance (ISO form CM 00 52 or AAIS form 745) that covers a lending institution for merchandise that has been financed through the institution and is held for sale by a dealer or vendor. Coverage is usually provided on an open perils basis.

flopper

Automobile. An insurance fraud term for a person who deliberately falls against the side of an automobile while it is turning at an intersection, then files a claim for injuries.

Florida Insurance Exchange

Insurer Operations.

see: Insurance Exchange of the Americas

flotage

Ocean Marine.

see: flotsam

flotsam

Ocean Marine. The floating wreckage of a ship or its cargo, including all cargo found on the shore between the high- and low-water lines. Ocean marine insurers today pay for *flotsam, jetsam, lagan,* and *derelict* without distinction.

synonym: flotage; *compare*: derelict, jetsam; *see*: lagan

flowchart

Risk Management. A risk exposure identification tool where a diagram indicates the step-by-step progression of values through an organization, or its transfer of money and securities. The values can be for such things as raw materials or the services used in the end product. The chart can identify or highlight the processing of each of the organization's products, locations of personnel and materials, flow of raw materials, transit exposures, and key machinery.

flower bond

Financial Planning. A special low-interest U.S. savings bond issued before March, 1971, at a discount that may be cashed in at par value in payment of federal estate tax if the decedent owned the bond at the time of death.

see: bond (*Financial Planning*), estate tax, par

flying club

Aviation. A general aviation rating classification for a nonprofit organization comprised of at least three persons who jointly own and operate an aircraft for pleasure use only.

compare: business and pleasure, fixed base operators, industrial aid operators; *see*: general aviation

foam

Loss Control. A fire extinguishing agent that is created by mixing a form of detergent with water. It is used to snuff out the fire by depriving it of oxygen and cooling it down with water. It is most effective on petroleum or flammable liquid fires.

see: class B fire, fire extinguisher, fire extinguishing system

focus

Property. As respects an earthquake, the point in the earth along a fault line where the slippage begins to occur. As energy is released from this point, it radiates outward in seismic waves.

compare: epicenter; *see*: earthquake

follow the fortunes

Reinsurance. A reinsurance contract provision that the reinsurer is bound by the ceding insurer's settlement decisions on claims covered by the reinsurance. The reinsurer therefore shares the ceding insurer's fortune, or fate, in regard to covered risks. In general, a reinsurer may avoid the obligation to pay its contractual portion of a claim settlement only if the cedent fails to exercise good faith (which implies a claim investigation appropriate to the circumstances) or if there is no reasonable basis for the cedent's conclusion that the claim is within the scope of the policy. This principle is often considered part of a reinsurance agreement even if not specified.

see: ceding insurer, reinsurance, reinsurer, uberrima fides

following form excess liability insurance

Liability. An excess liability policy that provides coverage identical to that provided by a specified primary liability policy. This term may also be applied to an umbrella policy that has been endorsed to provide coverage at least as broad as that provided by a specified primary policy.

compare: nonconcurrency; *see*: excess liability insurance, layering, umbrella liability insurance

following form excess property insurance

Property. An excess fire insurance policy that follows the terms and provisions of a specified primary policy. *Example*: A fire policy or other form written under exactly the same terms as a property insurance policy, providing the same coverage as other insurance on the same property.

compare: nonconcurrency; *see*: layering

following reinsurer

Reinsurance. A reinsurer participating in a large reinsurance contract that accepts the contractual terms negotiated by the lead reinsurer.

compare: lead reinsurer

Food and Drug Administration (FDA)

Organization. A federal agency within the Department of Health and Human Services that sets safety and quality standards for food, drugs, cosmetics, and other household substances sold as consumer products.

food rejection insurance

Ocean Marine. A form of ocean marine insurance that provides coverage against the risk of rejection of food at a port of entry by government authorities.

force majeure

General. An event or accident beyond any person's control. (French for "superior force"; same as the Latin term *vis major.*) It is often understood as natural disasters (or acts of God), but force majeure also includes mass acts of human agency, such as war and civil strife.

see: act of God, catastrophe loss, force majeure coverage, natural perils

force majeure coverage

International. Political risk insurance that indemnifies the insured for out-of-pocket expenses from the loss of a contract in a foreign country due to force majeure perils such as war or civil strife, flood or epidemic.

see: political risk insurance

Liability. Insurance—often in connection with a construction contract—that covers financial loss caused when commitments cannot be honored because of a force majeure event.

see: act of God, commercial impracticability, force majeure

forecasting

Risk Management.

see: loss forecasting

foreclosure

Law. A method of enforcing payment of a debt secured by mortgage or deed of trust by taking and selling the mortgaged property, with the proceeds paid to the creditor up to the amount of the outstanding debt.

see: attachment, default, deficiency judgment, mortgage

foreign agent

International. A person or office of an organization located in a foreign country that acts as the organization's legal agent but is not a branch or subsidiary.

compare: foreign branch, foreign subsidiary; *see*: agency, foreign correspondent

foreign branch

International. An office or facility of an organization that is located in a foreign country and is a separate but dependent part of the organization.

compare: foreign agent, foreign subsidiary

foreign corporation

International. A corporation chartered under the laws of a country other than where it is conducting business.

foreign correspondent

International. A firm or individual who acts as an organization's agent in a foreign country.

see: corresponding broker

foreign credit insurance

Financial Guaranty/International.

see: export credit insurance

Foreign Credit Insurance Association (FCIA)

International/Organizations. Members: Marine, property and casualty insurance companies. *Objectives*: Provides export credit insurance policies for overseas sales of goods and services and lessors of U.S. equipment. In cooperation with the Export-Import Bank, it insures exporters against the risk of nonpayment by foreign buyers for commercial or political reasons. *Founded*: 1962. *Headquarters*: New York, NY.

see: export credit insurance, combination foreign credit insurance policy, medium-term foreign credit insurance policy, overall master foreign credit insurance policy, short-term foreign credit insurance policy

foreign debt for equity swap

International. A method for creditors with substantial debt in a foreign country (usually a developing nation) to reduce their debt exposure. All or part of the debt is forgiven in exchange for an equity interest in a business or property located in the country.

see: foreign debt for equity swap insurance

foreign debt for equity swap insurance

International. A form of political risk insurance that insures a creditor against total or partial confiscation, expropriation or nationalization of an equity investment obtained in exchange for canceling foreign debts. The covered investment includes the investor's original investment, the investor's share of retained earnings, parental loans and loan guarantees, and net intercompany accounts receivable between the investor and the foreign entity.

see: foreign debt for equity swap, political risk insurance

foreign exchange rate
International.

see: exchange rate

foreign freight forwarder
International. A freight forwarder that acts as an exporter's agent for scheduling, routing, consolidating shipments, preparing documents, and providing marine and war risks insurance.

see: freight forwarder

foreign/home insurance
International.

see: home/foreign insurance

foreign insurer
Insurer Operations. An insurer or reinsurer is considered *foreign* in any U.S. state or territory other than its state of domicile or incorporation. In its home state, it is considered a *domestic* insurer.

compare: alien insurer, domestic insurer

foreign securities
International. Securities issued by a company that is incorporated in a foreign country and produces most of its business there; securities issued by a foreign government.

see: American Depository Receipt

foreign subsidiary
International. A corporation with its principal place of business in a foreign country or which is organized under foreign laws and is substantially owned or controlled by a domestic corporation.

compare: foreign agent, foreign branch

foreign trade zone
International. An area of a country that is designated free from the payment of import or export duties. The government often provides favorable tax treatment to foreign firms located within the area provided that goods shipped into and out of the area are not for domestic consumption, but will be shipped to another country.

synonym: free trade zone; *see*: maquiladoras

foreign voluntary workers' compensation coverage
Workers' Compensation. A manuscript workers' compensation policy endorsement that extends benefits to nationals of the United States who are hired or assigned to work indefinitely outside the country and are outside the jurisdiction of any compulsory workers' compensation or similar act.

see: compulsory compensation law, endemic disease coverage, manuscript policy

forensic expert
Law. An expert who assists the courts in applying specialized knowledge to legal principles and the facts of a case. (*Forensic* means pertaining to argumentation or legal proceedings.) There are specialists in forensic medicine, forensic pathology (dealing with diseases), forensic psychiatry (dealing with mental disorders), and forensic accounting (interpretation of accounting and financial records for the court).

see: expert witness, forensic liability insurance

forensic liability insurance
Professional Liability. A form of professional liability insurance for forensic experts and expert witnesses, such as litigation consultants and legal support specialists. Coverage is provided for third-party loss due to errors, omissions or negligence in the performance of professional duties. Coverage is excluded for bodily injury and property damage and is usually written on a claims-made basis.

see: forensic expert, professional liability insurance

forgery
Crime. The making or alteration of a document with a fraudulent intent; counterfeiting or signing a false signature to a negotiable instrument.

see: forgery bond, forgery or alteration coverage form

forgery bond
Surety. Insurance against loss due to alteration or forgery of negotiable instruments, checks, or other documents. '

synonym: check alteration and forgery insurance; *see*: alteration bond, lost instrument bond

forgery or alteration coverage form
Crime. A crime coverage form (ISO form CR 00 03, or form B) for loss involving checks, drafts, promissory notes, bills of exchange, and similar documents due to forgery or alteration of a covered instrument.

synonym: crime coverage form B; *see*: crime coverages, forgery bond

form
Insurer Operations. A document used to complete or create a section of an insurance policy.

see: ACORD forms, application, insurance contract

forms and scaffolding coverage
Property.

see: scaffolding and forms coverage

forthwith payment

General. A cash payment at the time of settlement to cover attorney's fees, costs, outstanding liens, or a payment to the plaintiff.

see: release

fortuitous event

Insurer Operations. An accidental, chance, unintended or unforeseen event. Insurance is protection against events of a fortuitous nature, not events that are intended by the insured.

see: accident, insurable risk, occurrence

forward contract

Financial Planning. The purchase or sale of a specific asset or commodity at a current price but with delivery and settlement at a future date; a financial derivative in the form of a tailor-made contract that is not traded on an organized exchange where the counterparties agree to exchange a specific asset for a fixed price at a future date.

compare: futures contract; *see*: counterparty, financial derivative

forward-looking statement

Financial Planning. A statement made by an officer or director of a corporation concerning the firm's future earnings potential or operations. These statements are encouraged by the Securities and Exchange Commission, but companies (especially new high-technology firms) whose stock value dropped after optimistic statements were often sued in strike suits during the 1980s and early '90s. Federal legislation in 1995 was intended to protect companies whose projections are not realized, provided cautionary language is used.

see: prospectus, strike suit

foundation coverage

Property. Coverage for a building foundation is excluded from commercial property policies but can be included by deleting the foundation exclusion and adjusting the insurable value. Most builders' risk policies include coverage for foundations.

see: builders' risk insurance

foundation exclusion clause

Property. A provision in a fire insurance policy that excludes the value of a building's foundation when determining the proper amount of insurance under a coinsurance clause.

see: coinsurance clause

foundering

Ocean Marine. The sinking of a disabled vessel below the surface of a navigable waterway.

compare: derelict

401(k) plan

Employee Benefits.

see: Internal Revenue Code § 401(k)

frame construction

Loss Control. A structure with outside support walls, roof and floors of wood or other combustible materials. The exterior walls may be covered with stucco or brick veneer and the interior walls with lath and plaster.

see: construction

franchise deductible

Personal. A deductible once popular in personal auto and homeowners policies. The deductible applies in small losses but is gradually reduced as the size of loss increases, so in a large loss the insurer provides first dollar coverage.

compare: flat deductible, percentage of value deductible; *see*: deductible

franchise insurance

Health/Life. A group insurance plan under which individual policies are issued to the employees of a common employer or the members of an association. Plan premiums are collected by the employer or association and remitted to the insurer. These plans are designed for small groups that would not qualify for true group coverage.

synonym: wholesale group insurance; *see*: group insurance

franchise marketing

Insurer Operations. The marketing of a personal lines products (e.g., homeowners, auto) to a large number of employees of an employer under a single plan of insurance with premiums payable by payroll deduction. The insurer retains the right of individual underwriting selection, so there is no group premium rate reduction.

compare: group marketing, mass marketing

fraternal benefit society

Health/Life. A life or health insurance company formed to cover members of an affiliated lodge, religious or social organization. Such companies are regulated less strictly than life insurance companies that offer coverage to the public at large.

see: insurance company

Fraternal Field Managers Association (FFMA)

Organizations. Members: Sales managers for fraternal life insurance societies. *Objectives*: Sponsors the designation of Fraternal Insurance Counselor (FIC) for representatives meeting education and production standards. *Founded*: 1935. *Headquarters*: Downers Grove, IL.

fraternal insurance

Health/Life. Life or health coverage developed for members of a lodge or fraternal order.

see: fraternal benefit society

Fraternal Insurance Counselor (FIC)

Organizations. A designation awarded by the Fraternal Field Managers Association after passing specified educational and production requirements.

see: Fraternal Field Managers Association

fraud

Law. The intentional misrepresentation or concealment of a material fact in order to induce another person to make or to refrain from making a contract. *Insurance fraud* is any willful deceit (such as filing a false claim) intended to result in a loss to an insurance company.

see: arson fraud, bull, deceit, capper, cow, flopper, fraud statement, squat, stager, swoop-and-squat, ten percenter

fraud statement

Insurer Operations. A statement required by many states to be included in an application or claim form. *Example:* "Any person who knowingly and with intent to defraud any insurance company or other person files an application for insurance or statement of claim containing any materially false information, or conceals, for the purpose of misleading, information concerning any fact material thereto, commits a fraudulent insurance act, which is a crime, and shall also be subject to a civil penalty not to exceed [$5,000] and the stated value of the claim for each such violation." (New York fraud statement for insurance other than automobile.)

see: application, claim, deceit, fraud, material fact

fraudulent delivery

Inland Marine. Coverage for a loss resulting from the fraudulent delivery of goods is included under inland marine coverage forms. The delivery or surrendering of goods to a party posing as an agent for the receiver is considered an invalid delivery and coverage applies under an inland marine form.

free alongside (FAS)

Ocean Marine. A term of sale providing that the shipper will place the goods to be shipped alongside a specific vessel or at a designated shipping point. The goods are the shipper's responsibility until they are alongside, at which time the responsibility passes to the consignee.

synonym: free alongside ship, free alongside vessel; *compare:* free on board

free alongside vessel

Ocean Marine.

see: free alongside

free and clear

General. The condition of property that is not mortgaged or title to which is unencumbered.

see: marketable title

free examination period

Health/Life.

see: free look period

free look period

Health/Life. A time during which a consumer may cancel a life or health insurance policy and receive a full refund of all premiums paid. In most cases, the free look period is ten days after delivery of the policy.

synonym: free examination period, free trial period

free of capture and seizure (FC&S)

Ocean Marine. An exclusion in ocean marine policies for loss to a vessel from capture or seizure or loss to a vessel's cargo from pirates or assailing thieves.

see: assailing thieves, enemy goods, ocean marine insurance, piracy (*Ocean Marine*)

free of particular average American conditions (FPAAC)

Ocean Marine. Coverage for a partial loss resulting from stranding, sinking, burning or collision with another vessel.

see: average, free of particular average

free of particular average English conditions (FPAEC)

Ocean Marine. A broader form of ocean marine free of particular average coverage (FPA). In addition to the FPA coverages, insurance is provided for a partial loss to the insured property if at any time during the voyage the vessel is stranded, sunk, burned, on fire or in a collision with another vessel.

see: average, free of particular average, ocean marine insurance

free of particular average (FPA)

Ocean Marine. An ocean marine policy provision where coverage is provided only if a total loss of the insured property occurs from an insured peril.

see: average, Janson clause, ocean marine insurance, particular average

free on board (FOB)

Inland Marine/Ocean Marine. A term of sale that the shipper (or seller) will place the goods on board a vessel, freight car, truck, or other means of transport, at which time the responsibility passes to the consignee (or buyer). Delivery charges are not included in the quoted sale price.

compare: free alongside, free on board destination

197

free on board destination

Inland Marine/Ocean Marine. A provision in the term of sale that the shipper (or seller) will be responsible for the goods until the consignee (or buyer) accepts them.

compare: free on board

free trade zone

Insurer Operations. A facility through which insurers can negotiate insurance policies without paying tariffs or taxes.

see: insurance exchange

International.

see: foreign trade zone

free trial period

Health/Insurer Operations/Life.

see: free look period

freedom of the seas

International/Ocean Marine. A doctrine in international law that the ships of any nation may travel through international waters without hindrance. Also, the right of ships of noncombatant nations to trade at will during wartime, except where blockades have been established.

freehold

Financial Planning/Title. An interest in real estate in fee simple or fee tail or for life.

see: fee simple, fee tail

freezing exclusion

Property. A property insurance policy exclusion for loss caused by the discharge of water or other substances from equipment when the insured does not maintain heat in the building or has not drained the equipment and shut off the water supply if heat cannot be maintained.

freight

Inland Marine/Ocean Marine. 1. Goods carried by a vessel or vehicle; goods transported as cargo by a commercial carrier, in contrast to mail, baggage and express.

2. A carrier's charge for transporting goods.

see: advance freight, cargo insurance, collect freight, guaranteed freight, prepaid freight

freight forwarder

Inland Marine/Ocean Marine. A firm that specializes in arranging the transportation of merchandise and completing the required documentation. Some forwarders pack or consolidate merchandise with other cargo for export to the same country.

see: customs broker, customs broker and freight forwarders' errors and omissions insurance, foreign freight forwarder, house waybill

frequency

Risk Management. The number of times an event occurs in a given period of time. *Frequency* is one factor used to evaluate and underwrite risks; another is *severity*. A series of low severity losses that occur at a relatively high frequency can be just as costly to an insurer (or to a self-insurer) as a single severe loss because of administrative expenses for each claim. In addition, sufficiently frequent losses in accumulation can produce a loss more severe than would otherwise be the case. Loss frequency should therefore be controlled, as frequency breeds severity.

see: probability analysis

frequency distribution

Risk Management. A statistical term for the arrangement of data in equal intervals to show the frequency of values; the number of times losses occur and their severity.

see: standard deviation

friendly fire

Property. A fire or combustion intentionally started for beneficial purposes and remaining within its intended confines. Insurance does not cover a friendly fire unless it accidentally spreads to unintended materials.

compare: hostile fire; *see*: fire

fringe benefit

Employee Benefits. An obsolete term first used during World War II by the War Labor Board to describe a benefit such as vacations, holidays, and pension that were considered supplementary to wages. The preferred term is *employee benefit*.

see: employee benefit

front-end load

Life.

see: premium load

front end load

Financial Planning. A fee or commission charged at the time a security is purchased, especially a mutual fund share.

compare: back end load; *see*: load, load fund, mutual fund, no load fund, net asset value

frontage

Liability. The length of the side of a plot of land that fronts on a street or road. It is sometimes used as a rating base for casualty insurance.

fronting

Insurer Operations. An agreement by an insurer to issue a policy on behalf of a reinsurer, captive insurer, self-insurer or another insurer. This fronting insurer assumes little or no loss exposure; instead, financial arrangements are made to guarantee claims administration and payments. The fronting insurer is usually paid a percentage of the premium. Fronting is done for a number of reasons, but is increasingly disfavored by regulators who contend fronting is not a true risk transfer.

see: acting insurer, fronting company

Reinsurance. An arrangement where an insurer (the fronting company) issues policies at the request of one or more other insurers with the intention of transferring the entire risk to the other(s) by a reinsurance agreement or otherwise. Many states expressly prohibit the transfer of insurance risk (i.e., substantially all of the fronting insurer's business or a particular line or class of business) from an authorized insurer to one that is neither an authorized insurer nor an approved reinsurer.

see: unauthorized reinsurance

fronting company

Insurer Operations. An insurer that issues policies with the intention of transferring most of the insured exposure through reinsurance or other means to unauthorized insurers or reinsurers or captive insurers.

see: authorized reinsurance, captive insurance company, fronting, funding of reserves

International. A domestically authorized insurer that issues a policy on behalf of an unauthorized foreign insurer. The foreign insurer then assumes the risk under a reinsurance agreement.

see: nonadmitted insurance

fronting loan

International. A loan from a domestic parent organization to a foreign subsidiary that is arranged through a financial intermediary, usually an international bank. The bank fronts for the parent in extending the loan to the foreign subsidiary.

frustration clause

Ocean Marine. An ocean marine provision that applies when war perils are insured, which states that a loss doesn't exist simply because of the termination (frustration) of a voyage due to an outbreak of hostilities. For a loss to exist, the goods must have suffered actual physical damage.

see: force majeure coverage, ocean marine insurance

full coverage

Insurer Operations. Coverage that pays for all insured losses in full. While this may be the intent of many coverages, frequently it is impossible to restore an insured to his or her exact situation before the loss.

see: indemnification

Full Disclosures Act

Regulation.

see: Securities Act of 1933

full interest admitted (FIA)

Ocean Marine. A phrase in ocean marine policies whereby the insurer agrees that the insured has the sole right to loss payments; an agreement that the insured is the only party with an insurable interest.

compare: as interest may appear; *see*: insurable interest, ocean marine insurance

full prior acts coverage

Professional Liability. Coverage under a claims-made policy for all acts that occurred before the policy was issued, unlike most claims-made policies, which have a retroactive date specifying the first date from which claims are recognized.

see: claims-made form, prior acts coverage, retroactive date

full reporting clause

Property. A provision in commercial property policies written with a reporting form which requires the insured to report the full value of insured property even if this value exceeds the policy limit. While this endorsement can provide a premium savings, if at the time of a loss it is determined that the full value had not been reported, a severe penalty is applied in the loss adjustment.

synonym: honesty clause

full service insurer

Insurer Operations. An insurer that writes a wide variety of coverages and sells to a large part of the total marketplace.

compare: market specialty insurer, product specialty insurer, selective specialty insurer; *see*: marketing

full tail

Liability.

see: maxi-tail

full trading account

Financial Planning. A trading account with a securities broker where the customer has authorized the broker or an investment advisor to make trades on the customer's behalf without prior approval.

see: churning, discretionary account

full value declared (FVD)

Inland Marine/Ocean Marine. A provision in a marine contract requiring that the shipper declare the full value of the merchandise to the carrier, at the time of shipment.

see: marine insurance

fully diluted earnings per share

Financial Planning.

see: earnings per share

fully earned at inception

Insurer Operations.

see: fully earned premium

fully earned premium

Insurer Operations. A policy provision that all or a specified portion of the premium is fully earned by the insurer when the policy is first issued. It is usually found only in excess and surplus lines policies. Even if a policy is canceled early in its term, the insurer retains the portion of the premium indicated under this provision. For example, a policy may provide that the premium is 25% fully earned at inception.

synonym: fully earned at inception; compare: flat cancellation; see: earned premium, surplus lines

fully funded

Employee Benefits. A pension plan is considered fully funded when there are sufficient assets to make all payments that are due at specific times. A fully funded plan provides assurance to the participants that they will receive their benefits even if the employer ceases business.

see: employee benefit plan, pension

fully insured status

Employee Benefits. The condition of having met Social Security requirements to obtain full retirement benefits, which are 10 years (40 quarters) of covered employment and attaining retirement age.

see: currently insured status, retirement age, Social Security

fully paid policy

Life. A life insurance policy with limited benefit payments where all benefits have been paid to the beneficiary.

functional building valuation endorsement

Property. A commercial property insurance endorsement (ISO form CP 04 38) that provides building coverage on the basis of functional replacement cost in the event of a total loss. The policy coinsurance requirement is eliminated, building ordinance coverage is included, and the building must be constructed at the same site unless relocation is legally required. In the event of a partial loss, the claims payment is based on the use of less costly material, if available, in the architectural style that existed before the loss.

see: functional replacement cost

functional obsolescence

Property/Risk Management. A plant, building or facility that has outlived it useful value because of antiquated equipment or impractical or outmoded design.

see: actual cash value, functional replacement cost, replacement cost, reproduction cost

functional personal property valuation (other than stock) endorsement

Property. A commercial property insurance endorsement (ISO form CP 04 39) that provides coverage on specified personal property on the basis of functional replacement cost and eliminates any coinsurance requirement for that property. The endorsement is principally used to insure older machinery or equipment that is no longer available. The loss settlement is based on the cost of replacement with the nearest equivalent machinery or the actual cost to repair or replace it, subject to the policy limit.

see: functional replacement cost

functional replacement cost

Property. Property insurance policies sometimes provide for loss adjustment on the basis of functional replacement cost, which is the minimum cost to replace the damaged property with property that performs the same functions, though it may be less expensive than the original. *Example*: A brick warehouse may be replaced with a concrete tilt-up building that functions the same and is less expensive.

compare: actual cash value, depreciated value, market value, replacement cost, reproduction cost, tax-appraised value; see: functional building valuation endorsement, valuation of potential property loss

fund states coverage

Workers' Compensation. In certain states and the Canadian provinces, workers' compensation insurance must be purchased as a separate policy through state-owned insurance funds. The monopolistic states are Nevada, North Dakota, Ohio, Washington, West Virginia, and Wyoming. The Commonwealth of Puerto Rico also operates a monopolistic fund. Fund states coverage provides this coverage, and can be added as part of an all-states endorsement.

see: all-states coverage, monopolistic state fund, workers' compensation insurance

fundamental analysis

Financial Planning.

see: financial ratios

fundamental risk

Risk Management. A risk of such a nature that it can affect a major segment of society, not just an individual or single entity. Examples: natural catastrophic exposures, such as earthquake and flood.

compare: particular risk; see: catastrophe, natural perils, risk

funded reserve

Accounting. A liability established on the books of

an organization which is offset by a reserve account funded by cash or other liquid assets for the payment of retained casualty losses. The funds held in the reserve account are not tax deductible until they are actually used to pay a casualty loss.

compare: unfunded reserve; *see*: casualty loss

funded spread loss plan
Risk Management.

see: spread loss plan

funding instrument
Employee Benefits. A trust agreement or an insurance contract stating the conditions under which a funding agency performs. It specifies the terms under which the funding agency will accumulate, administer, and disburse plan assets.

see: benefit funds, employee benefit plan

funding of reserves
Reinsurance. A method of providing security to a ceding insurer when reinsurance is obtained through an unauthorized reinsurer. The ceding insurer retains funds from the reinsurer in an amount equal to the outstanding loss reserves or unearned premium reserves.

synonym: outstanding claims account; *see*: fronting company, funds held account, unauthorized reinsurance, unearned premium reserve

funding standard account
Employee Benefits. An ERISA requirement that a bookkeeping account be maintained in which credits and debits are used to determine a balance. The credits and debits are determined from actuarial valuations of the plan's actual experience for the period. The objective is to identify funding deficiencies, which occur whenever the sum of negative entry amounts exceed the sum of positive entry amounts.

see: accumulated funding deficiency, Employee Retirement Income Security Act, minimum funding standard, unfunded actuarial accrued liability

funds held account
Reinsurance. Funds retained by a ceding insurer that represent the unearned premium reserve or the outstanding loss reserve applied to the business it cedes to a reinsurer.

synonym: funds withheld account; *see*: funding of reserves, loss reserve, unearned premium reserve

funds withheld account
Reinsurance.

see: funds held account

fur floater
Inland Marine. Personal furs insured on an all-risk

basis, under a personal articles floater or a scheduled personal property endorsement to a homeowner's policy.

compare: furriers' customer insurance; *see*: floater policy, personal articles floater, scheduled personal property endorsement

furnace explosion
Property. An explosion resulting from the accumulation of gases or unconsumed fuel within the combustion chamber of a fired vessel. Such an explosion is covered under a fire insurance policy rather than a boiler and machinery policy.

synonym: firebox explosion; *see*: explosion

furniture, equipment and supplies
Property. A miscellaneous classification of personal property owned by a business, often valued together for insurance purposes. It combines items of relatively low individual values.

see: personal property [1]

furriers' block
Inland Marine. Insurance coverage for fur garments belonging to a dealer or the fur department of a store. Coverage is written on an all-risk basis and includes fur garments of other dealers for which the insured is liable. Exclusions include furs of others accepted by the insured for storage; furs rented, leased or sold on an installment plan after delivery; furs at any exhibition; and furs worn by the insured or the insured's family.

see: furriers' customer insurance, furs coverage

furriers' customer insurance
Inland Marine. An inland marine form (AAIS form IM 707) that provides all-risk coverage on furs and garments trimmed with fur. The coverage is purchased by furriers, department stores, warehouses, and cleaners that accept such items for storage or service. Coverage for a declared value is provided for the customers' property, and customers are provided with receipts.

compare: fur floater; *see*: furriers' block, furs coverage, inland marine insurance

furs coverage
Personal. One of the nine classes of property that can be covered under a personal articles floater. Personal furs include any garments made of animal pelts and garments trimmed with fur or consisting principally of fur.

see: fur floater, jewelry, watches, furs—special limit, personal articles floater

fusible link
Loss Control. Two pieces of metal fused (linked) together, usually by bismuth, tin, lead or antimony. The link is designed to melt at a prescribed temperature, thereby allowing a sprinkler head or fire door

to automatically operate.

see: automatic sprinkler system

future service

Employee Benefits. The portion of a retirement plan participant's benefits that relate to the period of service after the effective date of the plan or after a change in the plan.

see: vesting, years of service

futures contract

Financial Planning. The purchase or sale of a standard quantity or quality of a specific asset or commodity at a specified price on a future date; a financial derivative in the form of a standard transferable agreement where the counterparties agree to exchange a commodity or financial asset for a fixed price at a future date. Futures are traded on regulated exchanges, while forward contracts are not.

compare: forward contract; *see*: catastrophe insurance futures contract, counterparty, currency futures contract, financial derivative, financial futures

G

gain and loss exhibit

Insurer Operations. An insurance company annual statement section that shows the company's gains, losses and policyholders' surplus for the year.

see: annual statement, policyholders' surplus

gambling

Risk Management. An undertaking of uncertain outcome; a speculative risk involving a chance of gain or loss. Insurance differs from gambling in that it presents no chance for gain on the part of the insured, and it eliminates or reduces an accidental or fortuitous loss.

compare: insurance; *see:* aleatory contract, pure risk, speculative risk

gap layer

Liability.

see: buffer layer

garage coverage form

Automobile. An Insurance Services Office policy (ISO form CA 00 05) that provides coverages for liability arising from garage operations, medical payments, automobile physical damage, and uninsured or underinsured motorists in a single contract for automobile dealers, service stations, auto repair shops and parking lots. The garage coverage form has several classifications of covered vehicles, coded by numbers, as follows:

21. Any auto: the broadest classification.

22. Owned autos only: vehicles owned by the insured, including any acquired during the policy period.

23. Owned private passenger autos only: vehicles defined as private passenger (for example, a sedan or station wagon). Coverage is not provided on vans or pickup trucks even if they are used only to transport people.

24. Owned autos other than private passenger autos only: vehicles not designed as private passenger vehicles (for example, pickup trucks, vans, truck-tractors), including newly acquired vehicles.

25. Owned autos subject to no-fault: coverage only for no-fault or personal injury protection on vehicles located in no-fault states.

26. Owned autos subject to compulsory uninsured motorist law: vehicles located in a state where uninsured motorist coverage is compulsory. The required coverage is provided under the policy form.

27. Specifically described autos: vehicles listed in the policy or supplementary schedule. Coverage is limited to 30 days for newly acquired vehicles.

28. Hired autos only: vehicles that are leased, rented or borrowed.

29. Nonowned autos used in the garage business: vehicles belonging to employees and partners or their household members, which are covered while being used for the insured's business purposes.

30. Autos left for service, repair, storage or safekeeping: customers' vehicles while in the insured's care.

31. Dealer's autos and autos held for sale by nondealers or trailer dealers: this category is only used to provide physical damage coverage, requiring other classifications with it. A further description of the coverage must be included on a supplementary schedule.

compare: business auto coverage form, truckers' coverage form; *see:* dealer class plan, direct excess coverage, direct primary coverage, driveaway collision, faulty work exclusion, garagekeepers' insurance, limited coverage for customers, no-fault insurance, nondealer, personal injury protection, uninsured motorist law

garagekeepers' extra liability

Automobile. An endorsement that extends a garagekeepers' liability insurance policy to provide coverage for any liability, regardless of the insured's legal liability as respects vehicles in the care, custody or control of the insured.

see: garagekeepers' liability insurance

garagekeepers' insurance

Automobile. Coverage of garage operators against

203

direct damage or legal liability for damage to vehicles in the insured's care, custody, or control. This coverage is included as part of the garage coverage form or as a separate endorsement (ISO form CA 99 37).

see: garage coverage form, garagekeepers' liability insurance, garagekeepers' extra liability

garagekeepers' liability insurance

Automobile. An obsolete form of insurance for a garage operator, protecting him or her against liability for damage to vehicles caused by specific acts while in the insured's care, custody, or control. This form has been replaced by the garagekeepers' coverage form.

compare: garagekeepers' insurance; *see*: garagekeepers' coverage form, garagekeepers' extra liability

garment contractors' floater

Inland Marine. A policy (AAIS form IM 638 or IM 637 for named perils coverage) that covers loss to clothing in the process of being manufactured while on the insured's premises, in transit, or temporally at other contractors' or subcontractors' locations on a broad named-perils or all-risk basis.

compare: furriers' block

gate guard

Loss Control.

see: movable barrier guard

gatekeeper

Health.

see: primary care physician

gender rating

Insurer Operations. A distinction used in developing rates that assumes that life expectancy, health costs and frequency of accidents differ between males and females. For example, women usually live longer than men, and young women are usually safer drivers than young men. However women have claimed that they have not received the premium reductions these statistics would support.

see: sex discrimination, uniform premium, unisex legislation

general agency system

Insurer Operations. An insurance distribution system where an insurer appoints a general agent to service the agents within a specified geographic area, rather than opening an insurance company branch office.

compare: direct writer; *see*: agent, general agent

general agent (GA)

Agency. An individual or entity authorized by an insurance company to be its exclusive representative in a particular geographic area for all or a specific line of business. Activities on behalf of the insurer may include marketing, appointing and supervising other agents, issuing policies, collecting premiums, and paying claims.

compare: managing general agent; *see*: agent, policywriting agent

General Agents and Managers Conference of National Association of Life Underwriters (GAMC-NALU)

Organizations. Members: Insurance general agents and managers. *Objectives*: Improving the management capabilities and the ability to sell life insurance products through research, education and a code of ethical practices. *Founded*: 1951. *Headquarters*: Washington, D.C.

general aggregate limit

Insurer Operations. The maximum limit payable for claims that occur under specified coverages during the policy period.

Liability. The highest amount an insured can recover under the ISO commercial general liability coverage forms for coverages A, B, and C. It excludes claims falling under the "products-completed operations hazard" provision.

see: aggregate limit, commercial general liability policy, products-completed operations insurance

general and insurance expenses

Insurer Operations. An insurance company annual statement section that shows expenses of the insurer, excepting commissions and taxes.

synonym: general operating expense; *see*: expense loading

general average adjuster

Ocean Marine. A marine specialist responsible for adjusting and providing the general average statement. Usually this individual is appointed by the shipowner or insurer and collects the general average deposit average deposit or obtains a general average guaranty from each party to the general average loss and authorizes release of cargo to the owners when the cargo is fully secured.

synonym: average adjuster; *see*: general average, general average contribution, general average deposit, general average guaranty, particular average

general average bond

Ocean Marine. A bond prepared by the general average adjuster binding the owner of the goods to pay a proportion of the general average.

see: average agreement, bond (*Surety*), general average

general average contribution

Ocean Marine. The amount that each party to a general average loss must contribute. This is determined by applying the general average percentage to each party's contributory value.

compare: general average deposit, general average guaranty; *see*: average agreement, general average

general average deposit

Ocean Marine. A cash deposit required by a general average adjuster from the owners of goods, to secure the payment of a proportion of the general average. The amount of the deposit is usually based on a percentage of the general average, and it is required in addition to the general average bond.

compare: general average, general average contribution, general average guaranty; *see*: general average adjuster, general average bond

general average (GA)

Ocean Marine. An ocean marine loss that occurs through the voluntary sacrifice of a part of the vessel or cargo, or an expenditure, to safeguard the vessel and its remaining cargo from a common peril. If the sacrifice is successful, all interests at risk contribute to the loss borne by owner of the sacrificed property based on their respective saved values. A party can insure their portion of such a loss under an ocean marine policy.

compare: particular average; *see*: average, contributory value, general average bond, general average contribution, general average deposit, general average guaranty, general average percentage, ocean marine insurance, York Antwerp Rules

general average guaranty

Ocean Marine. An insurer's written guaranty to a general average adjuster, guaranteeing payment of the proportion of general average finally assessed against the goods insured. This guaranty is usually accepted by the adjuster in lieu of a cash deposit and is additional security to a general average bond.

compare: general average contribution, general average deposit; *see*: average agreement, general average, general average adjuster

general average percentage

Ocean Marine. The total amount of a loss and expenses incurred as the result of a general average divided by the total amount saved as a result of general average, expressed as a percentage.

see: average agreement, general average

general aviation

Aviation. A term that includes all aviation except commercial airlines and military aviation. This includes pleasure aircraft, business (corporate) aircraft, air taxi operators, crop dusting, highway patrol aircraft, sports and instructional flying.

see: business and pleasure, fixed base operators, flying club, industrial aid operators

general contractor

General. An independent contractor who arranges, through subcontractors, for the completion of work under a contract with a property owner or developer.

see: independent contractor

general cover form

Property. An obsolete term used to identify a reporting form policy.

see: reporting form

general employer

Workers' Compensation. An employer who loans an employee to another (called a *special employer*) usually to assist in a specific job with the intent that when the job is completed, the employee will return to the first employer. The employee remains on the payroll of the general employer but works at the direction of the special employer.

see: borrowed employee, employee leasing, special employer

general obligation bond (GO bond)

Financial Planning. A municipal bond that is issued to finance public improvements and is repayable from taxes and guaranteed only by the credit and taxing power of the issuer.

see: municipal bond

general operating expense

Insurer Operations.

see: general and insurance expenses

general partners' liability insurance

Professional Liability.

see: limited partnership liability insurance

general partnership

Law.

see: partnership

general provisions

General.

see: additional provisions

general warranty deed

Title. A deed that not only conveys all of the grantor's interests in the property, but also warrants that if the title is defective or has a cloud (such as mortgage claims, tax liens, title claims, judgments, or mechanic's liens against it), the grantee may hold the grantor liable.

see: deed, defective title, warranty deed

Generally Accepted Accounting Principles (GAAP)

Accounting. A set of uniform accounting rules for recording and reporting financial data to accurately represent an organization's financial condition. These standards are endorsed by the Financial Accounting Standards Board, and their use is required by the Securities and Exchange Commission for corporations under its jurisdiction.

> *compare*: Statutory Accounting Principles; *see*: accounting, Financial Accounting Standards Board, financial statement

Insurer Operations. Stock insurers and some mutuals issue annual reports based on Generally Accepted Accounting Principles to their stockholders or policyholders, but use Statutory Accounting Principles, developed by the National Association of Insurance Commissioners, when reporting to state insurance departments.

> *see*: Statutory Accounting Principles

geographic limitation

Insurer Operations. An insurance policy provision that designates its region of coverage; for example, occurrences or claims made in a specific state (for a workers' compensation policy), in the United States and territories (for a property insurance policy) or worldwide (for a liability policy).

> *synonym*: coverage territory, territorial limitation; *see*: worldwide coverage

geological perils

Risk Management. Any naturally occurring potential causes of loss involving earth movement or gravity related events (e.g., earthquake or volcanic action).

> *compare*: economic perils, human perils; *see*: act of God, earthquake, natural perils, peril, volcanic action

gift tax

Financial Planning. A tax on the value of property transferred by gift, payable by the donor. A federal unified tax is assessed on the combined value of qualifying gifts and an estate so that estate taxes cannot be avoided by gifts made in anticipation of death.

> *see*: estate tax

glass breakage coverage

Property. Insurance under most broad and special property insurance forms for glass that is part of a building only. Coverage is usually limited to $100 per plate, pane or panel and is usually subject to a $500 per occurrence aggregate limit.

> *see*: glass coverage form

glass coverage form

Property. A commercial property form (ISO form CP 00 15) that covers the costs of replacement and incidental costs of building glass due to breakage or the accidental or malicious application of chemicals to the glass. The glass must be specifically listed in the declarations and includes its lettering, frame and ornamentation. Excluded from coverage by this form are stained glass, memorial windows, art glass, mosaic art, lenses, halftone screens and rotogravure screens.

> *synonym*: plate glass insurance; *see*: comprehensive glass insurance, glass breakage coverage

glass insurance

Property. Protection for loss of or damage to glass and its accessories.

> *see*: comprehensive glass insurance, glass coverage form, glass insurance 50/50 basis

glass insurance 50/50 basis

Property. An endorsement to a comprehensive glass policy that provides a 50% reduction in premium for what is in effect a deductible equal to the premium. The insured must bear a loss in an amount up to the premium paid before coverage is activated.

> *see*: comprehensive glass insurance, glass insurance

global broker

Agency/International. An insurance brokerage with a network of domestic and foreign offices that provides coordinated service on a worldwide basis regardless of where the business originates or where the client's risks are located.

> *compare*: domestic broker, international broker, multinational broker, transnational broker

global insurance program

International. A centralized and uniform insurance program that combines the parent organization's domestic insurance with the foreign locations' international insurance. Usually, a single master global insurance policy is issued and local underlier policies are issued in those countries that require admitted insurance. This approach is used more often with property insurance than with liability programs.

> *synonym*: global program; *compare*: controlled master insurance program; *see*: underlier policy

global program

International.

> *see*: global insurance program

"going bare"

Risk Management. An informal description of an uninsured organization or a firm without any type of insurance program or plan for an exposure that is normally insurable.

> *see*: passive retention

going concern value

Property/Risk Management. The value of an operating business, which is greater than the sum of its assets were they sold separately because it includes intangibles such as goodwill, operating efficiencies, management and employee quality, etc. Going concern value can be an important risk management factor.

compare: economic value, market value; *see:* intangible property (1)

goldware

Personal.

see: silverware

golf cart coverage

Liability. Unlicensed golf carts are covered under a commercial general liability policy. Coverage can be extended to any person who uses or is legally responsible for a golf cart that is loaned or rented from the named insured or from the insured's concessionaire by endorsement (ISO form CG 20 08).

see: commercial general liability policy, incidental motorized land conveyances endorsement

golfers' equipment coverage

Personal. One of the nine classes of property that can be covered under a personal articles floater. Golfers' equipment includes golf clubs, golf clothing and equipment except balls.

see: pair or set, personal articles floater

golf insurance

Inland Marine.

see: hole-in-one coverage

good driver discount

Personal. A premium discount granted on a personal auto insurance policy for a good driving record. In order to obtain the discount, a driver's record must be clear of moving violations or accidents for a period of time (usually three to five years).

see: chargeable offense, good student discount, safe driver plan

good faith

Law. Honest intent; the quality of conduct legally and ethically expected in a commercial transaction. All parties are to have honest motives, to intend full performance of their obligations as agreed, and to refrain from defrauding or taking unfair advantage of another party. In many relationships (e.g., the employment relationship, an insurance contract, etc.) there is a legally recognized "implied covenant of good faith and fair dealing," according to which each party must treat the other fairly and give as much consideration to the other party's interests as to its own.

compare: bad faith; *see:* uberrima fides

good student discount

Personal. A premium discount granted on a personal auto insurance policy for a students with a good academic record. Some statistical studies indicate that good students have fewer automobile accidents.

see: driver training credit, personal auto policy

good title

Title.

see: marketable title

goodwill

Accounting. An intangible asset maintained on the balance sheet of a business that represents its reputation or expected patronage; a value added to a business that is expected to earn a rate of return greater than the average in its industry. It is usually considered a capital asset that cannot be amortized since it lacks a specifiable useful life. *Example:* A famous brand name.

see: capital asset, intangible property

governing classification

Workers' Compensation. The workers' compensation rating classification that applies to the majority of an employer's payroll and that generally describes the insured employer's business. Excluding employees that qualify for one of the standard exceptions, the payroll is rated using the governing classification.

see: classification code, class rate, payroll, rate making

government insurance

General. An insurance program sponsored or provided by federal or state governments, such as Social Security, unemployment insurance, workers' compensation funds, or FAIR plans.

compare: public entity insurance; *see:* Fair Access to Insurance Requirements, National Flood Insurance Program, Social Security, unemployment compensation, workers' compensation insurance

Government National Mortgage Association participation certificate

Financial Planning. A security issued by the GNMA, an agency of the U.S. Department of Housing and Urban Development, in the form of a bond that matures in one to fourteen years for a minimum of $5,000. The securities, often called Ginnie Mae pass-throughs, represent an interest in a pool of mortgages. They increase the capital available in the mortgage market and are popular with institutional investors, such as insurance companies and pension funds.

see: bond (*Financial Planning*), mortgage-backed security

Governmental Accounting Standards Board (GASB)

Accounting. An accounting standards board formed to develop accounting standards for governmental entities. It is patterned after the Financial Accounting Standards Board, which develops accounting standards for private entities.

see: Financial Accounting Standards Board

governmental action exclusion

Property. An exclusion in most property insurance policies, denying coverage for losses occasioned by governmental seizure or destruction of property, except for destruction done to prevent the spread of fire.

see: civil authority clause, condemned building cancellation provision

grace period

Health/Life. A specified time (usually 30 days) after a premium payment is due, in which the insured may make the payment and keep the policy in force.

see: cancellation notice, lapse

graded commission

Agency. An agent's commission scale where the commission percentage rate varies by class of business and premium volume written.

synonym: unlevel commission; *compare*: flat commission; *see*: agent's commission, first-year commission, renewal commission

graded death benefit

Life. A provision usually found in juvenile life insurance policies where the benefits in the early years are less than the face amount of the policy and increase over time until they reach the face amount.

compare: jumping juvenile life insurance, lien plan; *see*: juvenile life insurance

graded premium

Life. A provision in some whole life insurance policies where the premiums are lower in the early years and increase over time until they become level for the remainder of the policy.

see: whole life insurance

grading schedule

Property. A schedule used by the Insurance Services Office for grading the fire protection provided by cities, towns and other fire districts. The schedule has ten grades or "protection classes," with "1" meaning the highest degree of protection and "10" unprotected. Factors are considered such as location of fire stations, firefighter training, water supplies, and building codes.

see: protection, protection class

graduated life table

Life. A mortality table that reflects such irregularities as an insufficient data base, use of a non-homogeneous data base, or statistics weighted too heavily toward particular years.

see: mortality table

graduated payment mortgage

Financial Planning/Mortgage Insurance. A mortgage on which the monthly payments are lower at the beginning and gradually increase to a fixed amount after five or ten years.

synonym: graded payment mortgage; *see*: mortgage, variable rate mortgage

grantee

Title. The buyer or transferee of a deed.

compare: grantor; *see*: deed

grantor

Title. The transferor or conveyer of property, especially of a deed, gift or annuity.

compare: annuitant, grantee; *see*: annuity, deed

greenmail exclusion

Professional Liability. An exclusion in some directors' and officers' policies for claims arising from the purchase of a corporation's own stock at above-market prices to resist a takeover attempt. Greenmail (modeled on *blackmail* with reference to the color of U.S. currency) is the above-market price paid by a takeover target company to buy back shares that have been acquired, and in return the acquirer agrees to stop the takeover attempt.

synonym: purchase of securities at a premium exclusion; *see*: directors' and officers' liability insurance, poison pill, tender offer defense expense insurance

Griffin Foundation for Insurance Education

Organizations. Members: Insurance companies, agents, brokers and others interested in the insurance industry. *Objectives*: Career development and scholarships for college students who take risk management and insurance courses. *Founded*: 1960. *Headquarters*: Columbus, OH.

gross combination weight (GCW)

Automobile. The maximum loaded weight for a truck-tractor and the semi-trailer(s) for which the truck-tractor was designed (as specified by the manufacturer).

compare: gross vehicle weight

gross earnings

Property. A coverage amount developed for business interruption insurance that essentially is calculated by subtracting the cost of goods sold from total sales. With the development of the business income coverage program, this concept was abandoned.

see: business income coverage form, gross earnings form

gross earnings form

Property. A property insurance lost earnings form that was widely used before the business income coverage form. The amount of insurance was based on the coinsurance percentage selected, which in turn reflected the expected length of time a business might be out of operation after a loss. The loss payment was based on expected normal earnings during the period needed for repairs, with no maximum time.

see: business income coverage form, earnings insurance form, gross earnings

gross hazard analysis (GHA)

Risk Management. An identification of the most serious risks to an organization. It involves inspection of the organization's operations and completion of a gross hazard analysis form, which includes such items as probable maximum loss estimate, frequency estimate, severity estimate, estimate of impact on earnings, detection methods, protection methods, contingency action time, salvageability and recommendations.

see: risk management

gross line

Insurer Operations. An amount of coverage written by an insurer on a single risk, including the insurer's net line and ceded reinsurance.

synonym: assumption, maximum line; *compare:* net line

gross negligence

Law. Negligence beyond the ordinary; a reckless or wanton disregard of the duty of care toward others.

see: degree of care, negligence

gross net earned premium income (GNEPI)

Insurer Operations/Reinsurance. A rating base for excess of loss reinsurance. It is the earned premium of a primary insurer for the lines of business covered by a reinsurer, minus cancellations, refunds and reinsurance premium paid to other reinsurers who are providing coverage on the same lines.

compare: gross net written premium income; *see:* earned premium

gross net written premium income (GNWPI)

Insurer Operations/Reinsurance. A rating base for excess of loss reinsurance. It is the written premium of a primary insurer for the lines of business covered by a reinsurer, minus cancellations, refunds and reinsurance premium paid to other reinsurers who are providing coverage on the same lines.

compare: gross net earned premium income; *see:* earned premium

gross premium

Insurer Operations. The entire premium charged by an insurer to a policyholder, including all of the insurer's expenses, estimated loss costs and profits.

see: premium

gross profits form

International.

see: British business interruption insurance

Property. A property insurance loss of earnings form that bases recovery on the prior year's sales amount. The indemnity period is the time it takes the insured's profit level to recover, subject to a maximum time, usually twelve months.

see: business income coverage form, earnings insurance form

gross vehicle weight (GVW)

Automobile. The maximum loaded weight for which a single vehicle is designed, as specified by the manufacturer.

compare: gross combination weight

ground coverage

Aviation. Physical damage insurance coverage on an aircraft hull, that applies when the aircraft is not in flight.

compare: flight coverage; *see:* in motion

ground fault circuit interrupter (GFCI)

Loss Control. A fast-acting circuit breaker that is sensitive to very low levels of current leakage to the ground. The interrupter is designed to limit electric shocks to a specified current and time duration value, to prevent serious injury.

see: electrical grounding

ground support insurance

Aviation. A form of satellite and space vehicle insurance that covers third-party liability claims from an occurrence associated with the launch of a satellite or space vehicle.

satellite and space vehicle insurance

ground-up loss

Insurer Operations. The total amount of loss sustained by an insurer before deductions are applied for reinsurance and any applicable deductible.

group accident and health insurance

Health. An insurance plan designed for a natural

group, such as employees of a single employer, or union members and their dependents. Insurance is provided under a single policy issued to the employer or union, with individual certificates issued to each participant or family unit.

see: accident and health insurance, group insurance

group anniversary rating date

Workers' Compensation. The month and day that the combined experience of a group of employers is initially used to rate individual members of the group and each annual anniversary thereafter.

synonym: normal anniversary rating date; *see*: anniversary rating date, experience rating modification factor, manual rates

group annuity

Employee Benefits. A master annuity contract issued in conjunction with an employee benefit plan providing for the issuance of individual annuity contracts to plan participants upon their retirement.

see: annuity, deferred group annuity, employee benefit plan

group captive insurance company

Risk Management. A captive insurance company established and owned by a group of companies engaged in similar businesses to underwrite their own collective risks. A group captive usually insures only its owners.

compare: association captive insurance company; *see*: captive insurance company, risk retention group

group certificate

Health/Life. An insurance coverage summary provided to participants in an employee benefit plan. The certificate confirms that a master policy has been issued to the employer and may be reviewed by the employee.

synonym: certificate of insurance; *compare*: group contract, master insurance policy

group contract

Health/Life. A master insurance contract issued to an employer or other entity that provides life or health coverage to a plan's qualifying participants. Individual group certificates are issued based on the group contract to indicate that the individual is covered.

synonym: master insurance policy; *compare*: certificate of insurance, group certificate

group credit life insurance

Life. Credit life insurance coverage that protects a lender (bank, credit union, credit card company) in the event that a debtor dies before repaying the

loan's balance. Coverage is written on all of a lender's debtors and recovery is limited to the outstanding loan balance. The premium for this coverage is paid by the lender.

see: credit life insurance, creditor beneficiary

group deferred annuity

Employee Benefits.

see: deferred group annuity

group deposit administration annuity

Health/Life.

see: deposit administration plan

group disability insurance

Health. An employee or association group insurance program that provides disability insurance coverage to each qualifying employee by issuing a certificate to a master plan contract. The coverage consists of the payment of a percentage of the plan participant's wages lost due to an illness or accident, subject to a maximum monthly payment.

see: disability, disability income insurance

group dividend plan

Workers' Compensation.

see: safety group dividend plan

Group Health Association of America

Organizations. Members: Group practice prepayment health plans and related organizations that support health maintenance organizations. *Objectives*: To conduct research, specialized education seminars, and conferences. *Founded*: 1959. Merged with American Managed Care and Review Association in 1995. *Headquarters*: Washington, D.C.

group health insurance

Health. An employee or association group insurance program that provides each qualifying plan participant with medical insurance coverage by issuing a certificate to a master plan contract. Generally, each employee is responsible for an annual deductible and some coinsurance portions of medical costs incurred, unless the plan uses a health maintenance organization or preferred provider organization.

see: coordination of benefits, group certificate, group contract, health maintenance organization, preferred provider organization, true group insurance

group I rates

Property. A classification for property insurance rates under the 1986 ISO Commercial Lines Program, for the perils of fire, lightning, explosion, sprinkler coverage and vandalism.

see: group II rates

group II rates

Property. A classification for property insurance

rates under the 1986 ISO Commercial Lines Program, for the perils of windstorm, hail, smoke, riot or civil commotion, aircraft, vehicles, sinkhole collapse, and volcanic action.

see: group I rates

group insurance

Employee Benefits. Insurance provided by an employer, association or other "natural" group (as opposed to a "fictitious" group, formed only for the purpose of purchasing insurance) to its employees or members by purchasing a master insurance contract under which individual certificates are issued. The cost of insurance under a group plan is usually lower than for individual policies because of lower acquisition and administrative expenses.

see: affinity group, association group insurance, deposit administration plan, fictitious group, franchise insurance, group annuity, group certificate, group contract, group credit life insurance, group disability insurance, group health insurance, group life insurance, group property and liability insurance, guaranteed issue, master insurance policy

group life insurance

Life. An employee or association group insurance program that provides each qualifying plan participant with life insurance by issuing a certificate to a master plan contract. Usually, annual renewable term policies are issued, but some plans provide permanent life insurance policies.

synonym: group term life insurance; *compare*: group permanent insurance; *see*: creditor group life insurance, employer group life insurance, facility-of-payment clause, labor union group life insurance, trustee group life insurance

group marketing

Insurer Operations. Promotion of a company's policies to a large number of individuals or organizations in a single insurance program at premiums lower than those that would be charged for similar persons or organizations not participating in the plan. Coverage is guaranteed for the members of the group, so there is no individual underwriting selection or individual proof of insurability.

compare: franchise marketing, mass marketing; *see*: safety group plans, trade association plans

group permanent insurance

Life. A group life insurance plan where participants may choose permanent life insurance coverage. Usually they are allowed to select from one of several forms of permanent insurance policies.

compare: group life insurance; *see*: permanent life insurance

group practice association

Health.

see: closed panel health maintenance organization

group property and liability insurance

Personal. An employee or association group insurance program that provides each qualifying participant with homeowners or automobile insurance. It is most often an elective employee benefit, fully paid for by the employee. The cost is usually lower than an individual policy, since the insurer can save on administrative expenses.

see: cafeteria benefit plan

group self-insurance

Risk Management. The combining together of several organizations, which may be too small to self-insure individually, into a large enough pool to allow them to formalize a self-insurance program.

see: pool, self-insurance

group term life insurance

Life.

see: group life insurance, term life insurance

growth fund

Financial Planning. A mutual fund that invests primarily in stocks that are expected to increase in value faster than most others (growth stocks), which generally reinvest profits rather than pay dividends to shareholders. Because growth stocks are riskier than most, the value of shares in growth funds is subject to fluctuation.

compare: fixed income fund, equity fund, hedge fund; *see*: mutual fund, stock (*Financial Planning*)

guaranteed annuity

Life.

see: fixed annuity

guaranteed annuity payments

Life. Annuity benefit payments that are not contingent upon how long the annuitant lives. If the annuitant dies, the payments are made to the decedent's estate.

synonym: certain payments; *see*: annuity

guaranteed bond

Financial Planning. A corporate or municipal bond with its interest or principal, or both, guaranteed by another corporation, such as an insurance company.

see: bond (*Financial Planning*), financial guaranty insurance, hospital bond guaranty insurance, industrial development bond guaranty insurance, municipal bond guaranty insurance

guaranteed continuable
Health/Life.

  see: guaranteed renewable

guaranteed cost
Insurer Operations. The fixed premium of an insurance policy based on the policyholder's exposures. No additional premium can be charged because of adverse loss experience.

  compare: experience rating plan, prospective rating plan, retrospective rating plan

guaranteed freight
Inland Marine/Ocean Marine. Freight that is not prepaid, but which is payable whether or not the merchandise arrives at the final port or destination.

  see: freight

guaranteed insurability
Health. An insurance policy option that at inception allows the insured the right to purchase additional benefits at a future date, such as additional disability income or higher medical expense benefit limits, without providing additional or updated evidence of insurability.

  compare: evidence of insurability, guaranteed issue; *see*: guaranteed renewable

Life. A life insurance policy option that may be purchased at inception that allows the insured to purchase additional amounts of life insurance without taking a physical examination or having to provide evidence of insurability. Generally, the provision requires the insured to increase the amount of insurance at a stated time (i.e., specified anniversary dates, upon the birth of a child).

guaranteed investment contract (GIC)
Life. An investment contract offered by a life insurance company that guarantees the repayment of principal and a compound interest return. It is frequently used to fund qualified pension plans.

  see: qualified plan, separate account guaranteed investment contract, synthetic guaranteed investment contract

guaranteed issue
Health/Life. A group insurance plan where the insurer does not require individual employees to provide evidence of insurability to obtain coverage. The amount of coverage provided is sometimes determined by the group size and distribution of ages. Some states require health insurers to offer basic coverage to small businesses on a guaranteed issue basis.

  compare: guaranteed insurability; *see*: basic benefits (2), evidence of insurability

guaranteed payout
Life. The sum of certain payments, i.e., guaranteed lump sums, annuities certain, and the payments generated during the certain period of a life-contingent annuity.

  see: certain period

guaranteed period
Life.

  see: certain period

guaranteed renewable
Health/Life. A policy provision that the insured has the right to continue the policy in force until the insured reaches a specified age. The insured must make premium payments in a timely manner, and the insurer may not unilaterally change the policy except for rate increases that apply to all policyholders in the relevant class of coverage.

  synonym: guaranteed continuable; *compare*: optionally renewable contract; *see*: guaranteed insurability, guaranteed issue, lifetime policy, noncancelable policy

guaranteed stock
Financial Planning. Stock of a corporation with its dividend payments guaranteed by another entity, such as an insurer. This usually involves preferred stock and is considered a dual security.

  see: financial guaranty insurance, stock

guarantor
Surety. The party who guarantees the actions or debts of another party. Under a surety bond, the surety is the guarantor.

  see: surety

guaranty
General.

  see: warranty

guaranty endorsement
Property/Reinsurance. A property insurance endorsement under which the reinsurer directly pays the mortgagee or policyholder in the event of the insurer's insolvency. The amount paid may be only the reinsurer's portion of the loss, or the reinsurer may agree to pay the entire loss.

  synonym: mortgagee endorsement; *compare*: cut-through endorsement; *see*: mortgagee, reinsurance

guaranty fund
Regulation. A fund created by statute in most states that guarantees the claim payments of state-domiciled insurance companies that become insolvent. The fund is created with assessments against the other insurers operating in that state. Most state guaranty funds operate on a post-insolvency basis; that is, the assessments are made following an insolvency. New York is an exception; there, the guaranty fund is prefunded by assessments.

  synonym: insolvency fund; *see*: American Trust

Fund, central loss fund, insolvency, liquidation, Lloyd's Premium Trust Fund, rehabilitation

guard

Loss Control.

see: barrier guard

guardian

Law. A person legally entrusted with custody of another's property or care of the person, most often a minor or an incompetent adult.

see: guardian ad litem

guardian ad litem

Law. A person appointed by the court during the course of litigation to protect the interests of a minor or an incompetent who is a party to the suit. The appointment automatically ends when the case is resolved.

see: guardian

guardian of the estate

Law. A person to whom the court has entrusted the custody and control of funds (e.g., periodic payments in a claims settlement) due to a minor (during minority) or an incompetent (during the period of incapacity).

see: guardian

Guertin laws

Life. Laws dealing with life insurance that are named after Alfred Guertin, former actuary for the New Jersey Insurance Department. The laws, initiated in 1947, apply to the valuation and nonforfeiture of life insurance policies and protect the insured's ability to recover from a life policy and obtain any equity built in the policy.

see: nonforfeiture benefit

guest law

Automobile.

see: guest statute

guest statute

Automobile. Generally, a passenger who has been invited to ride in a vehicle without any charge or expected payment has the right to bring suit against a negligent driver in the event of an accident. However, some states have laws that prohibit such a suit unless willful or wanton negligence is involved. The prohibition sometimes applies only to passengers who are close relatives of the driver.

synonym: guest law; *see*: assumption of risk, passenger hazard exclusion

guests' property—premises

Crime. A crime coverage (ISO form CR 00 13) developed under the 1986 Insurance Services Office crime program for hotels and motels which covers the insured's liability for damage or loss to guests' property anywhere within the insured's premises or outside the premises in the insured's possession.

synonym: crime plan 7; *see*: guests' property—safe deposit box, liability for guests' property—premises coverage form

guests' property—safe deposit box

Crime. A crime coverage (ISO form CR 00 12) developed under the 1986 Insurance Services Office crime program that provides coverage similar to the hotel safe deposit box liability form.

synonym: crime plan 6; *see*: hotel safe deposit box liability, liability for guests' property—safe deposit coverage form

guideline premium

Life. A premium defined in universal life insurance policies as the maximum premium payable that will qualify the policy as life insurance for federal income tax purposes.

see: universal life insurance

guiding principles

Insurer Operations. A set of principles developed by the Association of Casualty Surety Companies in 1963 that allocates liability between those insurers whose policies would respond to a loss and preserves protection for the insured. The complete name of the document is the *Guiding Principles—Casualty, Fidelity, Inland Marine—First-Party Property Losses and Claims.*

see: Association of Casualty Surety Companies

H

Hague Rules

Ocean Marine. A set of rules resulting from a 1921 conference at The Hague in Holland, concerning bills of lading for the carriage of goods by sea. In 1922, the rules were adopted by most countries to cover the carriage of goods by sea.

see: Carriage of Goods by Sea Act, Carriage of Goods by Water Act

hail

Property/Automobile. Precipitation in the form of ice pellets that occasionally are of sufficient size to cause severe property damage. Damage from hail is covered by most property and automobile physical damage forms.

see: crop hail insurance

hail insurance

Property.

see: crop hail insurance, windstorm and hail coverage

halon

Loss Control. A nontoxic, vaporizing liquid used in fire extinguishing systems. The vapor is injected into the room, depriving the fire of oxygen. It is most often used in computer and laboratory rooms, where foam or water extinguishing systems might do irreparable damage. Although these systems are still in use, production of new halon gas was discontinued in the United States as of January 1, 1994, due to its ozone depleting effects.

see: fire extinguishing system

hammer

Automobile.

see: bull

hangarkeepers' liability insurance

Aviation. Coverage for the owner or operator of an aircraft hangar, for damage to the aircraft of others while in the insured's custody for storage or repair.

see: airport owners' and operators' liability insurance

hard market

Insurer Operations. An insurance business cycle period when coverage is difficult for some insureds to obtain and premiums are high. Some coverages, such as professional liability, may not be available for some insureds during a hard market. Generally, *hard* markets are caused by heavy underwriting losses or extreme price competition, whereas a *tight* market is caused by a lack of capacity, such as when money is invested in places other than insurance companies.

compare: buyer's market, soft market, tight market; *see*: capacity, underwriting cycle

Harter Act

Ocean Marine. A federal statute adopted in 1893 concerning maritime ventures to and from U.S. ports which limits the responsibility of vessel owners for damage or loss due to navigational error if the vessel was properly equipped and manned and was a seaworthy vessel.

see: Carriage of Goods By Sea Act

hazard

Property. A condition or situation that creates or increases the probability or extent of a loss from a peril, such as unsafe or unclean conditions, cheap or flammable building materials, etc.

compare: exposure, peril, risk; *see*: moral hazard, morale hazard, physical hazard, substandard risk

hazard insurance

Risk Management. A term often found in contracts involving property (leases, mortgages) for commercial insurance against losses caused by fire, windstorms and other common insurable hazards (usually excluding earthquake and flood).

hazard logic tree analysis

Risk Management. A risk exposure analysis that links a loss exposure with the perils and hazards that may cause it. A diagram is developed that resembles a tree. At the top is an identified exposure under which are perils and hazards that could cause a loss to that exposure. It displays in a logical form the causal relationships between hazards and potential loss events.

see: exposure, fault tree analysis

hazard ranking system

Regulation. The principle screening tool used by the Environmental Protection Agency to evaluate risks to public health and the environment associated with abandoned or uncontrolled hazardous waste sites. The ranking system produces a score based on the potential of hazardous substances to spread through air, land, or ground water. Other factors are considered, such as the closeness and number of residents. The score is the primary factor in deciding whether the site should be on a national list of priorities for cleanup.

see: Comprehensive Environmental Response Compensation and Liability Act, hazardous substance, National Priorities List

Hazardous and Solid Waste Amendments
Regulation.
see: Resource Conservation and Recovery Act

Hazardous Materials Transportation Act

Regulation. Federal legislation adopted in 1975 that regulates the transportation of hazardous material. It provides the Department of Transportation with authority to promulgate regulations on safe transportation of hazardous materials.

see: Department of Transportation

hazardous substance

Loss Control. Any substance that potentially threatens human health or the environment. Typically, hazardous substances are toxic, corrosive, ignitable, explosive, or chemically reactive. The federal Environmental Protection Agency requires named hazardous substances to be reported if a specified quantity is emitted into the environment. The Occupational Safety and Health Administration also issues regulations concerning substances that may harm employees.

compare: hazardous waste; *see*: extremely hazardous substance

hazardous substance coverage

Property. A boiler and machinery policy coverage extension for additional expenses incurred by the insured for cleanup, repair, replacement or disposal of property that is declared by a governmental agency to be damaged, contaminated or polluted by a substance presenting health hazards. The expenses must be caused by a covered accident, and coverage is subject to a sublimit (e.g., $5,000). Higher limits may be available for an additional premium.

hazardous waste

Liability. Chemical or other products listed as hazardous waste pursuant to the Resource Conservation and Recovery Act. The materials are categorized according to their ignitability, corrosivity, reactivity and toxicity.

see: closure and post-closure insurance, Resource Conservation and Recovery Act, pollutant

Loss Control. Hazardous substances that are by-products of economic or consumer activity. Hazardous waste is usually classified as household wastes; agricultural wastes; mine site wastes; wastes from the combustion of fossil fuels; and wastes associated with the exploration, development or production of crude oil, natural gas, or geothermal energy.

compare: hazardous substance; *see*: hazardous waste disposal, hazardous waste manifest, listed waste, nonpoint sources, point source, reportable quantity

hazardous waste disposal

Loss Control. The final placement or destruction of toxic, radioactive, or other hazardous substances; surplus or banned pesticides or other chemicals; or polluted soils. Disposal may be accomplished through use of landfills, surface impoundments, land farming, deep well injection, ocean dumping, or incineration.

see: deep well injection, hazardous waste, incineration, land farming, secure chemical landfill

hazardous waste manifest

Regulation. The shipping document originated and signed by a hazardous waste generator that contains the information required by the Environmental Protection Agency and Department of Transportation. It travels with and is signed by all who interact with the waste, and is returned to the generator by the disposer.

see: hazardous waste, manifest

head office
Insurer Operations.
see: home office

health benefit plan

Health. Any program of direct health care services or indemnification of medical expenses offered by service providers or third-party payers—i.e., a health insurance policy, a health maintenance organization, preferred provider organization, health service contract sponsor, or an employee welfare benefit plan permitted under ERISA. The term does not usually include medical coverage under workers' compensation or automobile insurance.

see: health insurance, health maintenance organization, multiple employer welfare arrangement, preferred provider organization, third-party payer

215

Health Care Financial Management Association (HCFMA)

Organizations. Members: Professional society of health care financial executives and those in related fields. *Objectives*: Educational programs and annual examinations for the Fellow and Certified Manager of Patient Accounts. *Founded*: 1946. *Headquarters*: Washington, D.C.

Health Care Financing Administration (HCFA)

Health. The division of the U.S. Department of Health and Human Services that administers the Medicare program.

see: Medicare

health care provider

Health. Any person, professional association or entity duly licensed to render medical services to patients, including physicians, surgeons, nurses, dentists, pharmacists, physical therapists, optometrists, chiropractors, and other licensed practitioners of the healing arts; emergency medical technicians and persons employed by licensed practitioners who are directly involved in the delivery of health care services; and hospitals and clinics. The term is elastic and may include unconventional service providers, such as acupuncturists, herbalists, naturopaths, etc. Insurance policies and managed care plan contracts may not generally define an eligible provider more restrictively than the definition used to license that class of providers by the state where the service is provided.

synonym: provider; *see*: any willing provider law, fee for service, managed care (1), preferred provider organization, primary care physician

health indemnity plan

Health. Health insurance that reimburses the insured after paying his or her own medical expenses, minus any deductible or copayment.

synonym: hospital indemnity insurance; *see*: indemnification

health insurance (HI)

Health. Coverage for hospital, physician, and other medical expenses resulting from illness or injury. It also includes coverage for the accidental loss of life, limb or sight.

synonym: accident and sickness insurance, sickness insurance; *see*: accident insurance, accidental death insurance, disability income insurance, dismemberment benefit, experimental procedures exclusion, health benefit plan, hybrid health care, managed care, medical expense insurance, medically necessary

Health Insurance Associate (HIA)

Organizations. A professional designation given by the Health Insurance Association of America after successful completion of a five-part self-study program.

see: Health Insurance Association of America

Health Insurance Association of America (HIAA)

Organizations. Members: Health and accident insurance companies. *Objectives*: Promotes interests of health insurers through lobbying and industry information services. *Founded*: 1956. *Headquarters*: Washington, D.C. (Formed by a merger of the Bureau of Accident and Health Underwriters and the Health and Accident Underwriters Conference.)

see: Health Insurance Institute

Health Insurance Institute (HII)

Health/Organizations. Members: Representatives from the health insurance industry; usually members of the Health Insurance Association of America (HIAA). *Objectives*: Acts as the public relations arm of the HIAA. Relays health insurance information to consumers. *Founded*: 1956. *Headquarters*: Washington, D.C.

see: Health Insurance Association of America

health insurance purchasing cooperative

Health.

see: health purchasing alliance

health maintenance organization (HMO)

Health. A medical group practice plan that acts as both an insurer and health care provider. Group participants are entitled to services from participating physicians, clinics and hospitals for a flat monthly or quarterly fee.

compare: direct health care corporation, health indemnity plan, preferred provider organization; *see*: closed panel health maintenance organization, in-area emergency services, independent practice association, managed care, point-of-service plan, primary care physician

Health Maintenance Organization Act

Regulation. Federal legislation (U.S. Code Title 42, Chapter 6A, Subchapter XI) passed in 1973 and amended in 1988 that sparked the growth of health maintenance organizations. Employers with more than 25 employees must offer at least one of the two basic types of HMO plans (closed panel or independent practice).

see: health maintenance organization

health purchasing alliance

Health. A group of purchasers of health benefit plans (such as small employers or other group health insurance policyholders) that helps assess its members' needs and shops among competing plans. The alliance theoretically gives purchasers more access to information and more bargaining power than they would have individually and, therefore, better and lower-cost choices. A few states have state-chartered, nonprofit alliances to provide purchasing services to small employers and government agencies (for whom membership may be mandatory). Alliances do not directly provide insurance, bear any insurance risk, or form self-insurance plans among members.

synonym: health insurance purchasing cooperative; *see*: managed competition

health systems plan
General.
see: annual implementation plan

hearing level
Health/Loss Control. The deviation in decibels of an individual's hearing threshold from the zero reference of an audiometer.
see: decibel, noise level

hearing loss
Health/Loss Control.
see: hearing level

hearing officer
Law.
see: administrative law judge

hearsay
Law. Testimony in a legal proceeding that is not based on a witness's personal knowledge, but on matters told to the witness by another person; an out-of-court statement introduced in court to prove the truth of the statement. This form of evidence is not admissible in a court of law unless it falls within one of several recognized exceptions.
see: evidence, testimony

heavy timber construction
Loss Control/Property.
see: mill construction

hedge fund
Financial Planning. A highly speculative mutual fund that employs investment techniques such as the purchase of financial derivatives or the issuance of debt to increase investment leverage in the hope of obtaining large capital gains.
synonym: option fund, leverage fund; *compare*: fixed income fund, growth fund; *see*: capital gain (or loss), financial derivative, hedging, mutual fund

hedging
Financial Planning. Buying or selling a commodity futures contract or a security (particularly an option) in the direction opposite from the primary transaction as a protection against loss from price fluctuations. *Example*: A candy company that buys cocoa beans to make bonbons may at the same time sell cocoa beans, which the firm does not yet own, in the same quantity and at the same price in a futures contract with a delivery date near the time the bonbons will be ready to sell. By that time, if the price of cocoa beans (and therefore also bonbons) falls, the candy maker can buy the beans cheaply and sell them at the higher price specified in the futures contract. The profit from the commodity sale compensates for the loss on the bonbons. Similarly, should the price of cocoa beans rise, bonbons will sell for more, but this extra profit will be canceled in buying cocoa beans that the company must deliver under the futures contract. In a perfect hedge, the financial profit and loss would be equal, leaving only the manufacturing profit that represents the value added by turning cocoa beans into bonbons.
see: business risk, catastrophe insurance futures contract, financial risk, futures contract, hedge fund, option

hedonic loss
General. Deprivation of the pleasure or enjoyment of normal activities resulting from an accident or injury.
see: loss of consortium, noneconomic loss

herbicide applicator coverage
Liability.
see: pesticide or herbicide applicator coverage

hidden defect
Liability.
see: latent defect

high deductible health insurance
Employee Benefits/Health.
see: qualified higher deductible health plan

high pressure steam
Loss Control. Steam that is at a pressure in excess of 15 pounds per square inch.
compare: low pressure steam; *see*: boiler and machinery

high seas
Ocean Marine.
see: Death on the High Seas Act

high-yield bond
Financial Planning. A corporate bond or obligation (i.e., any evidence of debt, such as a note, debenture or commercial paper) that has a low rating by a securities rating agency, such as Standard & Poor's or Moody's. These bonds offer high yields but are more likely than others not to be repaid. Most states limit investments by insurance companies in obligations rated 3 or below in the *Securities Valuation Manual* of the National Association of Insurance Commissioners. On this scale, 3 is

217

medium, and 4, 5 and 6 are lower grade obligations.

synonym: high-yield high-risk obligation, junk bond, noninvestment grade obligation, lower grade obligation; *compare*: blue-chip stock; *see*: corporate bond, debt security, National Association of Insurance Commissioners, securities valuation, Valuation of Securities System, yield

high-yield high-risk obligation
Financial Planning.

see: high-yield bond

highly protected risk (HPR)
Property. Property insurance coverage for large commercial properties that are protected with automatic sprinkler systems and superior construction. Qualified insureds pay significantly lower premiums.

see: Factory Mutual System, Industrial Risk Insurers

Highway Loss Data Institute (HLDI)
Organizations. Members: Motor vehicle property and casualty insurers. *Objectives*: Provide consumers with insurance industry data about human and economic losses resulting from highway accidents. *Founded*: 1972. *Headquarters*: Arlington, VA.

hired autos
Automobile. Vehicles that are leased, rented or borrowed by the insured; a classification of covered vehicles under the business auto coverage form, garage coverage form, or truckers' coverage form.

compare: nonowned automobile; *see*: business auto coverage form, garage coverage form, rental reimbursement coverage, truckers' coverage form

hired autos liability coverage
Automobile. Coverage for liability arising out of the use of automobiles that are leased, rented or borrowed by the insured or its employees for business purposes.

compare: drive-other-car coverage, hired autos physical damage insurance

hired autos physical damage coverage
Automobile. Coverage for damage to automobiles that are leased, rented, hired or borrowed by the insured or its employees for business purposes. This coverage is usually purchased by an organization whose employees rent cars frequently, making it unnecessary to purchase collision damage waiver coverage from the rental car company. The autos must be rented in the organization's name.

compare: hired autos liability coverage; *see*: collision damage waiver

historic home insurance
Personal. A special homeowners policy for homes that are listed in or nominated for the Federal Register of Historic Places or are in a historic district designated by federal, state or local agencies. Coverage is written on a reproduction cost or modified replacement cost basis and can include valued coverage for such items as elaborate woodwork. The liability coverage is extended to include coverage for historic home tours.

see: dwelling policy, homeowners modified coverage form, replacement cost, reproduction cost

HIV positive
Health.

see: human immunodeficiency virus

hobbies or avocations
Life. Life insurance underwriters consider the leisure pastimes (hobbies and avocations) of prospective insureds in rating individual life policies. Some hobbies are so hazardous (e.g., auto racing or skydiving) that high premiums are required to issue a policy.

see: occupational hazard, substandard risk

hold harmless agreement
Law. A contract provision that transfers liability from one party to another; an agreement that one party will assume the other's liability arising under or because of the contract. Such agreements are frequently found in leases, sidetrack agreements and easements. There are three major types: *clarification* type—the parties provide that each will assume its own legal responsibility or will make only a small or reasonable transfer of responsibility from one party to the other; *moderate* type—one party assumes all legal liability except for the negligence of the other (this is considered the standard agreement); *severe* type—one party assumes all legal liability without regard to fault or negligence.

synonym: indemnity agreement; *see*: exculpatory provision, sidetrack agreement

holder in due course
Financial Planning. The person who has obtained a bill of exchange (such as a check, stock or bond) in a bona fide way for value. The instrument is taken free of previous defects in title.

see: holder in due course insurance, lender's holder in due course insurance, personal defense

holder in due course insurance
Financial Guaranty. Coverage for a creditor in the event that a consumer has a dispute with a vendor of a product or service purchased on credit, and the consumer/debtor refuses to make payments. In general, anyone (e.g., a financial institution) who purchases credit contracts underlying the sale of consumer goods is a "holder in due course." A 1976 Federal Trade Commission regulation makes a holder in due course subject to the same claims

that a buyer may assert against the seller.

compare: lender's holder in due course insurance

holding company

General. A business that confines its activities to owning stock in and supervising the management of other companies.

see: parent company

hole-in-one coverage

Inland Marine. A form of prize indemnification insurance which covers the insured (usually a tournament sponsor) should a hole-in-one be made on a specified hole on a golf course during a specified tournament. The policy warrants that certification of a hole-in-one must be made by at least two tournament officials prior to payment of a claim against the policy.

see: prize indemnification insurance

home day care coverage endorsement

Personal. A homeowners endorsement (ISO form HO 04 97) that covers home day care for insureds who regularly provide home day care services for compensation. This endorsement adds section II (personal liability and medical payments) exclusions for such things as riding draft or saddle animals, injury while getting into or out of a vehicle or watercraft, and injury to any employee of an insured arising out of the day care operation.

compare: home day care exclusion

home day care exclusion

Personal. An endorsement (ISO form HO 04 96) to the homeowners policy that specifically excludes coverage for home day care with respect to section II (personal liability and medical payments) and section I, coverage B (other structures). This exclusion is designed for insureds who regularly provide home day care services for compensation.

compare: home day care coverage endorsement; *see*: homeowners policy

home/foreign insurance

International. Insurance of an organization's business or property in a foreign country. "Home" refers to the country where the insured is domiciled and "foreign" to the territory where the risk or exposure is located. Many insurance companies have established special international departments to handle insurance of this type.

synonym: foreign/home insurance; *compare*: reverse flow insurance

home health care

Health. Health care provided in the home of the patient, usually by a private nurse or a state-licensed home health care agency. Services are usually limited to part-time or intermittent nursing care and physical or occupational rehabilitation.

see: house confinement

home office

Insurer Operations. The headquarters or principal office of an insurance company, where the chief executive officer and the senior executive staff are located.

synonym: head office; *see*: domestic insurer, domiciliary state

Home Office Life Underwriters Association (HOLUA)

Organizations. *Members*: Underwriters of legal reserve life insurance companies. *Objectives*: Offer education programs through the Academy of Life Underwriting for professional home office life underwriters. *Founded*: 1930. *Headquarters*: St. Paul, MN.

home protection insurance

Life.

see: mortgage protection insurance

home service insurance

Life.

see: industrial life insurance

homeowners basic form

Personal. A very limited homeowners policy (ISO form HO 00 01) which for that reason is not filed for use in many states. It is used primarily for owner-occupied dwellings. Under section I, it provides property coverage for the dwelling, other structures, and personal property for the named perils of fire or lightning, windstorm or hail, explosion, riot or civil commotion, aircraft, vehicles, smoke, vandalism, malicious mischief, theft, and glass breakage. Section II, liability coverage, is identical to all the other homeowners forms.

synonym: basic homeowners policy, homeowners policy form 1; *see*: homeowners policy

homeowners broad form

Personal. This homeowners policy (ISO form HO 00 02) is identical to the basic form except that the following additional named perils are covered: falling objects; weight of ice, snow, or sleet; accidental discharge from a plumbing, heating, air conditioning or sprinkler system or household appliance; sudden and accidental tearing, cracking, burning, or bulging of a steam or hot water heating system; freezing of a plumbing, heating, air conditioning or sprinkler system or a household appliance; sudden and accidental damage from artificially generated electricity; and volcanic eruption. Also, a number of the perils in the basic form (vehicles, smoke, glass breakage) are broadened. Section II liability coverage is identical to the other homeowners forms.

synonym: homeowners policy form 2; *see*: homeowners basic form, homeowners policy

homeowners contents broad form

Personal. This homeowners policy (ISO form HO 00 04) is used primarily for tenants of rented premises, as it only provides personal property coverage. Coverage of the dwelling and other structures is omitted. A limited amount of coverage is provided for additions and alterations the policyholder makes to the rented property. This limit may be increased by the "building additions and alterations increased limit" endorsement.

The contents broad form is identical to the basic form except that the following additional named perils are covered: falling objects; weight of ice, snow, or sleet; accidental discharge from a plumbing, heating, air conditioning or sprinkler system or household appliance; sudden and accidental tearing, cracking, burning, or bulging of a steam or hot water heating system; freezing of a plumbing, heating, air conditioning or sprinkler system or a household appliance; sudden and accidental damage from artificially generated electricity; and volcanic eruption. Also, a number of the perils in the basic form (vehicles, smoke, glass breakage) are broadened. Section II liability coverage is identical to the other homeowners forms.

synonym: homeowners policy form 4; *see*: homeowners basic form, homeowners policy

homeowners modified coverage form

Personal. This homeowners policy (ISO form HO 00 08) is for dwellings not considered eligible for replacement cost coverage, such as older ornate buildings and dwellings located in declining neighborhoods. There are three major areas where this form differs from the basic homeowners form: 1. rather than replacement cost, this form provides coverage on an actual cash value or repair cost basis; 2. the theft coverage is limited; 3. broadened coverages are not provided (e.g., personal property off the residence premises). Under Section I, it covers the dwelling, other structures, and personal property for the named perils of fire or lightning; windstorm or hail; explosion; riot or civil commotion; aircraft; vehicles; smoke; vandalism or malicious mischief; theft; and volcanic eruption. Section II liability coverage is identical to the other homeowners forms.

synonym: homeowners policy form 8; *see*: historic home insurance, homeowners policy

homeowners policy

Personal. An insurance policy designed to protect the owner or renter of a dwelling which combines property coverage for the dwelling structure, personal property coverage for the contents, and personal liability coverage. Numerous versions of homeowners policies exist, but most insurers use one of the six forms published by the Insurance Services Office or their own forms comparable to the ISO's. The ISO forms provide broad personal liability coverage for the owner or renter, including the spouse, children and relatives residing in the home. Numerous endorsements can be added, such as a personal articles floater for highly valued jewelry or furs, and an inflation guard endorsement to maintain adequate levels of insurance. All six forms use the following format (except the form for renters—homeowners contents broad form—which does not provide coverage for dwellings or other structures):

Section I coverages:
A—Dwelling
B—Other structures
C—Personal Property
D—Loss of Use
Additional Coverages
Section II liability coverages:
E—Personal Liability
F—Medical Payments to Others
Additional Coverages

The ISO forms differ in regard to property coverage only; all of the forms provide identical liability coverage.

see: actual cash value loss settlement roof surfacing endorsement, business pursuits endorsement, buildings and contents form, historic home insurance, home day care coverage endorsement, homeowners basic form, homeowners broad form, homeowners special form, homeowners contents broad form, homeowners modified coverage form, homeowners unit owners' form, homeowners policy—liability coverage, homeowners policy—property coverage, incidental farming personal liability endorsement, incidental motorized land-conveyances endorsement, increased limits on business property endorsement, inflation guard endorsement, mobile home policy, permitted incidental occupancies (residence premises) endorsement, personal property replacement cost endorsement, refrigerated property coverage endorsement, renters' insurance, residence employee, resident relative, scheduled personal property endorsement, sinkhole collapse endorsement, snowmobile endorsement, special computer coverage endorsement, special loss settlement endorsement, structure rented to others—residence premises endorsement, watercraft endorsement, windstorm or hail exclusion endorsement

homeowners policy—liability coverage

Personal. Most homeowners policies provide the liability coverage in Section II of the Insurance Services Office policy forms. The coverage is divided into sections E, F and Additional Coverages.

Many insurers modify the coverage in their homeowners forms.

Coverage E—Personal Liability provides coverage for defense and damages in the event that a claim or suit is brought against the insured because of bodily injury or property damage. Coverage is provided at the insured's premises and is extended to the personal (nonbusiness) activities of the insured homeowner or spouse, relatives of either, and others under the age of twenty-one in the care of the homeowner.

Coverage F—Medical Payments To Others provides reimbursement of reasonable medical expenses for injuries sustained by a third party as a result of the insured's activities, whether or not the insured is legally liable.

Additional Coverages include four extensions of coverage to the liability section: 1. *claim expenses,* such as premiums on bonds involved in a suit, loss of the insured's earnings up to $50 per day for assisting in the investigation or defense of a claim, interest on a judgment; 2. *first aid expense* to others who have a bodily injury claim against the insured; 3. *damage to property of others* replacement cost reimbursement up to $500 for property damage sustained by a third party; 4. *loss assessment* payment up to $1,000 for the insured's share of a loss assessment charged by a corporation or association of property owners.

compare: homeowners policy—property coverage

homeowners policy—property coverage

Personal. Most homeowners policies provide the property coverage in Section II of the Insurance Services Office policy forms. The coverage is divided into sections A, B, C, D, and Additional Coverages. A deductible ($100, $250 or more) usually applies to each Section I loss. Many insurers modify this coverage in their homeowners forms.

Coverage A—Dwelling provides a specified amount of coverage on the dwelling structure of the insured. Coverage is provided on a replacement cost basis (except for the homeowners modified form) if at the time of loss the limit of liability is 80% or more of the full replacement cost.

Coverage B—Other Structures covers other structures (garage, fences, storage sheds) on the premises that are set apart from the dwelling by clear space for a percentage (usually 10%) of the Coverage A limit.

Coverage C—Personal Property covers personal property at the insured residence for a set percentage (usually 50) and extends coverage to personal property owned or used by an insured off the premises for the greater of 10% of the Coverage C limit or $1,000. A number of special limits of liability (sublimits) apply to this coverage, such as $200 on money bank notes, bullion, and gold; $1000 on securities, accounts, deeds, evidences of debt; $2,500

on silverware or goldware; etc. Coverage is provided on an actual cash value basis.

Coverage D—Loss of Use provides coverage for a portion (between 10% and 40% of coverage A, depending on the policy form used) of the cost of additional living expenses that may result from damage to the residence or reimburses the insured for the fair rental value of the residence. Coverage lasts until the structure is repaired or replaced or until the insured permanently relocates.

Additional Coverages: depending on the homeowners policy form, some or all of the following additional coverages are provided: 1. debris removal; 2. reasonable repairs; 3. trees, shrubs, other plants; 4. fire department service charges; 5. property removed; 6. credit card, fund transfer card, forgery and counterfeit money; 7. loss assessment; 8. collapse; 9. glass or safety glazing material; 10. landlord's furnishings; 11. ordinance or law.

compare: homeowners policy—liability coverage; *see*: homeowners policy—special limits of liability, named perils, open perils, special loss settlement

homeowners policy—special limits of liability

Personal. The homeowners policy coverage section C (personal property) has a number of sublimits (e.g., money, electronic equipment, jewelry) that are listed in the form as "special limits of liability."

see: business property—special limit, electronic equipment—special limit, firearms—special limit, jewelry watches furs—special limit, money—special limit, securities—special limit, silverware—special limit, trailers—special limit, watercraft—special limit

homeowners policy form 1 (2, etc.)
Personal.

form 1: *see* homeowners basic form
form 2: *see* homeowners broad form
form 3: *see* homeowners special form
form 4: *see* homeowners contents broad form
form 6: *see* homeowners unit owners' form
form 8: *see* homeowners modified coverage form

homeowners special form

Personal. This homeowners form (ISO form HO 00 03) is used primarily for owner-occupied dwelling units. Under Section I, it covers the dwelling and other structures on an open perils basis and covers personal property on the broad named perils basis similar to the homeowners broad form. By endorsement, the personal property may be covered on an open perils basis. Section II liability coverage is identical to the other homeowners forms.

synonym: homeowners policy form 3, special homeowners policy; *see*: homeowners broad form, homeowners policy, open perils, personal property—special coverage

homeowners unit owners' form

Personal. A homeowners policy (ISO form HO 00 06) designed for residential condominium unit owners and cooperative apartment tenants. It is identical to the basic form except that the following additional named perils are covered: falling objects; weight of ice, snow, or sleet; accidental discharge from a plumbing, heating, air conditioning or sprinkler system or household appliance; sudden and accidental tearing, cracking, burning, or bulging of a steam or hot water heating system; freezing of a plumbing, heating, air conditioning or sprinkler system or a household appliance; sudden and accidental damage from artificially generated electricity; and volcanic eruption. Also, a number of the perils in the basic form (vehicles, smoke, glass breakage) are broadened. By endorsements, the personal property and the structures can be covered on an open perils basis. Section II liability coverage is identical to the other homeowners forms.

synonym: condominium unit owners' form, homeowners policy form 6; *see*: condominium, cooperative housing, homeowners policy

homestead

Property/Title. The right to land created by the construction of a home on a plot of land and the filing of a homestead with the appropriate local jurisdiction. An insurable interest is created by a homestead.

homogeneity

Insurer Operations. The quality of sameness or similarity among members of a group or class. In insurance, identification as one of a large group of homogeneous exposure units—allowing proper classification and rating of the risk, as well as spread of risk—is a condition that must be met before most insurers will provide coverage for a given risk.

see: homogeneous exposure units, insurable risk, spread of risk

homogeneous exposure units

Insurer Operations. Units that are alike in size, value, use, or other relevant characteristics, and so are similarly exposed to loss. Insurance underwriters evaluate a risk's characteristics, and place risks into classifications representing large numbers of similarly situated risks.

see: classification, insurable risk, rating class

honesty clause

Property.

see: full reporting clause

Honorable Order of the Blue Goose (HOBGI)

Organizations. Members: Individuals in insurance

sales, underwriting, and claims. *Objectives*: Fraternal organization that promotes information exchange. *Founded*: 1906. *Headquarters*: Elm Grove, WI.

horse and carriage liability

Liability. Insurance for horse-drawn carriages operated on public streets in a tour business or for special entertainment events. Coverage is similar to that provided by a commercial auto policy.

hospice

Health. A health facility that provides care for terminally ill individuals in a home-like setting. Admission is usually a few months prior to the patient's anticipated date of death and includes medical care and counseling. Hospice care may also include counseling for the patient's family.

see: custodial care, extended care facility, integrated care (2), residential care facility, skilled nursing facility

hospital benefits

Health. Benefits provided under an insurance policy for hospital charges that the insured has incurred because of a covered illness or injury.

see: hospital-surgical expense insurance

hospital bond guaranty insurance

Financial Guaranty. A form of guaranteed bond coverage for hospitals that guarantees the payment of principal and interest on hospital bonds should a bond issue default. The insurer's financial rating affords the bonds a higher investment grade than that of the issuer's rating.

see: financial guaranty insurance, guaranteed bond

hospital confinement insurance

Health. A limited form of health insurance that pays a stipulated daily, weekly or monthly benefit while an insured is confined to a hospital. The benefit is payable on an unallocated basis, without regard to the amount of actual hospital expense incurred.

synonym: hospital income insurance

hospital endorsement

Workers' Compensation. A special workers' compensation policy endorsement available in some states (California, Delaware, Pennsylvania) that can be attached to a policy issued to a hospital employer which provides reimbursement if the employer supplies complete statutory medical care to injured employees.

see: workers' compensation insurance

hospital expense insurance

Health.

see: hospital-surgical expense insurance

hospital income insurance
Health.
see: hospital confinement insurance

hospital indemnity insurance
Health.
see: health indemnity plan

hospital malpractice insurance
Professional Liability.
see: hospital professional liability insurance

hospital professional liability insurance
Professional Liability. Coverage for a hospital against claims for personal injury arising out of medical malpractice, error or mistake in rendering professional services. Coverage is usually written on a claims-made basis, though a few insurers provide occurrence coverage.
synonym: hospital malpractice insurance; *see:* medical malpractice

hospital-surgical expense insurance
Health. A limited form of health insurance that reimburses the insured for expenses directly related to hospitalization. This includes room charges, nursing, and surgical expenses resulting from the illness or injury of the insured.
synonym: hospital expense insurance, hospitalization insurance

hospitalization insurance
Health.
see: hospital-surgical expense insurance

host liquor liability
Liability. A special liability form that covers individuals or organizations (not engaged in the business of distilling, selling or distributing alcoholic beverages) that sponsor or host events where liquor is served. Coverage is provided for injury or damage caused by an intoxicated person to whom the insured served liquor. Host liquor liability is covered under a homeowners policy and the 1986 Insurance Services Office commercial general liability form.
compare: dram shop liability insurance; *see:* commercial general liability policy, homeowners policy

hostile fire
Property. An unintended fire, or a fire set intentionally that escapes an intended container or, though remaining in its container, becomes unusually or excessively hot. Fire insurance covers loss caused by hostile, not friendly, fire because insurance concerns the risk of fortuitous losses.
compare: friendly fire; *see:* fire insurance, fortuitous event

hotel safe deposit box liability
Crime. Coverage for an innkeeper from loss or damage to a guest's property kept in safe deposit boxes on the premises. Coverage is provided for the insured's legal liability, defense and supplementary payments.
compare: innkeepers' legal liability; *see:* guests' property—safe deposit box, liability for guest's property—safe deposit coverage form, safe depository direct loss coverage form

house confinement
Health. A health insurance contract provision requiring the insured to be confined to his or her residence in order to collect loss of income benefits.
see: confining illness, disability income insurance, home health care

house-to-house coverage
Inland Marine.
see: door-to-door coverage

house waybill
Aviation/Inland Marine. A waybill issued by a freight forwarder for air or truck shipments.
compare: master air waybill; *see:* freight forwarder, waybill

household and personal property
Personal.
see: condominium unit owners' form, homeowners policy—property coverage, personal property floater, renters' insurance

housekeeping
Loss Control/Property. A category of hazards that create or increase the probability of a loss. It is the general care, cleanliness and maintenance of a property.
see: hazard

Huebner Foundation for Insurance Education (HFIE)
Organizations. Members: Appointed trustees. *Objectives:* To strengthen the teaching of risk management and insurance at the collegiate level by providing pre-doctoral and post-doctoral fellowships at the Wharton Business School of the University of Pennsylvania and through publication of doctoral dissertations, research papers and sponsored lectures. *Founded:* 1940. *Headquarters:* Philadelphia, PA.

hull

Aviation. The fuselage, engine(s), wings, tail, rudder, and other major structural features of an aircraft.

see: hull coverage

Ocean Marine. The frame or body of the ship, exclusive of masts, yards, sails, and rigging.

see: hull policy

hull coverage

Aviation. An aviation contract that indemnifies the insured for damage to or loss of the hull of an aircraft.

synonym: aircraft hull insurance; *see*: aircraft insurance, hull

hull policy

Ocean Marine. An ocean marine contract that indemnifies the insured for damage to or loss of the hull of a ship, including most of the machinery attached to it.

see: hull, ocean marine insurance

hull syndicate

Ocean Marine. An association or group of ocean marine underwriters who have joined together to underwrite insurance on oceangoing vessels.

see: ocean marine insurance

human approach

Loss Control. A loss control technique that concentrates on modifying the habits of people in order to reduce loss frequency and severity. *Examples*: Driver safety programs and seat belt usage campaigns.

see: human factors engineering, job safety analysis

human factors engineering

Loss Control. A loss prevention technique that concentrates on the physical movements, working attitudes and physical condition of a work area.

see: ergonomics, human approach, job safety analysis

human immunodeficiency virus (HIV)

Health. The virus that causes acquired immune deficiency syndrome (AIDS). It may take several years for someone infected with the virus ("HIV positive") to develop the disease.

see: acquired immune deficiency syndrome, AIDS/HIV risk coverage

human life value (HLV)

Liability/Life. The monetary value of a human life, measured by determining the net present value of benefits that others (the decedent's spouse, dependents, partners, employers) might reasonably expect to receive from the future efforts of the individual whose life is being valued. This amount is used to calculate the benefit amount needed to replace lost future earnings of a wage earner, to set the amount of life insurance or the amount of a liability award or settlement.

synonym: economic value of an individual life

human perils

Property. One of three broad categories of perils (with *natural* and *economic*), meaning human acts and omissions, whether intentional or unintentional, that can cause a loss.

Risk Management. A general classification of perils that are or result from acts of people, such as arson, negligence or recklessness, discrimination, embezzlement, pollution, riot, sabotage, terrorism, theft, and vandalism.

compare: economic perils, natural perils; *see*: negligence, peril

Hunter disability tables

Health. Actuarial disability tables that indicate the rate of disability in a specific population, the rate of mortality among disabled people, and the probability of total and permanent disability.

see: morbidity table, mortality table

hurdle rate

Financial Planning. The minimum rate of return for an investment to be acceptable.

see: rate of return

hurricane

Property. A severe tropical storm originating over ocean waters with winds exceeding about 73 miles (119 kilometers) per hour, accompanied by rain, thunder, lightning and tidal surges. Hurricanes principally affect the islands and coastlines of the Caribbean Sea, the Gulf of Mexico, and the southern and mid-Atlantic United States. They also occur in the Pacific, where they are called *typhoons*.

synonym: typhoon; *compare*: tornado; *see*: hurricane insurance, meteorological perils, National Hurricane Center, natural perils

hurricane insurance

Property. Coverage of physical damage caused by the high wind, waves and flooding produced by a hurricane. In hurricane-prone areas, some insurers exclude wind and require insureds to buy "wind only" from a pool (or cede wind losses to the pool) and also require flood insurance.

see: beachfront coverage plan, hurricane

hybrid finite risk insurance

Financial Guaranty/Risk Management.

see: blended finite risk insurance

hybrid health plan

Health. A health benefit plan that combines elements of managed care and traditional indemnification for medical fees. Members are encouraged to use a health maintenance organization or similar provider network, but they can also choose a doctor outside the network and be reimbursed for a part of the cost. It is often called a *point-of-service plan.*

see: fee for service, health maintenance organization, managed care, out-of-network services, point-of-service plan, preferred provider organization

hypothecate

Law. To pledge property to secure a loan. Though title to the property is not transferred, hypothecation creates a right by the creditor to liquidate the property to satisfy the debt in the event of default.

see: assignment (*Law*), lien, mortgage

Ocean Marine. To pledge a vessel by a bottomry bond.

see: bottomry

225

I

identification
Risk Management.
see: risk identification

ignition temperature
Loss Control. The lowest temperature at which a flammable material will ignite.
see: flash point.

illegal employment
Health/Workers' Compensation. The hiring of people to perform tasks that are inherently dangerous or injurious to their health or morals or in violation of child labor or other laws governing employment. *Example*: Hiring minors as bartenders.

Health insurance policies frequently provide that the insurer is not liable for any injury sustained as a result of the insured's commission of a felony or being engaged in an illegal occupation. Illegally employed minors who are injured on the job are usually entitled to workers' compensation benefits greater than those for adults, and in some states they have the right to waive coverage under workers' compensation and pursue common law remedies.
see: child labor, common law, double compensation

Illinois Insurance Exchange (IIE)
Organizations. An insurance exchange created as a nonprofit corporation by the Illinois legislature in 1979. It opened for trading on November 20, 1981, and is the only one active of the three exchanges that operated in the United States during the 1980s. (The other two were in New York and Florida.)
see: insurance exchange

illness
Health. A physical or mental impairment of function; disease. Some insurance policies include pregnancy in their definition of illness.
see: bodily injury

immature policy
Liability. A liability policy written on a claims-made basis that has been in effect continuously for less than five years. The rates applied to immature policies are less than those for mature policies, because their period of claims exposure is less.
compare: mature policy; *see*: claims-made form

immediate annuity
Life. An annuity that commences benefit payments immediately after a specified interval (one month or one year). This type of annuity is nearly always purchased with a single premium.
compare: deferred annuity; *see*: annuity

immediate cause
Property. Property insurance policies may require an insured peril to be the immediate or proximate cause of a loss. A cause of loss is immediate if it has made actual contact with the covered property. When a peril is the immediate cause of loss, a direct loss by that peril has occurred.
compare: proximate cause; *see*: concurrent causation

immediate vesting
Employee Benefits. A pension plan participant's right to receive full benefits from a plan without a waiting period; an immediate, 100% vesting in a pension plan.
see: employee benefit plan, pension, vesting

immigrant bond
Surety. A bond that provides forfeiture of a penalty if a bonded alien does not honor visa terms or if the alien becomes a public charge.
synonym: alien bond

impaired asset
Accounting. An asset that is specifically pledged to secure liabilities and is not available to meet general obligations.
see: asset

impaired property

Liability. Property that has lost value because it contains a product or work that is defective or inadequate. Property impairment may provide the basis for a liability claim by the property owner against the supplier of the product or the work that causes the impairment.

see: bench error, defective product, product liability insurance

impaired risk

Insurer Operations.

see: substandard risk

impairment exclusion rider

Health. A rider attached to a health insurance policy that excludes losses arising from certain preexisting causes. For example, a heart attack might result in an exclusion for subsequent heart attacks.

see: preexisting condition, qualified impairment insurance, rider, substandard risk

impairment of capital

Insurer Operations. The depletion of a stock insurer's surplus account, forcing it to use its capital funds to meet liabilities. Some states allow a specific percentage of capital funds to be so used by insurers.

see: surplus

imperfect title

Title. A title to real estate that requires corrections before it can convey full and absolute ownership to another party, or a title that has not been properly recorded.

compare: marketable title; *see*: defective title, real estate, title

implied authority

Agency. Authority given by an insurance company to an agent that is not actually expressed or otherwise communicated. This allows the agent to perform all the usual and necessary tasks to sell and service an insurance policy and to exercise the agent's expressed authority.

compare: actual authority, agency agreement, expressed authority; *see*: agency

implied contract

Law. A relationship in which obligations are implied by conduct rather than expressed in writing.

see: contract

implied covenant of good faith and fair dealing

Law.

see: good faith

implied seaworthiness

Ocean Marine. The application for an ocean marine policy implies a warranty that the insured vessel's condition, its crew, and its equipment are prepared and competent to make the voyage covered by the policy.

see: implied warranty, ocean marine insurance

implied warranty

Law. Courts have sometimes ruled that a warranty exists, even though it is not explicitly stated, when the warranty is implied or inferred from the nature of the transaction and circumstances. *Example*: For the purposes of an ocean marine contract, a vessel is implicitly warranted to be seaworthy by the vessel owner/insured even if the warranty is not stated on the face of the policy.

compare: disclaimer, express warranty; *see*: implied seaworthiness, warranty

import credit

International. A commercial letter of credit issued to finance the importation of goods.

see: letter of credit

importers' embargo insurance

International. A form of political risk insurance that indemnifies an importer for losses caused by the government's embargo or license cancellation. This coverage can be written in conjunction with exporters' embargo insurance.

compare: exporters' embargo insurance; *see*: political risk insurance

imprest account

Risk Management. An account—usually established by a self-insurer or in a deductible liability plan—to pay for low-severity, high-frequency losses as they occur. As the account is depleted, additional funds must be deposited.

see: sinking fund

improvements and betterments

Property. Additions made to premises by a tenant that enhance the property value and that become part of the realty and therefore revert to the building owner upon termination of the lease. Both the property owner and the tenant may purchase insurance to cover loss or damage to improvements and betterments.

synonym: betterments; *compare*: personal property, real estate; *see*: fixture, improvements and betterments insurance, loss of use—value in improvements and betterments

improvements and betterments insurance

Property. Property insurance purchased by a building tenant to protect its interest in improvements and betterments it has made to the building. Many commercial property and renter policies automatically provide some limited coverage (10% of the policy limit) for improvements and betterments.

see: loss of use—value in improvements and betterments

imputed liability
Liability.
see: vicarious liability

in-area emergency services
Health. Emergency medical care rendered in the service area of a health maintenance organization. A typical HMO plan provision covers enrollees who are treated at any nearby emergency facility, rather than requiring them to go to a facility under contract with the HMO.

see: emergency medical services, health maintenance organization, out-of-network services

in flight
Aviation. For a fixed wing aircraft, the period of time that begins with the forward movement (in motion) of the aircraft through takeoff and continues until the aircraft stops its forward motion after landing. For rotor aircraft, the period of time from when the rotors begin to revolve under power until the rotors cease to revolve.

see: all risks—ground and flight, aviation insurance, in motion

in-force business
Health/Life. The total dollar amount of paid-up and current policies that a life or health insurer carries on its books. A life insurance company's in-force business is the aggregate of all policy face values in its portfolio; a health insurer's is its total premium volume.

synonym: life insurance in force

in-hospital medical expense
Health. A provision in some hospital insurance policies that extends coverage to pay for hospital physicians' services, such as hospital calls. This coverage is provided only while the physician is in the hospital and often excludes the physician's expenses for surgical procedures.

in kind
Property. A term used in many property insurance policies giving an insurer the option to replace damaged or stolen articles with new or equivalent ("in kind") replacements, instead of paying cash to the insured.

see: indemnification

in motion
Aviation. In aviation hull policies, the time when an aircraft is moving under its own power or momentum, including while in flight. The aircraft is not considered in motion at any other time. A rotor aircraft is considered in motion whenever its rotors

are moving under power.

see: aviation insurance, flight coverage, ground coverage, hull coverage, in flight

in orbit insurance
Aviation. Coverage for the failure of a satellite or space vehicle to operate successfully while in its ordinary orbit.

see: satellite and space vehicle insurance

in rem
Ocean Marine. Authority granted by an admiralty court to take or keep in custody a ship or other property until a claim has been decided or acceptable security has been substituted. A legal action "in rem" is one against the thing itself, rather than against a person (such as a vessel owner).

see: in rem endorsement

in rem endorsement
Ocean Marine. An endorsement to a marine policy adding coverage for suits brought against the vessel itself.

see: ocean marine insurance

in-trust policy
Inland Marine. An inland marine policy that insures specific items of property without regard to the insured item's location (for example, if stored temporarily in a warehouse) or in whose custody the insured items rest. In effect, the coverage follows the property.

synonym: consignment insurance, on-consignment policy; *see*: bailment, inland marine insurance, warehouse-to-warehouse coverage

inactive insurer
Insurer Operations. An insurer not engaged in the business of insurance, but whose charter still exists. The term excludes liquidated and insolvent insurers.

see: charter (*Law*), insolvency, liquidation

inactive risks
Insurer Operations. Risks not currently exposed to the hazards they are insured against.

incendiarism
Property.
see: arson

inception date
Insurer Operations.
see: effective date

Inchmaree clause
Ocean Marine.
see: Inchmaree perils

Inchmaree perils
Ocean Marine. An ocean marine coverage that

originated from a lawsuit in 1887 involving the vessel *Inchmaree*. The clause now is captioned "additional perils" and covers loss or damage to the property of the insured caused by bursting of boilers, breakage of shafts, or through any latent defect in the hull or machinery of the vessel. It also includes coverage for accidents in handling cargo, repairer's negligence and crew negligence as long as the damage is not a result of want of due diligence by the vessel owner.

synonym: additional perils, Inchmaree clause; *see*: ocean marine insurance

incidence rate

Loss Control/Workers' Compensation. A measurement of workers' compensation accidents that has replaced an older formula called the accident frequency. It is expressed as the number of incidents reported per a given number of hours worked. *Formula*: (number of accidents × 200,000) ÷ total hours worked during the year. (200,000 represents 100 employee-years, assuming an average work year of 2000 hours.)

see: accident frequency

incident report

General. A report prepared and issued by law enforcement officials following an automobile accident or crime.

accident report

Risk Management. A report prepared by an insured when an action or occurrence is likely to lead to a claim being filed.

see: notice of loss

incidental business

Personal. A homeowners or dwelling policy is usually only written on a structure that is primarily occupied as a residence. Exceptions are made to allow the insured to use part of the residence for incidental business purposes (for example, to maintain an office, private school or studio, or to provide limited home day care).

see: business pursuits endorsement, homeowners policy, permitted incidental occupancies

incidental contract

Liability. In older commercial general liability forms, an agreement for which coverage was automatically included, such as easement agreements, except in connection with grade crossings; agreements required by municipal ordinance, except in connection with work for the municipality; lease of premises agreements; sidetrack agreements; and elevator maintenance agreements. All other ("non-incidental") contracts required special contractual liability coverage.

see: commercial general liability policy, contractual liability insurance

incidental damages

Law. An award in a lawsuit for breach of contract in compensation for commercially reasonable expenses incurred as a result of the other party's breach, such as costs of inspecting and returning goods that do not conform to contract specifications.

see: damages

incidental farming endorsement

Personal.

see: farming personal liability endorsement

incidental medical malpractice liability insurance

Liability. A form of general liability coverage for injuries from negligently rendering or failing to render certain types of medical services by a person who is not in the health care profession—that is, the medical service is incidental or unrelated to the insured's business. For example, this coverage can apply to a first aid facility or infirmary operated by an employer. This coverage, once added to the comprehensive general liability policy by the broad form liability endorsement, is now included in the 1986 ISO commercial general liability policy.

see: commercial general liability policy, malpractice insurance, medical malpractice

incidental motorized land conveyances endorsement

Personal. An endorsement (ISO form HO 04 13) to the homeowners policies that provides liability coverage for certain types of motorized land conveyances, such as mopeds, motorized bicycles, and motorized golf carts. The vehicles must not be able to exceed 15 miles per hour, must not be subject to motor vehicle registration, may not be rented to others or used for business purposes, and may not be operated in a prearranged competition.

see: golf cart coverage, homeowners policy, snowmobile coverage

incidental occupancy

Personal.

see: incidental business, permitted incidental occupancies endorsement

incineration

Loss Control. A method of hazardous waste destruction by controlled burning at high temperatures.

see: hazardous waste disposal

income

Financial Planning. Revenue or accretions to wealth received from any source. For tax purposes, gross income includes the value of services performed for the taxpayer and other economic benefits, as well as wages, business profits, rent, and recognized returns on capital.

see: accrued income, adjustment income, average monthly wage, average weekly wage, business income coverage form, earned premium, extended business income, fixed income, gross earnings, investment income, net income, ordinary income, underwriting income

income approach appraisal

Financial Planning. A method used to appraise real estate for investment purposes which considers the expected income stream from the property. The property's projected expenses are subtracted from the projected income on an annual basis, and the result is multiplied by an assumed rate of return to determine the appraised value.

synonym: capitalization appraisal method; *compare*: cost approach appraisal, market approach appraisal; *see*: appraisal, rate of return, real estate

income average

Employee Benefits.

see: average monthly wage, average weekly wage

income bond

Financial Planning.

see: participating bond

income dividend

Financial Planning. A dividend paid by a mutual fund to its shareholders based on the fund's receipt of dividends, interest and short-term capital gains from the fund's investment portfolio.

see: capital gain (or loss), mutual fund

income replacement

Health/Workers' Compensation.

see: disability benefit, disability income insurance

income statement

Accounting. A statement of an organization's sales and expenses, showing profits or losses, usually for a period of one year.

synonym: profit and loss statement; *see*: financial statement, investment income, operating income, underwriting income

income stock

Financial Planning. A stock that usually does not appreciate much in value but pays steady dividends.

see: stock

incompetence

Law.

see: competence

incontestable clause

Health/Life. A provision in life and health insurance policies that once a policy has been in effect for a specified period of time (e.g., two years), an insurer can no longer contest statements in the policy application in order to deny claims or void coverage.

incorporeal interest

Property. A right to intangible property. An incorporeal interest provides the basis for an insurable interest.

see: insurable interest, intangible property (1)

increased cost of construction endorsement

Property. An endorsement that can be added to a property policy to cover any increased cost of repairs or construction resulting from the enforcement of any building, zoning or land use laws following damage by an insured peril. Under the ISO Commercial Property Program, this coverage has been incorporated into the ordinance or law coverage endorsement.

see: ordinance or law coverage endorsement

increased hazard

Property. A provision in a property insurance policy that releases an insurer from its obligations under its policy if a loss is caused by a hazard increased by any means within the insured's control or knowledge. Increased hazards must be materially greater than those contemplated when the policy was issued. *Example*: A moving and storage company begins using its warehouse to store explosives and combustible chemicals.

compare: aftercharge; *see*: change in occupancy or use, hazard, occupancy permit

increased limits on business property endorsement

Personal. An endorsement (ISO form HO 04 12) to a homeowners policy that increases the special limit of business property from $2,500 off premises and $250 on premises up to $10,000 in $2,500 increments.

see: business personal property—special limit, homeowners policy—property coverage

increased limits table

Liability. An actuarially developed table of factors, expressed in percentages, used by underwriters to increase rates for basic limits of liability to rates for higher limits. The tables take account of variations by time of exposure; for example, a table for premises liability exposures would show less of a rate increase than would a table for professional liability exposures.

see: base rate, basic limits, exposure unit, rate making

increasing annuity

Life. An annuity policy featuring payments that increase at a predetermined rate over the life of the contract. *Example*: An annuity that increases its monthly payment at an annual compound rate of 3%.

see: annuity

incurred but not reported (IBNR)

Risk Management. Losses occurring over a specified period that have not been reported to the insurer. IBNR losses are often calculated as a percentage of claims paid and claims outstanding and are reported in an insurer's annual report. Reinsurers establish IBNR reserves as a part of their rating plans under a facultative reinsurance treaty, lest an overly optimistic view of treaty results lead to further under-rating on a book of business. *Example*: Product liability losses are seldom reported during a policy year. This "tail" of claims will upset any rating plan, unless an IBNR reserve is established and factored into the profit picture.

see: expected losses, loss development factor

incurred loss ratio

Insurer Operations/Risk Management. The portion of an earned premium dollar that is spent on incurred losses.

see: incurred losses

incurred losses

Risk Management. Both paid and known reserved losses occurring within a specific period of time.

compare: incurred but not reported, loss reserve, paid losses; *see*: loss conversion factor, loss development factor

indemnification

Insurer Operations. Compensation or benefits payable under an insurance policy; a principle of insurance that an insured should be restored to the same financial position as before a covered loss. Insurance is not intended to allow the insured to make a profit, but to make the insured whole after a loss or injury.

compare: collateral source rule, gambling; *see*: damages, full coverage, pure risk

indemnify

Liability. Some casualty insurance policies provide that the insurer will indemnify or reimburse the insured for amounts the insured becomes legally obligated to pay, as opposed to making direct payment on behalf of the insured. Under this form of coverage, the insured must first make payment and then is reimbursed by the insurer.

compare: pay on behalf of; *see*: pure risk, reimbursement

indemnitee

General. A party receiving compensation from an indemnitor.

compare: indemnitor

Law. The person who is reimbursed under a contractual indemnity provision.

see: indemnity agreement

indemnitor

General. The party paying compensation to an indemnitee.

compare: indemnitee

Surety. A party entering into an agreement with a surety that should a principal on whose behalf a surety bond has been issued default, the indemnitor will assume the principal's obligations.

see: surety

Law. The person obligated to reimburse another under a contractual indemnity provision.

see: indemnity agreement

indemnity

General. Compensation for an incurred injury, loss or damage.

International. A coverage in many international or global nonadmitted insurance policies by which, if the nonadmitted insurer is prevented from defending the insured in a foreign country because local laws prohibit it, loss payments will be by indemnity rather than direct payments on behalf of the insured.

see: nonadmitted insurance, pay on behalf of

indemnity agreement

Insurer Operations. An insurance contract; an agreement to restore a party to its original financial position following an incurred loss or injury.

compare: valued coverage; *see*: indemnification, insurance contract, nonvalued policy

Law. A contract provision that one party will provide reimbursement for losses the other party may incur. Example: A lessee of data processing equipment agrees to indemnify the equipment's owner for any damage that may occur to it.

compare: hold harmless agreement; *see*: indemnitee, indemnitor

indemnity bond

Surety. A bond compensating an obligee if a principal fails to perform to the standards mutually agreed upon by the obligee and principal.

indemnity deductible workers' compensation plan

Workers' Compensation. A deductible workers' compensation plan under which the deductible applies only to workers' compensation indemnity (disability income) benefits, not to medical benefits.

compare: medical deductible workers' compensation plan; *see*: deductible workers' compensation plan, disability benefit

independent adjuster

Insurer Operations. An organization or a person, hired by an insurer, who is paid a fee for settling claims.

compare: public adjuster; *see*: claims adjuster

independent agency system

Agency. An insurance marketing system where independent agents sell and service insurance for one or more insurance companies. The agents are independent contractors who are compensated by commissions or fees and own the records and expirations of the policies issued through them.

synonym: American agency system; *compare*: captive agent, direct writer; *see*: agency company, broker, exclusive agency system, independent agent, Independent Insurance Agents of America, Professional Insurance Agents

independent agent

Agency. An independent contractor who sells insurance usually on behalf of more than one insurance company under the independent agency system. Independent agents operate their own business, own the records of the policies sold through them, and are compensated by commissions or fees rather than a salary.

compare: captive agent; *see*: agent, independent agency system

Independent Automotive Damage Appraisers Association (IADAA)

Organizations. Members: Professional automobile damage appraisal firms. *Objectives*: Promote the interests of independent auto damage appraisers, establish professional standards and exchange information. *Founded*: 1961. *Headquarters*: Naperville, IL.

independent contractor

Workers' Compensation. An individual or entity that agrees to perform specific work for another but is not subject to direction or management by, nor is an employee of, the person who contracted for the services. Independent contractors are not covered under an employer's workers' compensation policy.

see: acts of independent contractors, employee, general contractor, workers' compensation insurance

independent contractors' insurance

Liability.

see: owners' and contractors' protective liability

independent filing

Insurer Operations/Regulation. Application for an insurance rate or form submitted by an insurer to a state insurance department and not filed on its behalf by a rating organization.

see: rate making, rating bureau

Independent Insurance Agents of America Inc. (IIAA)

Organizations. Members: Agencies handling fire, casualty and surety insurance. *Objectives*: Promotes the common interests of independent insurance agents consistent with the best interests of the insurance buying public. Assists in developing the curriculum for the Accredited Adviser in Insurance designation. *Founded*: 1896. *Headquarters*: Alexandria, VA. (Until 1976, known as the National Association of Insurance Agents.)

see: Accredited Adviser in Insurance

independent insurance company

Insurer Operations. An insurance company that is not associated with another insurer or owned by an insurance holding company. Such insurers are generally specialty insurers or serve a limited geographic area.

compare: affiliated insurers; *see*: fleet of companies, pup company

independent practice association (IPA)

Regulation. One of two types of HMO approved by the Health Maintenance Organization Act. (The other is the *closed panel HMO*.) Under this type, the HMO has a network of nonexclusive contracts with individual physicians or medical groups to provide services to the HMO's members, usually in the physicians' own offices, and usually on a capitation fee basis. The physicians maintain their own private practices and thus can contract with more than one HMO and see regular fee-for-service patients as well.

synonym: network-model health maintenance organization; *compare*: closed panel health maintenance organization; *see*: capitation, health maintenance organization

index fund

Financial Planning. A mutual fund where the investment portfolio mirrors one of the various stock indexes. Example: A Standard & Poor's 500 indexed fund would hold the same stocks as those that make up the Standard & Poor's 500 index. An indexed fund usually has a lower administrative cost than a standard fund, as there is little or no portfolio management involved.

see: mutual fund

indexed life insurance

Life. A life insurance policy similar to a whole life policy, except that its face value varies according to a prescribed index of prices. The index may be applied automatically, or the insured may retain control of the index adjustment for an extra premium. As with most other whole life policies, a physical examination is not required.

see: whole life insurance

indexed limits

Insurer Operations. A policy valuation method used to guard against the effect of inflation whereby the insurer links the policy limit to a specified price index, such as the Department of Labor's Consumer Price Index. Such a provision is included in some international insurance policies covering risks in countries with high inflation. It automatically increases the policy limits.

see: indexing

indexing

International. The automatic adjustment of the property or liability values in an international insurance program to reflect the inflation rate in the country where the risk is located. This is done to avoid an average clause (coinsurance) penalty or an inadequate recovery in the event of a loss.

see: average clause, indexed limits

Reinsurance. An excess of loss reinsurance contract provision that adjusts the retention and limit provisions in accordance with changes in a published economic index (e.g., consumer prices).

see: excess of loss reinsurance, indexed limits, retention

Employee Benefits. The automatic adjustment of benefits in the course of payment to reflect changes in a consumer price index, cost of living index, or some other benchmark.

indicator post

Loss Control.

see: post indicator valve

indirect damage

Property.

see: consequential damage

indirect loss

Property.

see: consequential damage

individual account plan

Employee Benefits.

see: defined contribution plan, employee benefit plan

individual contract

Health/Life.

see: individual health insurance, individual life insurance

individual fidelity bond

Surety.

see: fidelity bond

individual health insurance

Health. A health insurance policy covering one person, as opposed to a group of people. It may include specified members of the insured's family.

compare: group health insurance; see: health insurance

individual level cost method

Employee Benefit. A method used to predict individual employee pension plan benefits at retirement age. Based on the projections, costs can be allocated on a level basis over a specified funding period.

see: employee benefit plan, pension

individual life insurance

Life. A life insurance policy covering one person, as opposed to a group of people. It may include specified members of the insured's family.

compare: group life insurance; see: life insurance

individual retirement account (IRA)

Employee Benefits. A federally approved tax deferred savings plan for individuals. The individual selects a plan administrator (a qualified financial institution or investment advisor), which establishes the plan on behalf of the individual, who may make payments to it up to $2,000 annually. There is a penalty for withdrawal of funds before age of 59½. Limitations apply to the establishment of the IRA when an individual is covered by an approved employer pension plan.

see: registered retirement saving plan, rollover individual retirement account

individual risk premium modification rating plan (IRPM rating plan)

Health/Life. A group insurance rating plan under which individual participants' premiums are lowered, based on the size of the group and premiums generated. The premium reduction is based on lower acquisition and administrative expenses resulting when a large number of participants are combined into a single contract.

compare: capitation, community rating, fee for service, single payer plan; see: base rate

Liability/Property. A large account rating plan where factors such as size of premium, spread of risk, superior construction, and quality of management are considered in determining the premium.

see: rate making

indoor pollution

loss Control.

see: sick building syndrome

233

industrial accident
Workers' Compensation.
see: occupational accident

industrial aid operators
Aviation. A general aviation rating classification that applies to corporations that own aircraft and employ full-time professional pilots.
compare: business and pleasure, fixed base operators, flying club; *see*: general aviation

industrial development bond guaranty insurance
Financial Guaranty. Financial insurance coverage for public entities that guarantees the prompt payment of principal and interest on industrial development bonds should a bond issue default. The insurer's financial rating affords the bonds a high-grade investment rating—often higher than the issuing party's rating—which makes the bonds more marketable and provides financing at a reduced cost.
see: financial guaranty insurance, guaranteed bond

Industrial Health Foundation, Inc.
Organizations. Members: Large employers. *Objectives*: A nonprofit research association of major industries. Staff scientists provide direct assistance to member companies in developing health programs. *Headquarters*: Pittsburgh, PA.

industrial health insurance
Health. A low-valued health insurance policy where the premium is collected by the salesperson directly at the home of the insured on a weekly or monthly basis.
see: industrial life insurance

industrial hygienist
Loss Control. A person, typically educated in engineering, chemistry, physics, or medicine, trained to recognize, evaluate and control health hazards in the industrial environment, particularly hazardous substances.
see: hazardous substance

industrial hygienist errors and omissions insurance
Professional Liability. A form of professional liability coverage for firms that test for unacceptable levels of hazardous materials or substances, such as asbestos, air contamination, bacteria, or hazardous chemicals. Coverage is written on a claims-made basis for damages from negligence, errors or omissions.
see: professional liability insurance

industrial insurance
Life.
see: industrial life insurance

industrial insured
Risk Management. An organization that buys its insurance through an employed insurance or risk manager or a continuously retained, full-time insurance consultant. Such insureds have minimum annual nonlife and health premiums of $25,000 per year and employ at least 25 persons on a full-time basis. Many state insurance codes, especially in surplus lines laws, exempt industrial insureds from requirements to purchase insurance only from a domestically authorized insurer.
see: surplus lines

industrial life insurance
Life. A low-valued life insurance policy with the premium collected by the salesperson at the home of the insured on a weekly or monthly basis.
synonym: debit insurance, home service insurance, industrial insurance, stipulated premium plan insurance, weekly premium insurance; *see*: debit, debit system, industrial health insurance, register

industrial property policy program
Property. A property insurance program that preceded the special multi-peril policy program. It was designed to insure manufacturers with two or more locations and could include coverage for buildings, stock, machinery and equipment. As an option, an insured could also cover improvements and betterments at leased locations.
see: special multi-peril program

Industrial Risk Insurers (IRI)
Insurer Operations/Property. A pool originally formed in 1890 by the major stock insurance companies, to compete with the Factory Mutual System on large industrial accounts that are protected by automatic sprinklers and meet certain other minimum protection requirements. The operation's name was changed to Industrial Risk Insurers in 1975 by the merger of the Factory Insurance Association and Oil Insurance Association.
compare: Factory Mutual System; *see*: highly protected risk

inefficacy coverage
Liability.
see: efficacy coverage

infant car carrier
Automobile. A restraining seat designed to protect a baby up to about 12 months of age in a car. It is padded and has a harness, and it should be anchored to the car seat with a regular seat belt.
see: child seat, passive restraint system

inflammable

Loss Control.

see: flammable

inflation

Financial Planning. A general rise in the price of goods and services, which may be caused by an excess of demand over supply (demand-pull inflation) or by increased costs of resources needed to produce goods and services (cost-push inflation).

see: appreciation, inflation factor, inflation guard endorsement, social inflation

inflation factor

Insurer Operations. A loading added during the development of insurance rates to cover increased claims costs due to anticipated increases in costs of medical care, building construction, vehicle repair, etc.

see: rate making

inflation guard endorsement

Property. An endorsement to a property policy that automatically increases the amount of insurance on buildings by a specific percentage (usually 1% or 2% per quarter). It is designed to offset the increased costs of replacing a building due to inflation.

synonym: automatic increase in insurance endorsement

Personal. An endorsement (ISO form HO 04 46) to the homeowners policy that provides an automatic specified increase (e.g., 3%) in the limits of liability for all section I (property) coverages on a pro rata basis during the policy period to avoid underinsurance due to inflation.

see: homeowners policy

infrared detector

Loss Control. A device used to trigger a burglar alarm; a detector that senses the body heat of an intruder who enters the protected area. A change in the protected area's normal heat profile sets off the burglar alarm.

see: burglar alarm

ingestion

Aviation. Under an aircraft policy, coverage for damage resulting from taking into its engine or power units foreign objects or substances (e.g., birds) that disable a plane enough to require immediate repair.

see: aviation insurance

ingress or egress clause

Property.

see: civil authority clause

inherent danger

Workers' Compensation. A danger intrinsic to a

job or conditions of work known to the employer or which the employer should have discovered by the exercise of reasonable care. The employer has a duty to warn employees of the danger and provide them with proper safety equipment and instruction.

inherent explosion

Loss Control/Property. An explosion arising out of characteristics inherent in or natural to an insured risk. *Example*: A dust explosion in a flour mill. Inherent explosion risks may be covered or not, depending on the coverage forms.

see: explosion

inherent vice

Inland Marine/Property. A quality within an object, material or property that results in its tending to deteriorate or destroy itself. Inherent vice is excluded by most property insurance policies. *Example*: The spoilage of fruit during storage or shipping would be excluded from a property policy. The destruction of unspoiled fruit by a fire, on the other hand, would be covered.

compare: deterioration

inheritance tax

Financial Planning.

see: estate tax

initial premium

Insurer Operations. The amount of premium charged at the time a policy is issued. This amount may be subject to adjustment during the policy term in case of changes in coverage, additional underwriting information, etc. In a participating policy, it is subject to a dividend.

compare: additional premium, return premium; *see*: deposit premium, estimated annual premium, net premium, participating policy, policy dividend, provisional premium

initial reserve

Insurer Operations. The first reserve established ("put up") by a claims adjuster when a covered claim has been reported.

see: claims adjuster, loss reserve

Life. A life insurance reserve established at the inception of each life policy year.

compare: mean reserve, terminal reserve; *see*: policy reserve

injunction

Law. A court order that restricts or prohibits an act, either for a limited time or permanently.

see: cease and desist, injunction bond

injunction bond

Surety. A bond written as the result of an injunction requiring a party to refrain from a particular act or course of conduct. There are two bond

235

forms: a *plaintiff's bond to secure* and a *defendant's bond to dissolve.*

see: defendant's bond to dissolve, judicial bond, plaintiff's bond to secure

injury

General. Any harm, impairment or loss, including bodily injury, nonphysical personal injury, property damage or other losses of an economic nature, and noneconomic losses.

see: bodily injury, damages, economic loss, noneconomic loss, personal injury liability

injury-in-fact theory

Law/Liability. A legal theory that policy coverage is triggered only at the point where a loss actually occurs, regardless of the time of exposure or whether the loss has become manifest. No liability is allocated to any policies that covered a long-term exposure at any time other than when the injury occurred.

compare: continuous trigger theory, exposure theory, manifestation theory; see: occurrence trigger, progressive loss

injury independent of all other means

Health. A health insurance policy provision covering an injury apart from any previous injury.

see: preexisting condition

inland marine

Inland Marine. Transportation of goods over land. The term now includes any goods in transit anywhere except on the high seas. The property must be movable or be included in the nationwide definition of marine insurance. Bridges and tunnels are also considered proper subjects for inland marine insurance, because they are instruments of transportation.

see: domestic goods in transit, inland marine insurance, Nationwide Marine Insurance Definition

inland marine floater policy—personal lines

Personal. A policy form (ISO form IPL 01 01) that provides the general conditions for the Insurance Services Office personal articles floater, personal property floater, and personal effects floater.

see: floater policy, inland marine insurance, personal articles floater, personal property floater, personal effects floater

inland marine insurance

Inland Marine. Coverage for property that involves an element of transportation. The property must be actually in transit, held by a bailee, at a fixed location that is an instrument of transportation, or be a movable type of goods that is often at different locations.

compare: ocean marine insurance; see: domestic goods in transit, inland marine, marine insurance

Inland Marine Underwriters Association (IMUA)

Organizations. Members: Insurers transacting inland marine insurance within the United States. *Objectives:* Promoting interest of the inland marine industry. Assists in developing the curriculum for the Associate in Marine Insurance Management designation. *Founded:* 1930. *Headquarters:* New York, NY.

see: Associate in Marine Insurance Management

inland waybill

Inland Marine.

see: waybill

innkeepers' legal liability

Liability. Legal liability of operators of inns, hotels and motels for the safekeeping of guests' property. Coverage for this exposure is available through an innkeeper's liability policy, which usually has a limit equal to the liability limit contained in the state's innkeeper's statute.

see: liability for guests' property—premises coverage form, liability for guests property—safe deposit coverage form

innocent market

Reinsurance. A term applied by professional reinsurers to inexperienced reinsurers or insurers who enter a new line of insurance or the reinsurance business with limited knowledge and commitment of resources because that line or business has been profitable for others.

see: market entrance reinsurance, professional reinsurer

inpatient

Health. The status of a patient who is admitted to a hospital and receives lodging and food as well as medical treatment. Health insurance policies have always covered most costs incurred during inpatient hospital stays, but only in recent times have most policies also covered outpatient services.

compare: outpatient; see: health insurance, hospital confinement insurance, hospital-surgical expense insurance

inrunning nip point

Loss Control. A dangerous rotating machine part or assembly that can seize and wind loose clothing, belts, hair, body parts, etc. It exists when two or more shafts or rolls rotate parallel to one another in opposite directions.

synonym: nip point; see: barrier guard, machine tool, point of operation

insanity

Law. A condition of mental derangement, psychosis, or incompetence that prevents a person from correctly perceiving the nature of his actions or appreciating legal rights or duties he is otherwise ordinarily expected or bound to know. The term is often used in a legal context, rarely in a medical or scientific context.

compare: competence, mental disorder, mental distress

insects, birds, rodents or other animals exclusion

Property. A special exclusion in all-risk or special form property policies for damage or destruction of property caused by insects, birds, rodents or other animals.

see: all-risk insurance, special form

inside adjuster

Insurer Operations. A claims adjuster who works almost exclusively inside the office and completes the claim adjustment process by telephone and mail. This form of adjusting is commonly used on third-party liability and workers' compensation claims.

compare: field adjuster; *see*: claim adjustment, claims adjuster

inside director

Financial Planning/Professional Liability. An employee, officer, or major stockholder of a corporation who is elected to the corporation's board of directors. A large number of inside directors in a corporation is a matter of concern to a directors' and officers' liability underwriter.

compare: outside director; *see*: directors' and officers' liability insurance

inside limits

Health. Limits for specific benefits of a health insurance policy that are less than the maximum policy benefits or that modify the policy benefits to some extent. *Example*: Hospital room benefits may be limited to a semi-private room for 90 days.

synonym: sublimits

insider

Financial Planning/Professional Liability. An individual who has information about a corporation that is not generally available to the public. This includes but is not limited to directors, officers, and shareholders who own 10% or more of the corporation's stock.

see: insider trading

insider trading

Financial Planning. Buying or selling corporate stock listed on a national exchange by an insider, or an insider's disclosure of privileged information ("tip") to benefit friends or relatives in their securities trading. Transactions by insiders must be reported monthly to the Securities and Exchange Commission. Trading on the basis of inside, or nonpublic, information is prohibited. Violations can result in civil and criminal penalties as well as disgorgement of profits.

see: insider, Securities and Exchange Commission

insolvency

General. An organization's inability to pay debts as they come due. Insolvency frequently results in bankruptcy or liquidation.

compare: bankruptcy; *see*: guaranty fund, liquidation, negative cash flow, rehabilitation, voidable preference

insolvency clause

Reinsurance.

see: cut-through clause

insolvency fund

Insurer Operations.

see: guaranty fund

inspection

Liability/Property. In property and casualty insurance, the insurer retains the right to make inspections and surveys relating to the insurability of the risk and the premiums charged. For example, the insurer may look for inherent structural defects and other hidden hazards. Inspections provide the opportunity to develop a loss prevention program for the insured.

Life. The verification of statements by a life insurance applicant, along with a summary of the applicant's financial, moral, and physical condition and any other relevant information, obtained through insurance investigators, agency personnel or an independent source. The product of this investigation is called an *inspection report*.

Loss Control. The in-person evaluation of an individual risk to determine whether it meets underwriting standards and to gather pertinent underwriting information. An inspection may be performed by an agent or by a loss control specialist employed by the insurer. It may result in recommendations for loss prevention.

Workers' Compensation. A workers' compensation insurer's verification of a payroll record. Workers' compensation premiums are based on the business's gross payroll, so inspection is the basis for the premium to be charged.

see: audit

inspection bureau

Organizations.

see: rating bureau

inspection report

Life/Workers' Compensation.

see: inspection

237

installation floater

Inland Marine. An inland marine policy written to cover machinery and equipment of all kinds during transit, installation, and testing at the purchaser's premises.

synonym: contractors' installation floater; *see*: floater policy, inland marine insurance, ripping and tearing insurance

installment refund annuity

Life.
see: annuity certain

installment sales floater

Inland Marine.
see: conditional sales floater

Institute of Home Office Underwriters (IHOU)

Organizations. Members: Home office life insurance underwriters. *Objectives*: Provides educational programs, such as examinations leading to the Fellowship in Academy of Life Underwriting. *Founded*: 1937. *Headquarters*: Atlanta, GA.

Institute of Life Insurance

Organizations.
see: American Council of Life Insurance

institutional investor

Financial Planning. A large investor, such as a mutual fund, pension fund, bank, investment company, or insurance company, that invests its own assets or assets held in trust either as its primary business or as an important secondary activity. Institutional investors account for a large portion of all securities traded on public exchanges and are major holders of insurance company stocks.

see: direct placement

institutional property

Property.
see: public and institutional property

instrumentalities of transportation and communication

Inland Marine. Part of the nationwide marine definition, describing means of communication and transportation—bridges, tunnels, and other similar instrumentalities, including auxiliary facilities and equipment. Other such properties are piers, wharves, docks, slips, dry docks and marine railways; pipelines; power transmission and telephone and telegraph lines; radio and television communication equipment; outdoor cranes; and loading bridges.

see: Nationwide Marine Insurance Definition

insurability

Insurer Operations. The risk-associated qualities of a person or entity that meet an insurer's underwriting standards and therefore make the insurer willing to offer coverage at a standard premium.

see: adverse selection, evidence of insurability, insurable risk

insurable interest

Insurer Operations. Any interest a person has in property that is the subject of insurance, so that damage to the property would cause the insured a financial loss or other tangible deprivation. Generally, an insurable interest must be demonstrated when a policy is issued and must exist at the time of a loss.

see: additional interest, as interest may appear, full interest admitted, incorporeal interest, loss payee

Life. The risk of financial loss that must be proved when a life insurance policy is purchased. Once a life insurance policy has been issued, the insurer must pay the policy benefit, whether or not an insurable interest continues to exist.

insurable risk

Insurer Operations. A risk that meets the following criteria: 1. The insured loss must have a definite time and place; 2. The insured event must be accidental; 3. The insured must have an insurable interest in the subject of coverage; 4. The insured risks must belong to a sufficiently large group of homogeneous exposure units to make losses predictable; 5. The risk must not be subject to a catastrophic loss where a large number of exposure units can be damaged or destroyed in a single event; 6. The coverage must be provided at a reasonable cost; 7. The chance of loss must be calculable.

compare: noninsurable risk; *see*: adverse selection, catastrophe loss, homogeneous exposure units, insurable interest, spread of risk, substandard risk

insurable value

Property. The total value of specific property to be covered by insurance, which is based on a property valuation method (e.g., actual cash value, replacement cost, functional replacement cost) recognized by insurance underwriters.

see: actual cash value, adjustable policy, functional replacement cost, replacement cost, reproduction cost

insurance

Insurer Operations. A contract whereby one person (insurer) agrees to indemnify or guarantee another (insured) against loss caused by a specified cause or future contingency in return for the present payment of premium.

synonym: assurance; *see*: aleatory contract, bottomry, business of insurance, commercial insurance, gambling, line (*General*), retention, risk transfer, tontine

Insurance Accounting and Systems Association (IASA)

Organizations. *Members:* Insurers, independent public accountants, actuarial consultants, management consultants, statisticians, statistical organization and other groups. *Objectives:* Promotes the research and development of insurance theory, practice and procedures, as applied to insurance accounting and statistics. *Founded:* 1928. *Headquarters:* Durham, NC.

insurance agency

Agency.

see: agency

insurance agent

Agency. The representative of an insurance company who is responsible for selling insurance products and providing services to policyholders. Agents have responsibilities in areas such as acceptance and binding of risks, notice, and other situations where the agent acts as the insurance company.

see: agency, agent's authority, agent's balances, agent's certificate of authority, agent's commission, agent's trust, agents' errors and omissions insurance, captive agent, independent agent

insurance agents' liability insurance

Liability.

see: agents' errors and omissions insurance

Insurance and Employee Benefits Division, Special Libraries Association

Organizations. *Members:* Insurance industry librarians. *Objectives:* Professional organization with interest in the collection and dissemination of insurance-related information. *Founded:* 1922. *Headquarters:* New York, NY.

insurance appraisal

Property.

see: appraisal

insurance archivist

Risk Management. An individual or firm who reconstructs an organization's insurance policy history for the purpose of filing claims based on those policies, usually involving pollution or product liability claims. In some cases, successful claims have been filed against insurers who provided coverage decades prior to the date the claim was filed, under policies that failed to clearly define their coverage term or limits.

synonym: insurance archaeologist; see: continuous trigger theory, exposure theory, manifestation theory

insurance broker

Agency.

see: broker

Insurance Bureau of Canada (IBC)

Organizations. *Members:* Insurance companies in Canada. *Objectives:* Provides a forum for discussion on all matters in the field of general insurance by its member insurance companies. Collects, analyzes and disseminates actuarial and statistical information. Studies legislation and engages in research and public relations activities. *Founded:* 1979. *Headquarters:* Toronto, Ontario

insurance carrier

Insurer Operations.

see: carrier, insurance company

insurance commissioner

Regulation. The senior official in a state's department of insurance or other insurance regulatory agency.

synonym: commissioner, director of insurance, superintendent of insurance; see: insurance department, insurance examiner

Insurance Committee for Arson Control (ICAC)

Organizations. *Members:* Insurance companies and insurance trade associations. *Objectives:* Work with law enforcement agencies and provide the public with information on arson. *Headquarters:* New York, NY.

insurance company

Insurer Operations. An organization that has been chartered by a governmental entity to transact the business of insurance.

synonym: assurance company, assurer, insurance carrier, insurer; see: alien insurer, carrier, cooperative insurer, domestic insurer, domiciled company, domiciliary state, enemy alien insurer, fleet of companies, foreign insurer, fraternal benefit society, insurance, insurance exchange, legal expense insurer, medical liability indemnity association, mutual insurance company, old line company, parent company, primary insurance company, proprietary insurer, quasi-insurance institutions, reciprocal insurance exchange, stock insurance company

insurance company as insured endorsement

Workers' Compensation. A special endorsement (NCCI form WC 00 03 04) to a workers' compensation policy issued to an insurance company. It makes clear that the policy covers compensation benefits for the company's employees (i.e., the insurer is the insured).

see: workers' compensation insurance

Insurance Company Education Directors Society (ICEDS)

Organizations. The former name for the Society of Insurance Trainers and Educators.

see: Society of Insurance Trainers and Educators

Insurance Conference Planners Association (ICPA)

Organizations. Members: Canadian insurance personnel involved in planning insurance conventions. *Objectives:* Sharing ideas on how to organize seminars and meetings to promote professionalism in the insurance industry. *Founded:* 1958. *Headquarters:* North Vancouver, British Columbia, Canada.

Insurance Conference Planners (ICP)

Organizations. Members: Insurance personnel involved in planning insurance conventions. *Objectives:* Sharing ideas on how to organize seminars and meetings to promote professionalism in the insurance industry. *Founded:* 1958. *Headquarters:* St. Paul, MN.

insurance consultation services

Risk Management. Survey, inspection or advisory services performed by insurers, agents or service contractors to reduce the likelihood of injury or loss.

see: inspection, loss prevention services

insurance contract

Insurer Operations. An aleatory contract between an insured and an insurer, who agrees to indemnify the insured for loss caused by specified events.

synonym: insurance policy; *see:* aleatory contract, application, attestation clause, contract, contract of adhesion, declarations, easy read, endorsement, entire contract provision, entire contract statute, evidence and duties provision, face, face amount, fine print, Flesch readability test, form, indemnity agreement, insuring agreement, jacket, manuscript policy, modification of contract, noncancelable policy, nonvalued policy, plain language laws, policy conditions

Insurance Contractors of America (ICA)

Organizations. Members: General contractors, special contractors, emergency service contractors, restoration specialists, etc., who specialize in property repair covered by insurance. *Objectives:* Promote the interests of contractors who do claims repair work for insurers. *Headquarters:* Newport Beach, CA.

Insurance Crime Prevention Bureau

Organizations. Members: Canadian insurance companies and underwriters. *Objectives:* Provides assistance to police and fire authorities in the detection, investigation and prosecution of insurance-related crimes. *Founded:* 1923. *Headquarters:* Toronto, Ontario, Canada.

see: Fire and Theft Index Bureau, Insurance Services Office, interinsurer claim service organization, Medical Information Bureau, National Automobile Theft Bureau, Property Insurance Loss Register

Insurance Crime Prevention Institute (ICPI)

Organizations. Members: Insurance companies. *Objective:* Investigates and seeks prosecution of fraud involving property and casualty insurance claims. *Founded:* 1970. *Headquarters:* Westport, CT.

see: interinsurer claim service organization

Insurance Data Management Association

Organizations. Members: Insurance company and production personnel involved in data management. *Objectives:* To promote and educate its members on data management. Awards the Certified Insurance Data Manager designation and the Associate Insurance Data Manager. *Founded:* 1983. *Headquarters:* New York, NY.

see: Associate Insurance Data Manager, Certified Insurance Data Manager

insurance department

Regulation. A state agency that is responsible for administering the laws regulating insurance, including the licensing of insurance companies, agents and brokers.

see: insurance commissioner, insurance examiner

Insurance Education Foundation, Inc.

Organizations. Members: Insurance companies and agents and brokers. *Objectives:* Educate public about insurance. Initial focus has been high school students. *Founded:* 1988. *Headquarters:* Indianapolis, IN.

Insurance Educational Association (IEA)

Organizations. Members: Insurance organizations. *Objectives:* Sponsors educational programs for insurance, risk management and financial services. *Founded:* 1876. *Headquarters:* San Francisco, CA.

see: Workers' Compensation Claims Professional

insurance examiner

Regulation. The insurance department representative assigned to audit the books or the market conduct of an insurance company.

see: examination, insurance commissioner, insurance department

insurance exchange

Insurer Operations. An insurance marketplace or organization patterned after Lloyd's of London, formed during the 1980s in New York City, Miami, Florida, and Chicago, Illinois. Exchanges were formed to write large or unique risks, generally on a surplus lines basis, and to write reinsurance business. Both the New York and Florida exchanges have suspended operations.

see: Illinois Insurance Exchange, Insurance Exchange of the Americas, Lloyd's of London, New York Insurance Exchange

Insurance Exchange of the Americas

Organizations. An insurance exchange created as a nonprofit corporation in Miami, Florida on October 1, 1979, that began trading on April 4, 1983. In February 1987, its management suspended all underwriting activity, and on March 18, 1988, the Florida Department of Insurance was appointed receiver of the exchange.

synonym: Florida Insurance Exchange; *see*: insurance exchange

insurance fraud
General.
see: fraud

Insurance Hall of Fame

Organizations. Members: Elected board of directors from the international insurance industry. *Objectives*: To recognize outstanding persons for their vision, integrity, innovation, enterprise and leadership in the insurance field. *Founded*: 1957. *Headquarters*: Columbus, OH.

see: International Insurance Society

insurance in force
Life.
see: in-force business

Insurance Industry Meetings Association (IIMA)

Organizations. Members: State and regional insurance company communication representatives. *Objectives*: Conducts seminars on insurance business techniques, sales practices and claims processing. *Founded*: 1980. *Headquarters*: St. Louis, MO.

Insurance Information Institute (III)

Organizations. Members: Property and casualty insurance companies. *Objectives*: Promotes interests of insurance companies by providing information

and educational services. *Founded*: 1959. *Headquarters*: New York, NY.

Insurance Institute for Highway Safety (IIHS)

Organizations. Members: Casualty insurance companies and trade associations. *Objectives*: A nonprofit research and information organization that works to reduce highway accidents and deaths. *Headquarters*: Arlington, VA

Insurance Institute for Property Loss Reduction

Organizations. Members: Property and casualty insurance companies. *Objectives*: To reduce deaths, injuries and loss of property resulting from natural perils of all types. *Founded*: 1993. *Headquarters*: Boston, MA. (Formerly, the National Committee on Property Insurance.)

Insurance Institute of America (IIA)

Organizations. The educational division of the American Institute for Property Casualty Underwriters.

see: American Institute for Property Casualty Underwriters, Associate in Risk Management

Insurance Institute of Canada (IIC)

Organizations. Members: Canadian insurance companies. *Objectives*: Maintains a uniform insurance educational program throughout Canada. This organization administers the examinations for the AIIC and FIIC designations in Canada. *Founded*: 1952. *Headquarters*: Toronto, Ontario.

Insurance Library Association of Boston

Organizations. Members: Insurers, brokers, law firms, consultants, adjusters, governmental agencies and academics. *Objectives*: Assist in risk management and insurance research. *Founded*: 1887. *Headquarters*: Boston, MA.

Insurance Loss Control Association (ILCA)

Organizations. Members: Loss prevention specialists for fire and casualty insurers. *Objectives*: Providing educational programs for loss prevention techniques. *Founded*: 1932. *Headquarters*: Indianapolis, IN.

insurance management

Risk Management. In contrast to risk management, insurance management is security-oriented management that deals with loss exposures almost exclusively through the use of insurance.

compare: risk management

Insurance Marketing Communications Association (IMCA)

Organizations. Members: Advertising, marketing, public relations and sales promotion executives of insurance companies. *Objectives*: Sponsors competition among members and presents annual awards for advertising excellence. *Founded*: 1923. *Headquarters*: Wellesley, MA. Known as the Insurance Advertising Conference until 1984.

insurance policy
Insurer Operations.
see: insurance contract

Insurance Premium Finance Association (IPFA)
Organizations. Members: Companies licensed to finance premiums for automobile and other liability coverage on an installment basis. *Objectives*: Promotes the exchange of information between members. *Founded*: 1961. *Headquarters*: Buffalo, NY.

Insurance Regulatory Examiners Society (IRES)
Organizations. Members: Insurance department personnel. *Objectives:* Awards the Accredited Insurance Examiner (AIE) and Certified Insurance Examiner (CIE) designations. Sponsors educational seminars for regulators. *Founded*: 1987. *Headquarters*: Overland Park, KS.

Insurance Regulatory Information System (IRIS)
Regulation. A system of scoring models designed to monitor the financial condition of insurance companies developed by the National Association of Insurance Commissioners in 1974. There are eleven ratios used to evaluate property/casualty insurers in the categories of profitability, liquidity, reserves, and overall financial condition. For life/health and fraternal insurers, twelve ratios are used to evaluate profitability, investments, changes in operations, and overall financial condition. A "usual range" is established for each ratio based on studies of failed and insolvent companies. For example, a large increase or decrease in net written premiums or the ratio of net written premiums to adjusted policyholders' surplus would cause a ratio to fall outside of the usual range.
see: annual statement, Financial Analysis and Solvency Tracking System, insolvency, National Association of Insurance Commissioners, risk-based capital

insurance representative
Agency/Insurer Operations. Producers and field representatives serving as agents, brokers, consultants, solicitors or adjusters. Also, sometimes used to refer to third-party administrators.
see: agent, broker, claims adjuster, third-party administrator

insurance risk
Insurer Operations.
see: risk

Insurance Services Office (ISO)
Organizations. Members: Rating bureaus, actuarial associations and other insurance research groups. *Objectives*: Provides statistical and actuarial information, policy forms and related services to insurers. Functions as an insurance advisory organization and statistical agent. Publishes rate manuals, plans, policy forms and endorsements and other materials. *Founded*: 1971. *Headquarters*: New York, NY.
see: commercial lines manual, Commercial Risk Services Inc., intercompany data

Insurance Society of New York (ISNY)
Organizations. Members: Insurance companies and brokers. *Objectives*: Serves as the parent organization of the College of Insurance. *Founded*: 1901. *Headquarters*: New York, NY.
see: College of Insurance

insurance to value
Property. Insurance coverage written at or near the value of the insured property; or the ratio that the amount of the insurance purchased bears to the value of the insured property.
see: coinsurance

Insurance Value Added Network Services (IVANS)
Organizations. Members: Property and casualty, life and reinsurance insurance companies. *Objectives*: Provides low cost, efficient electronic communications services between independent agencies and the insurance companies which they represent. IVANS provides a high speed, easy-to-use interface. *Founded*: 1983. *Headquarters*: Greenwich, CT.

insured
Insurer Operations. The person whose insurable interest is protected under an insurance policy; the one to whom or at whose direction an insurer reimburses losses, pays benefits, or provides services. The term is generally preferred to *policyholder.*
synonym: assured; *compare*: beneficiary; *see*: additional insured, automatic insured, derivative insured, first named insured, insurable interest, named insured

insured loss ratio
Reinsurance. The ratio that a reinsurer's percentage of losses incurred bears to premiums earned.
see: loss ratio

insured peril
Property. The danger to a property against which it is insured; a cause of loss that invokes coverage under a policy. For example, fire, explosion, wind and vandalism are insured perils under a typical

242

property insurance policy.

compare: exposure, hazard, peril, risk

insured's trailers not in insured's possession
Automobile. A classification of covered vehicles under the truckers' coverage form.

see: truckers' coverage form

insured variable annuity plan
Life. A variable annuity where the plan's units are tied to the investment results of a specific investment account managed by an insurance company.

see: variable annuity

insured vs. insured exclusion
Professional Liability. A coverage exclusion in many directors' and officers' liability policies for suits brought by the insured organization against its directors and officers. The exclusion is designed to eliminate claims arising from in-fighting between the corporation and its senior management.

synonym: cross liability exclusion

insurer
Insurer Operations.

see: insurance company

Insurers' Advisory Organization of Canada (IAO)
Organizations. Members: Canadian property and casualty insurance companies. *Objectives*: Provides rating, statistical, actuarial, policy form information and loss control engineering services on an advisory basis. *Founded*: 1883. *Headquarters*: Toronto, Ontario.

Insurers Rehabilitation and Liquidation Model Act
Regulation. A model law developed by the National Association of Insurance Commissioners to provide state insurance regulators with the power to deal with a financially troubled insurance company. The Act specifies the grounds for placing insurers in liquidation or in rehabilitation and establishes procedures when there are several insurance departments or claimants from several jurisdictions involved in the liquidation of an insurer. It also establishes the order in which an insolvent insurer's claimants and creditors will be paid.

see: liquidation, liquidation distribution, rehabilitation

insuring agreement
Insurer Operations. The section of an insurance contract containing the obligation of the insurer to pay covered claims, subject to specified conditions and exclusions.

synonym: insuring clause; *see*: exclusion, face,

insurance contract, policy conditions, policy declarations

insuring clause
Insurer Operations.

see: insuring agreement

intangible property
Property. 1. A right or possession of a nonphysical or abstract nature that has value, such as a copyright, patent, license, trademark, or goodwill of a business.
2. A financial asset having no intrinsic value but representing value, such securities, notes, accounts receivable, etc.

compare: tangible property; *see*: amortization, intellectual property, chose in action, personal property

integrated care
Health/Workers' Compensation. 1. A medical benefit program provided by an employer that coordinates workers' compensation insurance with group health coverage to provide seamless medical care to the employee without regard to where or when an injury or illness occurs. Two separate policies are issued, one for workers' compensation and one for health insurance, and claims processing is coordinated between the two. It is the stage just before 24-hour coverage.
2. A case management plan that combines medical care, nutritional services, custodial care, rehabilitation, and psychological counseling, often provided by extended (or long-term) care facilities.

compare: 24-hour coverage; *see*: arising out of and in the course of employment, case management, custodial care, skilled nursing facility

integration with Social Security
Employee Benefits. Employee pension plans are usually coordinated with Social Security benefits in compliance with regulations of the Internal Revenue Service. The offset method of integration is restricted to defined benefit plans. It allows the employer to subtract a percentage of the monthly retirement benefit payable to an employee. The integration method can be used with both a defined benefit plan or a defined contribution plan, which allows an employer to establish a basic level of compensation that must be funded. Actual benefits can be greater or less than this level, depending on the Social Security benefit level during the term of retirement.

see: defined benefit plan, defined contribution plan, pension, Social Security

intellectual property
Property. A form of intangible property consisting of documented, written or recorded knowledge, ideas, discoveries, product names, and problem-

solving techniques. Ownership is usually established by a copyright, patent, or trademark.

see: intangible property (1), intellectual property insurance, personal property, piracy (*Property*)

intellectual property insurance

Professional Liability. A broadened form of patent enforcement litigation insurance that expands coverage to include trademarks, copyrights, and computer software design. Coverage is written on a claims-made basis and usually has a coinsurance provision, e.g., 25%. Exclusions include liability for compensatory or consequential damages, fines, punitive damages, exemplary damages and multiple damages.

see: intellectual property, patent insurance, patent enforcement litigation insurance

intentional injury

Health. A self-inflicted or willful injury. Such injuries are generally not covered by health insurance policies.

synonym: willful injury; *see*: intentional loss, injury

intentional loss

Insurer Operations. Damage or destruction of property willfully caused with an intent to defraud an insurer, excluding arson fraud.

see: arson fraud

intentional tort

Law. The deliberate commission of an injurious act (e.g., assault, battery, defamation). Intentional torts are generally not insurable, with the exception of libel and slander.

see: libel, slander, tort

inter vivos trust

Financial Planning. An ordinary trust established by a person while living to manage and distribute assets to other living persons. (*Inter vivos* is Latin for "between the living.")

synonym: living trust; *see*: credit shelter trust, equitable title, personal trust, testamentary trust, trust

interchange insurance

Automobile. Insurance coverage for truckers who frequently trade trailers under an agreement that makes them responsible for any damage to a trailer in their care or custody. It covers the insured's liability for damage to a trailer not belonging to the insured.

synonym: trailer interchange insurance; *see*: trailer interchange agreement, truckers' coverage form

intercompany arbitration

Insurer Operations. Arbitration between two or more insurers as the result of a dispute over the responsibilities of each in the settlement of a loss. Each company is bound by the decision.

see: arbitration

intercompany data

Insurer Operations. Internal insurance company statistics shared by individual insurers through a bureau or rating organization.

see: Fire and Theft Index Bureau, Insurance Crime Prevention Institute, Insurance Services Office, interinsurer claim service organization, Medical Information Bureau, National Automobile Theft Bureau, Property Insurance Loss Register

intercompany transaction

Risk Management. A financial transaction among affiliated companies, including contributions to the reserve fund of a subsidiary by its parents.

see: affiliated insurers

interest

Financial Planning. The price for the use of money, expressed as a percentage of the amount borrowed; the charge paid by a borrower to a lender. The federal Truth in Lending Act requires the interest charge to be disclosed as an annual percentage rate in all consumer credit agreements.

see: compound interest, compounding, continuous compounding, net interest earned, prime rate, simple interest

Insurer Operations.

see: insurable interest

interest adjusted cost

Financial Planning/Life. A method of comparing the cost of life insurance to other investments, using the time value of money. Several different interest adjusted cost comparison methods are used, including the Linton yield method.

see: Linton yield method, time value of money

interest assumption

Employee Benefits. The expected rate of return on an employee benefit plan's assets.

see: employee benefit plan

Life. A minimum rate of return guaranteed on a life insurance policy which is used in calculating the policy's benefits.

interest free loan

Life. A policy loan option available under some universal life insurance policies for which no interest is charged.

see: policy loan, universal life insurance

interest option

Life. An option that a life insurance beneficiary

may select as a settlement by which policy proceeds are left on deposit with the insurer to accrue interest and are paid to the beneficiary annually. Subject to restrictions established by the insured, the beneficiary may withdraw all or part of the principal.

compare: fixed amount option, fixed period option, life income option, life income with period certain option; *see*: settlement options

interest rate swap

Financial Planning. A financial derivative in the form of a swap where the counterparties agree to exchange a fixed interest rate for a floating interest rate. This is a financial risk management technique used by organizations that could be affected by interest rate fluctuations.

see: counterparty, financial derivative, swap

interest-sensitive life insurance

Life. A life insurance policy that credits the policyholder with interest, based upon the investment return earned by the insurance company on all of the policies in a particular group.

interinsurance exchange

Insurer Operations.

see: reciprocal insurance exchange

interinsurer claim service organization

Insurer Operations. An organization established by insurers to compile and share information on fraudulent claims and disseminate claims information to the public.

see: Fire and Theft Index Bureau, Insurance Crime Prevention Institute, Insurance Services Office, Medical Information Bureau, National Automobile Theft Bureau, Property Insurance Loss Register

interior robbery policy

Crime. A crime insurance policy that covers only robberies within an insured's premises. Covered losses include loss of money, securities, personal property, and damage or destruction of real or personal property due to a robbery or attempted robbery.

interline endorsement

Insurer Operations. A policy endorsement applying to more than one part of a multiple line policy.

see: endorsement, multiple line policy

interlock

Loss Control. A device that interacts with another device or mechanism to govern succeeding operations. *Example*: Interlocked guards prevent machines from operating unless the guard has been moved to its proper place.

see: interlocked barrier guard

interlocked barrier guard

Loss Control. A barrier guard on machinery, such as a power press or drill, that is framed and interlocked with the power switch so that the operating cycle cannot be started unless the guard is in its proper position.

see: barrier guard, interlock

interlocking director

Financial Planning. An individual who serves as a director of two or more corporations. If the corporations are competitors, interlocking directorates generally violate antitrust laws.

see: director

intermediary

Reinsurance. An individual or firm that negotiates reinsurance contracts with reinsurers on behalf of an insurance company.

synonym: reinsurance broker, reinsurance intermediary; *see*: direct writer

intermediary clause

Reinsurance. A brokerage reinsurance contract provision that identifies the specific intermediary (broker) who negotiates the contract, communicates between the parties, and transmits funds. Occasionally, this clause provides that payment of premiums by the ceding insurer to the intermediary is deemed to constitute payment to the reinsurer(s) and payments by the reinsurer(s) to the intermediary is deemed to be payment to the ceding insurer.

see: intermediary, reinsurance

intermediate

Automobile. A commercial auto rating classification for vehicles that customarily operate within a radius of between 51 and 200 miles of the vehicle's garage location.

compare: local, long distance, radius of operation

intermediate disability

Employee Benefits.

see: permanent partial disability, temporary partial disability

intermediate excess reinsurance

Reinsurance. A property reinsurance arrangement that provides a layer of coverage over a relatively low underlying retention, exposing the ceding insurer to catastrophe losses in excess of the reinsurance contract limit.

see: excess of loss reinsurance, working cover

internal explosion coverage

Personal. This form of explosion coverage is unique to the dwelling policy basic form and requires that the explosion occur within the insured structure or in a structure containing covered personal property.

see: dwelling policy, explosion

internal financing

Risk Management. Funds that are made available for capital budgeting and working capital expansion through the normal operations of the firm; internal financing is approximately equal to retained earnings plus depreciation.

see: capital budgeting, working capital

internal rate of return (IRR)

Financial Planning/Risk Management. The average annual rate of return on an investment over a given number of years that makes the present value of future net cash flow equal the cost of the investment; the yield or interest rate that makes the present value of expected cash flow from an investment equal to the cost of the investment project.

see: capital budgeting, discount factor, discounted cash flow techniques, hurdle rate, present value, return on investment

Internal Revenue Code

Regulation. The federal tax statutes (U.S. Code Title 26), many of which have a material effect on insurance companies, policies, self-insurance, captive insurance, and employee benefit plans. The Internal Revenue Service, which is in the Treasury Department, issues regulations and letter rulings pursuant to the statutes.

Internal Revenue Code § 79

Life/Regulation. A federal tax statute that extends to employees tax benefits on the value of group whole life insurance policies provided by the employer. The benefit is provided by dividing the term and cash value elements of each policy, thereby taking advantage of the tax exemption on a specified amount of group term insurance plans and the special tax rate on the premium for insurance in excess of that amount.

see: group life insurance

Internal Revenue Code § 101

Regulation. A federal tax statute that excludes from gross income amounts received as proceeds from a life insurance policy and excludes the first $5,000 of employee death benefits paid by or on behalf of the employer.

see: tax benefits of life insurance

Internal Revenue Code § 104

Regulation. A federal tax statute that excludes from gross income amounts received in compensation for personal injuries or illness pursuant to workers' compensation, an award of damages or a legal settlement, or a disability pension or annuity from the armed forces. Amounts received through

accident or health insurance are also excluded if they are not attributable to employer contributions that were excluded from the employee's income and if they are not paid by the employer.

Internal Revenue Code § 125

Regulation.

see: flexible benefit plan

Internal Revenue Code § 303

Regulation. A federal tax statute concerned with stock redemption plans that specifies the procedure by which a corporation cancels or redeems its stock with funds from earnings or profits.

see: redemption

Internal Revenue Code § 401(k)

Employee Benefits/Regulation. A federal tax statute that governs establishment of an employer-sponsored retirement savings plan, allowing employees to invest pretax dollars that an employer can match on a proportional basis.

synonym: 401(k) plan; *compare*: individual retirement account, Keogh plan, stock purchase plan; *see*: employee benefit plan

Internal Revenue Code § 403(g)

Employee Benefits/Regulation. A federal tax statute that extends tax deferral to employees of tax-exempt organizations, such as public school districts, to pay for retirement annuity policies.

see: retirement annuity

Internal Revenue Code § 461(h)

Regulation. A federal tax statute that affects the way self-insureds treat their long-term structured obligations. Prior to its enactment, some self-insureds accrued the total of the future payouts and claimed that amount as a deduction in the tax year in which the settlement was concluded. The statute allows deductions only when economic performance occurs (i.e., each time a payment is made to the plaintiff).

see: self-insurance, structured settlement

Internal Revenue Code § 501(c)

Regulation/Risk Management. A federal tax statute that describes the corporations, clubs and other organizations that qualify as nonprofit and receive a tax exemption.

see: nonprofit organization

Internal Revenue Service bond

Surety.

see: federal bond

International Association for Financial Planning

Organizations. Members: Individuals involved in financial planning. *Objectives*: Assist members in increasing their expertise through education and the exchange of ideas. *Founded*: 1969. *Headquarters*: Atlanta, GA.

International Association for Insurance Law—United States Chapter

Organizations. Members: Insurance company executives, professors, attorneys, state insurance regulators and others interested in international and comparative aspects of insurance law. *Objectives*: Promote international collaboration in insurance law. *Founded*: 1963. *Headquarters*: Chicago, IL.

International Association of Classification Societies (IACS)

Organizations. Members: Ship classification societies, of which there are approximately 90. *Objectives*: Establish common standards for the classification of ships and audit member societies. *Headquarters*: London, England.

International Association of Defense Counsel (IADC)

Organizations. Members: Attorneys practicing defense trial law. *Objectives*: Sponsors research projects and annual legal writing competitions. Awards the Yancey Memorial Award for best article in its journal. Sponsors the Defense Counsel Trial Academy. *Founded*: 1920. *Headquarters*: Chicago, IL.

International Association of Health Underwriters

Organizations.

see: National Association of Health Underwriters

International Association of Industrial Accident Boards and Commissions (IAIABC)

Organizations. Members: Public and private workers' compensation specialists. *Objectives*: Exchange of information among workers' compensation administrators. *Founded*: 1914. *Headquarters*: Daytona Beach, FL.

international broker

Agency/International. An insurance brokerage based in one country that places and services insurance in more than one country.

compare: domestic broker, global broker, multinational broker, transnational broker; *see*: international organization

International Claim Association (ICA)

Organizations. Members: Claims executives and administrators of life, health and accident insurers. *Objectives*: Education and exchange of information among claims settlement professionals. *Founded*: 1909. *Headquarters*: Rock Island, IL.

see: Associate, Life and Health Claims

International Congress of Actuaries

Organizations. Members: Actuaries from approximately 24 countries. *Objectives*: To correlate the activities of actuarial associations in various countries, organize international conferences, and publish research and professional directories. *Headquarters*: Brussels, Belgium.

International Credit Insurance Association (ICIA)

Organizations. Members: Twenty insurers from 15 countries. *Objectives*: To promote uniform coverage in export credit insurance, investigating domestic export credit insurance conditions and comparing them in various countries, and to educate domestic exporters in many countries on how to buy export credit insurance. *Founded*: 1946. *Headquarters*: Zurich, Switzerland.

international development bank bond

International. A bond, note, or other obligation issued by an international development bank, such as the International Bank for Reconstruction and Development and the Asian Development Bank. Such bonds typically cover loans and grants to third-world countries to encourage those governments to raise their standard of living, increase international commerce, and adopt sound budget priorities.

International Foundation of Employee Benefit Plans (IFEBP)

Organizations. Members: Public and privately sponsored employee benefit plans, administrators, labor organizations, employer associations, benefit consultants, investment counselors and insurance consultants. *Objectives*: Maintains liaison with medical and hospital associations. Lobbies state and federal governments. Cosponsors the Certified Employee Benefit Specialist program. *Founded*: 1954. *Headquarters*: Brookfield, WI. Until 1973, known as the National Foundation of Health, Welfare and Pension Plans.

see: Certified Employee Benefit Specialist

international fund

Financial Planning. A mutual fund that invests in securities of corporations domiciled in different countries. These funds involve a currency risk, as the net asset value is affected by changes in the value of other currencies compared to the dollar.

see: mutual fund, net asset value

international insurance

International. Insurance of businesses or properties located in a country other than the insurer's. Many insurance companies have special international insurance departments.

see: global insurance program

International Insurance Advisory Council

Organizations.

see: International Insurance Council

International Insurance Council (IIC)

International/Organizations. Members: Companies and U.S.-licensed trade associations that are risk-bearing companies or insurers. *Objectives:* Promotes the business of international insurance and acts as a trade policy advocate representing U.S. insurers and reinsurers. *Founded:* 1946. *Headquarters:* Washington, D.C. (Until 1988, called the International Insurance Advisory Council.)

International Insurance Section, CPCU Society

Organizations. An interest section of the CPCU Society that provides information on developments in international and global insurance.

see: CPCU Society

International Insurance Seminars

Organizations.

see: International Insurance Society, Inc.

International Insurance Society, Inc. (IIS)

Organizations. Members: Professors of insurance of major universities and others in the insurance field. *Objectives:* Offers annual seminars to facilitate international economic development. *Founded:* 1959. *Headquarters:* Tuscaloosa, AL. (Before 1987, called International Insurance Seminars.)

international organization

International. A business organization that primarily does business in a single country but acquires a significant share of its resources or revenues from other countries.

compare: domestic organization, global organization, multinational organization

International Organization for Standardization

Organizations. Members: Experts in over 90 countries. *Objectives:* To establish standards for businesses to follow in their operations. In 1987 it developed the ISO 9000 standards, which have been adopted as the national standards for quality management and assurance by over 80 countries. *Founded:* 1979. *Headquarters:* Geneva, Switzerland.

see: ISO 9000

International Society of Certified Employee Benefit Specialists (ISCEBS)

Organizations. Members: Graduates of the Certified Employee Benefit Specialist program. *Objectives:* Promotes continuing education and professional development in the employee benefit field.

Founded: 1981. *Headquarters:* Brookfield, WI.

see: Certified Employee Benefit Specialist

International Union of Aviation Insurance (IUAI)

Organizations. Members: Five hundred private insurers operating in the aviation field from about 25 countries. *Objectives:* To hold annual conferences on aviation insurance and promote world insurance markets, exchange aviation insurance information, conduct loss prevention activities, and promote uniform insurance contract provisions in all countries. *Founded:* 1934. *Headquarters:* London, England.

International Union of Marine Insurance (IUMI)

Organizations. Members: Marine insurance associations from approximately 45 countries. *Objectives:* To hold annual conferences on marine insurance and promote world insurance markets, exchange marine insurance information, conduct loss prevention activities, and promote uniform insurance contract provisions in all countries. *Headquarters:* Zurich, Switzerland.

interpleader

Law. A legal motion to bring into court adverse claimants in order to determine rightful title to property that is in possession of a third person who does not claim ownership (e.g., an insurer or trustee). Insurers may interplead persons who claim insurance proceeds under different policies. The proceeds are held in deposit by the court until proper ownership is determined.

synonym: bill of interpleader; see: pleading, summons, trust

interstate carrier

Automobile. A trucking company that operates across state lines and is regulated by the Interstate Commerce Commission.

compare: intrastate carrier; see: Interstate Commerce Commission

Interstate Commerce Commission (ICC)

Regulation. A federal agency that regulates commerce between states, including the activities of trucking firms that transport goods across state lines. Regulations include standards of liability of truckers for cargo damage, which requires that they have insurance or post letters of credit or bonds.

see: financial responsibility law, interstate carrier, Interstate Commerce Commission endorsement

Interstate Commerce Commission endorsement

Inland Marine. A provision endorsed to a motor truck cargo or traveler's legal liability policy that guarantees that all losses to cargo will be paid by the insurer regardless of the perils insured by the policy. For losses not covered by the policy, but which are paid by the insurer pursuant to this endorsement, the common carrier must reimburse the insurer.

see: Motor Carrier Act endorsement

interstate experience modification
Workers' Compensation. A workers' compensation experience modification factor that applies to employers who have operations in several states where the National Council on Compensation Insurance is the rating bureau. This factor is applied to each state's manual premium to calculate the premium to be used on the policy in that state or to develop an overall combined multistate policy premium.

see: experience rating modification factor, National Council on Compensation Insurance, rating bureau

interstate experience rating
Workers' Compensation. A multistate experience rating program developed by the National Council on Compensation Insurance for employers with multistate operations. The experience of all the states is combined to determine the employer's experience modification.

see: experience rating modification factor, interstate experience modification, National Council on Compensation Insurance, rating bureau

intestate
Financial Planning. Dying without having made a legal will; a person who has died without leaving a will.

see: escheat, probate, will

intoxicating liquor bond
Surety.
see: alcohol bond

intra-family immunity
Law. A legal doctrine that a person is not liable to another member of the same family—i.e., is immune to suit by a family member. The purpose was to prevent collusive suits by related persons; however, courts have created exceptions.

see: family exclusion, liability coverage exclusion endorsement

intra vires
Law. Pertaining to an action within the proper authority or stated purposes of a corporation or corporate officer. (Latin for "within the power.")

compare: ultra vires

intrastate carrier
Automobile. A trucking firm that operates within a single state.

compare: interstate carrier

intrinsic value
Financial Planning. The difference between the market value of an underlying stock and the exercised option price.

see: option

intuitive trending
Risk Management. Loss forecasting that considers subjective or social variables such as shifts in demand, changed legal climate, or new loss control techniques as factors to modify loss forecasts.

see: loss trends, trending

invalidity
Health. A sickness or illness.

inventory
Property.
see: stock (*Property*)

inverse condemnation
Law. The taking of or reduction in the value of land by a government agency through the power of eminent domain without adequate compensation. *Example:* The acquisition of land for a new airport that diminishes the value of adjacent property.

see: condemnation, confiscation, eminent domain

Investment Advisers Act
Regulation. Federal legislation adopted in 1940 and amended in 1960 that requires persons or firms who receive compensation for providing securities investment advice to register with the Securities and Exchange Commission and follow standards established by the Commission to protect investors.

see: Securities and Exchange Commission

investment advisers' errors and omissions insurance
Professional Liability. A form of professional liability insurance for persons or firms that provide financial or investment advice that covers errors, omissions and negligent acts in the performance of professional duties. Coverage is excluded for the buying or selling of stock, bonds or other investments; security underwriting; libel and slander; dishonest acts or actual intent to deceive or defraud. Coverage is written on a claims-made basis.

see: errors and omissions insurance

investment annuity
Life. An annuity plan developed in conjunction with a bank or trust company using an irrevocable agreement with the institution to fund monthly retirement annuity income payments.

see: annuity

investment banker
Financial Planning. A person or firm that acts as

the middleman between a corporation issuing securities and the buying public. Generally, the investment banker buys the securities from the corporation and resells them to individuals and institutions.

synonym: underwriter; *see*: public offering, secondary offering

investment club

Financial Planning. An organization in which the members pool their funds to build up an investment portfolio larger than individual members could afford by themselves.

investment company

Financial Planning.

see: mutual fund

investment department

Insurer Operations. The employees and operations of an insurance company that handle the investments of company funds, including premium and claim reserves.

investment grade company

Financial Planning.

see: blue-chip stock

investment income

Insurer Operations. An insurance company's earnings from its investment portfolio, including interest, dividends, capital gains and rent.

see: cash flow underwriting, investment year method of allocating investment income, net interest earned

investment product sales exclusion

Professional Liability. An exclusion in many accountants' professional liability policies for claims arising from the sale of investment products, such as tax shelters and real estate limited partnerships. The exclusion can usually be deleted for an additional premium.

see: accountants' professional liability insurance

investment reserve

Insurer Operations. An insurance company balance sheet item that establishes a reserve to compensate for sudden, large reductions in the value of stocks, bonds or real estate held by the company in its investment portfolio.

see: mandatory securities valuation reserve, securities valuation

investment return insurance

Financial Guaranty. Insurance against the risk of loss for the value of the redeemable securities of an insured investor.

investment risk

Financial Planning.

see: financial risk

investment year method of allocating investment income

Insurer Operations. A method by which a life insurance company matches or allocates investment income to each of its policies, based on the date the premium was received for the policy.

invitation to bid

Surety.

see: advertisement to bid

invitee

Law. A person who enters the premises of another by the owner's request or inducement. Customers of a business are considered invitees. The one who invites has an obligation to maintain the property in a safe condition for any invitee.

compare: licensee, trespasser; *see*: attractive nuisance doctrine, degree of care

invoice

Inland Marine/Ocean Marine.

see: commercial invoice

involuntary conversion

Accounting. Loss of property as a result of theft, casualty, seizure or government condemnation. Income tax laws permit a gain from an involuntary conversion to be deferred if a qualifying reinvestment is made. A claimed loss may not exceed the lesser of the reduction in the affected property's fair market value or the owner's taxable income for the year in which the involuntary conversion occurred.

see: casualty loss, involuntary conversion option

involuntary conversion option

Accounting. A tax payment option for an insured upon receipt of a claim payment for a property loss. The taxpayer may elect either (1) to pay a capital gain tax on the excess of any payment over the damaged property's book value (adjusted tax basis) or (2) to defer a capital gain tax by using the excess claim payment to purchase replacement property. Replacement personal property must be purchased within 18 months and replacement real property within two years, and it must be similar or related in use to the damaged property.

see: capital gain (or loss), taxation of property insurance claims payments

iron safe clause

Inland Marine. A provision in some inland marine policies that requires the insured to keep all valuable papers and records in a safe when not in use. This is an archaic term, since safes are not necessarily made of iron today.

see: inland marine insurance

irrevocable beneficiary

Life. A life insurance policy provision by which the beneficiary cannot be changed unless the insured obtains the beneficiary's approval.

synonym: absolute beneficiary; *compare*: revocable beneficiary; *see*: beneficiary, trust

irrevocable life insurance trust

Financial Planning. A trust structured so that it is free from estate and income taxes. The trust receives the death benefits from a life insurance policy, which are either disbursed immediately or managed for the heirs.

see: estate tax, trust

irrevocable trust

Financial Planning. A trust that, once created, cannot be revoked or done away with by the individual who created the trust.

see: short-term reversionary trust

ISO 9000

Regulation. A set of international manufacturing and service standards developed by the International Organization for Standardization. The standards are developed by technical committees comprised of experts from over 90 countries. They are designed to help companies set up systems for the design, development, production, installation, testing, inspection and servicing of products. Compliance with these standards is now required in many contracts between suppliers and their customers. They are divided into four subsections: ISO 9001, ISO 9002, ISO 9003, and ISO 9004-1.

see: International Organization for Standardization, ISO 9000-1, ISO 9001, ISO 9002, ISO 9003, ISO 9004-1, National Bureau of Standards

ISO 9000-1

Regulation. The principal ISO guidelines for the ISO 9000 standards. In the United States it is the equivalent of ANSI/ASQC Q9000-1, titled *Quality Management and Quality Assurance Standards, Guidelines for Selections and Use*. It contains guidelines for the use of the other four standards in the 9000 series.

ISO 9001

Regulation. One of the subsections to the ISO 9000 standards. In the United States it is the equivalent of ANSI/ASQC Q9001, titled *Quality Systems, Model for Quality Assurance in Design, Development, Production, Installation and Servicing*. It contains guidelines for the design, development, production, installation, and servicing of products.

ISO 9002

Regulation. One of the subsections to the ISO 9000 standards. In the United States it is the equivalent of ANSI/ASQC Q9002, titled *Quality Systems,*

Model for Quality Assurance in Production, Installation and Servicing. This standard contains guidelines for the production, installation, and servicing of products.

ISO 9003

Regulation. One of the subsections to the ISO 9000 standards. In the United States it is the equivalent of the ANSI/ASQC Q9003, titled *Quality Systems, Model for Quality Assurance in Final Inspection and Testing*. It contains guidelines for the final inspection and testing of products.

ISO 9004-1

Regulation. One of the subsections to the ISO 9000 standards. In the United States it is the equivalent of the ANSI/ASQC Q9004-1, titled *Quality Management and Quality System Elements, Guidelines*. It contains guidelines for managers of an organization to follow in isolating their quality system. It is not a requirement itself, but it gives suggestions for effective quality management so that companies can be qualified to meet the ISO 9001, 9002, and 9003 requirements.

issuance date

Insurer Operations.

see: date of issue

issued business

Insurer Operations. Life insurance policies that have been sold and on which the premium has been paid, but which have not yet been delivered to the policyholder.

compare: delivered business, examined business, paid business, placed business, written business

item basis premium payment

Agency. A method of transmitting premium to an insurer where the premium does not have to be paid until it is actually collected by the agent from the policyholder.

compare: account current, statement basis premium payment; *see*: agency bill, premium

itemized premium charges

Insurer Operations. Separately identified charges for insurance coverages in a multi-peril policy; the specification of premiums in an agreement to finance the sale of property.

see: multi-peril policy

J

jacket
Insurer Operations.
see: policy jacket

Janson clause
Ocean Marine. A provision sometimes added to an ocean marine hull policy that the insurance is "free of particular average" if the amount of a partial loss equals or exceeds 3% of the insured value of the property covered, or should the vessel be stranded. The insured warrants that it will remain uninsured for this 3%.
see: free of particular average, particular average

jet ski insurance
Personal. Coverage for jet skis (inboard motorized small boats) is generally included under a standard homeowners policy including personal property coverage for up to $1,000, and liability coverage is included if the inboard motor is 50 horsepower or less. If the jet ski has over 50 horsepower or if coverage is excluded, special marine coverage is available for the hull and liability.
see: homeowners policy

jetsam
Ocean Marine. Goods purposely thrown overboard or jettisoned, either to save a ship or to keep the goods from sinking with a foundering ship. Technically, such cargo must then be brought ashore and above the high-water line, otherwise it remains "flotsam."
compare: flotsam, lagan; *see*: derelict, jettison

jettison
Ocean Marine. The voluntary dumping overboard of a vessel's cargo or gear in an effort to save it; a peril covered by ocean marine insurance.
see: ocean marine insurance

jewelers block insurance
Inland Marine. Inland marine insurance tailored to

the needs of wholesale and retail jewelers. Coverage is written on an open perils basis for the insured's entire stock of pearls, precious and semi-precious stones, jewels; jewelry, watches and watch movements; gold, silver, platinum, other precious metals, alloys; and the other stock common to the business of a jeweler, including items held in custody for others.
see: inland marine insurance, jewelers package policy

jewelers package policy
Inland Marine. A policy that is broader than the standard jewelers block and that includes all-risk coverage on all stock, property of others, furniture and fixtures and improvements and betterments. Coverage for a building and business interruption can be included.
see: jewelers block insurance

jewelry coverage
Personal. One of the nine classes of property that can be covered under a personal articles floater. Personal jewelry is defined as items of personal adornment composed in whole or in part of silver, gold, platinum or other precious metals and alloys, whether or not containing pearls, jewels, precious or semi-precious stones.
see: jewelry, watches, furs—special limit; pair or set; personal articles floater

jewelry floater
Inland Marine. A form of personal articles floater covering individual items of jewelry that are scheduled in the policy on an open-perils basis.
see: floater policy, personal articles floater, scheduled personal property endorsement

jewelry, watches, furs—special limit
Personal. The ISO homeowners policy coverage section C (personal property) has a "special limits of liability" provision on the theft of jewelry, watches, furs, precious and semi-precious stones.

The combined limit for these items is $1,000.
see: homeowners policy—special limits of liability, jewelry coverage

job hazard analysis
Loss Control.
see: job safety analysis

job safety analysis
Loss Control. The study of a job and its component parts to determine the hazards connected with it and the requirements or qualifications of those who perform it. This includes identifying hazards or potential accidents associated with each task and recommending measures to eliminate or prevent them.
synonym: job hazard analysis; *see*: human approach, human factors engineering

joint and several liability
Law. Liability arising from a contract or from a tort that applies to the responsible persons either separately (severally) or in combination (jointly), at the injured person's option. If a group of persons who default on an obligation or cause a loss are held jointly and severally liable either by terms of the contract or by operation of law, the claimant may sue either the group or any one member for the entire amount owed. This is a way to compensate an injured person if, for example, one or more liable persons are bankrupt or flee the jurisdiction.
see: joint liability, joint tortfeasors, several liability, tort

joint and survivor annuity
Life. An annuity contract that provides periodic payments during the lifetime of two individuals. The amount of the income benefit may decrease when the first annuitant dies. Joint and survivor contracts are usually written on spouses.
synonym: reversionary annuity, survivorship annuity

joint and survivorship option
Life. A life insurance policy benefit option that allows the policy cash value to be converted into a joint and survivor annuity.
see: cash surrender value, joint and survivor annuity

Joint Board for the Enrollment of Actuaries
Organizations.
see: Enrolled Actuary

joint control
Surety. When an estate is controlled jointly by a surety and a fiduciary (estate administrator or executor), funds are maintained in accounts that require the signatures of both. Joint control is used to reduce fraud when large estates are involved.
see: estate planning

joint insurance
Life.
see: joint life insurance

joint insured
Life. An individual insured under a joint life insurance policy.
see: joint life insurance
Crime. An endorsement (ISO form CR 10 43) that amends the named insured to schedule specific individuals or positions as respects the crime coverages provided by the various Insurance Services Office crime coverage forms.
see: crime coverages

joint liability
Law. The sharing of a legal obligation by two or more persons.
compare: several liability; *see*: joint and several liability, joint tortfeasors, market share liability

joint life and survivor annuity
Life. Life insurance coverage that converts to an annuity contract for two or more individuals (usually spouses), where the annuity benefits continue until the death of the last insured.

joint life and survivor insurance
Life. Life insurance coverage for two or more individuals where the death benefit is payable when the last surviving insured dies. Premiums on this type of policy are much lower than individual life policies because the period of time before the final benefit payment is longer.
compare: joint life insurance; *see*: second death insurance, tontine

joint life insurance
Life. Life insurance coverage for two or more individuals where the death benefit is payable upon the death of the first insured individual. Premiums on this type of policy are significantly higher than individual life policies because of the greater chance that one of two individuals will die.
synonym: joint insurance; *compare*: joint life and survivor insurance, second death insurance

joint loss agreement
Property. An endorsement to a boiler and machinery policy that prorates the policy limits with another property policy when both policies provide coverage on a similar basis. It is generally mirrored by an endorsement on the property policy. When a loss is payable, the insurer determines whether and to what extent it is a boiler and machinery or a property loss.
see: boiler and machinery insurance, firebox explosion, other insurance provision

joint mortgage protection insurance

Life. A decreasing term life insurance policy that insures two people. It provides coverage for an unpaid mortgage balance as it decreases throughout the mortgage period. The benefit is paid upon the first death, and the survivor usually has the right to apply for his or her own cash value policy without proof of insurability. If both insureds die within a 24-hour period, a double death benefit is usually paid.

see: mortgage protection insurance

joint tenancy

Law. The ownership of property by two or more persons where ownership passes to the survivor(s) upon one's death.

see: tenancy

joint tortfeasor release

Law. A settlement and release from further liability that applies to one tortfeasor and not to any other joint tortfeasors. It allows one or more tortfeasors to reach a settlement with the claimant without jeopardizing the claimant's right to seek additional recovery from the non-settling tortfeasors.

see: joint liability, release, tort

joint tortfeasors

Law. Two or more persons who unite in committing a tort.

see: joint liability, tort

joint underwriting association (JUA)

Insurer Operations. An organization of insurance companies formed with statutory approval to provide a particular form of insurance. JUAs are usually formed because voluntary market availability is lacking. They are generally allowed by regulators to establish their own rates and develop their own policy forms.

see: automobile shared market, extended health insurance, Fair Access to Insurance Requirements

joint venture

Law. An association of two or more individuals or companies to engage in a limited business transaction. Profits and losses are usually shared according to an agreed formula.

see: corporation, joint venture as insured endorsement, limited liability company, partnership

joint venture as insured endorsement

Workers' Compensation. A workers' compensation policy endorsement (NCCI form WC 00 03 05) that covers a joint venture and each partner in

his or her capacity as an employer of the joint venture's employees.

see: joint venture, workers' compensation insurance

joint venture political risk insurance

International. A form of political risk insurance designed to protect a corporation participating in a joint venture in a foreign country against political risks. This coverage was initially developed for joint ventures in Eastern Europe.

see: political risk insurance

joisted masonry construction

Loss Control. A structure with outside support walls made of incombustible masonry materials (concrete, brick, hollow concrete block, stone or tile) and a roof and floor made of combustible materials (e.g., wood). There are two sub-classes: ordinary construction and mill construction.

see: construction, ordinary construction, mill construction

Jones Act

Ocean Marine/Workers' Compensation. A federal law (U.S. Code Title 46, Chapter 18) that provides ships' crews with the same remedy available to railroad workers, that is, seamen may sue the employer/shipowner for injuries sustained through their fault or negligence. The Act applies to navigable waters used for international or interstate commerce.

see: cure, Longshore and Harbor Workers' Compensation Act, seaman's remedies

judgment

Law. A court's final decision or decree in a lawsuit.

compare: arbitration award; *see*: declaratory judgment, decree, default judgment, directed verdict, dismissal, injunction

judgment rates

Insurer Operations. Rates developed by an underwriter based on his or her experience and skills, rather than using actuarial analysis.

compare: manual rates; *see*: "A" rates, rate making, schedule rating

judicial bond

Surety. A general term applied to all bonds filed with a court.

see: appeal bond, bail bond, court bond, defendant's bond to dissolve, fiduciary bond, financial guaranty bond, injunction bond, plaintiff's bond to secure, plaintiff's replevin bond, security for expenses

jumping juvenile life insurance

Life. A life insurance policy designed for children that has a low initial face value ($1,000 or $2,000)

but increases significantly when the insured reaches a specified age, usually 21. The policy's annual premium remains the same throughout its term, and no medical examinations are needed after it is issued.

compare: graded death benefit; *see*: juvenile life insurance

junior mortgage
Financial Planning.
see: second mortgage

junk bond
Financial Planning.
see: high-yield bond

"junk science"
Law.
see: expert witness

jury duty reimbursement
Property. Business coverage that reimburses employers for a part (usually 80%) of wages paid to an employee during jury service.

just-in-time inventory system
Accounting. A practice of keeping inventory levels at or near zero by ordering just enough materials to satisfy immediate sales or production demands. This inventory method can result in significant contingent business income exposures.

see: business income coverage form, contingent business income coverage, stock (*Property*)

juvenile life insurance
Life. Insurance on children under 16 years old.
see: graded death benefit, jumping juvenile life insurance

K

Keene doctrine

Law/Liability. The judicial ruling concerning coverage for asbestos liability claims in the case of Keene Corp. v. Insurance Company of North America (D.C. Cir. 1981): 1. All insurers with policies in force between the time of initial exposure to asbestos and the manifestation of loss (or discovery of injury) must respond on behalf of the policyholder. This is the *continuous trigger* theory (also called the triple or multiple trigger), which invokes coverage at initial exposure, during continuing exposure, and upon manifestation of the disease. 2. All insurers responsible for coverage are liable for their full policy limits, not just their pro rata share. 3. The insured is allowed to select which potentially liable policy is to respond. The Keene principles are not uniformly accepted by courts across the United States.

compare: exposure theory, manifestation theory; *see*: asbestosis, continuous trigger theory

Keeton-O'Connell Plan

Automobile. An automobile no-fault plan proposed by two law professors, Robert Keeton and Jeffrey O'Connell, called "basic protection insurance." The plan sought to eliminate most auto liability lawsuits by requiring insurers to reimburse their own policyholders (up to $10,000 per person). The plan would permit regular tort claims only for noneconomic losses exceeding $5,000.

see: no-fault insurance

Kenney ratio

Insurer Operations. A property and casualty insurance company solvency guideline developed by the late Roger Kenney, an insurance journalist. A property and casualty insurer should not have written premiums greater than twice the sum of its capital and surplus.

Keogh plan

Employee Benefits. A retirement plan for self-employed individuals, permitted under the Keogh Act passed by Congress in 1962. It allows an individual

to make an annual tax deductible contribution to a retirement plan, up to a maximum limit of 25% of earned income (subject to a $30,000 maximum).

compare: individual retirement account

key employee insurance

Health/Life. A disability, life or health insurance program designed to protect an employer from the loss of an individual employee whose special skills or experience are vital to the firm. Policy proceeds are used to cover the firm's lost income and to locate and hire a replacement for the key employee.

synonym: key man insurance; *see*: cross purchase plan, overhead expense insurance, partnership insurance, personnel loss exposure, sole proprietorship insurance

key man insurance

Life.

see: key employee insurance

key personnel loss exposure

Risk Management. A risk of loss involving officers, directors, or employees with special skills or other characteristics of particular value to the organization, so that losing their services would cause significant lost revenue or extra expenses.

see: key employee insurance, personnel loss exposure

kidnap insurance

Crime. Insurance that provides compensation when a person (usually an employee) is seized and used to gain entry to a premises, to extract a ransom, or for the purpose of extortion. This coverage usually extends to the spouse and children of the covered individual.

compare: extortion insurance, kidnap-ransom-extortion insurance, terrorist insurance

kidnap-ransom-extortion insurance

Crime. Originally an insurance policy for financial institutions, it has been expanded for corporate executives and other wealthy persons or celebrities.

The policy reimburses the insured for the amount of a ransom paid, and the insurer may provide the assistance of professional negotiators to deal with the kidnappers. Coverage is written on a worldwide basis.

see: extortion insurance, kidnap insurance, ransom insurance.

L

labor and material bond
Surety. A bond that guarantees an owner (or general contractor) at a construction site that a contractor (or subcontractors) will pay for labor and material to be supplied. It protects the owner or contractor against liens from subcontractors, suppliers or laborers who are not paid.

synonym: payment bond

labor contractor endorsement
Workers' Compensation. A workers' compensation policy endorsement (NCCI form WC 00 03 20A) that covers an employer whose workers have been transferred to a labor contractor and then leased back to the former employer. The labor contractor is also covered for the leased employees.

see: employee leasing client endorsement, leased employee, multiple coordinated policy endorsement

labor contractor exclusion endorsement
Workers' Compensation. A workers' compensation policy endorsement (NCCI form WC 00 03 21) that covers only the direct (not leased) employees of a labor contractor. Leased employees are covered by the workers' compensation policy of the labor contractor's client.

see: leased employee

Labor-Management Relations Act
Regulation.
see: Taft-Hartley Act

labor union errors and omissions insurance
Professional Liability. A form of professional liability insurance for labor unions and their officers, former officers, executive board members, and other officials that provides coverage on a claims-made basis for legal expenses and liability for negligent acts, errors or omissions in the conduct of the organization's business.

see: errors and omissions insurance

labor union group life insurance
Life. Group life insurance issued to a labor union on the lives of union members for the benefit of persons other than the union.

see: group life insurance

laches
Law. Undue delay in asserting a right or privilege; specifically, undue delay in bringing a suit or complaint. Laches may be used as a defense if the defendant can prove a loss or prejudice caused by the plaintiff's delay or seeming acquiescence.

see: acquiescence, affirmative defense, estoppel, reservation of rights, statute of limitations, waiver

lacing detection system
Loss Control. A detection system used to trigger a burglar alarm. A closely woven pattern of metallic foil or fine brittle wire is placed on the surface of the protected area and covered by a panel. When the foil or wire is broken by an intruder, the detection circuit is interrupted, setting off the burglar alarm.

synonym: paneling detection system; *see*: burglar alarm

lading
Inland Marine/Ocean Marine.
see: bill of lading, freight

lagan
Ocean Marine. Loose cargo from a marine accident; goods thrown into the sea with a buoy attached, so they may be easily recovered later.

compare: derelict; *see*: flotsam, jetsam

land contract
Title. The sale of real property by a contract that conveys title from one party to another upon full payment of the purchase price. The title remains with the seller until the buyer has paid the entire

price, with the buyer taking possession of the property immediately following payment.

compare: mortgage

land farming

Loss Control. A method of disposing of hazardous waste by depositing it on or in the soil, where it is naturally decomposed by microbes.

see: hazardous waste disposal, secure chemical landfill

land surveyors' professional liability insurance

Professional Liability. A form of professional liability insurance for land surveyors that provides coverage for negligent acts, errors or omissions in the performance of their duties. Coverage is written on a claims-made basis.

see: professional liability insurance

landfill

Loss Control.

see: sanitary landfill, secure chemical landfill

landlords' protective liability endorsement

Liability. An endorsement (ISO form GL 99 02) available under the 1973 liability rating program that allowed a significant rate credit for buildings leased to a single lessee. The 1986 Insurance Services Office rating program eliminated the need for this endorsement, as rate credits previously allowed have been incorporated into new building and premises classifications.

lapse

Insurer Operations. Insurance policy termination due to the insured's failure to make premium payments.

see: cancellation notice, lapse ratio, reinstatement

Life. Life insurance policy termination due to nonpayment of premiums, with no nonforfeiture value.

see: nonforfeiture benefit

lapse ratio

Insurer Operations/Life. A ratio used by life insurers to determine the effectiveness of their marketing efforts. It is the ratio of the number of life contracts that have lapsed within a specified period of time to the number in force at the beginning of the period.

compare: persistency; *see*: termination rate

lapsed policy

Insurer Operations. An insurance policy that has been terminated because of the insured's failure to pay the premium.

larceny

Crime. In some jurisdictions, a theft other than one involving a forcible entry (burglary) or an actual or

threatened bodily harm (robbery). Many jurisdictions prefer the term *theft*.

see: burglary, embezzlement, forgery, pilferage, robbery, theft

large deductible plan (LDP)

Workers' Compensation. A deductible workers' compensation program designed for large employers, usually with multistate exposures. The size of the deductibles typically range from $100,000 to $1 million per occurrence. The insurer makes all payments as it does under a conventional policy, and the insured reimburses the insurer on a monthly or quarterly basis. The insurer also typically puts up security for the deductible exposure, such as a letter of credit.

see: deductible workers' compensations plans

large loss principle

Risk Management. A loss that would exceed a firm's ability to absorb it, so the risk of such a loss should be transferred through insurance.

compare: small loss principle; *see*: retention, risk transfer

larger settlement rule

Professional Liability. A judicial rule for allocating legal costs, including settlements or awards and defense costs, under directors' and officers' liability insurance. Allocation to the uninsured corporate entity is permitted only when its own acts, distinguished from those of the insured officers and directors, increased the settlement. The D&O insurer is responsible for all costs unless the corporation's or uninsured officers' actions increased the loss.

compare: relative exposure rule; *see*: allocation of defense costs, directors' and officers' liability insurance, entity coverage

laser endorsement

Liability. Any of a series of endorsements developed in conjunction with the Insurance Services Office claims-made commercial liability policy in 1986 that excludes specific accidents, products, or locations. Because the exclusions are very narrow, they were thought to resemble a laser.

see: claims-made form, commercial general liability policy

last clear chance

Law. The last reasonable opportunity to avoid an accident or injury. One who has the last clear chance to avoid an injury and fails to do so is usually held solely responsible, notwithstanding the injured person's own contributory negligence.

see: contributory negligence

last-in-first-out (LIFO)

Accounting. An inventory accounting method by which sales are considered to be from among the latest merchandise or inventory purchased or produced. This method minimizes inventory profits and losses. An understanding of inventory valuation methods is important in estimating business interruption losses.

compare: average cost; first-in-first-out; *see*: stock (*Property*)

latent defect

Liability. A hidden or dormant defect in a product that cannot be discovered by observation or a reasonably careful inspection.

synonym: hidden defect; *see*: active malfunction, bench error, defective product, product liability insurance

launch insurance

Aviation. A form of satellite and space vehicle insurance that covers physical loss or damage to a satellite or space vehicle while it is in the launch sequence. Coverage includes failure of the spacecraft to arrive at its designated orbit and failure of a satellite to perform properly once in orbit.

see: satellite and space vehicle insurance

laundry list

Professional Liability. An extensive list of past events that could trigger coverage under a claims-made liability policy that is being canceled or nonrenewed by the current insurer or is being replaced by another insurer.

see: claims-made trigger, professional liability insurance

law enforcement officers' professional liability insurance
Professional Liability.

see: police professional liability insurance

law of averages
Risk Management.

see: law of large numbers

law of large numbers

Risk Management. A principle that the larger the number of exposures considered, the more closely will reported losses equal the true probability of loss. This is the basis for the statistical expectation of loss, which determines premium rates.

synonym: law of averages; *see*: degree of risk, homogeneity, odds, probability analysis, pure risk, spread of risk

lawyers' professional liability insurance
Professional Liability.

see: attorneys' professional liability insurance

lay underwriter

Health/Life. A home office underwriter with extensive actuarial and medical knowledge.

layering

Liability/Property. A method of structuring policies covering a risk, so that each policy provides a layer of coverage. This technique is used in both liability and property coverages. *Example*: Policy A, a primary policy, provides $100,000 in coverage limits. Policy B provides $200,000 of coverage in excess of the Policy A limit. Policy C provides an additional $300,000, in excess of Policy B, for a total of $600,000. The advantage of layering is the additional spread of risk among insurers and the premium savings each company grants the insured.

see: buffer layer, divided coverage, following form excess liability insurance, following form excess property insurance, nonconcurrency, primary policy, quota share

LD₅₀

Loss Control. A measure of acute toxicity. It is the quantity of a substance (often, per unit of body weight) that constitutes a lethal dose to 50% of test animals. The lower the LD50, the more toxic the compound.

see: chronic toxicity

lead fee

Agency/Insurer Operations. Payment of a fee to another party for the referral of a prospective insured or customer.

lead insurance company

Insurer Operations. An insurer that leads a group of insurers and reinsurers in underwriting a large risk. The lead insurer usually assumes a large percentage of the risk for its own account.

see: lead underwriter

lead paint abatement bond

Surety. A performance bond designed for contractors who specialize in the removal of lead paint from buildings. This type of bond is usually available only from specialty bonding companies.

see: lead poisoning

lead paint abatement coverage

Liability. A form of pollution liability coverage for property owners or lead paint abatement contractors covering third-party bodily injury, property damage, and cleanup costs arising out of lead paint abatement.

see: lead poisoning

lead poisoning

Liability/Loss Control. Acute or chronic poisoning caused by the absorption of lead or any of its salts into the human body. Paint containing lead can cause injuries to children including brain damage. The only way to effectively reduce lead paint exposure to acceptable levels is by chemical removal, scraping, or encapsulating the painted surface with sheet rock or paneling.

see: lead paint abatement bond, lead paint abatement liability

lead reinsurer

Reinsurance. The primary participant among several reinsurers in a reinsurance contract, who is responsible for negotiating the terms of the contract. The lead reinsurer is usually the one assuming the greatest amount among the participating reinsurers.

compare: following reinsurer

lead underwriter

Insurer Operations. A Lloyd's term referring to the underwriter that leads on a Lloyd's slip. The lead underwriter is selected carefully, since the underwriter's prestige affects the number and dollar amounts for which other underwriters will participate.

see: slip

Leading Producers Round Table (LPRT)

Organizations. An award given annually by the National Association of Health Underwriters to producers who achieve certain levels of premium volume during the year.

see: National Association of Health Underwriters

lease payment insurance

Financial Guaranty. A form of credit insurance covering a lessor against nonpayment of rental installments by the lessee in a capital equipment or real estate lease transaction.

see: credit insurance

leased employee

Workers' Compensation. An employee who is sent by his or her employer to work for another organization and is under the exclusive control and direction of the management of the lessee organization. *Example*: A word processor sent by a temporary employment agency to work in a bank.

compare: borrowed employee; *see*: employee, employee leasing, employee leasing client endorsement, employee leasing client exclusion endorsement, labor contractor endorsement, labor contractor exclusion endorsement, leased workers coverage, multiple coordinated policy endorsement

leased property endorsement

Property. A commercial property insurance endorsement (ISO form CP 14 60) that allows leased personal property to be valued according to actual cash value or replacement cost to meet the lessee's requirements.

see: actual cash value, replacement cost

leased workers coverage

Liability. Employees provided through an employee leasing agency are included in the definition of "employee" under the commercial general liability policy.

see: commercial general liability policy, leased employee

leasehold

Law. A contract giving a person the right to use and occupy another's property; an interest in real estate held under a lease. The time period of the leasehold may be specified in writing or may be inferred from the manner of paying rent.

see: leasehold interest, tenancy

leasehold interest

Property. The right of a person (lessee) to occupy or use real property of the owner (lessor) for a specified time in return for the payment of rent or subject to other conditions. The lessee has an insurable interest in the property during the period of the lease.

see: insurable interest, leasehold interest coverage, leasehold profit interest

leasehold interest coverage

Property. A lessee's coverage for the loss that would result from the premature cancellation of a lease that requires less rent than would a new lease for similar property. Coverage is for the difference between the two rental amounts during the remaining lease term.

see: leasehold interest

leasehold profit interest

Property. Coverage for a lessee on leased space that is sublet to another for a higher rent than the lessee pays. The lessee recovers lost rental profit in the event of premature termination of the lease. Termination must be caused by an insured property loss.

see: leasehold interest

leasing or rental concerns—contingent coverage

Automobile. An endorsement (ISO form CA 20 09) to the business auto or truckers' coverage form for firms that lease or rent vehicles which provides contingent liability coverage in the event the lessee's or renter's auto liability coverage has lapsed or has inadequate limits. The company's liability as owner of the vehicle is also covered by this endorsement.

see: business auto coverage form, contingent liability, truckers' coverage form

leave of absence

Employee Benefits. An absence from employment authorized by the employer for a specified reason and period of time. Wages may or may not continue to be paid.

see: break in service, Family and Medical Leave Act, sabbatical, voluntary leave to meet business needs

ledger cost

Life. A life insurance policy's net cost, calculated by deducting the policy's cash value at a specific point in time from the premiums paid to that date, minus dividends paid on the policy.

see: dividend, life insurance

legal department

Insurer Operations. The employees and operations of an insurance company that are responsible for defending claims, drafting and reviewing contracts, monitoring changes in state insurance codes and regulations, and participating in industry lobbying activities.

legal expense insurance

Liability. Insurance, usually written on a group basis, covering attorneys' fees and related legal expenses for consultation, negotiations, and litigation. Benefits are scheduled for each type of legal service, and maximum benefit limits apply.

see: business legal expense insurance, legal expense insurer

legal expense insurer

Insurer Operations. An insurer that writes legal expense insurance. Regulators include in this category both commercial insurers and nonprofit organizations that operate legal expense service plans.

see: business legal expense insurance, legal expense insurance

legal expenses

Insurer Operations. Those legal expenses incurred in relation to the adjustment or settlement of a policyholder's claim.

see: claim expense, defense costs

legal liability indemnity association

Liability. An association of attorneys who form an inter-indemnity trust to mutually insure themselves against claims that may arise out of their legal practice.

see: malpractice insurance

legal list

Insurer Operations/Regulation. A list of securities, specified in insurance department regulations, in which pension funds and insurance companies are permitted to invest.

see: admitted assets

legal reserve

Life. Minimum reserves required by state law or regulation that life insurers must maintain to operate in that state.

see: reserve

legal reserve life insurance company

Life. A life insurance company that maintains reserves at least equal to the minimum prescribed by law or regulation in the state in which it does business. These reserves are based on actuarial formulas and are designed to allow the company to meet all of its financial obligations. An assessment life insurer, conversely, is permitted to assess its policyholders in the event of financial problems.

compare: assessment company; *see*: expense funds, old line company, reserve

legislated insurance coverage

Regulation. Coverages mandated by state or federal laws. *Examples*: Mandatory automobile liability insurance; earthquake insurance in California; crime insurance in New York; flood insurance to qualify for federally insured loans; and COBRA extension/conversion rights.

see: mandated benefits, minimum coverage clause, policy condition laws, standard provisions

lemon aid insurance

Automobile. Coverage indemnifying an auto dealer for a vehicle that is returned by a purchaser under the provisions allowed by state "lemon" laws, which permit a vehicle to be returned if it suffers persistent mechanical problems during its warranty period or other specified time.

lender's bond

Surety. A bond guaranteeing the completion of construction of a building or an improvement to a property, required prior to a lender or mortgagee advancing money to the owner or developer. After completion, the property replaces the bond as security for the loan.

synonym: completion bond; *see*: contract bond

lender's holder in due course coverage

Liability. Coverage usually provided in conjunction with a lender's single interest policy that indemnifies the lender for a loss sustained under Federal Trade Commission regulations, promulgated in 1976, that nullifies a lending institution's defense as a holder in due course of loans purchased by the institution from dealers or vendors. Prior to the change, the institution was immune from any dispute between the purchaser of an item and the seller. The regulation allows the purchaser to assert a claim against both the dealer or vendor and the holder in due course.

compare: holder in due course coverage; *see*: holder in due course, lender's single interest coverage

262

lender's pollution liability insurance

Liability. A form of pollution liability coverage for financial institutions who foreclose on property that is found to be contaminated by hazardous waste. Coverage is provided for government required cleanup of contamination that was present but undetected at the time the property was obtained. Coverage for remedial investigation, feasibility studies, and defense costs resulting from insured locations are included.

see: pollution insurance

lender's single interest coverage

Property. Coverage only for a lending institution's interest in property used as collateral for a loan in case the borrower does not have adequate coverage. A blanket limit of liability is provided for all outstanding collateral, and the premium is based on the outstanding loan balance, which must be periodically reported to the insurer. The amount of recovery is the lesser of the outstanding loan balance or the current value of the collateral. Coverage is not provided for any interest of the borrower.

see: collateral protection insurance, lender's holder in due course coverage, single interest coverage, skip-repossessed vehicle insurance

lending institution

General. Use of this term is generally restricted to public institutions such as public banks, savings and loan associations, and credit unions. Private organizations (such as investment bankers) are generally not included.

see: lender's bond, lender's holder in due course coverage, lender's pollution liability insurance, lender's single interest coverage

lessee

Law. A person who has a right to occupy real estate or use equipment belonging to another pursuant to a lease.

compare: lessor; *see:* leasehold, tenancy

lessees of safe deposit boxes coverage form

Crime. A crime coverage form (ISO form CR 00 10, or form I) providing burglary and robbery coverage for securities and property (other than money and securities) while located in a safe deposit box in a vault in a depository, leased or rented by the insured. The insurance covers insured property during the course of deposit or removal from the safe deposit box.

synonym: crime coverage form I; *see:* crime coverages, property other than money and securities, securities

lessor

Law. An owner of property who rents it to another under the terms of a lease.

compare: lessee; *see:* additional insured—lessor,

leasehold, tenancy

letter of credit (LOC)

General. A financial instrument issued by a bank that guarantees payment of a customer's drafts up to a stated amount. An LOC confers the bank's credit upon the holder. LOCs can be either "revolving" (periodically renewed for a specified amount) or "performance" (guaranteeing performance depending upon the beneficiary's needs).

see: evergreen clause

Reinsurance. A line of credit normally issued by a bank to a reinsurer, which can be drawn down to cover a liability. LOCs can cover the reserve for a loss or unearned premium in lieu of a cash deposit.

see: loss reserve, reinsurance, unearned premium reserve

level commission

Agency/Insurer Operations. An agent's commission structure where first-year and renewal commissions for a particular type of policy are the same.

synonym: flat commission; *compare:* unlevel commission; *see:* agent's commission

level death benefit option

Life. An option under universal life insurance allowing the beneficiary to choose either the face amount of the policy at the time of death or a stipulated percentage of the accumulation value, whichever is greater.

see: accumulation value, face amount, universal life insurance

level premium life insurance

Life. Whole life insurance where the premium remains the same for the policy's entire term. Under this plan, the premium is higher than necessary for the initial years of coverage, then is less than needed for the final years of coverage.

synonym: net level premium; *see:* net level premium reserve, whole life insurance

level term life insurance

Life. Term life insurance that has a constant face value from inception to expiration.

see: term life insurance

leverage fund

Financial Planning.
see: hedge fund

leveraged buyout (LBO)

Financial Planning. The purchase of a corporation or one of its subsidiaries by the use of a significant amount of debt supported by the target corporation's or subsidiary's assets and projected earning stream.

leveraged swap

Financial Planning. A highly speculative financial derivative in the form of a swap where the counterparties agree to exchange the difference between short-term and long-term interest rates.

see: counterparty, financial derivative, swap

liability

Accounting. In accounting, money or property owed or expected to be owed to another person.

see: assets, balance sheet, current liabilities

Law. An actual or potential legal obligation, duty, debt, or responsibility to another person; the obligation to compensate, in whole or in part, a person harmed by one's acts or omissions. Liability insurance policies provide coverage for an insured's legal liability, excluding criminal acts, most intentional torts, and breach of contract.

see: damages, liability insurance, negligence, strict liability, tort

liability control center

Risk Management. A central clearinghouse and coordination center established by an organization for disseminating information and monitoring liability claims. These facilities are usually established by organizations that are subject to professional or product liability claims.

see: loss control, product liability insurance, professional liability insurance

liability coverage exclusion endorsement

Personal. An endorsement (ISO form PP 03 26) to the personal auto policy clarifying that part A (liability coverage) does not include liability for bodily injury to any family member. This endorsement was added in 1993 because some state courts abolished the family immunity doctrine and have permitted family members to bring suit against each other.

see: family exclusion, family member, intra-family immunity, personal auto policy

liability for guests' property—premises coverage form

Crime. A crime form that provides coverage for the insured's legally imposed liability arising out of damage to guests' property while on the insured's premises or in the insured's possession.

synonym: crime coverage form L; *see:* crime coverages, innkeepers' legal liability

liability for guests' property—safe deposit coverage form

Crime. A crime form that covers the insured's legally imposed liability arising out of the loss or damage to guests' property while contained in a safe deposit box on the insured's premises. There is no limitation on the type of property that is covered.

synonym: crime coverage form K; *see:* crime coverages, hotel safe deposit box liability, innkeepers' legal liability

liability insurance

Liability. Insurance that provides indemnity or compensation for a harm or wrong to a third party for which the insured is legally obligated to pay. Usually, the injury or damage is caused by the insured's negligent acts or omissions, but in some situations the law imposes strict liability without regard to negligence, and this may also be covered by liability insurance.

see: casualty insurance, commercial general liability policy, damages, liability (*Law*), negligence, strict liability

Liability Insurance Research Bureau (LIRB)

Organizations. Members: Insurance companies. *Objectives:* Promote research about liability insurance exposures. *Headquarters:* Schaumburg, IL.

liability loss exposure

Liability/Risk Management. A potential loss to an organization from the possibility that a third party may file a lawsuit for negligence or breach of contract, whether or not the suit has merit. Substantial legal defense costs can result from this exposure even if no loss is proved.

see: accidental loss, liability insurance, negligence

liability-over suit

Workers' Compensation.

see: third-party over suit

Liability Risk Retention Act of 1986

Regulation. Federal legislation adopted in 1986 that expanded the provisions of the Product Liability Risk Retention Act of 1981. The primary changes were an expansion of risk retention groups and purchasing groups to all types of liability insurance (except personal liability and workers' compensation) and expansion of authorized groups able to form RRGs and PGs from only product manufacturers to almost all businesses.

synonym: Risk Retention Act; *see:* Product Liability Risk Retention Act of 1981, purchasing group, risk retention group

libel

Law. An untrue, defamatory written statement; a published writing that harms another's reputation, business, or livelihood.

compare: slander; *see:* advertising injury coverage, defamation, libel insurance, noneconomic loss, personal injury

libel insurance

Liability. Insurance providing coverage in the event that an insured without just cause intentionally publishes material or prints a picture that injures the reputation of another person.

compare: slander; *see*: advertising injury coverage, personal injury liability

liberalization clause

Insurer Operations. An insurance policy clause that extends broader legislated or regulated coverages to current policies if they do not affect premiums. An endorsement is not required.

license

Regulation. Legal authority granted by the state for a specified activity or business enterprise. State insurance departments grant licenses to insurance companys, agents, brokers, and other entities to transact insurance-related business within its borders.

see: admitted insurer, certificate of authority, certificate of convenience, licensee

Property. Intangible property in the form of contractual permission to market, sell, manufacture or reproduce a product or service, or to use a brand name, owned, patented, copyrighted or trademarked by another (the licensor).

see: intangible property (1), intellectual property, piracy (*Property*)

license bond

Surety. A bond guaranteeing that a person who has been issued a license will comply with the laws, regulations and ordinances associated with the issuance of the license.

see: permit bond

licensee

Agency/Insurer Operations. An individual or organization that has been approved by a state department of insurance to act as an insurance company, agent, broker, solicitor, consultant or other entity to conduct insurance-related business within that state.

see: admitted insurer, prelicensing education requirement

Liability. A person who enters or remains on another's premises with the express or implied consent of the owner for the licensee's own purposes, benefit, or convenience. Historically, the owner's standard of care owed toward a licensee was merely to refrain from reckless or wanton disregard for safety, and the licensee entered at his own risk. Today, the law generally requires a standard of due care or reasonable precaution.

compare: invitee, trespasser; *see*: degree of care

Property. A person or entity that has received a contractual license to market, sell, manufacture, or reproduce a product or service, or to use a brand name, owned by another (the licensor).

see: license (*Property*)

lien

Law. A claim or encumbrance on property by a creditor or a service provider pending payment of a debt; a creditor's conditional interest in property taken as security for a debt, or any similar right by operation of law.

see: encumbrance, hypothecate, mortgage, possessory lien, tax lien

lien plan

Life. A life insurance policy issued at a standard premium for a substandard risk, but with a provision that less than the face benefit amount would be paid in the initial years of coverage. This type of plan is illegal in many states.

compare: graded death benefit

life annuity

Life.

see: annuity

life care contract

Health. A contract entered into by older adults where occasional, simple medical services are provided in addition to room and board, for the duration of the resident's life, or for a period in excess of one year. The consideration for such a service is an entry fee, with or without subsequent, periodic charges.

synonym: life care provider; *see*: life care facility

life care facility

Health. A facility that provides board and lodging, nursing services, medical care, or other health-related services, pursuant to an agreement effective for the life of the individual or for a period in excess of one year.

synonym: continuing care facility; *see*: life care contract, residential care facility, skilled nursing facility

life care provider

Health.

see: life care contract

Life Communicators Association (LCA)

Organizations. Members: Specialists in the areas of life insurance advertising, sales promotion, public relations and corporate communications. *Objectives*: Conducts workshops for junior members. Distributes case histories describing activities of member companies. *Founded*: 1933. *Headquarters*: Des Moines, IA.

life expectancy

Life. The length of time a person of a given age can

be expected to live, based on mortality tables.

see: mortality rate, mortality table, normal life expectancy

life expectancy term insurance

Life. Term life insurance where the policy term is based on an individual's life expectancy, as opposed to a given period of time, such as five or ten years.

see: term life insurance

life income option

Life. A life insurance settlement option under which a beneficiary may have policy proceeds converted to a life annuity for the beneficiary. Annuity payments are made during the beneficiary's life in an amount determined by the life expectancy at the time the settlement is chosen.

compare: fixed amount option, fixed period option, interest option, life income with period certain option; *see*: settlement options

life income with period certain option

Life. A life insurance settlement option under which a beneficiary may have policy proceeds converted to a life annuity for the beneficiary, with the benefit period based on the beneficiary's life expectancy and payments that continue for that period of time whether or not the beneficiary lives.

compare: fixed amount option, fixed period option, interest option, life income option; *see*: settlement options

life insurance

Life. Insurance that pays a specified sum of money to designated beneficiaries if the insured person dies during the policy term.

compare: annuity; *see*: adjustable life insurance, cash surrender value, credit life insurance, decreasing term life insurance, deferred dividend policy, deferred life insurance, extended term life insurance, endowment policy, family income life insurance, family life policy, family maintenance life insurance, flexible premium life insurance, group life insurance, indexed life insurance, individual contract, industrial life insurance, interest-sensitive life insurance, joint life and survivor insurance, joint life insurance, jumping juvenile life insurance, level premium life insurance, level term life insurance, life expectancy term insurance, life insurance trust, limited payment life insurance, limited life insurance policy, monthly debit ordinary life insurance, multiple protection life insurance, National Service Life Insurance, ordinary life insurance, paid up at age life insurance, permanent life insurance, re-entry term life insurance, renewable term life insurance, savings bank life insurance, Servicemen's Group Life Insurance, single premium life insurance, split life insurance, survivor

life insurance, term life insurance, universal life insurance, universal variable life insurance, variable life insurance, variable premium life insurance, Veterans Group Life Insurance, whole life insurance

Life Insurance Agency Management Association (LIAMA)

Organizations. Members: Life insurance agency managers. *Objectives*: Seeks solutions to the problems of administering the agency force of a life insurer. *Founded*: 1945. *Headquarters*: Hartford, CT.

Life Insurance Association of America (LIAA)

Organizations. A former life insurance organization that served as the legislative relations arm for a large segment of the life insurance industry. It is now part of the American Council of Life Insurance.

see: American Council of Life Insurance

Life Insurance Company Office Management Association (LICOMA)

Organizations. Members: Administrative, management and staff personnel of life and health insurers. *Objectives*: Promote information exchange concerning life and health insurance company office operations. *Headquarters*: Oklahoma City, OK.

life insurance in force

Health/Life.

see: in-force business

Life Insurance Institute of Canada

Organizations. Members: Life insurers in Canada. *Objectives*: Encourages the development of a thorough knowledge of the business of life insurance. *Founded*: 1936. *Headquarters*: Toronto, Ontario.

Life Insurance Marketing and Research Association (LIMRA)

Organizations. Members: Life insurance companies. *Objectives*: Conducts market, consumer, economic, financial, manpower and human resources research. Provides executive and field management programs. *Founded*: 1916. *Headquarters*: Farmington, CT.

life insurance settlement modes

Life.

see: settlement options

life insurance trust

Life. A life insurance policy whose benefits are used to establish a trust that distributes the policy proceeds based upon the trust agreement.

see: accumulation trust, trust

Life Insurers Conference (LIC)

Organizations. Members: Multiple line and combined life, accident and health insurance companies. *Objectives*: Promotes the exchange of ideas among its members. Supports the member's interests in legislative and regulatory activities. *Founded*: 1910. *Headquarters*: Atlanta, GA.

life maintenance contract

Health/Life. A contract providing life, health and disability income coverages on condition that the subscriber maintain a healthy lifestyle. Healthful activities, such as exercise, diet, and stop-smoking programs may be included.

see: wellness program

Life Management Institute

Organizations. A unit of the Life Office Management Association that prepares and administers educational materials for the Fellow, Life Management Institute program. Upon successful completion of its examinations, the student receives the FLMI designation. It also assists in the development of the curriculum for the Associate in Insurance Accounting and Finance and the Associate in Research and Planning designations.

see: Associate in Insurance Accounting and Finance, Associate in Research and Planning, Fellow of the Life Management Institute, Life Office Management Association

Life Office Management Association (LOMA)

Organizations. Members: U.S. and Canadian life and health insurers. Associate members include life insurers in 32 countries. Affiliate members include firms providing professional support to member companies. *Objectives*: Provides educational programs; confers the Fellow, Life Management Institute (FLMI) designation upon individuals who pass a series of exams. *Founded*: 1924. *Headquarters*: Atlanta, GA

see: Associate, Customer Service; Associate, Life and Health Claims; Fellow of the Life Management Institute; Life Management Institute

life risk factors

Insurer Operations/Life. Information needed to underwrite a life insurance policy such as an individual's age, sex, weight, height, tobacco use, heredity, and occupation. Statistically, these factors are related to an individual's life span. Some jurisdictions prohibit sex and heredity from being used as rating factors.

see: discrimination, rate making

Life Safety Code

Loss Control. Guidelines published by the National Fire Protection Association for fire safety for specific types of buildings. These standards have been incorporated into, or are referred to by, most city or county ordinances in the United States.

see: National Fire Protection Association

life salvage

Ocean Marine. A claim against the owner of a vessel for a salvage award based upon the rescue of persons. Life salvage alone brings no salvage award, which is given out of property saved. However, someone who takes part in life-saving rescue operations during an accident that gives rise to the salvage of property may claim a share of the remuneration given to salvors of the vessel or cargo.

see: salvage

life underwriter

Life. A life insurance agent.

see: agent

Life Underwriter Political Action Committee (LUPAC)

Organizations. A life insurance lobbying organization created by the National Association of Life Underwriters.

see: National Association of Life Underwriters

Life Underwriter Training Council Fellow (LUTCF)

Organizations. The Life Underwriter Training Council and the National Association of Life Underwriters award this designation to life underwriters who have successfully completed the prescribed LUTC courses and are members of the NALU.

see: Life Underwriter Training Council, National Association of Life Underwriters

Life Underwriter Training Council (LUTC)

Organizations. Members: Life underwriters who take sales training courses sponsored by local life underwriter associations. *Objectives*: Provide vocational sales training and life underwriter educational programs. *Founded*: 1947. *Headquarters*: Washington, D.C.

Life Underwriters Association of Canada

Organizations. Members: Life insurance company underwriters in Canada. *Objectives*: Lobbies and educates those in the field of life insurance. Sponsors the Chartered Life Underwriter (CLU) designation in Canada. *Founded*: 1906. *Headquarters*: Don Mills, Ontario.

life underwriters' professional liability insurance

Professional Liability. A form of insurance agents' errors and omissions insurance for life insurance or general agents that provides coverage for liability for negligent acts, errors or omissions in the conduct of the business as an agent for the companies designated in a schedule attached to the policy. Coverage is provided on a claims-made basis.

see: agents' errors and omissions insurance

lifetime disability benefit

Health. Periodic payments under a disability benefit policy to replace lost income for the insured's entire disability period, if necessary for life.

see: disability income insurance

lifetime policy

Health/Life. A life insurance or disability policy that is noncancelable or is guaranteed renewable, usually for as long as the insured lives. Some policies of this type terminate when the insured reaches a specified age (e.g., 65).

compare: optionally renewable contract; *see*: guaranteed insurability, guaranteed renewable, noncancelable policy

lighter

Ocean Marine.

see: barge

lighter aboard ship (LASH)

Ocean Marine. An ocean vessel that carries specially designed barges.

see: barge

lightning

Property. A natural electrical discharge in the atmosphere from one cloud to another or from a cloud to the earth. It is an insurable peril, normally covered by a standard fire policy. It can ignite a fire, making it impossible to distinguish between lightning and fire as the cause of a loss.

see: causes of loss—basic form, fire insurance, New York standard fire policy, standing timer insurance

limit of liability

Insurer Operations. The maximum amount an insured may collect, or for which an insured is protected, under the terms of a policy.

synonym: amount of insurance, limits; *see*: aggregate benefits, aggregate limit, aggregate operations liability limit, aggregate product liability limit, aggregate protection liability limit, face amount, penalty, per cause maximum limit, per occurrence limit, per person limit

limit of liability rule

Property. A rule that allocates property insurance losses among insurers providing coverage on the same property.

see: contribution by limits, other insurance provision, pro rata liability clause

limitation of actions

Insurer Operations. A restriction on the period of time during which an insured may bring suit for a claim under a policy or during which legal rights are enforceable.

see: statute of limitations

limitations

Insurer Operations. Exceptions and limitations on the coverages provided by an insurance policy.

see: exclusion

limited coverage for customers

Automobile. A garage policy provision that limits liability coverage for customers of auto dealerships to the limits of the financial responsibility law in the state where the vehicle is principally garaged. This coverage does not apply if the customer has other applicable insurance.

see: dealer class plan, drive-away collision, garage coverage form

limited damage waiver (LDW)

Automobile.

see: collision damage waiver

limited form vendor's endorsement

Liability. An endorsement that extends a manufacturer's liability policy to include a vendor of the manufacturer's product as an additional insured against product liability claims. The limited vendor's endorsement excludes coverage for such things as the unauthorized sale or distribution of the product, acts that change the condition of the product, and failure to maintain the product in a merchantable condition.

compare: broad form vendor's endorsement; *see*: product liability insurance, vendor's endorsement

limited health benefit plan

Health. A health benefit plan that restricts covered services to a medical specialization or a group of related specializations, such as psychology and family counseling.

see: health benefit plan

limited liability company (LLC)

Law. A business organization that is not a corporation (though in a few states a corporate form is required) whose members have limited liability and actively participate in management. Members are taxed individually, as in a partnership; but limited liability for the entity's debts despite a member's active management differentiates an LLC from a partnership.

compare: corporation, partnership

limited license

Regulation. An agent's license conferring limited or restricted powers, such as one for a single line of business or for placement of out-of-state risks.

see: certificate of convenience, license

limited life and health insurer

Life. A life or health insurer that issues nonassessable policies with limited benefits.

see: nonassessable policy

limited life insurance policy

Life. A life insurance policy that pays benefits only if the insured dies from a specified cause (e.g., cancer or AIDS).

see: cancer insurance, specified disease insurance

limited partnership

Law. A partnership consisting of one or more limited partners (whose liability for partnership debts is limited to the amount invested) and one or more general partners (whose liability for partnership debts is unlimited). To create a limited partnership, a certificate must be filed with a state official. A limited partner may lose the shield of limited liability if he or she actively participates in the management of the business.

compare: limited liability company; *see*: limited partnership investor bond insurance, limited partnership liability insurance, partnership

limited partnership investor bond insurance

Financial Guaranty. A form of financial guaranty insurance that guarantees fulfillment of the obligations of a person investing in a limited partnership. If the person ceases making payments, the insurer will pay the outstanding amount in installments over the remaining payment period. The insurance is irrevocable and will remain in full force until all of the insured obligations are paid. *Example*: If the partnership has agreed to purchase a building, and each partner agrees to pay $1,000 a month for mortgage payments, this insurance would respond if one of the partners is unable to continue her required payments.

see: financial guaranty insurance

limited partnership liability insurance

Professional Liability. A form of directors' and officers' liability insurance that is amended to provide coverage for the general partners of a limited partnership. Coverage is provided for wrongful acts that affect the limited partnership, such as mismanagement, negligence, waste of partnership assets, and violation of securites laws. Coverage is usually provided on a claims-made basis.

synonym: general partners' liability insurance

limited payment life insurance

Life. A life insurance policy that covers the insured's entire life, with premium payments required only for a specified period of years.

see: paid up at age life insurance

limited risk health policy

Health. A health or Medicare supplement insurance policy often sold through newspaper or television advertising. Coverage is usually subject to low limits.

see: Medicare supplement insurance, newspaper policy

limited specified perils

Automobile. Automobile physical damage coverage for the specific perils of fire, lightning, explosion, theft, windstorm, or flood or the sinking, burning, collision, or derailment of any conveyance transporting the covered vehicle. This form of coverage can be provided by the use of the specified causes of loss endorsement.

compare: comprehensive coverage, fire coverage, fire and theft coverage, fire theft and windstorm coverage; *see*: specified causes of loss

limited theft coverage endorsement

Personal. An endorsement (ISO form DP 04 73) to a dwelling policy that adds theft coverage for personal property in the dwelling that is owned or used by the dwelling's owner. This coverage is designed for owners who do not occupy the dwelling and does not provide any coverage for tenants.

compare: broad theft coverage endorsement; *see*: dwelling policy

limits

Health/Life.

see: age limits

line

General. A class of insurance. Most insurers may be classified as either life and health or property and casualty. Sometimes three categories are used: life and health; fire and marine (which includes most property risks); and casualty (which includes most liability risks). Lines can also be classified according to whether the insured risks are primarily related to individuals and families (personal lines) or to businesses (commercial lines). State insurance regulators may employ any of these broad classes for some purposes, but more specific lines—automobile, homeowners, workers' compensation, life and annuity, health and accident, commercial liability, etc.—define the covered risks more clearly.

synonym: line of business; *see*: monoline policy, multiple line policy, package policy, risk classification

Insurer Operations. A term initially introduced at Lloyd's of London for the amount of liability assumed by an underwriter. A Lloyd's underwriter indicates the amount of liability assumed and initial acceptance on one line of a slip.

see: Lloyd's of London, slip

Reinsurance. The amount or limit of insurance that a reinsurer commits to a ceding company on a class of risks.

see: gross line, lines, net line

line card

Property. A property underwriter's record of the limits of liability written on a specific policy.

line guide

Insurer Operations.

see: line sheet

line of business

General.

see: line

line of credit

Risk Management. A prearranged borrowing limit established by an individual or organization with a financial institution.

synonym: credit line; *see*: commitment fee

line sheet

Insurer Operations. The schedule an insurer maintains to guide its underwriters as to the maximum amounts of insurance that can be written on different classes of risks.

synonym: line guide; *see*: rate card, underwriting

line slip

Insurer Operations.

see: slip

line underwriter

Insurer Operations. An underwriter who is responsible for evaluating individual applicants and policies subject to renewal.

synonym: desk underwriter; *compare*: staff underwriter; *see*: underwriter

lines

Insurer Operations. The amount of risk a reinsurer assumes, which is usually expressed in multiples of the net retention under a surplus treaty.

see: line (*Reinsurance*)

Link trainer

Aviation. A laboratory device that simulates flight conditions used to train pilots in the skills required for safe flying.

synonym: flight simulator

Linton yield method

Life. A method developed by actuary M. Albert Linton to measure the cost of life insurance. A comparison is made between a whole life policy and a decreasing term policy combined with an investment fund. The yield or return on the investment fund is compared to the cash value of the whole life policy after a specified time to determine which program should be selected.

see: interest adjusted cost

liquefaction

Property. In an earthquake, the percolation of subsurface water through unconsolidated soils such as sand, gravel, or silt, or the changing of unconsolidated soils into an unstable form to the point where it acts as a liquid and causes ground failure.

see: earthquake, ground failure

liquefied petroleum gas (LPG)

Loss Control. A compressed gas consisting of flammable light hydrocarbons (propane, butane, ethane or methane) and used as a fuel or as raw material for chemical synthesis.

liquidated damages

Law. The damages specified by contract in the event of a breach by one of the contracting parties.

see: breach, damages

liquidation

Regulation. The conversion of an insolvent organization's assets into cash in order to pay creditors. An insurance department takes this action after it has determined that an insolvent insurer cannot be rehabilitated. Its business is wound up, and any remaining assets are used to pay policyholder claims and other creditors.

see: insolvency, liquidation distribution, rehabilitation, seizure order, voidable preference

liquidation charge

Life. A penalty fee charged by an annuity or mutual fund for an early withdrawal of funds that have accumulated. The charge is made to allow the insurer or fund administrator to recover expenses associated with marketing and administration, which are higher in the initial years.

liquidation distribution

Regulation. The priority of disbursement of the assets of an insurer that has been declared insolvent and for which a liquidation order has been issued by a government regulator. Generally, but not necessarily, an insurer's assets are distributed among its creditors in the following order: 1. Regulator's oversight costs during the company's insolvency, liquidation or rehabilitation, including expenses of a state guaranty fund and attorney fees; 2. Wages owed to employees other than officers of the insurer (often for a certain period preceding the action that results in liquidation) and liens secured prior to regulatory proceedings; 3. Claims by policyholders and beneficiaries and covered liability claims against insureds; 4. Claims of general creditors and unsecured governmental claims for taxes; 5. Claims of guaranty association certificate holders, guaranty capital shareholders, surplus note holders, shareholders, members and other owners.

liquidation period

Life. The period during which an insurer makes annuity benefit payments, i.e., draws down or liquidates the accumulated annuity benefits. Depending on whether the annuity is a pure or refund annuity, the liquidation period ends either when all payments have been made or when the annuitant dies.

compare: accumulation period; *see:* pure annuity, refund annuity

liquidity

Risk Management. The ability of an organization to readily convert its assets into cash with little loss in the asset's value.

liquidity risk

Risk Management. The risk that an individual or organization may not have sufficient cash or other liquid assets to function normally.

see: business income coverage form, market risk

liquor bond

Surety.

see: alcohol bond

liquor liability coverage

Liability. Special liability coverage for insureds who are in the business of manufacturing, distributing, selling, or serving alcoholic beverages. For these insureds, liability can arise from such circumstances as contributing to the intoxication of an individual; furnishing alcoholic beverages to an underage person; or violating any statute, ordinance or regulation relating to the sale, gift, distribution or use of alcoholic beverages. (ISO form CG 00 33 and the claims-made form CG 00 34.)

see: alcoholic beverage liability insurance, dram shop liability insurance, liquor liability laws

liquor liability laws

Liability. State or local statutes ("dram shop acts") that establish the liability of a business that sells or serves alcoholic beverages to customers for injuries caused by intoxicated customers to third parties. Laws sometimes also include people who serve alcohol to guests.

see: dram shop liability insurance, liquor liability coverage

listed waste

Loss Control. A hazardous waste that that appears on the list of specific wastes considered to be hazardous pursuant to the Resource Conservation and Recovery Act.

see: hazardous waste, Resource Conservation and Recovery Act

litigation

Law. The attempt to resolve a dispute through proceedings in a court of law; a lawsuit.

compare: alternative dispute resolution, arbitration; *see:* civil law (1), defendant, plaintiff, pleading, process, tort

litigation bond

Surety.

see: court bond

livestock auction market form

Inland Marine. A specialized livestock insurance form covering a livestock auction market owner for livestock consigned to the market, from the point of origin to when the livestock is unloaded.

see: animal insurance, livestock floater

livestock commercial feedlot reporting form

Inland Marine. Specialized livestock insurance written on a monthly reporting form basis, covering livestock of others while in the insured's commercial feedlot.

see: animal insurance, livestock floater

livestock floater

Inland Marine. Coverage on farm or ranch animals (e.g., cattle, sheep, swine, horses, mules or goats) for death or destruction directly resulting from named perils such as fire, lightning, windstorm, earthquake, flood, attack by wild animals, drowning or accidental shooting. Exclusions often include quarantine losses or confiscation by civil authority.

compare: livestock mortality insurance; *see:* animal insurance, floater policy

livestock insurance

Inland Marine. Coverage for losses involving domestic farm or ranch animals, such as cattle or horses raised for profit. Included within this term are animal mortality and named perils property insurance coverages.

see: animal insurance, animal mortality insurance, livestock auction market form, livestock commercial feedlot reporting form, livestock floater, livestock mortality insurance, livestock transit insurance

livestock mortality insurance

Inland Marine. Specialized livestock insurance that provides the equivalent of life insurance coverage on such livestock as cattle, sheep, swine, horses, mules, goats or zoo animals. It provides coverage for death resulting from natural causes and all-risk coverage as respects physical perils, including acts of individuals other than the owner or employees of the owner.

compare: bloodstock insurance, livestock floater; *see:* animal insurance, breeder's policy, poultry insurance

livestock transit insurance

Inland Marine. Specialized livestock insurance covering the death or crippling of livestock while in transit by air, rail or truck.

see: animal insurance

living benefits

Life. An option under some life insurance policies by which the insurer provides discounted policy proceeds (face amount, cash value and dividends, if any) to a terminally ill insured. This permits the insured to meet extraordinary living, medical or hospice expenses.

synonym: accelerated death benefits; *see:* reverse-annuity mortgage, viatical settlement

living trust

see: inter vivos trust

living will

Health. A written statement by a legally competent adult instructing attending physicians to withhold or withdraw life-sustaining procedures in the event of a terminal health condition. The statement must be signed, dated, and witnessed by a person or persons having no interest in the declarant's estate. In effect, it limits what may be spent for medical treatment in order to preserve the individual's estate. State laws provide that withholding medical treatment pursuant to such a statement does not constitute suicide or assisting suicide.

synonym: natural death declaration; *see:* advance directive, brain death, do not resuscitate order

Lloyd's

Insurer Operations.
see: Lloyd's of London

Lloyd's association

Insurer Operations. A group of individuals formed to assume risks, patterned after the Lloyd's of London concept. Several Lloyd's associations exist in Texas and in other states.

see: Lloyd's of London

Lloyd's audit

Insurer Operations. An annual audit of the accounts of Lloyd's underwriters. It was begun in 1908 to assure the individual solvency of the underwriting accounts of all members of Lloyd's.

see: Lloyd's of London

Lloyd's broker

Insurer Operations. An individual—usually associated with a firm that is authorized to go onto the "floor" of Lloyd's of London—who negotiates contracts with a Lloyd's underwriter on behalf of clients seeking insurance coverage.

see: Lloyd's of London

Lloyd's member

Insurer Operations. An individual or corporation (after 1993) elected to membership of Lloyd's of London. Individually, they are insurers; collectively, they are Lloyd's. Members must have substantial worth (about $200,000 for Americans). They pledge their entire personal assets to pay Lloyd's claims; usually, they join with other members to form a Lloyd's syndicate.

synonym: names; *see:* Lloyd's of London, Lloyd's syndicate

Lloyd's names

Insurer Operations.
see: Lloyd's member

Lloyd's of London

Insurer Operations. The centuries-old insurance exchange that traces its beginnings to Lloyd's Coffee House in London. It provides insurance and reinsurance coverages through underwriting syndicates. The syndicates, a form of insurance company, are funded by individual members (or "names") who independently assume a proportionate part of the losses. The liability of the names is unlimited. The syndicates are managed by general managers who have underwriters on their staffs.

synonym: Lloyd's; *compare:* insurance exchange; *see:* American Lloyd's, American Trust Fund, Committee of Lloyd's, line, Lloyd's association, Lloyd's audit, Lloyd's broker, Lloyd's member, Lloyd's Premium Trust Fund, Lloyd's property first loss scale, Lloyd's Register of Shipping, Lloyd's syndicate, Lloyd's underwriter, London Form B, London market, London rig slip, open slip, slip, tribunalization

Lloyd's Premium Trust Fund

Insurer Operations. A trust fund established by Lloyd's of London into which Lloyd's underwriters must place premiums. The premiums are held until the end of a specified period (usually three years), and claims against the account are paid from this fund. At the end of this period, the underwriter is entitled to any profits that have been earned.

see: American Trust Fund, guaranty fund, Lloyd's of London

Lloyd's property first loss scale

Property. A scale frequently used by property underwriters in determining the allocation of premium between a primary and excess layer.

see: layering

Lloyd's Register of Shipping

Ocean Marine. A record of sea-going vessels maintained by Lloyd's in alphabetical order.

see: American Bureau of Shipping Record, Lloyd's of London

Lloyd's slip
Insurer Operations.
see: slip

Lloyd's syndicate
Insurer Operations. A group of persons at Lloyd's of London who have entrusted their business to a team of underwriters to underwrite on their behalf. Lloyd's syndicates are the source of underwriting capacity for obtaining coverage on a risk.
see: Lloyd's of London, Lloyd's underwriter

Lloyd's underwriter
Insurer Operations. An individual who is located on the floor of Lloyd's of London and acts on behalf of a Lloyd's syndicate to accept or reject risks submitted by Lloyd's brokers.
see: Lloyd's broker, Lloyd's of London, Lloyd's syndicate, underwriter

load
Financial Planning. The sales charge, commission or fee paid when purchasing or selling mutual fund shares.
see: back end load, breakpoint, front end load, load fund, low load fund, no load fund, mutual fund

load fund
Financial Planning. A mutual fund that charges its participants a commission (load), and sells its shares through an outside sales organization.
compare: low load fund, no load fund; *see*: mutual fund

loading
Insurer Operations.
see: expense loading

loading or unloading
Automobile/Liability. Liability coverage under a commercial automobile policy for bodily injury or property damage to others that may occur while merchandise or goods are on or in the insured's vehicle. Loading or unloading begins when goods are removed from the site where they were accepted for shipment and ends when the goods are delivered. Prior to loading and after unloading, liability coverage is provided by a commercial general liability policy or other form of premises liability policy.
see: business auto coverage form, commercial general liability policy, dual coverage

loan receipt
Life. A document signed by a policyholder that acknowledges that the funds from a life insurance policy loan have been received.

loan value
Life. The amount that a life insurance policyholder can borrow against a policy with a cash value provision.
see: cash surrender value, policy loan

local
Automobile. A rating classification in commercial automobile insurance for any vehicle not frequently operated beyond a 50-mile radius of the vehicle's garage location.
compare: intermediate, long distance, radius of operation

local agent
Agency. An agent that represents an insurance company in a specific geographic territory.
see: agent

local alarm system
Loss Control. Either a burglar or a fire alarm system that sets off an audible sound at the location where it is installed.
compare: auxiliary alarm system, central station alarm system, proprietary alarm system, remote station alarm system, water flow alarm

local underlier policy
International. An admitted insurance policy issued in the country where the risk exposure exists to support a controlled master or global insurance program. The policy is issued to comply with admitted insurance regulations and duplicates portions of the coverage provided by the master policy.
see: admitted insurance regulations, controlled master insurance program, fronting, global insurance program, master insurance policy

lock-out device
Loss Control. A locking device used during construction, maintenance or repair of a large engine or mechanical system to prevent activating a switch, valve, etc. Each worker on the project holds a unique key to a lock-out device, and the machine or system can be reactivated only after all workers have removed their lock-outs.

lockbox plan
Insurer Operations. An arrangement between an insurer or agent and a bank for insureds to send premium payments to the bank, which deposits the checks into the insurer's or agent's account. This speeds up the collection process and increases investment income.

locked-in clause
Financial Planning. A provision in some mortgages that prohibits prepayment of the monthly mortgage installments or charges a penalty for prepayment.
see: mortgage

loggers' property damage liability insurance

Liability/Property. A special coverage that combines standing timber property insurance and fire liability insurance. It is designed to protect a contractor logging on land owned by others. Coverage is provided for physical damage to or destruction of property of others, including loss of use arising out of an occurrence connected with logging. It also includes the cost to fight a fire caused by the logger's negligence.

see: fire damage liability, standing timber insurance

lognormal distribution

Risk Management. An actuarial distribution curve that is skewed to the right. If the logarithms of individual severities are calculated, they will fall into a normal distribution.

see: distribution curve

Loman Foundation

Organizations.

see: CPCU-Harry J. Loman Foundation

London form B

Liability. A property damage liability form developed in the London market that provides extremely broad coverage.

see: property damage liability coverage

London market

Insurer Operations. Lloyd's of London and English insurance companies with offices in London. Frequently, a Lloyd's broker's line slip will be completed using London market companies.

see: Lloyd's of London

London rig slip

Insurer Operations. An open slip on the London market that offers coverage for the physical damage exposures of offshore drilling platforms during construction and operations. It is the largest market for rig insurance, affording close to $800 million in coverage for any one risk, anywhere in the world.

see: Lloyd's of London, open slip

long distance

Automobile. A rating classification in commercial automobile insurance for a vehicle that is customarily driven at a distance of over 200 miles from its garage location.

synonym: long haul; *compare*: intermediate, local, radius of operation; *see*: zone rating

long haul

Automobile.

see: long distance

long hedge

Financial Planning.

see: buy hedge

long sale

Financial Planning. The selling of securities by an investor who owns them; a normal securities trade.

compare: short sale

long-tail liability

Liability. Liability for injuries that take many years before they become known to the insured and are reported as claims. Examples are product liability and medical malpractice claims.

see: continuous trigger theory, exposure theory, injury-in-fact theory, Keene doctrine, manifestation theory, occurrence trigger

long term agreement

International. A contractual agreement between an insurer and insured for a 3, 5, or 10 year policy period. Typically the agreement provides that the insurance contracts issued in conjunction with it are noncancelable by either party except for very limited conditions (e.g., material change in exposure). The agreement provides a premium rate discount and premium stability over the contract term. These contracts are designed to build a relationship between the insured and insurer. They are frequently issued in Austria and Italy.

long-term care facility

Health.

see: extended care facility, long-term care insurance

long-term care insurance

Health. Any insurance policy or rider intended to provide coverage for not less than twelve months for medically necessary diagnostic, therapeutic or personal care services provided in a setting other than an acute care unit of a hospital. Coverage is often subject to a daily limit (typically, from $40 to $80) and may be subject to a maximum period (e.g., 48 months).

see: custodial care, extended care facility

long-term debt

Accounting. A debt that extends beyond twelve months and is considered a long-term liability.

compare: short-term debt

long-term disability insurance (LTD)

Health. Coverage that provides an individual with monthly income payments during a period of disability in excess of 90 days due to a covered illness or accident. Most policies of this type terminate income payments at age 65.

see: disability income insurance

Longshore and Harbor Workers' Compensation Act (LHWCA)

Regulation/Workers' Compensation. A federal law (U.S. Code Title 33, Chapter 18) passed in 1927 that specifies the liability of employers for maritime employees other than ships' officers and crew members. The law applies to longshore workers when loading and unloading cargo and others "employed in maritime employment in whole or in part, upon the navigable waters of the United States." Amendments to the Act have extended this coverage to include seaside areas. (In 1984, the Act name was changed from "Longshoremen's and Harbor Workers' Compensation Act.")

see: Defense Base Act, Jones Act, Longshore and Harbor Workers' Compensation Act coverage endorsement, Nonappropriated Fund Instrumentalities Act, Outer Continental Shelf Lands Act

Longshore and Harbor Workers' Compensation Act coverage endorsement

Workers' Compensation. An endorsement (NCCI form WC 00 01 06A) that extends coverage under a workers' compensation policy to include benefits to employees designated by the Longshore and Harbor Workers' Compensation Act.

see: Longshore and Harbor Workers' Compensation Act, workers' compensation insurance

Longshore and Harbor Workers' Compensation Act rate change endorsement

Workers' Compensation. An endorsement (NCCI form WC 00 04 08) to a workers' compensation policy to indicate that rate changes for federal classification coverages have been approved by the rating bureau.

see: Longshore and Harbor Workers' Compensation Act, rating bureau, workers' compensation insurance

loss

General. A decrease or disappearance of value, especially if caused by an insured peril; the basis of a claim for indemnity from an insurer or for damages from another person.

see: consequential damage, economic loss, direct loss, injury, noneconomic loss, progressive loss

Insurer Operations. A claim either paid or payable; benefits paid pursuant to the insurer's policy obligations.

see: claim, expected losses, incurred losses, incurred but not reported, notice of loss, proof of loss

loss adjustment expense

Insurer Operations. The expense involved in settling a loss, excluding the actual value of the loss.

see: claim expense

loss assessment coverage

Property. Property insurance (ISO form CP 04 19) for a condominium unit owner, covering assessments charged by a condominium association for a loss to the property. The policy pays the amount of the assessment, if the loss is caused by an insured peril.

see: condominium commercial unit owners' coverage

loss assumption

Reinsurance.

see: assumed reinsurance

Risk Management.

see: retention, risk management, self-insurance

loss avoidance

Risk Management.

see: risk avoidance

loss clause

Property.

see: automatic reinstatement clause

loss constant

Insurer Operations. A charge included in the premium calculation for small risks to cover administrative expenses of writing low premium policies.

see: administrative expenses, minimum premium, minimum rate, rate making

loss control

Loss Control. Prevention and reduction of losses. An insured, often in consultation with an underwriter or loss control specialist, takes measures to reduce the frequency of losses and to minimize the financial impact or severity of a loss.

see: accident prevention, loss control specialist, loss prevention, loss reduction

loss control policy statement

Risk Management. A document—usually prepared by a risk manager or loss control specialist and often approved by a firm's officers or directors—that provides information about loss control objectives to management and employees.

see: risk management policy statement

Loss Control Section, CPCU Society

Organizations. An interest section of the CPCU Society that promotes innovative loss control techniques, new loss control applications, and relevant legislation.

see: CPCU Society

loss control specialist

Loss Control. A person charged with the responsibility of controlling losses, often called a *loss prevention engineer* or *safety consultant*. The title of loss prevention engineer is usually associated with property loss prevention. A safety consultant usually focuses on employee or public safety.

synonym: loss prevention engineer; *see*: Certified Safety Professional, loss control

loss conversion factor (LCF)

Liability/Workers' Compensation. A factor (e.g., 1.10, 1.15, 1.20) that is multiplied by incurred losses to cover claim adjusting expenses and the insurer's claim service. The resulting figure represents *converted losses*, a value often used in the calculation of retrospective rating and retention (dividend) plans.

compare: loss development factor; *see*: converted losses, incurred losses, retrospective rating plan

loss cost rating

Insurer Operations. A rating method developed by the Insurance Services Office to replace advisory (manual) rates. Loss cost rates provide an insurer with the portion of a rate not including expenses, other than loss adjusting expenses, or profit. They are based on past aggregate losses and loss adjustment expenses projected, through development, to their ultimate value and, through trending, to a future time. The expense and profit components to derive final rates must be added by the insurer, based on its own costs for these items.

synonym: advisory loss cost rating; *see*: manual rates, loss development, rate making, trending

loss damage waiver (LDW)

Automobile.

see: collision damage waiver

loss development

Insurer Operations/Risk Management. The increase or decrease in the value of losses that occurs between two loss evaluation dates.

see: loss development factor, trending

loss development factor (LDF)

Insurer Operations/Risk Management. A factor (expressed as a percentage) designed to correct errors in estimating the reserves for known but unsettled losses and to make an allowance for incurred but not reported losses.

compare: loss conversion factor; *see*: incurred but not reported, rate making, trending

Loss Executives Association (LEA)

Organizations. Members: Loss executives for insurance companies. *Objectives*: Exchanges information between members and liaison with independent adjusters. *Founded*: 1921. *Headquarters*: Parsippany, NJ.

loss expectancy

Insurer Operations. An underwriter's estimate of the losses that a large risk will generate during the next policy period, based on prior loss experience and projected exposure bases (e.g., receipts, payroll, vehicles). Consideration may be given to the potential reduction in losses from prevention activities or a change in the risk's operations.

synonym: loss pick

loss experience

Insurer Operations. A summary of losses for a specific insured, agency, territory or class of business.

synonym: experience; *see*: accident experience, loss run

loss exposure

Risk Management. A potential event that could result in a financial loss to an organization, caused by an identifiable peril.

see: liability loss exposure, peril, personnel loss exposure, property loss exposure

loss forecasting

Risk Management. A risk management tool for projecting future losses based on past loss patterns. Two methods are probability analysis and trend analysis.

see: probability analysis, trend analysis

loss frequency

Risk Management. The number of losses that occur during a specified period of time (usually one year).

synonym: claims frequency, loss rate; *compare*: accident frequency, accident severity, loss severity

loss frequency method

Risk Management. A method of projecting the number of future losses to occur in a specified time. It is used by underwriters to develop a basic premium on large accounts. To the basic premium are added the insurer's loading for expenses, profits and contingencies.

see: loss expectancy

loss limitation

Liability/Workers' Compensation. A factor or amount that limits the losses used to calculate the final premium in a retrospective rating plan or retention plan. This factor is designed to limit the adverse effect of a catastrophic loss on a plan's final premium calculation.

see: retrospective rating plan, stop loss

loss loading

Reinsurance. A method of calculating a reinsurance premium where pure losses are multiplied by a factor for inflation, expenses and other considerations.

loss of consortium

Law. Deprivation in some degree of the companionship, affection, sexual relations, or cooperation of a spouse due to an accident or injury.

see: hedonic loss, noneconomic loss

loss of income benefit

Workers' Compensation.
see: disability benefit

loss of income insurance

Health.
see: disability income insurance
Property.
see: business income coverage form

loss of market

Inland Marine/Ocean Marine. The inability to sell a product to prospective buyers. This is usually considered a business risk and is not covered by most insurance policies. A limited form of loss of market coverage is provided in marine insurance policies, where loss of market due to spoilage of goods can be covered when caused by an insured peril. Product recall and tampering insurance provide another limited form of this coverage.

see: business risk

loss of profits form

International.
see: British business interruption insurance

loss of time insurance

Health.
see: disability income insurance
Property.
see: business income coverage form

loss of use coverage

aviation. A form of aircraft hull coverage for the cost of renting or leasing a temporary substitute when the insured aircraft is damaged from an insured peril.

see: hull policy (*Aviation*)

loss of use—value in improvements and betterments

Property. Coverage for the loss of use of improvements made by a tenant in rented or leased property, which are destroyed and not replaced by the building owner.

see: improvements and betterments insurance

loss of use insurance

Property. Coverage for the loss of use of an insured's property, when it cannot be used for its intended purpose because of damage caused by an insured peril.

see: additional living expense insurance, business income coverage form, loss of use—value

in improvements and betterments, use and occupancy insurance

loss payable clause

Property. A property insurance policy provision that authorizes the insurer to make a loss payment to a person (loss payee) other than the insured to the extent that the loss payee has an insurable interest in the property.

compare: single interest policy; *see:* certificate of insurance, evidence of property insurance, loss payee, mortgagee clause, underlying insurance policy

loss payee

Property. The person named in a loss payable clause to whom insurance proceeds are to be paid in the event of damage to property. The loss payee must have an insurable interest. Loss payees include automobile lienholders and property mortgagees.

see: incorporeal interest, insurable interest, loss payable clause, mortgagee

loss pick

Insurer Operations.
see: loss expectancy

loss portfolio

Insurer Operations. The outstanding loss reserves on the books of an insurance company or self-insured organization.

see: loss portfolio transfer, loss reserve

loss portfolio transfer

Insurer Operations/Risk Management. The transfer of incurred losses to a third party. The assuming party hopes to profit by investing the sale price it has received over the length of time it requires to settle the claims it has assumed. Such transfers are undertaken by insurers or self-insureds in order to gain tax advantages, to clean up a financial statement, or to exit from a line or class of insurance.

see: portfolio runoff
Reinsurance.
see: portfolio reinsurance

loss prevention

Loss Control. Measures designed to reduce the probability that a loss will occur.

synonym: accident prevention; *see:* loss prevention services, loss reduction

loss prevention engineer

Loss Control.
see: loss control specialist

loss prevention services

Loss Control. Survey, consultation or loss control management services provided to policyholders by an insurer to reduce the likelihood of accidents.

see: inspection, insurance consultation services

loss rate

Insurer Operations/Risk Management.

see: loss frequency

loss ratio

Insurer Operations. A formula used by insurers to relate loss expenses to income. *Formula*: (incurred losses + loss adjustment expenses) ÷ earned premiums.

compare: combined ratio, dividend ratio, expense ratio; *see*: accident year statistics, burning ratio, earned premium, expected loss ratio, incurred losses, insured loss ratio, loss adjustment expense, underwriting margin

loss ratio reserve method

Insurer Operations. A method of evaluating losses and loss adjusting expenses as a percentage of premium. Past losses and loss adjusting expenses are evaluated to indicate the amount of reserves that must be maintained on future claims to adequately fund these expenses.

see: loss adjustment expense, reserve

loss reduction

Loss Control. A loss control measure designed to reduce the severity of loss occurrences.

synonym: accident prevention; *see*: loss prevention, loss severity

loss report

Insurer Operations.

see: loss run

loss reserve

Insurer Operations. An insurer's estimate of the amount an individual claim will ultimately cost. On an insurer's financial statement, it is the amount of estimated liabilities for known claims not yet paid and incurred but not reported claims.

synonym: claims reserve; *see*: incurred but not reported, incurred losses, reserve

loss reserve transfer

Insurer Operations.

see: loss portfolio transfer

loss retention

Risk Management.

see: retention

loss run

Insurer Operations/Risk Management. A printed report summarizing the losses that have occurred over a specific period of time and are valued as of a specific date.

synonym: claims report, loss report; *see*: accident

experience, loss experience

loss-sensitive insurance program

Insurer Operations. Insurance coverage for a specific insured where the final premium is based on the insured's losses.

see: experience rating plan, retrospective rating plan

loss severity

Risk Management. The amount of a loss.

synonym: claims severity

loss trends

Risk Management. Projections of future losses based on analysis of past loss patterns. Trends are used to determine the pure cost of protection and the resultant pure premium, contingency reserves, and whether the company should continue writing a specific type of policy, a line of business, or remain active in a particular geographic area.

see: pure premium, trending

losses

Insurer Operations.

see: incurred but not reported, incurred losses, loss reserve, outstanding losses, paid losses

losses paid

Insurer Operations.

see: paid losses

lost instrument bond

Surety. A type of surety bond bought by owners of stock certificates, bonds and similar financial instruments that guarantees replacement if an instrument is lost or destroyed. If a document reported as lost is later recovered, the owner is required to send it to the surety.

see: surety bond

lost or not lost clause

Ocean Marine. An obsolete ocean marine provision covering a vessel or cargo regardless of whether, at the time the coverage was accepted, there had already been a loss. This provision was needed because the owner of a vessel or cargo could not communicate with a foreign port or another vessel at sea before modern communication devices were available.

lost policy receipt

Insurer Operations. A form signed by a policyholder wishing to surrender a policy that has been lost. The signed and dated receipt then becomes evidence that the policy is no longer in force and releases the insurer from liability for coverage that would have been provided during the remaining term of the policy.

synonym: lost policy release

lost policy release
Insurer Operations.
   see: lost policy receipt

lost workday case rate
Loss Control. One of three commonly used measurements of an organization's level of employee safety. *Formula*: cases involving lost days in the year ÷ (annual employee hours ÷ 200,000). (200,000 represents 100 employee-years, assuming an average work year of 2000 hours.)
   compare: lost workday rate, recordable case rate

lost workday rate
Loss Control. One of three commonly used measurements of an organization's degree of employee safety. *Formula*: lost workdays per year ÷ (annual employee hours ÷ 200,000). (200,000 represents 100 employee-years, assuming an average work year of 2000 hours.)
   compare: lost workday case rate, recordable case rate

low load fund
Financial Planning. A mutual fund that charges its participants a low sales commission, which is called the *load*.
   compare: load fund, no load fund; *see*: mutual fund

low pressure steam
Loss Control. Steam at a pressure of no more than 15 pounds per square inch.
   compare: high pressure steam

lower explosive level
Loss Control.
   see: flammable limits

lower grade obligation
Financial Planning.
   see: high-yield bond

lucrative title
Title. A title to real estate that has been acquired with nothing given in exchange for it.
   compare: onerous title; *see*: real estate, title

lump sum option
Life. A life insurance provision to pay the benefit in a single sum rather than in installments.
   synonym: cash payment option; *see*: cash refund annuity, death benefit, settlement options

lump sum refund annuity
Life.
   see: cash refund annuity

M

machine guard

Loss Control.

see: barrier guard

machine tool

Loss Control. A powered machine, usually metalworking, for making the parts of other machines. Two general classes of machine tools are cutting tools (lathes, milling machines, grinders, drills, shapers) and forming tools (power press and breaks).

see: barrier guard, inrunning nip point, point of operation

machinery

Ocean Marine. The term used for apparatus that propels a ship, including the boilers, mechanical apparatus, refrigeration equipment and insulation, motors, generators and electrical equipment.

Property. Machines in general, or as a functional unit. For insurance purposes, there are three property definitions: boiler and machinery, fixed machinery, and mobile machinery.

compare: equipment; *see:* boiler and machinery, fixed machinery, mobile machinery

machinery and equipment

Property. Coverage that can be included under either a building or personal property policy, for items or equipment that are permanently installed at an insured premises (e.g., heating and air conditioning equipment, engines or shafting).

see: boiler and machinery insurance

machinery breakdown insurance

Property.

see: boiler and machinery insurance

MAERP Reinsurance Association

Liability. A group of over 120 mutual insurance company members that provide reinsurance for Mutual Atomic Energy Liability Underwriters (MAELU) and certain mutual fronting companies that write all-risk, first-party property insurance for nuclear facilities. It was originally called the Mutual Atomic Energy Reinsurance Pool and is now officially known as the MAERP Reinsurance Association.

synonym: Mutual Atomic Energy Reinsurance Pool; *see:* Mutual Atomic Energy Liability Underwriters

magnet location

Property. A large, well known store located near an insured business or in the same shopping mall that attracts customers to the insured's location.

see: contingent business income insurance, extra expense from dependent properties endorsement

mail coverage

Inland Marine. Coverage (ISO form CM 00 60) on valuable mail shipments, purchased by financial institutions such as banks and stock brokerage firms.

see: first class mail coverage, parcel post insurance, registered mail insurance

maintenance

Ocean Marine. A maritime term for room and board. It is one of a seaman's remedies while on a voyage.

see: cure, Jones Act, seaman's remedies

maintenance bond

Surety. A surety bond, usually posted by a contractor, against defects in workmanship or materials for a stated period (usually two years) after the acceptance of completed work.

see: faulty work exclusion

maintenance deductible

Insurer Operations. A deductible occasionally used in conjunction with an aggregate deductible. It applies only when the aggregate deductible limit is reached because of losses, and the insurer becomes responsible for further losses. Because processing many small claims is inefficient for an insurer, a small maintenance deductible applies to each loss

paid after the aggregate deductible is reached.
see: aggregate deductible, deductible

major hospitalization coverage

Health. Medical coverage for catastrophic hospital expenses, subject to a large deductible.
compare: comprehensive medical expense policy, major medical insurance

major medical insurance

Health. Medical coverage for catastrophic medical expenses, subject to a large deductible. Sublimits on services such as psychiatric care may be specified in the contract.
compare: basic medical expense, major hospitalization coverage; *see*: catastrophe policy, comprehensive medical expense policy, supplemental major medical insurance

makeup air

Loss Control. Clean exterior air supplied to a workspace to replace air removed by exhaust ventilation or other industrial processes.

malfeasance

Law/Professional Liability. Illegal or unethical conduct; wrongdoing beyond simple negligence. The term is found in public officials' professional liability policies.
compare: misfeasance, nonfeasance; *see*: public officials' liability insurance

malicious mischief

Property. The willful damage or destruction of another's property; a coverage included with vandalism.
see: vandalism and malicious mischief coverage

malingering

Health/Workers' Compensation. Pretending to be ill or disabled in order to avoid work and collect insurance benefits or receive such benefits longer than necessary.

malpractice

Professional Liability. Negligence or dereliction of a professional duty that results in an injury; the failure to exercise the customary degree of care, knowledge or skill of a practitioner in good professional. The practitioner is a person who provides services for which there are minimum standards of conduct, knowledge or skill (such as education or license requirements) generally accepted by the professional community.
see: malpractice insurance, medical malpractice

malpractice arbitration panel

Professional Liability. A group of arbitrators selected to hear and decide upon medical malpractice claims.
see: arbitration, medical malpractice, medical review panel

malpractice insurance

Professional Liability. Coverage of an individual or corporation for injury or loss to third parties arising from negligence or malfeasance in rendering professional services. Professional negligence (malpractice) is the failure to exercise the degree of care, knowledge or skill of the average practitioner in good professional standing under circumstances similar to those in which the injury occurred. The term *professional liability insurance* has the same meaning and is more often used outside the area of medical malpractice.
see: errors and omissions insurance, malfeasance, malpractice, negligence, professional liability insurance

managed care

Health. 1. The main alternative model of health care coverage to standard health insurance. While health insurance relies primarily on indemnity payments for services, managed care plans (e.g., health maintenance organizations and preferred provider organizations) rely on a network of contracts with health care providers and capitation fees or other cost controls.
2. The cost control methods (except traditional insurability criteria and benefit limitations) used by third-party payers, including utilization review, contracts with selected health care providers, financial incentives or disincentives for using specified providers or services, prospective payment schedules, case management, and payers' efforts to identify treatment alternatives for high-cost care. Traditional health insurers, as well as managed care organizations, use some of these methods.
see: any willing provider law, capitation, case management, health maintenance organization, independent practice association, managed prescription drug plan, out-of-network services, preferred provider organization, prospective payment system, utilization review

managed competition

Health. A system or process aimed at controlling health care costs and providing broader coverage by which purchasers (particularly employers) form alliances to choose among health benefit plans. The theory is that alliances give purchasers more negotiating power, and the competition among plan sponsors results in more efficiency and lower costs. Some reform legislation relying on the managed competition model also requires all health benefit plan sponsors to offer a standard package of basic benefits.
see: basic benefits (2), health benefit plan, health purchasing alliance

281

managed prescription drug plan

Health. A prescription drug plan that integrates preferred pharmacy networks, drug utilization review, and patient, pharmacist and physician education incentives. Some plans feature mail order pharmacy services.

see: managed care, preferred provider organizations, utilization review

management expense

Reinsurance. A formula-based deduction from a reinsurer's income or profit used to help defray the reinsurer's overhead expenses before calculation of a contingent commission.

see: ceding commission

managing general agent (MGA)

Insurer Operations. An agent authorized by an insurance company to manage all or a part of the insurer's business in a specific geographic territory. Activities on behalf of the insurer may include marketing, underwriting, issuing policies, collecting premiums, appointing and supervising other agents, paying claims, and negotiating reinsurance. Many states regulate the activities and contracts of managing general agents.

compare: general agent; *see:* agent

managing physician

Health.

see: primary care physician

mandated benefits

Health/Employee Benefits. A coverage or minimum benefit required by law to be included in any health policy issued by an insurer. Particular required coverages vary by state. Examples include cancer testing (e.g., mammography), fertility services (e.g., in-vitro fertilization), and chiropractic service.

compare: basic benefits (2), employer mandate; *see:* compulsory insurance

mandatory local reinsurance

International. The requirement in many countries that on specific lines of insurance all of the reinsurance must be placed through a monopolistic reinsurance facility that is usually controlled by the government. *Examples:* In Japan the government bureau is the exclusive reinsurer for auto insurance; in France the government reinsurer is entitled to write 4% of any private insurance transaction.

mandatory retirement

Employee Benefits.

see: compulsory retirement

mandatory securities valuation reserve

Regulation. A method of valuing life insurance company investments in stocks and bonds, established by the National Association of Insurance Commissioners. This valuation method is designed to moderate the effect of large swings in stock and bond values on an insurer's mandatory reserves.

see: investment reserve, risk-based capital, securities valuation

manifest

Ocean Marine. A document prepared by a vessel's master, listing all bills of lading by number and the type and quantity of all cargo carried by the vessel.

see: bill of lading, hazardous waste manifest

manifestation theory

Law/Liability. A legal doctrine that coverage for an injury or illness is invoked or triggered at the time the loss becomes apparent (i.e., when the symptoms of an illness are manifested or when a loss is or should have been discovered). This is similar to the way coverage is triggered under a claims-made policy. In cases of a long period of exposure to a hazardous condition during which several policies successively covered the risk, only the policy in force at the time a disease is detected is liable, not any policy in force during the hazardous exposure but before the disease developed, nor one in effect while the disease existed in an undiscovered, dormant state. Because of the seeming inequity of allocating 100% of the liability to a policy that may have been in effect for the shortest time among several policies covering a long-term exposure, a pure manifestation theory is applied less often than some other theories of coverage (i.e., the continuous trigger or exposure theory).

compare: continuous trigger theory, exposure theory, injury-in-fact theory; *see:* claims-made trigger, long-tail liability, progressive loss

manometer

Loss Control. A gauge that measures the pressure of gases and vapors.

manual

Insurer Operations.

see: rate manual

manual excess

Liability. A table contained in a rate manual that provides rate factors to increase basic limits to higher limits of liability.

see: rate making, rate manual

manual premium

Workers' Compensation. The premium developed by multiplying a published workers' compensation employee classification rate by each $100 of payroll for that employee classification.

compare: modified premium; *see:* standard premium

manual rates
Insurer Operations. Rates contained in a manual published by an insurer or rating organization for a unit of insurance.
compare: "A" rates, judgment rates; *see:* rate making, rate manual, state exception pages, state rate pages, state territorial pages

manufacturer's penalty insurance
Financial Guaranty. A commercial policy covering losses due to the unavailability of a product the insured has contracted to supply or manufacture. Coverage is purchased in amounts based on the contract between the insured and the buyer of the product. The objective is to protect the insured against responsibility for delays in completion due to non-delivery. Coverage is usually a percentage (i.e., 90%) of the penalty amount, but excludes coverage for delays due to a labor dispute.
compare: strike insurance; *see:* annual supply contract bond

manufacturer's selling price
Property. A method of valuing unsold finished goods: The actual cash value of finished stock manufactured by the insured equals that price (less all discounts and unincurred expenses) for which the stock would have been sold had not loss occurred.
see: actual cash value, selling price clause

manufacturer's selling price (finished stock only) endorsement
Property. A commercial property endorsement (ISO form CP 99 30) that amends coverage to include the profit that could have been earned on finished stock that is damaged by an insured peril.
see: manufacturer's selling price

manufacturers' and contractors' liability insurance (M&C)
Liability. A policy form previously available under the 1973 ISO liability rating plan. The form was designed for less desirable manufacturing and contracting risks to provide limited coverage (narrower than the comprehensive general liability form). The form excluded coverage for products and completed operations, independent contractors and structural alterations. The ISO 1986 liability rating plan does not include a similar form.
see: comprehensive general liability policy

manufacturers' output policy (MOP)
Inland Marine/Property. A single commercial property or inland marine policy that covers on an all risks basis damage to a manufacturer's, assembler's or processor's personal property during the manufacturing process, while it is temporarily off premises with a subcontractor, and loss to goods

being transported.
see: off-premises coverage

manuscript policy
Insurer Operations/Risk Management. An insurance policy designed or tailored for a large commercial insured; a unique coverage written at the request of a broker or a risk manager.
compare: contract of adhesion; *see:* insurance contract, modification of contract

map
Insurer Operations. A geographic chart or computerized representation used by an insurance underwriter to locate the area in which a risk is located. A detailed map, giving such details as elevation, soil conditions, terrain, proximity to other structures and to facilities such as airports or hospitals can be of great assistance in the underwriting process.
see: fire map; Sanborn Map Company, Inc.

maquiladoras
International. Light assembly plants (Spanish). As part of a Mexican government program to attract foreign investment and create jobs, foreign corporations build or partly finance plants in northern Mexico, where products are assembled from imported parts and are re-exported. The corporations receive special tax treatment and can take advantage of wage rates significantly lower than in the United States or Canada.
see: foreign trade zone, maquiladoras investment insurance

maquiladoras investment insurance
International. A form of political risk insurance that indemnifies an insured for total or partial confiscation, expropriation or nationalization of a maquiladora investment. Included coverages are such events as an embargo or license cancellation that may prevent importing raw materials into Mexico or exporting finished products.
see: maquiladoras, political risk insurance

margin
Financial Planning. The difference between the amount of a loan used to buy stock and the value of the stock, which serves as collateral on the loan. A percentage (ranging between 40% and 100%) is set by the Federal Reserve Board as the cash required to be maintained in relation to the value of securities purchased when a securities dealer maintains a margin account for a customer to buy securities on credit.
see: margin call

margin call
Financial Planning. A request for cash to be deposited into a margin account because the required

amount has fallen below the Federal Reserve Board standard.

see: margin

marine definition
Ocean Marine/Inland Marine.
see: Nationwide Marine Insurance Definition

marine insurance
Inland Marine/Ocean Marine. A broad term including ocean and inland marine insurance. The Nationwide Marine Insurance Definition, published by the National Association of Insurance Commissioners, includes imports, exports, domestic shipments, means of communications, and personal and commercial property floaters as marine insurance.

see: inland marine insurance, instrumentalities of transportation and communication, Nationwide Marine Insurance Definition, ocean marine insurance

marine insurance certificate
Ocean Marine. A certificate of insurance that is issued by the holder of an open cargo policy which indicates a specific shipment is insured under the policy. Periodically, copies of the certificate or a bordereau is provided to the open cargo policy underwriter.

see: bordereau, declarations, open cargo policy

Marine Mammal Protection Act
Regulation. Federal legislation adopted in 1988 that is similar to the Endangered Species Act except that it applies specifically to marine mammals, such as whales. It prohibits taking, possessing or trading of marine mammals or marine mammal products and limits methods used in commercial fishing.

see: Endangered Species Act

marine surveyor
Ocean Marine.
see: surveyor

Marine Syndicate B
Ocean Marine. An insurance syndicate created in 1920 by the Federal Maritime Commission. It is comprised of subscribing marine insurers who jointly underwrite certain American steamship vessel risks.

see: American Hull Insurance Syndicate, American Marine Insurance Clearinghouse

marital estate endorsement
Professional Liability. A directors' and officers' liability policy endorsement that includes the spouse of a director or officer in the term "insured" and includes coverage of claims for damages recoverable from marital community property, jointly

owned property, and property transferred to the spouse.

see: directors' and officers' liability insurance

marital tax deduction
Financial Planning. A deduction under the U.S. tax code that allows an estate to be transferred to the surviving spouse without incurring any federal estate tax.

see: estate tax, qualified terminable interest property trust

maritime
International/Ocean Marine. Navigation or commerce on the sea.
see: admiralty

maritime coverage endorsement
Workers' Compensation. An endorsement (NCCI form WC 00 02 01A) that extends coverage under a workers' compensation policy to include liability to employees covered by the Death on the High Seas Act. The maritime exclusion is deleted from the employers' liability section of the policy and the liability coverage is added.

see: Death on the High Seas Act, voluntary compensation maritime coverage endorsement

market approach appraisal
Financial Planning. One of three methods used to appraise real estate for investment purposes which considers prices recently paid for similar properties in the same geographic area and modifies these prices to reflect the physical conditions and specific location of the appraised property.

compare: cost approach appraisal, income approach appraisal; *see*: appraisal, real estate

market assistance plan (MAP)
Regulation. Assistance given by a state to insureds and producers in placing difficult lines of insurance (such as medical malpractice, private dwellings, day-care centers, and liquor liability coverage) in a cooperative effort with insurers. Some states require or request that insurers participate in setting up these underwriting pools. *Examples*: Many states set up MAPs to assist day care facilities find coverage during the early 1980s, when traditional market coverage disappeared.

see: assigned risk, Fair Access to Insurance Requirements, joint underwriting association

market entrance reinsurance
Reinsurance. Reinsurance placed in order to allow an insurer to enter a new line of business by spreading the risk to reinsurers until the premium volume on the new line is adequate to support it.

see: innocent market

market order

Financial Planning. An order to buy or sell securities at the most advantageous price available after the order reaches the trading floor.

see: delivery

market risk

Risk Management. 1. The risk of loss to an organization from new competitors, demand changes, etc.

2. The risk of loss to an organization from its being unable to buy or sell goods or services that it needs or provides in its customary marketplace at the usual terms and prices.

see: business income coverage form, liquidity risk

market share liability

Law. A legal doctrine that has been applied to products that harm consumers but cannot be traced to a single manufacturer. It imposes liability on all manufacturers of the product in proportion to their shares of the market for the product.

see: joint liability, joint tortfeasors, product liability insurance

market specialty insurer

Insurer Operations. An insurer that specializes in writing various types of property and liability insurance but to only one type of customer (e.g., florist package policies).

compare: full service insurer, product specialty insurer, selective specialty insurer; *see:* marketing

market value

Property. The price that a willing buyer would pay and a willing seller would accept in an arm's length transaction in a competitive (i.e., not monopolistic) market.

synonym: fair market value; *compare:* actual cash value, book value, depreciated value, economic value, going concern value, tax-appraised value; *see:* market value clause, replacement cost, reproduction cost, valuation of potential property loss

market value clause

Property. Occasionally, property insurance policies are endorsed to allow a loss to be adjusted based on the price a willing buyer would have paid for the damaged or destroyed property, prior to the loss.

compare: actual cash value, alcoholic beverages market value endorsement, market value stock endorsement, replacement cost

market value stock endorsement

Property. A commercial property coverage endorsement (ISO form CP 99 31) that amends coverage on goods held in stock to provide a loss settlement based on the stock's current market value.

This form excludes alcoholic beverages.

see: alcoholic beverages market value endorsement, market value clause

marketable title

Title. A title to real estate that is free and clear of liens or other title defects; a title that enables an owner to sell the property freely to others and which others will accept without objection.

synonym: clear title, good title, merchantable title; *see:* defeasance clause, defective title, free and clear, real estate, title

marketing

Insurer Operations. Promotion of an insurance company's policies and services to potential buyers. An insurer typically has a separate marketing department, which participates in product research and personnel training, as well as advertising.

see: full service insurer, market specialty insurer, marketing representative, mass marketing, product specialty insurer, selective specialty insurer, targer marketing

marketing representative

Agency/Insurer Operations. An individual employed by an insurer to promote business from agents in a specific territory.

synonym: field representative, special agent

masonry incombustible construction

Loss Control. A structure built with exterior walls made of masonry materials, such as adobe, concrete, stone, tile, or gypsum block. The floors and the roof are constructed of incombustible or slow burning materials.

see: construction, unreinforced masonry

mass marketing

Insurer Operations. Promotion of a company's insurance policies to a large number of individuals or organizations through an insurance plan at premiums lower than those that would be charged for similar persons or organizations not participating in the plan. The insurer retains the right of individual underwriting selection, which distinguishes this type of marketing from *group marketing.*

compare: franchise marketing, group marketing

Mass Marketing Insurance Institute (MMII)

Organizations. Members: Independent brokers, insurers and other companies who sell their products through mass marketing techniques. *Objectives:* Disseminating mass marketing information and techniques. *Founded:* 1969. *Headquarters:* Kansas City, MO.

mass underwriting

Insurer Operations. A method of underwriting that examines the demographic qualities of a group for its insurability, rather than the qualities of an individual.

see: mass marketing, underwriting

master

Ocean Marine. Under admiralty law, the captain of a ship.

master air waybill

Aviation/Inland Marine. An air waybill issued by an originating airline when more than one airline is involved with a shipment, or when a freight forwarder issues a house waybill.

see: air waybill, house waybill, waybill

master insurance policy

Insurer Operations. An original, complete insurance policy contract that is issued by an insurer with the understanding that certificates of insurance or underlying policies will be issued to others; for example, a master group health policy is issued to an employer while certificates are given to the employees. A master policy and underlying policies may be issued to a property owner to comply with requirements of a mortgage holder.

synonym: group contract; *compare*: certificate of insurance, group certificate, underlying insurance policy

International. A "stand alone" nonadmitted international or global policy that provides coverage on a primary basis or an international difference-in-conditions basis and is part of an overall program supported by local admitted policies. The policy provides a level of coverage that is typical in the insured's own country.

see: controlled master insurance program, difference in conditions insurance, global insurance program, nonadmitted insurance

master-servant endorsement

Workers' Compensation.

see: alternate employer endorsement

master-servant rule

Law. A legal principle that an employer is responsible for the acts of employees while performing their job duties.

see: employee, respondeat superior, vicarious liability

material fact

Law. A fact of such importance that without it a contract or other legal obligation would not have been made; a fact that would alter an underwriting decision or loss settlement.

Insurer Operations. A fact of such importance that were it revealed in an insurance application, the underwriting decision would have been different.

Such facts often come to light after a claims has been reported.

see: concealment, misrepresentation, warranty (1)

material misrepresentation

Law. The intentional concealment, distortion or fabrication of a material fact.

see: concealment, contribute-to-the-loss statute, election to avoid a policy, fraud, material fact, representation, warranty (1)

Material Safety Data Sheet (MSDS)

Loss Control. A compilation of information required under the Occupational Safety and Health Act that identifies the health and physical hazards, exposure limits, and precautions for a hazardous chemical. The Superfund law (CERCLA) requires facilities to submit an MSDS under certain circumstances.

synonym: chemical data sheet; *see*: Comprehensive Environmental Response Compensation and Liability Act, Occupational Safety and Health Act

materiality test

Accounting/Risk Management.

see: accountants' materiality test

maternity benefit

Health. Coverage for hospital, medical and surgical expenses of a mother during pregnancy and childbirth (or miscarriage or involuntary abortion) and care of the newborn. Many policies pay only a fixed amount, while others cover actual expenses. Childbirth coverage has historically been excluded in accident and sickness policies written on women, but it is commonly covered by hospitalization insurance and by employee group health policies.

see: flat maternity benefit, newborn, swap maternity, well baby coverage

mature

Employee Benefits. An employee group that has attained stability as to the distribution of age within the group. When it is mature, the group is close to having the same number of individuals of the same age year after year.

Life. A life insurance policy is said to mature when the policy benefits are payable, such as upon the insured's death or a specified benefit payment date.

compare: paid-up insurance; *see*: maturity date

mature policy

Liability. A claims-made insurance policy that has been in force continuously for at least five years with a retroactive date going back to the first claims-made policy. A mature claims-made policy is not eligible for rating credits assigned to immature policies.

compare: immature policy; *see*: claims-made form

maturity

Risk Management. A term used in loss forecasting for the time elapsed between a given insurance program year (usually inception) and the evaluation date.

synonym: age of development

maturity date

Life. The date a life insurance policy's benefits are payable because of the insured's death or because a specified benefit payment date has been reached.

see: policy period

maturity value

Life. The amount payable to the insured under a life insurance policy who has lived to a specified age; the amount due an insured at the end of an endorsement period.

compare: cash surrender value

Financial Planning. The amount, including principal and interest, that the holder of a bond, note, or mortgage is entitled to receive on the maturity date

maxi-tail

Liability. A provision of some claims-made policies that permits the insured an unlimited length of time to report a claim under the policy after its termination.

synonym: full tail, unlimited reporting period, unlimited tail; *see*: basic extended reporting period, claims-made form, extended reporting period, midi-tail, mini-tail, tail

maximum allowable concentration (MAC)

Loss Control. The concentration of an atmospheric contaminant during an eight-hour period below which it is unlikely that ill effects will be experienced by any except hypersensitive individuals.

maximum contaminant level goal

Regulation.

see: Safe Drinking Water Act

maximum disability income policy

Health. A noncancelable disability income insurance policy with a maximum limit of liability for any one claim, but no lifetime aggregate limit for multiple claims.

see: disability income insurance

maximum foreseeable loss

Loss Control/Property.

see: maximum possible loss

maximum line

Insurer Operations.

see: gross line

maximum period of indemnity

Property. An endorsement to the business income coverage form that deletes the required coinsurance. The coinsurance requirement is replaced with coverage for the actual loss sustained during the initial 120 days after a loss up to the policy limit.

compare: monthly limit of indemnity; *see*: business income coverage form

maximum plan limits

Employee Benefits. Maximum benefits payable to a health plan participant. Maximum limits can be categorized as a defined maximum limit, a per cause (disability) maximum limit, or an all causes maximum limit.

see: all causes maximum limit, health benefit plan, per cause maximum limit

maximum possible loss

Loss Control/Property. The worst possible loss that could occur under a policy. *Example*: Under a fire policy, the maximum possible loss would result from a fire in which the fire department does not respond, automatic sprinklers do not operate, and fire divisions fail.

synonym: maximum foreseeable loss; *compare*: probable maximum loss; *see*: automatic sprinkler system, fire division

maximum premium

Insurer Operations. The highest premium an insurer can charge for a policy that is subject to an audit or a unique rating plan.

see: audit, maximum retrospective premium

maximum probable loss

Loss Control/Property.

see: probable maximum loss

maximum retrospective premium

Liability/Workers' Compensation. The maximum premium that a policyholder would be required to pay under a retrospective rating plan, regardless of the amount of incurred losses. Usually, the maximum is expressed as a percentage of premium (e.g., 110%, 125%).

compare: minimum retrospective premium; *see*: retrospective penalty insurance, retrospective rating plan

McCarran-Ferguson Act

Regulation. Federal legislation (U.S. Code Title 15, Chapter 20) enacted in 1945 to permit the states to continue regulating the insurance business after the Supreme Court, in *U.S. v. South-Eastern Underwriters Association*, overruled the decision in

Paul v. Virginia, declaring insurance to be interstate commerce and therefore within Congress's constitutional authority to regulate. Under the Act, insurance is exempt from some federal antitrust statutes to the extent that it is regulated by the states. The exemption primarily applies to gathering data in concert for the purpose of ratemaking. Otherwise, antitrust laws prohibit insurers from boycotting, acting coercively, restraining trade, or violating the Sherman or Clayton Acts.

see: antitrust laws, Clayton Act, insurance department, Paul v. Virginia, Sherman Antitrust Act

McClintock table
Life. A life insurance mortality table developed by McClinton McClintock in 1896 based upon the experience of 15 U.S. life insurers.

see: mortality table

mean
Risk Management. The average value, computed by dividing the sum of a set of values by the number of values in the set. Though the mean is the mathematical average of a set of numbers, *mean, median* and *mode* may all be used in various contexts to indicate an average, typical or likely condition; however, they differ. *Example:* In the number set 1, 2, 2, 4, 5, 8, 13, the mean is 5 (35 ÷ 7); the median is 4 (the middle value); and the mode is 2 (the most frequent value).

synonym: arithmetic mean; *compare:* median, mode; *see:* central limit theorem

mean reserve
Life. A life insurance reserve that is based on the average of the initial reserve and the terminal reserve for a life insurance policy.

compare: initial reserve, terminal reserve

mechanic's lien
Property.
see: encumbrance

mechanical objects
Property. One of the four boiler and machinery object classifications for equipment covered under a policy. This classification (object definition no. 2 or ISO form BM 00 27) includes coverage for deep-well pump units; miscellaneous machines, gear wheels, and enclosed gear sets; engines, pumps, compressors, fans, and blowers; and wheels and shafts.

see: boiler and machinery insurance, object

media
Property. Tangible personal property consisting of the material on which data is recorded, such as magnetic tapes, disks, cards and programs.

compare: data; *see:* data processing coverage

median
Risk Management. A statistical term for the middle or most central value in a set of numbers; halfway between two outermost points.

compare: mean, mode

mediation
Law. A means of resolving disputes in lieu of litigation. The parties present their claims in a much less formal manner than required in a court to an individual or organization (mediator) acceptable to both parties. The mediator tries to persuade the parties to bargain their way to an agreement. The essence of mediation is to foster agreement between the parties rather than to impose a settlement.

compare: arbitration, litigation; *see:* alternative dispute resolution

mediator
Law. A person chosen or appointed to decide a controversy through mediation.

compare: arbitrator; *see:* mediation

mediators' errors and omissions insurance
Professional Liability.
see: arbitrators' errors and omissions insurance

Medicaid
Health. A state medical benefit program for persons, regardless of age, whose income and resources are insufficient to pay for health care. As of January 1, 1966, federal matching funds were provided to the states under Title XIX of the Social Security Act.

synonym: Title XIX of the Social Security Act; *compare:* Medicare

Medicaid Antidiscriminatory Drug Pricing and Patient Benefit Restoration Act (MADPA)
Health/Regulation. Federal legislation adopted in 1990 that requires pharmaceutical companies to provide their best prices to individuals covered under the Medicaid outpatient pharmacy program, guarantees that outpatients may have drug therapy consultations with their pharmacists, and requires that there be a drug therapy review before any prescription is dispensed.

medical benefit
Workers' Compensation. The payment of any medical, surgical or hospital expense incurred in treating an injury or illness suffered by an employee in the course of employment. Under workers' compensation laws, the employer is responsible for such payments.

compare: death benefit (*Workers' Compensation*), disability benefit; *see:* additional medical, arising out of and in the course of employment, medical benefits exclusion endorsement, medical benefits reimbursement endorsement, workers' compensation law

medical benefits exclusion endorsement

Workers' Compensation. An endorsement (NCCI form WC 00 03 06) to a workers' compensation policy that excludes coverage for medical benefit payments under the policy. It is used when an insured has been approved by the state as a self-insurer for such payments.

compare: medical benefits reimbursement endorsement; *see*: medical benefit

medical benefits reimbursement endorsement

Workers' Compensation. An endorsement (NCCI form WC 00 03 07) to a workers' compensation policy that excludes coverage for medical benefit payments under the policy unless the insurer is found responsible for such benefits; in that case, the insured must reimburse the insurer for the payments. The endorsement is used when an insured is not an approved self-insurer but has elected to pay its own medical benefits.

compare: medical benefits exclusion endorsement; *see*: medical benefit

medical cost containment

Health.

see: managed care (2)

medical deductible workers' compensation plan

Workers' Compensation. A deductible workers' compensation plan where the deductible applies only to workers' compensation medical benefits, not to indemnity (disability income) payments.

compare: indemnity deductible workers' compensation plan; *see*: deductible workers' compensation plan, disability benefit, medical benefit

medical emergency

Health. A sudden, unexpected deterioration in a person's medical condition that; if not treated immediately, could result in loss of life or limb or in a permanent impairment or dysfunction.

see: emergency medical services, in-area emergency services, triage

medical examination

General. A routine preventive examination or "check up" performed by a medical doctor to detect potential health problems.

Employee Benefits. 1. A medical examination of a prospective employee required and paid for by the employer to determine his or her ability to perform a particular job.

2. A periodic medical examination of an employee offered and paid for by the employer as an employee benefit.

Health/Life. A medical examination of an applicant or claimant required and paid for by a life or health insurer to determine acceptability for coverage or eligibility for benefits.

see: examined business, nonmedical insurance, paramedical examination

medical examiner

Health/Life. A public officer who makes postmortem examinations of bodies to determine the cause of death.

medical expense insurance

Health. Health insurance covering medical, surgical and hospital costs.

see: hospital-surgical expense insurance

medical expense limit

Liability. The highest amount recoverable under the ISO commercial general liability coverage form for medical payments to any one person—usually $1,000 or $5,000.

see: commercial general liability policy, medical payments coverage (*Liability*)

medical expense reversionary trust

Liability. A trust that a defendant establishes to make funds available for the future medical needs of the plaintiff. Funds remaining in the trust after the death of the plaintiff revert, in whole or in part, back to the defendant. Because the trust fund is used for medical expenses actually incurred, it avoids providing a windfall to the plaintiff's estate.

see: structured settlement, trust

medical expense threshold

Automobile.

see: threshold of injury

medical incident

Professional Liability. A term used in some medical malpractice policies meaning that all related acts or omissions in furnishing professional services to any one person is considered one medical incident.

Medical Information Bureau (MIB)

Organizations/Health. Members: Health and life insurers. *Objectives*: Serves as a central computerized data base for storing the health histories of persons who have applied for insurance from subscribing companies. *Founded*: 1938. *Headquarters*: Westwood, MA.

see: Fire and Theft Index Bureau, Insurance Crime Prevention Institute, Insurance Services Office, interinsurer claim service organization, National Automobile Theft Bureau, Property Insurance Loss Register

medical laboratories' professional liability insurance

Professional Liability. A form of professional liability insurance for medical laboratories that provides coverage for loss or injury caused by a biological, immunological or other therapeutic agent of the type customarily manufactured or sold by clinical laboratories, but only if prepared, sold, handled or distributed by the named insured at or from the designated premises. Coverage is usually written on a claims-made basis.

see: x-ray laboratories professional liability insurance

medical liability indemnity association

Liability. An group, corporation or inter-indemnity trust formed by physicians, hospitals or other health care providers. Such associations mutually insure against claims arising from any aspect of professional practice, including public liability and medical malpractice claims.

see: medical malpractice

medical licensing board

Professional Liability. A committee of physicians and other specialists in a field of medical practice who certify medical doctors as competent and able to practice medicine within their discipline. Also included are boards of medical osteopathic or podiatry examiners.

see: board certified physician

medical malpractice

Professional Liability. Negligence or wrongdoing by a medical practitioner; the failure to exercise the customary degree of care, knowledge or skill of a practitioner in good professional standing under circumstances similar to those that gave rise to an injury. The practitioner may be a physician, nurse, emergency medical technician, or other provider of health care services for which there are established standards of conduct, skill, knowledge or technique (such as education requirements, licensing, or specialist certification) generally accepted by the professional community.

see: board certified physician, incidental medical malpractice liability insurance, malpractice insurance, medical liability indemnity association, negligence

medical payments coverage

Automobile. Medical and funeral expense coverage for bodily injuries sustained from or while occupying an insured vehicle, regardless of the insured's negligence. Coverage is commonly limited to $5,000. Coverage in the business auto, garage or truckers' coverage form can be added by endorsement (ISO form CA 99 03). Coverage in a personal auto policy follows the insured, spouse and members of the household as passengers in other vehicles and as pedestrians if they are hit by a vehicle.

synonym: automobile medical payments; *see*: business auto coverage form, garage coverage form, personal auto policy, truckers' coverage form

Liability. Coverage for medical expenses of persons who sustain bodily injury at a commercial insured's premises or operations without regard to negligence. Medical expenses include first aid, surgery, x-rays, dental services, prosthetic devices, transportation by ambulance, and funeral services. This coverage is included in the commercial general liability policy as coverage part C.

see: commercial general liability policy, medical expense limit

medical payments—homeowners policy

Personal. Coverage provided under section II, coverage F of the homeowners policy. It includes medical expenses of persons who sustain bodily injury at an insured's premises without regard to negligence. Medical expenses include first aid, surgery, x-rays, dental services, prosthetic devices, transportation by ambulance, and funeral services. Most policies provide a $5,000 limit.

see: homeowners policy—liability coverage

medical review panel

Professional Liability. An advisory committee, usually established by the state, to review and determine the validity of medical malpractice claims prior to the filing of legal actions.

see: malpractice arbitration panel, medical malpractice

medical savings account (MSA)

Employee Benefits/Health. A trust account established for the benefit of an employee (or in a few states, established by an individual) to pay for qualified medical expenses. Where such plans are permitted, contributions, interest accumulations, and withdrawals applied to health costs are exempt from income taxes. The employer is usually required to purchase catastrophic health insurance coverage with a high deductible (e.g., not less than $2,000 per covered employee, though amounts vary by state). The high deductible results in a reduced premium, and the employer must use a part of this reduction to pay into the account. The employee may also contribute up to a maximum equal to the health insurance deductible. The account is managed by a qualified trustee, which may be an insurer, a financial institution, or an employer that maintains a self-insured health plan in compliance with ERISA. Returns of unspent funds and withdrawals from an account for any purpose other than paying qualified medical expenses become subject to income tax.

compare: flexible spending account; *see*: employee benefit plan, flexible benefit plan, qualified higher deductible health plan

medical service plan
Health. A plan by which medical services are rendered by participating physicians and other health personnel. The plan is funded from periodic payments made by the plan's members or subscribers.
see: health maintenance organization, preferred provider organization

medical treatment
Workers' Compensation. An employee injured in the scope of his or her employment is entitled to all necessary medical, surgical, and hospital treatment reasonably required to cure or relieve the effects of the injury. Under workers' compensation, the employee is not responsible for any of the expense associated with treatment.
see: workers' compensation law

medically necessary
Health. Health insurance policies usually limit coverage to treatments that are deemed necessary to restore a person to health, alleviate pain or prevent death. Most policies do not cover routine physical examinations or plastic surgery for cosmetic purposes.
compare: experimental procedures exclusion; *see*: elective surgery, health insurance

Medicare
Health. A federally administered program of hospital insurance (Part A) and supplementary medical insurance (Part B) primarily for people over 65, created by 1965 amendments to the Social Security Act. It also covers people of any age with permanent kidney failure and certain other disabilities. The Health Care Financing Administration in the U.S. Department of Health and Human Services reimburses hospitals and physicians for services to qualified patients. Part A (hospital insurance) coverage is automatic for all eligible people and is financed by a payroll tax on employers and employees. Part B (supplementary medical insurance) is a voluntary program of government-subsidized insurance requiring participants to make premium payments.
synonym: Title XVIII of the Social Security Act; *compare*: Medicaid; *see*: Medicare supplement insurance

Medicare supplement insurance
Health. Private insurance purchased by Medicare participants on a voluntary basis that is designed to fill the gaps in Medicare, such as coinsurance, deductibles and noncovered services (e.g., hospital

stays beyond a certain length).
synonym: medigap insurance; *see*: basic benefits (1), Medicare

medigap insurance
Health.
see: Medicare supplement policy

medium grade obligation
Financial Planning.
see: high-yield bond

medium-term foreign credit insurance policy
Financial Guaranty/International. A form of foreign credit insurance written by the Foreign Credit Insurance Association that provides coverage for 181 days to five years. It includes both commercial and political risks for up to 90% on sales of capital and quasi-capital goods solely of U.S. origin. Coverages are written on a case-by-case basis, and there is no requirement that the exporter insure all foreign sales.
see: export credit insurance, Foreign Credit Insurance Association, short-term foreign credit insurance policy

member
Workers' Compensation. A limb or organ of the human body. Parts of the body are usually listed in a state's workers' compensation laws under scheduled injuries.
see: scheduled injury

membership termination
Employee Benefits. Discontinuance of membership in an organization or group. Such termination usually includes cessation of eligibility under a group policy (e.g., due to termination of employment or other changing circumstances) as well as voluntary withdrawal from an organization.

memorandum clause
Ocean Marine. An ocean marine cargo policy provision that acts as a deductible and does not hold an underwriter responsible for a cargo loss until the loss exceeds a specified percentage of the cargo's value.
see: ocean marine insurance

mental disorder
Health. An emotional or organic mental impairment (usually excluding senility, retardation or other developmental disabilities, and substance addiction); a psychoneurotic or personality disorder; any psychiatric disease identified in a medical manual that describes or classifies such diseases (for example, the American Psychiatric Association's *Diagnostic and Statistical Manual*).
synonym: mental illness, nervous disorder; *compare*: insanity, mental distress

mental distress

Health/Law. A disturbing or miserable mental or emotional condition other than physical pain, such as fear, anxiety, depression or grief. Nearly all U.S. states impose liability for intentional infliction of mental distress (for example, by threatening violence to collect a debt); and a few states permit compensation for mental distress caused by negligence or recklessness.

synonym: emotional distress, psychiatric stress; *compare*: insanity, mental disorder; *see*: hedonic loss, noneconomic loss, personal injury

mental illness

Health.

see: mental disorder

mental-mental claim

Workers' Compensation. A workers' compensation claim based on an injury to or disorder of the mind with no associated physical injury or trauma.

Mercalli scale

Loss Control. A numeric scale with Roman numerals that describes the effects of an earthquake, reflecting local seismic destruction, as opposed to the Richter and moment-magnitude scales, which more scientifically estimate a quake's release of energy. The Mercalli scale is based on observations at the site and therefore reflects the effects of soil conditions, distance from the epicenter, etc.

synonym: modified Mercalli intensity scale of 1931; *see*: earthquake, moment-magnitude scale, Richter scale

mercantile open-stock burglary insurance

Crime. An obsolete crime form that covered a merchant's equipment and furniture from burglary and could be endorsed to include robbery and theft. This form has been replaced by the storekeepers' burglary and robbery form.

synonym: open-stock burglary policy; *see*: crime coverages, mercantile robbery insurance, mercantile safe burglary insurance, storekeepers' burglary and robbery coverage

mercantile robbery insurance

Crime. An obsolete crime form that covered loss by robbery committed on the premises of a merchant. This form has been replaced by the storekeepers' burglary and robbery form.

see: burglary, crime coverages, mercantile open-stock burglary insurance, mercantile safe burglary insurance, messenger robbery insurance, robbery, storekeepers' burglary and robbery coverage

mercantile safe burglary insurance

Crime. An obsolete crime form which provided coverage if a merchant's safe was forcibly entered.

This form has been replaced by the robbery and safe burglary form.

see: crime coverages, robbery and safe burglary form

merchantable title

Title.

see: marketable title

merger

General. The formation of one company from two or more companies.

see: articles of merger or consolidation, upstream merger, vertical merger

merger of plans

Employee Benefits. A merger or consolidation of two or more employee benefit plans. Such a merger usually requires that each participant receive benefits at least equal to those receivable without the merger or consolidation.

synonym: consolidation of plans; *see*: employee benefit plan, plan sponsor

merit rating

Insurer Operations. A rating system used in several types of insurance that bases premiums on the insured's particular loss record.

see: experience rating modification factor, experience rating plan, rate making

messenger

Crime. An individual who has care and custody of insured property away from the insured's premises. As respects crime insurance coverage, a messenger includes an insured, a partner of the insured, or an employee who has care and custody of insured property off the insured premises. An employee of an outside messenger service is not considered a messenger.

compare: custodian; *see*: messenger robbery insurance

messenger robbery insurance

Crime. A crime coverage for money and other property against robbery occurring off the premises of the insured business (e.g., an employee robbed on the way to make a bank deposit).

see: messenger, securities deposited with others coverage form

metallic foil

Loss Control.

see: window tape

meteorological perils

Property. A group of natural perils related to weather (e.g., wind, rain, hail).

compare: economic perils, geological perils, human perils; *see*: natural perils, peril

Mexican automobile insurance

Automobile. U.S. citizens who drive into Mexico may be subject to detention by Mexican authorities following an accident, because insurance policies issued by U.S. insurers do not satisfy Mexican financial responsibility laws. Short-term automobile policies issued by Mexican insurers may be purchased at most border crossings.

see: financial responsibility law, international market categories, Mexican extension endorsement

Mexico extension endorsement

Automobile. An endorsement that can be added to the business auto, garage or truckers' policies that extends liability coverage to vehicles driven in Mexico within 25 miles of the U.S. border. Nonadmitted insurance is not allowed in Mexico even with this endorsement, so a separate short-term policy should be purchased from a Mexican insurer. This coverage indemnifies an insured for defense and settlements in Mexico and provides coverage in excess of a policy issued by a Mexican insurer.

see: business auto coverage form, garage coverage form, Mexican automobile insurance, truckers' coverage form

microwave detector

Loss Control. A device used to trigger a burglar alarm; a motion detector that projects high-frequency radio waves, or microwaves, into the area to be protected. When the waves are interrupted by an intruder, the system's circuit is disrupted, setting off the alarm.

see: burglar alarm

midi-tail

Liability. A provision in some claims-made policies giving the insured an extended, but not unlimited, reporting period, usually longer than 60 days.

see: claims-made form, extended reporting period, maxi-tail, mini-tail, tail

Migrant and Seasonal Agricultural Worker Protection Act coverage endorsement

Workers' Compensation. An workers' compensation policy endorsement (NCCI form WC 00 01 11) that extends coverage for liability resulting from bodily injury sustained by a worker covered under provisions of the Migrant and Seasonal Agricultural Worker Protection Act.

see: domestic and agricultural workers exclusion endorsement

military service exclusion

Health/Life. An exclusion in most life and health insurance policies excluding payment of benefits for death or injuries caused by military service during time of war.

see: war clause, war risk accident insurance

mill construction

Property. A type of joisted masonry construction, which is used in older factories and warehouses. A mill building is constructed of heavy timbers and masonry walls with no concealed wall spaces. It is considered a superior class of construction for fire insurance purposes.

compare: ordinary construction; *see*: construction, joisted masonry construction

mill fever

Workers' Compensation.
see: byssinosis

Million Dollar Round Table (MDRT)

Organizations. Members: Life insurance agents who have sold $1 million or more in life insurance. *Objectives*: Recognize life insurance agents who meet the organization's qualifications. *Founded*: 1927. *Headquarters*: Park Ridge, IL.

mini-tail

Liability. A provision in some claims-made policies granting the insured a very limited (30 to 60 days) extended reporting period. The mini-tail provision will run concurrently with the midi-tail or maxi-tail.

see: claims-made form, extended reporting period, maxi-tail, midi-tail, tail

minimum amount policy

Life. A life insurance policy with a relatively high minimum face amount (e.g., $100,000, $300,000). The premium rate per thousand dollars of coverage may be lower than for policies with small face amounts because an insurer's administrative expenses do not increase proportionately with the face amount of a policy.

see: quantity discount

minimum benefit

Employee Benefits. A minimum amount that must be paid under a pension plan if the benefit formula produces a lesser amount. Usually, an employee must meet a required period of service to qualify for the minimum benefit.

see: benefit formula, pension, years of service

minimum coverage

Health.
see: basic benefits

minimum coverage clause

Insurer Operations. A provisions that, notwithstanding other terms or conditions of the policy, the coverage is deemed to be at least equal to the minimum required by state law.

see: mandated benefits, policy condition laws

minimum funding

Employee Benefits. An amount that an employer

293

must contribute to a defined benefit, money purchase, or target benefit pension plan. A penalty in the form of an excise tax is assessed if an employer fails to contribute the minimum amount.

see: defined benefit plan, money purchase plan, target benefit plan

minimum funding standard

Employee Benefits. For an approved pension plan, the lesser of: (1) the excess of the total charges to the funding standard account for all plan years (beginning with the first plan year to which the funding provisions apply) over the total credits to the account for those years, or (2) the excess of the total charges to the alternative minimum funding standard account for such plan years over the total credits to the account for those years.

see: accumulated funding deficiency, funding standard account, minimum funding

minimum group

Insurer Operations/Regulation. The minimum number of persons required to form a group insurance program under state law; the minimum number that an insurance company requires to issue a group policy.

see: discretionary group, fictitious group, true group insurance

minimum participation standards

Employee Benefits. Standards that apply to a single employer pension plan that bases eligibility for participation on age and service. The plan may not deny or delay participation beyond the time an employee achieves 25 years of age and has completed a year of credited service. If a plan provides full and immediate vesting of all accrued benefits, the denial of participation may be extended until the employee achieves 25 years of age and three years of credited service.

see: employee benefit plan

minimum premium

Insurer Operations. The lowest premium amount for which an insurance company will issue a policy or will include a particular coverage in a policy.

see: loss constant, premium

minimum premium plan

Health. A group insurance financing arrangement in which the employer is responsible for paying all claims (that is, it self-insures) up to an aggregate amount, and the insurance company pays for claims in excess of that amount. Administrative services and claims are usually handled by the insurer.

see: administrative services arrangement, self-insurance

minimum rate

Insurer Operations. The lowest premium rate that an insurer is willing to charge for a specific coverage regardless of available protection or credits; the rate applied to an insured in the lowest hazard category for the covered cause(s) of loss.

see: hazard, loss constant, rate making

minimum retirement age

Employee Benefits.

see: normal retirement age

minimum retrospective premium

Liability/Workers' Compensation. The minimum premium charged to a policyholder under a retrospective rating plan, even if there were no incurred losses. Usually, the minimum is expressed as a percentage of premium (e.g., 18%, 22%, or 30% of premium).

compare: maximum retrospective premium; *see*: retrospective rating plan

minor's compromise

Law. A proposed settlement of a minor's claim, which must be approved by a court.

see: settlement

mirror reserve

Reinsurance. In reinsurance accounting, an increase in liabilities by the reinsurer in an amount at least equal to the ceding insurer's reduction in liabilities (or reinsurance credit), so that the reinsurer's and cedent's aggregate unearned premium reserves or loss reserves remain equal to what would have been required of the original insurer had it retained the risk.

see: loss reserve, reinsurance credit, unearned premium reserve

miscellaneous hospital expenses

Health. Expenses involving hospital care other than room, board and doctors' fees, such as lab tests, drugs and radiology. Most hospital policies limit coverage for these expenses by scheduling the amounts covered or combining them for a an aggregate limit.

see: hospital-surgical expense insurance

miscellaneous medical professional liability insurance

Professional Liability. A form of professional liability insurance for practitioners, technicians, and various medical laboratories and firms which provides coverage for malpractice for miscellaneous medical professions such as chiropody, chiropractic, and dental hygiene. Coverage is on a claims-made basis.

miscellaneous type vehicle endorsement

Personal. An endorsement (ISO form PP 03 23) to

the personal auto policy that expands coverage to include motorcycles, mopeds and recreational vehicles, such as motor homes and golf carts, that are listed on the endorsement.

see: moped, personal auto policy

misdelivery of liquid products coverage

Liability. An endorsement (ISO form CG 22 66) that can be added to the commercial general liability policy to cover gasoline dealers or distributors, chemical distributors, anhydrous ammonia dealers, milk dealers, etc., who deliver a liquid product into a wrong receptacle or to a wrong address or deliver the wrong product.

see: commercial general liability policy

misdemeanor

Law. A crime less serious than a felony; a violation of law punishable by a fine or a relatively short term (up to six months) of confinement in jail.

compare: felony; *see*: criminal law

misfeasance

Law/Professional Liability. Negligence, incompetence, or the improper performance of a legal act. The term is found in public officials' professional liability policies.

compare: malfeasance, nonfeasance; *see*: negligence, public officials' liability insurance

misrepresentation

Law. A false oral or written statement made with an intent to deceive.

see: contribute-to-the-loss statute, election to avoid a policy, fraud, material misrepresentation, representation

misstatement of age

Life. An incorrect (usually lower) age given at the time a life insurance application is completed. When a misstatement of age is discovered after a policy is in force, the insurer adjusts the policy to apply the premium and coverage level appropriate to the correct age.

see: age-adjustment clause

mobile equipment

Automobile/Liability. Any land vehicle (including attached machinery or apparatus, whether or not self-propelled) that is not subject to motor vehicle registration. It also includes such vehicles or equipment when they are maintained for use exclusively on premises owned by or rented to the named insured, including the roadways immediately adjoining, or when they are designed for use principally off public roads, or vehicles or trailers whose sole

purpose is to transport equipment attached to subject vehicles (such as power cranes, concrete mixers, air compressors and generators). Liability arising from the operation of mobile equipment is usually covered by a general liability policy and is specifically excluded from automobile liability policies.

see: cherry picker, liability insurance

Property. Contractors' equipment, autos, aircraft, boats and ships, and other mobile machinery.

see: equipment floater, machinery

mobile home endorsement

Personal. An endorsement (ISO form MH 04 01) to the homeowners policy forms that provides coverage on a mobile home. Section I, property coverage, is changed from "residence premises" to "the mobile home" and other structures located on land owned or leased by the insured. Section II, liability coverage, is the same as the standard homeowners policy. To qualify for homeowners coverage, the mobile home must be at least 10 feet wide and 40 feet long.

see: homeowners policy, mobile home

mobile home policy

Personal. A package policy, similar to a homeowners policy, written on a permanently located mobile home.

see: homeowners policy

mobile machinery

Property. Machinery that is readily movable and often covered by inland marine insurance.

see: inland marine insurance, machinery

mode

Risk Management. The value with the highest probability; the most frequent or most likely outcome.

compare: mean, median

mode of premium payment

Insurer Operations.

see: premium payment mode

modification of contract

Insurer Operations. An agreement to change a standard insurance policy to include special provisions for large accounts or special programs. Modifications may be instituted by an underwriter to attract more business or by an insurer or broker to handle unique exposures.

compare: contract of adhesion; *see*: insurance contract, manuscript policy

modification rating

Property. A property insurance rating method by which published manual rates are modified or adjusted by a classification factor or experience factor to determine a final policy rate.

see: experience rating plan, merit rating, rate making, retrospective rating plan, schedule rating

modified cash refund annuity

Employee Benefits/Life.

see: modified refund annuity

modified fire resistive construction

Loss Control. Buildings where the exterior walls, floors, and roof are constructed of masonry or fire resistant material, with a fire resistant rating of one hour or more, but less than two hours.

see: construction

modified life insurance

Life. An ordinary life insurance policy with premiums adjusted so that during the first three to five years, the premiums are lower than a standard policy, and in subsequent years are higher than a standard policy.

see: graded premium, ordinary life insurance

modified Mercalli intensity scale of 1931

Loss Control/Property.

see: Mercalli scale

modified premium

Workers' Compensation. The manual premium developed for an employer multiplied by the employer's experience modification.

compare: manual premium; *see*: experience rating modification factor

modified prior approval rating

Regulation. One of four generally recognized methods of rate approval used by state regulators. This method requires prior approval of rates but allows new rates to go into effect immediately after filing without waiting for official approval.

compare: prior approval rating; *see*: file-and-use rating, open competition rating, rate regulation

modified refund annuity

Employee Benefits. A form of annuity commonly used by contributory pension or employee benefit plans where, if an employee dies after retirement, the beneficiary or estate will receive an amount equal to the accumulated value of the employee's own plan contributions, with or without interest up to their retirement date, less the total retirement benefits they received prior to death.

synonym: modified cash refund annuity; *see*: annuity

modular policy

Insurer Operations. A preprinted insurance policy of components constructed around a basic piece (such as a policy jacket) with several available forms that can be used in various combinations.

The Insurance Services Office's Commercial Rating Program uses a modular policy approach.

compare: package policy; *see*: Commercial Rating Program, preprinted policy, self-contained policy

molten material damage endorsement

Property. A commercial property endorsement (ISO form CP 10 60) that adds as a covered peril damage caused by molten material or heat from molten material that accidentally escapes from equipment. Coverage is excluded for the cost to remove or recover discharged material unless the discharge was cause by another insured peril.

moment-magnitude scale

Loss Control/Property. A measure of total energy released by an earthquake that scientists generally prefer to the Richter scale because it is more precise. It is calculated in part by multiplying the area of the fault's rupture surface by the distance the earth moves along the fault. A few well-known U.S. earthquakes show different readings between the Richter (R) and the moment-magnitude (M) scales:

earthquake	R	M
New Madrid, MO, 1812	8.7	8.1
San Francisco, 1906	8.3	7.7
Alaska, 1964	8.4	9.2
Northridge, CA, 1994	6.4	6.7

see: earthquake, Mercalli scale, Richter scale

money

Crime. As defined in crime insurance forms, money is currency, coins and bank notes in current use with a face value; traveler's checks and registered checks; and money orders held for sale to the public. Older policy forms also included bullion in the definition of money.

see: crime coverages, Eurodollars, exchange rate

money and securities broad form insurance

Crime. A crime insurance policy covering loss by theft, disappearance or destruction of the insured's money and securities inside the insured's premises or outside the insured's premises while in the custody of a messenger.

synonym: disappearance and destruction coverage form; *see*: crime coverages, theft

money damages

Law.

see: damages

money—special limit

Personal. The Insurance Services Office homeowners policy coverage section C (personal property) has a "special limit of liability" provision for coins, bank notes, bullion, gold other than goldware, silver other than silverware, platinum, and medals. Coverage is limited to $250.

see: homeowners policy—special limits of liability

money market fund

Financial Planning. A mutual fund that invests in short-term securities, such as Treasury bills and commercial paper, which are highly liquid and generally safe.

compare: short-term bond fund; *see*: mutual fund

money orders and counterfeit paper insurance

Crime. A form of crime insurance covering loss due to an acceptance in good faith of any money order that has been issued or is purported to have been issued by a post office or express company. Also covered is acceptance of counterfeit paper currency of the United States or Canada.

see: alteration bond, forgery bond

money purchase plan

Employee Benefits. A pension plan where the employer's contributions are assigned to a specific employee's account and his or her final benefits are based on the final funds in each individual's account.

compare: target benefit plan; *see*: employee benefit plan

monoline policy

Insurer Operations. An insurance policy that provides coverage for a single line of insurance.

compare: multiple line policy, package policy

monopolistic state fund

Workers' Compensation. A state-operated insurance fund where businesses are required to buy workers' compensation insurance from the state. Private insurers cannot operate in these monopolistic fund states: Nevada, North Dakota, Ohio, Puerto Rico, Washington, West Virginia and Wyoming.

compare: competitive state fund

monopoly insurance coverage

International. Compulsory insurance coverage that is only available from a government-owned or -operated insurer or entity.

see: compulsory insurance

monthly debit ordinary life insurance (MDO)

Life. Debit life insurance where premiums are collected (usually at the home of the policyholder) on a monthly basis.

see: industrial life insurance

monthly limit of indemnity

Property. An endorsement to the business income coverage form that deletes the coinsurance requirement and replaces it with a provision that recovery

is limited during each 30-day period to a preselected percentage of the business income limits. This form is designed for insureds having significant monthly income fluctuations.

compare: maximum period of indemnity; *see*: business income coverage form

moonlighting exclusion

Professional Liability. An exclusion in police professional liability policies for activities of an insured officer while working at a second job that may involve law enforcement activities.

see: police professional liability insurance

mooring

Aviation. A term found in aircraft policies for water-alighting aircraft, when they are on water and are anchored or moored, or during launching onto or hauling up from the water, except under its own power or momentum.

Ocean Marine. 1. A pier, wharf, or weighted buoy or other such device or structure to which a vessel is secured.

2. The act of securing a vessel to a mooring buoy, wharf, pier or dock by chains or ropes.

moped coverage

Personal. Coverage by endorsement to a personal auto policy for liability and physical damage arising from a moped. Often, the endorsement specifically excludes medical payments coverage. (A moped is a motorized bicycle that can be peddled or operated by its motor. In some states they are licensed for highway use; in others, they are licensed as bicycles.)

see: miscellaneous type vehicle endorsement, personal auto policy

moral hazard

Property. Circumstances of morals or habits that increase the probability of a loss from an insured peril. *Example*: An insured previously convicted of arson.

compare: morale hazard; *see*: hazard, neglect

morale hazard

Property. An increase in the hazards presented by a risk arising from the insured's indifference to loss because of the existence of insurance. *Example*: An insured fails to repair faulty wiring, believing it is less expensive to pay insurance premiums than to pay an electrician.

compare: moral hazard; *see*: hazard

morbidity

Life. The frequency of the incidence of disease, illness or sickness.

compare: mortality; *see*: morbidity table

morbidity assumption

Health/Life. A statistical projection of future illness, sickness, and disease.

compare: morbidity rate

morbidity rate

Health/Life. A rate of incidence of sickness to the number of well people in a given group of people (usually 100,000) over a specified period of time.

compare: morbidity assumption; *see*: expected morbidity

morbidity table

Health/Life. A table showing the number of individuals exposed to the risk of illness, sickness, and disease at each age, and the actual number of individuals who incurred an illness, sickness, and disease at each age.

compare: morbidity assumption, morbidity rate; *see*: Hunter disability table, natural premium

mortality

Life. The ratio of deaths to a specific population. The number of deaths resulting from specific types of illness or disease.

synonym: death rate; *see*: life expectancy, mortality table, normal life expectancy; *compare*: morbidity

mortality assumption

Life. An actuarial assumption of the probability of death at given ages.

synonym: death rate; *compare*: mortality rate

mortality rate

Life. The relationship of the frequency of deaths of individual members of a group to the entire group membership over a particular time period.

compare: mortality assumption; *see*: expected mortality, life expectancy

mortality savings

Life. The value to an insurer when expected mortality exceeds the actual experienced mortality.

see: expected mortality, loss experience

mortality table

Life. A table that indicates the number of individuals within a specified group of individuals (males, females, airline pilots, etc.), starting at a certain age, who are expected to be alive at succeeding ages. It is used to derive the "natural premium" for an individual life policy.

compare: morbidity table; *see*: American Annuitants Mortality Table, American Experience Table of Mortality, annuity table, Annuity Table for 1949, Commissioners Standard Ordinary Table,

graduated life table, increased limits table, McClintock table, National Fraternal Congress Mortality Rate Table, natural premium, select mortality table, smoker and nonsmoker mortality tables, special mortality table, ultimate mortality table, z table

mortgage

Financial Planning/Mortgage Insurance. A written instrument executed by a borrower (mortgagor) on behalf of a lender (mortgagee) that conveys title to real property to the lender pending repayment of the loan. Some mortgages, rather than conveying title, establish a lien in the lender's favor that permits taking title in the event of default.

compare: deed; *see*: acceleration clause, assumability clause, buy-down, conversion clause, default, defeasance clause, due-on-sale provision, encumbrance, locked-in clause, mortgage note, mortgagee, mortgagor, open-end mortgage, renegotiable rate mortgage, second mortgage, trust deed, variable rate mortgage

mortgage-backed security

Financial Planning. A security secured by a pool of mortgages and the income from the interest paid on the mortgage portfolio. Examples are securities issued by the Federal National Mortgage Association (FNMA, or Fannie Maes), by the Government National Mortgage Association (GNMA, or Ginnie Maes), and by the Federal Home Loan Mortgage Corporation (FHLMC, or Freddie Macs).

mortgage banker

Financial Planning/Mortgage Insurance. An organization that originates mortgage loans and sells them to investors. Either the banker's own funds or borrowed funds are used to back the mortgages until they are sold. Generally, the mortgage banker continues to service the loans that have been sold.

see: mortgage

mortgage bond

Financial Planning. A financial bond the payment of which is secured by a mortgage on property of the issuer. The bondholder therefore has a claim on specific property, rather than a claim on income only. It is the most common type of corporate bond.

see: bond (*Financial Planning*), debt security, corporate bond, mortgage

mortgage commitment

Mortgage Insurance. A written notice from a lending institution to a buyer that it will advance funds in a specified amount to purchase property.

mortgage correspondent

Mortgage Insurance. A lending institution agent who is authorized to process and service mortgage loans.

mortgage guaranty insurance

Financial Guaranty. Insurance purchased by a lender to provide indemnification in case a borrower fails, for whatever reason, to meet required mortgage payments. Typically, the mortgagee must report to the insurer when the mortgagor is two months in default. Should foreclosure be required, the mortgagee usually must acquire title to the property before the claim is paid.

> *compare*: mortgage insurance; *see*: financial guaranty insurance, mortgagor, mortgagee

mortgage impairment insurance

Mortgage Insurance. Coverage for lenders to protect their interest in property used to secure loans. Coverage is provided in the form of difference-in-conditions on the assumption that the borrower has purchased standard property insurance naming the lender as an additional insured. This policy covers the lender's interest in the property damaged by flood, wave wash, collapse or subsidence, and earthquake.

> *see*: difference in conditions insurance (*Property*)

mortgage insurance

Mortgage Insurance. A decreasing term life or disability policy purchased by a mortgagor that covers the unpaid mortgage balance as it decreases throughout the mortgage period. Benefits can be designed either to pay the entire balance due on a mortgage or to meet monthly payments upon the death or disability of the insured.

> *synonym*: mortgage redemption insurance; *compare*: mortgage guaranty insurance; *see*: credit health insurance, credit life insurance, mortgagee, mortgagor

Mortgage Insurance Companies of America (MICA)

Organizations. Members: Mortgage insurance companies. *Objectives*: Promotes interests of its members before state and federal regulatory agencies. *Founded*: 1973. *Headquarters*: Washington, D.C.

mortgage insurance premium

Mortgage Insurance. As respects Federal Housing Administration-backed mortgages, the payment made by a borrower to the lender for transmittal to the U.S. Department of Housing and Urban Development to defray the cost of the FHA mortgage insurance program and to provide a reserve fund to protect lenders against loss in insured mortgage transactions.

mortgage note

Mortgage Insurance. A written agreement to repay a loan. The agreement is secured by a mortgage, serves as proof of an indebtedness, and states the manner in which it is to be paid. The note states the amount of the debt that the mortgage secures and makes the mortgagor personally responsible for repayment.

mortgage redemption insurance

Health/Life.

> *see*: mortgage insurance

mortgagee

Mortgage Insurance. The person to whom property is mortgaged; the lender who takes a mortgage as collateral for a loan or other extension of credit.

> *compare*: mortgagor; *see*: loss payee, mortgage

mortgagee clause

Property. An endorsement attached to a fire or other direct damage policy that covers mortgaged property, specifying that the loss reimbursement will be paid to the mortgagee as the mortgagee's interest may appear; that the mortgagee's rights of recovery will not be defeated by any act or neglect of the insured; and giving the mortgagee other rights, privileges, and duties.

> *see*: certificate of insurance, loss payable clause, noncontribution mortgage clause, underlying insurance policy

mortgagee endorsement

Property.

> *see*: guaranty endorsement

mortgagor

Mortgage Insurance. A person who mortgages property to another; a borrower who pledges property in the form of a mortgage as collateral.

> *compare*: mortgagee; *see*: mortgage

morticians' professional liability insurance

Professional Liability. A form of professional liability insurance for morticians that covers a mortuary, funeral director and employees against malpractice claims arising from mortician or funeral services. Coverage is provided on a claims-made basis.

> *see*: deceased human body

Motor Carrier Act (MCA)

Automobile/Regulation. Federal legislation enacted in 1980 that enforces the financial responsibility requirements of carriers for hire of certain hazardous materials, which are listed in the Code of Federal Regulations (49 CFR 172.101 and appendices). Depending on the type of hazardous cargo, the insurance limit required under the Act is $750,000, $1 million or $5 million, and a Motor Carrier Act endorsement must be attached to the carrier's policy.

> *see*: financial responsibility law, hazardous materials, Motor Carrier Act endorsement

Motor Carrier Act endorsement (MCS-90)

Automobile. An endorsement required on a trucker's policy or business auto policy by the Interstate Commerce Commission (ICC) for firms that haul certain hazardous cargo. A copy of the policy with the MCS-90 endorsement is filed by the insurer with the ICC and makes the insurer strictly liable for any claim against the insured, subject to the policy limits, unless 30 days' notice of cancellation has been given to the ICC and the policy on file has been withdrawn. Until the policy is properly withdrawn, coverage remains in effect. Under this endorsement, the insured agrees to reimburse the insurer for any claims that are paid under the strict liability provision which would not be covered under the auto or truckers' liability policy.

see: business auto coverage form, hazardous materials, Motor Carrier Act, strict liability, truckers' coverage form

motor carrier coverage form

Automobile. A policy form (ISO form CA 00 20), introduced in 1994, that is similar to the truckers' coverage form. It is designed for motor carriers regulated by the Interstate Commerce Commission. The primary differences from the truckers' form pertain to the insured, contractual liability and other insurance provisions.

compare: truckers' coverage form

motor truck cargo insurance

Inland Marine. A form of inland marine insurance covering cargo while being transported in a truck. There are two basic forms. The *carrier's form* covers a common carrier's liability for damage to or destruction of a customer's property when that property is being transported as prescribed by the Federal Motor Carrier Act of 1935 and 1980. It does not insure against any loss for which the trucker is not legally liable. A truck is legally required to carry a minimum amount of coverage. The *owner's form* covers truck owners against loss or damage to their own property from covered perils while being transported.

synonym: carrier's form, owner's form; see: cargo insurance, Federal Motor Carrier Act, truckers' liability insurance

motor truck cargo radioactive contamination insurance

Inland Marine. A form of inland marine insurance covering a common carrier for damage or destruction due to radioactive contamination from commercial radioisotopes to property being transported.

see: motor truck cargo insurance, radioactive contamination insurance

motor vehicle record (MVR)

Automobile. The record maintained by a state motor vehicle department of a driver's accidents and traffic violations.

movable barrier guard

Loss Control. A barrier guard designed to enclose the point of operation of machinery or equipment completely, before the clutch can be engaged.

synonym: gate guard; see: barrier guard

movie completion bond

Surety. A form of surety bond that provides assurance to the financial backers of a motion picture that it will be completed on time.

see: surety bond

moving average rating method

Insurer Operations. A rate development method that smoothes out irregularities in data, such as exposure units that are not homogeneous, unrepresentative historical losses, adverse selection of data, social inflation and distortions resulting from misleading averages.

see: adverse selection, homogeneous exposure units

multi-employer plan

Employee Benefits. An employee benefit plan to which two or more employers contribute. Plan contributions by a participating employer must be detailed in a collectively bargained labor agreement. Within one year of enactment of a plan, it may irrevocably elect not to be treated as a multi-employer plan if it was categorized as a single employer plan for each of the last three years.

see: multiple employer welfare arrangement

multi-peril crop insurance (MPCI)

Property. An archaic term for what is now open perils crop insurance.

see: crop hail insurance, crop insurance, open perils crop insurance

multi-peril policy

Insurer Operations. A policy that covers more than one peril in a single contract.

see: commercial package policy, peril

multinational absolute liability

International.

see: multinational strict liability

multinational broker

Agency/International. An insurance brokerage with operations in a number of different countries but which has not developed the full service capabilities of a global broker.

compare: domestic broker, global broker, international broker, transnational broker

multinational organization

International. A business organization that has significant operations, investments, revenues from, or capital assets in countries other than its country of origin. There is typically far more local participation in and employment by a multinational organization than by companies that operate in or export to foreign countries but do not necessarily base management decisions on global factors.

compare: domestic organization, international organization; *see*: multinational strict liability

multinational strict liability

International. The application of the doctrine of strict liability to foreign subsidiaries or affiliated companies of U.S. corporations.

synonym: multinational absolute liability; *see*: strict liability

multiple coordinated policy (MCP)

Workers' Compensation. A method of insuring workers employed by an employee leasing firm. A master policy is issued to the employee leasing firm and separate policies are issued for each of the firm's clients by the same insurer. The employee leasing firm pays the premium and is responsible for maintaining all of the policies issued under the program.

see: employee leasing, multiple coordinated policy endorsement

multiple coordinated policy endorsement

Workers' Compensation. A workers' compensation policy endorsement (NCCI form WC 00 03 23) issued under a multiple coordinated policy program. The endorsement is added to the policies of all the clients of the employee leasing firm. It identifies the covered leased workers and excludes unidentified workers.

see: employee leasing client endorsement, labor contractor endorsement, leased employee, multiple coordinated policy

multiple coverage

Health.

see: duplication of benefits

multiple employer trust (MET)

Health. A legal trust formed by a health benefit plan sponsor to combine a number of small, unrelated employers for the purpose of providing group medical coverage on an insured or group self-insured basis.

see: group health insurance, multiple employer welfare arrangement, self-insurance

multiple employer welfare arrangement (MEWA)

Employee Benefits. A trust arrangement (formerly known as a multiple employer trust) for self-funding a corporate group benefit plan that covers medical and dental insurance and pensions. Generally, MEWAs are created by small employers. They are

regulated by the Department of Labor under the Employee Retirement Income Security Act, not state by insurance regulators.

compare: multi-employer plan; *see*: employee benefit plan, Employee Retirement Income Security Act

multiple enterprise

Workers' Compensation. An organization with more than one type of operation (e.g., an electrical contractor who does some plumbing), which therefore has one or more workers' compensation classification codes different from the governing classification.

compare: single enterprise; *see*: governing classification

multiple indemnity

Life. An increase of life insurance benefits by a stated multiple (double, triple) if death results from an accident. Some policies require more specific circumstances, such as an accident involving a public conveyance.

synonym: accidental death benefit, double indemnity; *compare*: double protection life insurance

multiple line law

Regulation. Legislation adopted in all states that allows an insurer to underwrite both property and casualty insurance. Prior to this legislation most states only allowed an insurer to be licensed for either property insurance or casualty insurance, but not both.

see: line

multiple line policy

Insurer Operations. A policy that insures more than one line of insurance, such as property and casualty. A package policy or the Insurance Services Office commercial lines policies are multiple line.

compare: monoline policy; *see*: interline endorsement, line, package policy

multiple location policy

Property. A policy that provides coverage on more than one location of the insured.

see: floater policy

multiple location rating plan

Property. A method to set premium rates on property insurance policies that cover five or more dispersed locations. It allows a credit for the reduced hazard because of the dispersed locations, and lower insurer expenses in writing a large amount of premium under a single policy.

synonym: premium and dispersion credit plan; *see*: premium discount, rate making

301

multiple of daily value deductible
Insurer Operations.

see: daily value deductible

multiple protection life insurance
Life. A life insurance policy that combines both term and whole life insurance, pays a multiple of the face amount during the term policy period, and converts to a whole life policy after a specified period of time. During the initial years—when both the term and whole life policies are in force—the multiple protection period is in effect.

see: term life insurance, whole life insurance

multiple retirement ages
Employee Benefits. Under some pension plans, ages at which an employee can retire and receive full benefits without a reduction or penalty.

see: deferred retirement, early retirement, normal retirement age, pension

multiple table extra premium
Health. A method of providing health insurance for insureds who are substandard risks. The insured is charged a multiple of a standard premium rate. The policy is issued without excluding particular risks from coverage.

see: substandard risk

multiple trigger theory
Law/Liability.

see: continuous trigger theory

municipal bond
Financial Planning. A financial bond issued by a county, municipality, or special district (e.g., water, school, port, or public transportation district). It is a long-term promissory note with interest payments exempt from federal income taxes.

see: bond (*Financial Planning*), general obligation bond, municipal bond guaranty insurance

municipal bond guaranty insurance
Financial Guaranty. Coverage that guarantees bondholders against default by a municipality. This form of financial guaranty was introduced in the early 1970s. Municipalities embraced it because their offerings took on the credit rating of the company that wrote the insurance, rather than their own ratings. It meant that most municipal bond offerings were elevated to AAA, and municipalities could raise money at lower interest. For investors, it made municipal bonds less risky.

see: financial guaranty insurance, guaranteed bond, municipal bond

municipal insurance
Insurer Operations. Insurance coverage for cities or municipalities.

see: public entity insurance

municipal lease payment insurance
Financial Guaranty. A form of financial guaranty insurance for firms that lease buildings or property to a municipal government. It guarantees the prompt payment of the lease should the governmental entity default on the lease payments. If the entity ceases making payments to the insured, the outstanding lease value will be paid by the insurer in installments over the balance of the lease period. The insurance is irrevocable and remains in full force and effect until all of the entity's lease obligations have been paid.

musical instrument dealers coverage
Inland Marine.

see: camera and musical instrument dealers' coverage

mutual aid agreement
Loss Control/Professional Liability. An agreement between a municipality or court and an adjacent public entity for law enforcement or fire protection assistance in case emergency response facilities are overtaxed by an incident. It is often called either a *mutual fire protection agreement* or a *mutual law enforcement agreement.* Many fire protection and law enforcement professional liability policies exclude contractual liability coverage with the exception of the liability assumed under mutual aid agreements.

synonym: mutual fire protection agreement, mutual law enforcement agreement; *see*: contractual liability insurance

mutual assent
General.

see: acceptance

Mutual Atomic Energy Liability Underwriters (MAELU)
Organizations. Members: Casualty insurance companies who write nuclear energy liability coverage. *Objectives*: Providing atomic energy liability insurance. *Founded*: 1956. *Headquarters*: Chicago, IL.

see: MAERP Reinsurance Association

Mutual Atomic Energy Reinsurance Pool
Liability.

see: MAERP Reinsurance Association

mutual benefit association
Insurer Operations. An association organized to provide benefits to its members under a plan that does not pre-fund the benefit (life insurance), but rather levies an assessment on members after a specific loss occurs.

mutual fire protection agreement
Loss Control/Professional Liability.

see: mutual aid agreement

mutual fund

Financial Planning. An investment company or trust that combines many investor's contributions, to invest in any one or a combination of stocks, bond, commodities, options, money market funds, precious metals or securities in foreign corporations. The funds are managed by professional money managers whose services would generally not be available to smaller investors.

synonym: investment company, mutual investment trust; *see:* asset allocation fund, balanced fund, breakpoint, closed-end mutual fund, corporate bond fund, equity fund, fixed income fund, government bond fund, growth fund, index fund, international fund, liquidation charge, load fund, low load fund, money market fund, net asset value, no load fund, open-end mutual fund, sector fund, short-term bond fund

mutual fund insurance

Financial Guaranty. A form of financial guaranty insurance that guarantees the repayment of the principal invested in a mutual fund.

see: financial guaranty insurance, mutual fund

mutual insurance company

Insurer Operations. An insurance company that has no capital stock, but is owned by its policyholders, who elect a board of directors or trustees through whom business is conducted. Any earnings belong to the policyholders and may be distributed to them as policy dividends or reduced premiums.

compare: reciprocal insurance exchange, stock insurance company; *see:* assessment mutual insurance company, bed pan mutual, demutualization, farmers mutual insurers, mutualization

mutual investment trust

Financial Planning.
see: mutual fund

mutual law enforcement agreement

Loss Control/Professional Liability.
see: mutual aid agreement

mutual mortgage insurance fund

Mortgage Insurance. A fund, managed by the Federal Housing Administration, that insures mortgages on homes, property improvement loans, and disaster relief loans.

see: mortgage guaranty insurance

mutual waiver

Law. A provision in some contracts that each party agrees to give up rights, claims or remedies against the other.

see: contract

mutualization

Insurer Operations. The conversion of an insurer's corporate ownership from a stock company to a mutual company, by buying back all the shares of stock and retiring them.

compare: demutualization; *see:* mutual insurance company

mysterious disappearance

Crime/Inland Marine. A disappearance of property without knowledge as to the place, time or manner of its loss. Losses that cannot be identified as to time and place are excluded from most all-risk property and inland marine policies.

see: all-risk insurance, disappearance, inland marine insurance

N

NAIC accreditation program
Regulation.
  see: Financial Regulations and Accreditation Program

nail
Automobile.
  see: cow

naive capacity
Insurer Operations. The potential underwriting capability in a particular line of business by insurers that do not customarily write that line; the entry of an insurer into a type of insurance (or reinsurance) with which it is not familiar, undertaken because it has been profitable for other insurers.
  see: capacity

name position bond
Crime. A fidelity bond that provides coverage in a specified amount for each employee holding a position listed in the bond schedule. *Example*: A $25,000 per position bond covering cashiers would cover a $100,000 loss caused by four cashiers; however, if four clerks were responsible for the same loss, there would be no coverage, as only cashiers were covered. If three cashiers and a clerk were responsible for a $100,000 loss, only $75,000 would be covered.
  compare: blanket fidelity bond, blanket position bond, name schedule bond

name schedule bond
Crime. A fidelity bond that provides coverage for an act by one or more employees specifically named in a schedule. Specific limits applying to each employee are listed in the schedule, as well.
  compare: blanket fidelity bond, blanket position bond, name position bond

named driver exclusion
Automobile/Personal. An endorsement added to an automobile policy that specifically excludes from all coverage losses involving a named individual. It is usually attached when the underwriter is aware of a problem driver who might be allowed to use an insured automobile (e.g., the son of the named insured) in the absence of this endorsement.
  see: automobile insurance, business auto coverage form, personal auto policy

named insured
General. An individual, business or organization that is specified in the declarations by name as the insured(s) under a policy. Other insureds may be covered without being named, but may be included for coverage as "insureds" or "additional insureds" by other provisions (e.g., the policy definitions). The named insured is responsible for premium payments, receipt of notices, and adjustment of losses.
Automobile. The named insured under a business auto policy is the insured designated on the declarations page, employees, and household members; individuals who work for an auto servicing, repairing, parking or storing business; partners and their household members; and other drivers using an insured vehicle with the permission of the named insured.
Aviation. Under an aircraft policy, the named insured is usually extended to include any person while using or riding in the aircraft and any person or organization legally responsible for its use, provided the actual use is with the express permission of the named insured.
Crime. Crime coverage forms that provide coverage for loss resulting from a dishonest or criminal act exclude coverage for acts committed by the named insured or its partners, whether they acted alone or in collusion with others. This does not exclude coverage for the dishonesty of employed corporate officers or other employees.
Liability. Under general liability policies, the named insured is required to maintain records of information necessary for premium computation, and the insurer is permitted to inspect the named insured's property and operations at any time. Only

a named insured may make agreements and representations as to statements in the policy declarations.

Property. Commercial property insurance policies have two classes of insureds: those who may file claims on their own initiative and in their own names, and those whose interests are protected only if the named insured chooses to apply the protection. The first class includes the named insured, the insured's legal representative, and named mortgage holders (for real property). The second class includes owners of property not owned by the insured whom the insured wants covered.

see: additional insured, broad named insured definition endorsement, insured, named insured—homeowners, named insured—personal auto, omnibus clause, policy declarations

named insured—homeowners

Personal. Under a homeowners policy, the named insured is usually extended to include the insured's spouse, and residents of the household who are relatives, and persons under age of twenty-one who are in the care of any other insured.

see: homeowners policy, named insured

named insured—personal auto

Personal. Under a personal auto policy, the named insured is extended to include the insured's spouse, any family member, and any person using the auto with the insured's permission.

see: family member, named insured, personal auto policy

named non-owned coverage endorsement

Personal. An endorsement (ISO form PP 03 22) to the personal auto policy that extends coverage for the use of non-owned autos to persons who do not have personal auto insurance because they do not own an automobile. This is needed when an individual is provided with an automobile by his or her employer, and the employer's insurance does not include personal auto coverage.

see: drive other car coverage, nonowned automobile, personal auto policy

named non-owner coverage

Automobile. An endorsement (ISO form PP 03 22) that can be added to an automobile policy that covers the individual operating any non-owned automobile or trailer. This type of coverage is needed by individuals driving employer-furnished cars who do not own vehicles themselves.

see: drive other car coverage

named perils

Property. Specified causes of loss covered under a property insurance policy. No coverage is provided for perils not listed.

synonym: specified perils; *compare*: all-risk insurance; *see*: broad form, open perils

names

Insurer Operations.
    see: Lloyd's member

NASDAQ

Financial Planning.
    see: over-the-counter

National Ambient Air Quality Standards

Regulation. Air quality standards established by the Environmental Protection Agency that apply to outside air.

see: Clean Air Act, National Emission Standards for Hazardous Air Pollutants, Prevention of Significant Deterioration

National Association of Bar-Related Title Insurers (NABRTI)

Organizations. Members: Title insurance companies known as "bar-related," which is a registered trademark of the association. *Objectives*: Promotes interests of its members. *Founded*: 1953. *Headquarters*: Chicago, IL. Until 1979, known as the National Conference of Bar-Related Title Insurers.

National Association of Casualty and Surety Agents

Organizations.
    see: Council of Insurance Agents and Brokers

National Association of Casualty and Surety Executives (NACSE)

Organizations. Members: Casualty and surety insurance company executives. *Objectives*: Promotes discussion of industry issues among insurance agents. *Founded*: 1911. *Headquarters*: Washington, D.C.

National Association of Catastrophe Adjusters, Inc. (NACA)

Organizations. Members: Catastrophe claims adjusters. *Objectives*: Promote the interests of the membership. *Founded*: 1976. *Headquarters*: North Richland Hills, TX.

National Association of Crop Insurance Agents (NACIA)

Organizations. Members: Service agents and insurance agencies selling federal all-risk crop insurance to farmers. *Objectives*: Disseminates information to its membership about crop insurance. *Founded*: 1981. *Headquarters*: Anoka, MN.

National Association of Fire Investigators (NAFI)

Organizations. Members: Fire investigators, insurance adjusters, firefighters, attorneys and related professions. *Objectives*: Improve the skills of those involved in investigating fires, explosions, arson, subrogation and fire prevention. *Founded*: 1961. *Headquarters*: Chicago, IL.

National Association of Fraternal Insurance Counselors (NAFIC)

Life/Organizations. Members: Sales personnel for fraternal benefit life insurance societies. *Objectives*: Promoting and educating the membership's sales force. *Founded*: 1950. *Headquarters*: Sheboygan, WI.

National Association of Health Underwriters (NAHU)

Organizations. Members: Insurance agencies and individuals engaged in the promotion, sale and administration of disability income and health insurance. *Objectives*: Sponsors educational seminars. Represents its members before federal and state legislators. *Founded*: 1930. *Headquarters*: Washington, D.C. (Formerly, International Association of Health Underwriters.)

see: Disability Insurance Training Council, Leading Producers Round Table

National Association of Independent Insurance Adjusters (NAIIA)

Organizations. Members: Claims adjusters and firms operating independently on a fee basis for all insurance companies. *Objectives*: Provides educational courses for adjusters and assists in developing the curriculum for the Associate in Claims. *Founded*: 1937. *Headquarters*: Chicago, IL.

see: Associate in Claims

National Association of Independent Insurers (NAII)

Organizations. Members: Independent property and liability insurance companies. *Objectives*: Operates as an independent statistical service that collects, compiles and files statistics. Develops simplified statistical plans. *Founded*: 1945. *Headquarters*: Des Plaines, IL.

National Association of Independent Life Brokerage Agencies (NAILBA)

Organizations. Members: Licensed independent life brokerage agencies that represent at least three insurers, but are not owned or controlled by an insurance company. *Objectives*: Promotes the interests of its member agencies. *Founded*: 1982. *Headquarters*: Washington, D.C.

National Association of Insurance Agents, Inc. (NAIA)

Organizations. The former name of the Independent Insurance Agents of America.

see: Independent Insurance Agents of America

National Association of Insurance Brokers, Inc. (NAIB)

Organizations. Members: Insurance brokers, primarily in the areas of commercial, industrial and institutional risks and related insurance. *Objectives*: Promotes the interests of the insurance brokerage industry. *Founded*: 1934. *Headquarters*: Washington, D.C.

National Association of Insurance Commissioners (NAIC)

Organizations. Members: State insurance regulators. *Objectives*: Promotes uniformity in regulation by drafting model laws and regulations for adoption by the states. Also provides support services to insurance departments such as examinations and statistical information. The organization holds four meetings each year to work on model laws and regulations and discuss other pertinent issues. *Founded*: 1871. *Headquarters*: Kansas City, MO.

see: Commissioners Standard Ordinary Table; McCarran-Ferguson Act; Insurers Rehabilitation and Liquidation Model Act; Schedule P; Statutory Accounting Principles; statutory earnings or losses

National Association of Insurance Women (NAIW)

Organizations. Members: Women in the insurance business. *Objectives*: Sponsors educational programs. Awards the Certified Professional Insurance Woman designation to qualified members who pass examinations. *Founded*: 1940. *Headquarters*: Tulsa, OK.

National Association of Life Companies (NALC)

Organizations. Members: Life and health insurance companies. *Objectives*: Promotes the interests of its members. *Founded*: 1955. *Headquarters*: Washington, D.C.

National Association of Life Underwriters (NALU)

Organizations. Members: Life insurance agents, general agents and managers. *Objectives*: Supports the principles of legal reserve life and health insurance. *Founded*: 1890. *Headquarters*: Washington, D.C.

see: Life Underwriter Political Action Committee, Life Underwriter Training Council Fellow

National Association of Mutual Insurance Companies (NAMIC)

Organizations. Members: Mutual fire and casualty insurance companies. *Objectives*: Gathering, compiling and analyzing information relating to insurance and reducing or preventing losses. *Founded*: 1895. *Headquarters*: Indianapolis, IN.

National Association of Professional Insurance Agents

Organizations. Members: Independent property and casualty agents. *Objectives:* Provide educational programs and support services. *Founded:* 1931. *Headquarters:* Alexandria, VA.

National Association of Professional Surplus Lines Offices (NAPSLO)

Organizations. Members: Brokerage firms and companies providing excess and surplus lines of insurance. *Objectives:* Provides services for its members, including conventions and educational seminars. Lobbies at the federal and state levels for its members' interests. *Founded:* 1975. *Headquarters:* Kansas City, MO.

National Association of Public Insurance Adjusters (NAPIA)

Organizations. Members: Public insurance adjusters. *Objectives:* Sponsors educational programs, certification, and rigid code of professional conduct for public adjusters. *Founded:* 1951. *Headquarters:* Baltimore, MD.

National Association of Securities Dealers (NASD)

Organizations. Members: Brokers and securities dealers. *Objectives:* Create rules for over-the-counter securities trading and standards of conduct for broker-dealers and underwriters; maintain its Automated Quotations system (NASDAQ) of reporting stock prices. *Founded:* 1938. *Headquarters:* Rockville, MD.

see: over-the-counter, registered representative

National Association of Surety Bond Producers (NASBP)

Organizations. Members: Insurance agents and brokers who write surety bonds. *Objectives:* Consider matters pertaining to contract bonds and assist in developing the curriculum for the Associate in Fidelity and Surety Bonding designation. *Founded:* 1942. *Headquarters:* Washington, D.C.

see: Associate in Fidelity and Surety Bonding

National Automobile Theft Bureau

Organizations.

see: National Insurance Crime Bureau

National Board of Fire Underwriters (NBFU)

Organizations. A now-defunct organization founded by fire insurance underwriters in 1866. The Board's main objectives were to promote fire prevention and property loss control. The NBFU was instrumental in developing the standard fire insurance policy. In the mid-1960s, the NBFU merged into the American Insurance Association; in the early 1970s, 30 rating bureaus formed the Insurance Services Office (ISO).

see: American Insurance Association, Insurance Services Office

National Building Code

Loss Control. A set of standard safety guidelines developed by the American Insurance Association. It is designed to be adopted by local governments, to provide uniformity in building construction.

National Bureau of Standards

Regulation. A division within the U.S. Department of Commerce that establishes minimum standards for manufacturing industries and products.

see: ISO 9000

National Commission on State Workers' Compensation Laws

Workers' Compensation/Regulation. A commission appointed by President Richard Nixon in 1971 to study the state workers' compensation systems. It recommended higher benefits, mandatory coverage, and unlimited medical care and rehabilitation benefits. After most states adopted the recommendations, premiums for the new benefits increased.

workers' compensation law

National Committee on Property Insurance

Organizations.

see: Insurance Institute for Property Loss Reduction

National Conference of Insurance Legislators (NCOIL)

Organizations. Members: Chairpersons or members of insurance or insurance-related committees in state legislatures. *Objectives:* Provide legislators with information to assist them in drafting laws regulating the insurance industry. *Founded:* 1969. *Headquarters:* Albany, NY.

National Convention of Insurance Commissioners

Organizations. The former name for the National Association of Insurance Commissioners.

see: National Association of Insurance Commissioners

National Coordinating Committee for Multiemployer Plans (NCCMP)

Organizations. Members: Trade unions, multiemployer pension and welfare funds and jointly administered employee benefit trusts. *Objectives:* Promotes and lobbies for improved retirement security. *Founded:* 1975. *Headquarters:* Washington, D.C.

National Council of Self-Insurers (NCSI)

Organizations. Members: Associations, companies

and others involved in or concerned with self-insurance and workers' compensation. *Objectives*: Promotes the interests of self-insurers or legally noninsured employers. *Founded*: 1945. *Headquarters*: Chicago, IL.

National Council on Compensation Insurance (NCCI)

Organizations. *Members*: Insurance companies that write workers' compensation insurance. *Objectives*: Collects statistics on the frequency and severity of job-related injuries (to establish a rate structure for member companies); files rate plans with insurance commissioners for member companies and generates forms and policies for member companies. *Founded*: 1923. *Headquarters*: Boca Raton, FL.

National Credit Union Administration (NCUA)

Organizations. An organization similar to the Federal Deposit Insurance Corporation that provides deposit insurance for credit union accounts.

see: Federal Deposit Insurance Corporation

National Crime Prevention Council (NCPC)

Organizations. *Members*: Citizen groups, governmental agencies, and law enforcement agencies. *Objectives*: Coordinate national strategy and provide information on crime prevention efforts. *Founded*: 1982. *Headquarters*: Washington, D.C.

National Crop Insurance Association (NCIA)

Organizations. An association that merged with the Crop Hail Insurance Actuarial Association in 1989 to form National Crop Insurance Services.

see: National Crop Insurance Services

National Crop Insurance Services (NCIS)

Organizations. *Members*: Insurers covering agricultural crops against hail, fire and other weather perils. *Objectives*: Serves as a statistical and rating organization. *Founded*: 1989. *Headquarters*: Overland Park, KS. Formed by a merger of the Crop-Hail Insurance Actuarial Association and the National Crop Insurance Association.

see: crop insurance, crop-hail insurance

National Emission Standards for Hazardous Air Pollutants

Regulation. Air quality emission standards of the Environmental Protection Agency for an air pollutant not covered by the National Ambient Air Quality Standards that may cause an increase in deaths or serious illnesses. Primary standards are designed to protect human health. Secondary standards are designed to protect public welfare.

see: Clean Air Act, National Ambient Air Quality Standards

National Employee Benefits Institute (NEBI)

Organizations. *Members*: Fortune 1000 corporations. *Objectives*: To reduce government regulation of employee benefits and to promote legislation and regulation favorable to their member's interests. *Founded*: 1977. *Headquarters*: Washington, D.C.

National Environmental Policy Act (NEPA)

Regulation. Federal legislation (U.S. Code Title 42, Chapter 55) adopted in 1970 and amended in 1990 that establishes the general policies and procedures for the federal government concerning the environment. It establishes the Council on Environmental Quality, requires that environmental values be considered in government decision making along with economic and technical factors, and requires federal agencies to submit environmental impact statements for proposed major projects.

see: Council on Environmental Quality

National Federation of Grange Mutual Insurance Companies (NFGMIC)

Organizations. *Members*: Grange insurance companies. *Objectives*: Provides reinsurance and promotes Grange mutual insurance. *Founded*: 1934. *Headquarters*: Glastonbury, CT.

national fire code

Property.

see: National Fire Protection Association

National Fire Protection Association (NFPA)

Organizations. *Members*: Business, industry, fire service, health care, educational groups and other institutions and people in the fields of insurance, government, architecture and engineering. *Objectives*: Sets fire safety standards, and serves as a clearing house of information concerning fire loss control. Publishes a national fire code. *Founded*: 1896. *Headquarters*: Quincy, MA.

National Flood Insurance Program (NFIP)

Property. A program administered by the Federal Insurance Administration that provides flood insurance under the National Flood Insurance Act of 1968. A number of private insurers are under contract to the NFIP to administer the program. These insurers issue the program's Standard Flood Insurance Policy, they are reinsured for 100% of any flood losses by the federal government, they collect the premium, and they adjust the losses. They receive a percentage of the premium for commissions, taxes, and allocated loss adjustment expenses.

see: Emergency National Flood Insurance Program, Federal Insurance Administration, Flood Disaster Protection, Flood Hazard Boundary Map, flood insurance, Flood Insurance Manual, flood insurance rate map, Regular National Flood Insurance Program

National Fraternal Congress Mortality Rate Table

Life. A mortality table prepared for fraternal insurers in 1898.

National Fraternal Congress of America (NFCA)

Organizations. Members: Fraternal benefit societies writing life, accident and health insurance. *Objectives*: To promote the general welfare of the fraternal benefit system by uniting fraternal benefit societies in all matters of mutual concern. *Founded*: 1913. *Headquarters*: Naperville, IL.

National Fraud Advisory Commission (NFAC)

Organizations. Members: Representatives of insurance, business, academia, labor, law, government, law enforcement and health care industry who have been appointed by the President of the National Council on Compensation Insurance. *Objectives*: A nonpartisan commission to educate key constituencies about the discovery and prevention of workers' compensation insurance fraud. *Founded*: 1992. *Headquarters*: Boca Raton, FL.

National Health Care Anti-Fraud Association (NHAFA)

Organizations. Members: Public and private agencies involved in health care and insurance. *Objectives*: Seeks to reduce health care fraud and costs. *Founded*: 1985. *Headquarters*: Washington, D.C.

national health insurance

Health/International. A form of health insurance in some countries, such as Great Britain and Canada, where all citizens are covered by a health insurance program administered by the national government and financed through taxes.

synonym: socialized health insurance; *see*: single payer plan

National Health Planning and Resource Development Act

Health.

see: annual implementation plan

National Institute for Occupational Safety and Health (NIOSH)

Regulation. A division of the U.S. Department of Health, Education and Welfare responsible for researching injury and illness arising from workplace hazards. As a result of its research, recommendations are made covering standards for employees' maximum exposures to hazardous substances.

see: Occupational Safety and Health Act

National Institute of Pension Administrators (NIPA)

Organizations. Members: Individuals with a minimum of one year's experience in pension administration. *Objectives*: Provides educational programs for the accreditation of pension administrators. *Founded*: 1983. *Headquarters*: Tustin, CA.

National Insurance Association (NIA)

Organizations. Members: U.S. insurance companies. *Objectives*: Exchanges information and ideas on common problems that especially affect the black community. *Founded*: 1921. *Headquarters*: Chicago, IL.

National Insurance Consumer Organization (NICO)

Organizations. Members: Consumer advocates. *Objectives*: Supports reform of unfair industry practices and marketplace abuses. Educates consumers about insurance. *Founded*: 1980. *Headquarters*: Alexandria, VA.

National Insurance Crime Bureau (NICB)

Organizations. Members: Property and casualty insurance companies and self-insured firms. *Objectives*: Stop crime and vehicle theft; maintains a computer data base used to fight crime. *Founded*: 1912. *Headquarters*: Palos Hills, IL. (Formerly, National Automobile Theft Bureau.)

see: Fire and Theft Index Bureau, Insurance Crime Prevention Institute, Insurance Services Office, interinsurer claim service organization, Medical Information Bureau, Property Insurance Loss Register

National Insurance Development Corporation (NIDC)

Reinsurance. A government corporation that provides reinsurance for private insurers that write riot and civil commotion insurance. Riot losses in major cities in the 1960s caused insurers to stop writing this coverage in certain urban areas, whereupon Congress created federal crime insurance and the National Insurance Development Corporation.

see: federal crime insurance program

National Insurance Producers Conference

Organizations. An organization of insurance broker and agent associations (e.g., the Independent Insurance Agents of America, National Association of Professional Insurance Agents, National Association of Insurance Brokers, etc.).

National Labor Relations Act

Regulation. Federal law (U.S. Code Title 29, Chapter 7) enacted in 1935 establishing the right of employees to organize and bargain collectively with employers, establish or work with labor organizations, and require other employees of the same employer to join a labor organization as a condition of employment. Many provisions were amended by the Taft-Hartley Act.

see: Taft-Hartley Act

National Oil and Hazardous Substances Contingency Plan

Regulation. Federal regulations that guide the inclusion of the sites to be corrected under the Comprehensive Environmental Response, Compensation and Liability Act.

see: Comprehensive Environmental Response Compensation and Liability Act

National Pollutant Discharge Elimination System

Regulation. A Federal Water Pollution Control Act provision that prohibits the discharge of pollutants into waters of the United States unless a special permit is issued by the Environmental Protection Agency, a state, or (where designated) an Indian tribal government.

see: Federal Water Pollution Control Act

National Priorities List

Regulation. A list of the most seriously contaminated hazardous waste sites in the United States. The list is provided for in the Comprehensive Environmental Response, Compensation and Liability Act and is updated annually by the Environmental Protection Agency. A hazardous waste site must be on the list to receive funding from the Superfund trust for remedial action.

see: Comprehensive Environmental Response Compensation and Liability Act, hazard ranking system, hazardous waste

National Safety Council (NSC)

Organizations. Members: Representatives from all kinds of industries. *Objectives*: Publishes and disseminates safety education material and statistics on accidents and workplace injuries. *Founded*: 1913. *Headquarters*: Itasca, IL.

National Service Life Insurance (NSLI)

Life. Life insurance underwritten by the federal government for those who served in the U.S. armed forces from 1940 to 1951.

synonym: United States Government Life Insurance

National Society of Insurance Premium Auditors (NSIPA)

Organizations. Members: Employees of insurance companies who are involved in field, administrative or support service policy auditing to determine insurance premiums. *Objectives*: Establishes uniform standards for auditing, promoting the interests of the members, and conducting research. Develops professional courses of study and proficiency test procedures and assists in developing the curriculum

for the Associate in Premium Auditing designation. *Founded*: 1975. *Headquarters*: Boys Town, NE.

see: Associate in Premium Auditing

nationalization

International. A government taking of property located within the country, after which the government controls the operation of the property.

compare: confiscation, deprivation, expropriation

Nationwide Definition and Interpretation of the Powers of Marine and Transportation Underwriters (NDIPMTU)

Inland Marine. The full title of the Nationwide Marine Insurance Definition.

see: Nationwide Marine Insurance Definition

Nationwide Inter-Company Arbitration Agreement

Insurer Operations. An agreement that covers controversies between insurance companies, including those involving policy coverage and interpretations, or subrogation. Participating companies agree that certain controversies must be submitted to arbitration.

see: arbitration, dual coverage, other insurance provision, subrogation

Nationwide Marine Insurance Definition

Ocean Marine/Inland Marine. A statement about the types of coverage that may properly be written on inland marine and ocean marine insurance forms. The National Association of Insurance Commissioners adopted a Nationwide Marine Insurance Definition in 1953 and revised it in 1976. This definition is used principally for classification purposes, rather than as a definition of underwriting powers. The majority of states have adopted the 1976 version, but the 1953 version is still in effect in some states.

synonym: marine definition, Nationwide Definition and Interpretation of the Powers of Marine and Transportation Underwriters; *see*: inland marine insurance, instrumentalities of transportation and communication, ocean marine insurance, transportation insurance

natural death declaration

Health.

see: living will

Natural Disaster Coalition, Inc. (NDCI)

Organizations. Members: Insurers, insurance industry associations, lenders, state emergency managers, firefighters and homeowner groups. *Objectives*: Reduce property losses and injuries from natural disasters. *Founded*: 1994. *Headquarters*: Washington, D.C.

natural expiry

Insurer Operations. The normal termination date of an insurance policy.

see: expiration date, policy period

natural perils

Property. One of three broad categories of perils (with *human* and *economic*), meaning forces or events of nature that can cause a loss, such as severe weather, earthquake, rot and rust, etc. These perils can also be called *acts of God*.

Risk Management. A general classification of perils including occurrences in the ordinary course of nature, such as drought, earthquake, erosion, fire of natural origin, flood, hail, mold, rust, sinkhole, temperature extremes, vermin, volcanic eruption and wind.

compare: economic perils, human perils; *see:* act of God, force majeure, geological perils, meteorological perils, peril

natural premium

Life. A life insurance premium developed from a mortality table, representing the amount of money that must be collected from each member of a group composed of the same age and sex in order to pay $1,000 for each death likely to occur in the group each year.

see: morbidity table, mortality table, pure mortality cost, pure premium

negative amortization

Financial Planning. A debt with installment payments less than the interest cost, so there is no amortization of the principal and the loan balance increases instead of declines.

see: amortization, payment cap

negative cash flow

Risk Management. A financial situation where a business's cash needs exceed its cash intake. Short periods of negative cash flow create no problem for most businesses, but long periods may require additional capital investment for a business to avoid insolvency.

see: cash flow, insolvency

negative film coverage

Inland Marine.

see: film coverage

neglect

Property. To disregard, leave undone, or fail to give proper attention; habitual carelessness. Most property insurance policies contain exclusions for losses caused by the insured's neglect.

compare: negligence; *see:* moral hazard

negligence

Law. The failure to exercise the care of a reasonably prudent or ordinarily careful person in the circumstances; a breach of the duty to act with care appropriate to the situation and the relationship of the persons, so as not to cause harm or loss.

compare: neglect; *see:* comparative negligence, contributory negligence, degree of care, gross negligence, liability (*Law*), res ipsa loquitur, tort

negotiable instrument

Financial Planning. A document signed by the maker or drawer that contains an unconditional promise or order to pay a definite sum of money on demand or at a specified time to the bearer or to order and does not contain any other promise, order, obligation, or power. *Examples:* checks, coupon bonds, and promissory notes.

see: demand deposit

negotiated contribution plan

Employee Benefits. A form of defined contribution plan, where a collective bargaining agreement establishes the amount of employer contributions. Frequently, these plans involve several employers and are administered jointly by the employer(s) and a union representing the employees.

see: collectively bargained contribution plan, employee benefit plan

neighbors and tenants liability

International/Property. Property insurance coverage for liability imposed by the Napoleonic code in France and by Islamic law for property damage and resulting financial loss caused by fire or other specified perils. The laws can impose a form of strict liability by an owner or tenant to neighbors, by a tenant to an owner, or by an owner to a tenant.

see: strict liability

neon sign floater

Inland Marine. Insurance that provides all-risk coverage on neon signs and automatic or mechanical electric signs. Each sign must be specifically listed on the policy. The form is not designed to cover billboards or ordinary fixed signs even if they are illuminated by attached electric lights.

see: floater policy

nervous disorder

Health.

see: mental disorder

net amount at risk

Life. The difference between a life insurance policy's face amount and its reserve or cash value.

see: cash surrender value, face amount

net asset value (NAV)

Financial Planning. The price calculated daily at

311

the market close for a mutual fund share. Shares are sold at NAV plus any sales charge (or front end load) and are redeemed at NAV minus any redemption charge (or back end load). *Formula*: (fund assets – fund liabilities) ÷ number of shares outstanding.

see: back end load, front end load, mutual fund, no load fund

net cash value
Life. The net amount of cash that the policyholder will receive from the insurer upon surrendering a life policy for its cash value. It is the cash value minus any policy loans, plus accumulated dividends.

see: cash surrender value, life insurance

net change
Financial Planning. The increase or decrease in the closing price of a stock from one trading day to the next.

net current assets
Accounting.

see: working capital

net income
Accounting. The balance of funds remaining after all of an organization's expenses are subtracted from gross sales; the excess of revenues over expenses; profit. Net income is the amount that can be distributed to an organization's owners or be kept as retained earnings.

see: financial statement, financial underwriting, retained earnings

net increase
Insurer Operations. The increase in an insurance company's business measured by premium volume during a specified period of time. It is calculated by adding the new and renewal policy premiums and subtracting the premium from lapsed and canceled policies.

net interest earned
Insurer Operations. The average interest an insurance company earns during a specified period of time. The amount is calculated prior to tax considerations by taking the interest earned on investments and subtracting investment expenses.

see: interest, investment income

net level premium
Life.

see: level premium life insurance

net level premium reserve
Life. A premium reserve established for level premium ordinary life insurance policies in their initial years of coverage, to offset inadequate premiums charged in later years. The reserve is based on the amount of excess premium charged in the initial years, plus the interest earned on the accumulated excess premium. As long as such a reserve exists for a policy, it comprises part of that policy's death benefit.

see: level premium life insurance

net line
Insurer Operations. The maximum amount of loss that an insurer is willing to retain on a particular risk without reinsurance.

synonym: retention; compare: remainder; see: gross line, line

Reinsurance. The amount of coverage retained by a ceding insurer on an individual risk (before a loss) or occurrence (after a loss).

synonym: net retained line; see: net retained lines clause, net retention

net loss
Insurer Operations. An amount of loss sustained by an insurer after deducting any recoveries, salvage and reinsurance.

see: net underwriting profit (or loss), ultimate net loss

net net income
Financial Planning. A term used in real estate investments, where the word *net* is repeated to indicate actual profits after *all* expenses are paid, including mortgage payments. It indicates whether or not the investment will generate a positive cash flow.

see: cash flow

net payment cost comparison index
Life. A comparison of the costs of life insurance policies at 10- and 20-year periods assuming premium payments continue until payment of the death benefit. This index is of value when the death benefit is considered more important than the cash surrender value.

compare: surrender cost comparison index; see: cash surrender value

net premium
Insurer Operations. Gross policy premium minus agent's or broker's commissions; the premium available to pay anticipated losses, prior to any loading for other expenses.

synonym: net single premium; compare: gross premium, pure premium; see: premium

Life. An initial participating life insurance policy premium minus policy dividends when the insured applies such dividends to pay part of the policy premium.

see: initial premium, participating policy, policy dividend

net premiums written

Insurer Operations. An insurer's retained premium income—direct or through reinsurance—minus payments made for reinsurance ceded.

see: premium, reinsurance premium

net present value method (NPV)

Financial Planning. A method of ranking investment proposals. The net present value is equal to the present value of future returns, discounted at the marginal cost of capital, minus the present value of the cost of the investment.

see: discount factor, profitability index, present value

net quick assets

Accounting/Surety. Net current assets minus inventory. It is of interest to surety underwriters because it indicates a business's ability to respond to financial obligations.

see: current assets, working capital

net retained liability

Reinsurance.

see: net retention

net retained line

Insurer Operations.

see: net line

net retained lines clause

Reinsurance. A provision in an excess of loss reinsurance contract that the agreement covers liability only on the insurer's net retention.

see: excess of loss reinsurance, line, net line, net retention

net retention

Insurer Operations. The amount of liability an insurer keeps for its own account and does not reinsure in any way.

synonym: first loss retention, net line, net retained liability; *compare*: remainder; *see*: net retention clause

net retention clause

Reinsurance. A provision in a reinsurance contract that indicates the amount the ceding company will retain and provides that the reinsurance obligations apply only to the business assumed by the reinsurer.

synonym: retainer clause; *see*: net line, net retained liability, net retention

net single premium

Insurer Operations.

see: net premium

net underwriting profit (or loss)

Insurer Operations. The amount (positive or negative) that results when policyholder dividends are subtracted from statutory profit or loss.

see: underwriting profit (or loss)

net worth

Accounting/Financial Planning. The total value of all assets minus liabilities. In a stock corporation, the amount of equity available to stockholders is the total common stock, capital surplus, earned surplus and accumulated retained earnings. Net worth is of interest to surety underwriters, since it indicates the ability of a business to respond to financial obligations.

see: book value (2)

net worth ratio

Financial Planning. A test of an organization's earning power based on its capitalization. It is a measure of what the stockholders earned from all sources as a percentage of their investment. *Formula*: net income + owner's equity. The higher the ratio, the more willing investors would be to invest in the company.

see: financial ratios, financial underwriting, owner's equity

network-model health maintenance organization

Health.

see: independent practice association

new for old

Ocean Marine. A provision contained in older marine policies that when damaged or lost equipment or parts are replaced with new, there is an agreed discount to represent the depreciation of the old items.

synonym: no thirds off; *see*: depreciation, repair or replace, replacement cost

New York Insurance Exchange

Insurer Operations. An insurance exchange that began operation in New York City in March 31, 1980 and ceased in 1987.

see: insurance exchange

New York standard fire policy

Property. A fire insurance form, initially drafted in 1918 and amended in 1943. Most states adopted it and required an insurer offering fire coverage to conform to the standard form until it was generally replaced by simplified language policies in the 1980s. It is still used in some areas but must be accompanied by other forms to constitute a complete modern policy. The policy covers fire, lightning, and the removal of property after a fire to protect it from further damage. It has 165 numbered lines describing the coverage.

synonym: standard fire policy; *see*: fire insurance, standard property policy

newborn
Health. A baby from the time of birth until its first discharge from the hospital or until 14 days old.
see: maternity benefit, well baby coverage

newly acquired
Automobile. A provision in a business auto policy that automatically covers a vehicle acquired since the policy was issued that either replaces a scheduled vehicle or adds to a fully covered fleet. The automatic coverage usually expires in 30 or 90 days, after which the insured must report the new vehicle to the insurer and add the vehicle to the policy.
see: business auto coverage form, nonfleet automatic

newly acquired aircraft
Aviation. A provision in many aviation policies that automatically extends coverage to newly acquired aircraft for a period of 30 days.
see: aircraft insurance, aviation insurance

newspaper policy
Health/Life. A limited health insurance policy, sold in the past by newspapers to increase circulation.
see: limited risk health insurance policy

niche marketing
Insurer Operations.
see: target marketing

nimble dividend
Insurer Operations. A dividend paid out of current earnings at a time when there is a deficit in earned surplus (or other financial account from which dividends might otherwise be paid). Some state statutes do not permit nimble dividends; they require current earnings to be applied against prior deficits, rather than being used to pay a current dividend. Some insurers occasionally pay nimble dividends to maintain a consistent dividend record.
see: dividend

nip point
Loss Control.
see: inrunning nip point

no-fault insurance
Automobile/Regulation. A system of compensation for auto accidents enacted by law in many states which requires indemnification to be made by the insured's own insurance company instead of the insurer of another driver who may be at fault in causing the accident. Legal liability or fault is not usually determined, but if injuries exceed a specified threshold, a legal action is permitted.
see: add-on no-fault benefits, Keeton-O'Connell

Plan, personal injury protection, threshold of injury

no load fund
Financial Planning. A mutual fund that does not charge its participants commissions (load). Shares are sold directly to the participant by the fund, and no outside sales organization is involved.
compare: load fund, low load fund; *see:* mutual fund

no par stock
Financial Planning. Stock stated to have no par value. Such shares are issued for the consideration designated by the board of directors, and the consideration is allocated to the capital stock account, unless the directors or shareholders determine to allocate a portion to capital surplus. As a result, in many respects no par shares do not differ significantly from par value shares.
see: par value

no-release settlement
Insurer Operations. The immediate settlement of a small claim by an insurer without obtaining a release from a potential claimant in order to maintain goodwill or avoid possible litigation.
see: release, settlement

no thirds off
Ocean Marine.
see: new for old

noise level
Loss Control. The amount of sound reaching a person's ear, measured in decibels (dB). Current U.S. requirements assign a sound level of 90 dB as a safe level during an eight-hour work day. Higher noise levels are permitted for short periods of time, ranging up to 115 dB for 15 minutes.
see: decibel, hearing level

nominal damages
Law. Money awarded in a lawsuit in order to vindicate a right or establish an interest when no substantial loss has resulted from another's wrongful act.
compare: punitive damages; *see:* damages

non-appearance insurance
Professional Liability. A form of entertainment insurance for movie and television producers that combines life and health insurance with casualty insurance to cover financial loss to a production company, theater, or event sponsor should a show be canceled or be unable to be performed at the scheduled time. The covered perils can include sickness, injury or death of a performer, flood,

snowstorm, windstorm, fire, epidemic or other catastrophic perils.

see: cast insurance, entertainment insurance

non-imputation provision
Professional Liability.

see: severability provision

non-original equipment manufacturer's replacement parts (non-OEM parts)
Automobile. Automobile replacement parts (also called *after-market replacement parts*) that were not manufactured by the original equipment manufacturer. Use of these parts by an insurer or repair shop to repair a damaged vehicle is restricted by legislation in some states.

see: functional replacement cost

nonadmissible assets
Insurer Operations.

see: nonadmitted assets

nonadmitted assets
Insurer Operations. Assets of an insurer that are not permitted by the state insurance department or other regulatory authority to be taken into account in determining an insurer's financial condition. Nonadmitted assets often include furniture, fixtures, agents' debit balances, and receivables over 90 days old.

synonym: nonadmissible assets; *compare*: admitted assets; *see*: annual statement, assets, Statutory Accounting Principles

nonadmitted insurance
International. Insurance written by an insurer that is not licensed or registered to do business in the country where the insured exposure exists. Often, a policy is issued directly to the insured's foreign parent and no local policy is provided. Premiums paid for these policies are often deductible as a business expense in the country where the insured exposure exists.

compare: admitted insurance

nonadmitted insurer
Insurer Operations. An insurance company not licensed to do business in a particular state.

compare: admitted insurer, fronting company

nonadmitted market
Insurer Operations. Insurers doing business in a state as nonadmitted insurers, that is, where such insurers are not licensed to sell and service their policies. Usually, such insurers can sell insurance in a state where they are not licensed only through excess and surplus lines brokers.

compare: admitted market; *see*: excess and surplus lines broker

nonadmitted reinsurance
Insurer Operations/Reinsurance.

see: unauthorized reinsurance

Nonappropriated Fund Instrumentalities Act coverage endorsement
Workers' Compensation. An endorsement (NCCI form WC 00 01 08A) to a workers' compensation policy that extends coverage to workers at sites specified in the endorsement that are subject to the Nonappropriated Fund Instrumentalities Act. The Act applies to civilian workers who provide services to the U.S. Armed Forces, such as post exchange (PX) services.

see: Nonappropriated Fund Instrumentalities Employees' Credit Act

Nonappropriated Fund Instrumentalities Employees' Credit Act
Regulation/Workers' Compensation. Federal legislation providing retirement and compensation benefits to people paid from so-called nonappropriated funds, who provide entertainment and retail goods and services to armed forces personnel on a military base.

see: Nonappropriated Fund Instrumentalities Act coverage endorsement

nonassessable mutual insurance company
Insurer Operations. A mutual insurance company with sufficient policyholders' surplus to cover projected losses and whose corporate charter and by-laws prohibit it from assessing its policyholders any funds in excess of initial premiums.

compare: assessment mutual insurance company; *see*: mutual insurance company, nonassessable policy

nonassessable policy
Insurer Operations. An insurance policy that prohibits an insurer from assessing the policyholder for any adverse loss or expense experience. The term is usually applied to policies issued by a nonassessable mutual insurer.

compare: assessment insurance; *see*: nonassessable mutual insurance company

nonassignable
Insurer Operations. An insurance policy that does not allow the policyholder to assign or transfer the policy to a third party. Most policies cannot be assigned without prior approval by the insurer.

see: assignment

noncancelable policy
Health. A health insurance policy that must be maintained in force by the insurance company for an extended period of time as long as its premiums are paid. Many states have adopted standards suggested by the National Association of Insurance

Commissioners which require that noncancelable health policies continue in force until age 50, or for at least five years when issued after age 44.

compare: guaranteed insurability, guaranteed renewable, optionally renewable contract; *see*: lifetime policy

noncomplying policy

Insurer Operations. An insurance policy that does not meet state insurance department requirements on premium rate or contents (e.g., mandatory coverage or wording).

see: insurance contract

nonconcurrency

Liability/Property. A lack of coordination between two or more policies that were intended to cover the same risk in different layers, creating coverage gaps. For example, policies in a layered program (umbrella or excess policies) may not agree with respect to policy effective dates or other provisions, triggering limits not expected by the insured or leaving an exposure uncovered.

compare: following form excess liability insurance, following form excess property insurance; *see*: Cromie rule, excess insurance, layering, nonconcurrent apportionment rules, umbrella liability insurance

nonconcurrent apportionment rules

Insurer Operations. Rules developed in 1963 by property and casualty insurance companies that provide a basis for determining how multiple policies with overlapping coverage should respond to a specific claim.

see: Cromie rule, nonconcurrency

noncontribution mortgage clause

Property. An endorsement that can be added to a commercial property policy if more than one policy is in force on a mortgaged property. The endorsement allows a mortgagee to require that in the event of a loss involving the property, the mortgagee's claim will not be apportioned with other policies and the lender's interest will be paid up to the limit of the policy to which this endorsement has been attached.

see: apportionment, loss payable clause, mortgagee clause

noncontributory group insurance

Employee Benefits. Insurance offered as part of an employee benefit plan with the entire premium paid by the employer, and employees contribute no part of the premium.

compare: contributory group insurance; *see*: employee benefit plan

nondealer

Automobile. A rating category for garage liability.

A firm that does not sell automobiles or motorized vehicles, but provides services and repairs them (e.g., repair shops, service stations, garages). This category also includes trailer and mobile home dealers even though they do sell mobile equipment that can be licensed for highway use.

see: garage coverage form

nondisabling injury

Health/Workers' Compensation. An injury that does not prevent a person from performing normal job duties and does not substantially interfere with daily living activities. Such an injury is not compensable under workers' compensation, but some disability policies provide benefits of 25% to 50% of one month's disability payment even though no income is lost.

see: disability income insurance, workers' compensation insurance

nondiscriminatory

Regulation. A standard of premium rates required by most state insurance regulations —that is, an insurer may not charge rates that unfairly discriminate against any segment of the population.

see: adequate, discrimination, equity (*Regulation*), excessive, rate making

nonduplication of benefits

Health. A provision in some health insurance policies that the insurer will not pay for benefits that are reimbursed by other insurance.

see: coordination of benefits

noneconomic loss

General. Harm or loss not of a financial or tangible nature resulting from an accident or injury. This includes pain and suffering; mental distress and emotional harm, such as lingering fear or grief; loss of reputation independent of lost employment or business earnings; noneconomic effects of a disability, such as loss of sensation or enjoyment of normal activities (hedonic loss); and loss of consortium, society or companionship.

compare: economic loss; *see*: damages, defamation, hedonic loss, loss of consortium, mental distress, personal injury liability

nonfeasance

Law/Professional Liability. Failure to perform, or complete neglect of, a required legal or contractual duty. The term is found in public officials' professional liability policies.

compare: malfeasance, misfeasance; *see*: public officials' liability insurance

nonfleet

Automobile. A business automobile rating classification that applies to a policy insuring fewer than

316

five self-propelled vehicles.

compare: fleet

nonfleet automatic

Automobile. Business or commercial automobile coverage that requires the insured to report newly acquired vehicles to the insurer within a certain number of days for coverage to remain in effect on those vehicles. A business auto policy provides basic coverage for newly acquired vehicles, but usually for a limited number of days.

compare: fleet automatic; *see*: business auto coverage form, newly acquired

nonforfeiture benefit

Life. A life insurance policy provision that an insured's equity in the policy cannot be forfeited; one of several options for the use of the cash value of a policy if it lapses for nonpayment of premiums. To recover policy equity, the insured may accept the cash surrender value, obtain extended term insurance, take a policy loan, or purchase reduced paid-up insurance. If none of these options is elected, a policy specifies one that is automatically effective.

see: cash surrender value, nonforfeiture extended term benefit, nonforfeiture loan value benefit, nonforfeiture reduced paid-up benefit

nonforfeiture cash surrender value benefit

Life.

see: cash surrender value

nonforfeiture extended term benefit

Life. A life insurance nonforfeiture benefit option to use the cash surrender value of the policy to pay the premium for an extended period of life coverage.

see: cash surrender value, extended term life insurance, nonforfeiture benefit

nonforfeiture loan value benefit

Life. A life insurance nonforfeiture benefit option to use the cash surrender value of the policy as collateral for a loan to the policyholder.

see: cash surrender value, nonforfeiture benefit, policy loan

nonforfeiture reduced paid-up benefit

Life. A life insurance nonforfeiture benefit option to use the cash surrender value of the policy to purchase a fully paid-up life policy for a lesser limit. The new policy limit is based on the insured's age and the policy cash surrender value.

synonym: reduced paid-up insurance; *see*: cash surrender value, nonforfeiture benefit

nonforfeiture value

Life.

see: nonforfeiture benefit

noninsurable risk

Insurer Operations.

see: uninsurable risk

noninsurance

Risk Management. A decision not to purchase insurance for a known exposure. Losses arising from such an exposure are not pre-funded or self-insured, but are absorbed as a business expense.

compare: insurance, passive retention, risk avoidance, risk transfer, self-insurance, underinsurance; *see*: small loss principle

noninsurance transfer

Risk Management. A risk management technique for shifting an organization's potential losses to others. Many alternatives are available that may be less costly than insurance, such as subcontracting part of a project or inserting a hold-harmless agreement in a contract.

see: hold harmless agreement, risk transfer

noninvestment grade obligation

Financial Planning.

see: high-yield bond

nonledger assets

Accounting. Assets that have not been received and have not been entered on the balance sheet, but are due and payable in the current year nonetheless.

nonlegal reserve life insurance company

Life.

see: legal reserve life insurance company

nonmedical insurance

Health/Life. A life or health insurance policy issued without requiring the applicant to take a medical examination, that is, it is based on the information in the insured's application.

compare: examined business; *see*: application, medical examination

nonoccupational disability

Health/Workers' Compensation. A disability that did not occur as a result of an individual's employment, but is nevertheless covered in a few states by workers' compensation.

compare: occupational accident, occupational disease

nonoccupational policy

Health. A provision in most health insurance policies that excludes coverage for injuries covered by workers' compensation or work-related injuries. Most health insurance policies are nonoccupational policies.

compare: workers' compensation insurance

nonowned aircraft liability insurance

Aviation. Liability coverage for an employer when

employees or agents use their aircraft on behalf of the employer. The coverage can be provided by an aviation policy, or by an endorsement to the commercial general liability policy. This is also a coverage included in many umbrella liability policies.

synonym: aircraft nonowned coverage

nonowned automobile

Automobile. A vehicle used for business purposes that is not owned, leased, hired or borrowed by the insured. *Example*: An employee's own auto used in making sales calls or deliveries for a commercial insured. Nonowned autos are a classification of covered vehicles under the business auto coverage form, garage coverage form, and truckers' coverage form.

> *compare*: hired automobile; *see*: business auto coverage form, garage coverage form, named non-owner coverage, nonowned automobile liability, truckers' coverage form

nonowned automobile liability

Automobile. Liability coverage for an employer when employees or agents use their own vehicles on behalf of the employer. The coverage can be provided by a commercial auto policy or endorsed to a commercial general liability policy.

> *synonym*: employers' nonownership liability; *compare*: drive other car coverage; *see*: business auto coverage form, commercial general liability policy, named non-owner coverage

nonowned trailers in insured's possession

Automobile. A classification of covered vehicles under the truckers' coverage form.

> *see*: truckers' coverage form

nonowned watercraft liability

Liability. Liability coverage for an employer when employees or agents use their watercraft on behalf of the employer. This coverage is usually endorsed to a commercial liability policy, but may also be provided by a separate policy.

> *synonym*: watercraft nonowned coverage

nonparticipating life insurance

Life. Life insurance that does not pay policy dividends. The premium is calculated to cover as closely as possible the anticipated cost of the insurance protection with no provision for dividends.

> *compare*: participating life insurance; *see*: participating policy, policy dividend

nonparticipating policy

Insurer Operations. An insurance policy that does not pay policy dividends.

> *compare*: participating policy; *see*: nonparticipating life insurance, policy dividend

nonpoint sources

Loss Control. Pollution sources that are diffused, do not have a single point of origin, or are introduced into a stream from no specific outlet. The commonly used categories of nonpoint sources are agriculture, forestry, urban, mining, construction, dams and channels, land disposal, and saltwater intrusion.

> *compare*: point source; *see*: hazardous waste

nonprofit insurer

Insurer Operations. An insurer that provides medical expense indemnification without a profit motive and is, usually, exempt from most insurer taxes. Blue Cross and Blue Shield plans have traditionally been organized as nonprofit corporations. A proposal to convert to for-profit status or to sell or transfer assets to a for-profit insurer may require the insurance commissioner's approval and may require a deposit into a state fund to meet continuing obligations for the public benefit and to compensate the state for taxes the entity would have paid but for its nonprofit status.

> *see*: Blue Cross and Blue Shield Association

nonprofit organization

General. An organization whose activities are not undertaken to generate profits and are exempt from federal and most state income taxes (except on earnings from activities unrelated to the organization's exempt or nonprofit purpose). Nonprofit organizations include charitable and religious groups, educational institutions, private foundations, trade associations, and labor unions.

> *synonym*: exempt organization; *see*: nonprofit insurer

nonproportional automatic reinsurance

Reinsurance. A reinsurance contract under which the reinsurer is obligated to automatically assume all or a large share of all losses up to a specified limit when these losses exceed the reinsured (ceding) company's retention limit.

> *see*: aggregate excess of loss reinsurance, nonproportional reinsurance; *compare*: excess of loss reinsurance

nonproportional facultative reinsurance

Reinsurance. A reinsurance contract that is issued to cover a specific policy or group of policies. The reinsurer is obligated to assume all or a large share of all losses for those policies, up to a specified limit, when losses exceed the reinsured (ceding) company's retention level.

> *see*: facultative reinsurance, nonproportional reinsurance

nonproportional reinsurance

Reinsurance. A reinsurance contract where the reinsurer is not involved in the direct sharing of risks.

The reinsurer is obligated only after the ceding insurer's loss payments exceed a predetermined amount, after which the reinsurer's share of subsequent losses is substantial or even total. The term *nonproportional* is used because the reinsurer's share of loss is not proportional to the share of original premiums.

> *compare*: aggregate excess of loss reinsurance; *see*: nonproportional automatic reinsurance, nonproportional facultative reinsurance

nonqualified plan

Employee Benefits. An employee benefit plan that is not qualified under Internal Revenue Service rules to receive federal tax deductions for employer contributions to fund the plan. Employers sometimes use this type of plan because it allows discriminatory coverage for certain employees, rewarding key personnel with special benefits—a practice not allowed under qualified plans. A nonqualified plan may be constructed so it is less expensive for an employer, since fewer employees are included for coverage.

> *compare*: qualified plan; *see*: employee benefit plan, top-heavy plan

nonresident agent

Agency. An agent domiciled in one state who becomes licensed to write insurance in another state. Agents who do business in more than one state require additional licenses to comply with legal requirements and to earn commissions in the states in which they do not have their principal offices.

> *compare*: resident agent; *see*: agent, countersignature

nonsmoker discount

Automobile/Life. A premium credit offered by some life insurers and some automobile insurers to insureds who do not use tobacco. For life insurance, the discount is based on the evidence that smoking causes premature death from cancer and heart disease. For auto insurance, the discount is based on evidence that nonsmokers are involved in fewer accidents.

> *see*: smoker and nonsmoker mortality tables

nonstandard policy

Insurer Operations. An insurance policy or contract developed by an individual insurer for its own use.

> *compare*: standard policy

nonsubscriber workers' compensation plan

Workers' Compensation. A system allowed in the states of Texas, South Carolina and New Jersey by which an employer may opt out of, or not subscribe to, the workers' compensation laws by filing the notices required by state insurance authorities. The employer must adequately provide for compensation of work-related injuries through another method.

nonvalued policy

Property. A policy that does not specify the amount of compensation for a loss. Loss reimbursements are calculated on an actual cash value basis.

> *compare*: limit of liability, valued coverage; *see*: insurance contract

nonvoting common stock

Financial Planning. Shares of common stock that do not include a right to vote, an unusual type of common stock. In some states nonvoting shares may be entitled to vote if a proposed corporate action would adversely affect that class of shares.

> *see*: common stock

nonwaiver agreement

Insurer Operations. A document signed by an insured shortly after a claim has been filed, stating that the participation of a claims adjuster in a loss adjustment does not waive the insurer's continued ability to deny coverage under the policy.

> *see*: estoppel, reservation of rights

noon clause

Property. An insurance policy provision starting coverage at noon, standard time. However, most property policies specify 12:01 a.m. as the effective time.

> *see*: policy period

normal anniversary rating date

Workers' Compensation.

> *see*: anniversary rating date

normal annuity form

Employee Benefits. A method of computing a pension plan's cost, assuming that retirement and plan benefits both begin on the first day of the month nearest the plan participant's retirement-year birthday, which is generally 65.

> *compare*: optional annuity form

normal life expectancy

Life. The number of years that a person is expected to live, statistically determined by sex and age.

> *see*: life expectancy, mortality table

normal loss expectancy (NLE)

Loss Control/Property. A maximum loss estimate developed for property insurance underwriters that assumes normal conditions at the time of loss. The estimate may be exceeded if unusual conditions exist, such as a delayed fire alarm, insufficient water supply, or delayed firefighting response.

> *compare*: probable maximum loss; *see*: above-normal loss, amount subject, segregation of exposure units

normal probability distribution

Risk Management. A statistical curve that is symmetrical and bell-shaped. It is often used to plot probable losses.

synonym: bell curve; *see:* probability analysis, symmetrical curve

normal retirement age

Employee Benefits. The age specified by a pension plan as the earliest at which an employee can retire without taking a reduction in pension benefits. To receive maximum benefits, an employee must have reached the minimum retirement age and must have worked a minimum number of years for the employer. Historically, the minimum age has been 65, but some plans provide earlier or later normal retirement ages.

synonym: minimum retirement age; *see:* deferred retirement, early retirement, normal annuity form, normal retirement date, retirement age, Social Security

normal retirement benefit

Employee Benefits. Under a pension plan, the greater of early retirement benefits or benefits payable upon normal retirement age.

see: early retirement, normal retirement age, pension

normal retirement date

Employee Benefits. Under a pension plan, the earliest date at which a plan participant qualifies for normal retirement; usually the later of the date on which the employee reaches minimum retirement age, or the date on which the employee has worked the minimum number of years for the employer as established under the plan.

see: normal retirement age, thirty and out

nose coverage

Liability.

see: prior acts coverage

not in motion

Aviation.

see: in motion

not otherwise classified (NOC)

Insurer Operations. A classification used in underwriting various lines of insurance when no specific classification applies. It is most often used in liability or workers' compensation rating and classification.

notary public errors and omissions insurance

Professional Liability. A form of professional liability insurance for persons certified as notary publics which covers claims arising from negligent acts, errors or omissions in the conduct of the notary business. Coverage is provided on a claims-made basis.

see: errors and omissions insurance

note

Financial Planning. A written promise to pay a debt.

see: bond (*Financial Planning*), commercial paper, debenture, debt security, floating rate note

notice of cancellation

Insurer Operations.

see: cancellation notice

notice of loss

Insurer Operations. A form or statement from an insured to an insurer, informing the insurer that events leading to a possible claim have occurred. The notice includes information as to how, when and where the loss took place. For a loss to be covered, a notice usually must be submitted to the insurer within a specified period of time.

synonym: notice to company; *see:* accident report, claim, incident report, nonwaiver agreement, proof of loss, reportable event

notice of occurrence

Liability. A provision in a liability or casualty insurance policy that requires the insured to inform the insurer of an occurrence (i.e., an event that could lead to a claim), including the time, place and circumstances. Other pertinent information must be given to the insurer or an authorized agent as soon as possible.

see: accident, cause of action, cause of loss, fortuitous event, occurrence

notice to company

Insurer Operations.

see: notice of loss

notification of change in ownership endorsement

Workers' Compensation. An endorsement (NCCI form WC 00 04 14) attached to a workers' compensation policy to advise the insured that a change in ownership must be reported in writing to the insurer within 90 days of the change.

see: change in ownership, workers' compensation insurance

novation

Law. 1. The substitution of a new contract or debt for an existing one, either between the same parties or between an original party and one who takes over the interests or rights of another original party, who is thereby released from contractual obligations. A novation requires the mutual consent of the parties, but consent may be implied from the circumstances.

2. In regard to corporations, the release of a promoter who is personally liable on a pre-incorporation contract when the corporation is formed and adopts the contract.

see: assignment, assignment and assumption, contract, promoter

nuclear energy liability insurance

Liability. A liability insurance policy that will respond to claims alleging bodily injury and property damage caused by nuclear material located on the company's premises or while in transit. Most liability policies exclude nuclear energy liability, so this coverage must be purchased separately.

see: American Nuclear Insurers, Price-Anderson Act

nuclear hazard exclusion

Property. A property policy exclusion that eliminates coverage for a loss caused by any weapon using atomic fission or fusion, or by any nuclear reaction, radiation or radioactive contamination, regardless of cause. However, a fire loss occurring after a nuclear incident is covered.

synonym: nuclear reaction exclusion; *see*: radioactive contamination insurance

nuclear pool

Liability.

see: American Nuclear Insurers, MAERP Reinsurance Association

nuclear reaction exclusion

Property.

see: nuclear hazard exclusion

Nuclear Regulatory Commission (NRC)

Regulation. A federal agency that regulates the nuclear power industry. The NRC also offers supplemental insurance for nuclear facilities, in addition to private insurance pools.

see: Atomic Energy Act

nuisance

Law. An obstructive, dangerous or offensive activity, object or condition of property that harms or disturbs others or interferes with the use and enjoyment of property either by particular persons or by the public at large.

see: attractive nuisance doctrine

nuisance value

Insurer Operations. An amount that an insurer will pay to settle a claim that may not be valid. Such values are sometimes set by insurers beforehand, and claim representatives are authorized to settle any claims within that amount unless a claim is

clearly fraudulent.

see: ex gratia payment

numerical exemption

Workers' Compensation. An exemption from workers' compensation requirements allowed to very small employers in a few states.

see: elective compensation law, workers' compensation law

numerical rating system

Life. An underwriting system that categorizes life insurance applicants by applying numerical values to certain demographic factors, such as physical condition, habits, morals and family history. The values for all factors are totaled, and applicants are then classified as preferred, standard, substandard or uninsurable.

see: preferred risk, rate making, standard risk, substandard risk, uninsurable risk

nurses' professional liability insurance

Professional Liability. A form of professional liability insurance for licensed nurses that covers injury claims arising from the nursing practice. Coverage is provided on a claims-made basis.

see: malpractice insurance, medical incident

nursing expense benefit

Health/Life. Medical expense coverage for nursing care required for a covered injury or sickness. The coverage is usually written to provide only for care by a private-duty registered nurse. Care by nurses who are hospital employees would be covered by ordinary health or hospital coverage.

nursing home

Health.

see: skilled nursing facility

Nursing Home Quality Reform Act

Health/Regulation. Federal legislation adopted in 1987 as part of the Omnibus Budget Reconciliation Act that establishes standards for the operation of nursing homes and prohibits discrimination against Medicaid recipients.

see: Medicaid, skilled nursing facility

O

oath

Law. A solemn, formal pledge to tell the truth by swearing on the Bible or invoking a deity.

compare: affirmation; *see*: evidence, testimony

object

Property. The term used in a boiler and machinery policy for the specific types or items of machinery or equipment that are covered by the policy. Usually, objects are grouped in classes; sometimes, specific objects are listed.

see: covered boiler and machinery property, object definition forms

object definition forms

Property. Under the ISO commercial property rating plan for boiler and machinery, there are six object groups, any one of which or in combination can be used to describe the objects covered in the policy. The groups are: 1. pressure and refrigeration objects; 2. mechanical objects; 3. electrical objects; 4. turbine objects; 5. comprehensive with production machinery; and 6. comprehensive without production machinery. The last two groups include all the objects covered in 1 through 4 plus any other machinery or equipment that is not excluded.

see: boiler and machinery insurance, comprehensive coverage (excluding production machines), comprehensive coverage (including production machines), electrical objects, mechanical objects, pressure and refrigeration objects, turbine objects

object protection

Loss Control. A form of burglar alarm detection where a specific important object such as a safe, filing cabinet, or expensive equipment is protected, as distinct from protecting an entire building or area.

see: burglar alarm

objective probability distribution

Risk Management. An actuarially based probability distribution that emphasizes or expresses reality, not personal opinions or feelings.

see: probability analysis

obligatory reinsurance treaty

Reinsurance. A reinsurance contract under which business must be ceded by the ceding company in accordance with contract terms and accepted by the reinsurer.

compare: facultative obligatory reinsurance treaty, facultative semi-obligatory reinsurance treaty

obligee

Surety. The individual, business or organization named in a surety bond in whose favor the obligor promises performance. The person, firm or corporation protected by the bond.

compare: obligor, principal, surety; *see*: bond

obligor

Surety. In a surety bond, the principal or party bound by the obligation. Under a surety bond, both the principal and the surety are obligors, as the surety must respond should the principal default.

compare: obligee; *see*: bond, principal, surety

occupancy

Property. In fire insurance underwriting, the type or character of the property and its intended use. Occupancy is an important consideration in determining both the appropriate amount of insurance and the premium rate.

compare: construction, exposure, protection; *see*: class rating

Automobile. Under an automobile policy, a person is said to occupy a vehicle while inside, upon, getting in or out, or getting on or off.

occupancy clause

Property. A clause in most builders' risk policies that suspends coverage if the building under construction is occupied or partially occupied before its completion or acceptance by the owner.

see: builders' risk insurance

occupancy permit

Property. An endorsement to a property policy allowing an occupancy that might otherwise suspend the policy or invalidate it.

see: change in occupancy or use, increased hazard, vacancy permit

occupational accident

Health/Workers' Compensation. An accident that arises out of and in the course of employment, which is covered by workers' compensation laws.

synonym: industrial accident; *compare*: nonoccupational disability; *see*: arising out of and in the course of employment, occupational disease, occupational hazard, workers' compensation law

occupational disease (OD)

Health/Workers' Compensation. An illness caused by exposure to adverse conditions inherent in an individual's occupation, frequently over a long period. Workers' compensation provides coverage for occupational diseases.

see: arising out of and in the course of employment, bioagent, black lung disease, brown lung disease, byssinosis, occupational accident, occupational hazard, silicosis, workers' compensation law

occupational hazard

Health/Workers' Compensation. A condition or circumstance inherent in a particular occupation that increases the chance of an accident or disease.

see: hobbies or avocations, occupational accident, occupational disease, substandard risk, uniform premium

Occupational Safety and Health Act (OSHA)

Regulation. Federal legislation (U.S. Code Title 29, Chapter 15) passed in 1970 that created safety and health standards on a national level. Department of Labor safety inspectors enforce the law. It also requires employers to keep records of job-related injuries and illnesses.

see: National Institute for Occupational Safety and Health, occupational accident, occupational disease

occurrence

General. An accident, sickness or other event that results in an insured loss.

Liability. An accident, including continuous or repeated events or exposure to a condition or substance that results in injury or damage; an act or related series of acts causing injury to persons or damage to property.

compare: accident; *see*: cause of loss, fortuitous event, notice of occurrence, occurrence policy

occurrence limit

Liability/Property. The maximum limit of insurance coverage for the payment of all claims arising from any one incident.

compare: aggregate limit, per person limit

occurrence policy

Liability. A liability policy for claims arising out of incidents that occur during the policy period, regardless of whether the policy is still in effect at the time the claim is made.

compare: claims-made form; *see*: exposure theory, occurrence trigger

occurrence trigger

Liability. Under an occurrence policy, coverage is invoked or triggered if a loss occurs during the policy period. Liability is assigned to the policy in force at the time of a covered loss, though an event or condition that eventually produces the loss may have existed at an earlier time when a different policy was in force.

compare: claims-made trigger, continuous trigger theory, manifestation theory; *see*: cause of loss, exposure theory, injury-in-fact theory, occurrence policy

ocean cargo insurance

Ocean Marine. A form of marine insurance covering goods lost or damaged during transport by water.

see: ocean marine insurance

ocean marine insurance

Ocean Marine. Coverage for these types of ocean transportation exposures: ships or hulls; goods or cargo; earnings (such as freight, passage money, commissions, or profit); and liability (known as protection and indemnity). This insurance may be purchased by the vessel owner or any party interested in or responsible for insurable property by reason of maritime perils.

see: boatowners' package policy, marine insurance, outboard motor and boat policy, protection and indemnity insurance, river marine insurance, wet marine insurance, yacht insurance

odd lot

Financial Planning. Less than 100 shares of a security, which is the number that makes up a trading unit on most exchanges.

compare: round lot

odds

General. The probability that one event will occur rather than another; a ratio expressing the probability of an outcome.

see: degree of risk, law of large numbers, probability analysis

off-duty exclusion

Professional Liability. An exclusion in some police professional liability policies for officers while they are not working on a regularly scheduled shift. This exclusion eliminates coverage for an officer who attempts to stop a crime while off duty.

see: police professional liability insurance

off-premises coverage

Property. A provision in some property insurance policies that (subject to limitations) extends coverage to personal property located away from the described premises for an amount less than the policy limit. Usually, coverage is for a specified amount ($10,000 to $50,000) or a percentage of the policy limit, subject to a maximum limitation.

compare: off-premises services—direct damage endorsement, off-premises services—time element endorsement; *see*: coverage extension, manufacturers' output policy

off-premises services—direct damage endorsement

Property. An endorsement (ISO form CP 04 17) to a commercial property policy that extends coverage to losses caused by the interruption of off-premises power or other utility services. The interruption must be caused directly by a covered peril to the power facility.

compare: off-premises coverage, off-premises services—time element endorsement; *see*: business income coverage form

off-premises services—time element endorsement

Property. An endorsement (ISO form CP 15 45) to a business income policy that extends coverage to losses caused by service interruption originating off-premises. The interruption must be caused by direct physical loss or damage by a covered peril to water supply, communications, or power services. Off-premises overhead transmission lines are excluded but can be included for an additional premium.

compare: off-premises coverage, off-premises services—direct damage endorsement; *see*: business income coverage form; power, heat and refrigeration deduction; overhead transmission lines coverage

off-set ground motion

Property. As respects an earthquake, the shaking of the ground caused by movement along a geological fault line in opposite directions, which can create a vibration effect on structures, causing them to collapse.

see: earthquake

off-site pollution liability insurance

Liability. Pollution or environmental impairment liability coverage for off-site third-party bodily injury and property damage resulting from pollution emanating from an insured site. These policies usually also include coverage for cleanup costs. Coverage is on a claims-made basis with exclusions for known pollution conditions existing prior to the inception of the policy and for intentional acts of pollution.

see: pollution insurance

off-site storage coverage

Property. A builders' risk policy extension that covers equipment, machinery, and materials intended to become a permanent part of the structure under construction.

see: builders' risk insurance

offer

Law. A proposal to enter into a reasonably specific agreement, inviting another person's consent; a contingent promise in exchange for another's act (e.g., making payment), forbearance, or return promise. It is one of the elements needed to form a legal contract, with acceptance, consideration, competent parties, and a legal purpose. An offer is not made merely by advertising or soliciting customers. Asking a prospective insured to complete an application is a solicitation. The offer of insurance consists in issuing a binder, which invites the insured's acceptance by paying the premium.

see: acceptance, binder, consideration, contract, offeree, offeror

offer to purchase

General.

see: binder

offered price

Financial Planning.

see: asking price

offering circular

Financial Planning. A document published by a corporation that is an abbreviated form of prospectus and contains information about the nature and objectives of an issue of securities. Except for private offerings under Regulation D, it must be filed with the Securities and Exchange Commission before it is distributed.

synonym: offering statement; *see*: prospectus, public offering, secondary offering

offering price

Financial Planning.

see: asking price

offering statement
Financial Planning.
    see: offering circular

office burglary and robbery insurance
Crime. A crime plan designed for business and professional offices that covers money, securities and other property against burglary and robbery inside the premises, and robbery of messengers outside the premises.
    synonym: crime plan 5; *see:* crime coverages, premises burglary coverage form

office personal property form
Crime. A commercial property insurance endorsement that provides coverage for all office equipment (whether or not owned), improvements made by the insured in leased office space, and valuable papers and documents.

officers' and directors' liability insurance
Professional Liability.
    see: directors' and officers' liability insurance

officers' protective policy
Ocean Marine. A policy providing all-risk coverage for the personal property of a ship's crew and passengers. This property is not covered by marine cargo insurance.
    see: cargo insurance

offset
Regulation. A cancellation or netting of mutual obligations to the extent of the smaller amount. In liquidation proceedings, offsets are often implemented if the insolvent corporation has a counterclaim against a creditor, but some offsets are prohibited in the interest of equal treatment of all creditors. Offsets are treated in detail in the Insurers Rehabilitation and Liquidation Model Act, which has been adopted by most states.
    synonym: setoff; *see:* liquidation
Insurer Operations. A form of other insurance provision that reduces one insurer's payment of a loss by the policy limits of all other insurance covering the same loss.
    see: other insurance provision

offset pension formula
Employee Benefits.
    see: integration with Social Security

offshore insurer
Insurer Operations/Risk Management.
    see: captive insurance company

ohm meter
Loss Control. An instrument used to measure the resistance of a material to an electric current.

oil and gas deficiency insurance
Financial Guaranty. A form of guaranteed performance insurance that indemnifies the insured if an oil or gas field's actual output falls short of engineering report projections. Coverage is generally limited to fields with proven reserves with at least three currently producing wells.

oil landmen's and lease brokers' errors and omissions insurance
Professional Liability. Errors and omissions coverage for oil landmen, who search for titles and purchase oil leases for clients.
    see: errors and omissions insurance

oil well liability
Liability. Coverage for contractors against bodily injury and property damage arising out of their ownership, operation or use of oil wells.
    see: blowout and cratering, platform insurance, saline contamination exclusion

Old Age, Survivors, Disability and Health Insurance
Employee Benefits/Health.
    see: Social Security

old line company
Life. A nonfraternal life insurance company that operates on a legal reserve basis. It is believed that the term grew from the early competition between the "new" fraternal insurance companies and the commercial insurance companies, who referred to themselves as old line legal reserve companies. Most fraternal companies now also operate on a legal reserve basis.
    synonym: old line legal reserve company; *see:* insurance company, legal reserve

old line legal reserve company
Life.
    see: old line company

Older Workers' Benefit Protection Act
Regulation. Federal legislation adopted in 1990 that governs early retirement plans, severance pay and disability benefits, health benefits, cost determinations, and waivers of age discrimination rights. When an employee benefit plan coverage varies according to the participant's age, equal benefits or equal costs must be provided to each participant.
    see: employee benefit plan

omissions clause
Reinsurance. A treaty reinsurance contract provision that should a ceding insurer fail to report a loss that would normally be covered, the reinsurer is

nonethless liable for the loss, provided the omission is unintentional.

see: treaty reinsurance

omnibus clause

Automobile. A standard automobile liability policy provision that extends coverage to others who may use an insured automobile with the insured's permission without specifically naming them in the policy.

on board bill of lading

Ocean Marine. A bill of lading issued by a steamship company that confirms the receipt of merchandise and its loading on board a vessel.

see: bill of lading

on-consignment policy

Inland Marine.

see: in-trust policy

on-deck cargo

Ocean Marine.

see: deck cargo

on-site pollution liability insurance

Liability. Pollution liability insurance coverage for on-site cleanup costs. These policies require a site assessment prior to issuance and usually are issued at the time of a property sale, foreclosure, merger or acquisition. Coverage can be written to protect against environmental liabilities arising from a currently owned property if a site assessment has been made. Coverage is on a claims-made basis with exclusions for known pollution conditions existing prior to the policy's inception and for intentional acts of pollution.

see: pollution insurance

one accident

property. As respects boiler and machinery insurance, one accident means the results of all accidents or accompanying accidents that occur, whether to one object or to more than one object or to part of an object.

see: boiler and machinery insurance

onerous title

Title. A title to real estate that has been acquired by paying a valuable consideration (money, service, assumption of obligations).

compare: lucrative title; *see*: real estate, title

open cargo policy

Inland Marine/Ocean Marine. A marine insurance policy primarily used to insure goods in transit. Once the policy is issued, it remains in force until canceled by either party. The policy usually indicates the types of goods to be insured, sets geographic limits, establishes a maximum limit of liability for any one shipment, and enumerates the perils insured against. Provisions also allow certificates of insurance to be issued by the insured, based upon the master policy. A monthly report of shipments is provided to the insurer, and it forms the basis for determining the premium.

see: cargo insurance, certificate of insurance, master insurance policy, open reporting form, warehouse-to-warehouse coverage

open competition rating

Regulation. An insurance market with minimal rate regulation, allowing insurers to charge the rates they wish, provided they are adequate to provide coverage and nondiscriminatory among insureds.

synonym: open rating; *see*: adequate, excessive, file-and-use rating, modified prior approval rating, nondiscriminatory, prior approval rating, rate making, rate regulation

open cover

Reinsurance. A reinsurance treaty under which a cedent may declare and reinsure risks of a certain category (e.g., a facultative obligatory reinsurance treaty).

see: facultative obligatory reinsurance treaty

open debit

Agency. A geographic territory of life and health insurers that is not serviced by an agent.

see: debit system

open-end mortgage

Mortgage Insurance. A mortgage with a provision that permits borrowing additional money in the future without refinancing the loan or paying additional finance charges. Open-end provisions often limit such borrowing to no more than the original loan amount.

see: mortgage

open-end mutual fund

Financial Planning. A mutual fund that issues its own shares to investors continuously and then redeems shares as required. Shares are not listed on any exchange, and participants buy and sell at a unit price based on the appraised value of the fund's total assets.

compare: closed-end mutual fund; *see*: mutual fund

open-end policy

Insurer Operations. A policy having no stated expiration date; it continues in effect until canceled. Many ocean cargo policies are written on this basis.

compare: perpetual insurance; *see*: policy period

open-end release

Insurer Operations/Law. A release given by a claimant with the understanding that the full value of the claim has not been determined and that additional payments may be made. Usually, the additional payments are for limited medical treatment or for property restoration that will be performed in the foreseeable future.

see: release

open-ended plan
Health.
    see: point-of-service plan

open enrollment
Health. 1. The period of time during which participants in a group health benefit plan have an opportunity to change from the type of plan in which they are enrolled to another (e.g., from traditional indemnity health insurance to a health maintenance organization or vice versa).

2. The period of time when uninsured employees and their dependents may elect to join a health insurance program without presenting evidence of insurability.

see: health benefit plan

open group actuarial cost method
Employee Benefits/Risk Management. A method of determining the cost of an employee benefit plan, where the actuarial present values associated with expected future entrants are considered.

see: actuarial cost method, employee benefit plan

open interest
Financial Planning. An order that has been placed for a financial derivative contract but has not yet been matched with a counterparty; the total number of outstanding commodity or option orders that have not been exercised or canceled.

see: counterparty, financial derivative

open loss loading
Insurer Operations/Workers' Compensation. A charge added by some workers' compensation insurers to the incurred value of all open claims to compensate for unanticipated expenses or inflation.

compare: expense loading

open perils
Property. A property insurance form that insures against any risks of loss that are not specifically excluded. This term is frequently used instead of "all risks."

see: all-risk insurance

open perils crop insurance
Property. Crop insurance coverage written under the jurisdiction of the National Crop Insurance Services. Under a crop insurance policy, the perils insured can include fire, hail, wind, flood, insects, and plant disease.

see: crop insurance, crop hail insurance, multi-

peril crop insurance, National Crop Insurance Services

open rating
Regulation.
    see: open competition rating

open reporting form
Property. A broad term for several forms of commercial property insurance that cover all types and locations of an insured's property in a single policy.

see: blanket insurance, manufacturers output policy, open cargo policy, stock throughput policy

open slip
Insurer Operations. A Lloyd's of London slip obtained by a broker that indicates an underwriter's pre-approval for any account that falls within specified requirements.

see: London rig slip, slip

open-stock burglary policy
Crime.
    see: mercantile open-stock burglary insurance

operating expenses
Accounting. Outlays for labor, supplies or resources to be consumed in one year or less; costs incurred in ordinary business operations other than depreciation or payments of debt.

compare: capital expenditures, operating income

operating income
Insurer Operations. The sum of the net investment income and net underwriting income in a reporting period.

compare: investment income, operating expenses, underwriting income; *see*: financial statement, net income

operating margin
Financial Planning. Operating earnings (before deducting depreciation, depletion, amortization, interest, and income tax) as a percentage of sales or revenues.

see: interest, depreciation

operating ratio
Financial Planning. A ratio that indicates the efficiency of management. *Formula*: operating expenses + net sales. The smaller the ratio, the greater the organization's ability to generate profit if revenues decrease.

see: financial ratios, financial underwriting

Insurer Operations.
    see: combined ratio

operations liability
Liability. Under a commercial general liability policy, the liability that arises from the activities of the

insured and his or her employees in the conduct of a business. It does not include completed operations liability. More commonly called *premises liability* or *premises-operations liability*.

see: commercial general liability policy, premises-operations liability

opportunity cost

Financial Planning. The cost of forgoing an economic opportunity because another is chosen; the difference between the maximum profit that could have been obtained from an alternative investment and the profit from the investment actually made.

see: return on investment

option

Financial Planning. The right to purchase (call option) or sell (put option) a stock at a specified future time and price.

see: call date, call option, call price, hedge fund, option writer, put option, warrant

Life. The right of an insured to choose the form in which payments are received from a life insurance policy.

see: nonforfeiture benefit, paid-up additions, settlement options

option fund

Financial Planning.

see: hedge fund

option writer

Financial Planning. The individual who initiates an option; the seller of an option.

see: option

optional annuity form

Employee Benefits. A provision in a pension plan that allows a participant to elect early retirement or to continue working past the normal retirement age. Employees who elect early retirement receive reduced benefits, and those who continue working usually receive enhanced benefits.

compare: normal annuity form; see: annuity, early retirement, normal retirement age

optional benefits

Health.

see: elective benefits

optionally renewable contract

Health. A group contract of health insurance allowing the insurer to terminate coverage (i.e., refuse to continue the policy) only at an anniversary or a premium-due date.

compare: guaranteed renewable, guaranteed insurability, lifetime policy, noncancelable policy

optometrists' professional liability insurance

Professional Liability. A form of professional liability insurance for optometrists that covers claims for injury arising from the insured's practice of optometry.

see: malpractice insurance, medical incident

oral contract

Law. A contract that is unwritten, or one written incompletely with some terms supplied by oral communication between the parties. An oral contract is usually enforceable provided it is not barred by the statute of frauds or similar legislation.

see: contract, parol evidence rule, statute of frauds

order bill of lading

Inland Marine. A bill of lading which is a negotiable document, with interest transferred from one party to another by endorsement. The shipper or buyer is the consignee.

see: bill of lading, certificate of insurance

ordinance

Law. A law enacted by a local government or municipality.

see: ordinance or law coverage endorsement, statute

ordinance or law coverage endorsement

Property. An endorsement (ISO form CP 04 05) that can be added to a property policy written on a replacement cost basis. It covers a building in the event that the enforcement of any building, zoning, or land use law results in loss or damage, any increased cost of repairs or reconstruction, or demolition and removal costs. This endorsement incorporates the coverages that were provided by the contingent liability from operation of building laws endorsement, the demolition cost endorsement, and the increased cost of construction endorsement.

synonym: building ordinance or law coverage; see: contingent liability from operation of building laws endorsement, demolition cost endorsement, increased cost of construction endorsement, ordinance or law exclusion, replacement cost

ordinance or law exclusion

Property. An exclusion in most property insurance policies for a loss or part of a loss caused by enforcing an ordinance or law regulating the construction, use or repair of any property or requiring the demolition of property, including the cost of removing debris.

see: civil authority clause, ordinance or law coverage endorsement

ordinance or law—increased period of restoration endorsement

property. A commercial property endorsement (ISO form CP 15 31) that extends the period of recovery under business income and extra expense coverages to the period of time required to comply with the building laws.

see: business income coverage form

ordinary agent

Agency/Life. An insurance agent who specializes in selling and servicing ordinary life insurance and who may sell other types of life insurance.

see: agent

ordinary construction

Loss Control. A type of joisted masonry construction; structures with masonry walls (brick, adobe, concrete, gypsum block, stone or tile) and wood floors and roofs that have concealed interior space. A fire spreads rapidly through this type of building.

compare: mill construction; *see:* construction, joisted masonry construction

ordinary income

Financial Planning. Income or revenue from sources other than the sale of capital assets. This includes wages and salaries, dividends and interest receipts, sales in the ordinary course of business, rents, and royalties.

see: capital asset, investment income, net income

ordinary life insurance

Life. A form of whole life insurance that is issued in multiples of $1,000, with premiums payable on a monthly, quarterly, semiannual or annual basis until the insured dies.

synonym: straight life policy; *see:* limited payment life insurance, modified life insurance, permanent life insurance, term life insurance, whole life insurance

ordinary payroll

Property. The payroll of an insured's employees (excluding officers, department managers, executives, contract employees and others). Ordinary payroll is a coverage provided by business interruption policies, depending or whether the ordinary payroll coverage endorsement or the ordinary payroll exclusion endorsement has been attached.

see: business income coverage form, ordinary payroll coverage endorsement, ordinary payroll exclusion endorsement, ordinary payroll limitation or exclusion

ordinary payroll coverage endorsement

Property. An endorsement that can be added to business interruption policies to provide coverage for the payroll of employees other than officers, executives, department managers, employees under

contract and other key employees, who are automatically included.

compare: ordinary payroll exclusion endorsement; *see:* business income coverage form

ordinary payroll exclusion endorsement

Property. An endorsement that must be added to some older business interruption policies to exclude coverage for the payroll of all employees except officers, executives, department managers, employees under contract and other important employees. Ordinary workers would not be paid.

compare: ordinary payroll coverage endorsement

ordinary payroll limitation or exclusion

Property. An commercial business income endorsement (ISO form CP 15 10) that eliminates or limits coverage (e.g., for 90 or 180 days) for the payroll of employees other than officers, executives, other key personnel or employees under contract.

organizational expenses

Accounting. The costs of organizing a corporation, including filing fees, attorneys' fees, and related expenses. Organizational expenses may also include the cost of raising the initial capital through the distribution of securities.

see: capital requirement

Organized Flying Adjusters (OFA)

Organizations. Members: Aircraft insurance adjusters, rated pilots or pilots with equivalent aircraft experience. Associate members include company claims personnel, manufacturers and general insurance members. *Objectives:* Promotes high standards in the processing of aviation insurance claims. *Founded:* 1958. *Headquarters:* Corpus Christi, TX.

original age

Life. The age of an insured on the inception date of a term life insurance policy.

see: attained age, term life insurance

original age option

Life.

see: retroactive conversion

orthodontic care

Health. Dental procedures to straighten the teeth, including diagnostic procedures and appliances to realign teeth. These services are often excluded or limited under a dental service plan.

see: dental service plan

orthotic appliance

Health. A mechanical device (for example, a brace) to correct any defect in form or function of the body.

other insurance

Insurer Operations. An insurance policy covering the same conditions and perils as an another policy.

see: concurrent insurance, excess insurance, other insurance provision

other insurance provision

Insurer Operations. A provision in a property, casualty or health insurance policy describing whether and how benefits are payable if more than one policy covers the same loss. There are three common types of other insurance provisions. The policy may provide that the insurer has no liability if other insurance is in effect; that the insurer is liable only for a proportional, or pro rata, share of a loss; or that the insurer is liable only when another policy's limits are exhausted—i.e., the coverage is excess of other insurance.

synonym: contribution clause; *see*: apportionment, coordination of benefits, excess insurance, exonerating provision, joint loss agreement, nonduplication of benefits, pro rata liability clause

other states insurance

Workers' Compensation. Coverage provided under Part Three of the workers' compensation policy that extends benefits to other states if the coverage has been indicated in the policy declarations. Coverage can be limited to specific states or be provided for all states if "all-states" is indicated. Coverage applies in the event the insured undertakes operations in any state not specifically designated in the policy and is required to pay compensation under that state's law. If the insurer is not allowed to pay the benefits directly, it will reimburse the insured for such benefits. Before 1983, this coverage had to be specifically endorsed to the workers' compensation policy.

see: all-states coverage, workers' compensation insurance

other-than-collision coverage (OTC)

Automobile.

see: comprehensive coverage

other valid insurance exclusion

Professional Liability.

see: failure to maintain other valid insurance exclusion

out-of-area services

Health. Health care services provided to a managed care plan member while outside the geographic service area. One way of covering out-of-area services is for managed care plans (e.g., HMOs) that offer similar services for similar fees and deductibles to enter reciprocal contracts whereby members of each plan may use providers and facilities of the other. This is an attractive arrangement for frequent travelers, students away from home covered by their parents' plan, and children of divorced families who often visit the noncustodial parent.

compare: out-of-network services; *see*: managed care (1)

out-of-court settlement

Law.

see: settlement

out-of-network services

Health. Services by health care providers who are not employed by or under contract with a managed care plan. Some plans require care to be provided only by physicians approved by the plan, and some allow a member to see physicians outside the plan subject to deductibles or coinsurance payments. Emergency medical care outside of the geographic area of a benefit plan is not considered out-of-network, but is usually specifically covered.

synonym: out-of-plan services; *compare*: out-of-area services; *see*: any willing provider law, health care provider, managed care (1), point-of-service plan

out-of-plan services

Health.

see: out-of-network services

out of trust

Agency. A term used when an agent's trust is inadequate to meet the payment of agent's balances. This can occur when an agent has made inadequate payments to the trust or illegally withdrawn funds from it.

see: agent's trust, bucking arrears

outage insurance

Property. Coverage for lost earnings caused by an insured peril that damages property and prevents machinery from operating.

see: business income coverage form

outboard motor and boat policy

Personal. A package policy similar to the personal auto policy that covers both physical damage and liability (including property damage and medical payments) arising out of the use of an outboard motor boat. Physical damage coverage includes the boat and associated equipment, such as boat carriers and trailers, fuel containers, electric starting equipment, and controls if they are supplied by the manufacturer as a part of the outboard motor. Usually, coverage for the battery is excluded. The policy is generally used to insure outboard motor boats less than 16 feet in length.

compare: outboard motor and boat policy, yacht insurance

outcomes program

Health. A managed health care plan that includes as a key feature the gathering and analysis of information about the results of prescribed treatments and procedures. An *outcome* is the patient's change in health status at a particular time following treatment (e.g., alleviation of symptoms, worsening of the condition, new symptoms, hospital admission, death). Sometimes, surveys of patient satisfaction are included in the data. The information is used to determine the most appropriate and cost-effective treatments of specific health conditions and to reduce unnecessary medical interventions.

see: case management, managed care

outdoor signs—theft extension

Crime. An endorsement (ISO form CR 15 21) that extends Insurance Services Office crime coverage forms to include outdoor signs at specified locations for loss resulting from theft. Vandalism coverage can also be included.

see: crime coverage form A (B, etc.)

outdoor trees, shrubs and plants endorsement

Property. A commercial property coverage endorsement (ISO form CP 14 30) that increases the coverage limit on outdoor trees, shrubs and plants. Without the endorsement, most commercial property policies have coverage of $250 per item and $1,000 per location for damage by the perils of fire, lightning, explosion, riot or civil commotion, or aircraft. Highly valued trees, shrubs and plants can be specifically scheduled on the endorsement and the location limit increased. The additional peril of vehicle damage can also be added.

Outer Continental Shelf Lands Act (OCSLA)

Regulation/Workers' Compensation. Federal legislation that extends Longshore and Harbor Workers' Compensation Act benefits to workers who are injured or die on the outer continental shelf, or upon fixed structures erected thereon, while engaged in oil or mineral exploration or development. The outer continental shelf is defined as "all submerged lands lying seaward and outside of the area of lands beneath navigable waters as defined in section 1301 of [Title 43, Public Lands] and of which the subsoil and seabed appertain to the United States and are subject to its jurisdiction and control."

see: Longshore and Harbor Workers' Compensation Act, Outer Continental Shelf Lands Act coverage endorsement

Outer Continental Shelf Lands Act coverage endorsement

Workers' Compensation. An endorsement (NCCI form WC 00 01 09A) that extends coverage under a workers' compensation policy to employees designated by the Outer Continental Shelf Lands Act and deletes the Outer Continental Shelf Lands Act exclusion from the employers' liability section of the policy.

see: Outer Continental Shelf Lands Act

outlier

Health. A patient who requires an unusually long stay in a hospital or unusually high-cost treatment compared to others in the same diagnosis related group—that is, the patient lies outside the statistical norm. The hospital can seek greater reimbursement than normally allowed under the prospective payment system.

see: diagnosis related group, prospective payment system

outpatient

Health. An individual who does not need overnight care in a hospital, but who receives diagnosis or treatment in a clinic, emergency room or health care facility.

compare: inpatient; *see*: ambulatory care facility

outpatient facility

Health.

see: ambulatory care facility

outside adjuster

Insurer Operations.

see: field adjuster

outside director

Financial Planning/Professional Liability. A person elected by shareholders to a corporation's board of directors who is not an employee, officer or major stockholder. Outside directors may include investment bankers and attorneys; people who attract business or investment to the company, make borrowing easier, or enhance the corporation's goodwill through their contacts or reputation (so-called "rainmakers"); and others who provide advice and services to management but who have a very limited direct interest in the corporation. The number of inside and outside directors is of concern to a directors' and officers' liability underwriter.

compare: inside director; *see*: directors' and officers' liability insurance

outside showcases or show windows as premises

Crime. An endorsement (ISO form CR 15 11) that extends Insurance Services Office crime coverage forms to include showcases or show windows outside of but adjacent to the building occupied by the insured.

see: crime coverage form A (B, etc.)

outsourcing analysis

Risk Management. A management tool to determine whether a particular function is more effectively performed within or outside the organization. Outsourcing is a firm's use of another firm or an outside person to perform a function not considered central to the firm's corporate purpose. The organization quantifies the value of performing the function itself compared to that of contracting with an outside person or firm whose business is to provide that particular service. The use of advertising agencies is an example of outsourcing, and many employers outsource the administration of their employee benefit programs.

see: benchmarking, performance assessment review, third-party administrator

outstanding claims account

Reinsurance.

see: funding of reserves

outstanding losses

Insurer Operations. Losses that have occurred that are known to an insurer but have not yet been settled.

compare: incurred but not reported; *see*: loss

outstanding premiums

Insurer Operations. Premiums due on issued policies or business that have not yet been received by an insurer.

see: premium

over-age insurance

Health. Health insurance coverage written for a person who is above the standard limit, which is usually 65 years.

synonym: extended health insurance

over-the-counter (OTC)

Financial Planning. The trading of securities by brokers among themselves rather than on an organized exchange; a security or securities not listed on an exchange, including stock of many companies not large enough to be listed. Trading rules for the over-the-counter market are made by the National Association of Securities Dealers. Prices from NASDAQ (the Automated Quotations system) are published daily along with New York Stock Exchange listings.

overall master credit insurance policy

Financial Guaranty/International. A foreign credit insurance policy written by the Foreign Credit Insurance Association that provides blanket political and commercial risks coverage. There is usually a

10% deductible on commercial risks and no deductible on political risks. Generally, all of an exporter's foreign sales must be insured.

see: export credit insurance, Foreign Credit Insurance Association

overhead expense insurance

Health. A form of health insurance that pays the overhead expenses of a business owner in the event of disability, such as rent, utilities, and employee salaries. Covered expenses usually do not include salaries, fees, drawing accounts, profits or other remuneration for the insured, nor is coverage provided for a family member, for a member of the insured's profession who substitutes during the disability, or for anyone sharing business with the insured or anyone employed to perform the duties of the insured.

synonym: disability overhead expense insurance; *see*: key employee insurance

overhead transmission lines coverage

Property. An off-premises utility service that can be specifically covered for a business income loss on a basis similar to the off-premises services—time element coverage, an endorsement that excludes coverage for overhead transmission lines.

see: off-premises services—time element endorsement, power interruption insurance

overinsurance

General. Insurance of a risk in an amount exceeding its reasonable value (e.g., actual cash value or replacement cost); excessive limits of coverage.

compare: underinsurance; *see*: stacking of limits, valued policy law

overlapping insurance

General. Duplicate coverage of a risk, involving at least two policies.

see: concurrent insurance, other insurance

overline

Reinsurance. 1. A risk that exceeds an insurance company's normal capacity, including automatic reinsurance treaties.

2. An insurer's agreement to provide insurance or a reinsurer's agreement to assume reinsurance in excess of normal capacity.

see: capacity, line

overriding commission

Agency/Insurer Operations. A commission paid to agents who have exclusive territorial or class-of-business agreements with an insurance company, for all policies written in their territory or for that class of business, even if the business is written by other agents.

see: agent's commission, compensation agreement

Reinsurance. A fee or percentage of premium that is paid to a party responsible for placing a retrocession of reinsurance.

synonym: overwriting commission; *see*: commission, retrocession

Overseas Private Investment Corporation (OPIC)

Insurer Operations. A federal program to provide political risk insurance on U.S. investments in developing countries. It insures against confiscation, expropriation, devaluation of currencies, war exposures, and other perils.

see: expropriation insurance, political risk insurance

overtime

Workers' Compensation. The wage increment paid to employees for working time in excess of a set limit. The standard in the United States is 8 hours per day and 40 hours per week. The part of a payroll that is designated as overtime remuneration should not be included for workers' compensation payroll purposes.

see: payroll

overwriting commission

Reinsurance.

see: overriding commission

owned automobile

Automobile. For automobile liability purposes, any automobile owned by the insured including non-owned trailers while attached to an owned auto.

owned autos

Automobile. A classification of covered vehicles under the business auto coverage form, garage coverage form, or truckers' coverage form.

see: business auto coverage form, garage coverage form, truckers' coverage form

owned autos other than private passenger

Automobile. A classification of covered vehicles under the business auto coverage form or garage coverage form.

see: business auto coverage form, garage coverage form

owned autos subject to compulsory uninsured motorist law

Automobile. A classification of covered vehicles under the business auto coverage form, garage coverage form, or truckers' coverage form.

see: business auto coverage form, compulsory insurance law, garage coverage form, truckers' coverage form

owned autos subject to no-fault

Automobile. A classification of covered vehicles under the business auto coverage form, garage coverage form, or truckers' coverage form.

see: business auto coverage form, garage coverage form, truckers' coverage form

owned commercial autos

Automobile. A classification of covered vehicles under the truckers' coverage form.

see: truckers' coverage form

owned private passenger autos

Automobile. A classification of covered vehicles under the business auto coverage form or garage coverage form.

see: business auto coverage form, garage coverage form

owner-controlled insurance program (OCIP)

Liability/Workers' Compensation. Insurance on large construction projects arranged by the owner or general contractor in such a way that all interests involved (those of the owner, general contractor, subcontractors, architect, engineer, and surveyors) are combined and insured under one policy with a single insurer. Generally, it includes workers' compensation, general liability, umbrella liability, and builders' risk insurance; occasionally, it is only workers' compensation. It is designed to reduce the project's overall insurance costs and provide a coordinated project safety program.

synonym: consolidated insurance program, wrap-up insurance program

owner's equity

Accounting. The interest in a business or property in excess of any claims or liens against it. As a balance sheet item, owner's equity is established by capital contributions to an organization by its owners for formation or expansion and includes profits (retained earnings).

see: balance sheet, capital, equity (*Financial Planning*), retained earnings

owner's form

Inland Marine.

see: motor truck cargo insurance

owners' and contractors' protective liability (OCP)

Liability. A stand-alone policy or an endorsement to a liability policy that covers claims for negligence by a contractor or subcontractor hired by the insured. Any vicarious liability of the owner-insured arising from a contractor's or subcontractor's activity is covered.

synonym: independent contractors' insurance; *see*: vicarious liability

owners, landlords, and tenants liability insurance (OL&T)

Liability. A policy form available under the 1973 ISO liability rating plan still used by some insurers. The form was designed for the less desirable owner, landlord or tenant risks to provide limited coverage (i.e., not as broad as the comprehensive general liability form). As it was limited to this premises liability coverage, the form did not include protection for other-than-designated premises, products and completed operations, independent contractors and structural alterations. The 1986 ISO liability rating plan does not include a similar form.

ownership change

Workers' Compensation.
  see: change in ownership

ownership of expirations

Agency/Insurer Operations. Property and casualty insurance policy expirations are considered the exclusive property of the independent agent producing the business, and an insurer cannot reveal this information to anyone other than the originating agent. Expirations of direct writing and exclusive agency companies usually belong to the insurance company.
  see: agency agreement

ownership provision

Life. A provision that allows policy ownership by a person other than the insured.

oxidation

Inland Marine/Loss Control/Ocean Marine. A physical or chemical change in metal (such as rusting) or a possible cause of spontaneous combustion in flammable materials.

P

P/E ratio
Financial Planning.
see: price/earnings ratio

package modification factor (PMF)
Insurer Operations. Under the Insurance Services Office's commercial rating plan and most company rating plans, a commercial package policy is eligible for a premium discount if it includes coverage for both property and premises and operations liability. A factor is applied to the normal rates to provide this premium modification.
see: premises-operations liability insurance

package policy
Insurer Operations. An insurance policy that includes two or more lines or types of coverage in a single contract. *Examples*: Homeowner's (including property and personal liability) and special multiple peril policies (including commercial property and liability).
see: coverage part, modular policy, multiple line policy

paid business
Life. A policy for which an application for coverage has been signed by the prospective insured, the medical examination has been completed, the initial premium payment has been tendered and accepted by the insurer, but the policy has not yet been delivered.
compare: delivered business, examined business, issued business, placed business, written business

paid claim count
Insurer Operations. The number of claims for which indemnity payments have been made and for which the claims files have been closed.
see: claim expense

paid expense
Insurer Operations. An amount paid for the costs associated with a claim, but not including insurance company claim handling expenses. It includes defense costs (such as attorneys' fees, filing fees, and expert witness fees).
synonym: allocated claim expense; see: claim expense

paid-in capital
Accounting. Money invested in a corporation by its owners, represented by shares of stock. On a corporation's balance sheet, paid-in capital amounts are reflected in owner's or stockholder's equity.
see: capital, owner's equity

paid-in surplus
Insurer Operations. Amounts paid in by stockholders in excess of paid-in capital, to meet policyholders' surplus requirements established by applicable state insurance codes. No stock is issued for paid-in surplus, rather it is usually accounted for as a form of stockholder's loan.
see: policyholders' surplus, surplus
Accounting. Money invested in a corporation by its owners for which no shares of stock are issued; rather, it is considered a loan to the corporation.

paid loss retrospective rating plan
Liability/Workers' Compensation. A conventional retrospective rating plan with an amended premium payment provision. The advance premium remains unchanged, but the insurer agrees to accept a substantially lesser amount in cash and, typically, a promissory note secured by an irrevocable letter of credit or surety bond for the balance. As claims are paid, the insured makes further payments to the insurer, usually on a monthly basis, until all claims are paid. The required letter of credit is usually adjusted periodically according to the value of open reserves.
see: cash flow program, retrospective rating plan

paid losses
Insurer Operations. The actual dollar total that has been paid on incurred losses by issuing checks or

335

drafts to claimants. Paid losses for a specified accounting period are the aggregate of such payments recorded on the books of the insurer within that period.

compare: incurred losses; *see*: loss

paid-up additions

Life. Some participating life insurance policies allow the policyholder the option to use policy dividends to purchase increments of permanent life insurance that are fully paid-up.

see: policy dividend, settlement options

paid up at age life insurance

Life. Life insurance coverage in force during the insured's entire lifetime, but premium payments cease at a specific age, when the coverage is fully paid up.

see: limited payment life insurance, paid-up insurance

paid-up insurance

Life. A life insurance policy that has all of its premiums paid but has not matured by either death or endowment.

compare: mature; *see*: endowment policy, paid up at age life insurance

pair or set clause

Inland Marine/Property. A provision in many property and inland marine policies that the insurer is not liable for the total value of a set of items if only one item has been lost, damaged or destroyed. The loss settlement is based on the proportion that the lost or damaged part bears to the total value of the set.

see: pair or set

pair or set

Property. For insurance purposes, a pair (e.g., earrings) or set (e.g., china place setting, golf clubs) is two or more items that are valued together. If one item is lost, the value of the remaining items is generally less than their value as part of the set. *Example*: A pair of antique salt and pepper shakers are valued at $2,000, and the salt shaker is destroyed. The pepper shaker may then be valued at $400 instead of $1,000. In an insurance loss settlement involving a pair or set, the value of the loss is based on the reasonable and fair proportion that the lost or damaged item bears to the total value of the pair or set.

compare: parts; *see*: pair or set clause

pallet

Inland Marine/Ocean Marine. A wooden or metal platform, usually about four feet square, for holding material in storage or during transport. Pallets permit moving stacked materials by fork lift. Because pallets hold the stock a few inches off the

ground and thereby reduce possible water damage, they are sometimes required by underwriters.

panel wall

Loss Control/Property. An exterior non-bearing wall in multiple-story buildings. The panel is one story in height and is supported at each floor level.

see: construction, curtain wall

paper losses

Ocean Marine. A form of cargo loss that does not involve a physical loss, but rather a loss due to the incorrect measurement of cargo during loading or unloading or other mistakes in documentation.

paper title

Title. Title of a property that is evidenced only by deeds or matters appearing on record.

see: certificate of title, title

par value

Financial Planning. The nominal or face value of a security. Par value has no relation to the market value of a share, but is an accounting value determined by dividing the total stated capital stock by the number of authorized shares. The assigned par is usually a very low value (e.g., $1; 10 cents). Dividends on preferred stock may be a percentage of the preferred stock's par value. Likewise, interest payable to bondholders is a percentage of the bond's par value.

compare: no par stock; *see*: common stock, preferred stock

paramedic

Health. An individual who has received professional training in routine and emergency medical care. Most states require paramedics to be licensed.

see: paramedical examination, paramedics' professional liability insurance

paramedical examination

Health/Life. A medical examination performed by a paramedic of a person applying for life or health insurance.

see: medical examination

paramedics' professional liability insurance

Professional Liability. Insurance for licensed paramedics, covering liabilities arising from their professional activities. The policy form is similar to a doctor's or nurse's malpractice liability policy. Coverage is usually on a claims-made basis.

compare: ambulance service malpractice insurance; *see*: malpractice insurance, medical malpractice

parapet

Loss Control. That portion of a solid masonry division or fire wall that extends through the roof.

see: fire division, fire wall

parasol policy

Property. A British term for a policy similar to a difference in conditions policy.

compare: bumbershoot, umbrella liability insurance; *see*: difference in conditions insurance

parcel post insurance

Inland Marine. Insurance to cover the interest of a shipper for loss against damage to or loss of property being transported by the U.S. Postal Service via parcel post, first class registered mail, registered air mail, certified mail or ordinary first class mail. Coverage can be provided either by the U.S. Postal Service or through private insurers.

compare: trip transit insurance; *see*: mail coverage, registered mail insurance

parent company

Insurer Operations. A company or holding company that owns other smaller companies.

compare: pup company; *see*: affiliated insurers, fleet of companies, holding company, subsidiary company

parol evidence rule

Law. A rule of law that prohibits evidence of any oral agreement between parties to a written contract if offered to modify the written provisions. When parties have recorded their agreement in writing (such as in an insurance policy), in the absence of mutual mistake, ambiguity, unilateral mistake of which the other party had knowledge, or fraud, an alleged parol (oral) agreement is not permitted to amend the written document.

see: evidence, oral contract, statute of frauds

part one

Workers' Compensation. The section of the workers' compensation policy that provides benefits required by the law of the employer's state. Prior to 1983 this coverage was provided under coverage A of the form.

see: workers' compensation insurance

part three

Workers' Compensation. The section of the workers' compensation policy that provides all-states coverage. Prior to 1983 this coverage had to be added by a separate endorsement.

see: all-states coverage

part two

Workers' Compensation. The section of the workers' compensation policy that provides employers' liability coverage. Prior to 1983 this coverage was provided under coverage B of the form.

see: employers' liability coverage

partial disability

Employee Benefits. A disability that prevents individuals from performing one or more functions of their occupation, but does not impair their capability of performing less demanding employment.

compare: permanent partial disability, permanent total disability, total disability; *see*: disability, temporary partial disability

partial disability insurance

Health. A disability income policy provision that provides partial benefit payments (usually 50% of the total disability limit) for a limited time period (usually six months) when the insured is partially disabled.

see: disability income insurance, partial disability

partial loss

Property. A loss to an insured property that does not completely destroy the property and is not extensive enough to be deemed a total loss.

compare: constructive total loss, total loss

partial pension plan termination

Employee Benefits. A method developed to allow employers to recapture excess pension plan assets by dividing a qualified plan into two parts, and then terminating one part. Generally, the employer buys annuities to pay retirees their benefits under the plan and then reclaim the excess assets.

see: pension, qualified plan

participant

Employee Benefits. An individual who is eligible for or covered under an employee benefit plan, a group insurance plan or a pension plan.

see: employee benefit plan

participate

Insurer Operations. To share in the writing of a risk with another insurer.

see: quota share

participating bond

Financial Planning. Corporate bonds that tie interest payments to the profitability of the corporation. Some provide for a fixed interest payment plus additional interest based on profitability.

synonym: income bond; *see*: corporate bond

participating life insurance

Life. Life insurance that pays policy dividends. The premium is calculated to provide a margin over the anticipated cost of the insurance protection. This margin is then returned as a policy dividend.

compare: nonparticipating life insurance; *see*: dividend (*Insurer Operations*), participating policy

participating policy

Insurer Operations. An insurance policy that distributes its dividends by cash payments, reduced premiums, units of paid-up life insurance, a savings program, or by the purchase of term insurance.

compare: nonparticipating policy; *see*: factoring, initial premium, net premium, participating life insurance, policy dividend

participating preferred stock

Financial Planning. Preferred shares entitled to share in excess profit distributions in addition to any fixed dividend they receive.

see: preferred stock

participating reinsurance

Reinsurance.

see: pro rata reinsurance

particular average

Ocean Marine. A method of loss allocation in the event that a portion of cargo, hull or freight is jettisoned at sea in order to save the remainder. The loss is borne entirely by the individual who owns the property that is damaged or sacrificed. The loss must be less than total and not subject to the provisions of general average. Some ocean marine policy forms provide limited coverage for a particular average loss.

compare: free of particular average, general average

particular risk

Risk Management. A risk of such a nature that it affects only a single individual or entity. A particular risk can be part of a fundamental risk. A natural catastrophe, such as an earthquake or flood, can affect a single individual and at the same time affect a whole community.

compare: fundamental risk; *see*: risk

partners, officers and others exclusion endorsement

Workers' Compensation. An endorsement (NCCI form WC 00 03 08) to the workers' compensation policy that specifically excludes a partner, officer or other individual who has elected under the state law not to be covered by workers' compensation benefits.

see: workers' compensation law

partnership

Law. An unincorporated association of two or more persons as co-owners of a business whose profits and losses are shared among the owners. Partners are personally liable for obligations of the partnership in both contract and tort. A *general partner* has managerial responsibilities and unlimited liability; a *limited partner* does not participate in management and has liability only to the extent of his or her capital contribution. The partnership entity is not subject to income tax; partners are taxed as individuals.

synonym: general partnership; *compare*: corporation, limited liability company; *see*: apparent partner, limited partnership, partnership financial bond, partnership insurance

partnership as named insured—nonownership liability coverage

Automobile. An endorsement to the business auto policy that excludes liability coverage for the individual partners and their families. It is used when partners want to avoid, for example, hazards created by teenage drivers or a partner with alcohol dependency.

see: business auto coverage form

partnership financial bond

Surety. A surety bond that guarantees that an individual investing in a private limited partnership will meet future financial obligations to the partnership.

see: limited partnership

partnership insurance

Health/Life. Life or health insurance coverage for a partnership that guarantees business continuity should one of the partners die or become disabled.

see: business insurance, cross purchase plan, key employee insurance, partnership

parts

Inland Marine/Property. For insurance purposes, parts are items used to make a more complex item. While the parts taken together usually have a greater value than when considered separately, the loss of one part is not considered for insurance purposes to affect the overall value of the complete item. If one part is damaged, the loss is based solely on the value of that part.

compare: pair or set

party

Law. An entity or individual who takes part in a legal proceeding as a litigant or in a commercial transaction as a person bound by a contract.

see: third-party liability

party wall

Loss Control. A wall shared by buildings constructed on either side of it.

synonym: common wall; *see*: adjoining building

passenger

Aviation. Any person who is in, on, boarding or disembarking an aircraft for the purpose of riding or flying on a flight or attempted flight. In its broadest interpretation, passenger includes pilots or crew members.

passenger bodily injury

Aviation. The basic aircraft liability policy specifically excludes coverage for claims arising out of injury to passengers; this must be added to the policy by a separate insuring agreement.

see: aircraft insurance

passenger hazard exclusion

Automobile. An endorsement frequently added to motorcycle policies that excludes coverage for claims against the insured driver for injury to a passenger.

see: guest statute

passenger yield

Aviation. The average revenue per mile paid by each passenger of an airline. *Formula*: total passenger revenues ÷ revenue passenger miles.

see: revenue passenger miles

passive restraint system

Automobile. One or more safety devices in a vehicle designed to prevent injuries in a collision by preventing occupants from being thrown into the windshield or other surfaces without requiring them to take deliberate action. Examples are air bags and automatic seat belts. Insurers encourage their use because they reduce the severity of injuries and are more reliable than manual devices, which occupants sometimes forget or refuse to fasten. Some insurers offer discounts on autos equipped with such devices.

see: air bag, automatic safety belt, child safety seat, infant car carrier

passive retention

Risk Management. The assumption of risk of loss (i.e., a person or firm does not purchase insurance or establish a fund to pay expected losses arising from an exposure) because of unawareness of the risk, the prohibitive cost of funding the exposure, or the insignificance of any possible loss.

compare: insurance, risk avoidance, risk transfer, self-insurance; *see*: noninsurance, retention

past service benefit

Employee Benefits. A credit allowed to a pension plan participant for a period of employment prior to the plan's commencement.

synonym: prior service benefit; *see*: past service liability

past service liability

Employee Benefits. An employer's obligation to fund pension benefits on newly created plans for employees who are qualified to participate prior to the plan's inception date.

see: past service benefit

patent

Law. A U.S. government grant to an inventor of the exclusive right to make and sell the invention for a nonrenewable period of 17 years.

compare: copyright, trademark, trade secret; *see*: patent insurance

patent enforcement litigation insurance

Professional Liability. Insurance for a holder of a patent against infringement by another person. Coverage is written on a claims-made basis and includes the cost of legal defense to enforce the patent. The policy includes a copayment provision, usually 25%. Excluded are liability for compensatory or consequential damages, fines, punitive damages, exemplary damages, and multiple damages.

compare: patent infringement liability insurance; *see*: intellectual property insurance

patent infringement liability insurance

Professional Liability. A form of professional liability insurance for manufacturers, users and sellers accused of infringing a patent holder's rights. Coverage is provided for defense and indemnity and can include profits and royalties that must be turned over to the patent holder. Coverage is written on a claims-made basis.

compare: patent enforcement litigation insurance

patent insurance

Professional Liability. 1. Insurance that protects a patent holder against loss due to infringement of a patent.

2. Liability insurance that protects the insured against infringement claims by a patent holder.

see: advertising injury coverage, patent enforcement litigation insurance, patent infringement liability insurance

Patient Self-Determination Act

Regulation. Federal legislation adopted in 1990 that requires most health care facilities to request from their patients information about their wishes (advance directives) about the use of medical interventions in the event that they lose decision-making capacity.

see: advance directive, do not resuscitate order, living will

pattern and die floater

Inland Marine. The pattern and die floater is seldom used today because patterns and dies are now usually covered under a property policy. The pattern and die floater ordinarily provides named perils coverage for patterns at owned and subcontractors' locations and all risks coverage for patterns and dies in transit. Patterns and dies (metal or plastic forms for molding materials) can represent a major investment for manufacturing concerns, and a loss can severely affect business income. They are often sent out to subcontractors, who use them to manufacture parts for the insured.

see: dies insurance, floater policy

Paul v. Virginia

Regulation. A U.S. Supreme Court case in 1869, ruling that an insurance policy did not constitute interstate commerce and therefore was not subject to federal regulation. It gave individual states the power to regulate insurance. This decision was effectively reversed in 1944 when the Supreme Court reinterpreted the Commerce Clause in the case of *United States v. South-Eastern Underwriters Association.* Congress then passed the McCarran-Ferguson Act to maintain the state regulatory framework that had evolved.

see: McCarran-Ferguson Act, South-Eastern Underwriters Association

pay on behalf of

Liability. Most liability insurance policies provide that the insurer will pay directly to the appropriate parties those sums that the insured becomes legally obligated to pay as damages. This term signifies that the insured need not first make payment and subsequently obtain reimbursement from the insurer.

compare: indemnification

payback period

Financial Planning. The length of time required for the accumulated net cash flow from an investment to equal the original cost of the investment. *Formula*: cost of investment ÷ annual net cash flow.

see: capital budgeting, cash flow, rate of return, return on investment

Reinsurance.

see: amortization period

payer benefit

Life.

see: payer disability

payer disability

Life. A rider attached to a life insurance policy to pay the premium for the insured if the payer dies or is disabled. When this rider is used, the payer of the policy is usually someone other than the insured person. It is often used on juvenile policies, where the payer is a parent.

synonym: death waiver, payer benefit

paymaster robbery insurance

Crime. Coverage against loss by robbery of payroll money while in the care of a custodian or carrier.

see: crime coverages

payment bond

Surety.

see: labor and material bond

payment cap

Financial Planning. A provision in some variable interest mortgages that limits the maximum monthly payment that can be charged during the life of the mortgage. A payment cap does not limit the amount of interest the lender is earning, so it may cause negative amortization of the mortgage.

see: cap, negative amortization, variable rate mortgage

payment certain

Life.

see: annuity certain

payout illustration

Employee Benefits. A computer-generated employee benefit schedule that indicates future periodic payments and cumulative payout figures.

payroll

Workers' Compensation. Total wages paid by an employer during the policy period. The rating base for workers' compensation insurance is the entire remuneration of the employees except for overtime pay and specific limits indicated in the rating manual for executive officers' remuneration, covered partners' remuneration, sole proprietor's remuneration, and specific classification limitations. The rating manual limitations vary by state.

see: overtime, payroll audit

payroll audit

Liability/Workers' Compensation. An examination and verification of an insured's records of employee compensation used in determining the final premium for certain lines of insurance, such as workers' compensation.

see: audit, initial premium, remuneration

payroll deduction insurance

Employee Benefits. Insurance coverage provided through an employer, where an employee authorizes all of the premium to be deducted from his or her salary. Initially, this plan was only used for term life insurance policies, but now it has been expanded to disability, homeowners, automobile, and legal expense insurance.

synonym: salary savings insurance; *see*: group insurance

peak season limit of insurance endorsement

Property. An endorsement (ISO form CP 12 30) providing additional coverage for seasonal risks (e.g., resorts, agricultural businesses) where greater inventories or a large percentage of a year's business is at risk during peak seasons. The peak season is defined by dates stated in the endorsement.

see: reporting form, seasonal risk

pecuniary damages
Law.
see: damages

peer review organization (PRO)
Health. 1. Any group of medical professionals or a health care review company that includes licensed medical professionals approved by the state insurance department to analyze the quality and appropriateness of care rendered to patients. PROs were formerly known as *professional standards review organizations.*

2. An organization with which the Health Care Financing Administration contracts to ensure that services covered by Medicare are medically necessary and reasonable, provided in the proper setting, and meet standards of professional quality. In the Medicare context, a synonymous term is *utilization and quality control peer review organization.*

synonym: professional standards review organization, utilization and quality control peer review organization; *see*: Health Care Financing Administration, Medicare, utilization review

penalty
Surety. The maximum amount for which an insurance company acting as a surety is held liable under a bond.

see: limit of liability, surety bond

pending and prior litigation exclusion
Professional Liability. An exclusion in many professional liability policies (e.g., directors' and officers', employment practices) for a claim arising from litigation that was pending before the inception or retroactive date of the policy.

synonym: prior litigation exclusion; *see*: directors' and officers' liability insurance, employment practices liability insurance, retroactive date

pending rate change endorsement
Workers' Compensation. An endorsement (NCCI form WC 00 04 04) that is attached to a workers' compensation policy if a rate change filing is under consideration by the rating bureau at the time the policy is issued. It advises the insured that rates other than those indicated in the policy may be applied at a future date.

see: workers' compensation insurance

pension
Employee Benefits. Money paid at regular intervals

as a retirement benefit. A retiree has to meet eligibility criteria under the retirement plan.

see: break in service, employee benefit plan, flat amount pension formula, pension trust fund, retirement age, simplified employee pension, Social Security, vesting

pension benefit formula
Employee Benefits.
see: benefit formula

Pension Benefit Guaranty Corporation (PBGC)
Regulation. A federal agency, administered by the U.S. Department of Labor, which was authorized by the Employee Retirement Income Security Act. It insures qualified and defined pension plans and protects vested pension benefits in those cases where the employer or pension trust is insolvent or otherwise unable to meet its commitments. Premiums are paid to the PBGC by employers, based on the number of employees in their plan.

see: Employee Retirement Income Security Act, pension, restoration of plan, vesting

pension liability
Employee Benefits. The total of all unfunded vested pension benefits that have accrued.

Pension Reform Act
Regulation.
see: Employee Retirement Income Security Act

pension trust fund
Employee Benefits. A trust fund holding the money contributed by an employer and, in some cases, employees to provide pension benefits. Contributions are paid to a trustee, who invests the funds, collects the interest and earnings, and disburses the benefits pursuant to the terms of the pension plan and the trust agreement.

see: pension

per capita
Financial Planning. The distribution of an estate among the deceased's beneficiaries on an equal, or individual, basis. If a life insured's beneficiaries are designated "children and grandchildren, per capita," grandchildren will share in the proceeds equally with surviving children (some of whom may die before the insured).

compare: per stirpes; *see*: beneficiary

per cause maximum limit
Health. Maximum benefits under a health insurance plan that apply separately to each accident or illness incurred by a covered participant. Policies with a per cause maximum limit do not have a maximum policy benefit limit.

see: inside limits, limit of liability, maximum

341

plan limits

per curiam

Law. A decision rendered "by the court" (usually an appellate court), rather than by a named judge. It requires unanimity among the judges, but not all unanimous decisions are given per curiam. Ordinarily, the opinion is brief, and the case raises no issues the judges consider to be of legal or social importance.

see: appellate court

per diem

General. Payment on a daily basis. (Latin for "by the day.")

see: per diem business interruption coverage

per diem business interruption coverage

Property. A business interruption coverage where the insured receives a specified amount of money for each day that the business is interrupted as the result of an insured peril. If the interruption is partial (i.e., some business can be transacted), the percentage of interruption is calculated and this percentage of the per diem amount is paid.

see: business income coverage form

per occurrence limit

Liability. A sublimit in some liability policies that caps the payment for all claims that arise from a single incident. Under the commercial general liability policy, a per occurrence limit applies to coverage A (bodily injury and property damage liability) and coverage C (medical payments).

see: commercial general liability policy, limit of liability

per person limit

Liability. A sublimit in some liability policies that caps the payment of a claim for any one person. Under the Insurance Services Office's commercial general liability policy, a per person limit applies to coverage B (personal and advertising injury liability) and coverage C (medical payments).

compare: aggregate limit, occurrence limit; *see:* commercial general liability form, limit of liability

per stirpes

Financial Planning. A method of distributing an intestate's estate or a deceased beneficiary's share of an estate. The allocation depends on the distributees' relationship to the intestate person or insured, rather than sharing on an equal basis. (Latin for "by roots," or by way of another.) *Example:* Shemp has a life policy for $120,000, naming as beneficiaries his brothers Moe and Curly. Curly dies, leaving heirs Trixie and Bubbles; then Shemp dies. A per stirpes distribution gives Moe $60,000, and Trixie and Bubbles together take Curly's share, or

$30,000 each.

compare: per capita; *see:* contingent beneficiary, intestate

percentage of loss deductible

Insurer Operations. A preset percentage deducted from the amount of a loss, usually subject to minimum and maximum amounts. *Example:* A 5% deductible applied to a $10,000 loss leaves the insured responsible for $500 of the loss.

compare: flat deductible, percentage of value deductible; *see:* franchise deductible

percentage of value deductible

Property. A deductible based on a percentage of the value of the property insured at the time of loss. Most earthquake and some flood insurance policies are written with this type of deductible. *Example:* A building valued at $120,000 with a 5% deductible at the time of loss would result in the insured being responsible for the first $6,000 of loss.

compare: flat deductible, percentage of loss deductible; *see:* earthquake insurance, first loss earthquake insurance, franchise deductible

percentage participation

Health. A condition in many health insurance policies, requiring that the insured pay a percentage of covered medical expenses. *Example:* A 10% participation requires the insured to pay 10% of a claim and the insurer to pay 90%.

compare: copayment; *see:* coinsurance

perfect title

Title. A title to real estate, free of any defects or encumbrances, which is properly recorded.

see: title

performance assessment review

Risk Management. A management tool to determine the efficiency of an operation, service or department. The firm's or operation's performance standards are compared with the industry average or the practices generally considered the best.

compare: benchmarking, outsourcing analysis

performance bond

Surety. A bond guaranteeing that one party (usually a contractor) will faithfully perform contractual obligations to another party.

see: bid bond, contract bond

peril

Risk Management. The potential cause of a loss. Perils include such things as fire, flood, wind, theft, negligence, errors and omissions, illness, accidents, and collision. Three major categories of perils are natural, human and economic.

synonym: cause of loss; *compare:* exposure, hazard, insured peril, risk; *see:* economic perils, human perils, natural perils

perils of the sea

Ocean Marine. A term in ocean marine contracts meaning perils that are peculiar to transportation by water, such as heavy weather, strandings, striking on rocks or on the ocean floor, collisions with other vessels, or contacts with floating objects such as logs or icebergs.

see: ocean marine insurance

period of restoration

Property. The period of time under business income coverage that is normally required for damaged property to be restored and during which, therefore, lost income is compensated. It is not the actual period of restoration, but rather the time typically required to restore the damaged property with property of similar quality. Time required for the insured to replenish supplies and restock merchandise is also considered.

see: business income coverage form, extended business income

periodic payment

Insurer Operations.

see: structured settlement

perishable stock

Property. A merchant's stock in trade that deteriorates or spoils if not maintained in a controlled climate, for example food, medicine or flowers. The term is used in spoilage coverage.

see: refrigeration maintenance agreement, spoilage coverage endorsement

permanent and stationary

Workers' Compensation. A stable health condition of a workers' compensation claimant so that the claimant will not benefit from further medical treatment.

see: workers' compensation insurance

permanent life insurance

Life. A general term for ordinary life and whole life insurance policies that remain in effect as long as their premiums are paid.

compare: term life insurance; *see*: ordinary life insurance, whole life insurance

permanent partial disability

Employee Benefits. A disability likely to prevent a person for the remainder of their life from performing one or more tasks of their accustomed occupation, but does not impair the ability to perform less demanding or other types of employment.

compare: partial disability, permanent total disability, total disability

Workers' Compensation. An inability to perform one or more, but not all, of the important duties of a the pre-injury occupation so that the worker's earnings ability is diminished throughout their working life. Such a disability can result from the loss, or loss of use, of a member of the body or a permanent impairment of function.

compare: permanent total disability, temporary partial disability, temporary total disability; *see*: able to earn, disability benefit

permanent total disability

Employee Benefits. A disability that prevents someone for the remainder of their life from performing the duties of any occupation; a permanent condition or impairment that leaves the person with no reasonable prospect of performing regular employment.

compare: partial disability, permanent partial disability, total disability; *see*: disability, presumptive disability

Workers' Compensation. An inability to perform any important occupational duties, preventing the injured worker from doing any kind of work for the remainder of his or her life. Such a disability can result from the loss, or loss of use, of both eyes, one eye and a limb, or two limbs. The weekly benefit for such a loss is a percentage of the employee's weekly wages, usually for the remainder of life.

compare: permanent partial disability, temporary partial disability, temporary total disability; *see*: able to earn, disability benefit

permit bond

Surety. A type of surety bond guaranteeing that the recipient of a permit will comply with the laws, regulations and ordinances associated with the use of the permit.

see: license bond, surety bond

permitted incidental occupancies endorsement

Personal. An endorsement (ISO form DP 04 20) to the dwelling policy that extends personal property coverage to include occupancies specifically listed on the endorsement (e.g., business office, music studio).

see: dwelling policy, incidental occupancies

permitted incidental occupancies (residence premises) endorsement

Personal. An endorsement (ISO form HO 04 42) to the homeowners policy that deletes the liability exclusions for business activities conducted on the residence premises of the insured. It also modifies the $2,500 business personal property special limit by including coverage for business "furnishings, supplies, and equipment" under coverage C.

see: business personal property—special limit, homeowners policy—property coverage

perpetual insurance

Property. A unique form of insurance on buildings. For a flat initial premium of sufficient amount, the insurer agrees to cover the building named in the policy without an expiration date. A few of these policies are still in force from the 1700s. Perpetual policies are generally assignable to subsequent owners of the covered property, and they often require endorsements for additional perils and to increase policy limits to the current value of the property.

compare: open-end policy

perpetual succession

Law. The continuation of a corporation's existence despite the death of any owner (shareholder) or any transfer of stock.

see: corporation

persistency

Insurer Operations. The percentage of insurance policies remaining in force or that have not been canceled for nonpayment of premium during their term.

compare: lapse ratio, termination rate

person

Law. In a legal context, either a natural person (a human being) or an artificial person (a corporation or other association with powers to sue and be sued, enter into contracts, etc.).

see: corporation

personal accounts of specified persons

Crime. A crime coverage form (ISO form CR 10 14) that extends forgery or alteration coverage to a loss that involves insured instruments associated with the personal accounts of the individuals named in the endorsement. Coverage is also extended to loss from forgery or alteration of the named individuals' personal checks.

see: forgery or alteration coverage form

personal and advertising injury liability

Liability. Coverage Part B of the Insurance Services Office commercial general liability policy, which combines both personal injury and advertising injury into a single insuring agreement and limit of liability.

see: advertising injury coverage, commercial general liability policy, per person limit, personal injury liability

personal articles floater

Personal. An Insurance Services Office policy (ISO form IPA 06 01) used in conjunction with the "inland marine floater policy—personal lines" to insure nine classes of personal property on a scheduled basis: 1. jewelry, 2. furs, 3. cameras, 4. musical instruments, 5. silverware, 6. golfer's equipment, 7. fine arts, 8. postage stamps, and 9. rare and current coins. This form is similar to the ISO homeowners scheduled personal property endorsement.

compare: personal effects floater, personal property floater; *see:* camera coverage, coin collections coverage, fine arts coverage, floater policy, furs coverage, golfers' equipment coverage, scheduled personal property endorsement, inland marine floater policy—personal lines, jewelry coverage, scheduled item, stamp collections coverage, silverware, unscheduled property floater

personal auto policy (PAP)

Personal. An insurance policy (ISO form PP 00 01) for the owners of private passenger vehicles. It combines physical damage insurance on the automobile with liability insurance for claims arising out of the ownership or use of the vehicle. Most insurers follow the ISO policy forms, though some have their own forms. The ISO forms provide liability coverage for the insured owner and extends coverage to include any family member and any person using the auto with the insured's permission. The policy has the following parts:

Part A—liability coverage
Part B—medical payments coverage
Part C—uninsured motorist coverage
Part D—coverage for damage to your auto
Part E—duties after an accident or loss
Part F—general provisions

There are four types of vehicles that can be covered under the policy: 1. any vehicle indicated in the policy declarations; 2. newly acquired vehicles (additional and replacement vehicles) for 30 days; 3. trailers owned by the insured; and 4. temporary substitute vehicles. Numerous endorsements can be added to meet special state financial responsibility requirements, personal operation requirements, or special equipment requirements.

see: audio visual and data electronic equipment and tapes records discs and other media endorsement, collision coverage, comprehensive coverage, coverage for damage to your auto (maximum limit of liability), medical payments coverage (*Automobile*), no-fault insurance, private passenger automobile, physical damage coverage, suspension of insurance endorsement, underinsured motorist coverage, uninsured motorist coverage

personal auto policy—liability coverage

Personal. Part A (liability coverage) of the personal auto policy obligates the insurer to pay damages for bodily injury or property damage for which any insured becomes legally responsible because of an auto accident, including the duty to settle or defend any claim or suit. Supplementary payments are included for the cost of bail bonds (up to $250), premiums on appeal bonds and bonds to release attachments, post-judgment interest, loss of earnings (up to $50 per day), and other reasonable expenses incurred at the insurer's request.

see: personal auto policy

personal contract

Insurer Operations. An insurance policy is a personal contract between an insurer and the insured. Each party relies implicitly on the other for disclosing critical information, and the insurer promises to indemnify the insured against certain events in return for the payment of premiums.

see: contract

personal defense

Law. A legal defense involving negotiable instruments, by which a party to such an instrument can avoid liability under the instrument because of their participation in or knowledge of certain transactions or facts. Such a defense is not valid against a holder in due course of the instrument.

see: holder in due course

personal effects

Property. Personal items with no business use or part of commercial operations. Commercial property insurance does not usually cover such items belonging to the insured, employees or others, but coverage can often be extended to personal effects for an additional premium.

compare: personal property

personal effects floater

Personal. An Insurance Services Office policy (ISO form IPE 16 01) used with the "inland marine floater policy—personal lines" to insure, on an unscheduled all-risk basis, personal effects that are usually carried by business travelers or tourists and their families. There are specific limitations ($100 for any one article and 10% of coverage limit) on the amount of coverage on such articles as jewelry, watches, articles consisting in whole or in part of silver, gold or platinum, and furs.

compare: personal articles floater, personal property floater; *see*: baggage coverage, camera coverage, coin collections coverage, fine arts coverage, floater policy, furs coverage, golfer's equipment coverage, inland marine floater policy—personal lines, jewelry coverage, musical instruments coverage, scheduled item, stamp collections coverage, silverware, unscheduled property floater

personal effects floater—$25 deductible endorsement

Personal. The standard no deductible coverage

under the personal effects floater form can be increased to $25 by endorsement (ISO form IPE 16 11).

see: floater policy, personal effects floater

personal income insurance

Health.

see: disability income insurance

personal injury (PI)

Liability. In the broadest sense, any harm to a person, whether physical or mental or an infringement of rights. However, insurers often distinguish between, and provide different coverages for, *bodily* injuries and *personal* injuries. The latter comprise infringements of rights, such as defamation (libel or slander), false arrest, invasion of privacy, etc.

compare: bodily injury; *see*: damages, defamation, mental distress, noneconomic loss, personal injury endorsement, personal injury liability

personal injury endorsement

Personal. An endorsement (ISO form HO 24 84) to the homeowners policies that expands the Section II coverage (personal liability) to include "personal injury" as well as "bodily harm, sickness or disease."

see: homeowners policy—liability coverage, personal injury

personal injury liability

Liability. Liability for personal injury to third parties, which includes both bodily harm and nonphysical, noneconomic harm. Injuries that are neither physical nor economic may include libel or slander, false arrest, discrimination, and invasion of privacy. These either cause psychological harm or are presumed to be damaging (as with defamation of character). The insurance covering this liability is automatically included in the Insurance Services Office's commercial general liability policy under coverage Part B.

compare: bodily injury liability; *see*: commercial general liability policy, damages, mental distress, personal and advertising injury liability, personal injury

personal injury protection (PIP)

Automobile. The bodily injury and related coverages required by state no-fault laws. Required benefits may include basic medical expenses, rehabilitation, lost earnings, funeral expenses, and survivors' benefits.

see: no-fault insurance, threshold of injury

personal liability endorsement

Personal. An endorsement (ISO form DL 24 01) to the dwelling policy that adds personal liability coverage; medical payments to others coverage; and additional coverages for claim expenses, first aid expenses, and damage to property of others, similar to but not as broad as provided in the ISO homeowners policies.

see: dwelling policy

personal lines

Insurer Operations. A general term for coverage of individuals or families, as opposed to *commercial lines*, which refers to business coverages.

compare: commercial lines

personal profit exclusion

Professional Liability. An exclusion in most directors' and officers' liability policies for claims based on or attributable to a director's or officer's personal profit or advantage to which they were not legally entitled.

see: directors' and officers' liability insurance

personal property

Property. Property other than real estate, or property that is movable or separable from real estate; for property insurance purposes, tangible property, which is often called "contents." Personal property may be used for business purposes and therefore may be covered by a commercial policy, while personal property not used for business purposes is generally covered only by personal lines policies (such as homeowners or renters' insurance).

synonym: chattel, personalty; *compare*: improvements and betterments, real estate; *see*: chose in action, equipment floater, intangible property, machinery and equipment, personal articles floater, personal effects floater, personal property floater

personal property—special coverage

Personal. The personal property perils covered under the homeowners special form can be broadened to "all risk of direct loss" by this endorsement (ISO form HO 00 15).

see: homeowners special form

personal property floater (PPF)

Inland Marine. Worldwide coverage on an all-risk basis for personal property owned, used or worn by the insured. Coverage extends to personal property of family members residing in the same household. Coverage is divided between blanket property and scheduled property sections.

see: floater policy

Personal. An Insurance Services Office policy (ISO form IPF 17 01) used with the inland marine floater policy—personal lines to create a personal property floater to insure, on an unscheduled all-risk basis, 13 classes of residential personal property. The following property can be insured on an unscheduled basis: 1. silverware; 2. clothing; 3. rugs; 4. musical instruments; 5. fine arts; 6. china and glassware (including bric-a-brac); 7. cameras; 8. guns and sporting equipment and supplies; 9. major appliances; 10. bedding; 11. furniture; 12. other personal property such as books, wines, liquors, foodstuffs, etc.; and 13. building additions and alterations.

compare: personal articles floater, personal effects floater; *see*: camera coverage, coin collections coverage, fine arts coverage, furs coverage, golfer's equipment coverage, inland marine floater policy—personal lines, jewelry coverage, musical instruments coverage, scheduled item, stamp collections coverage, silverware, unscheduled property floater

personal property floater—automatic increase in insurance

Personal. The personal property floater unscheduled property limit can be automatically increased by 1%, 1.5%, 2% or a selected percentage at the end of each 3-month period by attaching an endorsement (ISO form IPF 17 13, IPF 17 14, IPF 17 15 or IPF 17 16).

see: personal property floater

personal property floater—deductible endorsements

Personal. The standard $100 deductible under the personal property floater form can be increased to $250 or $500 by endorsement (ISO form IPF 17 11 or IPF 17 12).

see: floater policy, personal property floater

personal property of others

Liability/Property. Personal property (i.e., property other than real estate) that is damaged or lost while in the care, custody or control of a person other than the owner. Liability policies generally exclude coverage for such property, but coverage can be purchased for an additional premium. Many property forms provide limited coverage for personal property of others and allow additional coverage to be purchased.

see: bailment; care, custody or control

personal property replacement cost endorsement

Personal. An endorsement (ISO form HO 04 90) to a homeowners policy that provides replacement cost coverage on personal property, awnings, carpeting, household appliances, and outdoor equipment (including antennas). A number of items with special limits also qualify, such as jewelry, furs and fur-trimmed or fur garments, cameras, musical equipment, silverware, etc. There are four categories of items ineligible for replacement cost coverage: 1. antiques and fine arts; 2. memorabilia, souvenirs, collectors' items; 3. property not kept in good or workable condition; and 4. obsolete articles in storage or not being used.

see: business personal property—special limit,

homeowners policy—property coverage

personal protective equipment
Loss Control. Clothing or devices worn or used to protect various parts of the body. *Examples*: Hard hats, protective eyewear, gloves, etc.

personal surety
Surety. An individual, instead of an insurance company, who acts as a surety, guaranteeing the acts of another.
see: surety

personal theft insurance
Crime.
see: broad form personal theft insurance

personal trust
Financial Planning. An inter vivos trust where the owner of property gives it to another person to safeguard, hold, and use for a third party's benefit.
see: inter vivos trust

personal umbrella
Personal. A form of umbrella liability insurance for individuals and their families. It provides coverage for (1) excess liability over underlying liability coverage (homeowners, auto) and (2) some of the liability exposures excluded by underlying policies. The section 2 coverage often has a retained limit (the insured's responsibility, e.g., $5,000). There is no standard form, but generally the form requires the maintenance of underlying homeowners and auto liability policies with minimum combined single liability limits of $300,000 each.
see: umbrella liability insurance

personalty
Property.
see: personal property

Personnel Accreditation Institute
Organizations. A nonprofit research and accreditation institute formed by the American Society for Personnel Administration in 1948. It awards the Professional in Human Resources and Senior Professional in Human Resources designations.
see: American Society for Personnel Administration, Professional in Human Resources, Senior Professional in Human Resources

personnel loss exposure
Risk Management. The possibility of a reduction in the value or loss of services of persons who manage or work for an organization. Death, disability, retirement, or resignation are examples of perils that could cause a personnel loss.
see: key personnel loss exposure, loss exposure

pesticide or herbicide applicator coverage
Liability. An endorsement (ISO form CG 22 64) that can be added to the commercial general liability policy to provide coverage for exterminators, fumigators, crop spraying contractors, etc., who apply pesticides or herbicides. The endorsement modifies the pollution exclusion so it does not apply to these operations provided the insured meets all legal and regulatory standards, including license requirements.
see: commercial general liability policy, exterminator liability insurance, pollution exclusion

pet insurance
Inland Marine/Personal. A form of animal insurance that combines comprehensive, theft, animal mortality, and veterinary expense coverages for animals kept as household pets.
synonym: domestic pet insurance; *see*: animal insurance, exotic bird insurance

pet salon liability coverage
Liability. Coverage designed for pet salons and grooming establishments that clip nails or hair, or dock tails of cats and dogs. It provides liability coverage similar to that available for beauticians and barbers.

petition
Law. A written application to a court asking for it to exercise authority over a particular controversy.
see: complaint, pleading, summons

pewterware
Personal.
see: silverware

phantom stock plan
Employee Benefits. An employee benefit plan where the plan benefits are tied to the employing corporation's common shares. Actual shares are not utilized in funding the plan, rather "phantom shares" are assigned to each participant, and the value of their increase (or decrease), dividends and splits are accrued for their benefit. This allows the employees to participate in the corporation's results.
see: employee benefit plan, profit-sharing plan

pharmacists' professional liability insurance
Professional Liability. Coverage for employed pharmacists against claims for personal injury arising from malpractice, error or omission in rendering professional services.
compare: druggists' liability coverage; *see*: medical malpractice

photoelectric detector
Loss Control. A device used to trigger a burglar alarm. A beam of light (usually infrared) is projected across the area to be protected. If the beam is

interrupted by an intruder, the disrupted photoelectric circuit sets off the burglar alarm.

see: burglar alarm

photographers' errors and omission insurance

Professional Liability. A form of professional liability insurance for professional photographers that provides coverage on a claims-made basis for liability for invasion of privacy and errors or omissions, such as not taking photographs that were contracted for, misdelivery or nondelivery of proofs and finished photos.

see: errors and omissions insurance

physical damage coverage

Automobile. The part of automobile insurance that covers damage to the insured's property. Damage from perils such as collision, vandalism, fire and theft are included.

see: collision coverage; comprehensive coverage; fire coverage; fire and theft coverage; fire, theft and windstorm coverage

physical depreciation

Accounting.

see: depreciation

physical examination and autopsy provision

Health. A provision of some health insurance policies that allows the insurer to examine the insured during the pendency of a claim under the policy. In the event of the insured's death, the provision also allows an autopsy where not forbidden by law.

physical hazard

Loss Control. A hazard that results from material or structural features of a risk, as opposed to human or management factors.

see: hazard

physicians' and surgeons' equipment floater

Inland Marine. Coverage (ISO form CM 00 26 or AAIS form IM 650) on an all-risk basis for physicians and surgeons to cover medical, surgical and dental equipment and instruments (including tools, materials, supplies and scientific books) used in their profession. The policy may be extended to cover furniture, fixtures and tenants' improvements and betterments.

see: floater policy

physicians' professional liability insurance

Professional Liability. Coverage for physicians against claims for bodily injury arising from alleged malpractice, error or omission in rendering professional services. This coverage is usually written on a claims-made form.

see: malpractice insurance, medical malpractice,

physicians' surgeons' and dentists' professional liability insurance

physicians', surgeons' and dentists' professional liability insurance

Professional Liability. An Insurance Services Office liability program that includes policy forms and general rules for writing physicians', surgeons' and dentists' professional liability coverage. Coverage is available for each medical specialty.

see: dentists' professional liability insurance, malpractice insurance, medical malpractice, physicians' professional liability insurance

physiotherapists' professional liability insurance

Professional Liability. Professional liability insurance for physiotherapists that provides coverage on a claims-made basis for injury caused by a medical incident while rendering professional services.

see: malpractice insurance, medical incident

picketing

General. The presence outside an employer's business of employees or others to publicize a labor dispute, influence other employees or customers to withhold their work or business, or show a union's desire to represent the employees.

see: strike, strike insurance

pickling

Loss Control. The process of removing a coating of scale, oxide, or tarnish from metals by immersion in an acid bath to obtain a chemically clean surface.

pier and wharf additional covered causes of loss endorsement

Property. A commercial property coverage endorsement (ISO form CP 10 70) that extends coverage under a named perils form for properties located on or adjacent to a body of water to include the peril of collision of floating ice, objects or vessels. These perils are included under the broad form and all-risk forms.

see: causes of loss—broad form

pilferage

Crime. Petty theft; sneak thievery, especially of stored goods by someone with controlled or authorized access to the goods (e.g., employees at a warehouse, crew members of a ship).

see: theft

pilot and crew occupational disability insurance

Aviation/Health. Disability coverage for professional pilots and crew members when they are unable to perform their normal flight duties.

see: disability income insurance

pilot light

Loss Control. 1. A colored light on or near electrical equipment, indicating the equipment power is on or that it is in use.

2. A low flame in a gas-fired vessel or heater, which ignites the main heating elements when they are supplied with gas.

pilot warranty

Aviation. A warranty to an aircraft policy requiring that a covered aircraft be piloted by a specifically named pilot or by one meeting specified qualifications. The pilot's qualifications can be stated as a minimum number of flight hours, a number of hours in a specific type of aircraft, by a specific Federal Aviation Administration (FAA) flight rating, or a combination of these. An additional requirement is that a pilot must have a valid FAA license and medical certificates and operate the aircraft within the limits of the pilot's FAA rating.

see: aircraft insurance, warranty (2)

pipeline insurance

Inland Marine. Coverage, generally on an all-risk basis, for pipeline systems (including buildings, pipelines, meters and machinery, pumping stations and tanks).

see: platform insurance

piracy

Ocean Marine. Robbery or plunder of the property of a ship, especially on the high seas. It can include seizure of a ship's cargo by a mob from on shore or seizure of a ship by passengers.

see: assailing thieves, barratry

Property. The unauthorized commercial use, reproduction or distribution of intellectual property of another.

see: copyright, intellectual property, license (*Property*), patent, trademark

placed business

Life. An application for coverage that has been signed by the prospective insured, the medical examination has been completed, the initial premium payment has been tendered, and the policy has been delivered.

compare: delivered business, examined business, issued business, paid business, written business

placement

Agency. The process of binding or underwriting an insurance policy once an agent or broker has found a company to accept the risk.

see: underwriting

plain language laws

Regulation. Laws in many states that require insurance policies to be written in simple language, avoiding legal or technical terms.

see: easy read, Flesch readability test

plaintiff

Law. A person in a legal proceeding who accuses another of wrongdoing. In a civil suit, the plaintiff is the party alleging an injury or loss. In a criminal trial, the plaintiff is the government (or the people as a whole).

compare: defendant; *see*: civil law (1), claimant, criminal law

plaintiff's bond to secure

Surety. One of two forms of injunction bonds. As the result of a judicial process, an order granting an injunction may be conditioned upon the plaintiff furnishing a bond to indemnify the defendant against loss in the event it is finally decided that the injunction should not have been granted.

compare: defendant's bond to dissolve; *see*: injunction bond

plaintiff's replevin bond

Surety. A bond that guarantees that a plaintiff will pay damages or return property if the replevin action is defeated.

see: court bond, replevin

plan benefit formula

Employee Benefits.

see: benefit formula

plan sponsor

Employee Benefits. The entity or organization that sponsors an employee benefit plan; it may be a single employer, a group of employers (multiple employer trust), an employee organization (union), an association, committee or joint board of trustees.

see: employee benefit plan, merger of plans

plant age

Risk Management. An estimate of the average age of capital assets used in a business, derived by dividing accumulated depreciation at the most recent year end by the depreciation allowance in the most recent year.

Plant Closing Act

Regulation.

see: Worker Adjustment and Retraining Notification Act

plat

Title. A map or chart of a lot, subdivision or community drawn by a surveyor showing boundary lines, buildings, improvements on the land, and easements.

see: abstract plat

plate glass insurance

Property.

see: glass coverage form

platform insurance

Ocean Marine. Property and liability coverages written on an ocean marine form, for oil and gas drilling barges and platforms located offshore in an ocean or a lake.

see: oil well liability, pipeline insurance, saline contamination exclusion

play or pay

Health.

see: employer mandate

pleading

Law. A written statement or allegation by a party in a lawsuit filed with the court which constitutes a cause of action or a defense. A civil suit commences with the plaintiff's *complaint*, the first pleading. The defendant's initial pleading is an *answer* to the complaint, which may include a counterclaim. In some cases, further pleadings are made, including replies to counterclaims, crossclaims, or complaints and answers by third parties.

see: allegation, answer, complaint, counterclaim, demurrer, petition, summons

pleasure and business

Aviation.

see: business and pleasure

pleasure use

Automobile. An automobile rating classification for a vehicle not used for business purposes. Pleasure use includes driving to and from work.

compare: business use, drive to or from work, farm use

pluvious insurance

Property.

see: rain insurance

point

Financial Planning. 1. In stock trading, a $1 change in price.

2. In bond trading, a 1% change in value.

3. In mortgage lending, 1% of the principal amount. "Points" are a fee charged by the lender to increase the yield on a loan and to cover administrative or closing costs.

point of operation

Loss Control. The point of contact between the principal functional part of a machine or tool and the material or substance being worked on by the machine or tool.

see: barrier guard, inrunning nip point, machine tool, two-hand controls

point-of-service plan (POS plan)

Health. A health maintenance or preferred provider organization's program that allows members to seek treatment from providers outside the network (that is, providers not employed by or under contract with the organization) at a reduced benefit level, commonly 60% to 70% of in-plan coverage, or at a higher premium.

synonym: open-ended plan; *see*: health maintenance organization, hybrid health plan, out-of-network services, preferred provider organization

point source

Loss Control. A stationary location or fixed facility from which pollutants are discharged.

compare: nonpoint sources; *see*: hazardous waste

poison pill

Financial Planning. Any attempt by the current management of a corporation to discourage a hostile takeover by increasing the takeover cost, such as issuing new preferred shares carrying onerous redemption rights in the event of new corporate ownership.

see: greenmail exclusion, public exchange offer, tender offer, tender offer defense expense insurance, white knight

Poisson distribution

Risk Management. An actuarial distribution curve that is applied to independent, random events where the frequency is small compared to the number of exposure units.

see: distribution curve, probability analysis

police professional liability insurance (PPL)

Professional Liability. Coverage for law enforcement professionals on a claims-made basis for injurious acts, negligence, errors, and omissions.

synonym: law enforcement officers' professional liability; *see*: civil rights exclusion, off-duty exclusion

policy

Insurer Operations. The written forms, endorsements, riders and attachments that make up an insurance contract between an insured and insurer. A policy includes the terms and conditions of the coverage, the perils insured or excluded, the limits of insurance provided, the interests insured, the effective dates of the coverage, etc.

see: coverage form, coverage part, insurance contract, policy condition laws, policy conditions, policy declarations

policy anniversary

Insurer Operations. A date twelve months after the date when a policy is issued, or as specified in the declarations.

see: anniversary date, policy period

policy certification log

Agency. A log (ACORD form 26) used by an agent to keep a manual record or to prepare a hard copy of a computer record of all certificates of insurance issued for a single insured. The form summarizes the information contained in the individual certificates of insurance.

see: certificate of insurance

policy condition laws

Regulation. State regulations that require insurance policies issued in the state to include "statutory conditions." If a policy is issued that is inconsistent with provisions required by law, they will apply nonetheless. Occasionally, statutory conditions may be waived or modified by noting such a change in clear type with a different colored ink. The courts sometimes must decide whether such waivers or modifications are reasonable.

see: legislated insurance coverage, minimum coverage clause

policy conditions

Insurer Operations. The section of a policy or provisions in various places in the policy that indicate the general rules or procedures that the insurer and insured agree to follow under the contract.

synonym: condition; *see*: commercial common policy conditions, common policy conditions, exclusion, policy declarations

policy declarations

Insurer Operations. The section of an insurance policy containing basic underwriting information, such as the insured's name, address, a description of insured locations or receipts.

synonym: declarations; *see*: commercial common policy declarations, face, insuring agreement, policy conditions

policy dividend

Insurer Operations. Money paid to policyholders by a mutual insurer because of their ownership interest in the company. A stock insurer may also pay a policy dividend on participating insurance. The amount is based on savings in losses or expenses realized by the insurer on the participating class of business.

see: factoring, initial premium, paid-up additions, participating policy

policy fee

Insurer Operations. An amount sometimes charged in addition to the initial policy premium for issuing the policy. In many states, such a fee is illegal.

see: service fee, initial premium

policy jacket

Insurer Operations. The outer covering of an insurance policy, which often contains common provisions of the policy.

synonym: jacket; *see*: face, insurance contract

policy loan

Life. A loan from a life insurer to the owner of a policy that has a cash value. Such a loan is one of the usual nonforfeiture values of a life policy.

see: cash surrender value, delay clause, nonforfeiture loan value benefit, premium loan

policy period

Insurer Operations. The period during which an insurance policy provides coverage.

synonym: policy term; *see*: anniversary date, annual policy, duration of risk, effective date, expiration date, maturity date, natural expiry, noon clause, open-end policy, policy anniversary, term

policy period endorsement

Workers' Compensation. An endorsement (NCCI form WC 00 04 05) attached to a workers' compensation policy that is written for a period in excess of one year and sixteen days and does not consist of complete twelve-month periods. It advises the insured as to which period, the first or the last, is to be less than twelve months.

see: workers' compensation insurance

policy profile

Insurer Operations. A summary of an insurer's policies according to various characteristics (e.g., policy limits, premiums, coverages).

policy provision

Insurer Operations. Any term or clause of an insurance contract that describes its benefits, coverages, conditions, limits, exclusions, etc.

synonym: provision; *see*: insurance contract

policy release

Insurer Operations.

see: cancellation request/policy release

policy reserve

Life/Health. An amount set aside by an insurer specifically to fulfill the obligations of a policy. While such reserves may be calculated as an aggregate amount, covering many policies, it is assumed that each policy has a pro rata share of the total reserve. This reserve is for the increased claim rate encountered as the policyholder population ages.

synonym: active life reserve

policy term

Insurer Operations.

see: policy period

351

policy year

Insurer Operations. The 12-month period commencing with a policy's effective date or renewal date.

compare: calendar year, fiscal year; *see*: policy period

policy year experience

Insurer Operations. The losses incurred by a specific policy or line of business that was in force for a defined twelve-month period. In long-tail liability coverages, the incurred losses produced from a policy or line of business may not become known until several years after expiration of the defined policy period.

see: long-tail liability

policyholder

Insurer Operations. The party in whose name an insurance policy is issued; the first named insured.

compare: insured, named insured, policyowner

policyholder's equity

Life.

see: cash surrender value

policyholder's report

Insurer Operations. A form (ACORD form 225) used to obtain the actual amounts due from an insured when a general liability, workers' compensation or property policy has been issued on an estimated premium basis. The form is completed by the insured with necessary information (e.g., receipts, payroll, values) to rate the policy.

policyholders' surplus

Insurer Operations. The amount by which an insurance company's assets exceed its liabilities, as reported in its annual statement. For a stock insurer, the policyholders' surplus is the sum of its capital and surplus; for a mutual insurer, the policyholders' surplus equals the company's surplus.

synonym: surplus to policyholders; *see*: surplus

policyowner

Insurer Operations. An individual with an ownership interest in an insurance policy, especially life insurance.

compare: insured, named insured, policyholder

policywriting agent

Insurer Operations. An agent who is authorized to issue an insurer's policies.

see: agent, general agent, recording agent

political action committee liability insurance

Professional Liability. Coverage for political action committees, which raise funds for political candidates and parties. It provides liability protection for committee members, including exposures under federal campaign contribution laws.

political perils

Financial Guaranty/International. A group of perils under an export credit insurance policy including war, blocked currencies, and other governmental actions that make payment impossible.

compare: commercial perils; *see*: blocked currency, export credit insurance

political risk insurance

International. Coverage for an organization or activity for loss arising from confiscation or expropriation of property by a foreign government. Coverage can also be provided for loss due to a devaluation of currency. Political risk insurance can be provided by private insurers or governmental agencies.

see: deprivation insurance, evacuation expense, expropriation insurance, joint venture political risk insurance, Overseas Private Investment Corporation

pollutant

Liability. As used in most liability policies written after the mid-1980s, this term refers to any solid, liquid, gaseous or thermal irritant or contaminant, including smog, vapor, soot, fumes, acids, alkalines, chemicals and waste. *Waste* is further defined as materials to be recycled, reconditioned or reclaimed.

see: hazardous waste, pollution exclusion, pollution insurance

Property. A solid, liquid, gaseous or thermal irritant or contaminant, including smoke, vapor, soot, fumes, acids, alkalis, chemicals and waste. Since 1988 most property insurance policies have excluded damage from pollutants.

see: air pollutant, contaminant, pollutant cleanup and removal additional coverage, pollution insurance, thermal irritant, waste

pollutant cleanup and removal additional aggregate limit of insurance endorsement

Property. A commercial property insurance endorsement (ISO form CP 04 07) that covers pollutant cleanup and removal in excess of the coverage provided in the standard forms subject to a $1,000 minimum deductible.

see: pollutant clean up and removal coverage

pollutant cleanup and removal coverage

Property. A coverage limitation in most property insurance policies issued after 1988. Coverage is included for the removal (extraction) of pollutants from water or land at the described premises, provided the original release, discharge, or dispersal was caused by a covered cause of loss that occurred during the policy period. The cleanup and removal expense is paid only if the loss is reported within

180 days of the policy expiration date. This additional coverage usually has a modest sublimit of liability (i.e. $10,000).

synonym: contamination and pollution cleanup and removal coverage

pollution exclusion

Liability. A provision in the Insurance Services Office commercial general liability policy that denies coverage for bodily injury or property damage arising out of the actual, alleged or threatened discharge, dispersal, release or escape of pollutants. Occasionally, portions of this exclusion can be eliminated for an additional premium, or pollution coverage can be purchased in a separate policy. Prior to the 1986 CGL form, coverage was provided for pollution arising out of a sudden and accidental event.

see: commercial general liability policy, pollution insurance, pollution liability extension endorsement

pollution insurance

Property. A first-party coverage for contamination of insured property either by external or on-site sources.

Liability. Coverage for liability to third parties arising from contamination of air, water, or land due to the sudden and accidental release of hazardous materials from the insured site. The policy usually covers the costs of cleanup and may include coverage for releases from underground storage tanks. Intentional acts are specifically excluded.

synonym: environmental impairment liability insurance; *see*: aboveground storage tank pollution liability insurance, Comprehensive Environmental Response Compensation and Liability Act, environmental directors' and officers' liability insurance, environmental title insurance, off-site pollution liability insurance, on-site pollution liability insurance, point source, pollution exclusion, pollution liability extension endorsement, pollution liability—limited form, pollution prevention program, underground storage tank pollution liability insurance

pollution liability extension endorsement

Liability. An endorsement (ISO form CG 00 39) to the commercial general liability policy that deletes part of the pollution exclusion, thereby providing coverage for sudden and accidental pollution.

see: commercial general liability policy

pollution liability—broadened coverage for covered autos

Automobile. An endorsement (ISO form CA 99 48) to the business auto and truckers' policies that modifies the pollution exclusion to cover damages from the discharge of pollutants being hauled by a covered vehicle.

pollution liability—limited form

Liability. A policy form (ISO form CG 00 40) providing pollution liability coverage on a "claims-made" basis. Coverage for clean-up costs is excluded.

see: claims-made form, pollution insurance

Pollution Liability Insurance Association (PLIA)

Organizations. Members: Primary and reinsurance companies. *Objectives*: Promotes the availability of pollution and hazardous waste insurance. Policies are issued by member companies and reinsured through the association. *Founded*: 1982. *Headquarters*: Downers Grove, IL.

pollution prevention program

Loss Control. A loss prevention program designed to limit future environmental liabilities and reduce waste management expenses. Pollution prevention is required by the Resource Conservation and Recovery Act, and hazardous waste manifests require a statement that a pollution prevention program is in place for all hazardous waste shipped to and from a facility in the United States.

see: environmental audit, pollution insurance, Resource Conservation and Recovery Act

pollution product liability insurance

Liability. A coverage for liability resulting from pollution that fills the gap created by the pollution exclusion in the commercial general liability policy. It provides coverage for third-party injury, property damage and cleanup for pollution caused by the failure of the insured's products, such as valves, hoses, pipes and tanks.

see: commercial general liability policy, pollution exclusion, product liability insurance

polychlorinated biphenyls (PCBs)

Regulation. A class of chemicals that have been banned from manufacture and use in the United States. They were principally used in heavy electrical equipment, such as capacitors and transformers, as cooling agents. They can cause central nervous system damage, stomach and liver disorders, cancer and even death.

polygraph operators' liability insurance

Professional Liability. A form of professional liability coverage for polygraph operators that provides coverage on a claims-made basis for personal injury liability and defense coverage for disciplinary proceedings against the insured.

pool

Insurer Operations. A group of self-insurers, insurers or reinsurers that underwrites certain risks, with premiums, losses and expenses shared among members of the pool in predetermined ratios.

synonym: syndicate

port risk insurance

Ocean Marine. Coverage for a ship that remains in a port for a protracted period of time. The ship may move within the port limits, prepare for a voyage and load cargo, but coverage ceases when it leaves the port.

synonym: port risk only clause

port risk only clause

Ocean Marine.

see: port risk insurance

portability

Health. The right of an insured to carry health coverage to another job or place without having to prove insurability or losing coverage for preexisting conditions.

see: conversion privilege, evidence of insurability, preexisting condition

Employee Benefits. A pension plan provision that allows plan participants to change employers without changing the source from which benefits for both past and future accruals are to be paid.

see: pension

portfolio

Financial Planning. The financial assets (securities, bonds, bank deposits, notes, etc.) belonging to a single owner; an investor's entire holdings.

see: aggressive portfolio, bond (*Financial Planning*), defensive portfolio, note, security, stock (*Financial Planning*)

Insurer Operations. The insurance policies issued by an insurer; an insurance company's entire liability for in-force policies; the loss reserves held by an insurer.

see: loss portfolio, portfolio reinsurance, portfolio return, premium portfolio

Reinsurance. A reinsurer's book of business.

see: reinsurance

portfolio reinsurance

Reinsurance. The transfer of an entire portfolio of policies by a cession from a primary carrier to a reinsurer; the reinsurance of an entire line of business that a primary insurer no longer desires to write.

compare: portfolio return, treaty reinsurance; *see*: bulk reinsurance

portfolio return

Reinsurance. An insurer's reassumption of a specific line of ceded business from the reinsurer.

synonym: return of unearned premium, return portfolio; *compare*: portfolio reinsurance; *see*: recapture

portfolio runoff

Reinsurance. The continuing obligation of a reinsurer under a canceled reinsurance contract until all ceded premiums from the contract are earned and all losses paid.

see: earned premium

position schedule bond

Surety. A fidelity bond that provides coverage only for individuals filling specific positions for the insured, which are described in a schedule attached to the bond.

see: blanket position bond, fidelity bond, name position bond

possession

Law. The exclusive domain over and control of property, either as an owner or as a claimant to a qualified right in a property; custody.

see: adverse possession

possessory lien

Law. A lien with the right to retain possession of another's property as security for a debt or obligation. The lien continues only as long as possession is retained.

see: encumbrance, lien

post-closure

Loss Control. Regarding hazardous waste, the period of time following the closure of a hazardous waste management facility during which it must be monitored, generally 30 years. The facility must be maintained in a manner that minimizes the potential escape or runoff of hazardous waste, and the owner or operator must meet financial responsibility requirements.

see: closure, closure and post-closure insurance, financial responsibility law

post-FIRM rates

Property. A category of rates published in the National Flood Insurance Program Manual, applying to buildings located in a community qualifying for the regular flood program. Post-FIRM rates are used on building construction that started after December 31, 1974, or after the community's initial Flood Insurance Rate Map was published, whichever is later. These rates are lower than pre-FIRM rates.

compare: pre-FIRM rates; *see*: flood insurance rate map, National Flood Insurance Program

post indicator valve (PIV)

Loss Control. An automatic sprinkler system control valve that extends above the ground or through a wall for operating the sprinkler system. A target or indicator is visible through an opening in the post, which shows that the valve is open or shut.

synonym: indicator post

post-judgment interest

Law. Interest payable on court-awarded damages from the date of judgment until the damages are paid to the plaintiff.

compare: prejudgment interest; *see*: damages

post-mortem dividend

Life. A dividend paid under a participating life insurance policy that includes dividends earned from the last paid dividend date to the date of death.

see: participating policy

post-retirement funding

Employee Benefits. A pension funding method, prohibited by ERISA, where an employer would purchase an annuity or fund pension benefits only upon the retirement of a participant. ERISA requires all pension benefits to be funded on a current basis.

see: Employee Retirement Income Security Act

post-termination claim

Workers' Compensation. A workers' compensation claim that is filed by an employee after he or she has been terminated or released, including voluntary termination.

see: workers' compensation law

postage stamp collections coverage

Personal.

see: stamp collections coverage

postdate

General. To insert or place a later date on a document than the actual date on which it was executed.

compare: antedate

postdated check plan

Insurer Operations. A premium payment system no longer in common use whereby a policyholder provides the insurer with a series of postdated checks to make premium payments as they come due. This practice has been replaced by the preauthorized check plan.

compare: preauthorized check plan

posting notice

Workers' Compensation. A large bulletin usually required by state or federal law to be displayed in a conspicuous location on the employer's property indicating such things as workers' compensation benefits laws or benefits and laws applying to minimum wage and the employment of minors. The workers' compensation notice is usually provided by the workers' compensation insurer and indicates the carrier's name and information about benefits. The same type of notice must be displayed by a self-insured organization indicating that it is a qualified workers' compensation self-insurer.

see: workers' compensation insurance

potentially responsible party (PRP)

Regulation. An individual or organization, including owners, operators, transporters, or generators, who is potentially responsible for or contributed to contamination at a site identified pursuant to the Superfund law (CERCLA). Whenever possible, the Environmental Protection Agency requires PRPs to clean up hazardous waste sites they have created.

see: Comprehensive Environmental Response Compensation and Liability Act, hazardous waste

poultry insurance

Inland Marine. Coverage on poultry that insures against death directly and immediately resulting from fire or from named perils of fire and lightning, flood, or collision or overturn of a vehicle in which poultry is transported.

see: animal insurance, livestock mortality insurance

power, heat and refrigeration deduction

Property. A commercial property endorsement (ISO form CP 15 11) that allows the insurable limit for business income coverage to be reduced by the cost of utilities selected by the insured that will not be needed until damaged property is restored to operation. The endorsement is designed for businesses with high utility usage. Coverage cannot be excluded for the cost of minimum power and heat needed to maintain the premises or for utilities contractually required to be paid for even if not needed.

see: business income coverage form, off-premises services—time element endorsement

power interruption insurance

Property. Coverage that indemnifies the insured for lost earnings if power supplied by a public utility is interrupted by an insured peril.

see: contingent business income coverage, off-premises services—time element endorsement, overhead transmission lines coverage

power of attorney

Law. A written authorization given by one person or entity to a second party, to authorize the second party to act for and obligate the first to the extent set forth in the authorization.

see: attorney-in-fact

power plant insurance

Property. A form of boiler and machinery insurance that insures electrical generating stations against loss.

see: boiler and machinery insurance

pre-FIRM rates

Property. A category of rates published in the National Flood Insurance Program Manual applying to buildings located in a community that has qualified for the regular flood program. Pre-FIRM rates are used on building constructions that started on or before December 31, 1974, or before the community's initial Flood Insurance Rate Map was published, whichever is later. These rates are higher than post-FIRM rates.

compare: post-FIRM rates; *see*: flood insurance rate map, National Flood Insurance Program

pre-ignition insurance

Aviation. A form of satellite and space vehicle insurance that covers physical loss or damage to a satellite or space vehicle up to the time of the intended ignition of the launch vehicle.

see: satellite and space vehicle insurance

preaction automatic sprinkler system

Loss Control. An automatic sprinkler system that is similar to a dry-pipe system, but air pressure may or may not be used. The main sprinkler system control valve is opened by an actuating device, which permits water to flow to the individual sprinkler heads and the system then functions as a wet-pipe system. It is generally used in areas where piping systems are subject to mechanical damage and where it is important to prevent accidental discharge of water.

see: automatic sprinkler system, dry pipe automatic sprinkler system, wet pipe sprinkler system

preauthorized check plan

Insurer Operations. A premium payment system whereby the insured arranges with his or her bank and insurance company to have the payments made by electronic fund transfers, usually monthly, from the insured's account to the insurer's.

synonym: electronic funds transfer plan; *compare*: postdated check plan

preexisting condition

Health/Life. An illness or disability that existed before the effective date of a health or life insurance policy. Such a condition can result in cancellation of a policy or exclusion from coverage.

compare: substandard risk; *see*: aggravation of a previous condition, impairment exclusion rider, injury independent of all other means, portability, time limit

Workers' Compensation.

see: aggravation of a previous condition

preferred provider organization (PPO)

Health. A health benefit plan with contracts between the sponsor and health care providers to treat plan members. A PPO can also be a group of health care providers who contract with an insurer to treat policyholders according to a predetermined fee schedule. PPOs can range from one hospital and its

practicing physicians that contract with a large employer to a national network of physicians, hospitals and labs that contract with insurers or employer groups. PPO contracts typically provide discounts from standard fees, incentives for plan enrollees to use the contracting providers, and other managed care cost containment methods.

see: direct health care corporation, exclusive provider organization, health maintenance organization, managed care, prepaid group practice program

preferred risk

Insurer Operations. An insurable risk with underwriting characteristics that are superior to the standard risk.

see: standard risk

preferred stock

Financial Planning. A share or shares of ownership in a corporation with preferential rights over others in regard to the payment of dividends and distribution of assets upon liquidation. Preferred stock usually does not carry voting rights.

compare: common stock; *see*: callable preferred stock, convertible preferred stock, cumulative preferred stock, equity (*Financial Planning*), participating preferred stock

prejudgment interest

Law/Liability. Interest that accrues on a loss during a time prior to a court award of damages. Prejudgment interest is sometimes included in an award in cases of intentional wrongdoing. Most liability policies cover interest only from the time of a court decree until the date of payment. A few states require coverage for prejudgment interest calculated from a specified time (e.g., 60 days) following a demand for payment of a claim or a settlement offer in order to prevent the insurer from delaying settlement at the expense of the insured.

compare: post-judgment interest; *see*: damages

prelicensing education requirement

Agency/Regulation. An educational program that state laws require an agent or broker to complete before receiving a license.

see: licensee

preliminary prospectus

Financial Planning.

. *see*: red herring

preliminary term

Life/Insurer Operations. An accounting method for life insurers that does not require a terminal reserve to be established during the first year of a policy, making the policy more attractive to prospective buyers.

see: terminal reserve

356

premises

Aviation. As used in aircraft policies, the areas at an airport used for parking or storing aircraft.

see: aircraft insurance

Insurer Operations. A specified property, location or portion of a property designated for coverage in an insurance policy.

premises burglary coverage form

Crime. A crime coverage form (ISO form CR 00 06, or form E) providing coverage against actual or attempted robbery of a watchperson and actual burglary of property from an insured premises.

synonym: crime coverage form E; *see*: burglary, crime coverages

premises liability insurance

Liability. Liability insurance coverage for damage caused by accidents or occurrences arising from the condition, maintenance or upkeep of the insured's premises. Most basic premises liability policies provide this coverage.

see: owners, landlords and tenants liability insurance

premises-operations liability

Liability. Liability coverage for damage caused by accidents or occurrences arising from the condition, maintenance or upkeep of the insured's premises and from the insured's business operations. Most basic business liability policies provide this coverage.

compare: products-completed operations insurance; *see*: commercial general liability form

premises theft and outside robbery coverage form

Crime. A crime coverage form (ISO form CR 00 09, or form H) providing coverage against actual or attempted theft within or outside an insured premises. It also covers damage to the premises or its exterior resulting directly from an actual or attempted theft.

synonym: crime coverage form H; *see*: crime coverages, theft

premium

Insurer Operations. The price for coverage of a particular risk or set of risks described in the insurance policy during a specific period of time. The premium is the price (insured's cost) expressed as a periodic sum, while the *rate* is the price per unit of coverage (for example, the premium for each $100 of property value).

see: additional premium, adjustable premium, basic premium, deferred premium, deferred premium payment plan, deposit premium, direct bill, direct written premium, discounted premium, dividend, earned premium, earned reinsurance premium, estimated annual premium, excess loss premium factor, financed premium, fully earned premium, graded premium, gross premium, guideline premium, initial premium, itemized premium charges, Lloyd's Premium Trust Fund, maximum premium, maximum retrospective premium, minimum premium, minimum retrospective premium, multiple table extra premium, natural premium, net premium, net premiums written, outstanding premiums, policy fee, premium adjustment provision, premium deficiency, premium discount, premium financing, premium in force, premium income per share, premium load, premium note, premium payment mode, premium payment notice, premium portfolio, premium receipt, premium tax, premium written per share, premium written to surplus, provisional premium, pure premium, rate, reinsurance premium, reserve premium, restoration premium, retrospective premium, return of premium, return premium, risk premium, standard premium, step-rate premium, subject premium, unearned premium, unearned premium reserve, unearned reinsurance premium, uniform premium, unscheduled premium payments, valuation premium, vanishing premium, waiver of premium, waiver of restoration premium, whole dollar premium, written premiums

premium adjustment provision

Insurer Operations. A provision in or endorsed to some insurance policies that an initial or deposit premium is charged, but the final premium will be subject to adjustment during the period of coverage or at the end of coverage according to loss experience or change in the rating base.

see: audit provision, deposit premium, initial premium, retrospective rating plan

premium and dispersion credit plan

Property.

see: multiple location rating plan

premium audit

Insurer Operations.

see: audit

premium base

Insurer Operations/Reinsurance.

see: subject premium

premium deficiency

Insurer Operations. An amount by which anticipated losses, loss adjustment expenses, policyholder dividends, unamortized deferred acquisition costs and other underwriting expenses exceed the related unearned premiums and related future investment income.

see: premium deficiency reserve

premium deficiency reserve

Life/Regulation. A reserve sometimes required by state regulators of life insurers, when the gross premium is less than the valuation premium, because their experience reflects different loss statistics than current mortality tables.

see: Statutory Accounting Principles, statutory reserve

premium discount

Insurer Operations. A percentage reduction based on the size of the premium. The reason for a discount is that the proportionate cost of issuing and servicing a policy is generally less as the premium increases.

see: multiple location rating plan

premium discount endorsement

Workers' Compensation. An endorsement (NCCI form WC 00 04 06) that is attached to a workers' compensation policy to advise the insured that a premium discount has been applied. The endorsement schedule allows the discount be shown as a division of premium or as an average percentage.

see: premium discount, workers' compensation insurance

premium finance company errors and omissions insurance

Professional Liability. Errors and omissions coverage for insurance premium finance companies to pay damages in the event they allow an insurance policy to be incorrectly canceled or let a policy lapse.

see: errors and omissions insurance, premium financing

premium financing

Insurer Operations. The payment of premiums by a premium finance company (which may or may not be affiliated with an insurer), which then bills the insured in installments for a portion of the premium plus a finance charge. If the insured-debtor fails to make a payment, the finance company requests cancellation of the policy pursuant to an assignment of rights by the insured, and the lender receives the unearned premium refund.

see: deferred premium payment plan, unearned premium, financed premium, premium loan, return premium

premium in force

Insurer Operations. The total of initial premiums on all policies that have not expired or been canceled.

premium income per share

Insurer Operations. A financial measure of insurer strength, calculated by dividing premium income received by an insurer by the number of common shares outstanding at year-end.

compare: premium written per share

premium load

Life. The percentage of premium deducted from premium payments for universal life insurance policies, to cover policy expenses. Some policies are issued on a "no load" basis.

synonym: front-end load

premium loan

Life. A life insurance policy loan used to make premium payments.

see: policy loan, premium financing

premium note

Insurer Operations. A promissory note given by an insured to the insurer in lieu of a cash premium payment. Most jurisdictions consider the premium note and the insurance policy to be separate obligations with each being independently enforceable.

see: premium

premium offset

Life.

see: vanishing premium

premium payment mode

Insurer Operations. The method and frequency of paying the policy premium. *Examples*: Annually, or in quarterly or monthly installments; 10% deposit and 11 monthly installments; or a 20% deposit with monthly reports.

premium payment notice

Insurer Operations. An invoice from an agent or insurer to the insured, indicating that a premium is due by a specified date.

premium portfolio

Insurer Operations. The insurance policies that an insurer currently has in force.

see: portfolio

premium receipt

Insurer Operations. A receipt issued by an agent or insurer indicating that a premium payment has been received from the insured.

premium tax

Insurer Operations. A tax applied by many states to the gross premium written by an insurer on risks in that state. It is usually a percentage of premium, ranging from 1.5% to 6%.

premium to surplus ratio

Insurer Operations. One of the criteria used by the

National Association of Insurance Commissioners to evaluate an insurer. It is the relationship between the premiums written and the amount of policyholders' surplus and indicates the insurer's capacity to write business. *Formula*: net written premiums ÷ policyholders' surplus. If the ratio exceeds 3 to 1, it is considered out of bounds and subject to further review by regulators. The ratio for most major insurers is between 1.5 and 2.5 to 1.

see: capacity, policyholders' surplus

premium written per share
Insurer Operations. A financial measure of insurer strength, calculated by dividing the total premiums written by a property and casualty insurer during the year, by the number of common shares outstanding.

compare: premium income per share

premium written to surplus
Insurer Operations. The total premiums received from property and casualty policies sold during the year, divided by statutory net worth.

prenuptial agreement
Financial Planning. An agreement entered into by prospective spouses before marriage, usually to protect one of the spouses' assets or future inheritance, which establishes most of the terms of a financial settlement in the event of divorce.

prepaid expense
Accounting. A payment made for goods or services that have not yet been received.

see: current expensing

prepaid freight
Inland Marine/Ocean Marine. Freight for which the full bill of lading has been paid in advance. The freight is payable whether the goods are delivered or not, provided that the failure to deliver the goods resulted from causes beyond the carrier's control.

compare: collect freight; *see*: freight

prepaid group practice program
Health. An early form of preferred provider organization, where a group of physicians and dentists joined together to provide medical services for a predetermined fee.

see: preferred provider organization

prepared-bed bioremediation
Loss Control. A form of hazardous waste bioremediation where contaminated excavated soils are spread above ground over clay or nonpermeable liners surrounded by berms. The contaminated soil is regularly turned and sprinkled with water containing nutrients and, in some cases, bacteria.

see: bioremediation

preplanned impairment
Loss Control. All or a part of an automatic sprinkler system that is out of service due to work that has been planned in advance, such as repairs to the water supply or sprinkler system piping.

compare: emergency impairment; *see*: automatic sprinkler clause

preponderance of evidence
Law.
see: burden of proof

preprinted policy
Insurer Operations. An insurance policy obtained from an insurance service or advisory organization or developed by the insurer's own underwriting and legal staffs which is printed and stored until issuance to an insured.

see: advisory, organization, blank forms, modular policy, self-contained policy

present value
Financial Planning/Risk Management. The value today of a future monetary sum or cash flow; the amount that, if received now and invested at an assumed rate of return, equals a given future sum. A known or assumed future amount is discounted by a stipulated rate that might be received if invested over the period of time before the money is received. *Example*: At an assumed investment return of 20%, the present value of $10,000 receivable in one year is $8333.

synonym: actuarial liability; *see*: discount factor, discounted cash flow techniques, net present value method, profitability index, present value of sprinkler reduction, time value of money

present value of sprinkler reduction
Loss Control/Risk Management. A method used in risk management to evaluate the value of installing an automatic fire sprinkler system. The method compares the cost of installing the system today with the reduction in fire insurance premiums in the future. A formula is calculated to make the comparison on a present value of money basis, or on an organization's required rate of return basis.

see: automatic sprinkler system, present value

preservation of property
Property. The removal of items from the insured property to a temporary location for safekeeping following an insured loss or event. The cost is covered under almost all property insurance policies.

synonym: removal

pressure and refrigeration objects
Property. One of the four boiler and machinery object classifications used to describe the machinery covered under a policy. This classification (object definition no. 1 or ISO form BM 00 26) includes

coverage for boilers, fired vessels, and electric steam generators; unfired vessels; refrigerating and air conditioning vessels and piping; auxiliary piping; small compressing and refrigerating units; and air conditioning units.

see: boiler and machinery insurance, object

pressure vessel

Property. A container made to hold materials under pressure. Boiler and machinery policies divide such vessels into two categories: fired pressure vessels (such as boilers or gas water heaters) and unfired pressure vessels (such as air tanks, electric water heaters, steam cookers, and hydropneumatic tanks).

see: boiler and machinery insurance, object

presumed negligence

Law.

see: res ipsa loquitur

presumption of death

Life. The rebuttable presumption that someone has died when the person has been continuously absent and not heard from for a period of seven years.

presumptive disability

Health/Life. An insurer's assumption of an insured's total disability when the insured loses sight, hearing, speech or a limb. If such a disability occurs, the insurer generally assumes that the disability will continue for the insured's life.

see: permanent total disability

presumptive title

Title. A title to real estate that is presumed but questionable because it has arisen out of the simple possession of property without any apparent right, or claim of right, to hold and continue possession.

see: adverse possession, real estate, title

pretrial conference

Law. A conference held before a trial where the judge and the attorneys seek to clarify the issues and eliminate matters not in dispute.

Prevention of Significant Deterioration

Regulation. An Environmental Protection Agency program that requires state or federal permits for new or modified sources of air pollution. The permits are intended to restrict new emissions in areas where the current air quality exceeds the quality standards.

see: Clean Air Act, National Ambient Air Quality Standards, National Emission Standards for Hazardous Air Pollutants

Price-Anderson Act

Regulation. A federal law enacted in 1957 that requires owners or operators of nuclear facilities to provide proof of financial responsibility before they are licensed. The act limits a facility's liability to $700 million per nuclear accident.

see: Atomic Energy Act, financial responsibility law, nuclear energy liability insurance, Nuclear Regulatory Commission

price/earnings ratio (P/E)

Financial Planning. A stock's price divided by earnings per share, usually using the reported company profits for the last year; the multiple of per-share earnings that produces the stock price. It is reported daily in newspaper stock listings. When investors expect a company's profits to grow, they bid up the price of shares, which is reflected in a growing P/E ratio. *Example*: If a stock sells at $48 per share and had earnings per share of $4, its P/E ratio is 12 (48 ÷ 4).

see: earnings per share, financial ratios

price-to-book ratio

Financial Planning. The market price per share of common stock divided by the previous year's book value per share of common stock.

see: book value, financial ratios

Priestly v. Fowler

Workers' Compensation. A landmark case in the development of workers' compensation. This 1837 British court decision stated that an employer was not responsible for an employee's injury if it was caused by another employee. *Priestly* also laid the groundwork for the assumption of risk defense. This ruling changed the prior English common law that employers were responsible for injuries to their employees.

see: assumption of risk, common law defense, fellow servant rule, workers' compensation law

prima facie evidence

Law. Evidence that by itself establishes the claim or defense of a party if it is not rebutted or contradicted.

see: evidence

primary beneficiary

Life. The person designated as the first to receive the proceeds of a life insurance policy upon the death of the insured.

see: contingent beneficiary, secondary beneficiary

primary care physician (PCP)

Health. The medical doctor assigned to or selected by a member of a managed care plan as the practitioner who usually treats the member or authorizes treatment by specialists. Because of the primary care physician's role in referring patients to specialists, this doctor is sometimes termed the *gatekeeper*.

synonym: gatekeeper, managing physician; *see*: health maintenance organization, managed care

(1), preferred provider organization

primary earnings per share
Financial Planning.

see: earnings per share

primary insurance
Insurer Operations. 1. Insurance that responds first to a claim (i.e., it provides coverage on a first-dollar basis), sometimes subject to a deductible.
2. A low-limit policy over which excess or umbrella policies are issued.

synonym: underlying insurance; *compare*: excess insurance; *see*: layering, primary insurer, umbrella liability insurance, underlying limits

primary insurance amount (PIA)
Employee Benefits. Social Security benefits are considered primary insurance, over which private pension or medical plans build their benefits. The amount of Social Security primary insurance is determined by taking the average monthly wage and referring to the Social Security Wage Index, which translates it into a monthly benefit.

see: average monthly wage, Social Security Wage Index

primary insured
Insurer Operations. The first insured named in an insurance policy.

see: first named insured

primary insurer
Insurer Operations. The insurer that responds to a claim up to the applicable policy limit before any other insurer of all or part of the same risk becomes liable (e.g., an excess insurer).

see: excess insurance, primary insurance, underlying limits

Reinsurance. In the context of reinsurance, the ceding insurer.

see: ceding insurer, reinsurance

primary policy
Insurer Operations. The policy issued by the primary insurance company; the policy covering losses on a first-dollar basis; the policy covering the first or bottom layer in a layered program. To avoid multiple compensation for a loss covered by more than one policy, the policies assume liability in a specified order. The order varies by the type of loss and the coverages provided by the various policies in force. The first policy in order is sometimes called the primary policy.

see: apportionment, coordination of benefits, layering, primary insurer, other insurance provision

primary rating classification
Automobile. A classification needed to develop a rate for a vehicle to be covered, such as fleet or nonfleet, size, use, and radius of operation.

compare: secondary rating classification; *see*: fleet, nonfleet, radius of operation

prime rate
Financial Planning. The lowest or benchmark interest rate that a commercial bank charges its best customers—usually large, financially sound corporations. It is also the reference point for some types of adjustable rate loans. The prime rate reflects the costs that banks pay to borrow money; when a bank's own borrowing costs go down, the prime rate tends to decline.

compare: discount rate; *see*: interest

principal
Agency. A person who has authorized another (agent) to act on his or her behalf.

compare: agent; *see*: respondeat superior, vicarious liability

Surety. The debtor in a suretyship arrangement; the person or entity that purchases a surety bond.

compare: obligee, surety; *see*: obligor, suretyship

principal driver
Personal. The individual who uses a covered auto the greatest part of the time, regardless of ownership. Information on this person (primarily age and sex) is used for rating auto liability coverage.

see: personal auto policy

principal sum
Financial Planning. The capital sum of a debt, or the amount borrowed.

compare: interest

Health/Life. The amount specified in a disability income policy to be paid in the event of accidental death, dismemberment or loss of sight.

see: capital sum

principle of indemnity
General.

see: indemnification

prior acts coverage
Liability. Coverage that may be necessary for a person who has been uninsured or who has canceled a claims-made liability policy that does not provide an adequate claims discovery period. Insurance may be available from the new insurer or, occasionally, from a separate insurer who provides a policy only for claims arising from acts that occurred before the beginning of the policy period.

synonym: nose coverage; *see*: claims-made form, full prior acts coverage

prior approval rating
Regulation. The practice in some states of requiring the insurance commissioner's approval of premium rates and rate changes before the insurer may

implement them.

compare: file-and-use rating, modified prior approval rating, open competition rating, use-and-file rating; *see*: rate making

prior litigation exclusion

Professional Liability.

see: pending and prior litigation exclusion

prior service benefit

Employee Benefits.

see: past service benefit

prison guard captivity coverage

Liability. Coverage for prison guards that responds when they are seized as hostages or injured in a prison riot. It compensates the guard or family in case of injury or death.

private carrier

Automobile. A fleet of trucks owned by the shipper and used for carrying its own cargo (i.e., a firm's own fleet of trucks).

compare: common carrier, contract carrier; *see*: carrier

private passenger automobile

Automobile. An automobile used for personal purposes. To be covered by a personal auto policy, a vehicle must be owned by an individual and not be used to carry passengers for hire. For business auto classification purposes, private passenger automobiles are usually sedan and station wagon type vehicles, but also include pick-up trucks, panel trucks or vans not used for business purposes.

see: personal auto policy

privileged communication

Law. Communication between persons who are deemed to have a highly confidential relationship and who are legally protected, with some exceptions, from being compelled to testify against each other. *Examples*: Communication between spouses, attorney and client, priest and penitent, doctor and patient.

privity of contract

Law. The direct, private relationship between parties to a contract. Privity is usually required as between the plaintiff and defendant to maintain a suit. There are many exceptions; for example, a consumer of a defective product may sue the manufacturer either in tort or for breach of warranty though lacking the privity that exists between the manufacturer and the retailer.

see: contract

prize indemnification insurance

Inland Marine. A specialized inland marine coverage that pays for prizes offered at fund raising or sporting events. Frequently, the winners of large prizes are paid by underwriters in the form of an annuity over several years. The premium for this insurance is based on the odds faced by the insurer.

see: hole-in-one coverage, record fish coverage, tagged fish coverage

pro forma statement

Accounting. A financial or business projection according to certain assumptions. (Latin for "for the sake of form.")

see: financial statement

pro rata cancellation

Insurer Operations. An insurer's termination of a policy before the expiration date. Premiums returned to the insured are in proportion to the days remaining in the policy period, with no penalty because the insurer initiated the action.

compare: short-rate cancellation; *see*: cancellation, earned premium, return premium

pro rata distribution clause

Property. A penalty clause found in older property insurance policies which, if the insured is carrying inadequate coverage at the time of a loss, automatically distributes coverage on insured properties at various locations in the proportion that their values bear to the total of values on all properties insured.

synonym: distribution clause; *see*: average clause

pro rata liability clause

Property. A provision in most property insurance policies for the automatic division of a claim payment among two or more policies that cover the same claim. Each policy pays a share of the claim in the proportion of its limit of coverage to the total coverage limits on the property.

see: apportionment, assignment quota, other insurance provision

pro rata reinsurance

Reinsurance. A form of reinsurance where the reinsurer assumes an agreed percentage of the original losses and premiums of the ceding insurer.

synonym: participating reinsurance, proportional reinsurance; *see*: reinsurance

probability analysis

Risk Management. A mathematical description of the likelihood of a specific type of event; the ratio of a given outcome to the number of possible outcomes. The outcome of the forecast (or likelihood of an event occurring) is expressed as a number between zero (certain not to occur) and one (certain to occur).

see: degree of risk, law of large numbers, mean, median, mode, odds

probability of loss

Loss Control/Risk Management. The number of

security (crime) losses that occur during a specified period of time (usually one year). The term is used by security specialists and has the same meaning as the risk management term *loss frequency*.

see: loss frequency

probable maximum loss (PML)

Loss Control/Property. A maximum loss estimate developed for property insurance underwriters, which assumes an impairment to one sprinkler system exists at the time of loss. A PML estimate may include other adverse conditions, such as a delayed fire alarm, insufficient water supply or delayed firefighting response if such conditions seem reasonable.

compare: maximum possible loss, normal loss expectancy; *see*: above-normal loss, amount subject, segregation of exposure units

probate

Law. The legal procedure for proving that a document is the valid last will of the purported signer.

see: intestate, probate bond, probate court, will

probate bond

Surety. A fiduciary bond required by a probate court, to protect the administration of a will, estate or guardianship.

see: fiduciary bond, probate

probate court

Law. A court with specialized jurisdiction over the proof of wills, the settlement of estates, and guardianships.

see: probate, will

probationary period

Health. The period of time in a health insurance policy between the effective date and the first day of coverage for certain disabilities, illnesses or accidents.

synonym: excluded period

proceeding

Law. A judicial or administrative case, including any preliminary hearings.

see: due process of law

proceeds

Life. A life insurance policy's face value, including any additional benefits that may be payable at its maturity or upon the death of the insured.

see: face amount

process

Law. A summons or complaint, which begins a civil lawsuit, or other means by which a court exercises jurisdiction over a person or thing or compels a person to appear and respond to a pleading. *Abuse of process* is an action that departs from proper legal process or the use of a legal process

for an illegal or improper purpose, such as malicious or groundless issuance or service of a complaint (often called *vexatious litigation*).

see: complaint, litigation, pleading

processing endorsement

Ocean Marine. An endorsement to a cargo policy written on a warehouse-to-warehouse basis, that extends coverage while the merchandise is being processed at its destination.

see: warehouse-to-warehouse coverage

processor

Loss Control/Inland Marine. A business that is involved in the physical modification of a product, but which does not modify the fundamental nature of the product.

see: processor's policy

processor's policy

Inland Marine. An inland marine policy that provides coverage on goods that have been sent to another firm for processing. It covers damage to the goods while on the processor's premises and while in transit.

see: processor

producer

Agency. An insurance agent, solicitor, broker, or any other person directly involved in the sale of insurance.

see: agent, broker, producer-controlled insurer, solicitor

producer-controlled insurer

Agency/Insurer Operations. An insurer directly or indirectly owned or controlled by a producer (i.e., a broker, agent, solicitor, etc.). Many states require disclosure of such control when policies are solicited or procured so consumers know if the agent or broker is referring or recommending business to him- or herself.

see: producer, vertical integration

product contamination coverage

Liability. Coverage for the loss when the insured cannot sell a product designed for human consumption because it has been contaminated by any material that causes or threatens harm to health or causes or threatens damage, deterioration or loss of value to the product itself. This includes insects, vermin, bacteria, fungi, viruses or hazardous substances.

see: contaminant

product defect

Liability.

see: defective product

product extortion insurance

Liability. Coverage that indemnifies an insured for

a percentage of the loss incurred from the insured's payment of extortion, or for recalling a threatened or contaminated product, or destroying a contaminated product.

see: product recall expense insurance

product liability insurance

Liability. Coverage of a manufacturer's or seller's liability for losses or injuries to a buyer, user or bystander caused by a defect or malfunction of the product. When it is part of a commercial general liability policy, the coverage is often called *products-completed operations insurance.*

see: abnormal use, active malfunction, allergy and susceptibility, bench error, broad form product liability, clinical trials product liability insurance, completed operations insurance, defective product, design errors and omissions insurance, latent defect, market share liability, pollution product liability insurance, products-completed operations insurance, ripping and tearing insurance, state-of-the-art defense, strict liability, warranty (3)

Product Liability Risk Retention Act of 1981

Regulation. Federal legislation adopted in 1981 to facilitate the ability of product manufacturers to establish group self-insurance programs (risk retention groups) or group captive insurers for their product liability exposures and to purchase product liability insurance on a group basis (purchasing groups). The Act limited the states' control over insurance as respects product liability. A risk retention or purchasing group could be domiciled in one state, where it would be regulated, but it would be authorized to operate in all other states, exempt from most state insurance regulation and guaranty funds. The Act was amended by the Liability Risk Retention Act of 1986.

see: Liability Risk Retention Act of 1986, risk retention group, purchasing group

product liability safety committee

Risk Management. A committee established by a manufacturing firm to monitor the safety of products in development and assist in managing product liability losses. The committee members usually comprise various disciplines within the organization (e.g., chief executive officer, general counsel, risk manager, quality control manager, engineering representative). The committee also reviews existing products, labeling, consumer warnings, etc.

see: product liability insurance

product recall exclusion

Liability. A provision in commercial general liability policy forms (since 1966) that excludes from coverage the cost or expense incurred by an insured for the withdrawal, recall, inspection, repair, replacement, adjustment, removal or disposal of an insured's product. It is sometimes referred to as the "sistership" exclusion, because defective products that have already generated liability claims have "sister" products of the same production run or lot still in the hands of consumers.

synonym: sistership exclusion; *see*: commercial general liability policy, defective product, product liability insurance, product recall expense insurance

product recall expense insurance

Liability. Extra expense coverage that indemnifies the insured for the cost of recalling a product that is suspected of being defective and causing bodily harm to consumers. Coverage usually includes such expenses as communications, shipping charges, radio and television announcements, newspaper advertisements, hiring additional personnel, and destroying the product if necessary.

see: defective product, product extortion insurance, product tampering insurance

product specialty insurer

Insurer Operations. An insurer that specializes in writing only one line of business (e.g., auto insurance) without focusing on a particular customer market.

compare: full service insurer, market specialty insurer, selective specialty insurer; *see*: marketing

product tampering insurance

Liability. Coverage that protects a manufacturer whose product has been tampered with, threatening the safety or marketability of existing stock. It pays the cost of required inventory destruction, lost profits, business interruption and product rehabilitation. Coverage does not apply to third-party liability or extortion payments.

see: products-completed operations insurance, product extortion insurance, product recall expense insurance

product warranty inefficacy insurance

Liability. A form of product warranty that guarantees systems performance on newly constructed facilities. It guarantees that the system will perform at its engineer-designed level.

see: efficacy coverage, warranty (3)

products-completed operations aggregate limit

Liability. The total amount an insured can recover under the ISO commercial general liability coverage form for all claims arising under coverage Part A of the products and completed operations hazard during a single policy year.

see: aggregate limit, broad form product liability, commercial general liability form, general aggregate limit

products-completed operations insurance

Liability. Coverage against loss arising out of the liability of a manufacturer, merchant or distributor for injury or damage resulting from the use of a product; product liability coverage when part of a commercial general liability policy. Coverage also includes liability incurred by a contractor as the result of improperly performed work (construction or installation) after a job has been completed. This coverage can be included in the ISO commercial general liability policy under coverage Part A.

see: commercial general liability policy, completed operations coverage, defective product, product liability insurance, products-completed operations aggregate limit, state-of-the-art defense, your product, your work

Professional in Human Resources (PHR)

Organizations. A professional designation awarded by the Personnel Accreditation Institute after the applicant has passed a written examination, has sufficient college credits, and has met minimum experience requirements in human resource management.

see: Personnel Accreditation Institute

Professional Insurance Agents

see: National Association of Professional Insurance Agents

Professional Insurance Communicators of America (PICA)

Organizations. Members: Publication editors from mutual insurance organizations. *Objectives:* Reviewing and evaluating in-house publications; sponsoring educational programs and giving awards. *Founded: 1955. Headquarters:* Indianapolis, IN.

Professional Insurance Mass Marketing Association (PIMA)

Organizations. Members: Insurance companies, agencies and others servicing the insurance industry. *Objectives:* Promotes the marketing of insurance. *Founded:* 1975. *Headquarters:* Bethesda, MD.

professional liability insurance

Professional Liability. Coverage of a person or organization for injury or loss to third parties arising from negligence or malfeasance in rendering professional services. Professional negligence is the failure to exercise the degree of care, knowledge or skill of the average person in good professional standing under circumstances similar to those in which the injury occurred. The term *malpractice insurance* means professional liability coverage of medical malpractice. *Professional liability insurance* is also sometimes used instead of *errors and omissions insurance.*

see: architects' professional liability insurance, broadcasters' liability insurance, consent to settle provision, counsel selection provision, directors' and officers' liability insurance, educators' professional liability insurance, engineers' professional liability insurance, errors and omissions insurance, hospital professional liability insurance, malfeasance, malpractice insurance, negligence, professional service

Professional Liability Underwriting Society (PLUS)

Organizations. Members: Professional liability underwriters, managing general agents, brokers, surplus lines brokers, accountants and attorneys. *Objectives:* Nonprofit organization established to promote and develop the professional liability insurance industry through educational programs and seminars. *Founded:* 1993. *Headquarters:* Minneapolis, MN.

professional reinsurer

Reinsurance. A firm or intermediary whose business is mainly reinsurance and related services, as contrasted with insurance organizations that may sometimes assume reinsurance in addition to their main direct underwriting business.

see: innocent market, intermediary, reinsurance

professional standards review organization

Health.

see: peer review organization

professional service

Professional Liability. Work, assistance, information or advice performed or provided to another which is based on a recognized body of specialized knowledge or expertise. The major professions—medicine and surgery, nursing, law, accounting, architecture, engineering, teaching, etc.—require extensive formal education; emphasize a duty of service to the patient or client, rather than self-interested commercial gain only; and have a self-regulating code of conduct or ethics. Many commercial activities (including financial advice and insurance underwriting and counseling) have acquired some aspects of professionalism, such as special training requirements and ethical guidelines, which are intended to emphasize effective and honest service to consumers.

see: malpractice, professional liability insurance, special circumstances

profit and loss statement

Accounting.

see: income statement

profit center

Accounting. A unit of a large, decentralized firm

that has its own investments and for which a rate of return on investment can be calculated.

see: return on investment

profit commission
Reinsurance.

see: contingency commission

profit-sharing commission
Agency.

see: variable commission

profit-sharing plan
Employee Benefits. A benefit plan established by an employer to share the profits of the business with employees. A plan may qualify under federal laws and regulations for tax deductibility even if the employer does not have current accumulated profits, provided there is a definite formula for allocating plan contributions among participants and their beneficiaries for a fixed period, upon the attainment of a stated age, or upon an event such as the participant's retirement, disability, death or severance of employment.

see: employee benefit plan, phantom stock plan

profit-sharing provision
Reinsurance. A provision of some reinsurance contracts and most finite risk insurance contracts that, based on the program loss ratio or build-up of a claims fund, the insurer will allow some of its investment income to be credited to the insured.

see: finite risk insurance

profitability index
Risk Management. An index used to evaluate proposals for which net present values have been determined. The profitability index is determined by dividing the present value of each proposal by its initial investment. An index value greater than 1.0 is acceptable and the higher the number, the more financially attractive the proposal.

see: present value

profits and commissions insurance
Property. Coverage that protects an individual or firm from lost profit or commissions on a sold product due to damage to the product before its delivery to the buyer.

see: business income coverage, time element insurance

progressive loss
General. An injury, illness or property damage that occurs gradually over a long period of time rather than quickly, as from a sudden event. Long-term exposure to hazardous substances or pollution may result in a loss or disease with an indeterminate moment of onset.

synonym: continuous loss; *see*: continuous trigger theory, exposure theory, injury-in-fact theory, manifestation theory

prohibited list
Insurer Operations. An insurance company's list of the types or classes of risk it does not insure.

synonym: do not solicit list, undesirable list; *compare*: target risk; *see*: redlining, substandard risk

promissory warranty
Insurer Operations. A representation made by an applicant for insurance to an insurer as to a future event or condition for which the applicant takes responsibility. *Example*: A property insurance applicant warrants that an automatic sprinkler system will be maintained in proper working order.

see: protective safeguards clause, warranty (2)

promoter
General. A person who develops or takes the initiative in founding or organizing a business venture. If more than one promoter is involved in a venture, they are often called *co-promoters*.

promulgate
Insurer Operations. To establish, put into effect or implement insurance rates or forms. Rates and forms may be promulgated by insurers, rating bureaus, insurer organizations or state agencies (insurance departments or state rating bureaus).

see: rate making

Regulation. To develop or establish, put into effect or implement regulations and administrative rulings.

compare: enact

proof
Insurer Operations.

see: proof of loss

Law.

see: burden of proof, evidence

proof of loss
Insurer Operations. A sworn statement that usually must be furnished by the insured to an insurer before any loss under a policy may be paid. This form is usually used in the settlement of first-party losses and includes the date and description of the occurrence and the amount of loss.

synonym: statement of loss; *see*: affidavit of claim, notice of loss

property
Property. Real estate, buildings, objects or articles, intangible assets, or rights with an exchangeable

value of which someone may claim legal ownership.

see: buildings, intangible property, intellectual property, machinery, personal property, property insurance, real estate

property damage liability coverage
Liability. Coverage for the obligation to compensate another person for lost use or destruction or damage to that person's tangible property. This coverage is included in most personal and commercial liability policies along with bodily and personal injury coverages.

see: bodily injury and property damage liability

property first loss scale
Property.
see: Lloyd's property first loss scale

property insurance
Property. Coverage for real or personal property lost or damaged by a covered peril and, sometimes, consequential financial losses resulting from property damage. It is first-party coverage.

see: broad form property insurance endorsement, excess property insurance, fire insurance, first-party insurance, personal property, real estate

Property Insurance Loss Register (PILR)
Property. A list maintained by the American Insurance Association of all fire losses over $500,000. It is kept on a database that insurance companies may access to check for duplicate coverage.

see: American Insurance Association, Fire and Theft Index Bureau, Insurance Crime Prevention Institute, Insurance Services Office, interinsurer claim service organization, Medical Information Bureau, National Automobile Theft Bureau

Property Insurance Plans Service Office
Organizations. Organizations. *Members*: Insurance companies. *Objectives*: A nonprofit organization that compiles statistics, calculates rates, and provides technical services for property assigned risk plans. A division of the National Committee on Property Insurance. *Headquarters*: Boston, MA.

see: National Committee on Property Insurance

Property Loss Research Bureau (PLRB)
Organizations. Members: Mutual and stock insurance companies. *Objectives*: Sponsors property loss research. *Founded*: 1947. *Headquarters*: Schaumburg, IL.

property of others
Crime. An endorsement (ISO form CR 15 20) that expands the property covered by crime coverage forms to include the property of individuals or organizations other than the insured. This endorsement can also be used to limit coverage so that it

applies only to the property of others.

see: crime coverages

property other than money and securities
Crime. A term used in crime coverage forms to extend coverage to tangible property, except money and securities, with a monetary value. The crime coverage forms contain exclusions for many forms of property that would otherwise be included in this broad term.

see: crime coverages, money, securities

property transfer pollution insurance
Liability. An owner's or buyer's coverage of first-party cleanup costs for contamination discovered after the sale of property when cleanup is ordered by a governmental authority. Third-party bodily injury, property damage and cleanup may also be covered.

see: pollution insurance, remediation cost overrun insurance, remediation warranty insurance

proportional reinsurance
Reinsurance.
see: pro rata reinsurance

proposal
Agency. The written presentation of insurance terms, conditions and price presented by an agent to a client.

International. The term used in the London Market for an insurance application.

Proposition 103
Regulation. A ballot initiative approved by California voters in 1988 in an effort to reduce private passenger automobile rates. Provisions included a 20% rate rollback for auto insurance, homeowners, and commercial or municipal liability insurance; good driver discounts; an elected insurance commissioner; elimination of territorial (zip code-based) rating; elimination of the insurance industry's antitrust exemptions; allowing banks to sell insurance; allowing insurance agents to rebate commissions to insureds; legalizing group property and casualty insurance plans; and allowing policy cancellations by insurers only on the grounds of nonpayment of premiums, fraud or a substantial increase in the insured hazard. Some of these provisions were implemented, but the main rate rollback was overturned in court. Rates must be approved by the insurance commissioner and reductions may be ordered, but denying insurers a "reasonable" rate of return is an unconstitutional taking of property. The proposition triggered similar legislation in other states.

see: anti-rebate laws, good driver discount

proprietary alarm system
Loss Control. An alarm system owned, operated,

and maintained by the owner of the protected property. The alarm is received at a proprietary supervising station at the protected property, attended by security personnel.

compare: auxiliary alarm system, central station alarm system, remote station alarm system

proprietary insurer

Insurer Operations. An insurer formed to earn a profit for its owners. Examples are stock insurance companies, Lloyd's associations, and insurance exchanges.

compare: cooperative insurer; *see*: insurance exchange, Lloyd's associations, stock insurance company

proprietorship liability exclusion

Professional Liability. An exclusion in some physicians', surgeons' and dentists' professional liability policies for any activities arising out of their interest in the ownership of a hospital, clinic, or medical laboratory.

see: physicians', surgeons' and dentists' professional liability insurance

proration of benefits

Insurer Operations. The proportional division or adjustment of benefits between two or more insurance policies that cover the same loss.

see: contribution by limits, contribution by equal share, coordination of benefits, other insurance provision, pro rata distribution clause, pro rata liability clause

prospect

Agency. An individual or business that an agent or broker has screened and identified as a potential purchaser of insurance.

prospecting

Agency. Locating individuals or businesses that are potential buyers of insurance by obtaining referrals from clients, advertising, telephone solicitations or cold canvassing.

see: cold canvassing, marketing, prospect

prospective payment system

Health. The payment system for Medicare-covered services, which uses diagnosis related groups to establish payment rates in advance, regardless of the provider's actual cost of the services. The system gives providers an incentive to control costs.

see: capitation, diagnosis related group, Medicare, outlier

prospective rating plan

Insurer Operations. The most frequently used method of establishing insurance rates. A rate is developed in advance to be used on future policies. This rate is based on historical loss experience for similar exposures.

compare: retrospective rating plan

prospective reserve

Health/Life. A reserve amount designated as a liability for life or health insurers to pay the difference between projected benefits and projected premiums, including investment income.

prospectus

Financial Planning. A legal document published by a corporation or its officers that details the history and current status of an issue of securities. It is the principal document of a registered statement required by law to be furnished to investors before a public offering and must be filed with and approved by the Securities and Exchange Commission.

compare: offering circular; *see*: forward-looking statement, public offering, red herring, secondary offering

protected risk

Loss Control/Property. A property risk located within a fire protection district or area served by a recognized fire department.

see: grading schedule, highly protected risk, protection

protecting the treaty

Reinsurance. A ceding insurer's actions to prevent heavy losses to its treaty reinsurer, which might lead to increased reinsurance rates or decreased participation in a profit-sharing arrangement.

see: treaty reinsurance

protection

Property. The existence and nearness to an insured risk of firefighting facilities. Protection includes fire hydrants, adequacy and reliability of water supply, the number and quality of available firefighters, adequacy of equipment, etc.

synonym: fire protection; *compare*: construction, exposure, occupancy; *see*: class rating, grading schedule, protection class

protection and indemnity club (P&I club)

Ocean Marine. A quasi-assessable mutual insurance company formed by shipowners to provide indemnity insurance. The club establishes it own rules regarding notification of claims, the rights of club members, and club calls. Most clubs arrange reinsurance in the traditional reinsurance market.

see: assessment insurance, mutual insurance company

protection and indemnity insurance (P&I)

Ocean Marine. A broad form of marine liability insurance that covers the operator of a ship for such things as liability to crew members and other individuals on board the vessel, and for damage to fixed objects, such as docks, resulting from the insured's negligence.

see: ocean marine insurance

protection class

Loss Control/Property. A grade assigned to a fire protection district, usually expressed in a number between 1 (best) and 10 (worst).

synonym: class; *see*: grading schedule, protection

protective devices or services provision

Crime. An endorsement (ISO form CR 15 09) that requires the insured to maintain the protective devices (e.g., safe, burglar alarm) or protective services (e.g., watchperson) specified in the form at all times during the policy period. If the specified safeguard is not maintained, coverage is suspended.

protective safeguards clause

Property. A policy provision that voids coverage if the insured fails to exercise due diligence in maintaining protective safeguards such as automatic sprinklers or burglar alarms.

see: automatic sprinkler clause, promissory warranty

protective safeguards endorsement

Property. A commercial property endorsement (ISO form IL 04 15) that suspends or voids coverage if the protective safeguards (e.g., automatic sprinkler system) scheduled in the form are not maintained in good working order or the insured has knowledge that they are impaired.

Prouty exposure analysis

Risk Management. A risk exposure analysis method developed by Richard Prouty, a corporate risk manager, where exposures to loss are subjectively classified according to three categories of severity (slight, significant, severe) and four categories of frequency (almost nil, slight, moderate, definite) for comparison purposes.

see: exposure

provider

Health.

see: health care provider

provision

Insurer Operations.

see: policy provision

provisional premium

Insurer Operations. A premium based on a rough estimate of exposures, or using a provisional rate to issue a policy. The premium is subject to adjustment when additional information is available.

synonym: tentative premium; *see*: deposit premium, premium, provisional rate

provisional rate

Insurer Operations. A tentative rate used to issue a policy, subject to subsequent adjustment when sufficient information to develop a final rate is obtained.

synonym: tentative rate; *see*: provisional premium

proximate cause

Law. An act, event or omission that naturally and foreseeably results in a harm or loss, though it may not necessarily be the nearest or last cause; something that produces a harmful effect in a natural chain of causation unbroken by any intervening efficient cause.

compare: immediate cause; *see*: concurrent causation, sine qua non

Property. Most property insurance policies require an insured peril to be the immediate or proximate cause of a loss for coverage to apply. The loss must be a direct result of an insured peril.

proximity detector

Loss Control. A device used to trigger a burglar alarm. It uses an object (e.g., a safe, filing cabinet) as an antenna, electronically linked to an alarm control. When an intruder approaches or touches the object, its electrostatic field is disturbed, activating the alarm.

synonym: capacitance detector, electrostatic detector; *see*: burglar alarm

proxy

Financial Planning. A shareholder's written authorization to vote his or her stock on proposed corporate actions or in an election of directors; also, the person who holds or exercises the shareholder's authorization.

compare: voting trust; *see*: common stock, cumulative voting, dissenting shareholder, proxy soliciation machinery, statutory voting

proxy solicitation machinery

Financial Planning. A common description of the process whereby the incumbent management of a publicly held corporation is able to procure a favorable vote from shareholders on nearly any issue. This is based in part on the ability of management to use corporate funds to communicate with shareholders, in part on shareholders' trust in the expertise of management, and in part on close continuing consultation between executive officers and the largest shareholders.

see: proxy

psychiatric stress

Health.

see: mental distress

public adjuster

General. An organization or individual (other than a lawyer) who represents the insured in loss adjustments, charging a fee for settling claims with insurers.

compare: independent adjuster; *see*: claims adjuster

Public Agency Risk Managers Association (PARMA)

Organizations. Members: Risk and insurance managers from public agencies, private agencies and professionals. *Objectives*: Promotes the interests of those involved in risk management. *Founded*: 1974. *Headquarters*: San Jose, CA.

public and institutional property

Property. An obsolete property insurance rating program for government and nonprofit organizations. It provided reduced rates for these properties and very broad coverage.

see: public entity insurance

public auto

Automobile. A business auto policy classification for a vehicle used to transport members of the public for hire or pursuant to contract (e.g. taxicabs, limousines, school or church buses, van pool vans).

compare: private passenger automobile; *see*: business auto coverage form

public domain

General. Public or government-owned property.

see: eminent domain

public easement

Title. A right-of-way for use by members of the public at large.

see: dedicate, easement, inverse condemnation, public domain

public employee dishonesty coverage form (blanket)

Crime. A blanket employee dishonesty coverage form (ISO form CR 00 16, or form O), similar to the blanket employee dishonesty coverage form, that is designed for governmental entities and subdivisions, such as cities, counties, states, fire districts, transit authorities, public hospitals, public educational institutions, and boards of education.

synonym: crime coverage form O; *see*: blanket employee dishonesty coverage form, unauthorized advances coverage form

public employee dishonesty coverage form (per employee)

Crime. A per-employee dishonesty coverage form (ISO form CR 00 17, or form P), similar to the employee dishonesty coverage form, that is designed for governmental entities and subdivisions, such as cities, counties, states, fire districts, transit authorities, public hospitals, public educational institutions, and boards of education.

synonym: crime coverage form P; *see*: employee dishonesty coverage form, unauthorized advances coverage form

public entity insurance

Insurer Operations. Coverage for public entities such as municipalities, counties, state and federal governments and their agencies. Such entities have significant property and casualty exposures. Many of their exposures (such as police and fire department liability, road design and maintenance, public beaches and playgrounds) are unique and difficult to insure.

compare: government insurance; *see*: county clerks and recorders errors and omissions insurance, municipal bond guaranty insurance, public and institutional property, public official bond, public officials' liability insurance, sovereign immunity

public exchange offer

Insurer Operations. A corporation's attempt to acquire another corporation by offering its securities in exchange for the target corporation's voting shares. Usually, the takeover offer requires that a specified number of target corporation shares be presented for exchange.

compare: tender offer

public offering

Financial Planning. The sale of securities by an issuer (or a person controlling the issuer) to members of the public. Generally, any offering that is not an exempt private offering pursuant to the Securities Act of 1933 or similarly exempt under state blue sky laws is considered a public offering. Normally, securities to be offered must be registered with the Securities and Exchange Commission, and pertinent financial information must be disclosed to potential investors in a prospectus.

see: blue sky laws, offering circular, prospectus, secondary offering

public official bond

Surety. A surety bond that guarantees that a public official will faithfully perform his or her official duties and honestly manage funds entrusted to them. A law usually requires such a bond and prescribes the coverage.

synonym: federal official bond; *see*: state bonding fund, surety bond

public officials' liability insurance

Professional Liability. A form of professional liability insurance for a public entity and the persons who act on its behalf for errors, misstatements, omissions, neglect, or breach of duty. Policies sometimes describe the covered acts as *malfeasance, misfeasance,* or *nonfeasance*.

see: malfeasance, misfeasance, nonfeasance

public or livery exclusion

Personal. A personal auto policy exclusion of liability and medical coverage for a covered auto while it is used to transport members of the general public, whether or not a fee is charged (public or livery conveyance). The exclusion does not apply to a private car pool with shared expenses.

see: personal auto policy

public relations firm professional liability insurance

Professional Liability. A form of advertisers' insurance for firms who do marketing and advertising for clients which provides coverage on a claims-made basis for advertising liability, libel and slander, copyright infringement, and other forms of personal injury.

see: advertisers' and advertising agency liability insurance

Public Risk Management Association (PRIMA)

Organizations. Members: Risk, insurance and safety managers for cities, counties, villages, towns, school boards, water districts, utility districts and highway authorities. *Objectives:* Provides information on risk and safety management. Represents the members' interests before state and federal legislative bodies. *Founded:* 1978. *Headquarters:* Arlington, VA. Known as the Public Risk and Insurance Management Association until 1989.

public service exclusion

Professional Liability. An exclusion in some lawyers' professional liability policies for claims resulting from work associated with a public service position (not an attorney's pro bono work). The purpose is to preclude coverage for liabilities incurred while an attorney holds a public service position that is unrelated to his or her basic law practice.

see: lawyers' professional liability insurance

publishers' professional liability insurance

Professional Liability. A form of professional liability insurance for publishers that provides coverage on a claims-made basis for libel, slander, defamation, piracy of ideas or titles, infringement of copyright, unfair competition, and plagiarism.

see: copyright, libel, piracy (*Property*), slander

punitive damages

Law. Damages awarded in a civil lawsuit in order to punish wrongdoing of a greater culpability than simple negligence, without regard to compensating the plaintiff's actual loss. Punitive damages are intended as a deterrence. Some states prohibit insurance of punitive damages on the grounds that spreading the risk of punishment for willful misconduct lessens the deterrent effect. Some policies specifically exclude coverage for punitive damages, while others rely on state laws.

synonym: exemplary damages; *compare:* additur, compensatory damages

pup company

Insurer Operations. A subsidiary insurance company owned by a larger company.

compare: parent company; *see:* affiliated insurers, fleet of companies, subsidiary company

purchase date

Life. A specific date set for buying an annuity, which is used in calculating its cost.

see: annuity

purchase payment fund

Life.

see: active life fund

purchase securities at a premium exclusion

Professional Liability.

see: greenmail exclusion

purchasing group (PG)

Risk Management. An entity that offers insurance to groups of similar businesses with similar exposures to risk. (Personal lines and workers' compensation policies cannot be written by purchasing groups.) Such groups are exempt from most state laws or regulations, except for the state in which a group is domiciled. They were originally created, along with risk retention groups, by the Product Liability Risk Retention Act of 1981.

compare: risk retention group; *see:* Liability Risk Retention Act of 1986, Product Liability Risk Retention Act of 1981

pure annuity

Life. An annuity that pays a periodic income benefit for the life of the annuitant. Payments end when the annuitant dies. Premiums for a pure deferred annuity are considered fully earned as paid because they are discounted for the possibility of the annuitant's death during the payment (or accumulation) period. Should death occur before income payments begin, there is no premium refund.

compare: refund annuity; *see:* accumulation period, deferred annuity

pure captive

Risk Management. A captive insurance company that insures only its parent's business.

see: captive insurance company

pure financial loss coverage

International/Liability. A form of liability coverage in Germany, France and Spain that is similar to errors and omissions coverage in the United States. It provides coverage for a third party's loss of use of tangible property without the standard coverage triggers of bodily injury or property damage.

see: errors and omissions insurance

pure loss cost

Reinsurance. The ratio of reinsured losses incurred under a reinsurance agreement to the ceding insurer's subject earned premium for that agreement, before any loading factors are added.

synonym: burning cost

pure mortality cost

Life. The face amount of a life insurance policy, multiplied by a factor indicated on a mortality table. The result—the pure mortality cost—is the first element considered in developing a life insurance policy premium.

see: mortality table, natural premium

pure premium

Insurer Operations. That portion of the premium which covers losses and related loss expenses (i.e., includes no loading for commissions, taxes or other expenses).

see: expense loading, field expenses, general and insurance expenses, natural premium

pure risk

Risk Management. A risk involving the probability or possibility of loss with no chance for gain. A pure risk is generally insurable.

compare: speculative risk; *see*: indemnification

purging

Loss Control. The filling of a tank with water or inert gases, to remove toxic or flammable vapor or gases.

put option

Financial Planning. A contract granting the holder of stock the right to sell a given number of shares (usually in blocks of 100) at a specified price on or before a certain date. This is a hedging technique against the stock dropping in price, and the holder pays an option premium.

compare: call option; *see*: exercise price, hedging, option

pyramiding

Liability.

see: stacking of limits

pyramiding of limits

Life. The issuing of a credit life insurance policy to a consumer without canceling existing policies that duplicate coverage.

see: credit life insurance, overinsurance

Q

Q Schedule
Regulation.
    see: Schedule Q

qualified assignment
    Insurer Operations. A transfer of an obligation to make fixed periodic payments in compensation of a loss or injury—especially as part of a structured settlement—to an assignee, who then makes the payments. The assignment is "qualified" under Internal Revenue Code § 130 if the payments are excluded from income under Code § 104, the assignment does not involve an increase in the amount payable, the payments cannot be changed by the recipient, etc. Often, the person entitled to the payments releases the original obligor.
    see: Internal Revenue Code § 104, structured settlement

qualified higher deductible health plan
    Employee Benefits/Health. A health and accident insurance policy, group certificate or contract available to employers who establish a medical savings account (MSA) program for their employees. The policy covers medical or dental expenses eligible under the MSA in excess of a high deductible (e.g., not less than $2000 nor more than $5000) prescribed by law or regulation. The high deductible permits a premium reduction to the purchasing employer, who must apply part of the reduction to the MSA for the benefit of each employee who participates in the program. In several states that permit the tax-exempt MSAs, the required deductible is adjusted annually to reflect changes in an inflation index.
    synonym: high deductible health insurance; see: medical savings account

qualified impairment insurance
    Health. An endorsement attached to a health insurance policy that waives exclusion of an impairment for a policy applicant who would not otherwise

qualify for coverage.
    see: impairment exclusion rider, preexisting condition, substandard risk

qualified plan
    Employee Benefits. An employee benefit plan approved by the Internal Revenue Service, meeting requirements set forth in IRS Code § 401. Employer contributions to such plans are subject to favorable tax treatment.
    compare: nonqualified plan; *see*: employee benefit plan, profit-sharing plan

qualified terminable interest property trust (Q-TIP trust)
    Financial Planning. A trust under which a surviving spouse receives all income from trust assets. The income must be paid to the spouse annually. This acts to reduce any estate tax and provide for the surviving spouse. Often, this type of trust contains a provision that prohibits transfer of assets to another person but allows the surviving spouse to bequeath the remaining assets to one or more persons designated by the surviving spouse upon his or her death. This allows the estate to escape taxation on any assets remaining at the death of the surviving spouse.
    see: estate tax

quality control
    Loss Control. Procedures established to prevent or reduce the chance that products or services are negligently manufactured or performed.
    see: defective product

quality management and quality assurance guidelines
    Regulation.
    see: ISO 9000

quantity discount
    Life. Life insurance policy premium discount allowed on policies that are written with a large face

amount.
  see: minimum amount policy

quantity distance tables
Loss Control.
  see: American Table of Distances for Storage of Explosives

quarantine benefit
Health. A health coverage extension that reimburses lost wages while the insured is quarantined by health authorities.
  synonym: quarantine indemnity; *see*: disability income insurance

quarantine exclusion
Ocean Marine. Extra expenses resulting from a ship being ordered into detention or isolation by port authorities when it is suspected of carrying an infectious disease. These expenses are excluded from most marine insurance policies.
  see: marine insurance

quarantine indemnity
Health.
  see: quarantine benefit

quasi-contract
Law. A contract implied by law when no specific agreement exists between the parties, usually to prevent an unjust enrichment or an injustice considering the relationship and conduct of the parties.
  see: contract

quasi-insurance institutions
General. Government institutions (such as the Federal Insurance Administration and the Department of Health and Human Services) that have programs with some characteristics of private insurance.

quick assets
Surety. Assets that can be quickly converted into cash, such as trade receivables and marketable securities.
  see: current assets, quick ratio

quick-opening device
Loss Control. An approved device for a dry-pipe automatic sprinkler system, such as an accelerator or exhauster, that is used to speed up the system's operation.
  see: dry-pipe automatic sprinkler system

quick ratio
Risk Management. A measure of an organization's ability to expediently pay all of its current liabilities. *Formula*: quick assets (cash, trade receivables, marketable securities) ÷ current liabilities. The higher the ratio, the greater the immediate debt-paying ability.
  synonym: acid-test ratio; *see*: current liabilities,

financial ratios, financial underwriting, quick assets

quill pen law
Regulation. Legislation that requires records (e.g., medical records, workers' compensation or insurance claims) to be maintained in written form, rather than or in addition to electronic form.
  see: electronic claim

quit claim deed
Title. A deed against which any claim has been released or relinquished in the process of the conveyance of real estate to another party.
  see: deed

quota share
Property. A property insurance program where several policies share the exposure of a risk on a percentage, or quota, basis. *Example*: $1 million in fire insurance is split on a quota share basis, with Company A assuming 50% ($500,000), Company B assuming 30% ($300,000), and Company C assuming 20% ($200,000). The companies usually share the premium in the same proportion as the risk.
  synonym: assignment quota; *see*: participate, quota share reinsurance

quota share reinsurance
Reinsurance. A proportional or pro rata reinsurance treaty where the same proportion is ceded on all cessions. The reinsurer assumes a set percentage of risk for the same percentage of the premium, minus an allowance for the ceding company's expenses.
  see: excess of loss reinsurance, quota share, treaty reinsurance

quote
General.
  see: bid

R

racial discrimination
Liability.
   see: discrimination

racing exclusion
Automobile. An exclusion in some auto liability coverage forms for any automobile while it is being used in any professional or organized racing or demolition contest or stunt activity.

radiation
Loss Control. The emission and propagation of energy in the form of waves. It usually refers to electromagnetic radiation, such as gamma rays and ultraviolet rays, but may also apply to alpha and beta particles or heat waves.
   compare: radioactivity

radio or television antennas endorsement
Property. A commercial property endorsement (ISO form CP 14 50) that increases the coverage limit on radio or television antennas. Most commercial property policies cover radio or television antennas for a loss due to fire, lightning, explosion, riot or civil commotion, or aircraft, only up to $250 per item and $1,000 per location. Highly valued radio or television antennas can be specifically scheduled on the endorsement and the location limit increased. The covered perils can also be broadened.

radioactive contamination insurance
Property. Property insurance coverage for contamination of property from radioactive materials stored or used on the premises. Coverage is specifically excluded for radiation from nuclear reactors and nuclear fuel.
   see: motor truck cargo radioactive contamination insurance, nuclear hazard exclusion, shippers' radioactive contamination insurance

radioactivity
Loss Control. Spontaneous atomic disintegration accompanied by the emission of one or more types of radiation, such as alpha particles or gamma rays.
   compare: radiation

radius of operation
Automobile. A factor used in rating commercial trucks based on the distance traveled from the principal garage location. Risks are assumed to be greater for trucks traveling long distances (usually more than 50 miles), because of driver fatigue and higher speeds, than for those confined to a small area. It is customary to measure the radius by a straight line rather than by road miles.
   see: farthest terminal, intermediate, local, long distance, zone rating

railroad protective liability insurance
Liability. Insurance obtained by a contractor or a railroad on behalf of a contractor, naming the contractor and the railroad as insureds and covering the railroad against bodily injury and property damage sustained by the public, employees of the railroad, the general contractor or subcontractors. Coverage is also provided for physical damage to rolling stock and its contents and equipment.
   see: sidetrack agreement

Railroad Retirement Act
Employee Benefits. The federal Railroad Retirement Act of 1937 specifies death, retirement, disability and unemployment coverages for railroad employees. Retirement benefits are tied to Social Security cost-of-living increases.
   synonym: railroad retirement system

railroad retirement system
Employee Benefits.
   see: Railroad Retirement Act

railroad rolling stock insurance
Liability/Inland Marine. A package policy for a railroad that includes all-risk coverage on the rail cars and equipment, property damage liability to

the rail cars or equipment of others along the railway, and damage to property of others in the railroad's care, custody and control.

railroad sidetrack agreement
Liability.
see: sidetrack agreement

railroad subrogation waiver clause
Liability.
see: sidetrack agreement

railroad travel policy
Health/Life. A travel accident policy for a specific train trip sold in railroad stations through ticket agents or vending machines.
see: travel accident insurance

rain insurance
Property. Insurance that indemnifies an insured for financial loss caused by rain. Coverage is written for a specific period of time to cover a particular outdoor event, where financial success depends on the weather. The covered perils also include snow, sleet and hail.
synonym: pluvious insurance; *see*: weather insurance

raise
Loss Control. An exploratory mining tunnel, excavated upward, to reach an ore load.
see: adit, cross-cut

ranchowners personal liability form
Personal. An endorsement covering a rancher's liability arising out of a collision between an animal owned by the rancher that has escaped its enclosure and a motor vehicle not owned or operated by the insured or an employee of the insured. The collision must occur on a public highway and not while the animal was being transported in a vehicle.
see: animal insurance, farmowners personal liability form

ranchowners policy
Personal. A package policy for family-owned ranches patterned after a homeowners policy. Coverages include ranch dwellings (and their contents), barns, stables and other ranch structures.
compare: homeowners policy, farmowners policy

ransom insurance
Crime. Indemnification for payments made to kidnappers for the release of the insured or the insured's employee.
see: kidnap insurance

rate
Insurer Operations. The actuarially determined cost per unit of coverage that is applied to the rating basis (e.g., total payroll or total property value) to determine the insured's premium amount for the policy period.
see: premium, rate making, specific rate, tariff rate

Reinsurance. The unit or cost that is applied against the subject premium of the ceding company to develop a reinsurance premium.
see: reinsurance premium

rate card
Insurer Operations. A pocket-size card issued by an insurer to agents, listing rates for various coverages.
see: line sheet, rate manual

rate change endorsement
Workers' Compensation. An endorsement (NCCI form WC 00 04 07) attached to a workers' compensation policy used in multiple states to indicate that a rate change has been approved by a particular state rating bureau.
see: workers' compensation insurance

rate discrimination
Regulation. An illegal practice of applying different premium rates to consumers or risks that are in the same insurance class or that have the same general risk characteristics.
see: discrimination

rate making
Insurer Operations. The process of determining premiums by combining losses, expenses, and profit factors.
see: "A" rates, absorption rate, adequate, aftercharge, American Association of Insurance Services, annuity conversion rate, average blanket rate, Aviation Insurance Rating Bureau, base rate, building rate, bureau rate, class rate, contents rate, deviated rate, discretionary group, discrimination, driver training credit, empirical rate calculation, equity (*Insurer Operations*), excessive, expense constant, expense loading, experience rating plan, file-and-use rating, filing requirements, flat rate, flood insurance rate map, gender rating, governing classification, group I rates, group II rates, increased limits table, independent filing, individual risk premium modification rating plan, inflation factor, judgment rates, life risk factors, loss constant, loss cost rating, loss trends, manual excess, manual rates, merit rating, minimum rate, modification rating, modified prior approval rating, moving average rating method, multiple location rating plan, numerical rating system, open competition rating, paid loss retrospective rating plan, post-FIRM rates, pre-FIRM rates, prior approval rating, prospective rating plan, provisional rate, rate, rate

discrimination, rate manual, rate regulation, rating bureau, rating class, retrospective rating plan, schedule rating, short-rate table, specific rate, state rate pages, statistical agent, step-rate premium, tariff rate, territorial rating, zone rating

rate manual

Insurer Operations. A loose-leaf manual, periodically updated or revised, that contains rules, rates and other information prepared by an insurance company or rating bureau to develop premiums for insurance policies. Hard-copy manuals have been supplemented or replaced by electronic data (CD-ROMs, computer disks, electronic networks).

see: electronic rate manual, rate card, state exception pages, state rate pages, state territorial pages

rate of loss

Property.
see: time-loss unit

rate of natural increase or decrease

General. A census figure that is determined by subtracting the death rate from the birth rate. The rate of natural increase or decrease excludes changes in population due to migration.

rate of return

Life. A method developed by the Federal Trade Commission to compare the cost of various life insurance policies. *Formula*: Step 1. savings element = gross policy premium – pure cost of protection (mortality expectation) + policy dividends (if any). Step 2. Calculate the rate of return needed to match the savings element that must be accumulated in order to equal the cash value of the policy at some specified future date.

see: present value

Financial Planning. There are two methods of calculating rate of return: 1. the yield to maturity method, which is the current yield produced by a security based on its purchase price. *Formula*: current yield ÷ purchase price; 2. the current income method, which is the current yield produced by a security based on its current market value. *Formula*: current yield ÷ current market value.

see: financial ratios, hurdle rate, payback period, return on investment

rate on line

Reinsurance. Premium divided by total aggregate limit. It is used to judge rate adequacy for per-occurrence excess of loss reinsurance contracts.

see: excess of loss reinsurance

rate regulation

Regulation. Insurance rates are controlled through legislation established by each state. State laws usually require that insurance rates be adequate, equitable and not be excessive. Most states assign the responsibility of approving and monitoring insurance rates to its department of insurance. Generally, the development of rates and forms follows one or a combination of the following approaches: open competition rating, prior approval rating, modified prior approval rating, or file-and-use rating.

see: adequate, equity (*Insurer Operations*), excessive, file-and-use rating, modified prior approval rating, open competition rating, prior approval rating, rate making, ratification, use-and-file rating

rated policy

Life. A life insurance policy that is issued at a rate higher than standard to cover an individual classified as a substandard risk. The policy may also contain special limitations and exclusions.

synonym: rated up; *see*: substandard life expectancy, substandard risk

rated risk

Life.
see: rated policy

rated up

Life.
see: rated policy

ratification

Regulation. A formal approval by a state insurance department of rates or policy forms filed by insurers.

see: rate regulation

rating

Insurer Operations. The process of developing or applying classifications and statistical standards to a specific risk that will be covered by a policy to derive the appropriate premium.

see: expense loading, experience rating, homogeneous exposure units, judgment rates, loss cost rating, loss expectancy, loss frequency, manual rates, moving average rating method, pure premium, retrospective rating, schedule rating

rating bureau

Organizations. An organization, usually formed by or on behalf of a group of insurers, to develop rates. Membership in a rating bureau is sometimes mandatory for insurers that write a certain line of business. The bureau collects actuarial data and surveys individual risks.

synonym: inspection bureau; *see*: advisory organization, American Association of Insurance Services, bureau insurer, bureau rate, Insurance Services Office, National Council on Compensation Insurance

rating class
Insurer Operations. A group of risks that have the same general characteristics and that are placed into the same class for rating purposes. The same rate then applies to all risks in this class.

see: classification, homogeneous exposure units

ratio analysis
Financial Planning.

see: financial ratios

re-entry term life insurance
Life. A rider to an annual renewable term life insurance policy allowing the policyholder to periodically (every three or five years) re-apply for increased coverage at a reduced premium.

see: annual renewable term insurance, term life insurance

reaction distance
Automobile/Loss Control. The distance a motor vehicle travels from the time the driver sees a hazard, decides to slow down or stop, and applies the brakes.

compare: reaction time; *see:* braking distance, stopping distance

reaction time
Automobile/Loss Control. The time required for a driver to perceive a hazard and apply the brakes or turn the steering wheel.

compare: reaction distance; *see:* braking time, stopping time

readjustment income
Life. An estimate of the financial requirements of a family for a six-month period after the death or disability of its principal financial provider. This estimate is used as a benchmark in financial planning and recognizes that more funds than usual will be required during this period.

see: adjustment income, emergency fund

real chattel
Law. An item of personal or movable property annexed or connected to real estate.

see: chattel mortgage, personal property, real estate

real estate
General. Land and immovable structures attached to the land.

synonym: real property, realty; *compare:* improvements and betterments, personal property

real estate agents' errors and omissions insurance
Professional Liability. Coverage for a real estate agent against third-party claims for damages resulting from negligence in the performance for real estate services. Coverage is usually on a claims-made basis.

see: errors and omissions insurance

real estate investment trust (REIT)
Financial Planning. A financial intermediary that invests in income-producing real estate and mortgages. Under legislation passed in 1961, REITs were granted conduit tax treatment (the same as permitted to mutual funds), under which the part of earnings that is passed through to shareholders in the form of dividends is exempt from federal income taxes at the trust (or corporate) level, provided several conditions are met. Among the conditions are that at least 95% of otherwise taxable income must be distributed to shareholders, and specified percentages of both investments and gross income must be related to real estate.

real property
General.

see: real estate

realty
General.

see: real estate

reasonable and customary charge
Health. The usual fee charged in a geographic area by a medical provider for a specific medical procedure or service. The fee is based upon a consensus of what most other local hospitals, physicians or laboratories are charging for a similar procedure or service.

see: diagnosis related group, fee schedule

reasonable care
Law. The degree of care or prudence that a reasonable person would exercise under the circumstances.

see: degree of care, negligence

reasonable expectations doctrine
Law. A legal principle that insurance policy provisions capable of more than one interpretation should be construed in accordance with the objectively reasonable expectations of the insured.

see: ambiguity, contract of adhesion, contra proferentem, unconscionability

reassured
Reinsurance.

see: ceding insurer

rebate
Regulation. The return of a portion of an insurance agent's commission (or the giving of something

else of value) to induce someone to purchase insurance. Most states have anti-rebate laws.

see: anti-rebate laws, Proposition 103

recapture

Reinsurance. A ceding insurer's reacquisition of previously ceded insurance from a reinsurer.

see: portfolio return, reinsurance

recapture of plan assets

Employee Benefits. The return of all or a portion of an employer's contributions to a pension plan because of an Internal Revenue Service determination that the plan does not qualify or that portions of the plan do not qualify for tax considerations under provisions of the Revenue Code.

see: employee benefit plan

receivables

Accounting. The value of goods and services that are sold or provided to customers, but which are not yet paid for; total amounts due or collectible.

see: accounts receivable

Insurer Operations. In insurer operations, *receivables* is often used to refer to earned premiums not yet received.

see: earned premium

received for shipment bill of lading

Inland Marine/Ocean Marine.

see: dock receipt

recipient property

Property. Concerning contingent business income coverage, a location to which most of the insured's product is sold or shipped; a principal customer.

compare: dependent property; *see*: contingent business income coverage

reciprocal insurance company

Insurer Operations.

see: reciprocal insurance exchange

reciprocal insurance exchange

Insurer Operations. An insurance market of reciprocal agreements of indemnity among persons known as subscribers. The exchange is effected through an attorney-in-fact common to all persons. Subscribers agree to become liable for their share of losses and expenses incurred among all subscribers and authorize the attorney-in-fact to exchange insurance with the other subscribers, pay losses, invest premiums, recruit new members, underwrite new business, receive premiums and effect contracts of reinsurance.

synonym: exchange, reciprocal insurance company; *see*: assessment company, attorney-in-fact, insurance company

reciprocal legislation

Regulation. Legislation enacted by any two states, providing for mutual regulatory considerations. Most reciprocal laws deal with premium taxes and licensing requirements. For example, insurers domiciled in another state may be given favorable tax treatment if the insurer's domiciliary state does the same for insurer's domiciled in the first state. Reciprocal arrangements also exist with respect to offsets of payments due ceding insurers and reinsurers in cases of liquidation.

compare: retaliatory legislation, retaliatory tax

reciprocity

Reinsurance. The mutual exchange of reinsurance, whereby one reinsurer accepts (assumes) risk in exchange for the other company's acceptance of its ceded business.

see: reinsurance

record

Law. The official collection of all pleadings, exhibits, orders, and testimony from a hearing or trial.

see: certiorari, pleading

record date

Financial Planning. The date on which the ownership of securities is recorded in the corporation's stock book. This date establishes the shareholders voting and dividend rights.

see: dividend, record owner

record fish coverage

Inland Marine. A form of prize indemnification insurance that indemnifies the insured (usually the tournament sponsor) if a record-size fish is caught by a during a fishing tournament.

see: prize indemnification insurance, tagged fish coverage

record owner

Financial Planning. A person in whose name shares of stock are registered on the records of the corporation. A record owner is treated as the owner of the shares by the corporation, whether or not he or she is the beneficial owner of the shares.

see: record date

recordable case rate

Loss Control. One of three commonly used measurements of an organization's level of employee safety. *Formula*: disabling cases per year ÷ (annual employee hours ÷ 200,000). (200,000 represents 100 employee-years, assuming an average work year of 2000 hours.)

compare: lost workday case rate, lost workday rate

recording agent

Property. A policywriting agent for property insurance coverage.

see: agent, general agent, policywriting agent

recoverables

Insurer Operations. Money or any other item of value that an insurance company recoups through reinsurance, salvage, or by subrogation against a third party at fault.

see: reinsurance, salvage, subrogation

recovery

Health/Workers' Compensation. A person's restoration of health following an injury or illness.

see: rehabilitation (*Health/Workers' Compensation*)

Insurer Operations. 1. The rightful owner's regaining of possession of stolen property.

2. Property of which an insurer becomes the owner as a result of paying a loss.

Reinsurance. The amount an insurer receives from a reinsurer for a reinsured loss.

see: reinsurance

recurrent disability

Health. A disability that returns from time to time and has the same or a related cause.

see: aggravation of a previous condition, preexisting condition, recurring clause

recurring clause

Health. A provision in a health insurance policy that specifies the period of time required between two illnesses or disabilities for a new set of benefits to be available for the second illness or disability.

see: recurrent disability

red herring

Financial Planning. An advance copy of an initial offering prospectus that is filed with the Securities and Exchange Commission for approval. The words "not a solicitation, for information only" are printed in red on its face.

synonym: preliminary prospectus; *see*: prospectus

redeemable bond

Financial Planning.
see: callable bond

redeemable preferred stock

Financial Planning.
see: callable preferred stock

redemption

Financial Planning. The reacquisition of a security by the issuer pursuant to terms in the security. A security is called for redemption when the issuer notifies the holder that the redemption privilege has been exercised. If there is a conversion right, the shareholder typically has a limited period to decide whether to convert the redeemed shares into other common shares or to take the redemption cash price.

see: callable bond, callable preferred stock, redemption price

redemption fee

Financial Planning.
see: back end load

redemption price

Financial Planning. The price that must be paid by a corporation to redeem callable preferred stock; the price a bond issuer must pay to redeem a recallable bond or the amount to be paid on the bond maturity date; or the price a mutual fund must pay to redeem fund shares.

see: callable bond, callable preferred stock

redlining

Regulation. An underwriting practice of rejecting risks based on their geographic location. Most states prohibit this practice.

see: discrimination, prohibited list

reduced earnings

Employee Benefits. An employee's earnings after a disabling injury or illness. This amount is subtracted from the employee's pre-disability earnings to determine the amount of disability benefits payable.

see: able to earn, disability benefit, partial disability, wage loss

reduced paid-up insurance

Life.
see: nonforfeiture reduced paid-up benefit

reduction

Insurer Operations. A decrease in insurance policy benefits or limits because of a specific condition. A property policy may impose a sublimit on a specific location because of hazardous activities, or an accident policy may reduce benefits for a hazardous activity such as auto racing.

reduction of risk

Risk Management. A method of handling risk by the scope or volume of a firm's operations, or through the purchase of insurance. *Example*: A large outdoor advertising firm reduces its risk of lost revenue due to damaged billboards in a way that a small billboard company cannot because of its large number of dispersed exposure units. The scale of operations makes losses relatively predictable. Insurance reduces risk for the small company by combining a number of similar companies' risks into a more predictable group.

see: homogeneity, law of large numbers, spread of risk

referee

Law. An impartial person selected by parties in a dispute or appointed by a court to decide certain issues or determine facts and report to the court.

compare: arbitrator

reformation

Law. Revision or modification of a contract by a court because it was found to be incorrectly drawn and did not express the true intent of the parties; an equitable remedy to give expression to contracting parties' intent in cases of mutual mistake or, sometimes, unfair dealing.

see: contract, court of equity, unconscionability

refrigerated property coverage endorsement

Personal. An endorsement (ISO form HO 04 98) to the homeowners policy that provides $500 coverage (subject to a $100 deductible) for property in freezers and refrigerators caused by interruption of electrical service due to damage to the generating or transmitting equipment or by the unit's mechanical failure.

see: homeowners policy

refrigeration maintenance agreement

Inland Marine. A contractual service agreement between an insured and a refrigeration maintenance contractor for the contractor to check, repair and respond when called concerning a problem with the insured's equipment. Underwriters may require such an agreement in order to write coverage on perishable stock or to allow a rate credit.

see: perishable stock, spoilage coverage endorsement

refund annuity

Life. An annuity that returns all premiums (usually plus interest) to a designated beneficiary if the annuitant dies during the accumulation period.

compare: pure annuity; *see*: accumulation period (*Life*), annuity

regional office

Insurer Operations. An insurance company office that has greater authority than a branch office and is generally staffed to underwrite all lines of business in a specific geographic area.

compare: branch office, home office

register

Life. A listing or accounting of debit or industrial insurance policies.

see: industrial life insurance

registered bond

Financial Planning. A financial bond with the owner's name registered on the books of the issuing corporation, as with a stock share. For the bond to be negotiable, it must be endorsed by the registered owner.

compare: bearer bond; *see*: bond (*Financial Planning*)

registered mail insurance

Inland Marine. Coverage on an all-risk basis for loss of highly valued property (such as jewelry or watches) sent through the postal service.

see: mail coverage, parcel post insurance

registered mutual fund representative errors and omissions insurance

Professional Liability. Professional liability insurance for registered representatives of broker-dealers for third-party liability caused by negligence, errors or omissions in the sale of mutual funds or variable annuities. Coverage is usually written on a claims-made basis.

see: errors and omissions insurance, registered representative

Registered Record Administrator (RRA)

Organizations. A professional designation awarded by the American Health Information Management Association based on education and experience.

see: American Health Information Management Association

registered representative

Financial Planning. A person licensed by the National Association of Securities Dealers to sell securities to the public.

see: National Association of Securities Dealers

registered retirement saving plan (RRSP)

Employee Benefits. A program that allows citizens of Canada to accumulate retirement funds on a tax deductible basis. It is similar to the individual retirement account in the United States.

see: individual retirement account

registered tonnage

Ocean Marine. The tonnage on which an ocean marine policy's limit of liability is calculated in England. For sailing, it is the net registered tonnage; for steamers, it is the gross registered tonnage without deduction for engine room space.

see: ocean marine insurance

registrar

Financial Planning. A bank or trust company appointed by a corporation or other entity to maintain custody of the records of registered securities, including the names of the security holders and the distributions of earnings.

synonym: transfer agent

regression analysis

Risk Management. A statistical procedure for predicting the value of a dependent variable on the basis of knowledge about one or more independent variables.

Regular National Flood Insurance Program

Property. One of two national flood insurance programs. It requires the completion of a flood study of the community by the Federal Insurance Administration and publication of a Flood Insurance Rate Map. Once a community is approved, residents may purchase flood coverage in excess of the limits of the Emergency National Flood Insurance Program. The available coverages are: for a single family dwelling, $150,000 on the structure and $50,000 on contents; for a small business, $150,000 on the structure and $200,000 on contents.

compare: Emergency National Flood Insurance Program; *see:* National Flood Insurance Program

regulation

Regulation. Supervision of business and financial practices by a governmental entity.

see: agent's qualification regulations, emergency rules and regulations, insurance department, McCarran-Ferguson Act, rate regulation

Regulation A

Financial Planning/Regulation. A Securities and Exchange Commission regulation that provides a simplified registration procedure for small securities offerings.

see: public offering

Regulatory and Legislative Section, CPCU Society

Organizations. An interest section of the CPCU Society that informs members on legislative and regulatory developments on both state and national levels.

see: CPCU Society

Regulatory Information Retrieval System (RIRS)

Regulation. An on-line database developed by the National Association of Insurance Commissioners in 1983 to share information on persons and companies suspected of illegal or unethical activities in order to prevent their expansion.

see: National Association of Insurance Commissioners

rehabilitation

Health/Workers' Compensation. The attempt to restore the physical or mental capabilities and, therefore, earning ability of an injured employee or other person through physical therapy, counseling or education.

see: ability to earn, convalescent care, rehabilitation clause, vocational rehabilitation, workers' compensation law

Regulation. Supervisory action by an insurance department to restore a financially impaired insurance company. The affairs of the insurer are supervised by the insurance department either until it returns to financial stability or the decision is made to liquidate the company.

see: guaranty fund, insolvency, liquidation

rehabilitation clause

Health. A provision in many health and disability insurance policies for vocational rehabilitation of disabled policyholders.

see: vocational rehabilitation

reimbursement

Insurer Operations. Payment of an amount of money by an insurance policy in the event of a covered loss.

compare: pay on behalf of; *see:* indemnify

reinstatement

Insurer Operations. Restoration of a policy that has lapsed or has been canceled for nonpayment of premium.

see: lapse, cancellation

Life. Restoration of a life policy canceled due to nonpayment of premiums following expiration of the grace period. Past due premiums must be paid, and evidence of insurability may be required if there has been a long lapse period. Most states prescribe a standard policy provision that permits reinstatement of individual life policies up to three years from the cancellation date and reinstatement of annuities within a lapse period of one or two years.

synonym: revival; *see:* standard provisions

Reinsurance. Restoration of a reinsurance contract's limit to its full amount by a reinsurer after the payment of a large loss. Often, this requires the payment of additional premium.

see: reinsurance

reinsurance

Reinsurance. Risk transferred from one insurer to another; a contract whereby the assuming insurer (reinsurer) agrees to indemnify the ceding insurer (cedent) for all or part of the claim liabilities under policies issued by the ceding insurer, which pays the reinsurer a premium in return. By ceding some of its business, an insurer may write more business within its reserve or surplus requirements. Assuming insurers may cede risks to other reinsurers, which is called *retrocession.*

The two basic types of reinsurance are *facultative,* involving the transfer of individual risks, and *treaty*, involving the transfer of all risks in a class of business. The ceding insurer usually remains liable for policy claims, and the reinsurer must indemnify the cedent. In the less common *assumption reinsurance*, the reinsurer becomes directly liable for claims settlement.

synonym: assumed reinsurance; *compare*: retrocession; *see*: agency reinsurance, aggregate excess of loss reinsurance, aggregate working excess reinsurance, American Cargo War Risk Reinsurance Exchange, assumption reinsurance, authorized reinsurance, automatic reinsurance, bulk reinsurance, Cargo Reinsurance Association, Carpenter Plan, catastrophe reinsurance, ceded reinsurance, ceding insurer, certificate of reinsurance, cession, earned reinsurance premium, excess loss-ratio reinsurance, excess of loss reinsurance, facultative reinsurance, financial reinsurance, first surplus reinsurance treaty, flat rate, follow the fortunes, fronting, intermediary, MAERP Reinsurance Association, market entrance reinsurance, nonproportional reinsurance, obligatory reinsurance treaty, portfolio reinsurance, professional reinsurer, pro rata reinsurance, quota share reinsurance, recapture, reciprocity, reinsurance credit, reinsurance exchange, reinsurance premium, reinsurer, retrocession, stabilization reinsurance, surplus reinsurance treaty, surplus relief reinsurance, ticket reinsurance, treaty reinsurance, uberrima fides, unauthorized reinsurance, unearned reinsurance premium, withdrawal reinsurance

Reinsurance Association of America (RAA)

Organizations. Members: Property and casualty reinsurance companies. *Objectives*: Promotes the industry's interests by representing it before Congress and federal and state regulators. *Founded*: 1968. *Headquarters*: Washington, D.C.

reinsurance broker

Reinsurance.

see: intermediary

reinsurance capacity

Reinsurance. 1. The capacity for a particular reinsurer is the largest line it will commit to a risk; this may vary for casualty lines and property lines.

2. The capacity for a class of insurance (e.g., earthquake, offshore platforms) that is available in the world insurance market, including reinsurance markets.

3. A reinsurer's ability to accept risk, which may be limited by its policyholder's surplus.

see: capacity, overline

reinsurance clause

Reinsurance. A provision in a reinsurance contract that describes the business to be insured.

reinsurance commission

Reinsurance.

see: ceding commission

reinsurance credit

Regulation/Reinsurance. Credit allowed for ceded reinsurance premiums and losses recoverable on the ceding insurer's annual financial statement by reducing liabilities in the form of unearned premium and loss reserves or by increasing assets. For credit to be permitted, the reinsurance must be placed with a reinsurer approved or accredited by the state, and there must be a true transfer of insurance risk with no purpose of deception as to the ceding insurer's financial condition.

see: accredited reinsurer, annual statement, authorized reinsurance, ceding insurer, mirror reserve

reinsurance exchange

Reinsurance. An organized facility or market established by reinsurers having rules for the assumption or ceding of reinsurance between its participants.

compare: insurance exchange

reinsurance intermediary

Reinsurance.

see: intermediary

reinsurance premium

Insurer Operations/Reinsurance. An amount paid by the ceding insurer to the reinsurer in consideration for the liability assumed by the reinsurer.

see: net premiums written

Reinsurance Section, CPCU Society

Organizations. An interest section of the CPCU Society that promotes new and efficient reinsurance operations.

see: CPCU Society

reinsured

Reinsurance.

see: ceding insurer

reinsurer

Reinsurance. An insurer that assumes the liability of another insurer through reinsurance; the insurer to whom risk is transferred by a ceding insurer. Usually, the reinsurer has an obligation to indemnify the ceding insurer, which remains liable for claims on policies it has issued. In an assumption reinsurance arrangement, the reinsurer is substituted for the ceding insurer and becomes directly liable to policyholders.

compare: ceding insurer; *see*: accredited reinsurer, assumption reinsurance, retrocessionaire

rejection

Insurer Operations. The declination of a risk by an underwriter.

compare: acceptance; *see:* submitted business

relative exposure rule

Professional Liability. A rule governing allocation of directors' and officers' costs of legal liability and defense. A D&O claim involving both the insured directors or officers and the uninsured corporate entity is allocated between the parties if there is an independent basis for holding the entity liable, not derivative of or concurrent with the insured directors' or officers' liability.

compare: larger settlement rule; *see:* allocation of defense costs, directors' and officers' liability insurance, entity coverage

release

Insurer Operations/Law. 1. A document by which a legal right is discharged. It is an acknowledgment that the person signing it gives up specific rights or claims in exchange for a payment of compensation. 2. A document used by insurance adjusters to obtain a formal discharge by a claimant of any additional rights to recovery after a claim settlement.

see: drop check procedure, forthwith payment, joint tortfeasor release, no-release settlement, open-end release, special release, subrogation release

released bill of lading

Inland Marine. A bill of lading on which no stated value has been indicated, thereby limiting the carrier's liability to statutory amounts or to the specified rate per pound of merchandise shipped.

see: bill of lading

religious discrimination

Liability.

see: discrimination

remainder

Reinsurance. The amount a reinsurer assumes from a ceding insurer on an individual risk; the amount remaining after subtracting the ceding insurer's retention from the total insured risk.

compare: net line, net retention; *see:* reinsurance

remedial investigation

Loss Control. An in-depth study of a hazardous waste site to determine the nature and extent of contamination, establish criteria for cleanup, identify alternative remedial actions, and provide supporting technical and cost analyses of the alternatives.

see: hazardous waste

remediation cost overrun insurance

Liability. A form of pollution liability insurance for property owners to cover the cost of overruns for on-site cleanup and remediation expenses. This coverage is usually written in conjunction with pollution liability insurance for a specific site.

see: pollution insurance

remediation warranty insurance

Liability. A form of pollution liability insurance for property owners that provides coverage for pollution conditions discovered after environmental remediation has been completed. This coverage is generally written in conjunction with real estate transfer liability or remediation cost overrun coverage for sites that have been sold to third parties after cleanup.

see: pollution insurance, property transfer insurance, remediation cost overrun insurance

remote station alarm system

Loss Control. An alarm system that transmits the alarm from the protected premises to a remote location, such as a fire or police station.

compare: auxiliary alarm system, central station alarm system, local alarm system, proprietary alarm system

removal

Property. A term that has been replaced in most modern property policies by *preservation of property.* The cost of removing insured property for purposes of protecting it from further loss is generally covered by property insurance.

see: preservation of property

remuneration

Liability/Workers' Compensation. The salary or other earnings of employees, which make up the payroll of an organization. It is often used as a rating base and includes regular earnings, piece work payments, and overtime.

see: exposure unit, payroll audit

renegotiable rate mortgage (RRM)

Financial Planning. A mortgage with an interest rate that can be modified by the lender at specified intervals (e.g., three or five years). Usually the increase or decrease must remain within a specified range and may be tied to an index.

compare: variable rate mortgage; *see:* mortgage

renewable and convertible term life insurance (R&C)

Life. Term life insurance usually issued for a period of one or five years that can be renewed for additional terms or can be converted to a permanent or cash value policy. It is usually used for persons with short-term, high-value needs, such as to cover a short-term business loan.

see: convertible term life insurance, renewable term life insurance

renewable term life insurance

Life. Term life insurance that may be continued beyond its original term by acceptance of a premium for a new policy term without evidence of insurability.

see: annual renewable term insurance, guaranteed renewable, renewable and convertible term life insurance, term life insurance

renewal

Insurer Operations. The act or process of maintaining insurance in force by issuing a new policy to replace an expiring policy or the issuance of certificates or endorsements extending the term of an expiring policy.

see: anniversary date, annual renewal agreement, renewal certificate

renewal certificate

Insurer Operations. A form notifying the insured that an insurance policy is renewed on the same terms as the expiring policy.

see: renewal

renewal commission

Agency/Insurer Operations. A commission paid to an agent or broker for premiums on policies that have been renewed.

compare: first-year commission; *see:* agent's commission, graded commission, unlevel commission

rent insurance

Property.

see: rental value insurance

rental cost reimbursement

Inland Marine. A coverage that can be added to a contractor's equipment floater to cover the rental cost of temporary replacement equipment if the insured equipment is damaged by an insured peril. Usually this coverage is written with a waiting period deductible (e.g., 24 hours).

see: contractors' equipment floater

rental income insurance

Property. A form of property insurance that pays the owner of a building for the amount of lost rent due to damage from an insured peril. The form also covers the tenant of a building for rent that must be paid even if the premises cannot be occupied.

compare: rental value insurance

rental reimbursement coverage

Automobile. Coverage that can be endorsed to an automobile policy that pays for a rental vehicle if the policyholder's car is disabled by a covered loss.

(ISO form CA 99 23 for commercial auto coverage; form PP 03 02 for private passenger auto coverage.)

see: business auto coverage form, personal auto policy, temporary substitute automobile, transportation expense coverage

rental value insurance

Property. A form of property insurance that covers the use interest of owners occupying their own building or tenants in a building. For a building owner, it pays to secure other facilities similar to the damaged building or pays the amount the owner would have received if the building were leased to others. For a tenant, it covers any excess rent required to secure comparable facilities.

synonym: rent insurance; *compare:* rental income insurance

renters' insurance

Personal. A personal property and liability package designed to protect a renter. It combines broad coverage on personal property with broad personal liability coverage. It is similar to a homeowners policy, except there is no property coverage for the structure itself.

compare: rental income insurance, rental value insurance; *see:* homeowners contents broad form

reorganization

Financial Planning. The restructuring of a financially troubled organization. A firm's assets are restated to reflect their current market value or may be written off altogether, and the firm may sell or dispose of unprofitable operating units.

see: bankruptcy, rehabilitation

repair or replace

Inland Marine. A condition commonly found in inland marine policies that refers to the insurer's right to settle a loss by repairing or replacing damaged property with property of like kind and quality.

see: new for old

repatriation coverage

International/Workers' Compensation. Coverage that can be provided by a manuscript endorsement to a workers' compensation policy or a separate accident insurance policy for transportation expenses of a sick or injured employee from a foreign country home for medical care. These expenses may be great because many airlines do not allow a sick or injured person on regularly scheduled flights, requiring the use of a chartered flight.

see: endemic disease coverage, manuscript policy

repetitive motion injury

Health/Workers' Compensation. An injury or disorder that results from repeated movements, usually by an employee in the performance of work, that puts unusual strain on a part of the body.

synonym: repetitive strain syndrome; *see*: carpal tunnel syndrome, cumulative trauma, ergonomics disorder

repetitive strain syndrome

Health/Workers' Compensation.

see: repetitive motion injury

replacement cost

Property. Valuation of property according to the cost of replacing it with property of a like kind and quality; the cost to replace property at its current price with no deduction for depreciation.

compare: actual cash value, depreciated value, economic value, functional replacement cost, market value, reproduction cost, tax-appraised value; *see*: new for old, replacement cost insurance, replacement cost—secondhand market, valuation of potential property loss

replacement cost—secondhand market

Property. Valuation of property according to the cost of replacing it with used, restored or rebuilt property of an equivalent model or type. This valuation method is most often used with manufacturing machinery.

see: replacement cost

replacement cost insurance

Property. Insurance that compensates property owners for losses on a replacement cost basis.

see: depreciation insurance, replacement cost

replacement policy

Insurer Operations. A policy that has been issued to replace one currently in force.

replacement ratio

Agency/Life. A ratio used by life insurers and their agents to determine the amount of new insurance premium that must be developed to replace lost premium. The ratio can be developed based on the number of new to lost policies, or based on policy face amounts lost to the face amounts of new policies.

replevin

Law. A plaintiff's recovery of goods claimed to be wrongfully taken after posting security pending trial of the matter in court. The plaintiff is bound to return the property if defeated in the court action.

see: plaintiff's replevin bond

replevin bond

Surety.

see: plaintiff's replevin bond

reportable event

Insurer Operations. A loss from any insured peril. An insured is obligated to report such losses to the insurer or its representative as soon as possible.

see: accident report, incident report, notice of loss

reportable quantity

Loss Control. As respects hazardous waste, the quantity that triggers a report under the Comprehensive Environmental Response, Compensation and Liability Act or the Clean Water Act. A release in an amount that exceeds the reportable quantity must be reported to the National Response Center, the state emergency response commission, and community emergency coordinators for the potentially affected areas.

see: Comprehensive Environmental Response Compensation and Liability Act, hazardous waste

reported claims count

Risk Management. The number of claims reported by an insured to an insurance company.

reporting arrangement

Automobile. A reporting form method of arranging automobile physical damage under a garage policy. This method of coverage provides a maximum limit of liability for all vehicles, basing the premium on a rate applied against reports of monthly or quarterly values at risk.

see: garagekeepers' insurance

reporting form

Insurer Operations. A form that must be completed by a policyholder on a periodic basis (monthly, quarterly) to report that period's exposure basis (receipts, payroll, units produced), which is used to determine the premium to be charged.

A reporting form property policy requires the insured to report property values that frequently vary during the policy period. This arrangement usually results in lower premiums, since coverage does not have to be purchased for the maximum exposure during the year; instead the premium is based on the actual or average exposure. Often policies written on this basis have a penalty provision for late reporting.

synonym: value reporting form; *see*: adjustable policy, business income premium adjustment, full reporting clause, peak season endorsement, seasonal risk

reporting policy

Property.

see: adjustable policy

repossessed autos

Automobile. An endorsement (ISO form CA 20 19)

386

to the business auto policy designed for banks or finance companies to provide liability and physical damage coverage on autos that are repossessed. Coverage continues until a vehicle is sold.

see: business auto coverage form

representation

General. A response to questions or a statement made on an application for insurance that the applicant indicates as true and the underwriter relies upon to issue a policy.

see: application, misrepresentation, warranty (1)

representative

Agency. An agent of a direct writing insurance company.

see: direct writer

representative suit

Law.

see: class action, derivative suit

reproduction cost

Property. Valuation of property according to the cost of replacing it with identical property at the same location. Loss adjustment is only occasionally provided on this basis. The insurer then must replace a damaged or destroyed building, for example, using existing blueprints and specifications.

compare: actual cash value, depreciated value, functional replacement cost, market value, replacement cost, tax-appraised value; *see*: historical home insurance, valuation of potential property loss

request for proposal

Surety.

see: advertisement to bid

res ipsa loquitur

Law. A legal doctrine that, given the circumstances and the undisputed facts, the defendant's negligence is presumed. (Latin for "the thing speaks for itself.") When the cause of an injury does not ordinarily occur without someone's negligence, and the cause is shown to be under the defendant's control, this doctrine shifts the burden of proof to the defendant to rebut the presumption of negligence. *Example*: Ollie, standing on the sidewalk, is hit by a crate that fell from Stan's truck. Stan's negligence is presumed unless contrary facts are proved.

synonym: presumed negligence; *see*: burden of proof, negligence

rescission

Law. The cancellation or undoing of a contract and restoration of the parties to the position they occupied before the contract. A party may ordinarily rescind a contract in cases of fraud, misrepresentation or duress by the other party and, in some cases,

where a breach renders the contract worthless.

see: duress, fraud, misrepresentation, void

reservation of rights

Insurer Operations. An insurer's written notification to the insured stating its right to affirm or deny coverage for a claim that appears questionable. However, the insurer agrees to defend the insured.

see: acquiescence, duty to defend, nonwaiver agreement, waiver

reserve

Accounting/Insurer Operations. Funds set aside by an insurance company to assure that it can cover future liabilities; the total unpaid amount of claims that have been reported at a specific accounting date.

see: balance sheet reserves, deficiency reserve, expense reserve, funding of reserves, initial reserve, investment reserve, legal reserve, loss ratio reserve method, loss reserve, mandatory securities valuation reserve, mean reserve, net level premium reserve, policy reserve, premium deficiency reserve, prospective reserve, reserve premium, self-insurance reserve, statutory reserve, tabular-value reserve method, technical reserves, terminal reserve, unearned premium reserve, valuation reserve, voluntary reserve

reserve premium

Insurer Operations. A premium collected in addition to the regular premium to offset unexpected claims. It is calculated as a proportion of the policy premium and maintained in a separate reserve account. To the extent it is not used to pay losses, it is returned to the policyholder with interest. No insurance company expenses are charged against the premium, with the exception of unexpected losses and state premium taxes.

see: premium

residence employee

Workers' Compensation. A person hired by the owner of a private residence to do domestic work. In some states, workers' compensation coverage for such an employee must be included in a homeowner's or renter's policy.

see: domestic

residence premises three or four family dwelling endorsement

Personal. An endorsement (ISO form HO 04 44) to the homeowners policy that modifies the definition of "residence premises" to include three-family and four-family dwellings. The endorsement provides both property and liability coverage for the owner-occupant of such a dwelling.

see: homeowners policy

resident agent

Agency. An agent who is domiciled in the state where he or she does business.

compare: nonresident agent; *see*: agent, countersignature

resident relative

Personal.

see: family member

residential care facility

Health. An inpatient facility that provides custodial care.

compare: skilled nursing facility; *see*: custodial care

residual disability income insurance

Health. A policy providing benefits for loss of income following disability, rather than the inability to perform the duties of an occupation. It is an important coverage for a professional whose disability may cause a business interruption with a loss of clients, even though recovery from the disability is complete.

compare: disability income insurance

residual markets

Insurer Operations. Specialty insurance markets or facilities designed to assume risks that are generally unacceptable to the normal insurance market. Such markets include assigned risk plans, government insurance programs, and aviation or nuclear pools.

see: assigned risk, Fair Access to Insurance Requirements

residual value

Accounting. The value of leased property at the end of the lease term.

see: residual value insurance

residual value insurance

Financial Guaranty. A form of financial guaranty insurance that protects a lessor against unexpected declines in the market value of leased equipment (automobiles, aircraft, heavy machinery) upon termination or expiration of the lease agreement.

see: equipment value insurance, financial guaranty insurance, residual value

Resolution Trust Corporation (RTC)

Regulation. A corporation formed by Congress in 1989 to replace the Federal Savings and Loan Insurance Corporation and respond to the insolvencies of about 750 savings and loan associations. As receiver, it sold assets of failed S&Ls and paid insured depositors. In 1995 its duties, including insurance of deposits in thrift institutions, were transferred to the Savings Association Insurance Fund.

see: Federal Deposit Insurance Corporation, Savings Association Insurance Fund, Securities Investor Protection Corporation

Resource Conservation and Recovery Act (RCRA)

Regulation. Federal legislation (U.S. Code Title 42, Chapter 82) adopted in 1976 and substantially amended in 1984 by the Hazardous and Solid Waste Amendments. It is the statutory basis for the Environmental Protection Agency to establish a comprehensive program to control hazardous waste from its generation to its final disposal. The identifies wastes by toxicity and production characteristics, specifies on-site management and storage procedures, limits duration and method of storage, requires pollution prevention, prescribes personnel training content and frequency, establishes treatment, storage and disposal parameters, and specifies shipping requirements.

see: closure and post-closure insurance, Comprehensive Environmental Response Compensation and Liability Act, Emergency Planning and Community Right-to-Know Act, Environmental Protection Agency, listed waste, pollution insurance, pollution prevention program

respondeat superior

Law. A legal rule that the principal or employer is liable for harms done by agents or employees while acting within the scope of their agency or employment.

see: agency, master-servant rule, principal (*Agency*)

rest cure

Health. Custodial care at a sanitarium or nursing home.

see: custodial care

restoration of plan

Employee Benefits. The act of restoring a pension plan that has been terminated to its previous status by funding all or a portion of the plan's previous assets. Such a restoration must be approved by the Pension Benefit Guaranty Corporation.

compare: recapture of plan assets; *see*: Pension Benefit Guaranty Corporation

restoration of vested benefits

Employee Benefits. An Employee Retirement Income Security Act provision allowing employees of a pension plan who are less than 50% vested to buy back retirement benefits lost because contributions are withdrawn.

see: employee benefit plan, Employee Retirement Income Security Act

restoration premium

Insurer Operations. A premium that must be paid by the policyholder to restore benefit limits following their exhaustion by the payment of claims. Most policies do not reduce the limits because of claim payments, but some London market policies and bonds contain such a provision.

compare: automatic reinstatement clause; *see:* aggregate limit, first loss insurance, premium

restrictive covenants

Title. Conditions placed in a deed to real property by private parties that limit the use of the land and are binding on subsequent purchasers. Occasionally, covenants are limited to the original buyer and seller (personal covenants). Restrictive covenants are encumbrances and may affect the value and marketability of title. Covenants that violate the law or public policy, such as racial restrictions on selling property, are unenforceable.

see: encumbrance, covenants for title

retail credit report

Insurer Operations. A report used by insurers as an underwriting tool to determine an applicant's financial condition. These reports are developed and supplied by credit reporting agencies. Most states require that an applicant for insurance be notified if the insurer requests a retail credit report.

see: bankruptcy, Fair Credit Reporting Act

retail use

Automobile. A business use auto rating classification that applies to vehicles used for pickup or delivery of property to consumers.

compare: business use, commercial use, pleasure use, service use

retained earnings

Accounting. The sum of an organization's profits during its existence minus all dividends paid.

synonym: earnings retained; *see:* balance sheet, capital, common equity, financial statement, owner's equity

retainer

Law. An initial fee or deposit paid to secure an attorney's services in a particular case.

compare: contingent fee agreement

retainer clause

Reinsurance. A nonproportional reinsurance contract provision that specifically limits coverage

under the contract to business that the ceding insurer retains for its own account.

synonym: net retention clause; *see:* nonproportional reinsurance

retaliatory legislation

Regulation. State legislation that imposes fees, taxes, license requirements, or other obligations on specified categories of other states' residents (e.g., agents, insurers) equal to those that another state imposes on the domestic state's residents when doing business in the foreign state.

compare: reciprocal legislation; *see:* domestic insurer, foreign insurer, retaliatory tax

retaliatory tax

Regulation. The tax imposed by retaliatory legislation.

compare: reciprocal legislation; *see:* retaliatory legislation

retention

Insurer Operations/Workers' Compensation. A portion of premium retained by an insurer for expenses associated with the issuance of a workers' compensation policy, such as administration, overhead, profit, and loss control, for dividend calculation.

see: dividend, retention plan

Reinsurance. The amount of liability that an insurer does not reinsure, but retains for its own account.

see: reinsurance

Risk Management. The planned assumption of risk by an insured through deductibles, policy retentions, or self-insurance. The insured's reason for a risk retention is usually to reduce expenses and improve cash flow, to increase control of claims reserving and claims settlements, or to fund losses that cannot be insured.

synonym: loss assumption, loss retention, net line, risk assumption, risk retention; *compare:* noninsurance, passive retention; *see:* accountants' materiality test, diversification, insurance, large loss principle, risk avoidance, risk retention techniques, risk transfer, small loss principle

retention and limits clause

Reinsurance. A provision in excess of loss reinsurance contracts that the reinsurer will pay all claims in excess of the ceding insurer's retained limit (retention) up to the reinsurer's limit of liability.

see: excess of loss reinsurance, retention

retention limit

Liability. The amount an insured must pay before a liability policy with a self-insured retention will respond to a loss. In regard to an umbrella policy, it is the amount an insured must pay for a loss not

389

covered by an underlying policy, before the umbrella policy will respond.

see: deductible, retention, self-insured retention

retention plan
Insurer Operations/Workers' Compensation. A form of participating policy where the dividend is based on the insurer's retention and the insured's converted losses.

compare: sliding scale dividend plan; *see*: converted losses, dividend (*Insurer Operations*), participating policy, retention

retention ratio
Insurer Operations. A ratio used by an insurer to evaluate underwriting and policyholder service performance. *Formula*: number of renewed policies ÷ number of expired policies (during a specific period of time). An unfavorable ratio indicates problems such things as poor claims service or noncompetitive pricing.

compare: success ratio

retired life fund
Life.
see: annuity purchase fund

retirement age
Employee Benefits. The age at which a participant in a pension plan becomes eligible to receive pension benefits.

see: Age Discrimination in Employment Act, compulsory retirement, deferred retirement, delayed retirement credit, early retirement, normal retirement age, pension, Social Security, thirty and out

retirement annuity
Life. An insurance contract that does not contain an element of pure insurance. The death benefit of the contract is based on the remaining reserve or the premium paid, without interest, whichever is larger.

see: annuity

Retirement Equity Act
Regulation. Federal legislation of 1984 that amended the Employee Retirement Income Security Act to provide greater pension equity for working women and surviving spouses.

see: Employee Retirement Income Security Act

retirement income endowment policy
Life. An endowment policy designed to generate a large enough cash value to produce a specified life income beginning at a given age. The policy cash value in the later years exceeds the original death benefit.

synonym: super endowment policy; *see*: cash surrender value, endowment policy

retirement income policy
Life. A deferred annuity policy that does not provide any life insurance coverage and begins paying benefits at a specified age. The premium, minus the insurer loading, is accumulated with interest to fund the periodic annuity payments.

see: accumulation period, deferred annuity

retiring from a line
Insurer Operations. The withdrawal of an insurance company from a line of business by canceling or non-renewing policies.

see: line

retroactive aggregate excess of loss agreement
Reinsurance. A reinsurance contract that provides an aggregate stop loss coverage for unknown losses that occurred within a specified time (e.g., calendar year, accident year) or for known losses that have occurred but fall outside the scope of the current traditional reinsurance program. The coverage is designed to protect an insurer's current year's results from the impact of adverse loss development or prior accident years' losses, or to smooth the results of periods of abnormally adverse loss frequency in generally predictable loss layers.

see: aggregate excess of loss reinsurance

retroactive conversion
Life. Conversion of a term life insurance policy to a cash value policy, using the term policy's original inception date rather than the date of conversion.

synonym: original age option; *see*: cash surrender value, term life insurance

retroactive date
Liability. A date stipulated in a claims-made liability policy declarations section as the first date of incidents covered by the policy. The retroactive date is designed to provide coverage for claims resulting from incidents that take place prior to the current policy term. Renewal claims-made policies usually have the retroactive date of the first policy issued to the insured. When this is not done, there is a gap in coverage.

see: claims-made form, claims-made trigger

retroactive extension
Liability. An extension of the terms of an insurance policy back to a past time.

see: retroactive date

retroactive period
Workers' Compensation. A provision in many state workers' compensation laws that if a covered disability continues past a specified time, the benefits will be paid retroactively to the date of injury, including any waiting period.

see: waiting period

retrocedent

Reinsurance. A reinsurer who cedes a portion of the business it assumes to another reinsurer.

compare: retrocessionaire; *see*: ceding insurer, retrocession

retrocession

Reinsurance. The transfer of assumed reinsurance to another reinsurer; the further spreading of a large risk assumed by a reinsurer among other reinsurance companies.

see: overriding commission, reinsurance

retrocessionaire

Reinsurance. A reinsurer who assumes reinsurance from another reinsurer.

compare: retrocedent; *see*: reinsurer, retrocession

retrofit

Loss Control. To adjust or upgrade a structure or equipment in order to meet current standards. *Example*: Retrofitting a building with a new type of support to meet current earthquake standards.

retrospective penalty insurance

Liability/Workers' Compensation. A separate insurance policy, written in conjunction with a retrospective rating plan policy, that protects the policyholder against having to pay a penalty or extra premium in excess of the standard retrospective premium in the event of an adverse loss ratio. This is sometimes called a *Chinese retro* and is illegal in some states.

see: maximum retrospective premium, retrospective rating plan

retrospective premium

Insurer Operations. The final premium developed under a retrospective rating plan.

see: retrospective rating plan

retrospective rating plan

Insurer Operations. A method of establishing a premium on large commercial accounts. The final premium is based on the insured's actual loss experience during the policy term, subject to a minimum and maximum premium, with the final premium determined by a formula. Under this plan, the current year's premium is based on the current year's losses, although the premium adjustments may take months or years beyond the current year's expiration date. The rating formula is guaranteed in the insurance contract. *Formula*: retrospective premium = converted loss + basic premium × tax multiplier. Numerous variations of this formula have been developed and are in use.

compare: adjustable premium, experience rating plan, maximum retrospective premium, paid loss retrospective rating plan, prospective rating plan; *see*: basic premium, converted losses, excess loss premium factor, loss-sensitive insurance program, retrospective penalty insurance, tax multiplier

Reinsurance. A reinsurance contract rating formula where the final premium is based on the primary carrier's loss experience over a specified period of time.

return commission

Agency. The portion of a commission that has been received by an agent that must be returned to an insured as the result of cancellation, rate adjustment, deletion or reduction in coverage, or an error in calculation of the initial premium.

compare: flat cancellation, pro rata cancellation, short-rate cancellation

return of cash value

Life. A life insurance policy provision stating that if death occurs during a certain period of time, the policy will pay its cash value, in addition to the face amount.

compare: return of premium; *see*: cash surrender value

return of premium

Insurer Operations.

see: return premium

Health. A provision in a health insurance policy providing for the payment of a benefit equal to the sum or a stated percentage of all the premiums paid, less claims paid, if the claims paid over a stated period of time do not exceed a fixed percentage of the premiums paid.

Life. A life insurance policy provision that the death benefit paid will be the face amount, plus the sum of all the premiums paid, should death occur within a specified period of time after inception of the policy.

compare: return of cash value

return of unearned premium

Reinsurance.

see: portfolio return

return on equity ratio

Financial Planning. A financial analysis ratio that measures the rate of return on the owner's investment. *Formula*: net income ÷ shareholders' equity.

see: financial ratios

return on investment (ROI)

Financial Planning. A frequently used financial analysis ratio that indicates both an investor's return on investment and whether the volume of income generated is adequate relative to the amount of capital invested in the organization. *Formula*: net income ÷ total assets. The higher the ratio, the greater the profitability.

see: financial ratios, internal rate of return, opportunity cost, payback period

return portfolio
Reinsurance.

see: portfolio return

return premium (RP)
Insurer Operations. The portion of the premium returned to an insured as the result of cancellation, rate adjustment, deletion or reduction in coverage or an error in calculation of the initial premium.

synonym: return of premium; *compare*: additional premium, initial premium; *see*: flat cancellation, pro rata cancellation, short-rate cancellation, unearned premium

revenue passenger miles
Aviation. A measure of airline traffic. Each revenue passenger mile represents one revenue-paying passenger flying for one mile.

see: available seat miles, passenger yield

Revenue Reconciliation Act
Regulation. Federal legislation of 1993 that among other things established a 15-year period of depreciation for intangible assets, including insurance agents' goodwill and expirations.

see: depreciation, intangible property (1)

reverse-annuity mortgage (RAM)
Financial Planning. A quasi-annuity whereby a homeowner receives lifetime monthly payments from a lender based on the value of the property and the homeowner's life expectancy. Upon the death of the homeowner, title to the house automatically transfers to the lender. It is an especially useful technique for elderly persons, who usually own their homes free and clear, since it allows them to benefit from the equity in their homes while guaranteeing them a place to live.

see: annuity, living benefits

reverse flow insurance
International. Coverage of a foreign organization's business or property located in the country of the insurer's domicile. Many U.S. insurance companies have special departments to concentrate on this business because of increasing foreign investments.

compare: home/foreign insurance

reverse mortgage
Financial Planning. A form of mortgage whereby the lender makes monthly or periodic payments to the borrower. Interest accrues on these payments over the years, and the borrower does not have to repay the loan and interest until he or she sells the property or dies. Upon sale of the property, the lender recovers all the cash the borrower received

from the loan, plus interest.

see: mortgage

reverse stock split
Financial Planning. A proportional decrease in the number of a corporation's outstanding shares. A corporation may decide to decrease the number of shares, increasing the market value of each, in order to attract a different type of investor.

compare: stock split

reversionary annuity
Life.

see: joint and survivor annuity

revival
Insurer Operations/Life.

see: reinstatement

revocable beneficiary
Life. A life insurance policy in which the owner reserves the right to revoke or change the beneficiary.

compare: irrevocable beneficiary; *see*: beneficiary

Richter scale
Loss Control. The Richter scale measures the amount of energy released by an earthquake. It is a logarithmic scale, so each whole number on the scale indicates an earthquake ten times more powerful than the preceding number. An earthquake reading 1.5 is the smallest tremor that people can feel, though most tremors that small are not felt.

see: earthquake, Mercalli scale, moment-magnitude scale, seismograph

rider
Insurer Operations. An attachment that modifies an insurance policy or a bond, often by adding or excluding various coverage.

synonym: attachment, waiver; *compare*: endorsement

right of dissent
Financial Planning.

see: dissenting shareholder

right of exoneration
Surety. A surety's right of recourse against a principal who defaults on its obligations. After a principal defaults and the surety performs under the terms of a bond, most bonds provide the surety with a right to recover from the principal the amounts that the surety was required to pay.

see: surety bond

right to die
Life.

see: advance directive, living will

RIMSNET

Organizations. A computer network established by the Risk and Insurance Management Society (RIMS) in 1987. It provides an electronic forum for news and information of concern to risk managers, brokers, and insurance service vendors.

see: Risk and Insurance Management Society, Inc.

riot

Property. A general disturbance or a public assembly of a group of people who commit acts of violence or threaten violence. Riot is an insurable peril under most basic property insurance policies and is substantially the same as *civil commotion.*

see: riot and civil commotion coverage

riot and civil commotion coverage

Property. Insurance for property damaged caused by riot or civil commotion, which are usually combined because there is no meaningful distinction between them. The coverage also includes damage caused by striking employees who occupy the insured's premises.

compare: civil commotion exclusion; *see:* riot

ripping and tearing insurance

Liability. A liability insurance coverage that reimburses a contractor for the cost of labor required for the destruction and removal of a defective product that the contractor had installed. Coverage can also be included for the cost of restoring the structure to the condition that existed before the defective product was removed.

see: defective product, product liability insurance

risk

Insurer Operations/Risk Management. The possibility or chance of loss or injury; the property or person exposed to damage or injury; an insurance company's uncertainty regarding the ultimate amount of any claim payment (underwriting risk) or uncertainty regarding the timing of claim payments (timing risk), or both.

synonym: uncertainty; *compare:* exposure, hazard, peril; *see:* assigned risk, business risk, degree of risk, dynamic risk, financial risk, fundamental risk, insurable risk, pure risk, risk classification, risk transfer, speculative risk, static risk, substandard risk

risk-adjusted discount rate

Financial Planning. The discount rate applicable to a particularly risky (uncertain) stream of income; the risk-free rate of interest, plus a risk premium appropriate to the level of risk attached to the particular income stream.

see: discount factor, discounting, risk premium

Risk and Insurance Management Society, Inc. (RIMS)

Organizations. Members: Corporate risk, insurance and employee benefits managers. *Objectives:* Sponsors educational programs. Promotes risk management concepts. *Founded:* 1950. *Headquarters:* New York, NY. (Originally, the National Insurance Buyers Association until 1954, when the name was changed to the American Society of Insurance Management. The current name was adopted in 1975.)

see: RIMSNET, Spencer Educational Foundation

risk appraiser

Life. A life insurance company employee responsible for deciding whether an application for life insurance coverage should be approved or rejected, or if alternative coverage should be offered.

see: risk classification, underwriter

risk assumption

Risk Management.

see: retention

risk avoidance

Risk Management. The elimination of a loss exposure by ceasing or never undertaking an activity that produces the exposure. In making this decision, the person or organization must weigh the potential value of the activity against the potential loss.

synonym: loss avoidance; *see:* diversification, opportunity cost, retention, risk control techniques, risk transfer

risk-based capital

Insurer Operations. Minimum capital and surplus standards for insurance companies that depend on the insurer's business risks, especially the risks of its underwriting and investment activities. Many states have adopted the complex formulas developed by the National Association of Insurance Commissioners, which contain separate standards for property/casualty insurers and life/health insurers. Failure to maintain minimum capital and surplus adequate to support the insurer's particular risks may subject it to regulatory action by the state insurance commissioner.

see: capital, investment reserve, surplus

risk classification

Insurer Operations. An underwriting function of determining the characteristics of an insurance applicant or the applicant's property or activities that have value in determining the probability of loss. Classification is the basis for determining whether a risk should be accepted for insurance and at what premium. Insurers modify, drop or add classifications according to their claims experience, striving for homogeneity of risk within each class while

keeping the number of classes to a practical limit.
see: risk appraiser, underwriting

Workers' Compensation. The placing of employees into various job classifications to determine the rate that should be used to develop a workers' compensation policy premium.
see: workers' compensation insurance

risk control
Risk Management. Techniques or programs used to reduce the total amount of physical damage, injury or loss should an event occur that results in a fortuitous loss.
see: loss control, loss prevention, risk management process

risk control techniques
Risk Management. Risk management techniques to minimize the frequency or severity of accidental losses or to make accidental losses more predictable.
see: duplication of exposure units, loss prevention, loss reduction, risk avoidance, risk control, risk transfer, segregation of exposure units

risk distribution
Risk Management. The transfer of the risk or potential liabilities of a third party (insured) by an assuming insurer or other organization (e.g., pool, captive) to other parties (insureds) for which the assuming insurer or organization has also assumed risk or potential liabilities.

risk financing
Risk Management. Techniques or methods used to provide funds to pay for losses due to fortuitous events.
compare: noninsurance; *see*: captive insurance company, insurance, retention, self-insurance

risk identification
Risk Management. The first of the five steps in the risk management process, in which potential sources of loss are identified by conducting complete examinations of possible events that could occur by negligence, oversight or accident.
synonym: identification; *see*: risk management process

risk management
Risk Management. The procedures used to identify, assess, control and finance accidental loss; management of the pure risks to which an organization might be subject; the application of resources to reduce and finance identified loss exposures.
compare: insurance management; *see*: gross hazard analysis, loss control, pure risk, risk management process

risk management audit
Risk Management. A systematic evaluation of an organization's exposure to risks, insurance coverages or retentions as they relate to those risks, and how the organization is coordinating its risk management program, including any necessary recommendations for improvements.
see: risk identification, risk management process

risk management consultant
Risk Management. An individual or firm that provides risk management and insurance consulting—e.g., risk management audits, policy analysis, feasibility studies, etc.—on a fee basis. As a rule, the risk management consultant does not sell insurance, and so maintains its independence and objectivity. Usually such an individual holds a CPCU (Chartered Property Casualty Underwriter) or ARM (Associate in Risk Management) designation.
see: Associate in Risk Management, Chartered Property Casualty Underwriter, Society of Risk Management Consultants

risk management manual
Risk Management. A manual developed for an organization—usually by its risk manager, risk management consultant, or broker—which includes a risk management policy statement, a description of all insurance contracts purchased by the organization, and procedures to report changes in exposures, and claims.
compare: risk management policy statement

risk management policy statement
Risk Management. A statement developed and approved at a high management level within an organization for the following purposes: 1. to commit top managers to the risk management function; 2. to disseminate risk management information throughout the organization; 3. to set a standard against which the firm's risk management performance can be judged.
see: automobile use policy statement, loss control policy statement, risk management process

risk management process
Risk Management. The risk management process is a series of steps: 1. identifying and analyzing loss exposures; 2. measuring loss exposures; 3. selecting the technique or combination of techniques to be used to handle each exposure; 4. implementing the techniques chosen; and 5. monitoring the decisions made and making appropriate changes.
see: feasibility study, insurance, risk control, risk financing, risk identification, risk management, risk management audit, risk transfer

Risk Management Section, CPCU Society
Organizations. An interest section of the CPCU

Society that examines techniques, developments, and legislation of interest to risk managers, benefit plan sponsors, and consultants.

see: CPCU Society

risk premium
Financial Planning. The difference between the rate of return on a particularly risky asset, and the rate of return on an asset without risk, with the same expected life.

see: rate of return, return on investment, risk-adjusted discount rate

risk premium insurance
Life.

see: annual renewable term insurance

risk quantification
Risk Management. The measurement criteria used to evaluate loss frequency and loss severity.

see: loss frequency, loss severity

risk retention
Risk Management.

see: retention

Risk Retention Act
Regulation.

see: Liability Risk Retention Act of 1986

risk retention group (RRG)
Regulation. A group self-insurance program or group captive insurance company formed under provisions of the Liability Risk Retention Act of 1986, by or on behalf of businesses joined to insure their liability exposures. Such a group is exempt from most state laws, rules or regulations except for the state in which it is domiciled.

see: association captive insurance company, group captive insurance company, Liability Risk Retention Act of 1986

risk retention techniques
Risk Management. An organization can retain risk by one or more of the following techniques: current expensing of losses, funded loss reserves, unfunded loss reserves, borrowing funds to pay losses, or using a captive insurer.

see: captive insurance company, loss reserve, retention

risk securitization
Financial Planning. The use of securities or financial contracts (i.e., stocks, bonds, commodities, financial futures) to transfer the risk of accidental loss, which is usually transferred through insurance.

see: act of God bond, catastrophe insurance futures contract, financial derivative, financial futures, risk transfer

risk transfer
Risk Management. A risk control technique that involves the contractual shifting of a pure risk from one party to another. An example is the purchase of an insurance policy, by which a specified risk of loss is passed from the policyholder to the insurer. Other examples are the hold harmless clauses in many contracts, contractual requirements to provide insurance coverage for another party's benefit, and reinsurance.

compare: noninsurance, passive retention, retention, risk avoidance, self-insurance; *see*: hold harmless agreement, insurance, noninsurance transfer, reinsurance, risk control techniques, risk management process

river marine insurance
Ocean Marine. Ocean marine insurance coverage for vessels operating on inland waterways.

see: ocean marine insurance

robbery
Crime. The taking of another's property by using violence or threats.

see: theft

robbery and safe burglary coverage form— money and securities
Crime. A crime coverage form (ISO form CR 00 18, or form Q) designed for financial institutions that provides coverage for money and securities lost in a robbery or safe burglary at a designated premises or in the care and custody of a messenger.

synonym: crime coverage form Q; *see*: messenger, robbery, safe burglary insurance

robbery and safe burglary coverage form— property other than money and securities
Crime. A crime coverage form (ISO form CR 00 05, or form D) covering robbery and burglary from a safe inside the insured premises and robbery of messengers outside the premises.

synonym: crime coverage form D; *see*: robbery, safe burglary insurance

rollover individual retirement account
Employee Benefits. An individual retirement account created for the purpose of receiving funds distributed from a qualified pension plan, usually without incurring any tax liabilities. Some restrictions exist on the amount, frequency and timing of these rollovers with respect to their tax exempt status.

see: individual retirement account, tax free rollover

roof surfacing endorsement
Personal.

see: actual cash value loss settlement roof surfacing endorsement

round lot

Financial Planning. One hundred shares of a security, which is the number that makes up a trading unit on most exchanges.

compare: odd lot

rule of 72

Financial Planning. A method for estimating how soon inflation will halve a sum of money or what rate of return is needed to double an amount by a specified time. To approximate the number of years when an amount of money will be worth only half of what it is today, divide 72 by the rate of inflation. To approximate what rate of return is needed to double an amount of money in a specified time, divide 72 by the number of years the money is to be invested. *Example*: Investing for 12 years requires an interest rate of 6% to double the investment because $72 \div 2 = 6$. (Alternatively, dividing 72 by a known interest rate produces the number of years.)

run-off cancellation

Reinsurance. A reinsurance contract termination provision requiring the reinsurer to remain liable for losses under reinsured policies in force at the date of termination as a result of occurrences after the date of termination.

compare: cut-off provision; *see*: cancellation

running down clause

Ocean Marine. Liability coverage that can be added to an ocean marine hull policy for damage caused by a collision with another vessel.

synonym: both to blame collision clause, collision clause

Rural Electrification Administration endorsement

Workers' Compensation. A workers' compensation policy endorsement (NCCI form WC 00 03 09) that provides that the Rural Electrification Administration will receive its required copy of a policy issued to a rural utility and any notice of its cancellation.

Rural Electrification Administration—joint insured

Crime. A crime policy endorsement (ISO form CR 10 40) required by the Rural Electrification Administration when a utility is an "REA borrowing corporation" which amends several crime policy provisions to protect the REA in the event of an employee dishonesty loss.

Rural Electrification Administration— regulations

Crime. A crime policy endorsement (ISO form CR 10 39) required by the Rural Electrification Administration when a utility is an "REA borrowing corporation" which amends several crime policy provisions to comply with REA regulations.

S

sabbatical

Employee Benefits. A paid leave of absence to an employee at recurring intervals to lessen employee burnout or allow employees to acquire additional professional skills. College professors have traditionally been granted leave for a year or a semester every seven years to do research, write for publication, redesign courses, etc. Upon return from this form of leave, the employee resumes his or her previous duties.

see: Family and Medical Leave Act, leave of absence

saddle animal liability

Liability. Coverage for saddle animals ridden at riding schools, dude ranches and resorts can be included under the commercial general liability policy, but the exposure is usually insured separately under a special liability policy and excluded from the general liability policy. This endorsement (ISO form CG 20 14) to the commercial general liability policy extends coverage to include any person or organization who uses or is responsible for an animal as an additional insured.

see: commercial general liability policy

safe

Crime. A container, usually metal, for storing valuables and designed to be opened only by an authorized person.

see: iron safe clause, robbery and safe burglary coverage form—property other than money and securities, safe burglary insurance, vault

safe burglary insurance

Crime. Coverage against the taking of covered property from within a locked safe or vault inside a premises, or the actual taking of the safe or vault from the premises. Some older forms of the coverage required that there be visible signs of forcible entry.

see: mercantile safe burglary insurance

safe deposit box coverage

Crime. Coverage for a bank or savings and loan from liability for loss to property in a safe deposit box against burglary from the box or against robbery from within the vault containing the box or the customers' section of the safe deposit department. Money is excluded from coverage but may be added by an endorsement.

compare: safe depository direct loss coverage form; *see*: hotel safe deposit box liability, safe depository liability coverage form

safe depository direct loss coverage form

Crime. A crime coverage form (ISO form CR 00 15, or form N) that provides direct damage coverage for securities and property of customers (other than money and securities) that have been entrusted with an insured safe depository facility that is not a financial institution (e.g., a hotel). Money may be included for coverage by endorsement.

synonym: crime coverage form N; *compare*: safe deposit box coverage; *see*: crime coverages, hotel safe deposit box liability, money, property other than money and securities, securities

safe depository liability coverage form

Crime. A crime coverage form (ISO form CR 00 14, or form M) that provides liability coverage for loss of a customer's securities and property other than money and securities while in an insured safe depository facility.

synonym: crime coverage form M; *see*: safe deposit box coverage

Safe Drinking Water Act

Regulation. Federal legislation of 1974, amended in 1986, that establishes maximum contaminant levels for drinking water. It establishes an underground injection control program and provides for Environmental Protection Agency and state enforcement of its provisions.

see: Environmental Protection Agency, Water Quality Improvement Act

safe driver plan

Automobile. An automobile insurance rating plan that assigns points to insureds for traffic violations and some accidents. Those without any violations or accidents pay the base rate; surcharges are imposed on those with points.

see: chargeable offense, good driver discount, merit rating

safe-place-to-work laws

Workers' Compensation. Labor statutes in many states, similar to the federal Occupational Safety and Health Act, that require the facilities or job sites of all employers to be constructed, equipped and operated to provide reasonable and adequate protection for the lives, health and safety of employees. On large construction projects, the general contractor is usually responsible for compliance with the safe-place-to-work laws.

see: Occupational Safety and Health Act

safety

Loss Control. The elimination or reduction of hazards to prevent accidents and injuries.

see: hazard, job safety analysis, safe-place-to-work laws, safety audit, safety can

safety audit

Loss Control. A systematic study and inspection of an organization's operations to identify existing and potential hazards and recommend actions to reduce or eliminate the hazards.

see: job safety analysis

safety can

Loss Control. A container, up to five gallons in capacity, approved by an accredited safety organization for handling flammable liquids. It is fitted with a spring-closing lid and spout cover that remain closed when not in use but will relieve internal pressure from extreme heat.

safety group dividend plan

Workers' Compensation. A large number of similar risks that are combined into a single plan. The loss experience is pooled for dividend purposes. Dividends are distributed to all participants in the group if the plan is profitable during the policy period.

synonym: group dividend plan; *see*: dividend

safety group plan

Insurer Operations/Loss Control. A form of commercial mass marketing where the insurance product is available to any firm in a selected industry provided the firm meets the insurer's underwriting requirements and agrees to undertake specific loss control measures.

see: mass marketing

salamander

Loss Control. A portable oil-fired heater used at construction sites or in large warehouses.

salary continuation plan

Employee Benefits. A plan to continue an employee's salary to a spouse or other beneficiary for a specified time after the employee's disability or death. This type of plan is usually funded by disability or life insurance.

see: disability income insurance

salary savings insurance

Life.

see: payroll deduction insurance

sale and lease-back agreement

Financial Planning. An agreement by an owner to sell property with the understanding that the new owner will lease it back to the first. This provides cash to the first owner, depreciation for the new owner, and shifts the risk of loss to the new owner.

sale of company exclusion

Professional Liability. An exclusion in some directors' and officers' liability policies for claims arising from the sale of the company or large portions of its assets or stock to directors or officers.

see: directors' and officers' liability insurance

sales representative

Agency.

see: special agent

salesperson's samples floater

Inland Marine. Inland marine coverage for business firms covering loss or damage to samples used by their sales personnel on an all-risk basis.

see: floater policy, inland marine insurance

saline contamination exclusion

Liability. An endorsement (ISO form CG 22 47) to a commercial general liability policy insuring oil drilling risks, excluding coverage for contamination of underground resources caused by pumping saline water into wells to increase the recovery of oil.

see: commercial general liability policy, oil well liability, platform insurance

salvage

Insurer Operations. Property recovered from an insured loss with the title transferred to the insurer. The insurer then sells the property to recover part of the paid loss.

Ocean Marine. 1. The amount realized from the sale of damaged or recovered merchandise.

2. Services rendered by the rescuers of a ship or

cargo.

see: life salvage, recoverables, salvage charges, salvor

salvage charges

Ocean Marine/Property. Payment by the property owner to a salvor following the salvage or recovery of property. Frequently, the amount is determined by a court based on the value of the salvaged material and the salvor's expenses.

see: salvage, salvor

salvage loss

Ocean Marine. The difference between the amount raised at a salvage sale and the insured value. This is important when an insured and an insurer cannot agree on the value of damaged goods, because it is used to determine the actual value of the salvage.

see: salvage sale

salvage sale

Ocean Marine. The public sale of damaged property recovered by salvage.

see: salvage loss

salvor

Ocean Marine. A person who saves property from loss or damage; one involved with salvaging property.

see: salvage

Sanborn Map Company, Inc.

Property. The Sanborn Map Company was formed in 1866 to provide fire maps for the insurance industry. The maps were used for basic underwriting of property insurance and to monitor accumulations of insurer liability in specific geographic areas. By the mid-1950s, Sanborn maps covered most U.S. cities and towns with a population over 2,500. Most insurers have stopped using the maps because of the high cost of maintaining them and the use of computers, however they are sometimes used to identify potential pollution exposures because they show the historical occupancies of particular locations (e.g., types of factories prone to pollution).

see: fire map

sanitary landfill

Loss Control. A disposal site where nonhazardous wastes are spread in layers and compacted to a small volume. Cover material is applied at the end of each operating day. Site designers consider the effects of rain and surface water runoff and the permeability of the underlying geological layers.

compare: secure chemical landfill

satellite and space vehicle insurance

Aviation. Special coverages for lost expenses to

launch or operate a satellite or spacecraft that malfunctions. There are four types of satellite insurance: pre-ignition, launch, in orbit, and ground support.

see: ground support insurance, in orbit insurance, launch insurance, pre-ignition insurance

satisfaction of judgment

Law. In a lawsuit, a party's compliance with a court's final judgment that includes an order to pay damages.

see: damages, post-judgment interest

Savings Association Insurance Fund

Regulation. A deposit insurance fund for savings and loan associations administered by the Federal Deposit Insurance Corporation. It assumed the functions of the Resolution Trust Corporation in 1995.

see: Federal Deposit Insurance Corporation, Federal Savings and Loan Insurance Corporation, Resolution Trust Corporation

savings bank life insurance

Life. Life insurance that is permitted to be sold by mutual savings banks in certain states such as New York, Connecticut, and Massachusetts.

savings element

Life. The cash value accumulation within a life insurance policy that is considered the policy's savings element. The insured can borrow against this accumulation in some policies; it is returned to the policyholder if the policy is canceled or has reached maturity.

see: cash surrender value

savings plan

Employee Benefits. A profit-sharing benefit plan established and administered by an employer. The plan requires a certain rate of contributions by participating employees, which are withheld from salary. The employer contributes matching funds out of profits.

synonym: thrift plan; *see*: Internal Revenue Code § 401(k), profit-sharing plan

scaffolding and forms coverage

Property. A builders' risk coverage extension for scaffolds and forms at the insured premises that are to be used in the construction project. Often this coverage is subject to a sublimit.

see: builders' risk insurance

scale order

Financial Planning. An order to trade securities that specifies the maximum number to be traded at specified price levels.

see: delivery

schedule

Health.

see: fee schedule

Inland Marine. A list of the items (such as jewelry, furs, silverware or cameras) covered by an inland marine floater policy. For each item listed there is a description and a value indicated.

see: floater policy, inland marine insurance

Property. A list of buildings, structures and contents covered by a property policy covering multiple locations.

schedule bond

Crime. A surety or fidelity bond listing the various covered principals by name or position.

see: name position bond, name schedule bond

Schedule P

Regulation. A loss reserve development schedule, considered to be the most important, in the National Association of Insurance Commissioner's annual statement for a property and casualty insurance company. It includes reserve development for auto liability, other liability, workers' compensation, package policies, ocean marine, aircraft, and boiler and machinery and consists of three parts: cumulative loss experience by accident year—the basis used to determine the minimum statutory reserve; the historical development of incurred losses; and comparison of the claims settlement experience of the last seven accident years.

Schedule Q

Regulation. A schedule that life insurers doing business in New York must file with the insurance department. It includes a list of all life insurance selling expenses and places a limit on commissions paid to agents.

synonym: Q Schedule

schedule rating

Insurer Operations. A method of developing property and liability insurance premiums by applying debits or credits within established ranges for various characteristics of the risk, which are either above or below a schedule of standards.

see: "A" rates, account premium modification plan, judgment rates

scheduled coverage

Inland Marine/Property. Coverage that insures items of property that are specifically listed. The schedule indicates amount of insurance applicable to each item.

compare: blanket insurance; *see*: schedule, scheduled item

scheduled employee dishonesty

Crime.

see: employee dishonesty coverage form

scheduled injury

Workers' Compensation. A permanent injury to a designated part of the body by amputation or loss of use, loss of vision or hearing, etc. An injury may be scheduled in a state workers' compensation law for a specific income benefit regardless of whether the worker suffers a loss of earning power.

see: disability benefit, workers' compensation law

scheduled item

Inland Marine/Property. An insured item specifically listed in the policy for which an amount of insurance is indicated.

see: scheduled coverage

scheduled personal property endorsement

Personal. An endorsement (ISO form HO 04 61) to the homeowners policy that allows the insured to obtain higher limits on an all-risk basis for specified highly valued personal property (jewelry, furs, cameras, musical instruments, silverware, golfer's equipment, fine arts, stamps and coins). This endorsement has its own insuring agreements, exclusions and conditions and is the equivalent of adding the ISO personal articles floater to the homeowners policy. Special sublimits apply to many of these items in the homeowners form.

compare: coverage C increased special limits of liability; *see*: homeowners policy—special limits of liability, personal articles floater

school board liability

Professional Liability.

see: board of education liability insurance, educators' professional liability insurance

scrub tower

Loss Control. A piece of equipment that removes airborne impurities by passing exhaust gases or dust through a system of fine water spray or through wet slats that collect the impurities.

scuppers

Loss Control. Openings in a building wall covered by hinged metal flaps that allow water to flow through, reducing the weight and preventing possible collapse. Scuppers may be put at floor level to allow water from sprinklers to flow through and may be put in parapet walls above roof level to allow rain to run off in the event the roof drains are clogged.

see: automatic sprinkler system, sprinkler leakage coverage

seaman's remedies

Ocean Marine. Maritime law provides ship's crew members with a right to wages until the end of the voyage or period of hire, and to board and care during that time.

see: cure; Jones Act; wages, maintenance and cure

seasonal risk

Insurer Operations. A business that operates on a seasonal basis, such as a farm or resort hotel, where there is little or no exposure for part of the year; a risk with seasonal fluctuations in insured exposures (changes in inventory or sales, increased or decreased use of facilities, etc.). Underwriters must take account of seasonal risk changes.

see: peak season endorsement, reporting form

seat belt

Automobile. A lap or shoulder belt in a vehicle designed to prevent the occupant from striking the windshield or other interior surfaces in the event of a collision. A manual lap belt must be fastened by the occupant, whereas an automatic shoulder belt fastens by itself when the door is closed. The latter is an example of a passive restraint device.

see: passive restraint system

second beneficiary

Life.

see: secondary beneficiary

second career

Workers' Compensation. The theory sometimes applied to workers' compensation claims by professional athletes that benefits for permanent disability should be paid only for the anticipated remaining length of the athletic career rather than to normal retirement age. The rationale is that the athlete would have found other employment after retiring from sports.

see: permanent partial disability, workers' compensation insurance

second death insurance

Life. Life coverage on two individuals that pays the benefit upon the death of the second insured.

compare: joint life insurance; *see*: joint life and survivor insurance, survivor life insurance

second injury fund

Workers' Compensation. A state fund (known in New York as the *special disability fund*) established to pay additional benefits (for example, beyond a limited number of weeks) for aggravation of an injured employee's prior condition. The employer of a permanently impaired worker is responsible only for compensating the most recent injury. The policy goals are to fairly apportion liability for compensation benefits and to overcome reluctance to hire handicapped or disabled workers.

synonym: subsequent injury fund; *see*: aggravation of a previous condition, recurrent disability,

workers' compensation law

second mortgage

Financial Planning. A mortgage that is subordinate or junior to the first mortgage. A first mortgagee's interest in the property has priority over the interest of a second mortgagee.

synonym: junior mortgage, subordinate mortgage; *see*: mortgage, senior debt

second surplus treaty

Reinsurance. A reinsurance treaty used in writing large industrial risks where the limits of liability are too large to be covered by a first surplus treaty.

see: first surplus reinsurance treaty

secondary beneficiary

Life. 1. The person who becomes the beneficiary of a life insurance policy or annuity in the event that the primary beneficiary survives the insured but dies before receiving all entitled proceeds or installments. Insofar as permitted under the policy or annuity contract, the secondary beneficiary succeeds to the rights of the primary beneficiary; however, settlement options available to a secondary beneficiary are often more limited.

2. Often also used as a synonym for *contingent beneficiary*, i.e., the person designated to receive life or annuity benefits in the event that the primary beneficiary dies before the insured.

synonym: second beneficiary; *see*: contingent beneficiary, primary beneficiary, settlement options

secondary offering

Financial Planning. The sale of large blocks of securities by institutional shareholders rather than by the issuing corporation, which usually requires the services of investment bankers to stabilize the price; a redistribution of securities.

see: investment banker, public offering

secondary rating classification

Automobile. A classification by type of industry needed to complete the rating of a commercial vehicle after the primary factors have been determined. The industry classifications are contractors, dump trucks, farming, food delivery, logging and lumbering, specialized delivery, transmit mixers, trucking, waste disposal, and all others.

compare: primary rating classification

seconded employee

Workers' Compensation.

see: borrowed employee

sector fund

Financial Planning. A mutual fund that invests in the stocks of a specific industry, such as utilities, technology or health care.

see: mutual fund

secure chemical landfill

Loss Control. A hazardous waste disposal site designed to minimize the chance of releasing the hazardous substances into the environment.

compare: sanitary landfill; *see*: hazardous waste disposal, land farming

secured creditor

Financial Planning. A creditor with an interest in the specific assets of a debtor which is supported by documentation.

see: security interest

securities

Crime. As defined in crime insurance forms, securities are both negotiable and non-negotiable instruments or contracts representing money, and evidence of debt issued in connection with credit or charge cards not issued by the insured.

see: crime coverages, security

Securities Act of 1933

Regulation. Federal legislation (U.S. Code Title 15, Chapter 2A) that requires registration of securities issued in interstate commerce and full disclosure of information concerning the financial condition of the issuer. The definition of securities includes variable annuity and variable life insurance policies.

synonym: Full Disclosures Act; *see*: security

securities analyst

Financial Planning. An individual who investigates the financial soundness and probable future value of securities and the issuing corporations, usually specializing in one industry, one market segment, or one type of security.

synonym: analyst

Securities and Exchange Commission liability insurance

Professional Liability. Coverage for securities underwriters or issuers of stock sold in secondary offerings. It covers third-party liability imposed under the Securities Act of 1933, the Securities Exchange Act of 1934, or a similar state common or statutory law on securities.

see: Securities Act of 1933

Securities and Exchange Commission (SEC)

Regulation. A federal agency created as part of the Securities Exchange Act of 1934 to regulate issuers of securities, securities firms, investment firms and investment advisors.

see: Securities and Exchange Commission liability insurance, security

securities deposited with others coverage form

Crime. A crime coverage form (ISO form CR 00 11, or form J) providing theft, disappearance or destruction of securities deposited with others, such as banks, trust companies, public officials or stockbrokers, while the securities are inside the custodian's premises or are being conveyed outside by employees of the custodian.

synonym: crime coverage form J; *see*: crime coverages, securities, theft

securities—special limit

Personal. The Insurance Services Office homeowners policy coverage section C (personal property) has a "special limits of liability" provision as respects securities, accounts, deeds, evidences of debt, letters of credit, notes other than bank notes, manuscripts, personal records, passports, tickets and stamps. The combined coverage for these items is limited to $1,000 including research costs. This limit applies to these categories regardless of the medium (such as paper or computer software) on which the material exists.

see: homeowners policy—special limits of liability

Securities Investor Protection Corporation (SIPC)

Regulation. A nonprofit corporation created by Congress in 1970 under the Securities Investor Protection Act that provides insurance to protect the assets of client accounts held by registered securities broker-dealers. The maximum coverage for cash and securities in a client account is $500,000 with a sublimit of $100,000 on the amount of cash.

see: Federal Deposit Insurance Corporation, Savings Association Insurance Fund

securities valuation

Insurer Operations/Regulation. A method used by state insurance regulators to value securities on the books of insurance companies. Bonds meeting certain credit requirements are carried at face value, plus or minus any purchase discount or premium. Preferred stock is valued at cost and common stock at market price. The National Association of Insurance Commissioners values impaired securities, such as bonds in default.

see: high-yield bond, investment reserve, mandatory securities valuation reserve, Valuation of Securities System

Securities Valuation Manual

Financial Planning.

see: high-yield bond

securitization

Financial Planning.

see: risk securitization

security

Financial Planning. A document issued in bearer or registered form, such as a note, stock, option, bond, debenture, certificate of deposit, certificate of interest or participation in an oil, gas or mining title or lease, or warrant.

see: bond (*Financial Planning*), capital stock, commercial paper, debenture, debt security, option (*Financial Planning*)

security for expenses

Surety. A statutory requirement of certain plaintiffs in a derivative suit to post a surety bond from which defendants may be reimbursed for their expenses if they prevail. It was designed as a protection against strike suits.

see: judicial bond, strike suit

security interest

General. An interest by a creditor in personal property or fixtures which secures payment or performance of an obligation.

see: secured creditor

seedmens' errors and omissions insurance

Professional Liability. Coverage that protects seed growers, seed dealers, wholesalers, seed packagers, seed brokers and any other individual or firm that handles seeds against losses arising from errors or omissions in germination tests, failure to germinate, mislabeling of seeds and similar claims.

see: errors and omissions insurance

seepage exclusion

Property. A property insurance exclusion for losses arising from continuous or repeated seepage or leakage of water or steam from an insured system occurring over a period of more than 14 days. It is designed to eliminate claims for rotting of floors or support structures.

segregation of exposure units

Risk Management. A risk control technique to prevent a catastrophic economic loss by physically arranging an organization's activities and resources so they cannot all be lost in a single event. This is commonly accomplished by constructing separate fire divisions at a plant site or by using multiple plants.

see: fire division, probable maximum loss, risk control techniques

seismograph

Loss Control. An instrument to measure and record vibrations and tremors within the earth.

see: earthquake, Mercalli scale, moment-magnitude scale, Richter scale

seizure order

Regulation. A court order directing an insurance

commissioner to take possession and control of the property, accounts, records and other items of an insurer.

see: liquidation

select mortality table

Life. A mortality table based only on individuals that have recently purchased life insurance policies; such individuals historically produce lower mortality rates because they are younger and have had better medical care than older policyholders.

see: mortality table, special mortality table

selection of risk

Insurer Operations. The practice of an insurer to select, through underwriting, better risks over poorer risks.

see: substandard risk, underwriting

selective specialty insurer

Insurer Operations. An insurer that specializes in writing various types of property and liability insurance to specific customers (e.g., school or church package policies).

compare: full service insurer, market specialty insurer, product specialty insurer; *see*: marketing

self-administered plan

Employee Benefits/Health. A qualified employee benefit plan funded and administered by the employer rather than an insurer. Such plans are not subject to regulation by state insurance departments and need not provide coverages required in health insurance plans. Instead, these plans are regulated by the federal government through the Employee's Retirement Income Security Act.

see: employee benefit plan, Employee Retirement Income Security Act

self-contained policy

Insurer Operations. A single, complete insurance policy that contains all of the agreements, terms and conditions between the insured and the insurer.

see: modular policy, pre-printed policy

self-inflicted injury

Life/Health/Workers' Compensation. An intentional injury a person causes to him- or herself. Generally, such an injury is not covered by a health plan or a workers' compensation policy, since it is not an accident; but suicide is often covered by a life insurance policy after a specified time period.

self-insurance

Risk Management. The planned assumption of risk instead of purchasing insurance. An organization develops a program for identifying, evaluating and funding its losses. It is often used for workers' compensation, where losses are fairly predictable. Smaller losses that occur frequently are a better subject for self-insurance than large infrequent losses. Self-insurance programs are frequently structured to retain losses up to a specific limit, and insurance is purchased above that level. Most states regulate self-insurance as they do insurance, requiring certificates of self-insurance for compulsory coverages such as auto liability and workers' compensation.

compare: noninsurance, passive retention, risk transfer; *see*: captive insurance company, excess insurance, group self-insurance, self-insured retention

Self-Insurance Institute of America (SIIA)

Organizations. Members: Actuaries, attorneys, adjusters, insurance consultants, corporations, employers, insurers, risk managers, third party administrators and others interested in self-insurance. *Objectives*: Promotes self-insurance concepts, plans and interests. Supports educational programs. *Founded*: 1981. *Headquarters*: Santa Ana, CA.

self-insurance reserve

Risk Management. Funds set aside by an organization to cover liability for future claims under its self-insurance program.

see: reserve, self-insurance

self-insured retention (SIR)

Liability/Risk Management. A potential loss assumed by an organization—that is, not insured. The SIR differs from a deductible because the insured performs all the functions normally undertaken by an insurance company for losses within the SIR, including claims adjusting and audits, funding and paying claims, and complying with applicable state and federal laws and regulations.

see: effective retention, retention, umbrella liability insurance

selling price clause

Property. A property policy provision that pays at selling price (realized market value) losses to finished stock that is sold but not delivered. This includes the insured's profit. Normally, such stock would be valued at its production or replacement cost, whichever is lower.

see: manufacturer's selling price

selling price or processing charge coverage form

Crime. An endorsement (ISO form CR 15 25) that amends Insurance Services Office crime coverage forms to include coverage for the insured's processing fees or the insured's profit on merchandise that is ready for sale.

see: actual cash value, crime coverages

Senior CPCU Section, CPCU Society

Organizations. An interest section of the CPCU Society that addresses retirement planning, second-

career options, and other issues of interest for senior citizens.

see: CPCU Society

senior debt

Financial Planning. Debt that has preference over other debt; the first layer of various layers of debt.

see: second mortgage

Senior Professional in Human Resources (SPHR)

Organizations. A professional designation awarded by the Personnel Accreditation Institute after the applicant has passed a written examination, has sufficient college credits, and has acquired extensive experience in human resource management.

see: Personnel Accreditation Institute

separate account guaranteed investment contract

Life. A form of guaranteed investment contract (GIC) where the assets supporting the contract are held in a dedicated account segregated from the insurer's general account and, theoretically, insulated from claims by other policyholders. This form of GIC is participating in nature, and the credited interest rate is reset periodically based on the portfolio's investment performance and cash flow. The insured has significant control over the investment characteristics of the underlying portfolio, including credit quality and choice between a targeted duration portfolio and a fixed payout date.

see: guaranteed investment contract, synthetic guaranteed investment contract

separate limits

Insurer Operations. Multiple specific limits of liability contained within a single insurance policy, each applying to a specific coverage.

see: limit of liability

separation of insureds

Liability. A condition in liability policies obligating an insurance company to provide a separate defense for each insured and to settle each claim or suit against each insured independently.

see: duty to defend

sequential approach

Loss Control. A method of examining potential business income losses by following the activities or operations of a business from where they begin (raw materials, or telephone order) to where they end (delivery of a finished product or completion of a service).

see: business income coverage form

servant

Liability/Workers' Compensation. A person whose conduct is under the control of another (the master or principal).

see: agency, employee, master-servant rule

service

Employee Benefits. In the employee benefit context, employment for wages; compensated labor.

see: service adjustment, years of service

service adjustment

Employee Benefits. An increase or decrease in years of service credited to an employee when pension benefits are calculated.

see: employee benefit plan, pension, years of service

service fee

Agency. A fee paid directly to an insurance broker for services rendered. In many states, fees to brokers are illegal, or are illegal if they are combined with a commission.

compare: agent's commission; *see*: policy fee

service insurance corporation

Insurer Operations. An organization that sponsors an insurance or prepayment plan with benefits in services rather than money, with or without the incidental payment of indemnity under certain circumstances.

see: Blue Cross Plan, Blue Shield Plan, health maintenance organization, legal expense insurer

service plan

Health. An insurance plan that provides services rather than indemnity benefits.

see: Blue Cross Plan, Blue Shield Plan, dental service plan

service provider

Insurer Operations. A person or organization whose profession or business function is to provide insurance services to covered individuals, e.g., a health maintenance organization.

see: health maintenance organization, service insurance corporation

service use

Automobile. A business use auto rating classification that applies to vehicles when they are used for the transportation of employees, tools, equipment or supplies to or from a job site.

compare: business use, commercial use, farm use, pleasure use, retail use

Servicemen's Group Life Insurance (SGLI)

Life. Life insurance underwritten by private insurance companies for members of the U.S. Armed Forces on active duty. Policies are issued based on standard mortality tables, with the federal government providing reimbursement for any increased risk from the individual's military duty. Upon leaving active duty, the SGLI policy can be converted

to either a Veterans Group Life Insurance Policy or to a standard policy based on the veteran's current age.

see: Veterans Group Life Insurance

servicing broker

International. A broker located in the country of an organization's foreign subsidiary that provides the local service requirements under an international insurance program and reports to the controlling broker.

see: account executive, controlling broker

servicing facility

Insurer Operations. Offices designated to process claims on the behalf of a joint underwriting association or a guaranty association.

see: guaranty fund, joint underwriting association

servicing insurer

Insurer Operations. An insurer designated to process claims for a joint underwriting association or a guaranty association.

see: guaranty fund, joint underwriting association

setback

Title.

see: building line

setoff

Insurer Operations/Regulation.

see: offset, setoff clause

setoff clause

Insurer Operations. An insurance policy provision that reduces the amount of an insured's recovery for a loss by amounts that are recovered from other sources stipulated in the policy.

compare: salvage, subrogation; *see*: offset, other insurance provision

settlement

Insurer Operations. An agreement between a claimant or beneficiary to an insurance policy and the insurance company as to the amount and method of a claim or benefit payment.

synonym: out-of-court settlement; *see*: consent to settle provision, minor's compromise, settlement options, structured settlement, viatical settlement

settlement options

Life. A life insurance policy provision that indicates how proceeds from the policy are or may be paid to a living insured or to beneficiaries. These options are a lump sum or cash payment option; fixed amount option where payments are made monthly until all proceeds and interest are paid; fixed period option; life income option; or interest option where payments of interest on proceeds left with the insurer are made.

synonym: life insurance settlement modes; *see:* dividend option, fixed amount option, fixed period option, interest option, life income option, life income with period certain option, lump sum option

settlor

Financial Planning. The maker of a trust; the person whose property is placed in trust for the benefit of another.

synonym: trustor; *see:* trust

severability of interest

Insurer Operations. A provision in some insurance policies and applications for insurance that each insured or applicant will be treated as if separately covered under the policy, or the knowledge of each applicant is separate from the others.

synonym: cross liability clause

severability provision

Professional Liability. A provision in some directors' and officers' liability policies or policy applications that the wrongful act or knowledge of one director or officer is not imputed to any other director or officer for the purpose of applying the policy exclusions. Without this provision, the action of one director or officer could eliminate coverage for the others.

synonym: non-imputation provision

several liability

Law. Full responsibility by each of a group of persons for an injury caused or an obligation owed by the group. For example, each of several persons may individually promise the performance required in a contract.

compare: joint liability; *see:* joint and several liability

sex

Insurer Operations.
see: gender rating, sex discrimination

sex discrimination

Health/Life. The use of the insured's sex to determine premium rates. Most states permit a limited use of sex-distinct rating classifications for life and health insurance, but coverage cannot generally be denied on account of sex. For example, if dependent coverage is available under a group insurance policy for the spouse of an employee of one sex, dependent coverage cannot be denied for the spouse of an employee of the other sex.

see: gender rating, risk classification

Liability. The illegal refusal by an employer to hire or promote an individual because of gender.

see: discrimination, sexual harassment, unisex legislation

sexual harassment

Liability. Conduct or speech of a sexual nature that has the purpose or effect of creating an intimidating, hostile or offensive work environment; unwelcome, repeated advances or other sexual conduct that, explicitly or implicitly, makes the response a condition of a person's employment, promotion or compensation or requires a quid pro quo. Sexual harassment is a violation of Title VII of the U.S. Civil Rights Act; employers who commit or knowingly permit harassment are subject to legal action.

see: discrimination, employment practices liability insurance, sexual harassment defense coverage, unfair labor practices

sexual harassment defense coverage

Liability. Coverage on a claims-made basis for an employer's legal costs in sexual harassment lawsuits or administrative proceedings. This coverage is included in employment practices liability policies and is seldom written as a separate policy.

see: employment practices liability insurance, sexual harassment

shareholder

Financial Planning. A person or entity that owns stock in a corporation. Dividends are paid to this person.

synonym: stockholder; *see:* common stock, dissenting shareholder, dividend (*Financial Planning*), preferred stock

shareholder derivative suit

Law.
see: derivative suit

Sherman Antitrust Act

Regulation. Federal legislation (U.S. Code Title 15, Chapter 1) passed in 1890 that prohibits a monopoly or restraint of trade in interstate commerce. It did not apply to the insurance industry because the Supreme Court had ruled in *Paul v. Virginia* (1869) that insurance was not interstate commerce and thus not subject to federal regulation.

see: antitrust laws, Clayton Act, McCarran-Ferguson Act

ship charters liability insurance

Ocean Marine.
see: charters liability insurance

shipper

Inland Marine/Ocean Marine.
see: consignor

shippers' radioactive contamination insurance

Inland Marine. Inland marine coverage available to shippers of radioactive materials (except those who ship radioactive waste and nuclear reactor fuel), insuring against direct loss or damage caused by radioactive contamination.

compare: motor truck cargo radioactive contamination insurance; *see*: radioactive contamination insurance

shop right

Liability. An employer's nonexclusive, irrevocable, nonassignable license to use an invention or discovery by an employee who has used employment time or the employer's facilities for the invention or discovery.

see: patent, trade secret, trademark

shore risk clause

Ocean Marine. An extension of an ocean marine cargo policy to provide coverage for onshore perils such as fire, sprinkler leakage, collapse of docks, flooding and damage from accidents during ground transportation.

see: cargo insurance

short form bill of lading

Inland Marine/Ocean Marine. A bill of lading in summary form that does not spell out all obligations and responsibilities of the parties to the bill. It is not generally used unless the shipper is familiar with a carrier's tariff.

see: bill of lading

short line railroad liability insurance

Liability. Special liability coverage for railroads that operate over a short distance, generally less than 100 miles. Coverage includes general liability, damage to foreign rolling stock, bill of lading insurance, and Federal Employers' Liability Act coverage.

synonym: tourist railroad liability insurance; *see*: railroad insurance

short-rate cancellation

Insurer Operations. The termination of a policy contract before the expiration date at the request of the insured. Premiums returned to the insured are not in direct proportion to the days remaining in the policy period because of fixed expenses incurred by the company.

compare: pro rata cancellation; *see*: cancellation, return premium

short-rate table

Insurer Operations. A table used to calculate the refund due on a policy canceled by the insured prior to its full term. The table displays a percentage of earned premiums that include a component for policy administration and other services, and a pro rata component based on the number of days the policy has been in force.

see: short-rate cancellation

short sale

Financial Planning. The sale of securities before they are purchased in the belief that they will decrease in value when they are actually purchased for delivery.

compare: long sale

short tail

Liability. As respects liability insurance, the liability where claims become known within a short period of time (i.e., during the policy period or within 12 months of expiration).

compare: long tail

short-term bond fund

Financial Planning. A mutual fund that invests in bonds that mature in a relatively short time, usually one or two years.

compare: money market fund; *see*: mutual fund

short-term debt

Accounting. Debt that is due within twelve months and therefore is considered a current liability.

compare: long-term debt; *see*: total debt

short-term disability

Health. A disability that impairs an injured party's earning capacity for a short time, usually less than 90 days.

see: disability

short-term disability insurance (STD)

Health. Disability coverage for a period of two weeks to two years. Coverage in excess of two years is considered long-term disability insurance.

compare: long term disability insurance; *see*: disability income insurance

short-term foreign credit insurance policy

International. A form of foreign credit insurance policy written by the Foreign Credit Insurance Association that provides coverage for losses up to 180 days on commercial credit with deductibles of 10% or more. Political risks are insured with deductibles of 5% or more on sales of any product of which at least 50% is produced in the United States. Coverage is required on all or most foreign shipments.

see: export credit insurance, Foreign Credit Insurance Association, medium-term foreign credit insurance policy

short-term reversionary trust

Employee Benefits. A form of trust frequently used prior to the Tax Reform Act of 1969 to defer taxes. An irrevocable trust was established for a minimum of ten years, and upon termination the principal was returned to the grantor. This usually allowed the earnings on the principal to be taxed at the beneficiary's tax rate, instead of the higher tax rate of

407

the grantor. This tax deferral arrangement is no longer allowed.

see: irrevocable trust, tax bracket shifting, trust

sick building syndrome

Loss Control. The accumulation of air pollutants or contaminants, such as asbestos, radon, acetic acids, organic gases or microorganisms inside a building, making a significant number of its occupants ill. When this occurs, an office building's air conditioning system must be cleaned and redesigned to circulate adequate air from outside. A private house may require a sealing layer to block gases rising from the earth.

synonym: indoor pollution, tight building syndrome

sickness insurance

Health.

see: health insurance

sidetrack agreement

Liability. A contractual hold-harmless agreement between a railroad and a property owner pertaining to the use of a sidetrack leading to the property owner's premises. The railroad requires that the property owner assume certain liabilities in exchange for constructing the sidetrack, such as liability for damaged goods or bodily injury resulting from use of the sidetrack. The contractual liability resulting from a sidetrack agreement is provided automatically under the Insurance Services Office commercial general liability forms.

see: commercial general liability policy, hold harmless agreement

sign coverage

Inland Marine. An open perils form (ISO form CM 00 28 or AAIS form IM 663) that can be endorsed to commercial property or inland marine policies to cover neon, fluorescent, automatic, or mechanical electric signs and lights.

synonym: sign floater

sign floater

Inland Marine.

see: sign coverage, neon sign floater

silent alarm

Loss Control.

see: burglar alarm

silicosis

Health/Workers' Compensation. A disease of the lungs caused by the inhalation of silica dust. Silicosis is a common condition among coal miners.

compare: asbestosis; *see*: black lung disease, brown lung disease, occupational disease

silverware

Personal. 1. Silverware is a class of personal property specifically included in homeowners policies. Coverage for theft is usually limited ($2,500).

2. One of the nine classes of property that can be covered under a personal articles floater. It includes silverware, silver-plated ware, goldware, gold-plated ware and pewterware, including flatware, hollowware, tea sets, trays and trophies made of or including silver, gold or pewter, except pens, pencils, flasks, smoking implements or jewelry.

see: homeowners policy—special limits of liability, personal property floater, silverware—special limit

silverware—special limit

Personal. The Insurance Services Office homeowners policy coverage section C (personal property) has a "special limits of liability" provision regarding the theft of silverware, silver-plated ware, goldware, gold-plated ware and pewterware. The combined coverage for these items is limited to $2,500.

see: homeowners policy—special limits of liability

simple interest

Financial Planning. Interest that is earned on the initial principal, without compounding.

compare: compound interest; *see*: interest

simplified application

Health/Life. A life or health insurance application that contains no detailed questions about the applicant's history of medical treatment.

see: application, preexisting condition

simplified earnings form

Property. An older, rarely used form for loss of earnings coverage for small businesses, that provides reimbursement when a property is destroyed and a business is unable to continue. The inability of the business to continue must be as a result of a direct loss. Coverage under such a policy protects income and is subject to a monthly limitation.

see: earnings insurance form

simplified employee pension (SEP)

Employee Benefits. An individual retirement account (IRA) funded by an employer or jointly funded by the employer and the employee. Under the Tax Reform Act of 1986, such plans may be used as an alternative to 401(k) plans when 25 or or fewer employees are involved. Any employer contributions must be included as income to the employee, but an offsetting deduction to the IRA, subject to the maximum contribution limit, is allowed on the employee's tax return. Employees benefit from these plans, as employer contributions are vested immediately and investment decisions rest completely with the employee.

compare: Internal Revenue Code § 401(k); *see*: individual retirement account, Keogh plan

simultaneous death
Life/Regulation.
see: uniform simultaneous death act

sine qua non
Law. A necessary element in the chain of causation of an injury or loss, so that the loss would not have occurred (or not to the same extent) but for an act or omission of the defendant. (Latin for "without which not.") The plaintiff must prove that the injury was a natural or proximate result of the defendant's negligent act. Though a defendant may have acted negligently, if the injury would have resulted in any case from another efficient cause, the defendant's negligence is not a sine qua non.

see: concurrent causation, negligence, proximate cause

single annuitant
Life. An annuity that pays benefits until the annuitant dies.
synonym: single life annuity; *see*: annuity

single enterprise
Workers' Compensation. A business that has a single operation or a number of operations that fall into a single manual classification.
compare: multiple enterprise; *see*: classification, classification code, manual rates

single entity condominium
Property. A condominium unit in which all values—such as carpets, cabinets, electrical fixtures, and appliances—contained at the time it is sold to the first purchaser are owned by the condominium association.
synonym: "all in" condominium; *compare*: bare wall condominium; *see*: condominium forms

single interest coverage
Property. An insurance policy that protects only the interests of one party, usually the named insured. *Example*: Physical damage coverage on a car bought with a loan that covers the insurable interest of the lending institution, and not that of the driver.
see: lender's single interest coverage

single life annuity
Life.
see: single annuitant

single limit
Automobile/Liability.
see: combined single limit

single payer plan
Health. A method of paying health care providers whereby all fees are paid by a government or a designated administrator. The government establishes standard fees without regard to the providers' actual service costs in particular cases. This is the system used in Canada.
compare: all-payer system; *see*: health care provider, national health insurance

single premium life insurance
Life. A life insurance policy with the entire premium paid in a lump sum at the policy's inception.

single risk cargo insurance
Ocean Marine. A cargo policy issued on a single shipment of goods.
synonym: special risk insurance, trip transit insurance; *compare*: open cargo policy

sinkhole collapse endorsement
Personal. An endorsement (ISO form HO 04 99) to the homeowners policies that replaces the sinkhole and earth movement exclusion with coverage for direct property loss caused by the peril of sudden settlement or collapse of earth supporting the property when the settlement or collapse results from subterranean voids created by action of water on limestone or similar rock formations.
see: homeowners policy

sinkhole coverage
Property. A coverage included in property insurance policies issued in areas subject to this exposure, such as Florida. It covers loss or damage caused by the sudden sinking or collapse of land, which is due to the action of subsurface water on soft rock formations. Coverage does not include the cost of filling sinkholes and the collapse of the land into man-made underground cavities.
see: earth movement coverage, sinkhole collapse endorsement

sinking fund
Financial Planning. A fund established by regular deposits from current earnings for paying off a long-term debt, redeeming debt securities or preferred stock issues.
Risk Management. A fund established by a self-insurer to cover large losses when they occur. As losses are paid, the fund is replenished to maintain a specified amount.
see: imprest account, self-insurance

sistership exclusion
Liability.
see: product recall exclusion

skewed curve
Risk Management. An actuarial term that refers to

the shape of a distribution curve that is not symmetrical. Most curves involving loss projections are skewed to the right because of the small chance for large losses.

synonym: asymmetrical curve; *compare:* symmetrical curve; *see:* distribution curve

skilled nursing facility

Health. A non-hospital, non-acute care facility staffed and equipped to provide skilled nursing care, physical and occupational rehabilitation, and custodial care, but not generally to treat mental diseases. Since the 1980s, generally used instead of *extended care facility.*

synonym: nursing home; *compare:* acute health care facility, convalescent care, custodial care, transitional care facility; *see:* extended care facility, integrated care (2)

skip-repossessed vehicle insurance

Property. Coverage on cars or trucks taken as collateral by lending institutions, often included with lender's single interest coverage. It covers the loss on a vehicle that supports a loan in default when the vehicle cannot be located for repossession—the borrower/owner has "skipped"—within a certain time (usually 90 to 180 days). The recovery amount is the remaining loan balance or the current value of the vehicle, whichever is less.

see: lender's single interest coverage

slander

Law. Oral defamation; a defamatory spoken statement or gesture.

compare: libel; *see:* advertising injury coverage, defamation, noneconomc loss, personal injury liability

sliding scale commission

Reinsurance. A reinsurance contract commission formula that is designed to reward a ceding insurer for a profitable loss ratio. The reinsurer pays a ceding insurer a commission that varies inversely with the loss ratio, subject to a minimum and maximum commission rate.

see: ceding commission, loss ratio

sliding scale dividend plan

Workers' Compensation. A workers' compensation program designed for small or medium size employers who generally do not qualify for a retention plan. The amount of the dividend, generally expressed as a percentage of premium, is governed by the insured's loss ratio.

see: dividend; *compare:* retention plan

slip

Insurer Operations. An application submitted by a broker to the underwriters at Lloyd's of London, which when accepted by underwriters of syndicates, becomes a binder of insurance.

synonym: line slip; *see:* line, Lloyd's of London, open slip

small business boiler and machinery broad coverage form

Property. A boiler and machinery policy (ISO form BM 00 45) that provides broad, inflexible coverage for small businesses. It covers damage to the following types of objects, which are common to small businesses: boilers, pressure vessels, process boilers, and air conditioning and air compressing units. It can be endorsed to include coverage for spoilage. It also provides business interruption and extra expense coverage for 25% of the policy limit.

see: boiler and machinery insurance, business interruption insurance, extra expense insurance

small loss principle

Risk Management. A risk management principle that small losses can be absorbed more efficiently as normal business expenses through deductibles or through self-insured retentions than through insurance, since insurers add expense loadings (for profit, administrative and selling expenses, etc.) to the basic premium.

compare: large loss principle; *see:* noninsurance, retention

small quantity generator

Loss Control. In reference to hazardous waste, a facility that produces less than 1,000 kg/month of hazardous wastes and no more than 1 kg/month of acutely hazardous wastes. A small quantity generator is conditionally exempt from most Resource Conservation and Recovery Act regulations if it generates no more than 100 kg/month of hazardous wastes.

see: hazardous waste, Resource Conservation and Recovery Act

smoke coverage

Property. Coverage under basic property insurance policies for damage caused by smoke from an unfriendly fire (as opposed to damage caused by fire or combustion itself). Damage from agricultural smudge pots or industrial operations, for example, would not be covered because the smoke source is *friendly* fire or combustion.

see: friendly fire, hostile fire

smoker and nonsmoker mortality tables

Life. Mortality tables that show the different mortality rates for tobacco smokers and nonsmokers.

see: mortality table, nonsmoker discount

snow insurance

Property.

see: rain insurance, weather insurance

snowmobile coverage

Automobile. Coverage (ISO form CA 20 21) that can be endorsed to an automobile policy that covers physical damage to snowmobiles on a named perils or all-risk basis.

Personal. An endorsement (ISO form HO 24 64) to the homeowners policy that extends coverage under Section II (personal liability and medical payments) to snowmobiles scheduled on the endorsement. Coverage does not apply to snowmobiles that are subject to motor vehicle registration, used to carry paying passengers, used for a business purpose, rented to others, or operated in any organized competition.

see: homeowners policy—liability coverage, incidental motorized land conveyances endorsement

social inflation

Risk Management. A general rise in insurance claim costs resulting from generous jury awards, more liberal treatment of claims by workers' compensation appeal boards, legislated benefit increases, and changing legal concepts of tort and negligence that benefit plaintiffs.

see: inflation, mandated benefits

social insurance

General. Any compulsory insurance program to benefit a large percentage of the population. The typical social insurance program is administered and enforced by government and is intended to ensure that a common type of loss (e.g., loss of income due to illness, injury or old age) does not impoverish large numbers of people. Social Security and workers' compensation are examples.

see: basic benefits (2), Social Security, Supplemental Security Income, voluntary insurer, workers' compensation law

Social Security

Employee Benefits. The social insurance program enacted by the Social Security Act of 1935 (U.S. Code Title 42, Chapter 7) and amendments (also called Old Age, Survivors, Disability and Health Insurance). Benefits are funded by both employer and employee taxes under the Federal Insurance Contributions Act. The program includes pension benefits, survivor benefits upon an employee's death, and benefits for workers younger than retirement age who are physically disabled. Early retirement age under Social Security is 62. Full retirement age ranges from 65 years for people born before 1938 to 67 years for people born after 1959. The general view is that the pension program is inadequate as a retiree's sole income, but is merely supplemental to the individual's private pension plan, insurance or annuity, and other investments.

synonym: Old Age, Survivors, Disability and Health Insurance; *see*: blackout period, currently insured status, early retirement, Federal Insurance Contributions Act, fully insured status, integration with Social Security, pension, retirement age, Supplemental Security Income

Social Security integration

Employee Benefits.

see: integration with Social Security

Social Security offset

Employee Benefits.

see: integration with Social Security

Social Security Wage Index

Employee Benefits. A Social Security Administration table of the amount of Social Security benefits payable to a participant or the primary insurance amount that will be paid monthly based on the average monthly wage.

synonym: wage index; *see*: average monthly wage, primary insurance amount, Social Security

socialized health insurance

Health.

see: national health insurance

Society for Human Resource Management (SHRM)

Organizations. Members: Human resource personnel and industrial relations executives. *Objectives*: Professional organization to promote human resource management. *Founded*: 1948. *Headquarters*: Alexandria, VA.

Society for Risk Analysis (SRA)

Organizations. Members: Risk assessment professionals. *Objectives*: Study risks posed by technological development on a scientific basis; disseminate pertinent information. *Founded*: 1982. *Headquarters*: McLean, VA.

Society of Actuaries (SOA)

Organizations. Members: Professional society of those trained in the application of mathematical probabilities to the design of insurance, pension and employee benefit programs. *Objectives*: Sponsors a series of examinations leading to the designation of Fellow or Associate within the Society. *Founded*: 1949. *Headquarters*: Schaumburg, IL.

see: Associate in Society of Actuaries, Fellow of the Society of Actuaries

Society of Certified Insurance Counselors (SCIC)

Organizations. Members: Licensed agents, brokers, solicitors, corporate risk managers and insurance faculty of accredited colleges or universities. *Objectives*: Organizes examinations and certifications. *Founded*: 1969. *Headquarters*: Austin, TX.

Society of Fire Protection Engineers (FPE)

Organizations. Members: Fire protection engineers. *Objectives*: To advance fire protection engineering and allied fields, maintain a high ethical standard among its members, and foster fire protection engineering education.

Society of Insurance Accountants (SIA)

Organizations. Members: Insurance accountants, statisticians, actuaries and others interested in insurance accounting procedures and use of data processing equipment. *Objectives*: To provide a forum for discussion of accounting statistical and related problems, an interchange of ideas and for the dissemination of information to its membership. *Founded*: 1960. *Headquarters*: Hollowville, NY.

Society of Insurance Research (SIR)

Organizations. Members: Industry personnel actively involved in insurance research. *Objectives*: Promote insurance research concepts and methodology; assists in developing the curriculum for the Associate in Research and Planning designation. *Founded*: 1970. *Headquarters*: Marietta, GA.

see: Associate in Research and Planning

Society of Insurance Trainers and Educators (SITE)

Organizations. Members: Individuals, teachers and others engaged in educating and training those in the insurance industry. *Objectives*: Furthering the education and training of insurance within the industry. *Founded*: 1953. *Headquarters*: Greenbrae, CA. (Formerly, the Insurance Company Education Directors' Society.)

Society of Professional Benefit Administrators (SPBA)

Organizations. Members: Independent third-party contract employee benefit plan administration firms. *Objectives*: Promotes public understanding and acceptance of contract administration. *Founded*: 1975. *Headquarters*: Chevy Chase, MD.

Society of Risk Management Consultants (SRMC)

Organizations. Members: Independent risk management and insurance consultants. *Objectives*: Promotes professional standards for risk managers and insurance consultants. *Founded*: 1984. *Headquarters*: New York, NY. Formed in 1984 by the merger of the Insurance Consultants Society and the Institute of Risk Management Consultants.

Society of State Filers (SSF)

Organizations. Members: Persons involved in required state filings and associated regulatory requirements, with emphasis on property-casualty insurance. Associate members include service organizations, consultants, attorneys, etc. *Objectives*: To educate members on requirements and methods

and provide advice to state regulators. *Headquarters*: Kansas City, MO.

soft market

Insurer Operations. A period during the insurance underwriting cycle when coverage is readily available and underwriters must actively compete for business. Generally, there are significant rate reductions, and higher limits of liability and new coverages are available.

compare: hard market, tight market; *see*: buyer's market, underwriting cycle

software coverage

Property.

see: data processing coverage

soil testing exclusion

Professional Liability. An exclusion in some architects' or engineers' professional liability policies for claims based on soil tests that assess the feasibility of building a proposed structure on a specific parcel of land.

sole proprietors, partners, officers, and others coverage endorsement

Workers' Compensation. A workers' compensation policy endorsement (NCCI form WC 00 03 10) that extends coverage to sole proprietors, partners, officers, or others who elect to be covered under the state's workers' compensation law. The persons making the coverage election must be specifically listed on the endorsement.

see: workers' compensation insurance

sole proprietorship insurance

Health/Life. Life and disability insurance designed for an owner of a small business. It provides benefits to family members adequate to continue operations of the business or arrange for its sale.

see: key employee insurance

solicitor

Agency. An individual employed or contracted by an agent to solicit, but not to conclude, contracts of insurance on behalf of the agent.

see: agent, broker, producer

solid waste

Regulation. Under the Resource Conservation and Recovery Act, any garbage, refuse, or sludge from a waste treatment plant, water supply treatment plant, or air pollution control facility, and other discarded material, including solid, liquid, semi-solid, or contained gaseous materials resulting from industrial, commercial, mining, agriculture or community activities.

see: Resource Conservation and Recovery Act

sonic boom

Property. The shock wave and noise resulting from

an aircraft or missile exceeding the speed of sound. Most property policies cover damage from this peril.

South-Eastern Underwriters Association

Regulation. A property insurance rating organization that brought a lawsuit leading to the 1944 U.S. Supreme Court decision that insurance is interstate commerce within the meaning of the Constitution and is therefore subject to federal regulation. As a result, Congress passed the McCarran-Ferguson Act, which preserves the regulatory authority of the states in the absence of specific preemptive congressional action.

see: McCarran-Ferguson Act, Paul v. Virginia

sovereign immunity

Liability. A governmental body's exemption from civil suits. In order to make a remedy available to injured persons while preserving the government's ability to freely make decisions in the public interest, the federal government and many states and municipalities have waived immunity from being sued in some circumstances.

see: Federal Tort Claims Act, public entity insurance

spacecraft insurance

Aviation. Insurance on rockets and satellites designed for voyages in outer space.

see: satellite and space vehicle insurance

special acceptance

Reinsurance. An agreement by a reinsurer to make an exception to a reinsurance contract, allowing a specific risk not ordinarily covered under the contract to be included.

see: reinsurance

special agent

Agency/Insurer Operations.

see: marketing representative

Life. An individual who has an exclusive agreement with an insurer to sell and service life insurance in a particular area.

synonym: sales representative

Property. An old term for a marketing or sales representative of property insurance.

see: state agent

special cargo policy

Ocean Marine. A policy used in the shipping of merchandise that is similar to a certificate of insurance, except that it is an entire insurance policy and not subject to the underlying terms of an open policy when title has been transferred to a third party.

see: cargo insurance

special circumstances

Agency. Representation by an insurance agent to a customer that he or she is a skilled specialist (i.e., CLU, CPCU, expert, consultant, advisor, or professional), creating a higher duty or standard of care than usual. When special circumstances exist, the agent has a duty to take affirmative actions, such as giving advice on insurance coverage, rather than merely to follow the customer's instructions.

see: agency, professional service

special computer coverage endorsement

Personal. An endorsement (ISO form HO 04 14) used with a homeowners policy that does not include personal property coverage on an open perils basis to cover computers and peripheral equipment on an open perils (all-risk) basis. Coverage does not include computer tapes and disks.

see: data processing coverage, homeowners policy—property coverage, open perils

special damage

Property.

see: consequential damage

special disability fund

Workers' Compensation.

see: second injury fund

special employer

Workers' Compensation. An employer who borrows an employee from another (the general employer), usually to assist in a specific job with the intent that when the job is completed, the employee will return to the first employer. The employee remains on the payroll of the general employer but works at the direction of the special employer.

see: borrowed employee, employee leasing, general employer

special event liability insurance

Liability. A form of entertainment insurance tailored for special events or holidays with large potential loss exposures because of large crowds. Coverage can be provided as premises liability, grandstand erection and use, defamation by a speaker or performer, product liability arising out of the sale of food or souvenirs, and medical expenses.

see: entertainment insurance

special form

Property. A property form that insures against all risks of direct physical loss that are not specified as exclusions or limitations. Any accidental loss is presumed covered unless the insurer shows that it was caused by an excluded peril.

see: all-risk insurance

special homeowners policy

Personal.

see: homeowners special form

special industry class

Automobile. A classification code that applies to commercial vehicles that is indicated in the ISO rate manual.

see: secondary classification

special loss settlement endorsement

Personal. An endorsement (ISO form HO 04 56) to the homeowners policy that changes the loss settlement provision for full replacement cost if at least 80% coverage is maintained to a lesser percentage (i.e. 50%, 60%, 70%). This is sometimes required by an insurer to avoid a moral hazard when the replacement cost far exceeds the current market value of the dwelling.

see: homeowners policy

special mortality table

Life. A mortality table developed for purchasers of annuities which reflects the fact that people who purchase annuities have a longer life expectancy than the population as a whole.

see: mortality table, select mortality table

special multi-peril program (SMP)

Liability/Property. A combination or package policy for commercial risks that, since 1986, has been replaced by the commercial package policy. The program included at least property and liability coverages, with optional coverages for crime and boiler and machinery.

see: commercial package policy, industrial property policy program, special personal property form

special package automobile policy

Automobile. An obsolete automobile policy form created in the 1960s that provided a single limit of liability for bodily injury and property damage and a corresponding limit for medical payments. Physical damage coverage could be included as a separate item.

see: personal auto policy

special personal property coverage endorsement

Personal. An endorsement (ISO form HO 00 15) that, when attached to the homeowners special form, provides all-risk coverage on personal property.

see: homeowners special form

special personal property form

Property. A form used in the special multi-peril program that provided all-risk coverage on business-use personal property. It has largely been replaced by the building and personal property coverage form. It was once the broadest coverage available for the personal property of a business.

see: building and personal property coverage

form, special multi-peril program

special release

Law. A release drafted to suit the particular circumstances or to provide less than a full release, such as where joint tortfeasors or minors are involved in a claim settlement.

see: joint tortfeasor release, release

special risk

Insurer Operations. A risk that, due to its unusual nature, high hazard of loss, or other special circumstance, may be exempted from applicable rate filing requirements.

see: insurable risk, specialty insurer, uninsurable risk

special risk insurance

Ocean Marine.

see: single risk cargo insurance

specialty insurer

Insurer Operations. An insurance company that covers a narrow spectrum of risks, often involving unusual, substandard or difficult-to-place risks.

see: market specialty insurer, product specialty insurer, selective specialty insurer, substandard risk

specific excess workers' compensation insurance

Workers' Compensation. Insurance coverage for organizations that self-insure their workers' compensation benefits. It indemnifies the insured for claims on a per-occurrence basis in excess of a specific retention ($50,000, $100,000, $250,000), subject to a maximum that can range from $1 million to statutory benefits. Coverage is based on the those provided by a standard worker's compensation policy.

compare: aggregate excess workers' compensation insurance

specific insurance

Property. A policy that covers a specific kind or unit of property, in contrast to a policy that covers all property at one or more locations on a blanket basis. Generally, a specific policy is considered primary coverage in the event of overlapping policies.

compare: blanket insurance; *see*: primary insurance

specific limit

Insurer Operations. The maximum amount that an insurer will pay per item or per occurrence for a loss associated with a particular incident, item or class of property within a single insurance policy.

see: limit of liability

specific performance

Law. A remedy sought by a plaintiff to compel the

defendant to comply with the conditions of a contract existing between them, rather than to accept damages for a breach of the contract.

compare: damages; *see*: contract

specific rate

Property. A published rate (as opposed to a tariff rate) that applies to an individual location or building.

compare: average blanket rate, class rating, tariff rate; *see*: rate

specific reinsurance

Reinsurance.

see: facultative reinsurance

specifically described autos

Automobile. A classification of covered vehicles under the business auto coverage form, garage coverage form, or truckers' coverage form.

see: business auto coverage form, garage coverage form, truckers' coverage form

specified causes of loss

Automobile. An endorsement (ISO form CA 99 14) to the business auto, garage or truckers' policy to provide physical damage coverage for the specific perils of fire, lightning, explosion, vandalism, theft, windstorm, flood, or the sinking, burning, collision, or derailment of any conveyance transporting the covered vehicle.

compare: comprehensive coverage, fire coverage, fire and theft coverage, fire theft and windstorm coverage; *see*: business auto coverage form, garage coverage form, truckers' coverage form

Personal. A limited form of physical damage coverage under a personal auto policy for the same perils as in the case of a commercial auto policy.

compare: collision coverage, comprehensive coverage, limited specified perils

specified disease insurance

Health/Life. Health insurance coverage that is limited to specific diseases named in the policy. These policies usually provide high limits of coverage for illnesses that typically require lengthy, expensive treatment.

synonym: dread disease insurance; *see*: acquired immune deficiency syndrome, cancer insurance, extra percentage tables, living benefits, viatical settlement

specified perils

Property.

see: named perils

specimen policy

Insurer Operations. A sample policy used to discuss its provisions with a prospective insured.

see: comparison statement

speculative risk

Risk Management. A risk for which it is uncertain as to whether the final outcome will be a gain or loss. Gambling is a speculative risk. Generally, speculative risks cannot be insured.

compare: pure risk; *see*: gambling

Spencer Educational Foundation

Organizations. An educational foundation created by the Risk and Insurance Management Society in 1979 to assist outstanding students in risk management. Scholarships for undergraduate and graduate students are funded up to $7,500 by corporate and individual donors.

see: Risk and Insurance Management Society, Inc.

spendthrift trust clause

Life. A life insurance policy provision that prevents a beneficiary from assigning, encumbering or creating a lien against the proceeds. Creditors of the beneficiary may not claim any part of the proceeds before the beneficiary is paid.

see: beneficiary

sphygmomanometer

Health. An apparatus used to measure arterial pulse.

see: blood pressure

Spill Prevention Control and Countermeasure Plan

Regulation. An oil and hazardous wastes spill prevention plan required by the Federal Water Pollution Control Act for on-shore facilities to prevent spills from reaching navigable waters. An organization that fails to prepare and maintain such a plan is subject to a penalty of $5,000 per day.

see: Federal Water Pollution Control Act

split deductible

Insurer Operations. A combination of two or more deductibles within a policy, with each applying to a different form of coverage. *Example*: A property policy with a $5,000 deductible on fire losses, $100,000 deductible on flood losses, and $250,000 deductible on earthquake losses.

see: deductible

split dollar insurance

Health. Disability income insurance jointly paid for by an employer and an employee. The employer pays for the basic or primary level of coverage, and

415

the employee pays for an extended period of coverage.

see: disability income insurance

Life. Life insurance jointly paid for by an employer and employee or by a parent and a child. The ownership right and death proceeds of the policy may also be divided between the parties paying the premium.

see: contributory group insurance

split funding

Employee Benefits. A pension plan funding arrangement using both insured (or allocated) and uninsured (unallocated) assets. The allocated portion (insurance and annuity contracts) guarantees income, while the unallocated portion provides the pension fund trustee with investment flexibility in search of higher yields.

see: pension trust fund

split life insurance

Life. A combination of annuity and term insurance, where the term insurance is based on a factor of the installment annuity premium paid.

compare: double protection life insurance

split limits

Automobile/Liability. Separately stated policy limits for different coverages. The limits may be stated per person, per occurrence, or per policy period, or may be split between bodily injury and property damage. *Example*: An auto liability policy with limits of $200,000/$500,000/$100,000 has a maximum of $200,000 bodily injury coverage for each person, $500,000 for bodily injury per accident, and $100,000 for property damage liability per accident.

compare: combined single limit

spoilage coverage endorsement

Property. A commercial property coverage endorsement (ISO form CP 04 40) that covers perishable stock for damage resulting from a mechanical breakdown, a power outage, or a refrigerant contamination.

compare: consequential damage endorsement; *see*: perishable stock, refrigeration maintenance agreement

spoliation

Insurer Operations. Alterations made to an insurance policy by a nonparty to the contract. Such alterations do not affect the contract if the original terms can be ascertained with certainty.

see: alteration

sponsor corporation coverage

Professional Liability. A coverage that can be included in a directors' and officers' liability policy for directors and officers of the corporation (sponsor) when serving with another corporation at the request or on behalf of the sponsor corporation.

see: directors' and officers' liability insurance

spontaneous combustion

Loss Control. The self-ignition of combustible material through chemical action (e.g., oxidation) of its constituents.

sporting event abandonment insurance

Liability. A form of entertainment insurance that provides coverage to anyone with a financial interest in a sports event that is canceled or postponed due to catastrophic perils, such as an air or common carrier crash or epidemic disease that injures key participants. Coverage can be written for a single game or an entire season, and the amount of recovery is based on estimated gate, radio and television receipts.

synonym: sporting event cancellation insurance; *see*: entertainment insurance

spouse's benefit

Employee Benefits. Benefits payable to the spouse of a worker after retirement or death, such as benefits under the Federal Retirement Equity Act, the Social Security Act, or through a special provision by an employer.

see: blackout period, dependent

spray powers

Financial Planning.

see: sprinkling powers

spread

Financial Planning. The difference between the bid price and offering price of a security.

spread loss plan

Risk Management. A form of banking plan involving a long-term contract of insurance (3 to 10 years), under which an annual premium is paid based on projected losses and the insurer's expense loading. The final premium is based on a retrospective rating formula, which, if the premium and investment income exceeds the losses and loading over the life of the plan, is returned to the policyholder. In the event losses exceed funds accumulated in this plan, the insurer loans the insured funds to pay losses up to the policy limit and increases the annual premium over the remainder of the plan to repay the funds loaned.

synonym: funded spread loss plan; *see*: banking plan, chronological stabilization plan, finite risk insurance

spread loss reinsurance

Reinsurance.

see: Carpenter Plan

spread of risk

Risk Management. A principle of insurance that insurers need to accept homogeneous exposure units spread over a wide geographic area, with the knowledge that only a given number of risks will result in claims or losses. This dispersion of exposure units allows insurers to project expected losses from the entire body of insureds, lessens the potential for catastrophic losses that could occur to exposure units close to each another, and allows for the development of rates.

see: homogeneity, law of large numbers, reduction of risk

spreadsheet

Risk Management. A worksheet of entries (usually numerical values) arranged in rows and columns to show the relationship between two variables. Spreadsheets are widely used to display business information, and risk managers use them to track exposure and claim information in a form that can be easily updated.

sprinkler leakage coverage

Property. Coverage of damage to a building or contents caused by leakage or discharge from an automatic sprinkler system, or caused by the fall or collapse of tanks that are part of the system. Coverage is included under the Insurance Services Office commercial property basic, broad, and special coverage forms. Many property forms exclude coverage if sprinkler leakage is caused by an earthquake or volcanic action.

compare: water damage clause; *see*: automatic sprinkler system, discharge of any substance, earthquake sprinkler leakage coverage, scuppers

sprinkler leakage liability insurance

Liability. A liability coverage that protects the insured should a sprinkler leakage loss occur on rented premises or on premises loaned to the insured. Coverage applies when an automatic sprinkler system discharges or leaks water or other substances as the result of the insured's negligence.

compare: water damage liability; *see*: automatic sprinkler system

sprinkling powers

Financial Planning. A trust that allows the trustee discretion over the distribution of the trust income. The trust income may be distributed by the trustee to the surviving spouse or children according to their needs.

synonym: spray powers; *see*: trust

squat

Automobile. An insurance fraud term for a type of contrived collision. A driver who has stopped at an intersection begins to move, then hits the brakes, causing the car behind to rear-end the first. The driver then files a medical claim against the other's insurance company. Drivers who strike other vehicles from the rear are usually presumed to be at fault.

compare: swoop-and-squat

stabilization reinsurance

Reinsurance. Reinsurance designed to assist in smoothing an insurer's overall operating results from year to year, or to stabilize year-end results.

stabilization/solidification bioremediation

Loss Control. A form of bioremediation where materials are added to the affected soil to reduce a contaminant's toxicity, solubility and mobility.

see: bioremediation

stacking of limits

Liability. The application of two or more policies or coverages to the same loss or occurrence, resulting in higher combined limits of liability. A typical situation involves a claimant injured as a passenger in a collision with an uninsured vehicle. If several injured persons sustain losses in the same accident exceeding the statutory minimum uninsured motorist coverage, either by statute or common law a claimant may be permitted to combine ("stack") the uninsured motorist coverages of both the passenger-claimant's own auto policy and the insured driver's policy. Stacking is also an issue in pollution and product liability claims for damage that has occurred over many years where it is impossible to determine which policy applies to a specific claim.

synonym: pyramiding; *compare*: layering; *see*: dual coverage, joint and several liability, other insurance provision, overinsurance

staff adjuster

Insurer Operations. An individual employed by an insurance company to settle claims with or for policyholders of the company.

see: claims adjuster

staff-model health maintenance organization

Health.

see: closed panel health maintenance organization

staff underwriter

Insurer Operations. An underwriter who assists in the formulation of an insurance company's overall underwriting policy and in the implementation of that policy.

compare: line underwriter; *see*: underwriter

stager

Automobile. An insurance fraud term for a driver who participates in a staged accident intended to result in a fraudulent claim.

stamp and coin dealers' insurance

Inland Marine. A special inland marine coverage designed for stamp and coin dealers, written on an all-risk basis. Coverage includes the time that the insured items are in transit.

see: inland marine insurance

stamp collections coverage

Personal. One of the nine classes of property that can be covered under a personal articles floater. It includes postage stamps (including due, envelope, official revenue, match, and medicine stamps); covers; locals; reprints; essays; proofs; and other philatelic property. Coverage is also provided for books, pages, and mountings, whether or not owned by the insured. Special exclusions relating to stamps are fading, creasing, denting, scratching, tearing or thinning; transfer of colors, inherent defect, dampness, extremes of temperature, or depreciation; being handled or worked on; and the disappearance of individual stamps.

see: personal articles floater, stamp and coin dealers insurance

stamping office

Insurer Operations.
see: audit bureau

standard deviation

Risk Management. An arithmetic mean of the differences between each outcome and the average of all outcomes within a set. It is utilized by actuaries to indicate the degree of dispersion that exists between a set of outcomes.

synonym: standard variation; *see:* frequency distribution

standard exceptions

Workers' Compensation. Workers' compensation classifications (e.g., clerical office, outside sales) that are separately rated regardless of the governing rating classification.

see: governing classification

standard fire policy ·

Property.
see: New York standard fire policy, standard property policy

standard limit

Liability.
see: basic limits

standard of proof

Law.
see: burden of proof

standard policy

Insurer Operations. An insurance contract used by a group of insurers that is approved by state insurance regulators or prescribed by law.

see: standard provisions

standard premium

Liability. A factor used in a retrospectively rated casualty program. It is the premium developed for the risk at standard rates (i.e., the premium that would apply if no retrospective plan were to be used).

Workers' Compensation. A factor used in a retrospectively rated workers' compensation program. The standard premium is generally derived by multiplying the workers' compensation rates by the applicable payroll amounts, to which the insured's experience modification factor is then applied.

see: basic premium, manual premium, modified premium, retrospective rating plan

standard property policy (SPP)

Property. A property policy (ISO form CP 00 99) that has in effect replaced the New York standard fire policy as the basic property insurance form. However, because of its very limited named-perils coverage, it is generally used only on substandard risks and is not designed to be used with the Insurance Services Office commercial package program.

see: commercial package policy, fire insurance, named perils, New York standard fire policy, substandard risk

standard provisions

Insurer Operations/Regulation. Provisions of an insurance policy that are in common use by most insurers or required by legislation.

see: minimum coverage clause, policy condition laws, reinstatement, standard policy

standard risk

Insurer Operations. A risk that is considered by the underwriter as a basis by which to judge other risks. Material deviations from the standard risk result in higher or lower rates based on the degree of deviation, and a risk that deviates too far may be rejected.

synonym: average risk; *compare:* preferred risk, substandard risk

standard variation

Risk Management.
see: standard deviation

standing timber insurance

Property. Coverage on living trees that are of a commercially harvestable quality (having a minimum diameter, not diseased, etc.) or on all living trees in an area of reforestation. The insured value is determined by the current price for standing timber. Coverage is limited to the perils of fire and lightning. Since most fires occur in spring and summer months, the policy premium is considered fully earned if coverage is provided at any time during those seasons. It is used by investors and timber owners seeking financing to secure their interests and the interests of lenders.

see: Christmas tree lot insurance

standpipe system

Loss Control. A series of pipes running through a building to supply water to fire hoses, allowing firefighters to operate in a large or high-rise building without having to pull in hoses. One type is directly connected to a water supply (wet system); another requires connecting a fire hose to a receptor outside the building to provide water (dry system).

see: automatic sprinkler system, dry pipe automatic sprinkler system, wet pipe automatic sprinkler system

stare decisis

Law. A legal principle that courts generally follow the decisions of former cases. (Latin for "stand by what is decided.")

see: common law

state agent

Agency. An obsolete term either for an agent with an exclusive agreement to represent an insurer in a specific state, or for a senior special agent.

see: agent, special agent

state bonding fund

Surety. A fund maintained by a state for the bonding of public employees.

see: public official bond

state disability plan

Health.

see: statutory disability income insurance

State Emergency Response Commission

Regulation. A commission required in each state by the Superfund Amendments and Reauthorization Act, Title III. The commission designates the emergency planning districts, appoints local emergency planning committees, and supervises and coordinates their activities.

see: Emergency Planning and Community Right-to-Know Act, Superfund Amendments and Reauthorization Act

state exception pages

Insurer Operations. Rating manual pages that contain special rating provisions or exceptions to the general rules for policies issued in a particular state or territory.

see: manual rates, rate manual

state fund

Insurer Operations/Workers' Compensation. A state government-operated insurance facility used to insure workers' compensation benefits. Some states have monopolistic funds that require employers to purchase coverage from them, while other state funds compete with private insurers.

see: competitive state fund, monopolistic state fund, workers' compensation law

state-of-the-art defense

Law/Liability. A product liability defense that a manufacturer should not be liable for harm caused by a product that met the best prevailing standards of design, performance and safety at the time it was manufactured (i.e., the product represented the state of the art).

see: defective product, product liability insurance

state rate pages

Insurer Operations. Rating manual pages containing base rates for the coverages available in a particular state or territory.

see: manual rates, rate manual

state territorial pages

Insurer Operations. Rating manual pages that indicate codes for each rating territory (city, county, zip code) in a state. These pages are used to locate base rates.

see: manual rates, rate manual

stated amount

Automobile. A method of writing automobile physical damage coverage where the limit that can be recovered in the event of a total loss cannot exceed the amount of insurance specified for the vehicle. It is used for older vehicles whose value after a loss might be difficult to establish.

compare: actual cash value; *see*: valued clause, valued coverage

Property. An amount of insurance scheduled in a property policy that is not subject to any coinsurance requirement in the event of a loss. The amount scheduled is the maximum amount of insurance available in the event of loss.

see: agreed value

statement basis premium payment

Agency. A method of transmitting insurance premiums by an agent to an insurer. The insurer is responsible for preparing a periodic statement of the premiums due (minus commission) from the agent, who is then responsible for transmitting that amount to the insurer.

compare: account current, item basis premium payment; *see*: agency bill, premium

statement blank

Regulation.

see: annual statement

statement of changes in financial position

Accounting. A section of the financial statement that summarizes the cash flow or working capital of an organization that brings about changes in the assets, liabilities, and equity of the owners in the period between two consecutive balance sheets. It reveals certain aspects of an organization's financing and investment activities, whether or not these affected the balance sheet or other working capital.

see: financial statement

statement of loss

Insurer Operations.

see: proof of loss

statement of opinion

Accounting. The opinion of a certified public accountant as to the financial condition of an organization as expressed by its financial statement. The opinion is in one of three forms: unqualified (or "clean"), which means no exceptions were found; qualified, which means that the financial statement fairly represents the organization's condition except for some important uncertainties that cannot be determined at this time; or adverse, which means the statement is unacceptable to the accountant.

see: financial statement, Statutory Accounting Principles

statement of policy information

Life. An annual statement or document issued for universal life insurance policies that indicates all transactions (premiums, death benefits, interest credited, etc.) that occurred during the year.

see: universal life insurance

statement of values

Property. A property insurance form used when coverage is written on a blanket basis or when the insured has selected the agreed value optional coverage. It lists all insured locations and the buildings, personal property, and business income values for each covered item at a location. The form is used to develop a blanket rate and must be signed by the insured if coverage is on an agreed value basis.

see: agreed value, option clause, blanket rate

statewide average weekly wage (SAWW)

Workers' Compensation. A periodically prepared report, indicating the average state-wide weekly wages paid over a specific period of time. This report is used to determine the adequacy of workers' compensation benefit levels.

see: average weekly benefits

static electricity

Loss Control.

see: electrostatic discharge

static risk

Risk Management. A risk that arises from the normal course of business activities and does not involve changes in the environment or technology. Static risk can only result in a loss.

compare: dynamic risk; *see*: risk

statistical agent

General. A person or organization that prepares statistical studies used in rate making.

see: rating bureau

statistics

Risk Management. A branch of mathematics dealing with the collection, analysis, interpretation and presentation of masses of numerical data; a collection of quantitative data. A leading branch of statistics is actuarial science, which deals with insurance loss probabilities.

see: actuarial science

statute

Law. A law enacted by Congress or by a state legislature.

see: ordinance

statute of frauds

Law. A law that requires certain types of contracts to be written in order to be enforced. Contracts involving most interests in real estate, agreements that are not to be or cannot be performed within one year, and the sale of goods exceeding a certain value (e.g., $500) are included.

see: contract, oral contract

statute of limitations

Law. A law limiting the time within which a claim may be asserted in court. Expiration of the time period negates the plaintiff's right of action.

see: laches

Statutory Accounting Principles (SAP)

Accounting. Statutory requirements based on criteria established by the National Association of Insurance Commissioners in regard to the preparation of an insurer's financial statements required to be filed with a state insurance department. Compared to Generally Accepted Accounting Principles, they are more regulatory by nature and give a more conservative depiction of an insurer's financial condition.

compare: Generally Accepted Accounting Principles; *see*: accounting, Financial Accounting Standards Board, financial statement

statutory combined ratio
Insurer Operations.
see: combined ratio

statutory conditions
Regulation.
see: policy condition laws

statutory disability income insurance
Health. Compulsory disability income coverage for injuries or illnesses not arising out of employment which must be provided by employers in a few states (e.g., California, Hawaii, New Jersey, Puerto Rico). This coverage fills the gap between workers' compensation (payable only if a disability arises out of employment) and unemployment compensation (payable only if a person is not disabled and is seeking work).
synonym: state disability plan; *see*: disability benefit law, unemployment compensation disability insurance

statutory earnings or losses
Regulation. An insurer's earnings or losses as indicated on the National Association of Insurance Commissioners convention blank.
see: annual statement

statutory reserve
Regulation. A reserve maintained by an insurer in order to comply with requirements for such reserves mandated by state law. These reserves are required to guarantee that an insurer can pay policyholder claims.
see: reserve

statutory underwriting profit (or loss)
Insurer Operations. Premiums earned minus losses and expenses.
see: underwriting profit (or loss)

statutory voting
Financial Planning. The predominant method of shareholder voting, under which shareholders are permitted to cast all their votes either for or against each candidate for the board of directors. *Example*: With three board members to be elected, a shareholder with 100 shares may cast 100 votes either for or against each director. Under the less common *cumulative voting* rule, the shareholder would be permitted to cast 300 votes for one director, 150 votes for each of two directors, or 100 votes for each of the three.
compare: cumulative voting; *see*: common stock, dissenting shareholder, proxy

step-rate premium
Health/Life. A life or health insurance policy that has built-in rate increases that are based on reaching certain ages or numbers of years in force.

stevedore
Ocean Marine/Workers' Compensation. An individual or firm who works at or is responsible for loading or unloading a ship in port.
see: stevedores' liability insurance

stevedores' liability insurance
Liability. Liability coverage that protects a stevedore against loss or damage to vessels or cargo arising out of loading or unloading operations.
see: stevedore

stipulated premium plan insurance
Life.
see: industrial life insurance

stipulation
Law. 1. A voluntary agreement to any fact or issue raised by parties to a lawsuit or a contract.
2. A requirement or essential condition in a contract, or a demand for an essential condition.
see: contract

stock
Financial Planning. A certificate of ownership in a corporation or any number of equity (ownership) shares in a corporation; a contract between the issuing corporation and shareholders conferring an equity interest in the corporation, the right to participate in profits, and if the corporation is dissolved, a claim to corporate assets.
see: common stock, dividend, equity (*Financial Planning*), preferred stock
Property. Merchandise held in storage or for sale, including supplies used in packing or shipping and raw materials used in making finished goods; goods on hand in inventory.
synonym: inventory; *see*: finished stock

stock dividend
Financial Planning. The issuance of additional common shares of stock on a pro rata basis to common stockholders.
see: dividend (*Financial Planning*), stock split

stock insurance company
Insurer Operations. An insurance company formed as a corporation that is owned and controlled by stockholders, usually for profit. Initial capital is contributed by stockholders, to whom profits are distributed as dividends. Policies are issued at a fixed cost, and should losses exceed premiums received, the stockholders' investment and equity must make up the difference.
synonym: capital stock insurance company; *compare*: mutual insurance company

stock purchase plan

Employee Benefits. An employee benefit plan allowing workers to buy shares of stock in the corporation. The firm contributes a specified percentage of employee contributions.

compare: deferred stock grant; *see*: employee benefit plan

stock split

Financial Planning. An increase in the number of a corporation's outstanding shares of a particular class of stock by substituting a number of shares for each one, resulting in a proportionately lower market value per share. The most common reason for doing this is to remove high share price as a barrier to potential investors.

compare: reverse stock split; *see*: stock dividend

stock throughput policy

Inland Marine/Ocean Marine. A personal property insurance form developed in the London market covering the personal property of manufacturers, processors, importers/exporters or assemblers anywhere in the world on an all-risk basis. Coverage can include machinery, electronic data processing, equipment, furniture and fixtures, and raw materials. The policy is a combination of ocean cargo, inland marine, and personal property coverages. The premium is usually based on a rate applied to the insured's annual sales.

stockbrokers' errors and omissions insurance

Professional Liability. A form of professional liability insurance for investment banking firms for stockbrokers that provides coverage on a claims-made basis for losses arising from negligent acts, errors or omissions in purchasing or selling securities for the accounts of customers.

see: errors and omissions insurance

stockholder

Financial Planning.

see: shareholder

stop loss

Insurer Operations. Any provision in a policy limiting the maximum claim amount payable. It may take the form of a maximum aggregate limit payable or a maximum limit payable for any one event.

see: limit of liability, loss limitation

stop loss reinsurance

Reinsurance.

see: aggregate excess of loss reinsurance

stopgap coverage

Workers' Compensation. Coverage that can be provided by an endorsement to a workers' compensation or to a general liability policy. It provides a multistate employer with employers' liability insurance. This coverage is needed for an employer with employees in a state where workers' compensation coverage is only available through a monopolistic state fund that does not provide employers' liability coverage.

see: monopolistic state fund

stopping distance

Automobile/Loss Control. The distance a motor vehicle travels from where the driver perceives a need to stop to the actual stopping point.

compare: stopping time; *see*: braking distance, reaction distance

stopping time

Automobile/Loss Control. The time required for a vehicle to be brought to a complete stop after the driver perceives a hazard that requires stopping. It is the sum of the driver's reaction time and the car's braking time.

compare: stopping distance; *see*: braking time, reaction time

storekeepers' broad form

Crime. A crime coverage plan developed under the 1986 ISO crime program which is designed for small storekeepers, providing all-risk coverage on money and securities, depositor's forgery, limited employee dishonesty coverage, plus nine specific crime coverages on the same basis as a storekeeper's burglary and robbery policy.

synonym: crime plan 3; *see*: crime coverages, storekeepers' burglary and robbery coverage

storekeepers' burglary and robbery coverage

Crime. A crime coverage plan that requires coverage forms D and E (premises burglary and robbery and safe burglary forms) and combines seven different burglary and robbery coverages for storekeepers in a single form. The selected limit of liability applies separately to each of the coverages, which include safe burglary, damage caused by robbery and burglary, robbery of a guard, burglary of merchandise, robbery inside and outside the insured premises, kidnapping to force the opening of a premises, and theft of money and securities from a messenger.

synonym: crime plan 4; *see*: crime coverages, premises burglary coverage form, robbery and safe burglary form, storekeepers' broad form

straight deductible

Insurer Operations. A deductible expressed as a specific dollar amount.

see: deductible

straight life policy
Life.
see: ordinary life insurance

straight line depreciation
Accounting. Depreciating a capital asset by the same amount each year over the asset's useful life. The cost (or other valuation basis) minus salvage value is divided by the number of years the asset is expected to remain useful and efficient.
compare: accelerated depreciation; *see*: depreciation, capital asset

stranded
Ocean Marine. A ship that has run aground.

strict liability
Law. Liability for injury to others without regard to fault or negligence, arising from inherently dangerous activities (which may have economic or social value). It also may apply to defective or unreasonably dangerous products, provided the product reaches or affects the injured person without having been altered by another. Some states also impose strict liability for some violations of criminal law or public policy. *Examples*: Strict liability may attach to harm done by a person's pet poisonous snake or by a demolition contractor's use of explosives.
synonym: absolute liability; *see*: negligence

strike
General. A concerted work stoppage or slowdown by a group of employees for the purpose of forcing the employer to accede to a demand regarding wages, working conditions, employee benefits, or the collective bargaining process.
see: collective bargaining, employee benefit plan, picketing, strike insurance

strike insurance
Property. Insurance designed to protect employers from lost income caused by labor disruptions.
compare: manufacturer's penalty insurance; *see*: strikes riots and civil commotions exclusion

strike-slip fault
Loss Control. A geological fault where each side slips past the other without significant vertical motion. This is the most predominant type of fault in the United States. It is one of three types of fault, along with blind thrust and thrust faults.
compare: blind thrust fault, thrust fault; *see*: earthquake

strike suit
Law/Professional Liability. A shareholder derivative suit filed against corporate directors and executives soon after a fall in the firm's stock value. These suits usually involve high-technology firms and are filed in the form of a class action by law firms that closely monitor stock price changes. Often, the allegation is that the officers and directors made overly optimistic forward-looking statements concerning the firm's income or operations which were relied upon by investors.
see: class action, derivative suit, forward-looking statement, security for expenses

strikes, riots and civil commotions exclusion (SR&CC)
Ocean Marine. A marine policy clause that excludes coverage for losses caused by acts of strikers, locked-out workers or persons taking part in labor disputes, riots or civil commotions, or for losses that are directly caused by persons acting maliciously. This exclusion may be deleted for an additional premium.
see: marine insurance

stripped building cancellation provision
Property. A form of vacant property exclusion found in some property insurance policies that allows the insurer to cancel coverage with prior written notice (usually of five days) if the building's salvageable fixtures have been or are being removed and are not being replaced.
see: vacancy permit, vacant

structure rented to others—residence premises endorsement
Personal. An endorsement (ISO form HO 04 40) to the homeowners policy that covers scheduled residential structures on the insured's premises that are rented to others. It modifies the liability exclusions to extend liability coverage to the rented residence.
see: homeowners policy

structured settlement
Insurer Operations. A claim settlement involving periodic payments for a specific number of years or for life in cases where special medical care must be provided. Often such payments are funded by an annuity, and because the time value of money is contemplated in the settlement, a structured settlement is usually less costly to an insurer or self-insurer than a lump sum settlement.
synonym: periodic payment; *see*: Internal Revenue Code § 461(h), medical expense reversionary trust, qualified assignment, settlement

student accident insurance
Health. A form of group accident insurance designed for students. Coverage is provided on a blanket basis for accident medical reimbursement, accidental loss of life, and accidental dismemberment or loss of sight. Two main types of plans are offered: one provides coverage only during the school year while on the school premises or while

attending a school sponsored event; the other provides 24-hour coverage. Often, coverage for students while playing on athletic teams is excluded but may be added for an additional premium or through a separate team sports accident policy.

see: accident insurance, team sports accident insurance

sub-agent

Agency. An agent who reports to another agent or to a general or managing general agent, and not directly to an insurer.

see: agent, managing general agent, solicitor

sub-broker

Reinsurance. A reinsurance broker (intermediary) from whom another reinsurance broker is able to obtain reinsurance business.

see: intermediary

sub-contractor

General. An independent contractor who does not work directly for the property owner, but works for or through a general contractor. Typically, a general contractor uses several specialty sub-contractors on a project.

compare: general contractor; *see*: independent contractor

subacute health care facility
Health.

see: transitional care facility

Subchapter S

Financial Planning. A tax option under the Internal Revenue Code that permits certain closely held corporations to be taxed in a manner similar to that applicable to partnerships. Under Subchapter S, corporate income is taxable directly to shareholders whether or not it is actually distributed to them. Subchapter S was designed to eliminate the double taxation problem; however, the provisions of Subchapter S are complex and create a number of unique problems that are not present in the tax treatment of partnerships.

see: close corporation, partnership

subject premium

Reinsurance. The premium of a ceding insurer to which a rate is applied, to develop the premium due to a reinsurer for reinsurance coverage.

synonym: base premium, premium base, underlying premium; *see*: premium

sublease

General. A lease by a tenant or lessee of part or all of a leased premises. The tenant or lessee retains some rights or interests under such an arrangement.

see: tenant's legal liability

sublimit

Insurer Operations. A smaller limit of coverage for a specified type of loss while a general limit applies to all covered losses.

see: limit of liability

sublimits
Health.

see: inside limits

submitted business

Insurer Operations. An insurance application that is in the insurer's review and approval process.

see: acceptance, rejection

subrogation

Insurer Operations. The right of a person to assume a legal claim of another; the right of a person who has paid a liability or obligation of another to be indemnified by that person; an insurer's substitution in place of the insured in regard to a claim against a third party for indemnification of a loss paid by the insurer.

see: recoverables, subrogation release, subrogation waiver, subrogee, subrogor

Surety. The right of a surety to seek indemnification for a bond loss from the principal or any other party liable for the loss. It is also called *right of exoneration*.

see: right of exoneration

subrogation release

Insurer Operations. A document executed by an insured upon receiving a claim payment that assigns the insured's right of recovery against any other responsible party for the loss to the insurer.

see: release, subrogation

subrogation waiver

Property/Liability. The named insured's intentional relinquishing of any right to recover damages from another party who may be responsible. Commercial insurance policies recognize a written subrogation waiver issued prior to a loss.

see: subrogation, waiver of subrogation rights clause

subrogee

Insurer Operations. A person who assumes the rights or claims of another (the subrogor) against a third party; an insurer who takes its insured's right to recover from a third party.

see: subrogation

subrogor

Insurer Operations. A person who transfers his or her rights or claims agains a third party to another (the subrogee); an insured who, usually in accepting a benefit payment, assigns to the insurer the insured's right to recover from a third party.

see: subrogation

subscribers agreement

Regulation. Basic documents organizing reciprocal, and occasionally, assessment mutual insurers.

subscription policy

Insurer Operations. Insurance on a risk using a single policy form to which two or more insurers subscribe for a share of the coverage. Their participation can be expressed either as a percentage of the coverage or a specified amount.

see: participate

subsequent injury fund

Workers' Compensation.

see: second injury fund

subsidence

Property. Sinking or settling of land caused by heavy rains or man-made caverns. Subsidence does not include earth movement caused by an earthquake.

see: earthquake, sinkhole coverage, subsidence coverage

Liability. An excluded coverage in most liability policies.

subsidence coverage

Liability. Coverage that can be endorsed to a general liability policy or purchased as a separate policy by a developer or contractor. It provides coverage for the unexpected subsidence of land, causing damage to the homes or buildings on it.

compare: sinkhole coverage

subsidiary

Law. A corporation that is legally separate from, but at least most of whose stock is owned by, another corporation (the parent).

see: corporation

subsidiary company

Insurer Operations. A company wholly owned by another company.

compare: parent company, holding company; *see*: affiliated insurers, pup company

substance abuse

Health. The excessive use of alcohol or drugs, especially involving psychological or physical dependency and detrimental health effects.

synonym: drug addiction; *see*: alcoholism

substandard life expectancy

Life. Life expectancy of an individual that is materially less than indicated on a standard mortality table.

synonym: age "rate up;" *see*: rated policy, substandard risk

substandard risk

Insurer Operations. A risk that is considered by the underwriter as not meeting normal underwriting standards. While many insurers avoid such risks, some specialize in them. Such a risk may be written at a surcharged rate. *Example*: An applicant for life insurance has a family history of heart disease and likes to go hang gliding.

synonym: impaired risk; *compare*: preexisting condition, standard risk; *see*: accommodation line, classified insurance, hobbies or avocations, occupational hazard, qualified impairment insurance, rated policy, substandard life expectancy, uninsurable risk

success ratio

Insurer Operations. A ratio used by an insurer to evaluate underwriting competitiveness. *Formula*: number of new policies written ÷ number of submissions quoted (for a specified period of time). An unfavorable percentage indicates such things as noncompetitive pricing or overly restrictive coverage. On the other hand, a high success ratio may indicate inadequate pricing or broader coverage than is being provided by other insurers.

compare: retention ratio

successor life rider

Life. A guaranteed insurability option designed to enhance traditional survivor life insurance policies. When one of the individuals covered under the policy dies, the survivor can increase his or her original face amount by a predetermined amount without evidence of insurability.

see: guaranteed insurability, survivor life insurance

sue and labor clause

Ocean Marine. An ocean marine policy provision that covers expenses reasonably incurred by the policyholder or its agents to protect insured property from further harm and to assist in recovering the damaged property to minimize the loss.

suicide

Life.

see: self-inflicted injury

summons

Law. A legal document notifying the defendant of a complaint and requiring him to appear in court and answer the complaint.

see: answer, complaint, summons and complaint

summons and complaint

Law. A summons that has been combined with the plaintiff's initial pleading (complaint) and requires an answer from the defendant.

see: answer, complaint, pleading, summons

super endowment policy
Life.
see: retirement income endowment policy

Superfund Act
Regulation.
see: Comprehensive Environmental Response Compensation and Liability Act

Superfund Amendments and Reauthorization Act (SARA)
Regulation. Federal legislation of 1986 that expanded the Comprehensive Environmental Response, Compensation and Liability Act. Among its provisions, it places an increased emphasis on the evaluation and remediation of the impact of hazardous waste on plant and animal habitat. It includes the Emergency Planning and Community Right-to-Know Act.
see: Comprehensive Environmental Response Compensation and Liability Act, Emergency Planning and Community Right-to-Know Act, Environmental Protection Agency, State Emergency Response Commission

superintendent of insurance
Regulation.
see: insurance commissioner

superseded suretyship rider
Surety. An endorsement or a provision in a fidelity bond that supersedes one that has been canceled, providing that the new bond covers a loss that occurred while the old bond was in force and that would have been covered under that bond had it been discovered within the discovery period. Coverage is limited to the amount provided by the previous bond.
see: fidelity bond

supplemental extended reporting period
Liability. A provision in many claims-made liability policies allowing an insured to purchase an additional time (12 months to unlimited) during which claims occurring may be reported. The Insurance Services Office commercial liability claims-made form provides an unlimited time in which to report claims.
see: basic extended reporting period, claims-made form, commercial general liability policy

supplemental major medical insurance
Health. Medical insurance providing coverage for expenses not covered by a basic medical plan. It usually has no deductible or copayment.
see: copayment, deductible, major medical insurance

Supplemental Security Income (SSI)
Employee Benefits. A program of the Social Security Administration that provides monthly payments from general U.S. Treasury funds to people with limited incomes and assets. The program is designed to assist citizens over 65 years of age and people of any age who are blind or disabled.
see: Social Security

supplementary contract
Life. An agreement between a life insurance company and a policyholder or beneficiary by which the insurer retains the cash sum payable under the policy and makes payments in accordance with the settlement option chosen.
see: settlement options

supplementary payment
Liability. A benefit payment under a liability policy in addition to the basic coverages provided by the policy. The cost of bail bonds or prejudgment interest are examples of supplementary payments.
see: commercial general liability policy, prejudgment interest

surety
Surety. The individual or entity that guarantees the legal liability for the debt, default, or failure to perform a duty (such as an appearance in court) of a principal.
compare: obligee, principal; *see*: guarantor, obligor, surety bond

Surety Association of America (SAA)
Organizations. Members: Insurers writing fidelity, surety and forgery bonds. *Objectives*: Classifying risks, rates, minimum premiums and rating plans. Preparing forms, provisions, terms and riders. Making filings with regulatory authorities. *Founded*: 1908. *Headquarters*: Iselin, NJ.

surety bond
Surety. A promise by a professional surety insurer to pay should the principal default or commit a wrongful act. A written guaranty that a party will perform an expressed obligation.
see: bond (*Surety*), obligee, obligor, surety

Surety Bond Guaranty Program
Surety. A program developed by the Small Business Administration (SBA), by which the SBA acts as a guarantor of bonds issued by a surety company to minority contractors.
see: surety bond

suretyship
Surety. The function of being a surety. It is the obligation of a surety to pay the debts of or answer for the default of another. A three-party contract is the

basis for a suretyship: One party (surety) undertakes to answer to a second party (obligee) for the debt or default of a third (principal) resulting from the third party's failure to pay or perform as required by an underlying contract or legal obligation.

see: obligee, obligor, principal (*Surety*), surety bond

surgical expense insurance
Health. A health insurance policy that covers costs of surgery.

surgical schedule
Health.
see: fee schedule

surplus
Accounting. On a financial statement, the amount by which assets exceed liabilities.

see: policyholders' surplus

Reinsurance. The portion of a reinsurer's risk that remains after deducting the ceding company's retention.

see: surplus reinsurance treaty

surplus deposit
Insurer Operations. A deposit maintained by reciprocal subscribers in lieu of an assessment liability.

surplus lines
Insurer Operations. Insurance placed with an insurer that is not admitted (not licensed) to do business in a particular state, but permitted because coverage is not available through licensed insurers. Insurance commissioners often maintain a list of eligible surplus lines insurers.

synonym: excess lines; compare: unauthorized insurance; see: admitted insurer, excess and surplus lines broker

surplus lines broker
Agency. A broker licensed and authorized by a state to conduct business within the state on behalf of nonadmitted insurers.

see: excess and surplus lines broker, nonadmitted insurer, surplus lines

surplus note
Insurer Operations. A debt instrument in the form of a note or an option to issue a note within a specified period of time by an insurer. The terms of the instrument provide that in the event of catastrophe losses that adversely affect the insurer's loss ratio, the insurer may forego all or part of the note repayment based on that loss ratio. Because of the note holder's risk of loss, these debt instruments pay a higher than normal rate of return. This form of note allows an insurer to pay catastrophe losses without

a material effect on its policyholders' surplus.

see: act of God bond, catastrophe loss, debt security, policyholders' surplus

surplus reinsurance treaty
Reinsurance. A reinsurance treaty where the reinsurer automatically assumes a layer of each risk in excess of the ceding company's retention. Generally, the layer assumed by the reinsurer is a multiple of the ceding company's retention.

see: first surplus reinsurance treaty, second surplus treaty

surplus relief reinsurance
Reinsurance. A portfolio reinsurance contract where an admitted reinsurer assumes a ceding company's business to relieve stress on the cedent's policyholder surplus. The portfolio transfer allows the ceding insurer to recapture the equity in unearned premium reserves on the business ceded.

compare: loss portfolio transfer; see: portfolio reinsurance

surplus share
Reinsurance.
see: surplus relief reinsurance

surplus to policyholders
Insurer Operations.
see: policyholders' surplus

surrender
Life. The relinquishing of a life insurance policy by the owner for its cash surrender value.

see: accumulation value, cash surrender value, surrender charge, surrender cost comparison index

surrender charge
Life. A provision in some annuities that the insurer may impose a charge for a withdrawal of funds before a specified time. The charge may be as much as 10% and applies during the first five to ten years of the annuity. The period for making a surrender charge usually begins with the original contract date, but it sometimes also applies to subsequent payments.

see: annuity, bonus yield, surrender

surrender cost comparison index
Life. A comparison of the costs of life insurance policies over 10- and 20-year periods. This index is of value when the cash surrender value is considered more important than the death benefit.

compare: net payment cost comparison index; see: cash surrender value

surrender value
Life.
see: cash surrender value

survey

Inland Marine/Ocean Marine. 1. The examination of damaged cargo after a marine loss to determine the cause and extent of damage.

2. The inspection of a ship's hull to determine its insurability or, after a loss, to determine the cause and extent of damage.

see: surveyor

surveyor

Ocean Marine. An individual who performs inspections of marine cargoes and hulls, generally for insurance purposes.

synonym: marine surveyor; *see:* survey

surviving company

General. The corporation that remains after an acquisition, consolidation or merger.

see: articles of merger or consolidation, merger

survivor life insurance

Life. A life insurance policy that is written to cover two or more individuals with the policy benefits payable only after all of them die. It is used as a vehicle to fund estate taxes upon the deaths of both spouses, or to fund the continuation of a business in the event its principals die.

see: joint and survivor option, successor life rider, tontine

survivorship annuity

Life.

see: joint and survivor annuity

survivorship benefits

Employee Benefits. Benefits paid to a survivor of a retiree who was receiving a pension. Survivorship benefits are based on a formula contained in the plan.

synonym: benefits of survivorship; *see:* employee benefit plan, pension

Life. A retirement income benefit for an insured's survivor which is set according to a predetermined formula.

synonym: benefits of survivorship

suspect

Agency. An individual or business that an agent or broker has identified as a potential buyer of insurance. The objective is then to convert the suspect into a prospect.

compare: prospect

suspension of coverage endorsement

Automobile. An endorsement (ISO form CA 02 40) to the business auto policy that allows an insured to request coverage to be suspended if the vehicle is out of service for more than 30 days. Using this endorsement reduces the premium charged for the suspended vehicle.

compare: suspension of insurance endorsement; *see:* business auto coverage form

suspension of coverage provision

Property. A boiler and machinery policy provision that allows an inspector or other representative of the insurer to suspend coverage when a covered object is found to be in, or exposed to, a dangerous condition. Before the suspension is effected, the insurer must provide the insured a written notice, which can be issued immediately during an inspection. Once the suspension is effective, it can be lifted only by an endorsement to the policy.

see: boiler and machinery insurance, object

suspension of insurance endorsement

Personal. An endorsement (ISO form PP 02 01) to the personal auto policy that allows an insured to request coverage to be suspended if the vehicle is out of service for more than 30 days. Using this endorsement reduces the premium for the suspended vehicle.

compare: suspension of coverage endorsement; *see:* personal auto policy

swap

Financial Planning. A financial contract (usually on a stock exchange) where the counterparties exchange a series of cash flows in the future, for example, the swap of fixed interest rate payments for floating rate payments.

see: counterparty, currency swap, interest rate swap, leveraged swap, swap option

swap maternity

Health. Maternity coverage that is provided at the beginning of a group health insurance plan but terminates for pregnancies in progress upon the plan's termination. This is the reverse of the way coverage is usually provided—hence *swap* maternity.

see: maternity benefit

swap option

Financial Planning. An option to enter into a swap on or before a specified time in the future.

see: option (*Financial Planning*), swap

swoop-and-squat

Automobile. An insurance fraud term for a type of contrived collision. A vehicle pulls into another's path and slams on its brakes, causing the other vehicle to rear-end it. The riders in the front vehicle then file fraudulent claims for whiplash.

compare: squat

symmetrical curve

Risk Management. An actuarial term for a distribution curve where the mean, median and mode have the same numerical value; a bell-shaped curve of mathematical values.

synonym: bell curve; *compare*: skewed curve; *see*: distribution curve, mean, median, mode, normal probability distribution

syndicate

Insurer Operations. Insurers or reinsurers that have joined or become associated to underwrite a risk or risks. They usually take agreed shares of premiums, expenses, profits and losses. A syndicate is often formed to underwrite large risks that are beyond the ability of a single member to insure.

synonym: pool; *see*: insurance exchange, Lloyd's syndicate

synthetic guaranteed investment contract

Life. A form of guaranteed investment contract (GIC) that provides insureds with industry diversification and enhanced credit quality over a traditional GIC. Generally, the insured retains ownership of a portfolio of highly rated fixed income securities. The synthetic GIC provider agrees to accommodate benefit payments and other qualified withdrawals at book value and the return of principal on a specified date.

see: guaranteed investment contract, separate account guaranteed investment contract

system performance guaranty insurance

Financial Guaranty. A form of financial guaranty patterned after efficacy insurance. Coverage is provided for a seven- to ten-year term on large industrial construction projects, guaranteeing that the project will perform to a specified percentage of its designed output. Coverage includes the cost to repair or replace part of the project to bring it up to the designed output and any resulting loss of use and resulting litigation. Each policy is specifically tailored to the project to be insured.

see: efficacy coverage

T

table of allowances
Health.
   see: fee schedule

tabular mortality
Life. Expected mortality as indicated in a mortality table.
   see: mortality table

tabular plan
Liability/Workers' Compensation. A retrospective rating plan in which the factors (i.e. basic, minimum, maximum) used in the rating formula are indicated in a table. The factors vary, depending on the risk's premium size and prior loss experience.
   see: retrospective rating plan

tabular value reserve method
Life. A life insurance reserving method that uses a mortality table to indicate the reserve that applies to the rating of specific insureds.
   see: reserve

tacit renewal
International/Regulation. A provision required in insurance policies issued in some countries for automatic annual renewal on the same contractual terms and conditions unless the insured notifies the insurer of the intent to cancel by a specified time before the renewal date (usually 30, 90 or 180 days).
   see: renewal

Taft-Hartley Act
Employee Benefits/Regulation. Federal legislation that amended the National Labor Relations Act of 1935. Among other things, it defines unfair labor practices, grants individual employees the right to sue union or company officials for unfair labor practices, restricts closed shops, and prohibits secondary boycotts. It also prohibits employers from making direct contributions to unions for employee benefits, but allows employee contributions to be paid to a separate benefit trust fund managed by the union.
   synonym: Labor-Management Relations Act; *see*: National Labor Relations Act, unfair labor practices

tagged fish coverage
Inland Marine. A form of prize indemnification insurance that indemnifies the insured (usually the tournament sponsor) should a tagged fish be caught by a participating fisherman during a specified fishing tournament.
   see: prize indemnification insurance, record fish coverage

tail
Liability. 1. Liability that exists after the expiration of a policy.
   2. Outstanding liability claims that are not yet known to an insured or insurer.
   see: claims-made form, incurred but not reported, tail coverage

tail coverage
Liability. Coverage that can be purchased after the expiration of a claims-made liability policy that extends for a period of time, with or without limit, the right to report events that occurred before the policy was terminated.
   see: claims-made form, extended reporting period

takeover attempt insurance
Professional Liability.
   see: tender offer defense expense insurance

tangible property
Property. Physical property, such as land, buildings, machinery and equipment, timber and other growing crops, mineral resources, and merchandise. This is one of the two risk exposure categories for property, with *intangible property*.
   compare: intangible property; *see*: personal property, real estate

target benefit plan

Employee Benefits. A defined contribution plan that is structured so benefits may change according to the investment performance of the pension plan assets. Plan contributions are set at a level to fund a target benefit, such as 30% of compensation, using acceptable mortality and interest rate assumptions.

compare: money purchase plan; *see*: employee benefit plan, defined contribution plan

target marketing

Insurer Operations. The concentration of a marketing effort to a specific client base, business or industry (e.g., senior citizens, electronics industry) by developing an extensive understanding of the target customers' needs and exposure and designing coverages and services for them. A specialized class of business or exposures is often called a "target" or "niche" market.

synonym: niche marketing; *compare*: mass marketing; *see*: affinity group, marketing

target risk

Insurer Operations/Agency. 1. A large account that is considered a target for competing brokers or insurance companies.

2. Prospective buyers of insurance classified according to various demographics such as age, sex, and type of insurance.

compare: prohibited list, uninsurable risk

General. A risk that is large, hazardous, or generates sizable premiums.

Reinsurance. A risk that involves a concentration of values—such as a bridge, tunnel, or art collection—that could produce an exceptionally large loss. Such risks will frequently be excluded from treaty reinsurance and must be reinsured on a facultative basis instead.

see: facultative reinsurance, treaty reinsurance

tariff rate

Insurer Operations. A rate developed by rating organizations for a general category of property or liability insurance.

compare: specific rate

International. An insurance rating system used in some countries that requires an insurer to use a prescribed rating schedule, terms and conditions with no deviation. Often the rates are higher than what would be available from a nonadmitted insurer and the terms and conditions are more restrictive.

tax accounting

Accounting. Financial information provided in a manner prescribed by the Internal Revenue Service for the purpose of preparing an income tax return. There may be differences from customary corporate accounting, such as the establishment of unfunded or funded reserves for retained casualty losses which can not be deducted for income tax purposes.

see: accounting, funded reserve, unfunded reserve

tax-appraised value

Financial Planning. The value of real or personal property based on the valuation established by a government tax assessor.

compare: actual cash value, depreciated value, fair market value, functional replacement cost, market value, replacement cost, reproduction cost; *see*: valuation of potential property loss.

tax audit insurance

Professional Liability. Insurance that was designed to reimburse taxpayers for expenses of having their tax return prepared by an attorney or an accountant, and the Internal Revenue Service disallowed claimed deductions. The IRS objected to this coverage on the grounds that it encouraged taking unjustified deductions, and it was discontinued.

see: tax preparers' errors and omissions insurance, tax shelter legal expense insurance

tax avoidance

Financial Planning. The reduction or avoidance of income tax liability by legally permitted methods. Also, the nonpayment of taxes attached to the purchase of taxable goods and services by not purchasing them.

compare: tax deferral, tax evasion

tax benefits of life insurance

Financial Planning/Life. The two principal tax advantages of purchasing life insurance are tax deferral of the buildup of earnings in whole life policies and annuities, which go untaxed, and tax-free death benefits of a life insurance policy.

see: Internal Revenue Code § 101, Tax Equity and Financial Responsibility Acts

tax bracket shifting

Financial Planning. A method of reducing taxes for a family by shifting income from one family member in a high tax bracket to another in a lower bracket. The family members must file separate tax returns.

see: irrevocable trust, short-term reversionary trust

tax deferral

Financial Planning. Arrangement of financial affairs in order to postpone tax liability until a time when the taxpayer anticipates having lower taxable income.

compare: tax avoidance, tax evasion; *see*: deferred stock grant

431

tax deferred annuity (TDA)

Life. A retirement program for employees of a public school system or a qualified charitable organization, permitted under § 403(b) of the Internal Revenue Code.

see: Internal Revenue Code § 403(b)

Tax Equity and Financial Responsibility Acts (TEFRA)

Employee Benefits/Life. Federal legislation enacted in 1982 and '83 that altered the traditional taxation of life insurance and life insurance companies. It increased the corporate tax rate on life insurance companies, redefined flexible premium life insurance so that it no longer provides favorable tax benefits, and reduced the estate tax exclusion for a retirement plan death plan benefits to a maximum of $100,000. It also lowered pension plan contributions and benefits, specified that certain loans from plans are to be treated as distributions, and repealed special Keogh plan and Subchapter S restrictions.

see: tax benefits of life insurance, Tax Reform Act of 1984

tax evasion

Financial Planning. The illegal nonpayment of taxes, such as underreporting income or claiming invalid deductions.

compare: tax avoidance, tax deferral

tax factor

Liability/Workers' Compensation.

see: tax multiplier

tax free rollover

Employee Benefits. ERISA and IRS provisions allowing an individual to transfer funds within a 60-day period from a qualified pension plan to an IRA or from an IRA to a qualified pension fund or from one IRA to another. No tax payment is required for withdrawing funds if they are transferred within 60 days.

see: Employee Retirement Income Security Act, rollover individual retirement account

tax interruption insurance

Property. A form of contingent business income coverage for a public entity that insures against a large fire, windstorm, or other disaster that destroys a leading industry, convention or entertainment center that contributed a sizable portion of the community's tax income.

see: contingent business income coverage

tax lien

Financial Planning. A claim on real or personal property for the satisfaction of taxes.

see: lien

tax multiplier

Liability/Workers' Compensation. A factor applied in retrospective rating plans to cover the insurer's costs for licenses, fees, assessments and taxes that the insurer must pay on collected premiums. The factor varies by state, and sometimes is a composite of several state factors.

synonym: tax factor; *see*: retrospective rating plan

tax planning

Financial Planning. The systematic structuring of discretionary income, expenses and investments to enhance after-tax wealth. Frequently, life insurance annuities and employee benefit plans can be used to increase after-tax income through their tax-deferral features.

see: exemption, marital tax deduction, qualified terminable interest property trust, tax avoidance, tax deferral

tax preparers' errors and omissions insurance

Professional Liability. Coverage for losses due to errors or omissions of persons who prepare tax returns for others for a fee, including incorrect or incomplete preparation of forms, calculation errors, and erroneous advice. Coverage is usually written on a claims-made basis.

see: errors and omissions insurance

Tax Reform Act of 1976

Employee Benefits/Regulation. Federal legislation that extended tax credit provisions for employee stock ownership plans contained in the Tax Reduction Act of 1975. These were used as temporary rules and regulations for implementation of the Employee Retirement Income Security Act of 1974.

see: Employee Retirement Income Security Act

Tax Reform Act of 1984

Life/Insurer Operations. Federal legislation that included provisions to tighten the life insurance tax provisions of the Tax Equity and Financial Responsibility Acts of 1982 and 1983. This act further raised the corporate tax on life insurance companies and broadened the definition of life insurance to include all life insurance contracts, not just those with flexible premiums. The act also addressed redistribution of the tax burden between mutual and stock life insurance companies.

see: Tax Equity and Financial Responsibility Acts

Tax Reform Act of 1986

Employee Benefits/Regulation. Federal legislation that eliminated many tax shelters and deductions previously allowed. It also reduced individual and corporate tax rates. It restricted personal tax deductions for individual retirement accounts, restricted use of corporate sponsored 401(k) payroll deduction plans, and increased corporate expenses to start and maintain pension plans. An alternative minimum tax for corporations originated with this Act and has had a material effect on insurance company tax payments.

see: individual retirement account

tax relief liability

International. A policy or an endorsement to an international or global insurance policy that provides coverage for the difference between the insured's normal tax rate in a foreign country and the tax rate applied to insurance proceeds brought into the country because of a nonadmitted policy loss payment in that country.

see: global insurance program, international insurance

tax shelter

Financial Planning. An investment or employee benefit structured to provide a tax savings by reducing taxable income or creating losses to offset taxable income.

see: Tax Reform Act of 1986

tax shelter legal expense insurance

Professional Liability. Coverage designed for partnerships, syndicates and joint ventures established to provide tax shelter benefits to investing members. It reimburses the group's legal expenses if the Internal Revenue Service challenges any claimed deduction, credit, investment loss, etc., that affects the amount of taxes owed. The insurance does not cover additional assessed taxes or penalties.

see: tax audit insurance

taxation of business income loss payments

Accounting. Business income insurance proceeds pay for profits that were not realized plus continuing expenses; therefore, like profits, these payments are subject to taxation.

compare: taxation of uninsured business interruption insurance losses; *see*: business income coverage form

taxation of interest on life insurance dividends

Life. Interest earned on participating life insurance policy dividends, left on deposit with the insurance company, that is subject to taxation.

see: dividend accumulation

taxation of property insurance claims payments

Accounting. Property insurance proceeds are generally taxed as ordinary income to the extent that

they exceed the book value of the damaged property. It is sometimes possible to defer taxation if the property is replaced with similar property.

compare: taxation of uninsured property losses; *see*: involuntary conversion option

taxation of uninsured business interruption losses

Accounting. Uninsured business interruption losses are not considered casualty losses and are therefore not tax deductible; unindemnified business interruption losses simply represent lost income.

compare: taxation of business income loss payments

taxation of uninsured property losses

Accounting. Uninsured business property losses are generally considered casualty losses and are therefore tax deductible, but only up to the amount of book value at the time of loss. When the book value is zero, no deduction is allowed.

compare: taxation of property insurance claims payments

taxes and utilities cancellation provision

Property. A provision in some property insurance policies that allows cancellation with prior written notice (usually five days) by the insurer if the property taxes on the insured building are more than one year overdue or if the building has not been supplied with heat, water, electricity or sewer service for 30 or more consecutive days.

team sports accident insurance

Health. A form of group accident insurance designed for student athletes and members of youth sports teams. Coverage is provided on a blanket basis for accident medical reimbursement, accidental loss of life, and accidental dismemberment or loss of sight. The policy limit may range from $1,500 to $10,000 per covered participant and may be primary or excess over other available insurance.

see: accident insurance

Technical and Miscellaneous Revenue Act

Regulation. Federal law of 1988 that amended the Consolidated Omnibus Budget Reconciliation Act (COBRA). It made a number of technical changes including (1) modifying the penalties for noncompliance with COBRA, (2) providing definitions and rules concerning distributions, excess distribution requirement, IRA rollovers, and vesting schedules for pension and profit-sharing plans, and (3) increasing the federal excise tax on excess pension assets that result from termination of qualified plans.

see: Consolidated Omnibus Budget Reconciliation Act

technical reserves
Insurer Operations/Reinsurance. Reserves made for future underwriting liabilities on an insurance or reinsurance account.

telephone fraud coverage
Crime. A special crime coverage to protect organizations from losses due to theft of telephone time. Coverage is provided when persons other than employees or other representatives of the organization fraudulently charge calls to the organization's phone access number.

see: crime coverages

television closed circuit breakdown insurance
Property. Coverage that indemnifies a sponsor of a closed circuit telecast (a seminar, sporting event, etc.) for loss of revenues because of interruption of service for technical reasons that necessitates the refund of admissions.

see: entertainment insurance

temperature extremes exclusion
Property/Inland Marine. A provision in all-risk property and inland marine policies, excluding coverage for loss from extremes of temperature to such things as fruits, vegetables, and living plants.

temporary admission
International.
see: admission temporaire

temporary disability benefits
Employee Benefits. Benefits in the form of income payments to a sick or disabled worker who is not receiving workers' compensation benefits. Often these benefits are prescribed by state legislation.

see: disability benefit law

temporary employment agency errors and omissions insurance
Professional Liability. A form of professional liability insurance for firms that provide employees on a temporary basis to employers. Coverage is provided on a claims-made basis for losses due to errors and omissions in representing an individual's qualifications, or for discrimination or defamation of character.

see: errors and omissions insurance, professional liability insurance

temporary life annuity
Life. An annuity that makes income payments for a limited time (e.g., five years). Payments cease after the stipulated period or upon the annuitant's death.

see: annuity

temporary life annuity due
Life. An annuity with a limited number of income payments. Payments cease after the stipulated number have been made or upon the annuitant's death.

see: annuity

temporary partial disability
Health/Workers' Compensation. An injury to an employee that impairs his or her ability to work for a limited period of time. The impairment is such that the individual is able to perform limited employment duties and is expected to fully recover.

synonym: intermediate disability; *see*: partial disability

temporary structures coverage
Property. A builders' risk extension of coverage for impermanent structures, such as sheds, small storage buildings, or offices located on a construction job site while working on an insured construction project.

see: builders' risk insurance

temporary substitute aircraft
Aviation. A provision in many aviation policies that automatically extends coverage to a temporary substitute for an insured aircraft that is being repaired or serviced or has been damaged or destroyed.

temporary substitute automobile
Automobile/Personal. A rented or borrowed auto for an insured to use while the insured's damaged vehicle is being repaired. Part of the cost of a temporary car is usually covered by an auto insurance policy.

see: rental reimbursement coverage, transportation expense coverage

temporary total disability
Health/Workers' Compensation. An injury to a worker that results in an inability to perform employment duties for a limited period of time, but full recovery is expected.

see: total disability

ten day free look
Health/Regulation. Many state insurance departments require that a prospective insured have ten days to examine a health insurance policy during which it can be returned without any obligation.

ten percenter
General. The middleman in a fraudulent scheme to increase or hasten an insurance settlement. (The term comes from the typical kickback received from the settlement.) Usually, the ten percenter learns of pending cases from a corrupt claims adjuster. He then seeks a bribe from a claimant's attorney in order to expedite a settlement by passing part of the bribe to the adjuster. The attorney receives a higher fee from an inflated settlement, and using a ten percenter to broker the deal can make it

difficult for the insurer to detect the adjuster's misconduct. The claimant may never know of the fraud.

see: capper, claims adjuster, fraud, public adjuster, settlement

ten year averaging
Employee Benefits. A tax provision, repealed by the Tax Reform Act of 1986, that could be used to reduce income taxes on lump sum distributions from qualified pension or retirement plans by averaging the payment over ten years. Averaging is now limited to five years.

ten year vesting
Employee Benefits. A rule in the Employee Retirement Income Security Act that allowed employers to require ten years of service of an employee before being vested in a pension plan. The Tax Reform Act of 1986 reduced the vesting period to five years.

synonym: cliff vesting; *see*: Employee Retirement Income Security Act, Tax Reform Act of 1986, vesting

tenancy
Law. The possession or occupancy of real estate pursuant to a lease or payment of rent.

see: joint tenancy, leasehold, tenancy by entirety, tenancy in common, tenant's legal liability

tenancy by entirety
Law. The ownership of property by spouses together. If one dies, the property passes to the other. Neither can sell or transfer the property without the other's consent.

see: tenancy

tenancy in common
Law. The ownership of property by two or more individuals that do not have the right of survivorship. If one tenant dies, the property passes to that person's estate and not to the other tenant.

see: tenancy

tenant's legal liability
Law. A tenant is usually legally obligated to compensate the owner for damage to the property, including the structure and permanent fixtures.

see: liability (*Law*), tenancy

tender offer
Financial Planning. A formal offer or bid to buy shares of a corporation at a specific price, usually greater than the current market value.

compare: public exchange offer; *see*: tender offer defense expense insurance

tender offer defense expense insurance
Professional Liability. Coverage for legal costs to defend a corporation from a hostile takeover attempt. This coverage is usually provided by the London market.

, *synonym*: takeover attempt insurance; *see*: greenmail exclusion, poison pill, tender offer

tentative premium
General.
see: provisional premium

tentative rate
General.
see: provisional rate

term
Insurer Operations. The length or period of time during which an insurance policy or bond is in force.
see: policy period

term health insurance
Health. A contract of health insurance that makes no provision for renewal or termination other than by expiration of the policy term.

term life insurance
Life. Life insurance in effect for a specific length of time (e.g., 5 or 10 years). If the insured survives beyond that period, coverage ceases. Unlike a whole life policy, this type of policy does not build up any cash or nonforfeiture values.

compare: life expectancy term insurance, permanent life insurance, whole life insurance; *see*: automatically convertible term life insurance, convertible term life insurance, cost-of-living rider, decreasing term life insurance, extended term life insurance, level term life insurance, life expectancy term insurance, re-entry term life insurance, renewable term life insurance

term policy
Insurer Operations. An insurance contract written for a period of more than one year.

term rate
Insurer Operations. The rate for a term policy.
see: term rule

term rule
Insurer Operations. A rule in rate manuals concerning discounts for policies that are issued for a time longer than one year.
see: rate manual, rate making

terminal dividend
Life. An additional dividend paid to a life insurance policyholder when a policy terminates. Such a dividend is usually paid only after a minimum in-force period of 10 to 20 years.

see: dividend (*Insurer Operations*)

terminal funding

Employee Benefits. The funding of a pension plan by an employer in a lump sum upon retirement of an employee. The Employee Retirement Income Security Act eliminated this funding method for qualified pension plans and requires current funding of future pension liabilities.

see: Employee Retirement Income Security Act

terminal reserve

Life. A life insurance reserve that is established at the end of each life policy year.

compare: initial reserve, mean reserve; *see:* preliminary term

termination

Insurer Operations. The cancellation of an insurance policy by an insurer for nonpayment of premium.

see: cancellation

Life. Ceasing coverage on a whole life insurance or endowment policy for nonpayment of premium prior to its expiration date.

see: lapse

termination rate

Insurer Operations. An insurer's ratio of policy cancellations or lapses to total policies in force.

compare: persistency; *see:* lapse ratio

territorial limitation

Insurer Operations.

see: geographic limitation

territorial rating

Insurer Operations. A method of using geographic areas to assist in the classification of risks and subsequent setting of rates. This process assumes geographic location is a significant factor in loss experience.

see: rate making

terrorist insurance

Property. Coverage that can be added to a worldwide property insurance program to provide insurance against destruction of property by terrorists.

see: kidnap-ransom-extortion insurance

tertiary beneficiary

Life. The life insurance beneficiary designated as the third person to receive policy proceeds. No benefits are payable to this beneficiary if either the primary or secondary beneficiary is alive.

see: primary beneficiary, secondary beneficiary

test modifier

Workers' Compensation. An experience modification that has been developed by someone other than a workers' compensation rating bureau (usually by the accounts broker or current insurer) that is used

to estimate what the bureau modifier will be when it is issued.

see: experience rating modification factor, rating bureau

testamentary trust

Financial Planning. A trust established by the terms of a will to become effective upon probate of the will. The testator (maker of the will) can change its provisions, but when the person dies, the testamentary trust becomes irrevocable.

see: inter vivos trust, trust

testator

Financial Planning. The maker of a will.

see: intestate, will

testimony

Law. Any statements made by a witness in a legal proceeding under oath or affirmation. Testimony may be given by statements in court or by deposition.

see: deposition, evidence, expert witness, hearsay

testing and research laboratory errors and omissions insurance

Professional Liability. Errors and omissions coverage for laboratories involved in testing and research. Coverage is provided subject to complete information on the nature of the testing and research performed.

see: errors and omissions insurance

testing coverage

Property. A builders' risk coverage, occasionally available from an underwriter, for the testing of specified structures, machinery or equipment associated with the insured construction project. Coverage can include hydrostatic, pneumatic, or mechanical testing and is usually limited to a specified period (e.g., 30 or 60 days).

see: builders' risk insurance

testing exclusion

Property. A boiler and machinery policy exclusion that suspends coverage while a covered object is undergoing testing. Coverage remains in force before and after testing.

see: boiler and machinery insurance

Thaisoi

Health/Life. The name of an ancient Greek benevolent society that is considered one of the forerunners of modern life and health insurance.

see: insurance

theatrical property coverage

Inland Marine. Inland marine coverage (ISO form

436

CM 00 29 or AAIS form IM 785) for props, costumes, etc., used by a theatrical company or production. Generally, such events are scheduled in the policy declarations.

theft
Crime. The taking or deprivation of property from its rightful owner. Theft includes burglary, robbery and embezzlement.

see: burglary, crime coverages, embezzlement, forgery, larceny, pilferage, robbery

theft, disappearance and destruction of money and securities coverage form
Crime. A crime coverage form (ISO form CR 00 04, or form C) that covers loss by theft, disappearance, or destruction of the insured's money and securities inside the insured's premises as well as outside the insured's premises while in the custody of a messenger.

synonym: crime coverage form C; *see:* crime coverages

theory of probability
Risk Management.
see: probability analysis

thermal irritant
Property. A pollution exclusion that was added to most property insurance forms issued after 1988. It is the damaging effect when heated gas or water is discharged into the atmosphere or a body of water and causes injury to humans, vegetation, fish or animals.

see: pollutant cleanup and removal additional coverage, pollution exclusion

third-party administrator (TPA)
Risk Management. A claims administrator or insurance company that processes claims on behalf of a self-insured organization or multiple employer welfare arrangement or manages workers' compensation claims for an employer. The administrator is a third party because it is neither the self-insurer nor an insured (claimant or payee). Services may include processing claims (including audits, adjusting, and negotiating settlements), record keeping, self-insurance certification, and notification of excess insurers.

synonym: administrative agent; *see:* benefits manager, claims processing, deposit administration plan, multiple employer welfare arrangement, self-insurance

third-party administrators' professional liability insurance
Professional Liability. Liability coverage for third-party administrators against claims alleging negligent errors or omissions.

see: professional liability insurance, third-party

administrator

third-party beneficiary
Law. An individual or entity that is not a party to a contract but possesses an enforceable right under it; a beneficiary under an insurance policy.

see: beneficiary

third-party liability
Liability. The obligation to compensate another person harmed or injured by a negligent or wrongful act or omission. A person other than the parties to a liability policy (i.e., not the insurer nor the policyholder) is a third party. When an insured (the first party) causes a loss, the insurer (the second party) assumes the insured's liability up to the policy limit.

compare: first-party insurance; *see:* negligence

third-party over suit
Liability/Workers' Compensation. A lawsuit in which an injured worker has sued a third party (a person other than the employer or a fellow employee), and the third party in turn sues the employer. For example, a worker may claim that an injury resulted from defective equipment, but the equipment manufacturer (the third party) claims the injury resulted from the employer's misuse of the equipment or negligent disregard of safety instructions. The manufacturer's suit against the employer is a third-party over suit and is covered by employer's liability insurance.

synonym: action over, liability-over suit; *see:* employers' liability insurance

third-party payer
Health. The insurance company or other health benefit plan sponsor that pays for medical services provided to a patient. The patient and the health care provider are considered the primary two parties.

thirty and out
Employee Benefits. A pension plan option allowing a participant to retire after completing 30 years of service, regardless of age.

see: retirement age

thirty-year cap
Employee Benefits. A pension plan provision that reaches maximum benefit or accumulation levels after 30 years of credited service.

3-D policy
Crime.
see: dishonesty disappearance and destruction policy

three-fourths loss clause
Property/Ocean Marine. An obsolete clause once

contained in property and marine policies, providing that an insurer's maximum loss would be three-fourths of the actual cash value of the property. In effect, this clause imposed a 25% deductible.

three percent rule

Employee Benefits. A rule used in vesting pension plan benefits. The participant's accrued benefit must be at least equal to 3% of the participant's normal projected retirement benefit for each year of participation, with a maximum of 100% after 33 ⅓ years of participation.

see: pension, unit credit actuarial cost method, vesting

threshold of injury

Automobile. Under some no-fault insurance laws, the degree of personal injury from an auto accident that entitles the person to bring suit. A person may be allowed to sue, for example, if medical expenses exceed $2,500 or if the accident resulted in death, disfigurement or permanent disability.

synonym: medical expense threshold; *see*: no-fault insurance, personal injury protection

thrift plan

Employee Benefits.

see: savings plan

thrust fault

Loss Control. One of three type of geological faults (with blind thrust and strike-slip). One side of the fault rides up over the other. This vertical motion can cause especially violent shaking.

compare: blind thrust fault, strike-slip fault; *see*: earthquake

ticket policy

Health.

see: travel accident insurance

ticket reinsurance

Reinsurance. A method of indicating the placement of reinsurance on a policy, where a form is attached to the daily report indicating the details of any reinsurance that has been effected.

tickler

Agency/Insurer Operations. A system used by agents and underwriters to remind them of actions that must be taken.

see: expiration card, expiration file

tidal wave

Property.

see: tsunami

tie-in sale

Regulation.

see: tying arrangement

tight building syndrome

Loss Control.

see: sick building syndrome

tight market

Insurer Operations. A period of time during the underwriting cycle when there is little or no insurance capacity. It is distinguished from a *hard* market by a lack of policyholders' surplus, as opposed to being created by that segment of the underwriting cycle when heavy losses and extreme price cutting create a lack of capacity. Occasionally, a tight market occurs toward the end of a calendar year when underwriters have used their allocated surplus, particularly as on the London market.

compare: hard market, soft market; *see*: underwriting cycle

time and distance reinsurance

Reinsurance. A form of reinsurance that was introduced in Lloyd's which guarantees specific payments for anticipated claims at specific times based on the initial premium paid and the investment returns expected by the reinsurer. The concept is similar to a life insurance annuity in that a limit and specific payout pattern are selected at the outset. This form of contract has evolved into what is now termed finite risk insurance or reinsurance contracts.

see: finite risk insurance

time charter

Ocean Marine. The hiring of a ship with the vessel owner's crew managing and navigating the vessel, but its cargo capacity taken by the hirer for a specified period of time for carriage of goods or passengers. The vessel may be hired, or chartered, to sail anywhere in the world or anywhere within stipulated geographic limits on as many voyages as can be fitted into the charter period.

see: charter party

time deductible

Property. A deductible that can be applied to property or boiler and machinery business income coverage, expressed as a period of time (e.g., 24 hours) during which the insurer is not responsible for any business income loss or lost value of machinery.

see: deductible

time deposit

Financial Planning. An interest-bearing account with a financial institution that must remain on deposit for a specified period of time to receive the full interest available. Early withdrawal can result in penalties, such as lost interest or interest paid at a lower rate. The depository institution may also impose a waiting period before funds are released.

compare: demand deposit; *see*: certificate of deposit

time element insurance

Property. Insurance that provides coverage when a direct property loss results in an indirect or consequential loss, such as loss of earnings or increased expenses. Coverage is usually tied to the loss of earnings or increased expenses over a specific period of time.

see: business income coverage form, extra expense insurance, profits and commissions insurance

time limit

Health. A statutory provision in most states applying to individual health insurance policies. An insurer has a period from the policy inception date (usually two years) in which to deny a claim on the basis of an adverse physical condition that existed at the time the insured completed the application but which the insured did not reveal. The period may be shortened if the insurer used a simplified application containing no detailed questions about the insured's medical history.

see: material misrepresentation, preexisting condition, simplified application

Insurer Operations. The period of time (90 to 120 days) allowed for a proof of loss or notice or claim to be completed.

synonym: certain defenses; see: proof of loss

time-loss unit

Property. The amount of economic loss for each unit of time that the insured's business production is interrupted or curtailed. This is a consideration in adjusting a business income loss.

synonym: rate of loss; see: business income coverage form

time value of money

Risk Management. The possible investment return on money received immediately. Compound interest tables indicate the value between two points in time.

see: discount factor, present value

title

Title. A document that constitutes evidence of a legally exclusive possession of property.

see: absolute title, abstract of title, accession, accretion, adverse title, certificate of title, chain of title, clear title, clear title of record, cloud on title, covenants for title, defective title, deed, environmental title insurance, equitable title, imperfect title, lucrative title, marketable title, onerous title, paper title, perfect title, presumptive title, title by descent, title insurance, title search, title standards

title by descent

Title. A title to real estate that has been legally

transferred to the heirs of a deceased owner.

see: real estate, title

title guaranty company

Title. A business that does real estate title searches to determine whether any defects or encumbrances are recorded and gives the buyer of the property a guaranty of the title.

compare: title insurance company; see: real estate, title, title search

title insurance

Title. A class of insurance that provides coverage for the risk that the title to real estate may be found to contain defects. Indemnification is provided to the property owner for losses resulting from such defects.

see: environmental title insurance, title, title insurance company, Torrens system

title insurance company

Title. An insurance company chartered to write only title policies. Historically, these companies have operated in limited geographic areas because of the need to review documents at local halls of records.

see: abstract of title, chain of title

title search

Title. The examination of records on file with the governmental agency that maintains real estate ownership documents to determine whether title to a property is valid or if there are any defects to the title.

see: defective title, real estate, title

title standards

Title. Many states have standards by which a title to real estate may be evaluated to determine if it is defective or marketable.

see: defective title, marketable title

Title XIX of the Social Security Act
Health.

see: Medicaid

Title XVIII of the Social Security Act
Health.

see: Medicare

tontine

Life. An early form of life insurance that is now illegal. It is named after the Italian, Lorenzo Tonti, who during the 17th century established a state lottery to raise money for the French government in which the oldest survivor would collect the funds. It later developed into an agreement where several participants placed an amount of money in escrow with the understanding that after an agreed period of time, survivors would share the accrued proceeds. Tontines are now illegal, as they had the unintended effect of encouraging participants to assure that they were the surviving party by arranging the early demise of other participants.

see: insurance, joint life and survivor insurance

top-heavy plan

Employee Benefits. An employee benefit plan that primarily benefits highly compensated employees, top executives or owners of a business. It is difficult for a top-heavy plan to qualify for favorable tax treatment.

see: employee benefit plan, nonqualified plan

tornado

Property. A rotating column of wind, accompanied by a funnel-shaped cloud. It produces very violent and destructive winds (up to 300 mph) that travel in a narrow path. It is a natural peril that occurs principally in the Midwest and Southwestern United States.

synonym: cyclone, twister; *see*: National Severe Storms Forecast Center, natural perils, windstorm and hail coverage

Torrens system

Title. A form of title insurance whereby a county recorder or county clerk provides a written guarantee of clear title when a property is transferred. The guarantee is based on the fact that the county recorder registers the title and maintains the deed records. Under this system, a transfer fee is charged, a part of which is used to finance an insurance fund to indemnify losses in the event the county recorder makes an error.

see: title insurance

tort

Law. A wrong or harm other than breach of contract; breach of a noncontractual duty toward another person which causes harm or loss. The same action may be both a tort, for which a private person may seek compensation, and a crime, punishable by the state. A tort can be either intentional (such as battery) or unintentional (such as negligence, the broadest general category of torts). Intentional torts are not usually covered by insurance—libel and slander are exceptions—because insurance generally transfers the risk only of accidental or fortuitous events and because insurance of willful misconduct undermines the deterrent effect of the law.

see: civil law (1), intentional tort, liability, negligence, tortfeasor

tortfeasor

Law. A person who commits a tort; one who causes a harm or loss for which a civil remedy may be sought.

see: tort

total disability

Health/Workers' Compensation. A disability that prevents a worker from continuously performing any part of his or her occupation and that does not allow them to perform any other employment.

see: disability, partial disability, permanent partial disability, permanent total disability

total loss

Insurer Operations. A loss payment by an insurer that equals the maximum insurance policy limit.

see: actual total loss, constructive total loss

Ocean Marine/Property. The complete destruction of insured property; property that has disappeared or has been damaged irreparably or so there is no salvageable or reparable value. A total loss usually signifies the maximum settlement under the terms of a policy.

synonym: actual total loss; *compare*: partial loss; see abandonment clause, constructive total loss, total loss only clause

total loss only clause (TLO)

Ocean Marine. Ocean marine insurance that responds only if a vessel or cargo is a complete loss. Partial losses are not covered.

see: constructive total loss, ocean marine insurance, total loss

total return

Financial Planning. Return on investment, including capital gain or loss and dividend disbursements expected over the next three to five years, divided by the recent stock price and expressed as an average annual rate of growth.

tour operators' errors and omissions insurance

Professional Liability. Insurance for organizations that organize and market travel tours by contracting with motor coach operators, airlines, cruise ship lines, hotels and restaurants. Coverage is provided on a claims-made basis for losses arising from negligence, errors, omissions or bankruptcy of outside tour operators.

see: errors and omissions insurance, travel agents' liability insurance

tourist railroad liability insurance
Liability.

see: short line railroad liability insurance

towing and labor costs coverage

Automobile. An optional automobile coverage (ISO form PP 03 03) that can be added to the physical damage coverage that provides reimbursement up to a specified limit for towing or on-site labor

440

costs.

see: personal auto policy

toxic

Loss Control. A substance that is poisonous to the human body. There are degrees of toxicity—from mildly toxic, to highly or deadly toxic.

see: acute toxicity, LD50

Toxic Substances Control Act

Regulation. Federal legislation enacted in 1976 that regulates commercial manufacturing, processing and distribution of chemical substances. Every industrial corporation is required to compile an inventory of existing stocks of commercial chemicals, and manufacturers must advise the Environmental Protection Agency of plans to produce any chemical not listed in the initial inventory. It authorizes the EPA to order testing to determine health or environmental effects of a substance.

see: Environmental Protection Agency

trade association plan

Insurer Operations. A form of commercial mass marketing where the insurance product is available to any member firm of a trade association who meets the insurer's underwriting requirements. The insurance is usually available at a reduced premium and has coverage enhancements.

see: mass marketing

trade basis combined ratio

Insurer Operations. A combined ratio used by the insurance industry and financial analysts to evaluate an insurer. It differs from the traditional *combined ratio* by compensating for the fact that a growing insurer's earned premiums lag behind written premiums. *Formula*: 1. (incurred losses + loss adjustment expense) ÷ (earned premiums + incurred underwriting expenses); 2. this result ÷ written premiums.

compare: statutory combined ratio; *see*: combined ratio

trade fixtures

Property. A form of personal property owned and used by a business tenant, such as display counters or shelves, which the tenant may remove (or may be obligated to remove) when the premises are vacated.

compare: improvements and betterments; *see*: fixture

trade libel

Liability.

see: commercial speech, libel

trade name

Professional Liability. The name used for merchandise or services by an organization to distinguish it from similar goods or services sold or performed by others. It is a form of intangible property and is usually trademarked.

see: intangible property (1), trademark

trade secret

Law/Property. An invention, process, pattern or formula that has not been patented but provides an advantage to a business over competitors because they do not know of it. The owner may bring an action to enjoin or seek damages for the fraudulent divulgence or receipt of a trade secret, but it may freely be used if the secret is discovered through analysis of a product or independent discovery. It may have an insurable value.

compare: trademark; *see*: copyright, intangible property (1), patent

trademark

Law/Property. The exclusive legal right granted by the federal government to own and use a distinctive word, logo or symbol that indicates ownership or origin of merchandise or services. It is a form of intangible property that may have an insurable value.

compare: copyright, patent, trade secret; *see*: intangible property (1)

trading loss exclusion form

Crime. An endorsement (ISO form CR 10 04) that excludes coverage under the Insurance Services Office crime coverage form for an employee dishonesty loss arising from securities or commodities trading.

see: employee dishonesty coverage form

trailer interchange agreement

Automobile. A written agreement that transfers a trailer containing cargo from one trucker to another for the continuation of a trip. Commonly, the agreement requires the trucker using the trailer to reimburse the one who owns the trailer for any damage while it is in his or her possession.

see: interchange insurance

trailer interchange insurance

Automobile.

see: interchange insurance, trailer interchange agreement

trailers—special limit

Personal. The Insurance Services Office homeowners policy coverage section C (personal property) has a "special limits of liability" provision as respects trailers not used with watercraft. The limit is $1,000.

see: homeowners policy—special limits of liability, watercraft—special limit

trailing dividend yield

Financial Planning. The total of the dividends declared over the last 12 months, divided by the recent price.

see: dividend yield

transacting insurance

Regulation. A term in state insurance laws for carrying on the business of insurance, usually including the solicitation, inducement, negotiation or advising of an individual concerning coverage or claims.

see: business of insurance

transaction exposure

International. The foreign exchange gain or loss resulting from international business transactions.

see: exchange rate

transfer agents' errors and omissions insurance

Professional Liability. Errors and omissions insurance for securities transfer agents. A transfer agent acts for a corporation in transferring stock from one owner to another, usually a bank or trust company. Coverage includes loss from securities forgery, erasure guaranty, and voluntary destruction of stock records.

see: errors and omissions insurance

transfer of business

Insurer Operations. An arrangement by sale, reinsurance, merger, consolidation or assumption, under which the business of one insurer is transferred to another one.

see: portfolio reinsurance

transfer of coverage

Employee Benefits. Transfer of coverage under a group policy or benefit plan from one carrier to another, including transfer under an optional choice enrollment plan.

transfer of risk

Risk Management.

see: risk transfer

transit insurance

Inland Marine. Insurance covering loss or damage to goods while they are being transported.

see: cargo insurance, door-to-door coverage, trip transit insurance

transition program

Insurer Operations. A program implemented in conjunction with the 1986 Insurance Services Office's Liability Rating Plan to compensate for large

premium differences on mercantile premises and operations coverages. Such coverages are now rated on gross sales. Formerly rated on square footage, the program set upper and lower amounts for premium changes caused solely by an exposure base change.

transitional care facility

Health. A short-term comprehensive skilled nursing or rehabilitation facility for patients who no longer need full acute hospital care. The care differs from long-term skilled nursing care in that there are more intensive levels of medical intervention and comprehensive rehabilitation services.

synonym: comprehensive outpatient rehabilitation facility, subacute health care facility; *compare*: skilled nursing facility

transnational broker

International. An insurance brokerage with central operations located in two different countries. This is usually the stage prior to becoming a global broker.

compare: domestic broker, global broker, international broker, multinational broker

transportation expense coverage

Automobile. Coverage under an automobile policy's physical damage section for the cost of substitute transportation should the covered vehicle be stolen.

see: rental reimbursement coverage, temporary substitute automobile

transportation facilities

Inland Marine. Facilities such as a bridges, piers, wharves, loading facilities, or pipelines that are covered by inland marine insurance.

see: instrumentalities of transportation and communication

transportation insurance

Inland Marine/Ocean Marine. Insurance that covers merchandise or goods in the course of transit by air, rail, truck, barge or ship from a starting location to a final destination.

see: cargo insurance, inland marine insurance, ocean marine insurance, transit insurance, trip transit insurance

transportation ticket insurance

Health.

see: travel accident insurance

traumatic injury

Health. A physical or mental injury caused by an external force to an individual's body, as distinguished from a disease.

see: bodily injury

travel accident insurance

Health. A form of accidental death, dismemberment and disability insurance commonly sold at airports. Coverage is issued in conjunction with a common carrier (airline, train) ticket and is limited to travel periods during the trip. The term *transportation ticket insurance* was once used to describe this insurance, because coverage was provided in the form of an additional stub on the traveler's ticket.

synonym: ticket policy, transportation ticket insurance; *see*: air travel insurance, railroad travel policy

travel agents' liability insurance

Professional Liability. Coverage for travel agents against claims arising out of negligent acts, errors and omissions committed by the insured, or persons for whose acts the insured is legally liable. Coverage usually includes employees, tour guides and tour directors under contract. Coverage applies worldwide for accidents or occurrences such as canceled hotel or tour reservations, lost luggage and misleading travel brochures.

treasurer

General. The executive financial officer of a business enterprise or organization entrusted with the receipt, care and disbursement of funds.

compare: chief financial officer, controller

Treasury bill

Financial Planning. A U.S. Treasury security that matures in 90 days to one year, issued for a minimum of $10,000 and multiples of $1,000 thereafter up to $1 million per issue. It is issued at a discount price determined by auction, and the return is based on the holding period.

see: Treasury security

Treasury bond

Financial Planning. A U.S. Treasury security issued for a period of 10 years or longer in minimum denominations of $1,000 at a fixed interest rate.

see: bond (*Financial Planning*), Treasury security

Treasury note

Financial Planning. A U.S. Treasury security issued at a fixed rate for a term of one to 10 years and issued for a minimum of $1,000.

see: note, Treasury security

Treasury security

Financial Planning. A form of debt issued by the U.S. government. The main types are Treasury bills, Treasury notes, and Treasury bonds.

see: debt security, Treasury bill, Treasury bond, Treasury note

treasury stock

Financial Planning. Common stock that has been issued by a corporation and then reacquired from stockholders and held by the corporation for its own use.

see: capital stock, common stock

treatment, storage and disposal facility (TSDF)

Loss Control. A hazardous waste site regulated by Environmental Protection Agency or a state environmental quality agency under the provisions of the Resource Conservation and Recovery Act for the treatment, storage, or disposal of hazardous waste.

see: closure and post-closure insurance, hazardous waste, Resource Conservation and Recovery Act

Treaty of Paris

Ocean Marine.

see: enemy goods

treaty reinsurance

Reinsurance. An automatic reinsurance agreement between the ceding insurer and the reinsurer by which the reinsurer is bound to accept all risks ceded to it, usually for one year or longer.

compare: facultative reinsurance; *see*: aggregate excess of loss reinsurance, automatic reinsurance, Carpenter Plan, catastrophe reinsurance, excess of loss reinsurance, omissions clause, quota share, special acceptance

trend analysis

Risk Management. A loss forecasting technique that identifies past loss patterns and uses them to forecast future losses.

see: effective retention, trending

trending

Risk Management. The adjustment of historical statistics (both premiums and losses) to current levels or expected future levels in order to reflect measurable changes in economic and demographic forces and to make past data useful for determining current and future expected cost levels.

compare: probability analysis; *see*: age-to-age factor, cumulative factors, intuitive trending, trend analysis

trespasser

Law. An individual who enters the property of another without permission.

compare: invitee, licensee; *see*: attractive nuisance doctrine, degree of care

triage

Health. The sorting or classifying of patients according to the nature and severity of their illness or injury in order to set priorities for treatment. It is done at the site of an accident or at an emergency care facility when the number of patients temporarily strains available resources.

see: emergency medical services, medical emergency

tribunalization
Insurer Operations. The process of approval at Lloyd's, by a committee of five persons, of a correspondent (usually in the United States) who is sponsored by a Lloyd's broker. Once approved, the correspondent can bind coverage and issue certificates of coverage on behalf of Lloyd's.

see: Lloyd's of London

trick and device exclusion
Automobile. An exclusion in some automobile dealers' physical damage policies that eliminates coverage for losses due to fraudulent acts, such as a customer stealing a car under the pretense of test-driving or paying for a car with a bad check.

synonym: false pretense exclusion; *see*: conversion, embezzlement, or secretion exclusion; false pretense coverage

trigger
Liability.

see: coverage trigger

trip cancellation insurance
Liability.

see: charter fare protection insurance

trip transit insurance
Inland Marine. Insurance on a single shipment of property for a specific trip on a common carrier. It specifically excludes shipments via the U.S. Postal Service, which is not a common carrier.

synonym: single risk cargo insurance; *compare*: parcel post insurance

triple A
Organizations.

see: American Automobile Association

triple A tenant
Financial Planning. A prestigious and financially strong tenant, who often acts as an anchor tenant—i.e., one who attracts other tenants of good quality.

synonym: AAA Tenant; *see*: anchor tenant

triple indemnity
Life.

see: multiple indemnity

triple protection policy
Life.

see: double protection life insurance

triple trigger theory
Law/Liability.

see: continuous trigger theory, Keene doctrine

truckers' coverage form
Automobile. An Insurance Services Office policy (ISO form CA 0012) providing liability, physical damage, medical payments, and uninsured or underinsured motorist coverages for a trucker. It has ten classifications of covered vehicles, coded by numbers, as follows:

41. Any auto: the broadest classification, providing coverage for owned, hired, and nonowned vehicles.

42. Owned autos only: vehicles owned by the insured, including any acquired during the policy period, plus liability coverage for nonowned trailers connected to a power unit owned by the trucker.

43. Owned commercial autos.

44. Owned autos subject to no-fault: coverage only for no-fault or personal injury protection on vehicles located in no-fault states.

45. Owned autos subject to compulsory uninsured motorist law: vehicles located in a state where uninsured motorist coverage is compulsory. The required coverage is provided under the policy form.

46. Specifically described autos: vehicles listed in the policy. Coverage is limited to 30 days for newly acquired vehicles.

47. Hired autos only: vehicles that are leased, rented or borrowed.

48. Nonowned trailers in insured's possession.

49. Insured's trailers not in insured's possession.

50. Nonowned autos: vehicles of employees or partners while used for business purposes.

compare: business auto coverage form, garage coverage form

truckers' down-time insurance
Automobile. Lost earnings insurance for truckers that provides coverage when a tractor or trailer cannot be operated because of a collision, fire or other insured peril. The coverage has no daily limitation, and is an "actual loss sustained" form. Coverage can include payments on a financed unit and the cost to lease a replacement unit while a damaged one is being repaired.

see: earnings insurance form

truckers' insurance
Automobile.

see: bobtail coverage, interchange insurance, motor truck cargo insurance, motor truck cargo radioactive contamination insurance, truckers' coverage form, truckers' down-time insurance, truckers' liability insurance

truckers' liability insurance
Automobile. Coverage insuring a trucker against liability arising out of damage to cargo in his care, custody or control (i.e., while being transported in an insured vehicle).

see: motor truck cargo insurance

truckers' occupational accident insurance
Health. A form of group accident coverage for truckers who operate as independent contractors principally to a single trucking company. The program is arranged by the trucking company and may be required before the owner-operator can haul for the company. It is designed to prevent workers' compensation claims by the trucker. Coverage is provided for work-related injuries and generally follows the state's workers' compensation benefit schedule.

see: arising out of and in the course of employment, workers' compensation law

true group insurance
Automobile. An insurance program organized through an employer, union or association, offering all employees personal automobile insurance regardless of their types of vehicles or driving records. This can result in a savings to employers, but the underwriter usually reserves the right to exclude bad drivers (those with a number of points or chargeable offenses) or to write them on a substandard basis.

see: chargeable offense

Health/Life. An insurance program through an employer, union or association that accepts all group members for coverage regardless of physical condition. This generally results in a savings for employees, but the underwriter usually reserves the right to cover some employees on a substandard basis.

compare: fictitious group; *see*: discretionary group, group health insurance, minimum group

trust
Financial Planning/Law. An agreement whereby a person (settlor) transfers property to another person or entity (trustee) to hold and manage for the benefit of another (beneficiary).

see: accumulation trust, agent's trust, American Trust Fund, beneficiary of trust, charitable lead trust, charitable remainder trust, credit shelter trust, inter vivos trust, irrevocable trust, life insurance trust, Lloyd's Premium Trust Fund, medical expense reversionary trust, multiple employer welfare arrangement, personal trust, qualified terminable interest property trust, short-term reversionary trust, testamentary trust, trust agreement, voting trust

trust agreement
Financial Planning. The legal agreement that documents the rules that are to be followed by a trustee in administering assets in a trust.

see: trust

Life. A life insurance policy rider indicating how policy proceeds are to be distributed.

trust and commission clause
Property. A provision in many property insurance policies extending coverage to property of others held by the insured in trust, on commission, for storage, for repairs, or for other reasons.

see: care, custody or control

trust deed
Title. A deed of land to a trustee as security for performance of an obligation. The trustee has the power to sell the land in case of default on the obligation.

synonym: deed of trust; *see*: deed, mortgage

trust departments' errors and omissions insurance
Professional Liability. Coverage for trust departments of banks against loss due to breach of duty, negligence, errors or omissions in the administration of estates or trusts or in managing real or personal property.

see: errors and omissions insurance, fiduciary bond

trust position ratio
Agency. A financial ratio used to evaluate the ability of an insurance agency to promptly pay their insurers. *Formula*: (cash + premium receivables) ÷ (premiums payable + pre-billed payables).

see: agency bill, agent's trust, collection ratio

trustee
Financial Planning. A person or institution who holds the title to property conveyed by another person (the settlor) in trust for the benefit of a third person (beneficiary).

see: trustees' and fiduciaries' errors and omissions insurance

trustee group
Employee Benefits. A group insured under a policy issued to the trustees of a fund established by two or more employers; one or more labor unions or a combination of employers and labor unions.

trustee group life insurance
Life. Group life insurance issued to a trustee for two or more employers in the same industry, for two or more unions, or for joint employer-union funds for the benefit of the employees or members.

see: group life insurance

445

trusteed assets

Financial Planning. Assets that have been placed in trust with a financial institution for a specific purpose. *Example*: An insurance agent's premium trust accounts.

see: trust

trustees' and fiduciaries' errors and omissions insurance

Professional Liability. Errors and omissions coverage, permitted under the Pension Reform Act of 1974, that protects trustees and fiduciaries who directly or indirectly exercise control over pensions or employee benefits. The insurance may be purchased with assets of the plan or trust in order to protect the plan and its fiduciaries.

see: employee benefit plan, errors and omissions insurance

trustor

Financial Planning.

see: settlor

tsunami

Loss Control/Property. A large sea wave produced by underwater seismic activity (earthquake or volcanic eruption). It can travel through the ocean at up to 600 mph.

see: flood, Pacific Tsunami Warning System

tuition and fees insurance

Property. A commercial property business income endorsement (ISO form CP 15 25) that indemnifies a school, college or university for lost tuition and fees caused by a direct loss from an insured peril.

see: business income coverage form

turbine objects

Property. One of the four classifications of machinery or equipment covered under a boiler and machinery policy. This classification (object definition no. 4 or ISO form BM 00 29) includes a rotary engine or part thereof powered by pressurized water or steam passing over a series of curved vanes on a central rotating spindle. Generally, turbines are used to generate electrical power.

see: object

turnkey insurance

Professional Liability. A professional liability coverage for general contractors, architects or engineers involved in a specific construction project under a turnkey construction contract, a design or build construction contract, or a project management team construction contract. Turnkey insurance combines design error and omissions and completed operations coverages.

see: completed operations coverage, design errors and omissions

turnover rate

Employee Benefits. A rate or frequency by which employees terminate employment with an employer for reasons other than death or retirement. The rate is expressed as a percentage of those leaving to the total number of those employed over a stated period of time.

see: payroll

24-hour coverage

Employee Benefits/Health/Workers' Compensation. An employee health benefit program that links group health insurance with workers' compensation insurance in a single program to cover employees without regard to where or when an injury or illness occurs. The plan uses the same carrier or health care delivery system (e.g., a health maintenance organization) to treat the employee regardless of the source of injury or illness.

compare: integrated care (1); *see*: group health insurance, workers' compensation insurance

twister

Property.

see: tornado

twisting

Regulation. An attempt by an agent or broker to persuade an insured, through misrepresentation, to cancel an existing policy and replace it with another policy.

see: anti-coercion law, misrepresentation

two-hand controls

Loss Control. Devices for a machine that require simultaneous application of both hands to operate the control, so the operator's hands are kept out of the point of operation while the machine is operating.

see: point of operation

tying arrangement

Regulation. An agreement between a seller and a purchaser that the sale of a product is contingent upon the purchase of another product or service of the seller. Tying the sale of insurance to another product or service is widely prohibited, which in some states includes combining unrelated forms of insurance coverage.

synonym: tie-in sale; *see*: unfair trade practices

typhoon

Property.

see: hurricane

U

uberrima fides

Insurer Operations/Reinsurance. (Latin for "utmost good faith.") In insurance contracts, it is expected that both parties (insurer and insured, or cedent and reinsurer) have entered into the contract in good faith, have disclosed all material facts, and intend to carry out their obligations.

It has been said that reinsurance especially requires the utmost good faith. Reinsurance premiums must be lower than the initial premium for ceding insurers to have an incentive to reinsure, and assuming reinsurers cannot incur costs of evaluating risks and handling claims if they are to charge lower premiums than the initial insurer. Cedents and reinsurers must therefore be completely honest for long-term relationships to be maintained and the reinsurance market to remain viable.

compare: caveat emptor; *see*: follow the fortunes, good faith, reinsurance

UL listed

Loss Control.

see: Underwriters Laboratories, Inc.

ultimate mortality table

Life. A mortality table based on the experience of a book of insurance policies that compensates for adverse selection by eliminating the experience of those policies that were issued within the past five to ten years.

see: adverse selection, mortality table

ultimate net loss (UNL)

Insurer Operations. The sum of all costs that an insured or insurer is legally obligated to pay as the result of a claim, including judgments or compromises, legal, medical and investigation expenses, minus any salvage, subrogation and reinsurance.

see: net loss, net underwriting profit (or loss)

ultra vires

Law. An action outside the proper authority or purposes of a corporation or corporate officer. (Latin for "beyond the power.") Courts generally validate ultra vires acts so persons who rely on a corporation's apparent authority do not incur losses unfairly.

compare: intra vires

ultrasonic detector

Loss Control. A burglar alarm trigger that emits an ultrasonic wave pattern into the area to be protected. When the wave pattern is disrupted by an intruder, the burglar alarm operates.

see: burglar alarm

umbrella liability insurance

Liability. A special liability policy that serves three main functions: provide high excess coverage over a primary or underlying liability policy; provide broader coverages than the primary liability policy, usually excess of a self-insured retention; and provide a drop-down feature that automatically replaces coverage provided by underlying policies when they are reduced or exhausted by losses. Ordinarily used for commercial risks, umbrellas have also been developed for personal lines. The form was first introduced in the United States by Lloyd's around 1947, but umbrellas are offered today by many American liability insurers.

compare: bumbershoot, excess liability insurance, parasol policy; *see*: drop-down provision, personal umbrella, self-insured retention

umpire

Law. A term used instead of *arbitrator* in some contracts.

see: arbitration, arbitrator

unallocated benefit

Health. A health insurance policy provision that sets a maximum amount of reimbursement for the costs of all extra miscellaneous hospital services without specifying or scheduling the amount that will be paid for each type of service.

compare: fee schedule

unallocated claim expense

Insurer Operations. An expense that cannot be assigned to and recorded with a specific claim. This includes claim department operating expenses such as rent, heat and electricity, and other overhead expenses.

synonym: unallocated loss expense; *compare*: allocated claim expense; *see*: claim expense

unallocated funding agreement

Employee Benefits. An agreement found in a pension plan providing that money paid into the plan that is not currently allocated to purchase retirement benefits cannot be commingled with any other funds. Such funds are not allocated to a specific plan participant, but can be used when a plan participant retires, to purchase an annuity policy for that individual or pay benefits directly to the participant.

see: employee benefit plan

unallocated loss expense

Insurer Operations.

see: unallocated claim expense

unauthorized advances coverage form

Crime. A crime coverage form (ISO form CR 10 06) that amends the employee dishonesty coverage forms to provide coverage specifically for fraternal orders and labor unions and to exclude any loss resulting from unauthorized advances to members for delinquent dues or assessments.

see: employee dishonesty coverage form

unauthorized computer access coverage

Crime. A special crime coverage designed for organizations with an unauthorized computer access exposure. Coverage is provided for financial and extra expense losses that result from the illegal entry to the insured's computer system whether or not there was an intent to achieve financial gain. Coverage is provided for both first- and third-party losses.

see: computer fraud coverage form

unauthorized insurance

Insurer Operations. Insurance written by an insurer not licensed by the country or state where the coverage is provided.

compare: surplus lines; *see*: unauthorized insurer, unauthorized reinsurance

unauthorized insurer

Insurer Operations. An insurer neither licensed nor approved as a surplus lines insurer or a reinsurer neither licensed nor approved in a particular jurisdiction.

compare: admitted insurer; *see*: nonadmitted insurer, surplus lines, unauthorized insurance, unauthorized reinsurance

unauthorized reinsurance

Insurer Operations/Reinsurance. Insurance risk transferred to a reinsurer that is neither admitted to write insurance directly in the state of the primary insurer nor approved to assume reinsurance. State insurance regulators do not permit credit for unauthorized reinsurance in the ceding insurer's annual statement.

synonym: nonadmitted reinsurance; *compare*: authorized reinsurance; *see*: fronting, funding of reserves, reinsurance credit

unbundled services

Risk Management. Certain services performed by the insurer, such as claims administration, claims adjusting and loss control, are automatically included in the purchase of a policy. For large policyholders, some insurers provide a policy that excludes some or all of these services, which are provided either directly by the insured or by a third-party contractor.

unconscionability

Law. Unfairness or one-sidedness in a contract to such a degree that it is legally unenforceable or its validity is limited by a court to the provisions that are fair and reasonable.

see: contract, contract of adhesion

uncontrolled insurance program

International. An international insurance program with no central point of control. The parent organization's foreign subsidiaries have the authority to select coverages, deductibles, and limits and purchase insurance locally.

compare: controlled master insurance program, coordinated program, global insurance program

underground exclusion

Liability. An exclusion under the 1973 Insurance Services Office's liability rating program that applied to businesses involved in operations like grading, paving, excavating, drilling, burrowing, filling, back-filling or pile driving. The exclusion denied coverage for property damage to underground wires, pipes, cables, sewers, etc., caused by such operations. The coverage could be purchased back for an additional premium.

see: blasting and explosion exclusion, collapse exclusion, XCU exclusions

underground storage tank pollution liability insurance

Liability. Pollution liability insurance for owners of underground storage tanks that covers third-party bodily injury, property damage and cleanup expense for claims arising from the release of hazardous materials from a specifically insured tank. A site assessment is required before policy issuance.

Coverage is on a claims-made basis with exclusions for known pollution conditions existing prior to the policy's inception and for intentional acts of pollution.

see: aboveground storage tank pollution liability insurance, pollution insurance

underinsurance

Risk Management. The purchase of insurance with limits inadequate to meet policy coinsurance requirements, or the failure to purchase insurance in amounts sufficient to cover a large loss.

compare: noninsurance, overinsurance

underinsured motorist coverage

Automobile. Coverage that may be endorsed to an auto policy to pay damages for bodily injury to its own insured, in excess of the insurance of another motorist who is legally liable for such damages but who has inadequate liability coverage.

compare: uninsured motorist coverage

underlier

Reinsurance.

see: underlying limits

underlier policy

International.

see: local underlier policy

underlying insurance

Insurer Operations.

see: primary insurance

underlying insurance policy

Insurer Operations. A policy providing coverage below an umbrella or excess policy in a layered program.

see: master insurance policy

Property. A policy required by mortgage holders that duplicates portions of the coverage provided by a master policy.

compare: single interest policy; *see*: certificate of insurance, layering, loss payable clause, master insurance policy

underlying limits

Insurer Operations. The limits of insurance or reinsurance in place before the next level or layer of insurance or reinsurance takes effect.

synonym: underlier; *see*: layering

underlying premium

Reinsurance.

see: subject premium

underwriter

Insurer Operations. An individual skilled in the process of selecting risks for an insurance company. The term originated in London at the Lloyd's Coffee House, where a person willing to provide insurance protection signed their name beneath a description of the protection to be provided and thereby became an under-writer.

see: Chartered Life Underwriter, Chartered Property Casualty Underwriter, lay underwriter, lead underwriter, line underwriter, Lloyd's underwriter, risk appraiser, selection of risk, staff underwriter, underwriting, underwriting department

Life. A life insurance agent.

see: agent, risk appraiser

Financial Planning.

see: investment banker

underwriters' fire patrol

Property. In the past, insurers had their own fire brigades or patrols that fought fires on their insured's properties. Insurers often competed for business on the basis of their fire patrols. A policyholder's property had a fire mark to identify which patrol protected it. In some communities the insurers joined together to maintain a single patrol to protect the entire community.

synonym: fire brigade; *see*: fire mark

Underwriters Laboratories, Inc. (UL)

Loss Control/Organizations. Members: A nonprofit testing laboratory sponsored by the National Board of Fire Underwriters. *Objectives*: Test various materials, products, devices and appliances for safety. Products that meet safety standards are certified as "UL Approved" and may bear such a label. *Headquarters*: Northbrook, IL.

Underwriters Laboratories of Canada (ULC)

Organizations. Members: Canadian insurance companies. *Objectives*: Maintains and operates laboratories and a certification service for examining, testing and classifying devices, construction materials and methods to determine their fire and safety characteristics. *Headquarters*: Scarborough, Ontario, Canada.

underwriting

Insurer Operations. The process of reviewing applications for coverage and the information contained therein. Those that are accepted must then be classified by the underwriter according to the type and degree of risk, and appropriate rates are assigned for the exposure. The steps of the underwriting process are: 1. Gather information; 2. Identify, develop, and evaluate alternatives; 3. Select an alternative; 4. Implement the decision; and 5. Monitor the exposure. Underwriting often involves a subjective evaluation.

compare: placement; *see*: account underwriting, adverse selection, benefit of selection, class underwriting, classification, mass underwriting, risk classification, underwriting audit

underwriting audit

Insurer Operations. An insurance company management tool used to determine if established underwriting standards are being followed by individual line underwriters. A team of staff underwriters usually reviews selected files and makes an underwriting audit report.

see: line underwriter, staff underwriter

underwriting cycle

Insurer Operations. An insurance business cycle, where rates and premiums (and therefore profits) alternately rise and fall, rather than growing smoothly. Causes of these cycles are interest rate and stock market fluctuations, flow of excessive new capital into the insurance industry during profitable years, social and economic inflation, catastrophic losses, and competition.

see: buyer's market, cash flow underwriting, hard market, soft market, tight market

underwriting department

Insurer Operations. The employees and operations of an insurance company that are responsible for evaluating applications and determining whether a policy should be issued, and if so, its terms, conditions and rates.

see: underwriting

underwriting income

Insurer Operations. The gain or loss by an insurance company from the business of insurance. *Formula:* earned premium – (incurred losses + loss adjusting costs + other incurred underwriting expenses + policyholder dividends).

compare: underwriting profit (or loss); *see:* underwriting income per share

underwriting income per share

Insurer Operations. Statutory underwriting profit adjusted for the equity in the amount transferred to or from the unearned premium reserve divided by the number of common shares outstanding at year end.

see: underwriting profit (or loss)

underwriting margin

Insurer Operations. The difference between 100% and the sum of the loss and expense ratios in property/casualty underwriting. It may be either positive (indicating an underwriting profit) or negative (indicating an underwriting loss).

see: expense ratio, loss ratio

underwriting profit (or loss)

Insurer Operations. Money earned or lost by an insurer in its underwriting operations, as distinguished from money earned or lost in the investment of assets. *Formula:* earned premiums –

(losses + loss adjusting expenses + other underwriting expenses).

compare: underwriting income; *see:* cash flow underwriting, net underwriting profit (or loss)

Underwriting Section, CPCU Society

Organizations. An interest section of the CPCU Society that promotes information and study of underwriting theory and techniques.

see: CPCU Society

undesirable list

Insurer Operations.

see: prohibited list

unearned premium

Insurer Operations. The amount of premium remaining after deducting the earned premium from written premium; the portion of a premium representing the unexpired part of the policy period. Since coverage has not yet applied to the unexpired period, the insurer has not yet earned that portion of the premium.

compare: earned premium; *see:* return premium

unearned premium reserve

Insurer Operations. The sum of all the premiums representing the unexpired portions of the policies or contracts that the insurer or reinsurer has on its books as of a specific point in time.

compare: earned premium; *see:* funding of reserves, premium, unearned premium

unearned reinsurance premium

Insurer Operations/Reinsurance. The amount of reinsurance premium remaining on a reinsurance contract for the period of time the policy must continue in force.

compare: earned reinsurance premium; *see:* premium

unemployment compensation

Employee Benefits. A state or federal program funded by payroll taxes that pays weekly income benefits for a limited time (e.g., 26 weeks) to workers who are temporarily unemployed but are able to work and actively seeking work.

see: unemployment compensation disability insurance, unemployment insurance

unemployment compensation disability insurance (UCD)

Health. State legislation imposing liability on employers to provide weekly benefits to employees that sustain off-the-job accidents or sickness. Injured employees eligible for workers' compensation benefits are ineligible for the disability benefits under this program.

see: statutory disability income insurance, unemployment compensation

unemployment insurance

Liability. Federal legislation allows qualified non-profit organizations to self-insure their unemployment compensation obligation. Some insurers provide coverage for this obligation on a stop-loss or excess-of-loss basis.

see: unemployment compensation

unfair claims practice

Regulation. Deliberate action taken by an insurer to avoid paying claims to insureds. Many states have passed laws patterned after model legislation developed by the National Association of Insurance Commissioners in response to these actions, requiring that insurance claims be handled fairly and that insurers communicate honestly with insureds.

see: bad faith, entire contract statute

unfair discrimination

Regulation.

see: discrimination

unfair trade practices

Insurer Operations/Regulation. With respect to insurers and their agents, unfair trade practices usually include boycott, coercion, intimidation, bad faith, price fixing, and other noncompetitive actions.

see: anti-coercion law, bad faith, twisting, tying arrangement, unconscionability, unfair claims practice

unfired pressure vessel

Property.

see: pressure vessel

unfired vessels

Loss Control. Any vessel normally operated under pressure or vacuum, but not directly heated by fire or fuel gases. Electrically heated pressure vessels are classified as unfired vessels.

unfunded actuarial accrued liability

Employee Benefits. The excess of an employee benefit plan's actuarial accrued liability over the actuarial value of the plan's assets.

see: actuarial valuation, employee benefit plan, funding standard account, minimum funding

unfunded reserve

Accounting. A liability entered on the books of an organization for which funds have not been set aside to offset the liability. An unfunded reserve is used to reflect casualty losses on the organization's financial statement but cannot be used to reduce its income tax liability. Many organizations that self-insure establish either funded or unfunded reserves.

compare: funded reserve; *see*: casualty loss

uniform bill-patient summary

Health. A written statement from a medical service provider documenting both the billing and the medical information.

see: Uniform Billing Form

Uniform Billing Form

Health. A standard hospital services billing form that provides the basic data required by most third-party payers to process claims. The form is also known as UB-82, UB-92, or Health Care Financing Administration form 1450.

see: Health Care Financing Administration

Uniform Commercial Code (UCC)

Regulation. A business code that has been adopted as law in most states. The UCC governs commercial transactions (sale of goods, ownership) concerning personal property.

see: personal property

uniform forms

Insurer Operations. Policy forms developed by industry organizations for general use, such as ACORD and ISO forms.

see: ACORD forms, Insurance Services Office, standard policy

uniform hospital discharge data set

Health. A recommended hospital discharge abstract, developed by the Uniform Hospital Abstract Subcommittee of the U.S. National Committee on Vital and Health Statistics.

see: Uniform Billing Form

Uniform Individual Accident and Sickness Policy Provisions Act

Health/Regulation. Model legislation developed by the National Association of Insurance Commissioners that has been adopted by all states. It requires certain provisions in all health insurance policies, such as provisions on beneficiary changes, submission of proof of loss, policy reinstatement, and a grace period.

see: standard provisions

uniform premium

Health/Life. A rating system used by life and health insurers that does not distinguish among applicants for such usual rating classifications as age, sex, or occupation. All applicants receive the same rates.

see: age discrimination, gender rating, occupational hazard

uniform provisions

Health.

see: Uniform Individual Accident and Sickness Policy Provisions Act

Life. Life insurance policy provisions that are required by state law to be contained in all policies. Some latitude is usually allowed as to the exact wording, but the provisions must be contained in substance.

see: standard provisions

uniform simultaneous death act

Life/Regulation. Legislation adopted in most states providing for the transfer of benefits when an insured and the beneficiary of a life insurance policy die simultaneously or within a short time of each other in a common accident where it cannot be determined who died first. The law presumes that the insured survived the beneficiary. Therefore, the policy benefits are paid to a secondary beneficiary or, if none is designated, to the insured's estate.

see: common disaster clause, secondary beneficiary

uniform straight bill of lading

Inland Marine/Ocean Marine.

see: waybill

unilateral contract

Law.

see: contract of adhesion

uninsurable risk

Insurer Operations. A risk where there is no insurable interest; a risk where the potential for loss is so great it does not meet the definition of insurance; a risk where insurance is prohibited by public policy or is illegal.

synonym: noninsurable risk; *see*: insurance, special risk, substandard risk

uninsured motorist coverage

Automobile. Coverage that must be offered to insureds in many states and which, when added to an automobile policy, pays damages for bodily injury to its own insured for which an uninsured motorist is legally liable but unable to pay.

synonym: family protection endorsement; *compare*: unsatisfied judgment fund; *see*: underinsured motorist coverage, uninsured motorist law

uninsured motorist law

Automobile. State legislation in most states requiring insurers who write automobile insurance to offer all of their policyholders protection against uninsured motorists.

see: uninsured motorist coverage

union shop

Employee Benefits. A place of employment where the employer may hire non-union employees, but after a short period of time (usually 30 days) new employees must become members of the union or be discharged.

unique impairment

Life. A life insurance underwriting term denoting substandard or uninsurable risks such as physical,

moral or financial conditions that are below normal underwriting criteria.

see: substandard risk, uninsurable risk

unisex legislation

Regulation. Legislation that prohibits distinguishing between males and females in insurance rates or coverages. It requires that for a given class of insurance, all individuals regardless of sex must be offered the same rates and coverages.

see: gender rating, sex discrimination, uniform premium

unit credit actuarial cost method

Employee Benefits. The calculation of pension plan benefits based on the accumulation of "benefit units," which are based on such things as salary and service years. A plan's normal cost for a year is based on the sum of (1) the present value of units accumulated by plan participants during the current year and (2) the present value of accrued benefits credited to participants for service prior to the present year.

synonym: accrued benefit cost method, accumulated benefit cost method; *see*: actuarial cost method, pension, vested benefit

unit statistical filing

Workers' Compensation. A printed form or electronic file for each employer by the National Council on Compensation Insurance or a state workers' compensation rating bureau that contains all the information needed to establish a workers' compensation experience modification for the employer (e.g., payroll, claims information).

see: experience rating modification factor, National Council on Compensation Insurance, payroll, rating bureau, workers' compensation experience rating work sheet

United States Government Life Insurance (USGLI)

Life.

see: National Service Life Insurance

universal life insurance

Life. A form of life insurance in which the policyholder may periodically change the death benefit and modify the amount or timing of premium payments. The insurance company's policy expenses and other charges are specifically disclosed to the policyholder and are deducted from the premium. The balance of the premium is used to pay mortality charges, and any remaining funds are credited to the policy and earn interest at rates that usually are tied to U.S. Treasury issues or money market rates.

synonym: flexible premium adjustable life insurance; *compare*: universal variable life insurance; *see*: accumulation value, additional deposit privilege, current assumption whole life insurance, guideline premium, interest free loan, level death benefit option, statement of policy information, unscheduled premium payments

universal mercantile system

Property. A rating system for property insurance risks that is no longer in wide use. It has been replaced by a new system developed by the Insurance Services Office.

universal variable life insurance

Life. A form of life insurance that combines the features of universal life insurance and variable life insurance. The policyholder may direct the insurer as to which investment vehicle excess premiums and interest are to be invested. These investment vehicles are separate accounts and may include equity securities, bonds, or real estate. This policy is considered a replacement for standard universal life insurance, which ties investment income to U.S. Treasury securities and money market rates.

compare: universal life insurance

University Risk Management and Insurance Association (URMIA)

Organizations. Members: Colleges and universities with insurance and risk management offices. *Objectives*: Promote the exchange of ideas and information about sound insurance and risk management. *Founded*: 1966. *Headquarters*: Birmingham, AL.

unlevel commission

Agency/Insurer Operations. A system where an agent's commissions are higher the first year an insurance policy is written, then reduced on anniversary or renewal billings. Designed to encourage the development of new business, this system has been criticized as encouraging unnecessary replacement policies, particularly Medicare supplement policies for elderly customers.

synonym: graded commission; *compare*: level commission; *see*: agent's commission, first-year commission, Medicare supplement insurance, renewal commission

unlimited reporting period

Liability.
see: maxi-tail

unlimited tail

Liability.
see: maxi-tail

unlisted security

Financial Planning. A security that is not traded on a stock exchange.

unoccupied

Property. A building that is furnished but in which nobody resides. Some property insurance policies suspend coverage if a building is unoccupied for more than a specified time, usually 60 or 90 days.

compare: vacant; *see*: vacancy permit, vacant or unoccupied cancellation provision

unreinforced masonry

Loss Control. A form of brick construction used in older buildings where the brick was set with lime or lime-sand mortar and no steel reinforcing rods were used between the rows of brick. This type of construction is very susceptible to earthquake damage.

see: construction, earthquake, masonry incombustible construction

unrepaired damage cancellation provision

Property. A provision in some property insurance policies that allows cancellation with prior written notice (usually five days) by the insurer if repairs to the building for damage from a covered cause of loss have not begun or have not been contracted for within 30 days of the loss payment.

unreported claims

Insurer Operations. A claim that has occurred but has not yet been reported to the insurer. Insurers account for such claims by establishing an incurred but not reported reserve.

see: incurred but not reported

unsatisfied judgment fund (UJF)

Automobile. A fund established in some states to reimburse people injured in auto accidents who have been unable to collect awards for damages against those responsible for the loss.

compare: uninsured motorist coverage

unscheduled premium payments

Life. A universal life insurance policy provision that allows a policyholder to make additional, unscheduled premium payments at any time in order to build equity in the policy investment feature.

see: universal life insurance

unscheduled property floater

Inland Marine. An inland marine policy that provides blanket coverage on all property of a specified classification (such as household furnishings or tourist luggage), usually on an all-risk basis.

compare: scheduled coverage; *see*: floater policy, inland marine insurance

unsecured bond

Financial Planning.
see: debenture

up-stream merger

Risk Management. A merger of a subsidiary corporation into its parent.

see: merger

upper explosive level (UEL)
Loss Control.
   see: flammable limits

uprising
Property. An insurrection, revolt or rebellion. Losses resulting from such an event are often excluded from property insurance policies.
   see: riot and civil commotion coverage

upset coverage
Inland Marine. A coverage that can be added by endorsement to a contractor's equipment floater to cover cranes. Coverage is for the damage caused to the equipment if it is upset or overturned, provided the equipment does not exceed its maximum rated load.

Urban Development Act of 1970
Crime. An act of Congress that established the Federal Crime Insurance Program to provide coverage for business owners and residents located in high crime areas. The program is administered by private insurers under the direction of the Federal Insurance Administration.
   see: federal crime insurance program

use-and-file rating
Regulation. The practice in some states of permitting insurers to implement new rates for a brief period (usually 30 days) before filing them with the insurance commissioner, who may disapprove the rates if not in compliance with legal requirements.
   compare: file-and-use rating, prior approval rating; *see*: rate making, rate regulation

use and occupancy insurance (U&O)
Property. Coverage for lost income under a boiler and machinery policy; also, an obsolete term for business income insurance. Use and occupancy insurance covers an insured business for loss of use of equipment caused by an insured peril.
   see: boiler and machinery insurance, business income coverage form

use limitation
Aviation. An aircraft policy exclusion that excludes coverage if the aircraft is used for a purposes other than those indicated in the policy's purpose of use classification.
   see: aircraft insurance, business and pleasure, fixed base operators, flying club, general aviation, industrial aid operators

usual, customary and reasonable fee
Health.
   see: reasonable and customary charge

utilization and quality control peer review organization
Health.
   see: peer review organization

utilization review
Health/Workers' Compensation. An examination of the medical necessity, economic appropriateness and quality of care provided by a health care facility to its patients. It may be conducted either by an internal staff committee or by an external, independent review organization. For workers' compensation purposes, a utilization review may also apply to rehabilitation and retraining services.
   see: case management, managed care, peer review organization

utmost good faith
Insurer Operations.
   see: good faith, uberrima fides

V

vacancy permit

Property. Consent from a fire underwriter for an insured to maintain coverage on a building that has been vacant or unoccupied beyond the limitation period (usually 90 days) specified in a policy; an endorsement (ISO form CP 04 50) issued by an insurer after the insured gives notice that the property will be vacant beyond a specified time which waives a vacancy cancellation. Usually, the permit is granted free of charge when the structure is in an area with satisfactory fire protection.

compare: change in occupancy or use; *see*: unoccupied, vacant or unoccupied cancellation provision, "while" clauses

vacant

Property. A building devoid of any personal property used in the operations or activities usually conducted within it.

compare: unoccupied; *see*: occupancy, vacancy permit

vacant or unoccupied cancellation provision

Property. A property insurance policy provision that if an insured building is vacant or unoccupied for a number of consecutive days (usually 90), coverage may be canceled by the insurer with prior written notice (usually five days) unless a vacancy or unoccupancy permit is obtained from the insurer.

see: vacant, vacancy permit, unoccupied

validation period

Life. The time required for a life insurer to amortize the expense of a new life insurance policy. Because expenses such as commissions, file setup, and medical examinations create higher first-year expenses than those for future years, these costs are amortized over several years.

see: amortization

valuable papers and records insurance

Inland Marine. An inland marine policy (ISO form CM 00 67 or AAIS form IM 661) covering property such as blueprints, manuscripts, maps, historical documents, and business records on an all-risk basis.

see: inland marine insurance

valuation

General. Assessment of the value or worth of something, usually by appraisal; the determination of the value of insured property.

see: actual cash value, agreed value, appraised value, business interruption value, depreciated value, economic value, functional replacement cost, going concern value, insurance to value, market value, replacement cost, reproduction cost, tax-appraised value, valuation of assets, valuation of loss, valuation of potential property loss

Insurer Operations. The determination of insurance company claims reserves needed to pay future claims.

see: actuarial valuation

Life. The determination of a life insurance company's policy reserve.

see: asset share value, policy reserve, tabular value reserve method, valuation premium

valuation method

Insurer Operations. The procedure used by claims adjusters in determining that a loss has occurred and establishing the economic value of the loss.

see: valuation of loss

valuation of assets

Regulation. The assets of an insurance company are valued according to rules promulgated by state insurance departments. These rules are based on guidelines developed by the National Association of Insurance Commissioners' Committee on Valuation of Securities. Valuation criteria require that an insurer's real estate be valued at book value, its common stock be valued at market value (at year-end for annual statement purposes), investment-quality bonds at amortized value, and preferred stock at original cost.

see: mandatory securities valuation reserve, securities valuation, Valuation of Securities System

valuation of loss

Insurer Operations. The procedure followed by an insured to establish the value of a property loss. The valuation of some losses requires subjective interpretation, as they involve partial damage or lost items for which valuation support is unavailable.

see: valuation method

valuation of potential property loss

Risk Management. The risk management task of identifying and valuing property loss exposures. The value assigned to each risk may be based on replacement cost, actual cash value (physical depreciation considered), original cost, depreciated value, market value, or tax appraised value, depending on its current use and the organization's financial structure. Once loss exposures are identified and valued, funding for a potential loss, including transfer of risk, can be developed.

see: actual cash value, depreciated value, fair market value, functional replacement cost, market value, replacement cost, reproduction cost, tax-appraised value, valuation, valuation method

Valuation of Securities System (VOS)

Regulation. An on-line database maintained by the National Association of Insurance Commissioners to help monitor insurers' solvency which contains a list of securities held by insurers along with historical data beginning with 1989, for financial review purposes. The database also has individual portfolios of the 250 subscribing insurance companies.

see: high-yield bond, insolvency, National Association of Insurance Commissioners, securities valuation, valuation of assets

valuation premium

Life. A rate for a life insurance policy that is based on the reserves the insurer must maintain to meet state insurance department standards. The reserves on a class of policies are valued so there will be sufficient assets to pay all claims in full, and then a rate for the policies is developed based upon this value. Some insurers deviate from the valuation premium rate in light of favorable experience or updated mortality tables. If this is done, the insurer must establish a deficiency reserve in the event the rate is inadequate.

see: deficiency reserve

valuation reserve

Accounting. An accounting reserve established to anticipate a decrease in an asset's value; a depreciation reserve to protect an insurer against wide swings in the price of securities.

see: reserve

value reporting form

Property.

see: reporting form

valued bill of lading

Ocean Marine. A bill of lading issued by the carrier, indicating the amount that the shipper has declared as the value of merchandise. The carrier will be held liable for the amount indicated if the carrier is found responsible for loss or damage to the shipment.

synonym: ad valorem bill of lading; *see*: bill of lading

valued business interruption insurance

Property. Coverage for a stated amount of lost earnings for each day due to an insured peril.

compare: maximum period of indemnity, monthly limit of indemnity; *see*: business income coverage form

valued clause

Automobile/Property. A provision in some automobile and property insurance policies stating the value of each insured item.

see: stated amount

valued coverage

Insurer Operations. Insurance coverage that pays a specified amount for a covered item in the event of a total loss. Valued coverage applies to personal property that has been specifically scheduled (e.g., 1995 GMC truck, painting of Hawaii by Roslie Rupp Prussing). In general, a policy may be considered valued which pays an amount not directly related to the extent of loss. In this sense, a life insurance policy is valued, because it pays a specified sum rather than attempting to restore an insured to the same financial position as before the loss.

compare: indemnity agreement, nonvalued policy; *see*: limit of liability, scheduled coverage, stated amount

valued policy law

Regulation. A regulation adopted in some states to discourage insurers from selling more insurance than needed on a property. It requires that in the event of a total loss, all insurers must pay the face amount of the policy, regardless of the traditional role of indemnity—to restore on indemnitee to his or her original position—unless fraud or arson is involved.

see: overinsurance

values

Life. Shorthand for *nonforfeiture values* among life insurers.

see: nonforfeiture benefit

vandalism

Property. Willful or malicious destruction or defacement of another's property; a coverage included with malicious mischief insurance.

see: vandalism and malicious mischief coverage

vandalism and malicious mischief coverage (V&MM)

Property. Insurance of losses due to vandalism and malicious mischief, which is usually provided by an endorsement to a fire insurance policy. Basic homeowners and commercial property insurance forms include this coverage with no special endorsement.

see: malicious mischief, vandalism

vanishing premium

Life. A life insurance policy with large premium payments in its initial years that are used to quickly build up cash value. After an adequate cash value is accumulated, remaining premium payments are made by borrowing against the policy's cash value.

synonym: premium offset

variable annuity

Life. An annuity where the accumulation and benefits are expressed as "accumulation units" or "benefit units" rather than fixed monetary amounts. The annitant pays level premiums to purchase units of varying value. Unit values are based on a combination of actuarial factors, the value of the investment portfolio of the insurer's variable annuity account (which comprises premiums and accumulations from all or a class of variable annuities), and an inflation index. When the annuity matures, the annuitant's credited units are converted to a number of income units that determine the monthly payments. The annuitant assumes the investment risk, while the insurer assumes only expense and actuarial risks, in the hope that income payments will maintain more stable purchasing power (i.e., keep pace with inflation) than would payments under a conventional annuity.

see: accumulation period, annuity, cost-of-living variable annuity plan, equity variable annuity plan, insured variable annuity plan

variable commission

Agency. A commission paid to agents in addition to their normal commission. It is usually based on the agent's loss ratio and volume of business and is used to motivate agents to write preferred risks and more business.

synonym: bonus commission, contingent commission, profit-sharing commission

variable life insurance

Life. Life insurance with benefits tied to the return of a specific portfolio of securities. Often, the policyholder may select from several portfolios with different investment characteristics. The policy offers a fixed premium and a minimum death benefit. The higher the investment return, the higher the benefit or surrender value of the policy.

compare: fixed annuity, universal life insurance, universal variable life insurance; *see*: indexed life insurance

variable premium life insurance

Life. A life insurance policy that allows the insured to vary the premium payments subject to certain limitations. The policy benefits and cash value vary with the premium payments. The most common form of variable premium life insurance is the universal life policy.

compare: variable life insurance; *see*: universal life insurance, universal variable life insurance

variable rate mortgage

Financial Planning. A mortgage on which the interest rate charged by the lender may be adjusted in accordance with a stipulated cost-of-funds index (e.g., New York prime rate).

synonym: adjustable rate mortgage; *compare*: fixed rate mortgage, renegotiable rate mortgage; *see*: discount (1), payment cap

vault

Crime. A fortified room or compartment for the safekeeping of valuable property.

see: safe

vehicle damage coverage

Property. Part of the coverage under most basic property insurance policies, usually combined with aircraft damage coverage. Coverage is for damage caused by direct physical contact between an insured property and a vehicle and extends to damage caused by objects thrown from passing vehicles. Damage caused by a vehicle owned by the insured or a tenant of the insured is excluded.

see: aircraft damage coverage

vendee

General. The buyer of property.

compare: vendor

vendor

General. The seller of property.

compare: vendee; *see*: vendor's endorsement

vendor's endorsement

Liability. An endorsement (ISO form CG 20 15) that extends a manufacturer's commercial general liability policy to cover designated vendors as additional insureds for bodily injury or property damage arising out of the manufacturer's products.

Coverage may be on a blanket basis (for all vendors) or may specify certain vendors only.

see: broad form vendor's endorsement, commercial general liability policy, limited form vendor's endorsement

venture

Ocean Marine. An undertaking, such as the voyage of a vessel.

see: adventure, common venture

verdict

Law. The decision of a jury in a trial.

see: burden of proof, directed verdict

vertical integration

Agency/Insurer Operations. Generally, the combination of different levels of business operations under common management or control (for example, combining the manufacture and the retail distribution of a product).

In insurance, the ownership of an insurance company by an agent or broker, or the ownership of an agency or brokerage by an insurer, in an attempt to reduce the costs of marketing insurance products.

see: producer-controlled insurer, vertical merger

vertical merger

Risk Management. A merger between a corporation and one of its major suppliers or customers.

see: merger

vested benefit

Employee Benefits. A benefit that has been fully credited to an employee without further requirements, including continued employment.

see: employee benefit plan, vesting

vested commissions

Agency/Insurer Operations. Commissions due an insurance agent on renewal policies regardless of the agent's continued employment by the insurer or agency.

see: agent's commission

vesting

Employee Benefits. A pension plan participant's right to receive benefits from employer contributions to a plan even if the participant changes jobs. All employee contributions made to a plan are fully vested at the time they are made. Employer contributions are vested according to a schedule contained in the plan.

see: conditional vesting, deferred vesting, employee benefit plan, future service, immediate vesting, pension, three percent rule, vested benefit, vesting schedules

vesting schedules

Employee Benefits. The Tax Reform Act of 1986 established two minimum vesting schedules for pension plans: 100% vesting after a plan participant has completed five years of service; or 20% vesting after completing three years of service and 20% additional vesting each year thereafter, with 100% vesting achieved in seven years.

see: ten-year vesting, vested benefit, vesting

Veterans' Administration

Organizations.

see: Department of Veterans Affairs

Veterans Administration hospital

Health. A hospital operated by a branch of the Department of Veterans Affairs (formerly the Veterans' Administration) for those who served in the U.S. armed forces. Most health insurance policies exclude expenses in VA hospitals because they are provided without cost.

see: Department of Veterans Affairs

Veterans Group Life Insurance (VGLI)

Life. Life insurance offered to veterans that were covered by a Servicemen's Group Life Insurance policy during active duty. The coverage is a five-year nonrenewable term policy that can be converted to individual permanent life issued through an insurer participating in the program.

see: Servicemen's Group Life Insurance

veterinarian professional liability insurance

Professional Liability. Insurance for veterinarians that covers losses or injury resulting from negligence or errors in rendering professional services.

see: pet insurance, pet salon liability coverage

viatical settlement

Health/Life. The sale of a life insurance policy by a terminally ill insured. The purchaser, usually a non-insurance investment type of company, pays a portion of the policy value to the insured and is named the beneficiary. Intending to profit from the policy proceeds, the purchaser pays the premiums until the policyholder dies. Some state laws require a minimum purchase price relative to the policy face amount to prevent taking unfair advantage of terminally ill people. The insured who sells the policy is called the *viator*. (Derived from the Latin word *viaticum*, meaning money and supplies given to Roman officials before a journey to distant parts of the empire.)

see: living benefits

vibration detector

Loss Control. A burglar alarm trigger device that uses a highly sensitive piezoelectric crystal or microphone to detect the sound pattern that an object, such as a hammer or drill, would generate on the protected surface (a safe or vault). When a vibration is detected, the burglar alarm is set off.

see: burglar alarm

vicarious liability

Law. Liability attributed to a person who has control over or responsibility for another who negligently causes an injury or otherwise would be liable. Whenever an agency relationship exists, the principal is responsible for the agent's actions. The negligence of an employee acting within the scope of employment is attributed to the employer.

synonym: imputed liability; *see*: agency, master-servant rule, negligence, principal, respondeat superior

vis major

General. An event or accident beyond any person's control. (Latin for "superior force"; same as the French term *force majeure*.) It is often understood as an "act of God," but it can include mass acts of human agency, such as war and civil strife, as well as natural disasters.

see: act of God, force majeur coverage, natural perils

vision care insurance

Health. Health insurance coverage for eye examinations and eyeglass or contact lens prescriptions.

vocational rehabilitation

Workers' Compensation. A form of rehabilitation designed to assist an injured worker who is unable to return to the occupation held at the time of the injury. It may include such services as job counseling, retraining or placement assistance.

see: rehabilitation clause

void

Law. A contract that does not have and never had legal force; null. Such a contract creates no legal obligations by either party and is treated as if it never existed.

compare: voidable; *see*: contract, rescission

voidable

Law. A contract that can be nullified at the option of one or more of the parties; a contract void as to one party but not the other pending the remedy of a defect. *Example*: A contract between an adult and a minor (who lacks legal competence to make a contract) is voidable by the minor; however, if the minor attains legal age and ratifies the contract, or if it is ratified by a person legally responsible for the minor, the contract is valid and enforceable by the adult.

compare: void; *see*: contract, election to avoid a policy, rescission

voidable preference

Law. A transfer of property by an insolvent debtor to a creditor within four months of a petition for bankruptcy, depriving other creditors of their proportional recovery. The transaction can be set aside and the property returned to the bankrupt's estate. This is a provision of the federal Bankruptcy Act, and similar state laws apply to insolvent insurers.

see: bankruptcy, insolvency, liquidation

volcanic action

Property. A violent explosion in a vent in the earth's crust (eruption), which results in the flow of lava, discharge of ash and dust, volcanic blast or shock waves. The term does not include loss from any form of earth movement. Coverage for loss by volcanic action is provided in most property insurance forms. Coverage does not extend to the cost of removing ash, dust, or particulate matter that does not cause direct physical loss or damage to the insured property.

compare: volcanic eruption, *see*: earth movement coverage

volcanic eruption

Property. The earth movement associated with a volcanic action including the eruption, explosion or effusion. Coverage for this peril is specifically excluded from property insurance forms but is included with earth movement and earthquake coverage.

compare: volcanic action; *see*: acid rain, earth movement coverage, earthquake insurance

voluntary compensation

Workers' Compensation. Some state workers' compensation laws allow an employer to voluntarily provide compensation benefits for employees not covered by the law. Examples of such employment are domestic servants, farm laborers, persons employed exclusively in a foreign country, or those employed in an area of federal jurisdiction.

see: voluntary compensation and employers' liability coverage endorsement, voluntary compensation maritime coverage endorsement, workers' compensation law

voluntary compensation and employers' liability coverage endorsement

Workers' Compensation. An endorsement (NCCI form WC 00 03 11A) to a workers' compensation policy that provides statutory coverage for employees who do not fall under a state's workers' compensation act, such as farm workers. It provides that the insurer will pay statutory benefits to the insured in exchange for the injured worker releasing the employer and the insurer from further liability. If the employee does not sign a release, any further compensation under the endorsement ceases.

see: release, voluntary compensation, workers' compensation law

voluntary compensation maritime coverage endorsement

Workers' Compensation. An endorsement (NCCI

form WC 00 02 03) to a workers' compensation policy that can be attached only in conjunction with the maritime coverage endorsement. It provides that the insurer will offer an injured master or crew member of a covered vessel a settlement based on the statutory workers' compensation benefits specified in the endorsement. If the settlement offer is refused, coverage is then provided under the employers' liability section of the maritime coverage endorsement.

see: maritime coverage endorsement

voluntary employee contribution plan

Employee Benefits. A pension plan where participants may elect to make regular contributions to the plan by payroll deductions. Under most qualified plans, such employee contributions are tax-deferred.

see: qualified plan

voluntary insurance

General. Insurance coverage not required by law.

compare: compulsory insurance, social insurance; *see*: voluntary insurer

voluntary insurer

Insurer Operations. An insurer offering voluntary insurance, as opposed to social insurance (i.e., Social Security, unemployment compensation). Voluntary insurers include private insurers, cooperatives, governmental agencies and self-insurers who can offer a wide spectrum of coverages.

voluntary leave to meet business needs

Employee Benefits. An unpaid leave of absence agreed to by the employee for the purpose of temporarily reducing an organization's operating expenses.

see: Family and Medical Leave Act, leave of absence

voluntary plan termination

Employee Benefits. Ending a pension plan at the election of an employer or sponsor. The employer has the right to change or terminate a pension plan at any time; however, the termination must meet requirements of the Employee Retirement Income Security Act. Assets must be distributed to the participants according to federal guidelines.

see: Employee Retirement Income Security Act

voluntary reserve

Insurer Operations. A reserve established by an insurer from its policyholders' surplus that is not required by statute. Such a reserve is often used for the payment of future policyholder dividends, or to indicate financial strength. Generally, it appears as a liability on the insurer's financial statement but is not deductible for tax purposes.

compare: statutory reserve; *see*: balance sheet

reserves, policy reserve

volunteer public safety officers

General. Members of volunteer fire departments, rescue squads or ambulance corps.

volunteer workers' coverage

Liability. An endorsement that can be added to the commercial general liability policy (ISO form CG 20 21) for hospitals, nonprofit organizations, etc., to include as additional insureds volunteer workers acting at the direction of the named insured. Volunteer status may be lost in some circumstances even though the individual receives no wages if meals, training, tuition credits, etc., are offered in exchange for services.

see: church members', officers' and volunteers' coverage; commercial general liability policy

voting trust

Financial Planning. A trust created by an agreement among shareholders to transfer legal title to their voting stock to a trustee authorized to vote the stock as a unit.

compare: proxy; *see*: cumulative voting, statutory voting

voyage

Ocean Marine. A vessel's complete journey, from home port through all of its ports-of-call back to home port; the journey of a cargo consignment from its origin to the warehouse of its final destination.

see: venture, voyage charter, voyage clause

voyage charter

Ocean Marine. The hiring of a ship's cargo capacity for a single voyage from one port to another. The vessel owner supplies the crew.

compare: bareboat charter; *see*: charter party

voyage clause

Ocean Marine. A clause in some ocean marine policies that limits the period of coverage to the time it takes for a voyage. A voyage can be comprised of a single trip or a number of trips grouped together.

see: voyage charter

W

wage index
Employee Benefits.
see: Social Security Wage Index

wage loss
Workers' Compensation. A workers' compensation concept, initiated by Florida in 1979, that ties employee recoveries from disability to actual economic loss, rather than to projections of the loss.
see: average weekly wage loss, reduced earnings

wages, maintenance and cure
Ocean Marine. An admiralty law principle indicating the care to which a sick or injured crew member is entitled. Wages are to continue during the seaman's injury or illness up to the time a voyage ends. For vessels operating year round and on inland waterways, wages are not to be paid beyond one year, the end of a contract, or the period of illness, whichever is shortest. A lawsuit must be brought by the seaman to recover earnings beyond this period of time. The term *maintenance* means rehabilitation and a proper living environment for the seaman, and *cure* refers to medical treatment, usually free of charge.
see: cure, Jones Act, maintenance, seaman's remedies

waiting period
Health. Under a disability policy, the period of time between the beginning of a policyholder's disability and the beginning of the policy's benefits.
synonym: elimination period; see: disability income insurance
Property. Under a boiler and machinery policy's loss of use coverage, the waiting period is a form of deductible and is usually specified in time (hours or days) before which the policy will not respond to a loss.
see: deductible
Workers' Compensation. Workers' compensation laws prescribe a period of time before disability

benefits may be paid. Most laws provide retroactive coverage if the disability extends beyond a certain time. No waiting period applies to medical benefits.
see: disability benefit, medical benefit, retroactive period, workers' compensation law

waiver
Health/Life. A policy rider excluding coverage for specified disabilities or injuries that normally would be covered by the policy.
Insurer Operations. The nullification or replacement of a policy provision by actions or statements of the issuing insurer's agent or employee that the insured relies upon.
see: acquiescence, estoppel, laches
Law. The intentional, voluntary act of relinquishing a known right, claim or privilege.
see: collision damage waiver, subrogation waiver, waiver of inventory clause, waiver of premium

waiver of inventory clause
Property. A provision in many property insurance policies that waives the requirement to provide an inventory of undamaged property. The waiver applies if a loss is under a specified amount (usually $10,000) or less than 5% of the amount insured.

waiver of our right to recover from others endorsement
Workers' Compensation. A workers' compensation policy endorsement (NCCI form WC 00 03 13) that waives the insurer's right to recover from a third party specifically named in the endorsement who may have contributed to a covered worker's injury. *Example*: A building owner hires a contractor to remodel the building and does not want to be responsible for any injuries to employees of the contractor. The endorsement is added to the contractor's policy, waiving the insurer's right to recover any paid claims from the building owner in a subrogation action.
see: subrogation

waiver of premium

Health/Life. A provision in some life insurance policies that forgives premium payments when the insured is disabled for more than six months.

synonym: disability waiver of premium; see: disability income insurance, waiver of restoration premium

waiver of restoration premium

Insurer Operations. A provision found primarily in policies issued in the London Market that reinstates the face amount of a policy without payment of an additional premium in the event a claim is paid.

Surety. A provision contained in a surety bond that automatically reinstates full coverage after payment of a loss without the payment of an additional premium.

see: surety bond

waiver of subrogation rights clause

Property/Liability. An endorsement issued by an insurer that waives its right of subrogation against a third party. It is usually requested by an insured in conjunction with a lease.

see: subrogation, subrogation waiver

war clause

Health/Life. A provision in a life insurance policy that excludes coverage for death or injury caused by acts of war. Some policies contain an absolute war exclusion applying to any insured, while others apply only to members of the armed forces serving in a war zone.

see: military service exclusion, war risks accident insurance

war damage insurance corporation

Insurer Operations. A reinsurance program developed by the federal government during World War II to cover private property in the United States from war damage.

war risk accident insurance

Health. Coverage for accidental death, dismemberment or disability for civilians who enter areas with an on-going conflict or risk of war.

war risks insurance

Ocean Marine. Coverage on ships or cargo against loss or damage by enemy action and against damages sustained in fighting such an action. The perils of war are excluded from most policies.

warehouse receipt

Inland Marine. A document issued to a bailee by a warehouseman for goods stored in the warehouse. Regulated by the Uniform Commercial Code, such receipts have a degree of negotiability.

see: bonded warehouse, Uniform Commercial Code, warehouse receipts losses exclusion form

warehouse receipts losses exclusion form

Crime. An endorsement (ISO form CR 10 05) that amends Insurance Services Office employee dishonesty forms to exclude coverage for any loss arising out of the fraudulent signing, issuing, canceling, or failing to cancel a warehouse receipt or any papers connected with it.

see: employee dishonesty coverage form, warehouse receipt

warehouse-to-warehouse coverage

Inland Marine/Ocean Marine. A clause that can be added to inland and ocean marine policies extending the policy to cover property in transit from the shipper's warehouse to the consignee's warehouse.

see: cargo insurance, in-trust policy, processing endorsement

warehouseman

Liability/Surety. A person in the business of storing goods belonging to others.

see: warehousemen's bond, warehousemen's liability coverage

warehousemen's bond

Surety. A surety bond provided by a warehouseman that guarantees that goods stored in a warehouse will be delivered upon presentation of a receipt.

see: surety bond

warehousemen's liability coverage

Liability. Coverage for a warehouseman or bailee that covers liability for loss, destruction or damage to property in the insured's warehouse. A major exclusion is a loss caused directly or indirectly by fire, which must be covered separately.

see: care, custody or control

warrant

Financial Planning. An option to buy a security, usually a common stock, at a set price (the exercise price) on an established future date. A warrant establishes no claim on either the equity or the profits of a company.

see: equity (*Financial Planning*), option (*Financial Planning*)

warranted no known or reported losses (WNKORL)

Insurer Operations/Reinsurance. A statement included in an application for insurance or reinsurance coverage to be back-dated that the applicant is not aware of any loss that has occurred between the requested inception date of the contract and the date of the application.

see: antedate, application

warranty

General. 1. A statement to the insurer by an insured upon which the validity of the policy depends. The insurance contract is not binding unless the warranty statement is literally true. This is called an *affirmative warranty.* Traditionally, warranties appear either expressly or by reference on the face of the policy, and noncompliance is a complete defense for the insurer because a warranty is presumed to be material (of such substance or importance that the insurer relied upon it). On the other hand, *representations* may appear in documents collateral to or supporting the policy or may be oral; they are required to be substantially true but not absolutely so; and they must be proved to be material to relieve the insurer of its policy obligations. The strict rules of warranty have been modified in many states. Some statutes require that an insurance applicant's statements be deemed representations rather than warranties; or a court may interpret a description of insured property as a general identification rather than a warranty, so the insurer may not deny a claim only because the property did not continue to meet the description in every detail.

2. A promise by an insured as to a future event or condition during the policy term, such as maintaining fire sprinklers or burglar alarms in working order. This is called a *promissory warranty.*

3. A statement by the manufacturer or seller that a product is free of defects and will perform the functions for which it is sold. A product warranty includes a promise to repair or replace it or to refund the purchase price if a defect is discovered under normal conditions of use. In this sense, a warranty is a promise of indemnity against defects, while *insurance* is a promise of indemnity against loss or damage from perils unrelated to the product itself.

compare: disclaimer; *see:* contribute-to-the-loss statute, extended warranty agreement, implied warranty, representation

warranty company

Property.

see: warranty fire

warranty deed

Title. A deed that guarantees a freehold in writing by the grantor and the grantor's heirs or successors.

see: deed

warranty fire

Property. A type of insurance used for substandard and accommodation fire risks, where there is a capacity problem. Coverage is divided on a pro rata basis with a licensed domestic insurer and the London Market. The domestic company issues an insurance policy that contains all the terms and conditions of coverage and is known as a "warranty company." The London Market insurers agree to follow the terms and conditions of the warranty company.

warranty of authority

Agency. The implied warranty that an agent does possess the authority that the agent purports to possess.

see: agent's authority, expressed authority, implied authority

warranty of fitness for a particular purpose

Law. A warranty given by or legally imputed to a seller of goods when the seller knows or can infer from the circumstances the specific purpose for which the goods are being purchased and represents to the buyer that the goods are suitable for that purpose.

compare: warranty of merchantability; *see:* warranty (3)

warranty of merchantability

Law. A warranty given by or legally imputed to a seller of goods that they are fit for the ordinary, customary or general purposes for which they are used.

compare: warranty of fitness for a particular purpose; *see:* warranty (3)

warranty of title

Law. A warranty, often implied or legally presumed, that a seller has proper title to goods being sold or that the seller has authority from the true owner to transfer title to a buyer.

Warsaw Convention

Aviation/International. An international agreement, originally ratified by 42 countries in 1929, that defines the liabilities of airlines operating between countries and over international waters. Many other countries have since signed the agreement. The Warsaw limitations do not apply if it can be proved that an accident was caused by willful misconduct of the airline or crew.

waste

Property. A pollutant added to the pollution exclusion that was added to most property insurance forms issued after 1988, meaning damaged, defective, superfluous, or unwanted materials and including materials to be recycled, reconditioned or reclaimed.

see: pollutant cleanup and removal additional coverage, pollution exclusion

waste-to-energy plants

Property.

see: alternative energy plants

watchman warranty clause

Crime/Property.

see: watchperson warranty clause

watchperson warranty clause

Crime/Property. A warranty clause that provides a rate credit on burglary and fire policies when the insured agrees to maintain a watchperson on duty at the insured premises.

synonym: watchman warranty clause

water back-up and sump overflow coverage

Personal. Coverage for water that backs up through sewers or drains or that overflows from a sump can be added to the dwelling policy by this endorsement (ISO form DP 04 95).

see: dwelling policy

water damage coverage

Property. Coverage for the accidental discharge or overflow of water or steam from a plumbing, heating or air-conditioning system or domestic appliance, but only when it is the direct result of broken or cracked pipes, fittings, parts, or fixtures in the system or appliance. The cost of tearing out and replacing any part of the covered building to make repairs is also covered. It is included in property policies covering broad causes of loss.

compare: sprinkler leakage coverage

water damage liability

Liability. A property damage liability coverage for an insured tenant when damage results from negligently caused leakage or overflow of water.

compare: sprinkler leakage liability insurance

water exclusion clause

Property. A provision in most property insurance policies that excludes loss resulting from flood, backup of sewers or drains, and underground water.

water pollution liability

Ocean Marine. A shipowner's responsibility to pay for cleanup of water pollution caused by discharges of oil or other polluting or hazardous substances.

see: Water Quality Improvement Act, Water Quality Insurance Syndicate

Water Quality Improvement Act

Ocean Marine/Regulation. Federal legislation of 1970 that requires the owners of vessels to clean up or cover the cost of cleaning up water polluted by discharges from their vessels.

see: Safe Drinking Water Act, water pollution liability, Water Quality Insurance Syndicate

Water Quality Insurance Syndicate

Ocean Marine. A marine syndicate established in 1971 to insure shipowners for water pollution liability.

see: water pollution liability, Water Quality Improvement Act

water resource insurance

Property. Coverage of lost earnings for small hydroelectric power plants in the event that daily water flow at the site is reduced by drought or other natural disturbances.

see: natural perils, rain insurance

water supply service

Property. An off-premises utility service that can be covered for a business income loss with an off-premises utilities coverage endorsement. Coverage is extended to pumping stations and water mains.

see: off-premises services—time element

watercraft endorsement

Personal. An endorsement (ISO form HO 24 75) to the homeowners policy that modifies the watercraft exclusion to cover specified watercraft. Coverage is excluded for liability arising from the operation of watercraft in a prearranged race or similar competition, unless the competition is for sailing vessels (with or without auxiliary power) or is a predicted log cruise.

see: watercraft exclusion, watercraft—special limit

watercraft exclusion

Personal. A homeowners policy exclusion of watercraft that exceed a certain size (usually 26 feet in length or 25 horsepower).

see: watercraft endorsement, watercraft—special limit

watercraft—special limit

Personal. The Insurance Services Office homeowners policy coverage section C (personal property) has a "special limits of liability" provision as respects watercraft, including trailers, furnishings, equipment and outboard engines or motors. The combined coverage for these items is limited to $1,000.

see: homeowners policy—special limits of liability, trailers—special limit, watercraft endorsement, watercraft exclusion

watercraft nonowned coverage

Liability.

see: nonowned watercraft liability

watered stock

Financial Planning. Corporate stock that has been reduced in value by issuing shares without a proportionate contribution of capital or by issuing par value shares for less than par.

see: bonus shares, par value

waterflow alarm

Loss Control. A device for an automatic sprinkler system that sends an alarm signal if there is any flow of water from the system equal to or greater than that from a single sprinkler head.

see: local alarm system

wave damage insurance

Property. Insurance for property loss due to the perils of high waves or overflow from tides.

wave wash

Property. Property damage caused by the action of large waves.

see: wave damage insurance

waybill

Inland Marine/Ocean Marine. A bill of lading usually issued by airlines and trucking companies, indicating the merchandise to be transported, as well as shipping instructions.

see: air waybill, bill of lading, master air waybill

wear and tear exclusion

Property. An exclusion in most property insurance policies for a reduction in the value of property due to normal use.

see: deterioration, depreciation

weather insurance

Property. Insurance for the sponsor of an outside event, a resort operator, or a manufacturer of a product that depends on specific weather conditions (rain, snow, freeze, sun) for sales. Coverage includes losses from the cancellation of outdoor events or from reduced sales of specified products or services.

compare: entertainment insurance; *see*: rain insurance

wedding presents floater

Inland Marine. A property floater policy providing all-risk coverage on wedding presents before and after the wedding, usually not for more than 90 days after the wedding date.

see: floater policy, inland marine insurance

weekly compensation

Workers' Compensation.

see: average weekly benefits

weekly premium insurance

Life.

see: industrial life insurance

weight of ice, snow or sleet insurance

Property. Coverage of buildings and contents for damage directly attributed to the weight of ice, snow or sleet on the structure.

welding screen

Loss Control. A portable screen made of fire resistant materials designed to control flying welding or metal cutting sparks and shield non-welders from the welding glare.

welfare and pension plan ERISA compliance (blanket) coverage form

Crime. An endorsement (ISO form CR 10 27) that amends the blanket employee dishonesty coverage form to satisfy Employee Retirement Income Security Act requirements as respects welfare and benefit plan bonding.

see: employee benefit plan, employee dishonesty coverage form, Employee Retirement Income Security Act

welfare and pension plan ERISA compliance (scheduled) coverage form

Crime. An endorsement (ISO form CR 10 28) that amends the employee dishonesty coverage form to satisfy Employee Retirement Income Security Act requirements as respects welfare and benefit plan bonding.

see: employee benefit plan, employee dishonesty coverage form, Employee Retirement Income Security Act

Welfare and Pension Plans Disclosure Act

Regulation. Federal legislation passed in 1958 that requires pension plan administrators to file a plan description with the Labor Department for all plans covering 25 or more participants. A description must be made available to plan participants and must include a benefit schedule, type of administration, and a copy of plan documents. An annual financial statement must be included for plans with more than 100 participants.

see: employee benefit plan, Employee Retirement Income Security Act

well baby coverage

Health. Coverage for pediatric preventive health care from birth to age 2. A premature baby is not considered a well baby.

see: maternity benefit, newborn

wellness program

Health. A program of incentives by an employer to encourage employees to maintain a healthy lifestyle. It may include education about diet, sponsorship of stop-smoking and drug or alcohol programs, a company gym, or partial reimbursement of dues at an off-site gym. A wellness program may cut the employer's overall health-related costs by bringing down insurance premiums and absenteeism.

see: life maintenance contract

Western Insurance Information Service (WIIS)

Organizations. Members: Property/casualty insurers and agents. *Objectives*: Nonprofit consumer educational and information organization on property and casualty insurance. *Founded*: 1952. *Headquarters*: Englewood, CO.

wet marine insurance

Ocean Marine. Ocean marine insurance that covers ships and cargoes.

see: ocean marine insurance

wet pipe automatic sprinkler system

Loss Control. An automatic sprinkler system where all piping is filled with water under pressure and released by a fusible mechanism in the sprinkler head.

compare: dry pipe automatic sprinkler system; *see*: automatic sprinkler system

wharfingers' liability insurance

Liability. Special coverage for owners and operators of landings or wharves. The contract combines bailee protection, liability for damage to hulls and cargo in the custody of the wharf operator, and coverage for third-party liability for damage to property in the custody of the wharf operator.

see: care, custody or control

what if

Surety.

see: as if

"while" clauses

Property. Coverage suspension provisions found in older property insurance policies, such as "while" the property is vacant.

see: vacant

white knight

Financial Planning. A person or company who helps a corporation resist an unfriendly takeover.

see: poison pill, tender offer

whole dollar premium

Insurer Operations. A round-off of an insurance premium to a whole dollar. Premium calculations of 50 cents or less are dropped, while those of 51 cents or more are rounded to the next dollar.

see: premium

whole life insurance

Life. Life insurance in effect for the entire life of the insured (provided premiums are paid). In most cases, no physical exam is required.

compare: endowment policy, term life insurance; *see*: limited payment life insurance, nonforfeiture benefit, ordinary life insurance, permanent life insurance

wholesale group insurance

Life/Health.

see: franchise insurance

will

Financial Planning. A legal document by which a person provides for the disposition of his or her estate, to take effect at the time of death. It may also designate a guardian for the person's children. The maker of a will is called a *testator*.

see: intestate, estate tax, probate

willful injury

General.

see: intentional injury

window switch

Loss Control.

see: contact switch

window tape

Loss Control. A device used to trigger a burglar alarm. A thin metallic foil is affixed to the glass surface of a door or window. Breaking the glass ruptures the foil, which interrupts the burglar alarm detection circuit and sets off the alarm.

synonym: metallic foil; *see*: burglar alarm

windstorm

Property. A wind of velocity sufficient to damage buildings and structures. Areas subject to hurricanes and tornadoes present the greatest windstorm loss potential.

see: windstorm and hail coverage

windstorm and hail coverage

Property. Coverages usually included together in basic property policies. Windstorm includes tornadoes, hurricanes, cyclones and other high winds. Historically, this coverage has been part of the extended coverage endorsement, but now is frequently included as part of the basic coverages. In areas where windstorms are common coverage may be excluded and available only for an additional premium.

synonym: hail insurance; *see*: crop hail insurance, windstorm or hail exclusion endorsement

windstorm or hail exclusion endorsement

Personal. An endorsement (ISO form HO 04 94) to the homeowners policy that excludes coverage for the perils of windstorm or hail. This exclusion does not apply to coverage D (loss of use).

see: homeowners policy, windstorm and hail coverage

Wisconsin state life insurance fund

Life. A life insurance program for residents of Wisconsin. Premiums are paid into a state fund, and policies participate in cash dividends. There is a $10,000 coverage limit, and the fund employs no agents or solicitors.

see: participating policy

with average

Ocean Marine. Coverage that can be added to an ocean marine policy that is free from particular average conditions. Partial loss or damage to the property insured by the basic named perils is recoverable in full.

compare: with average if amounting to 3%; *see*: particular average

with average if amounting to 3%

Ocean Marine. Coverage that can be added to an ocean marine policy that, in addition to being free from particular average conditions, covers partial losses caused by the basic perils named in the policy, provided that the amount of the partial loss is equal to or exceeds 3% of the insured value of the property coverage.

compare: with average; *see*: particular average

withdrawal reinsurance

Reinsurance. Reinsurance ceded to allow the ceding insurer to withdraw from a line of business, a geographic area, or a production source.

see: ceding insurer

Women Leaders Round Table (WLRT)

Organizations. Members: Women life insurance agents who sell a specified amount of life insurance. *Objectives*: Recognizes women life insurance agents who meet specified annual premium volume requirements. *Headquarters*: Washington, D.C.

see: National Association of Life Underwriters

Women Life Underwriters Confederation (WLUC)

Organizations. Members: Life and health underwriters. *Objectives:* Developing educational opportunities; providing peer support and sales motivational techniques. *Founded*: 1987. *Headquarters:* Reston, VA.

work and materials clause

Property. A provision in many property insurance policies that allows an insured to maintain on the premises the work and materials required in the operation of the insured's business. This clause prevents the policy from being voided under an increased hazard provision.

see: increased hazard

work program clause

Reinsurance/Surety. A provision in a contractor's bond reinsurance policy that the primary carrier's retention is a specified level of an insured contractor's total volume of work, rather than an individual contract or bond amount.

work you performed exclusion

Automobile.

see: faulty work exclusion

Worker Adjustment and Retraining Notification Act (WARN Act)

Regulation. Federal law (U.S. Code Title 29, Chapter 23) adopted in 1988 that requires an employer with 100 or more full-time employees to provide 60 days' notice if a plant is to be shut down and will result in 50 or more employees losing their jobs in any 30-day period. If the employer has two or more shut-downs of less than 50 employees each but which together total over 50, the 30-day period is extended to 90 days unless the employer demonstrates that the shut-downs were separate and distinct and not an attempt to evade the Act.

synonym: Plant Closing Act

workers' compensation catastrophe reinsurance

Reinsurance/Workers' Compensation. A catastrophe excess of loss reinsurance policy purchased by a ceding insurer to cover workers' compensation claims in excess of a retained limit.

see: excess of loss reinsurance, workers' compensation insurance

Workers' Compensation Claims Professional (WCCP)

Organizations/Workers' Compensation. A professional designation granted by the Insurance Education Association. Candidates must successfully complete eight college-level courses in workers' compensation claims and related subjects. Six hours of continuing education are required each year.

see: Insurance Education Association

workers' compensation excess insurance

Workers' Compensation.

see: aggregate excess workers' compensation insurance, specific excess workers' compensation insurance

workers' compensation experience rating work sheet

Workers' Compensation. A printed form that is completed by the National Council on Compensation Insurance or a state workers' compensation rating bureau. The formulas on the form are calculated with information from an employer's unit statistical filing to develop the workers' compensation experience modification.

see: experience rating modification factor, National Council on Compensation Insurance, rating bureau

workers' compensation insurance (WC)

Workers' Compensation. Insurance that covers an

employer's responsibility to compensate injuries, illnesses, disabilities or death of employees, as prescribed by state workers' compensation laws; coverage provided by Part I (prior to 1986, section A) of the standard workers' compensation policy (NCCI form WC 00 00 00A). The insurance ordinarily covers legally imposed employers' liability for medical and surgical treatment, disability benefits, rehabilitation therapy, and survivors' death benefits.

synonym: coverage A; *compare*: employers' liability insurance, nonoccupational policy; *see*: deductible workers' compensation plan, designated workplace exclusion endorsement, domestic and agricultural workers exclusion endorsement, dual capacity doctrine, exclusive remedy, Federal Employers' Liability Act, insurance company as insured endorsement, labor contractor endorsement, medical benefits exclusion endorsement, maritime coverage endorsement, notification of `change in ownership endorsement, partners officers and others exclusion endorsement, second injury fund, sole proprietors partners officers and others coverage endorsement, 24-hour coverage, voluntary compensation, workers' compensation law

workers' compensation law

Workers' Compensation. All states require employers to pay benefits to employees with injuries or illnesses arising out of and in the course of employment (except for designated categories of employees). Benefits are scheduled in the laws, which also generally prohibit an employee from suing the employer for common law damages. Workers' compensation laws ensure that employees receive adequate medical treatment and at least some compensation for injuries suffered on the job; at the same time, the liability of employers is limited. The basic categories of benefits are medical care, partial reimbursement for income lost due to disability, rehabilitation therapy if required, and survivors' benefits in case of an employee's death.

compare: disability benefit law; *see*: arising out of and in the course of employment, common law defense, death benefit (*Workers' Compensation*), disability benefit, medical benefit, rehabilitation, scheduled injury, workers' compensation insurance

working capital

Accounting. Total current assets minus total current liabilities. Working capital (or net current assets) includes such current assets as cash and government securities, receivables, and inventories, minus such current liabilities as accounts payable, current taxes, dividends payable, short-term bank notes, and the portion of long-term debt that comes

due over the next 12 months.

synonym: net current assets; *see*: internal financing

working cover

Reinsurance. An excess of loss reinsurance contract written directly over a policy with a low retention causing frequent penetration of limits.

synonym: working layer; *see*: excess of loss reinsurance

working layer

Reinsurance.

see: working cover

Risk Management. One of the three layers to which losses are normally assigned. It is the first or primary layer, representing losses that occur with enough regularity that they may be funded or planned for within the organization's operating budget.

compare: buffer layer, catastrophe layer

Worldwide Assurance for Employees of Public Agencies (WAEPA)

Organizations. Members: Federal civilian employees. *Objectives:* Providing group life, accidental death and dismemberment and dependent group life insurance coverage to the federal civilian employees at reasonable costs. *Founded*: 1943. *Headquarters*: Falls Church, VA.

worldwide coverage

Liability/International. A provision in some liability policies or in an endorsement that extends coverage worldwide. Some policies provide that the insurer must indemnify the insured for the cost of defense and settlements, and others provide coverage only if a suit against the insured is brought in the United States or Canada.

see: geographic limitation

worry factor

Risk Management. A part of risk management analysis that assigns a monetary value to each risk management alternative based on the uncertainty of that choice compared to the others. The value is subjective, based on senior management's comfort with the alternative. This worry factor is then factored into any cash flow analysis comparing the various alternatives.

see: net present value method, profitability index, risk management process

wrap-up insurance program

Liability/Workers' Compensation.

see: owner-controlled insurance program

writ

Law. A document containing a court order.

write
Insurer Operations.
see: underwriting

written business
Insurer Operations. Insurance on which an application has been filed but for which a policy has not yet been delivered or the first premium has not yet been paid.
compare: delivered business, examined business, issued business, paid business, placed business

written premiums
Insurer Operations. The aggregate amount of premiums written by an insurer during a specified period of time, including both earned and unearned premiums.
compare: earned premium; *see*: premium, unearned premium

wrongful abstraction
Crime. In crime insurance policies, the illegal removal of property. It includes all types of burglary, robbery and theft.
see: crime coverages, theft

wrongful calling of bid guaranty insurance
International. A form of political risk insurance that protects an exporter or contractor against the arbitrary and unfair call of a bid bond.
see: political risk insurance

wrongful calling of guaranty insurance
International. A form of political risk insurance that protects an exporter or contractor against the arbitrary and unfair call of its guaranties (e.g., standby letters of credit, on-demand bonds) by a foreign government, or a rightful call when nonperformance is caused by a foreign or domestic government action.
see: political risk insurance

wrongful death
Law. A death caused without legal justification. The beneficiaries of the deceased person may bring a lawsuit for wrongful death on the basis of negligence or intentional wrongdoing.
see: negligence, tort

wrongful discharge or discrimination legal expense insurance
Liability. Coverage that provides an employer reimbursement for legal expenses to defend suits by employees alleging wrongful discharge, discrimination or sexual harassment.
see: discrimination, employment practices liability insurance, sexual harassment, unfair labor practices

wrongful employment practices insurance
Professional Liability.
see: employment practices liability insurance

X-Y-Z

x-ray laboratories professional liability insurance

Professional Liability. A form of professional liability insurance for x-ray laboratories that provides coverage on a claims-made basis for claims arising from taking and analyzing x-rays.

   see: medical laboratories professional liability insurance

x table

General. A term referring to drafts of rate tables under development.

XCU exclusions

Liability. The Insurance Services Office rating program for the 1973 comprehensive general liability policy included classifications for organizations with operations particularly exposed to explosion (X), collapse (C), and underground (U) hazards. For such organizations, the classification code means a particular hazard is excluded from the policy unless included for an additional premium. The 1986 CGL program does not include these rating factors, and the form has been revised to automatically cover the XCU exposure.

   synonym: explosion, collapse, and underground exclusions; *see:* blasting and explosion exclusion, collapse exclusion, commercial general liability policy, underground exclusion

yacht

Ocean Marine. A relatively small ocean-going vessel, usually in excess of 26 feet, characterized by a sharp prow and graceful lines. It is primarily used for pleasure and may be propelled by means of sails, or by steam or motor power.

   see: watercraft exclusion, yacht insurance

yacht insurance

Ocean Marine. A special policy insuring yachts, cabin cruisers, inboard motorboats and sailing ships. Most policies cover the hull, sails, fittings, furniture, provisions, machinery and equipment. The policy is valued, and full insurance value is required. Usually written on an all-risk basis for hull coverage, to named perils forms are also used.

   compare: boatowners' package policy, outboard motor and boat policy

yearly renewable term

Life.

   see: annual renewable term insurance

years of service

Employee Benefits. The time credited to a pension plan participant for employment with the plan sponsor. Some plans require continuous employment, while others have rules crediting participation in the event of breaks in employment.

   see: employee benefit plan, future service, vesting

yield

Financial Planning. The return on an investment, expressed as a percentage of its cost or market value.

   see: annual yield, cumulative rate of return, dividend yield, earnings yield

York Antwerp Rules

Ocean Marine. A set of rules, initially agreed upon in 1890 and last revised in 1950, by which ocean marine general average losses are adjusted.

   see: general average

your product

Liability. A term used in simplified language liability policies for manufactured goods or products sold, handled, distributed, or disposed of by the insured. It includes containers in which the product is shipped and warranties or representations made with respect to the product's fitness, quality, durability, or performance.

   compare: your work; *see:* product liability insurance, products-completed operations insurance

your work

Liability. A term used in simplified language liability policies for work or operations performed by, or on behalf, of the insured, including materials, parts, or equipment furnished in connection with the work. It includes warranties or representations made with respect to its fitness, quality, durability, or performance.

compare: your product; *see*: product liability insurance, products-completed operations insurance

youth group accident insurance

Health. A form of group accident insurance for members of a youth group (e.g., Boy or Girl Scouts, etc.). Coverage is provided on a blanket basis for medical expenses, accidental loss of life, and accidental dismemberment or loss of sight. Members are covered only while at the location of a group meeting or at a group-sponsored event.

see: accident insurance, blanket insurance

z table

Life. A life insurance mortality table developed from major life insurer experience from 1925 to 1934. This was the forerunner of the Commissioners Standard Table.

see: Commissioners Standard Ordinary Table, mortality table

zone rating

Automobile. A method used to rate commercial auto policies, where units are larger than a light truck and are operated over 200 miles in distance from the garage location.

see: farthest terminal, long distance, radius of operation

zone system

Regulation. A method for the triennial examination of insurers developed by the National Association of Insurance Commissioners. Examination teams are assembled from the insurance departments located in a specified region of the United States, and the results of the audit are accepted by all insurance departments.

see: examination, National Association of Insurance Commissioners

Abbreviations and Acronyms

Listed below are abbreviations and acronyms for terms and organizations described in the *Glossary.*

A&H	accident and health insurance
AAA	American Academy of Actuaries
	American Agents Association
	American Arbitration Association
	American Automobile Association
	Association of Average Adjusters of the United States
AACI	American Association of Crop Insurers
AADC	American Association of Dental Consultants
AAI	Accredited Advisor in Insurance
	Alliance of American Insurers
AAIMC	American Association of Insurance Management Consultants
AAIS	American Association of Insurance Services
AALU	Association for Advanced Life Underwriting
AAMGA	American Association of Managing General Agents
ABA	American Bar Association
ABS	American Bureau of Shipping
ACAS	Associate of the Casualty Actuarial Society
ACCI	American Corporate Counsel Institute
ACLI	American Council of Life Insurance
ACORD	Agency-Company Organization for Research and Development
ACRS	accelerated cost recovery system
ACS	Associate, Customer Service
ACSC	Association of Casualty and Surety Companies
ACV	actual cash value
ACWRRE	American Cargo War Risk Reinsurance Exchange
AD&D	accidental death and dismemberment
ADA	Americans with Disabilities Act
ADEA	Age Discrimination in Employment Act
ADR	alternative dispute resolution
	American Depository Receipt
ADS	American Depository Shares
ADTA	Association of Defense Trial Attorneys
AEIA	American Excess Insurance Association
AFSB	Associate in Fidelity and Surety Bonding
AHIMA	American Health Information Management Association
AHIS	American Hull Insurance Syndicate
AIA	American Institute of Architects
	American Insurance Association

AIAF	Associate in Insurance Accounting and Finance
AIC	Associate in Claims
AIDM	Associate Insurance Data Manager
AIDS	acquired immune deficiency syndrome
AIHA	American Industrial Hygiene Association
AIHSA	American Insurers Highway Safety Alliance
AIM	Associate in Management
AIME	average indexed monthly earnings
AIMU	American Institute of Marine Underwriters
AIP	annual implementation plan
AIPSO	Automobile Insurance Plans Service Office
AIRAC	All-Industry Research Advisory Council
AIRB	Aviation Insurance Rating Bureau
AIS	Associate in Insurance Services
AISG	American Insurance Services Group, Inc.
ALC	American Life Convention
ALCM	Associate in Loss Control Management
ALHC	Associate, Life and Health Claims
ALIC	Association of Life Insurance Counsel
ALOS	average length of stay
AMEMIC	Association of Mill and Elevator Mutual Insurance Companies
AMIC	American Marine Insurance Clearinghouse
AMIF	American Marine Insurance Forum
AMIM	Associate in Marine Insurance Management
AMW	average monthly wage
ANI	American Nuclear Insurers
ANL	above-normal loss
ANSI	American National Standards Institute
AP	additional premium
APA	Associate in Premium Auditing
APIW	Association of Professional Insurance Women
APL	automatic premium loan
APS	attending physician's statement
ARAC	Atmospheric Release Advisory Center
ARe	Associate in Reinsurance
ARIA	American Risk and Insurance Association
ARIS	Alien Reporting Information System
ARM	adjustable rate mortgage
	Associate in Risk Management
ARMI	Associated Risk Managers International
ARP	Associate in Research and Planning
ART	Accredited Record Technician
	annual renewable term insurance

ASA	American Surety Association
	Associate in Society of Actuaries
ASCLU & ChFC	American Society of Chartered Life
	Underwriters and Chartered Financial Consultants
ASIS	American Society of Industrial Security
ASM	available seat miles
ASME	American Society of Mechanical Engineers, Inc.
ASO	administrative services only
ASPA	American Society of Pension Actuaries
	American Society of Personnel Administration
ASSE	American Society of Safety Engineers
ATLA	Association of Trial Lawyers of America
ATRA	American Tort Reform Association
AU	Associate in Underwriting
AWW	average weekly wage
B&M	boiler and machinery insurance
BCBSA	Blue Cross and Blue Shield Association
BCSP	Board of Certified Safety Professionals of the Americas, Inc.
BFPD	broad form property damage
BI	bodily injury
BOP	business owners' policy
BPP	building and personal property coverage form
BTN	Brussels Tariff Nomenclature
CAPP	Conference of Actuaries in Public Practice
CARE	Concerned Alliance of Responsible Employers
CAS	Casualty Actuarial Society
CATV	community antenna television liability insurance
CCIA	Consumer Credit Insurance Association
CCIC	Conference of Casualty Insurance Companies
CCS	Certified Coding Specialist
CD	certificate of deposit
CDW	collision damage waiver
CEB	Council on Employee Benefits
CEBS	Certified Employee Benefit Specialist
CEQ	Council on Environmental Quality
CERCLA	Comprehensive Environmental Response, Compensation and Liability Act
CFP	Certified Financial Planner
CFTC	Commodity Futures Trading Commission
CGL	commercial general liability policy
	comprehensive general liability policy
CHCM	Certified Hazard Control Manager
ChFC	Chartered Financial Consultant

CHIAA	Crop-Hail Insurance Actuarial Association
CICA	Captive Insurance Companies Association
CIDM	Certified Insurance Data Manager
CIRB	Crop Insurance Research Bureau
CLU	Chartered Life Underwriter
CMPA	Certified Manager of Patient Accounts
CNHI	Committee for National Health Insurance
COB	coordination of benefits
COBRA	Consolidated Omnibus Budget Reconciliation Act
COGSA	Carriage of Goods by Sea Act
COGWA	Carriage of Goods by Water Act
CPA	Certified Public Accountant
CPCU	Chartered Property Casualty Underwriter
CPL	comprehensive personal liability policy
CPP	commercial package policy
CRA	Cargo Reinsurance Association
CRC	Chemical Referral Center
CRS	Commercial Risk Services, Inc.
CSIO	Centre for the Study of Insurance Operations
CSL	combined single limit
CSO Table	Commissioners Standard Ordinary Table
CSP	Certified Safety Professional
D&O	directors' and officers' liability insurance
DAP	deposit administration plan
dB	decibel
DB&C	dwelling, buildings and contents form
DCF	discounted cash flow techniques
DDD	dishonesty, disappearance and destruction policy
DEFRA	Deficit Reduction Act
DI	double indemnity
DIC	difference in conditions insurance
DIL	difference in limits insurance
DITC	Disability Insurance Training Council
DMIC	Direct Marketing Insurance Council
DOHSA	Death on the High Seas Act
DOT	Department of Transportation
DPA	Designated Planning Agency
DPP	deferred premium payment plan
DR	daily report
DRG	diagnosis related group
DRI	Defense Research Institute, Inc.
DVP	delivery versus payment
E&O	errors and omissions insurance
E&S	excess and surplus lines broker

EA	Enrolled Actuary
EAP	estimated annual premium
EBRI	Employee Benefit Research Institute
EC	extended coverages
ECC	Eastern Claims Conference
ECF	extended care facility
ECFC	Employers Council on Flexible Compensation
ECO	extra-contractual obligations
EEL	emergency exposure limit
ELP	excess loss premium factor
EMT E&O	emergency medical technicians' error and omissions insurance
EPA	Environmental Protection Agency
EPLI	employment practices liability insurance
ERIC	ERISA Industry Committee
ERISA	Employee Retirement Income Security Act
ERP	emergency response plan
	extended reporting period
ESOP	employee stock ownership plan
EXIM Bank	Export-Import Bank
FAA	Federal Aviation Administration
FAIR plan	Fair Access to Insurance Requirements
FAP	family automobile policy
FAS	free alongside
FASB	Financial Accounting Standards Board
FAST	Financial Analysis and Solvency Tracking System
FC&S	free of capture and seizure
FCAS	Fellow of the Casualty Actuarial Society
FCIA	Foreign Credit Insurance Association
FCIC	Federal Crop Insurance Corporation
FCPL	farmers' comprehensive personal liability policy
FDA	Food and Drug Administration
FDIC	Federal Deposit Insurance Corporation
FELA	Federal Employers' Liability Act
FEMA	Federal Emergency Management Agency
FFMA	Fraternal Field Managers Association
FIA	Federal Insurance Administration
	full interest admitted
FIC	Fraternal Insurance Counselor
FICA	Federal Insurance Contributions Act
FICC	Federation of Insurance and Corporate Counsel
FIFO	first-in-first-out
FIFRA	Federal Insecticide, Fungicide and Rodenticide Act
FIRM	flood insurance rate map

FLMI	Fellow of the Life Management Institute
FM	Factory Mutual System
FOB	free on board
FOC	Fire Office Committee forms
FPA	free of particular average
FPAAC	free of particular average American conditions
FPAEC	free of particular average English conditions
FPE	Society of Fire Protection Engineers
FSA	Fellow of the Society of Actuaries
	flexible spending account
FSLIC	Federal Savings and Loan Insurance Corporation
FSPA	Fellow of the Society of Pension Actuaries
FTC	Federal Trade Commission
FVD	full value declared
GA	general agent
	general average
GAAP	Generally Accepted Accounting Principles
GAMC-NALU	General Agents and Managers Conference of National Association of Life Underwriters
GASB	Governmental Accounting Standards Board
GCW	gross combination weight
GFCI	ground fault circuit interrupter
GHA	gross hazard analysis
GIC	guaranteed investment contract
GNEPI	gross net earned premium income
GNWPI	gross net written premium income
GO bond	general obligation bond
GVW	gross vehicle weight
HCFA	Health Care Financing Administration
HCFMA	Health Care Financial Management Association
HFIE	Huebner Foundation for Insurance Education
HI	health insurance
HIA	Health Insurance Associate
HIAA	Health Insurance Association of America
HII	Health Insurance Institute
HIV	human immunodeficiency virus
HLDI	Highway Loss Data Institute
HLV	human life value
HMO	health maintenance organization
HOBGI	Honorable Order of the Blue Goose
HOLUA	Home Office Life Underwriters Association
HPR	highly protected risk

IACS	International Association of Classification Societies
IADAA	Independent Automotive Damage Appraisers Association
IADC	International Association of Defense Counsel
IAIABC	International Association of Industrial Accident Boards and Commissions
IAO	Insurers' Advisory Organization of Canada
IASA	Insurance Accounting and Systems Association
IBC	Insurance Bureau of Canada
IBNR	incurred but not reported
ICA	Insurance Contractors of America
	International Claim Association
ICAC	Insurance Committee for Arson Control
ICC	Interstate Commerce Commission
ICEDS	Insurance Company Education Directors Society
ICIA	International Credit Insurance Association
ICP	Insurance Conference Planners
ICPA	Insurance Conference Planners Association
ICPI	Insurance Crime Prevention Institute
IEA	Insurance Educational Association
IFEBP	International Foundation of Employee Benefit Plans
IHOU	Institute of Home Office Underwriters
IIA	Insurance Institute of America .
IIAA	Independent Insurance Agents of America Inc.
IIC	Insurance Institute of Canada
	International Insurance Council
IIE	Illinois Insurance Exchange
IIHS	Insurance Institute for Highway Safety
III	Insurance Information Institute
IIMA	Insurance Industry Meetings Association
IIS	International Insurance Society, Inc.
ILCA	Insurance Loss Control Association
IMCA	Insurance Marketing Communications Association
IMUA	Inland Marine Underwriters Association
IPA	independent practice association
IPFA	Insurance Premium Finance Association
IRA	individual retirement account
IRES	Insurance Regulatory Examiners Society
IRI	Industrial Risk Insurers
IRIS	Insurance Regulatory Information System
IRPM rating plan	individual risk premium modification rating plan
IRR	internal rate of return
ISCEBS	International Society of Certified Employee Benefit Specialists

ISNY	Insurance Society of New York
ISO	Insurance Services Office
IUAI	International Union of Aviation Insurance
IUMI	International Union of Marine Insurance
IVANS	Insurance Value Added Network Services
JUA	joint underwriting association
LASH	lighter aboard ship
LBO	leveraged buyout
LCA	Life Communicators Association
LCF	loss conversion factor
LDF	loss development factor
LDP	large deductible plan
LDW	limited damage waiver
	loss damage waiver
LEA	Loss Executives Association
LHWCA	Longshore and Harbor Workers' Compensation Act
LIAA	Life Insurance Association of America
LIAMA	Life Insurance Agency Management Association
LIC	Life Insurers Conference
LICOMA	Life Insurance Company Office Management Association
LIFO	last-in-first-out
LIMRA	Life Insurance Marketing and Research Association
LIRB	Liability Insurance Research Bureau
LLC	limited liability company
LOC	letter of credit
LOMA	Life Office Management Association
LPG	liquefied petroleum gas
LPRT	Leading Producers Round Table
LTD	long-term disability insurance
LUPAC	Life Underwriter Political Action Committee
LUTC	Life Underwriter Training Council
LUTCF	Life Underwriter Training Council Fellow
M&C	manufacturers' and contractors' liability insurance
MAC	maximum allowable concentration
MADPA	Medicaid Antidiscriminatory Drug Pricing and Patient Benefit Restoration Act
MAELU	Mutual Atomic Energy Liability Underwriters
MAP	market assistance plan
MCA	Motor Carrier Act
MCP	multiple coordinated policy
MCS-90	Motor Carrier Act endorsement
MDO	monthly debit ordinary life insurance
MDRT	Million Dollar Round Table

MET	multiple employer trust
MEWA	multiple employer welfare arrangement
MGA	managing general agent
MIB	Medical Information Bureau
MICA	Mortgage Insurance Companies of America
MMII	Mass Marketing Insurance Institute
MOP	manufacturers' output policy
MPCI	multi-peril crop insurance
MSA	medical savings account
MSDS	Material Safety Data Sheet
MVR	motor vehicle record
NABRTI	National Association of Bar-Related Title Insurers
NACA	National Association of Catastrophe Adjusters, Inc.
NACIA	National Association of Crop Insurance Agents
NACSE	National Association of Casualty and Surety Executives
NAFI	National Association of Fire Investigators
NAFIC	National Association of Fraternal Insurance Counselors
NAHU	National Association of Health Underwriters
NAIA	National Association of Insurance Agents, Inc.
NAIB	National Association of Insurance Brokers, Inc.
NAIC	National Association of Insurance Commissioners
NAII	National Association of Independent Insurers
NAIIA	National Association of Independent Insurance Adjusters
NAILBA	National Association of Independent Life Brokerage Agencies
NAIW	National Association of Insurance Women
NALC	National Association of Life Companies
NALU	National Association of Life Underwriters
NAMIC	National Association of Mutual Insurance Companies
NAPIA	National Association of Public Insurance Adjusters
NAPSLO	National Association of Professional Surplus Lines Offices
NASBP	National Association of Surety Bond Producers
NASD	National Association of Securities Dealers
NAV	net asset value
NBFU	National Board of Fire Underwriters
NCCI	National Council on Compensation Insurance
NCCMP	National Coordinating Committee for Multiemployer Plans
NCIA	National Crop Insurance Association
NCIS	National Crop Insurance Services
NCOIL	National Conference of Insurance Legislators
NCPC	National Crime Prevention Council

NCSI	National Council of Self-Insurers
NCUA	National Credit Union Administration
NDCI	Natural Disaster Coalition, Inc.
NDIPMTU	Nationwide Definition and Interpretation of the Powers of Marine and Transportation Underwriters
NEBI	National Employee Benefits Institute
NEPA	National Environmental Policy Act
NFAC	National Fraud Advisory Commission
NFCA	National Fraternal Congress of America
NFGMIC	National Federation of Grange Mutual Insurance Companies
NFIP	National Flood Insurance Program
NFPA	National Fire Protection Association
NHAFA	National Health Care Anti-Fraud Association
NIA	National Insurance Association
NICB	National Insurance Crime Bureau
NICO	National Insurance Consumer Organization
NIDC	National Insurance Development Corporation
NIOSH	National Institute for Occupational Safety and Health
NIPA	National Institute of Pension Administrators
NLE	normal loss expectancy
NOC	not otherwise classified
non-OEM parts	non-original equipment manufacturer's replacement parts
NPV	net present value method
NRC	Nuclear Regulatory Commission
NSC	National Safety Council
NSIPA	National Society of Insurance Premium Auditors
NSLI	National Service Life Insurance
OCIP	owner-controlled insurance program
OCP	owners' and contractors' protective liability
OCSLA	Outer Continental Shelf Lands Act
OD	occupational disease
OFA	Organized Flying Adjusters
OL&T	owners, landlords, and tenants liability insurance
OPIC	Overseas Private Investment Corporation
OSHA	Occupational Safety and Health Act
OTC	other-than-collision coverage
	over-the-counter
P&I	protection and indemnity insurance
P&I club	protection and indemnity club
PAP	personal auto policy
PARMA	Public Agency Risk Managers Association
PBGC	Pension Benefit Guaranty Corporation

PCBs	polychlorinated biphenyls
PCP	primary care physician
P/E	price/earnings ratio
PG	purchasing group
PHR	Professional in Human Resources
PI	personal injury
PIA	primary insurance amount
PICA	Professional Insurance Communicators of America
PILR	Property Insurance Loss Register
PIMA	Professional Insurance Mass Marketing Association
PIP	personal injury protection
PIV	post indicator valve
PLIA	Pollution Liability Insurance Association
PLRB	Property Loss Research Bureau
PLUS	Professional Liability Underwriting Society
PMF	package modification factor
PML	probable maximum loss
POS plan	point-of-service plan
PPF	personal property floater
PPL	police professional liability insurance
PPO	preferred provider organization
PRIMA	Public Risk Management Association
PRO	peer review organization
PRP	potentially responsible party
Q-TIP trust	qualified terminable interest property trust
R&C	renewable and convertible term life insurance
RAA	Reinsurance Association of America
RAM	reverse-annuity mortgage
RCRA	Resource Conservation and Recovery Act
REIT	real estate investment trust
RIMS	Risk and Insurance Management Society, Inc.
RIRS	Regulatory Information Retrieval System
ROI	return on investment
RP	return premium
RRA	Registered Record Administrator
RRG	risk retention group
RRM	renegotiable rate mortgage
RRSP	registered retirement saving plan
RTC	Resolution Trust Corporation
SAA	Surety Association of America
SAP	Statutory Accounting Principles
SARA	Superfund Amendments and Reauthorization Act
SAWW	statewide average weekly wage
SCIC	Society of Certified Insurance Counselors

SEC	Securities and Exchange Commission
SEP	simplified employee pension
SGLI	Servicemen's Group Life Insurance
SHRM	Society for Human Resource Management
SIA	Society of Insurance Accountants
SIIA	Self-Insurance Institute of America
SIPC	Securities Investor Protection Corporation
SIR	self-insured retention
	Society of Insurance Research
SITE	Society of Insurance Trainers and Educators
SMP	special multi-peril program
SOA	Society of Actuaries
SPBA	Society of Professional Benefit Administrators
SPHR	Senior Professional in Human Resources
SPP	standard property policy
SR&CC	strikes, riots and civil commotions exclusion
SRA	Society for Risk Analysis
SRMC	Society of Risk Management Consultants
SSF	Society of State Filers
SSI	Supplemental Security Income
STD	short-term disability insurance
TDA	tax deferred annuity
TEFRA	Tax Equity and Financial Responsibility Acts
TLO	total loss only clause
TPA	third-party administrator
TSDF	treatment, storage and disposal facility
U&O	use and occupancy insurance
UCC	Uniform Commercial Code
UCD	unemployment compensation disability insurance
UEL	upper explosive level
UJF	unsatisfied judgment fund
UL	Underwriters Laboratories, Inc.
ULC	Underwriters Laboratories of Canada
UNL	ultimate net loss
URMIA	University Risk Management and Insurance Association
USGLI	United States Government Life Insurance
V&MM	vandalism and malicious mischief coverage
VGLI	Veterans Group Life Insurance
VOS	Valuation of Securities System
WAEPA	Worldwide Assurance for Employees of Public Agencies
WARN Act	Worker Adjustment and Retraining Notification Act
WC	workers' compensation insurance
WCCP	Workers' Compensation Claims Professional

WIIS	Western Insurance Information Service
WLRT	Women Leaders Round Table
WLUC	Women Life Underwriters Confederation
WNKORL	warranted no known or reported losses

Policy and Endorsement Forms

Listed below are standard forms that provide some of the coverages and exclusions described in the *Glossary*. Many form names are defined terms; in other cases, you are referred to a term that differs somewhat from the form label. In the order listed here, the forms are prescribed by the following organizations:

Insurance Services Office (ISO)

National Council on Compensation Insurance (NCCI)

American Association of Insurance Services (AAIS)

Agency-Company Organization for Research and Development (ACORD)

miscellaneous forms.

Insurance Services Office (ISO) forms

BM 00 25	boiler and machinery coverage form see: boiler and machinery insurance
BM 00 26	object definitions no. 1—pressure and refrigeration objects see: pressure and refrigeration objects
BM 00 27	object definitions no. 2—mechanical objects see: mechanical objects
BM 00 28	object definitions no. 3—electrical objects see: electrical objects
BM 00 29	object definitions no. 4—turbine objects see: turbine objects
BM 00 30	object definitions no. 5—comprehensive coverage (excluding production machines) see: comprehensive coverage excluding production machines
BM 00 31	object definitions no. 6—comprehensive coverage (including production machines) see: comprehensive coverage including production machines
BM 99 25	boilers, fired vessels and electric steam generators—limited coverage
CA 00 01	business auto coverage form
CA 00 05	garage coverage form
CA 00 12	truckers' coverage form
CA 00 20	motor carrier coverage form
CA 02 40	suspension of insurance see: suspension of coverage endorsement
CA 20 01	additional insured—lessor
CA 20 21	snowmobiles see: snowmobile coverage
CA 25 01	broad form products coverage see: broad form product liability

CA 25 03	false pretense coverage
CA 99 03	auto medical payments coverage
	see: medical payments coverage
CA 99 10	drive other car coverage—broadened coverage for named individuals
	see: drive other car coverage
CA 99 23	rental reimbursement coverage
CA 99 37	garagekeepers coverage
	see: garagekeepers' insurance
CA 99 48	pollution liability—broadened coverage for covered autos—business auto and truckers coverage forms
	see: pollution liability—broadened coverage for covered autos
CA 99 60	audio, visual and data electronic equipment coverage
CG 00 01	commercial general liability coverage form
	see: commercial general liability policy
CG 00 02	commercial general liability coverage form (claims-made coverage)
	see: commercial general liability policy
CG 00 33	liquor liability
	see: liquor liability coverage
CG 00 34	liquor liability—claims-made
	see: liquor liability coverage
CG 00 39	pollution liability
	see: pollution liability extension endorsement
CG 00 40	pollution liability—limited form
CG 03 00	deductible liability insurance
CG 20 02	additional insured—club members
	see: club members' coverage
CG 20 08	additional insured—users of golfmobiles
	see: golf cart coverage
CG 20 14	additional insured—users of teams, draft or saddle animals
	see: saddle animal liability
CG 20 15	additional insured—vendors
	see: vendor's endorsement
CG 20 21	additional insured—volunteer workers
	see: volunteer workers' coverage
CG 20 22	additional insured—church members, officers and volunteer workers
	see: church members', officers' and volunteers' coverage
CG 21 42	exclusion—XCU-A
	see: XCU exclusions
CG 21 43	exclusion—XCU-B
	see: XCU exclusions

CP 04 40	spoilage coverage endorsement
CP 04 50	vacancy permit
CP 10 10	causes of loss—basic form
CP 10 20	causes of loss—broad form
CP 10 30	causes of loss—special form
CP 10 39	earthquake sprinkler leakage
CP 10 40	causes of loss—earthquake form
CP 10 41	earthquake inception extension endorsement
CP 10 60	molten material
	see: molten material damage endorsement
CP 10 70	pier and wharf additional covered causes of loss endorsement
CP 12 30	peak season limit of insurance endorsement
CP 14 30	outdoor trees, shrubs and plants endorsement
CP 14 50	radio or television antennas endorsement
CP 14 60	leased property endorsement
CP 15 08	business income from dependent properties—broad form
	see: contingent business income coverage
CP 15 09	business income from dependent properties—limited form
	see: contingent business income coverage
CP 15 11	power, heat, and refrigeration deduction
CP 15 15	business income report/work sheet
	see: business income report and work sheet
CP 15 20	business income premium adjustment
CP 15 25	tuition and fees
	see: tuition and fees insurance
CP 15 29	electronic media and records endorsement
CP 15 31	ordinance or law—increased period of restoration endorsement
CP 15 34	extra expense from dependent properties endorsement
CP 15 45	off-premises services—time element endorsement
CP 99 05	distilled spirits and wines market value
	see: alcoholic beverages market value endorsement
CP 99 30	manufacturers' selling price (finished stock only) endorsement
CP 99 31	market value—stock
	see: market value stock endorsement
CR 00 01	employee dishonesty coverage form (coverage form A—blanket)
	see: employee dishonesty coverage form
CR 00 02	employee dishonesty coverage form (coverage form B—schedule)
	see: employee dishonesty coverage form

CR 00 03	forgery or alteration coverage form (coverage form B)
	see: forgery or alteration coverage form
CR 00 04	theft, disappearance and destruction of money and securities coverage form
CR 00 05	robbery and safe burglary coverage form—property other than money and securities
CR 00 06	premises burglary coverage form
CR 00 07	computer fraud coverage form
CR 00 08	extortion coverage form
CR 00 09	premises theft and outside robbery coverage form—property other than money and securities
	see: premises theft and outside robbery coverage form
CR 00 10	lessees of safe deposit boxes coverage form
CR 00 11	securities deposited with others coverage form
CR 00 12	liability for guests' property—safe deposit box form
	see: guests' property—safe deposit box
CR 00 13	liability for guests' property—premises coverage form
	see: guests' property—premises
CR 00 14	safe depository liability coverage form
CR 00 15	safe depository direct loss coverage form
CR 00 16	public employee dishonesty coverage form (coverage form O—per loss)
	see: public employee dishonesty coverage form (blanket)
CR 00 17	public employee dishonesty coverage form (coverage P—per employee)
	see: public employee dishonesty coverage form (per employee)
CR 00 18	robbery and safe burglary coverage form—money and securities
CR 10 04	exclude trading loss
	see: trading loss exclusion form
CR 10 05	exclude warehouse receipts losses
	see: warehouse receipts losses exclusion form
CR 10 06	exclude unauthorized advances, required annual audit
	see: unauthorized advances coverage form
CR 10 09	add faithful performance of duty
	see: faithful performance of duty
CR 10 12	credit, debit, or charge card forgery
CR 10 14	include personal accounts of specified persons
	see: personal accounts of specified persons
CR 10 15	add schedule excess limit of insurance for specified employees
	see: excess coverage for specified employees

CR 10 27	welfare and pension plan ERISA compliance (blanket) coverage form
CR 10 28	welfare and pension plan ERISA compliance (scheduled) coverage form
CR 10 39	Rural Electrification Administration—regulations
CR 10 40	Rural Electrification Administration—joint insured
CR 10 43	joint insured
CR 15 07	include automotive products in outside containers
	see: automotive products in outside containers
CR 15 09	protective devices or services provision
CR 15 11	include outside showcases or show windows as premises
	see: outside showcases or show windows as premises
CR 15 20	property of others
CR 15 21	theft of outdoor signs
	see: outdoor signs—theft extension
CR 15 23	extend definition of premises to include portion of grounds enclosed by fence or wall
	see: extended definition of premises to include portion of grounds enclosed by fence or wall
CR 15 25	include selling price or processing charge
	see: selling price or processing charge coverage form
CR 15 33	excess bank burglary and robbery
DL 24 01	personal liability endorsement
DP 00 01	dwelling property 1—basic form
	see: dwelling policy basic form
DP 00 02	dwelling property 2—broad form
	see: dwelling policy broad form
DP 00 03	dwelling property 3—special form
	see: dwelling policy special form
DP 04 20	permitted incidental occupancies endorsement
DP 04 69	dwelling—earthquake
	see: earthquake
DP 04 72	broad theft coverage endorsement
DP 04 73	limited theft coverage endorsement
DP 04 95	water back-up and sump overflow
	see: water back-up and sump overflow coverage
GL 99 02	landlord's protective liability
	see: landlords' protective liability endorsement
HO 00 01	homeowners 1—basic form
	see: homeowners basic form
HO 00 02	homeowners 2—broad form
	see: homeowners broad form
HO 00 03	homeowners 3—special form
	see: homeowners special form

IPF 17 01	personal property floater
IPF 17 11	personal property floater—$250 deductible endorsement
	see: personal property floater—deductible endorsements
IPF 17 12	personal property floater—$500 deductible endorsement
	see: personal property floater—deductible endorsements
IPF 17 13	personal property floater—automatic increase in insurance
IPF 17 14	personal property floater—automatic increase in insurance
IPF 17 15	personal property floater—automatic increase in insurance
IPF 17 16	personal property floater—automatic increase in insurance
PP 00 01	personal auto policy
PP 02 01	suspension of insurance endorsement
PP 03 03	towing and labor costs coverage
PP 03 02	increased limits transportation expenses coverage
	see: rental reimbursement coverage
PP 03 08	coverage for damage to your auto (maximum limit of liability)
PP 03 13	coverage for audio, visual and data—electronic equipment and tapes, records, discs and other media
	see: electronic equipment coverage
PP 03 22	named non-owner coverage
PP 03 23	miscellaneous type vehicle endorsement
PP 03 26	liability coverage exclusion endorsement

National Council on Compensation Insurance (NCCI) forms

WC 00 00 00A	workers' compensation
	see: workers' compensation insurance
WC 00 01 01A	Defense Base Act coverage endorsement
WC 00 01 02	Federal Coal Mine Health and Safety Act coverage endorsement
WC 00 01 04	Federal Employers' Liability Act coverage endorsement
WC 00 01 06A	Longshore and Harbor Workers[1] Compensation Act coverage endorsement
WC 00 01 08A	Nonappropriated Fund Instrumentalities Act coverage endorsement
WC 00 01 09A	Outer Continental Shelf Lands Act coverage endorsement
WC 00 01 11	Migrant and Seasonal Agricultural Worker Protection Act coverage endorsement
WC 00 02 01A	maritime coverage endorsement
WC 00 02 03	voluntary compensation maritime coverage endorsement
WC 00 03 01A	alternate employer endorsement
WC 00 03 02	designated workplace exclusion endorsement
WC 00 03 03B	employers[1] liability coverage endorsement
	see: employers' liability insurance
WC 00 03 04	insurance company as insured endorsement
WC 00 03 05	joint venture as insured endorsement

WC 00 03 06	medical benefits exclusion endorsement
WC 00 03 07	medical benefits reimbursement endorsement
WC 00 03 08	partners, officers and others exclusion endorsement
WC 00 03 09	Rural Electrification Administration endorsement
WC 00 03 10	sole proprietors, partners, officers and others coverage endorsement
WC 00 03 11A	voluntary compensation and employers[1] liability coverage endorsement
WC 00 03 13	waiver of our right to recover from others endorsement
WC 00 03 15	domestic and agricultural workers exclusion endorsement
WC 00 03 19	employee leasing client endorsement
WC 00 03 20A	labor contractor endorsement
WC 00 03 21	labor contractor exclusion endorsement
WC 00 03 22	employee leasing client exclusion endorsement
WC 00 03 23	multiple coordinated policy endorsement
WC 00 04 01A	aircraft premium endorsement
WC 00 04 02	anniversary rating date endorsement
WC 00 04 03	experience rating modification factor endorsement
WC 00 04 04	pending rate change endorsement
WC 00 04 05	policy period endorsement
WC 00 04 06	premium discount endorsement
WC 00 04 07	rate change endorsement
WC 00 04 08	Longshore and Harbor Workers[1] Compensation Act rate change endorsement
WC 00 04 11	assigned risk premium differential endorsement
WC 00 04 12	contingent experience rating modification factor endorsement
WC 00 04 13	assigned risk premium surcharge endorsement
WC 00 04 14	notification of change in ownership endorsement

American Association of Insurance Services (AAIS) forms

IM 660	accounts receivable coverage form see: accounts receivable insurance
IM 637	garment manufacturers named perils coverage see: garment contractors' floater
IM 638	garment manufacturers coverage see: garment contractors' floater
IM 650	physicians and dentists equipment coverage see: physicians' and surgeons' equipment floater
IM 661	valuable papers and records coverage form

	see: valuable papers and records insurance
IM 663	neon and electric sign coverage
	see: sign coverage
IM 700	camera or musical instruments dealers coverage
	see: camera and musical instrument dealers' coverage form
IM 707	fur dealers coverage
	see: furriers' customer insurance
IM 745	floor plan coverage
	see: floor plan insurance
IM 785	theatrical property coverage

ACORD forms

26	policy certification log
27	evidence of property insurance
35	cancellation request/policy release
50	automobile insurance identification card
75-S	binder
76	binder log
225	policyholders' report

miscellaneous forms

Financial Institution form 24	banker's blanket bond
HCFA form 1450	Uniform Billing Form